Career Education

A Functional Life Skills Approach

Third Edition

Donn E. Brolin

University of Missouri–Columbia

Merrill, an imprint of
Prentice Hall
Englewood Cliffs, New Jersey   Columbus, Ohio

Library of Congress Cataloging-in-Publication Data

Career education : a functional life skills approach / Donn E. Brolin.—3rd ed.

p.   cm.

Rev. ed. of: Career education for handicapped individuals / Charles J. Kokaska, Donn E. Brolin. c1985.

Includes bibliographical references and indexes.

ISBN 0-02-315062-9

1. Handicapped—Education—United States. 2. Career education—United States. 3. Handicapped—United States—Life skills guides.   I. Kokaska, Charles J. Career education for handicapped individuals. II. Title.

LC4813.K65   1995

371.9'044—dc20   94-45749

CIP

Cover photos: Merrill/Larry Hamill (top and bottom); Todd Yarrington (middle)

Editor: Ann Castel Davis

Production Editor: Linda Hillis Bayma

Copy Editor: Luanne Dreyer Elliott

Photo Editor: Anne Vega

Text Designer: STELLARViSIONS

Production Buyer: Laura Messerly

Electronic Text Management: Marilyn Wilson Phelps, Matthew Williams, Jane Lopez, Karen L. Bretz

Illustrations: Jane Lopez

This book was set in Transitional 511 BT by Prentice Hall and was printed and bound by R.R. Donnelley & Sons Company. The cover was printed by Phoenix Color Corp.

© 1995 by Prentice-Hall, Inc.
A Simon & Schuster Company
Englewood Cliffs, New Jersey 07632

Earlier editions, entitled *Career Education for Handicapped Individuals*, © 1985 by Macmillan Publishing Company and © 1979 by Merrill Publishing Company.

Photo credits: Gloria Braxton-Davis and Linda Ortman, pp. 288, 297; Pat Burch, pp. 54, 83, 179, 302, 307, 321, 328, 336, 382, 405, 417; Terri Chasteen, p. 378; Patricia Clay, p. 309; Norman Gysbers, p. 355; Inkster, Michigan Public Schools, p. 63, Beverly Lavender, p. 419; Bob Muller, p. 152; Linda Ortman, pp. 269, 421; Carol T. Powers/The White House, p. 25; Barbara Schwartz, p. 235; Barbara Schwartz/Merrill and Prentice Hall, pp. 3, 391, 427; Melody Thurman-Urbanic, p. 215; Anne Vega/Merrill and Prentice Hall, pp. 39, 117, 145, 345; Tom Watson/Merrill and Prentice Hall, p. 91; Mike Wehmeyer, p. 110; Randall D. Williams, p. 164; Diane Wisniewski, pp. 300, 402; Todd Yarrington/Merrill and Prentice Hall, p. 205. Photos on pp. 13, 136, 410, and 425 were supplied by the author.

Printed in the United States of America

10 9 8 7 6 5 4 3 2 1

ISBN: 0-02-315062-9

Prentice-Hall International (UK) Limited, *London*
Prentice-Hall of Australia Pty. Limited, *Sydney*
Prentice-Hall of Canada, Inc., *Toronto*
Prentice-Hall Hispanoamericana, S. A., *Mexico*
Prentice-Hall of India Private Limited, *New Delhi*
Prentice-Hall of Japan, Inc., *Tokyo*
Simon & Schuster Asia Pte. Ltd., *Singapore*
Editora Prentice-Hall do Brasil, Ltda., *Rio de Janeiro*

This book is dedicated to my mother, Marion O. Brolin, a wonderful teacher to her children, grandchildren, and hundreds of others, and to the memory of my father, Herbert C. Brolin, a remarkably kind, unpretentious, and courageous man. I will be forever grateful to them both for their love, support, and encouragement to pursue a career that has been of great satisfaction and, hopefully, has resulted in an important contribution to enhancing the quality of life of persons who have special learning needs.

Foreword

Robert S. Muller of Steelcase, Inc., Grand Rapids, Michigan, is responsible for Employee Community Relations and ADA Implementation. Born with cerebral palsy, Bob has been an inspiration to countless numbers of people, with and without disabilities, by demonstrating how to overcome the many barriers associated with having a severe disability. Among Bob's numerous achievements are appointment by the President to the National Council on Disability, adjunct professor at Aquinas College in Grand Rapids, national and international lecturing on disability, and numerous national awards for his many contributions. On July 26, 1990, he participated in the special events associated with the signing of the Americans with Disabilities Act of 1990, legislation that he helped to formulate. Bob and his wife Carol have raised three children and live in Grandville, Michigan.

Everyone is born with the potential for successful career functioning and to be a productive worker. Work is the most important and central adult activity in our society. It is how everyone, including those with disabilities, is judged as being successful after completing the educational program. Thus, the success of students with disabilities, on completion of their education, depends greatly on the ability of educators, supportive parents, community agencies, and employers to prepare these students with the skills, understanding, and career opportunities that are needed to become independent, productive, happy, and tax-paying adults.

The provision of a career education approach to teach important functional life skills is critically important to the successful transition of students from school to work and community living. The "transition from school to work" movement was launched in the 1980s, thanks to the passage of Public Law 98–199, The Education of the Handicapped Act Amendments of 1983, Section 626. In addition, the Carl Perkins Vocational Education Act (PL 98–524) provided further impetus to the movement. And more recent legislation has spurred the implementation of this important area even further.

This third edition of *Career Education: A Functional Life Skills Approach* provides professionals with a specific approach and techniques for providing students with disabilities and disadvantages, and others who are not destined for higher education, a more practical education that will result in successful adult adjustment. The book provides educators in training and those professionals already in the field with the direction for implementing an effective career education program. Four important subjects are covered to achieve this goal: family and community resources, instructional planning, instructional delivery, and implementation.

Too many students with disabilities and other learning difficulties continue to experience limited career opportunities after they leave school. Too many educators are using outdated approaches, parents become only minimally involved or committed, and local community resources, including service agencies, are not fully engaged in the cooperative and collaborative spirit that is necessary to help these children to become independent and successful citizens and employees. Much has been written and professed in recent years about the need to provide students with a more appropriate education. With the rapid changes that are occurring in the job market of today, it is critical for us to develop to the maximum degree possible the abilities of each and every student, so they develop appropriate career development goals, personal and social skills, employability skills, and all the other skills they will need to become contributing members of their community.

Preface

Meeting the needs of children and youth who have learning difficulties that are due to one or more disabilities and/or disadvantaged situations is a major concern of educators, parents, legislators, and others concerned about these individuals and their future quality of life and community adjustment. Over the past 30 years, significant legislation has been passed to provide substantial funds to expand and improve educational services that will better prepare these students for successful community assimilation. Many innovative and effective field-validated curricular methods and materials have been developed during this period for teaching students with special learning needs. Educators now have at their disposal a vast amount of literature, training materials, and programs that provide the concepts and information needed for implementing effective instruction and services.

What then is the outcome of the educational system's efforts after 30 years of progressive actions? Have local educational agencies responded to the hue and cry for reform and restructured their programs to better meet the needs of their students? Are students now leaving school prepared to live and work in their communities as contributing rather than dependent citizens? Or, are most schools still providing, or emphasizing even more, the traditional standard academic-oriented curriculum that presents unwarranted stress, frustration, and failure experiences for these students? If so, why don't schools make the changes to meet the needs of these students?

These and many other questions and issues regarding the education of students with learning difficulties and disabilities are presented in this book. The overall contention presented is that most schools have not changed substantially enough to meet the needs of these students and the legislative intent of Congress and government agencies. Consequently, most students with special learning needs are still ill prepared to function adequately in their community after leaving the educational system. Unfortunately, most end up dependent on society for their livelihood despite their potential to become independent, functioning persons.

Attitudes must change! Educators, parents, agency workers, employers, and the general public must believe that almost every student with serious academic learning difficulties can be prepared to function as a productive citizen who can live and work successfully in the community and that it is their joint responsibility to ensure that the student's potentials are realized. It is my firm belief that such a goal is totally attainable *if* these individuals are given a more substantive educational program that emphasizes an appropriate blend of academic and functional skills instruction. Such a program must begin during the elementary years and require the active involvement of the student's family to the extent possible and many local community resources. The program can be built on the concepts of career education, an educational movement and approach that was first conceived in the 1970s but which has yet to be widely adopted by the majority of school districts. As the old adage goes, "Everyone is for change, unless it is they that have to do it!"

In this book, a comprehensive functional life skills curriculum model and framework is presented. This curricular approach—*Life-Centered Career Education* (LCCE)—has evolved over more than 20 years and has stood the test of time. Numerous school districts throughout the country have adopted the model and are using its methods and materials to provide a more functional life skills approach that will eventually lead their students to a successful transition to community living and working. Examples of the efforts of several schools are presented. In addition to the LCCE approach, several other models and curriculum materials and resources are covered so the reader may consider and secure further information on them if they appear warranted for possible use.

For over two decades, several close colleagues have supported the concepts and curriculum approach that are presented in this book. My good friend, Professor Emerita Iva Dean Cook, West Virginia Graduate College, has taught practically every special educator in her state the LCCE approach and has contributed two chapters in this book besides providing her opinions about its content. I am deeply indebted to Iva Dean for her unwavering support, assistance, and continual prodding over the years. Professor Emeritus Oliver (Bud) Kolstoe, University of Northern Colorado, should be given credit for initiating the concepts of functional skills and career education into the special education field. Bud has been the pioneer of our field, a close friend and ally, a hero to career development professionals, and a supporter to those, like myself, who have continued his earlier efforts. Professor Gary N. Clark, University of Kansas, is one of the most outstanding and highly respected innovators in the area of transition, functional skills, and career development. Gary has supported my efforts since 1970, when he first provided consultative services to my first federal special education curriculum development project. He has never stopped providing the support and advice I've needed to expand and improve my curriculum research and development activities while he has been contributing immensely himself to the transition/career development literature and field.

I am also particularly indebted to Jean Boston and her organization, The Council for Exceptional Children (CEC), for their belief in the importance of the LCCE approach and for publishing the materials for the field; to long-time colleagues, Professors Charles Kokaska (co-author of the previous editions of this book), Bruno D'Alonzo, Rick Roessler, and Bob Loyd; and to the other contributors to this book, especially my brother James Brolin, Sharon Davis, Sharon Field, and Stephen Thomas. I also want to thank one of my heroes, Bob Muller, for writing the Foreword and contributing much information to Chapter 6, on business and industry involvement. Despite his being born with a severe disability, Bob, his family, friends, teachers, and employers have clearly demonstrated that any disability can be overcome with proper support, love, perseverance, and of course, educational opportunities. Bob is truly an inspiration to me.

One final colleague who has had an important impact on my efforts is the "father of career education for all students," Distinguished Professor Kenneth B. Hoyt, Kansas State University, and former director of the U.S. Office of Career Education. Ken has been an invaluable source of information over the years and has enthusiastically endorsed and supported the LCCE curriculum approach for all students. Appreciation is also extended to the reviewers of the second edition of this text who made suggestions for this one: Ruth Cox Buehler, Millersville University; Jerald F. Etienne, University of Cincinnati; Janice Ferguson, Western Kentucky University; Patrick Grant, Slippery Rock University; and Kathy Peca, Eastern New Mexico University. And last, but not least, special thanks are extended to Ann Davis, administrative editor, Linda Bayma, production editor, and Luanne Dreyer Elliott, copy editor, for their patience, encouragement, and competence in making this publication a reality.

If the purpose of education is to prepare all students to realize their potentials so they can function successfully in society, schools will need to provide flexible options to meet the needs of those who have learning difficulties. This includes many students with disabilities, disadvantages, and others for whom the standard academically oriented curriculum is not feasible without modifications. These individuals can become productive citizens if educators and others spend the time and effort to restructure their programs and attitudes appropriately. The contents of this book provide the guidelines and specific information to interface with the academic curriculum, a comprehensive, functional life skills approach (K–12) for students who need such an approach to become productive and independent members of their community.

Donn E. Brolin

Contents

Chapter 2

A Functional Skills Curriculum Approach   39

Chapter 3

Life-Centered Career Education Curriculum   63

Chapter 6

Business and Industry Involvement   145

Part ...3   Instructional Planning   177

Chapter 7

Functional/Career Assessment   179

Chapter 8

Individualized Educational and Transition Planning   205

Iva Dean Cook, Carol Opperman, and Melody Thurman-Urbanic

Point of View: Jean N. Boston   208

Chapter 9

Instructional Materials and Resources   235

Iva Dean Cook, Carol Opperman, and Melody Thurman-Urbanic

Point of View: Robert J. Loyd   236

Part ...4   Instructional Delivery   267

Chapter 10

Daily Living Skills   269

Chapter 11

Personal–Social Skills   307

Chapter 12

Occupational Guidance and Preparation   345

Part ...5   Implementation   389

Chapter 13

Career Education Programs   391

Chapter 14

Issues and Future Directions   427

Appendix A

Cooperative Agreement Between the Department of Education and the Division of Rehabilitation Services, State of West Virginia   451

Appendix B

List of Professional Organizations   457

Appendix C

LCCE Performance Test 17   461

Part 1

Introduction

Chapter 1

Education of Students with
Special Learning Needs

Chapter 2

A Functional Skills Curriculum Approach

Chapter 3

Life-Centered Career Education Curriculum

Chapter 1

Education of Students with Special Learning Needs

Preliminary Questions About the Topic

1. What proportion of students drop out of school each year and fail to graduate from high school?

2. Approximately what proportion of American students have special learning needs?

3. What is the adult adjustment outcome of most students with special learning needs after they leave the educational system?

4. Name three major forces that can effect positive educational change in American schools.

5. What have been the results of the more recent court cases that have addressed the right of students with disabilities to be educated in the regular classroom?

6. What major special education legislation has mandated that transition services be documented and provided to all students in special education services?

7. What federal legislation was passed in the 1990s that reflects the growing national concern and need for more career development efforts in our schools?

8. What is meant by "full inclusion," and how does it differ from the Regular Education Initiative (REI)?

9. What is the 20/20 Analysis approach promoted by Reynolds and his associates?

10. Overall, how would you characterize the present state of the art in this country relative to the education of students with special learning needs, especially those with disabilities?

Approximately 25%, or 12½ million, of the students in American schools have special learning needs. These students are generally described as those who have various types of disabilities or are disadvantaged, in essence, students who are at risk. Approximately 5 million (10%) students have disabilities, and 7½ million (15%) can be considered disadvantaged. *Students with disabilities* are those who are classified as having specific learning disabilities, speech or language impairments, mental retardation, serious emotional disturbance, multiple disabilities, hearing impairments, orthopedic impairments, other health impairments, visual impairments, deaf-blindness, autism, and traumatic brain injury. Almost half of these children have specific learning disabilities (U.S. Department of Education, Office of Special Education Programs, 1993). *Students who are disadvantaged* are those who are economically, socially, or academically disadvantaged; are reluctant learners; are substance abusers; are pregnant; or have a criminal record. These and many other students with special learning needs present a formidable challenge to educators who are responsible for providing them with an education that will appropriately meet their needs and learning styles.

In 1990, the Bush administration established six National Education Goals to be attained by year 2000:

1. Every American child must start school prepared to learn, sound in body, and sound in mind.
2. The high school graduation rate in the United States must increase to no less than 90%.
3. All students in grades 4, 8, and 12 will be tested for progress in critical subjects.
4. American students must rank first in the world in achievement in mathematics and science.
5. Every adult must be a skilled, literate worker and citizen, able to compete in a global economy.
6. Every school must be drug-free and offer a disciplined environment conducive to learning (Bush, 1991).

The Clinton administration continued this effort and established their Goals 2000: Educate America, a U.S. Department of Education project to encourage and support grassroots, community-wide efforts to reach the National Education Goals.

This book devotes primary attention to individuals in need of special services and consideration to keep them in school to prepare them for successful community adjustment. In the opinion of many experts and educators in American schools, many students—including those who fall into the disadvantaged, disabled, and disruptive categories—need a more functional life-centered educational emphasis if they are to become responsible, contributing members of their families and communities and the labor force. These students' needs must also be addressed in relation to the six national goals. The approach advanced in this book is intended to provide a needed direction for reaching these goals.

This chapter begins with a discussion of expert opinion and research that supports those who believe there is a critical need to make significant changes in the educational system on behalf of students with special learning needs. Some of the major forces that effect positive educational change in the United States are presented and followed by a discussion of some major recent legislation enacted to better meet the life skills and career development needs of these students. The final section describes recent educational restructuring to integrate students into the mainstream of their entire school program. Final comments on the state of the field along with suggestions for class activities conclude the chapter.

THE NEED TO CHANGE

The definition of an appropriate educational program for students in American schools continues to be debated nationwide. In past decades, many educational concepts and movements have come and gone. Unfortunately, as the debate continues, large numbers of students leave school to become unproductive and unsuccessful. Dropout rates remain about the same as 20 years ago, discipline and drug problems are dramatically increasing in most schools, the number of students who end up in correctional facilities is rising, and unemployment and underemployment continue to be major problems for these individuals as adults.

 What should be the primary purpose of education?

A fundamental question or issue that must be resolved by educational policymakers and decision makers is, What should be the primary purpose of education? Is it to teach primarily the basic academic/literary skills and the enrichment/content subjects and then expect all students to be able to acquire the other skills needed for living and working on their own? Or, is it *to purposely teach every student what they need to learn, while they are in school, to become a productive member of their community?* Inspection of most school districts' philosophy of education statements will probably reveal the latter, although the curriculum content may focus primarily on the former.

The six National Education Goals for 2000 clearly reflect a sincere recognition by the federal bureaucracy for the purpose of educating all students to become productive members of society, especially goal 5, "Every adult must be a skilled, literate worker and citizen, able to compete in a global economy." However, the educational system will need to truly accept these goals and restructure its services and programs to meet the many pressing and contemporary adult adjustment needs of all its students—including those who have special learning needs.

 The proportion of students who drop out of school is very alarming.

6

Point of View

Our nation has made great strides in providing quality programs for persons with disabilities, but it has many frontiers to cover before comprehensive transitional needs of students with disabilities are met.

Approximately 20 years ago, Public Law 94–142 mandated a free and appropriate public education in the least restrictive environment. More recently, The Individuals with Disabilities Education Act (IDEA) included the requirement that the Individualized Education Program (IEP) include transition services before or by the time they are age 16. The law also requires that children with disabilities be educated with children who are not disabled and that students not be removed from the regular environment except when their disability is such that they cannot be satisfactorily educated in regular classes with use of supplementary aids and services. Thus, in the past 20 years, we have moved from a most restrictive environment of separate schools and classes to that of a least restrictive environment—full inclusion.

Education is of little value to students with disabilities, regardless of where it occurs, unless they can participate in the family, community, and the world of work—become partially or totally self-sufficient—on exiting the school. Neither legislative mandates nor the least restrictive placement options will necessarily improve the preparation of students to make this transition. Only the dedication of educators, support staff, parents, and the community to a well-planned, functional, outcome-based curriculum will resolve the problems and issues faced by students with disabilities.

Four key elements of transition, which must be addressed in transitional planning, are (a) systematic career/vocational education and training throughout the early, middle, and secondary school years; (b) effective work by cooperative and interagency teams; (c) parent, consumer, and employer involvement in the transition-planning process; and (d) community and professional awareness and support of multiple employment options. Education must address these elements and prepare those with disabilities for transition.

It is not easy to prepare some students for this success, but it is our responsibility to strive to educate all students to their maximum ability.

Iva Dean Cook is Professor Emeritus of Special Education, West Virginia Graduate College, Institute, West Virginia, and a former president of the Division on Career Development and Transition, The Council for Exceptional Children.

The Dropout Problem

One of the best gauges of the impact of the educational system on its students is what happens after they leave school. A revealing indicator is the number of students who drop out of school and never graduate. Unfortunately, the news is tragic.

Approximately 25% or more of the students from general education will not complete high school. A high proportion of these students are those who are called at-risk or disadvantaged students. In some cities, the dropout rates of inner-city children exceed 40% (Hahn, Danzberger, & Lefkowitz, 1987).

The *Fourteenth Annual Report to Congress on the Implementation of the Individuals with Disabilities Act* (IDEA) (U.S. Department of Education, Office of Special Education Programs, 1992), using data secured from the National Longitudinal Transition Study (NLTS) of Special Education Students, noted that students with disabilities drop out of school at a significantly higher rate than other secondary students. In addition, for the youth who at ages 15 to 20 left their secondary schools, the following was reported:

- 43% of those with disabilities, including those who were expelled or suspended, became dropouts. This compared with 24% in the general population.
- A fairly high absenteeism and course failure rate was found for a large proportion of the students, although many did graduate despite not learning sufficient academic and other skills.
- Significant relationships were found between aspects of students' school programs and student outcomes. For example, a more occupationally oriented curriculum with a wide range of meaningful experiences is more positive (Wagner, 1991).

The *Fifteenth Annual Report to Congress* (U.S. Department of Education, Office of Special Education Programs, 1993) noted a slightly lower dropout figure of 39%. This report also noted that the federal special education agency is now funding several dropout-prevention projects to promote new approaches to keeping students with disabilities in school.

Students labeled as having a learning disability have been found to have a particularly high dropout rate. The *Fifteenth Annual Report to Congress* (U.S. Department of Education, Office of Special Education Programs, 1993) noted a 22.2% rate. Zigmond and Thornton (1985) found a rate of 54%. In reviewing studies later, de Bettencourt and Zigmond (1990) identified absenteeism, discipline problems, and poor achievement as significant predictors of dropout. They raised serious doubts about the appropriateness of traditional required mainstream classes taken at the high school level. Lichtenstein (1993) followed the progress of four dropouts who were identified as having a learning disability. Lichtenstein identified the major reasons for dropping out as low self-esteem and the students' feelings that further schooling would be too anxiety provoking and humiliating. He noted that these students were not really "losers" or "failures" but rather victims of inadequate secondary programming and transition planning.

It should be apparent that *the educational system is not effectively meeting the needs of many different types of students through the standard curriculum.* With the tremendous increase in the proportion of immigrants entering American schools each year with different life experiences, skills, and problems, even greater dropout and other problems will result unless more relevant functional curriculum approaches are made available. For those students in special education programs, Kaufman, Kameenui, Birman, and Danielson noted,

> children with disabilities are not dropping out of special education, they are dropping out of school. These children are failing more frequently in regular than special education classes. Significant numbers are being arrested in their communities and, after leaving school, are not engaged in employment, education, or other productive activities. (1990, p. 109)

These writers, most of whom were employed by the federal Office of Special Education Programs, based their conclusions on national data received by the U.S. Department of Education.

"Children with disabilities are not dropping out of special education, they are dropping out of school."

Kaufman et al. (1990)

More specific and recent studies on the postschool employment and community adjustment of students with various disabilities and other learning problems are presented next.

The Postschool Adjustment Problem

Only 25% of all secondary students will actually graduate from college. For the majority of students, the journey from school to work consists of a rough passage of several years of dead-end, low-paying jobs. Most employers want mature individuals with work experience, not someone just out of high school or who is a dropout. Thus, it is no wonder that one third of all young people fail to find stable employment by the time they reach the age of 30 (Winters, 1993).

Many follow-up studies of the postschool adjustment of former students receiving special education services have been conducted over a period of several decades. In the 1980s, a substantial number of studies were conducted with generally similar results. For the most part, the studies revealed an unsatisfactory outcome for the majority of former students. Only about one third of these individuals could be considered as leading a relatively satisfactory life. These studies will not be identified or reviewed here, because they have been reported in numerous other publications and are now relatively dated. Instead, a review of some of the more recent and significant studies reported in the 1990s are described.

Research has found that most students lack sufficient functional skills.

The NLTS, conducted by SRI International, has provided the most comprehensive investigation of numerous aspects of student outcome (Wagner et al., 1991). SRI International studied 8,000 former special education students, ages 13 to 21, and secondary special education students in the 1985 to 1986 school year. The students were followed for a 5-year period to provide important information about their transition from school to early adulthood. Some of the most important findings of their research follow:

- The proportion of persons falling into the 11 disability categories who were employed full-time 1 year or more out of school was 29.2%. Persons with learning disabilities were employed the most (37.9%); those with multiple disabilities, orthopedic impairments, and visual impairments were employed the least (1.3%, 1.3%, and 10%, respectively).
- The average wage of the former students was $4.35 per hour. Those with learning disabilities earned the most ($4.63); those with visual impairment and mental retardation earned the least ($3.12, $3.68); those classified as orthopedically impaired, health impaired, multidisabled, and deaf–blind accounted for too few cases to report.
- Although the former students' ability to perform self-care skills was rated very well by their parents in 86.4% of the cases, only 40.4% of the entire group was rated able to adequately perform functional mental skills, such as looking up telephone numbers, using a telephone, counting change, telling time, and reading common signs. Those who were particularly deficient in this area were classified as being deaf–blind, multidisabled, visually impaired, mentally retarded, and deaf.
- The social experiences of these young adults were also quite limited, becoming more so the longer they were out of school.

These data do not present an impressive outcome for the majority of students in special education. For years, experts in the field have noted that if students with learning problems are properly trained, the vast majority can become independent, productive, and contributing members of their communities. Apparently, however, they have not yet been given this opportunity. SRI data revealed that only approximately 27% had received any postsecondary education 3 to 5 years after leaving the secondary school, compared to 68% of those without disabilities.

 "Although people with mental retardation have successfully demonstrated their capacities for gainful employment, few are actually integrated into the work force with people who have no disability."

Sharon Davis (1993)

In 1993, The Arc, a national organization on mental retardation, issued its "A Status Report to the Nation on Inclusion in Employment of People with Mental Retardation" (S. Davis, 1993). Based on her review of recent studies and other data, Davis concluded that although people with mental retardation have successfully demonstrated their capacities for gainful employment, few are actually integrated into the work force with people who have no disability. She noted the emergence of some positive trends, in that many persons who previously were steered toward sheltered (workshop) employment are now recognized as being capable of supported or competitive employment. She attributed much of this improved state of affairs to recent federal legislation (i.e., the Rehabilitation Act Amendments of 1992, the Americans with Disabilities Act of 1990, and the Job Training Partnership Act of 1987) and greater awareness by employers of the capabilities of these individuals. However, Davis concluded that people with mental retardation still face many barriers to successful adjustment: the failure of the public education system to adequately prepare them for work, the false perceptions and beliefs about their work capabilities held by many employers and families, and the work disincentives existing in federal entitlement programs.

Sitlington and her associates conducted a number of statewide follow-up studies in Iowa to determine the adult adjustment of former students with different disabilities 1 and 3 years after leaving the educational system (Frank & Sitlington, 1993; Sitlington & Frank, 1993; Sitlington, Frank, & Carson, 1991). Some major findings from these studies follow:

- Three years after graduation, only 18.5% of 322 persons with mental disabilities interviewed met the low criteria of successful adult adjustment, and only 3.9% met the high criteria for success.
- Only 11% of the students with learning disabilities met high standards of success, and an additional 27% met the low criteria 3 years out of school.
- Dropouts experienced the least number of gains in adult adjustment.
- The longer individuals are out of school, the less we can attribute to the impact of the educational program.
- Only 0% to 10% of individuals who were labeled either behaviorally disordered, learning disabled, or mentally disabled were successful by stringent criteria, and 25% to 50% did not even meet minimal adult adjustment criteria.

These important findings in a state that is known for its excellent educational programs reflect the challenge that still lies before us.

Schools are experiencing a tremendous increase in students who are disruptive and dangerous to both students and teachers. "Youth with behavioral disorders experience a high dropout rate; as a result many of these students never have access to training designed to prepare them for meaningful careers" (Bullis & Gaylord-Ross, 1991). These writers noted that very few follow-up studies have tracked these persons and documented their experiences. Indications are, however, that these individuals have limited success and that a career education curriculum focus is badly needed if they are to learn the social and vocational skills needed for the workplace.

The Change Problem

The majority of students with special learning needs still encounter significant difficulties in achieving successful employment, independent living, and social relationships after leaving the educational system. Although their status will improve somewhat over time, and some will become successful, the majority will most likely become either unemployed or substantially underemployed and low-paid members of the secondary labor market. They will tend to be dependent on their families, many will get in trouble with the law, and they will have limited friendships and recreational outlets.

 "External pressure exerted on an organization to change its basic structure will, for as long as that pressure is applied, cause the organization to bend and assume a new shape. Once the pressure is removed, the organization will reassume its original shape!"
Kenneth B. Hoyt (1976) speaking on "The Marshmallow Principle"

Although our nation continues to be a nation at risk, greater recognition for the need to accomplish true educational reform is even stronger today than in the 1980s, when numerous studies and reports were released by many prestigious professional groups concerned about the deteriorating nature of the educational system. Even though many professionals responsible for educational change and improvement were responsive to the need for change, others failed to heed the cry, believing they alone really understood what was best for their local district. Consequently, little substantive change occurred.

In many school districts, dedicated administrators, teachers, counselors, and others are trying to respond to the many needs of their students. Unfortunately, many of these dedicated educators are not always supported by the significant others (parents, other educators, agency personnel, community resource people) on whom change is dependent. In several school districts, exemplary programs have evolved to demonstrate it can be done if the will is there. Much remains to be accomplished, however, if the majority of students in American schools are to get an education that will help them to realize their potentials to achieve a satisfying life-style and career that will benefit them and their community.

MAJOR FORCES EFFECTING EDUCATIONAL CHANGE

How can change really happen? Who are the major instigators of significant and positive change for persons who need special educational services? Certainly, many professionals working in the field are continually trying to improve the quality and quantity of services to children, youth, and adults. Major change, however, must come from society as a whole. Public awareness of the problems and their remedies are important stimulants. Education and other human service systems depend on taxpayers. Unfortunately, with numerous forces vying for government money (i.e., military, space program, welfare, labor department, health care), even the greatest needs often go relatively unheeded.

In the case of persons with special learning needs, three distinct forces have fostered change to enhance their educational, employment, and accessibility potential: parents and advocacy organizations, the legal system, and federal and state legislation. Each of these forces interact to bring about educational change.

Parents and Advocacy Organizations

It is appropriate to begin a discussion of major forces for educational change with a review of the numerous organizations that have been founded by the parents of individuals with disabilities. Such organizations date back to the founding of the National Society for Crippled Children in 1921. But the biggest surge of progress was made in 1949 to 1950, when the National Association for Retarded Children (now The Arc) and the United Cerebral Palsy Association were organized within a few months of one another. Membership in such organizations is open to parents, students, and professionals and numbers in the hundreds of thousands.

These organizations were created by parents as a response to public inaction manifested by the absence of school programs, treatment centers, or even skilled personnel who were interested in working with children with disabilities. A well-known example of the parents' efforts can be found in the story of the beginnings of the New York State Cerebral Palsy Association. A parent advertised daily in several local newspapers that those individuals who were interested in receiving help should call or write to her (Killilea, 1960). There are numerous examples of parents seeking each other out to receive and provide solace and find answers to basic questions about their children's condition and future. Today, these organizations also function as viable representatives of individuals with disabilities in affecting political and social action.

The parent organizations had initial problems in working with professionals. Parents were forced into combined action because very little was being provided by agencies employing doctors, teachers, and psychologists. At first, these problems forced parents to rely on themselves for counsel and direction; in time, they learned to use the professionals' skills as the parent organizations continued to expand their role and influence. Numerous parent groups now have professionals as consultants and members of their board of directors, although the parents still control the overall intent and direction of policy.

Parents' strongest drive and accomplishments have been to promote legislation from the local level through the statehouses and Congress. Several organizations have active legislation committees that monitor the progress of bills, organize attempts to lobby on behalf of favorable legislation, produce witnesses during committee hearings, and function as a source of information to its members, legislatures, and representatives of the media. These efforts have been rewarded. Repeated laws that support the rights of individuals with disabilities have been passed at all levels of government.

Parent groups have been a major force in improving education for persons with disabilities.

Parent groups have also served other purposes, such as the following:

1. Organized educational facilities and services when public schools or agencies were unavailable.
2. Promoted public awareness and support for programs and efforts to assist individuals with disabilities.
3. Supported parents through counseling, guardianship plans, respite care programs, and medical services.
4. Promoted research into causes, treatment, education, and other aspects of the individual's life.
5. Sponsored training for teachers, teacher aides, community leaders, doctors, and other individuals who may be involved in care, education, and treatment.
6. Built permanent structures for sheltered workshops, day schools, and diagnostic centers.
7. Developed programs for such necessary functions as daily care, mobility, recreation, leisure, and raising a family.

Finally, parent groups have established themselves as advocates by representing individuals with disabilities as plaintiffs in litigation involving public agencies. One of the most prominent suits, *Pennsylvania Association for Retarded Children v. Commonwealth of Pennsylvania,* is reviewed later in the chapter. The case and decision have been termed landmark, and it is appropriate that a parent organization was so intimately involved in a decision that affirmed the constitutional right of every child to an education.

In the 1980s, the federal government made funds available for states to institute parent centers to work on behalf of persons with disabilities. Private nonprofit organizations can apply for grants through a separate competition for the purpose of providing training and information to parents of infants, toddlers, children, and youth with disabilities and persons who work with parents. The centers assist parents in the following:

1. Better understand the nature and needs of the child's disabling condition.
2. Provide follow-up support for their child's educational program.
3. Communicate more effectively with special and regular educators, administrators, related services personnel, and other relevant professionals.
4. Participate fully in educational decision-making processes such as their child's individualized education program.
5. Obtain information about the range of options, programs, services, and resources available at the national, state, and local levels.
6. Understand the provisions for educating children with disabilities under the federal law. Every state has at least one federally funded parent center of this nature. These centers are an important addition to improving the educational efforts on behalf of children and youth with disabilities.

The Courts and Important Litigation

As important as the doctor, teacher, or psychologist may be in the history of special education, the lawyer and judge are not to be forgotten. Since 1960, legal suits and judicial decisions have had a direct effect on the education, training, care, and protection of individuals with disabilities.

The Supreme Court decision in *Brown v. Board of Education of Topeka Kansas* (1954) set a major precedent in litigations involving the right of every citizen to an education. The court ruled that state laws could not permit segregation of students on racial grounds and that the doctrine of "separate but equal" education facilities was unconstitutional. The court stated:

> In these days it is doubtful that any child may reasonably be expected to succeed in life if he is denied the opportunity for an education. Such an opportunity, where the state has undertaken to provide it, is a right which must be made available to all on equal terms.

Although racial discrimination was the prominent concern in the *Brown* case, the Supreme Court's ruling helped to establish arguments used in labor cases involving individuals with disabilities who had been denied equal education because of the unfounded belief that they would not be able to profit from it and contribute to society.

Hobson v. Hansen (1968) was one of the first litigations that included special education within the broader context of segregation and labeling of children. Judge Skeley Wright ruled that the five-part track system used in grouping students was unconstitutional, because it deprived students who were black or from lower socioeconomic families of an opportunity to experience equal educational service. The school system was unable to demonstrate that the system allowed students to advance within and across the tracks or that instruction at the lower levels was meeting the needs of the students. The *Hobson* case established additional precedent for future right-to-education suits in the following ways:

1. It established that school districts had to provide evidence that programs yielded adequate results. It was not enough for school districts to *intend* to design adequate programs for students.
2. It indicated that placement of students into appropriate programs had to be substantiated by adequate procedures and supporting evidence. The courts would not accept procedures that violated the constitutional right of the child or tests that were inappropriate for the intended educational objectives.
3. It forced the field of special education to examine its unwilling partnership in de facto segregation and the practice of placing students into categories of disability.

A third major decision was reached in *Pennsylvania Association for Retarded Children v. Commonwealth of Pennsylvania* (1971). On behalf of the parents of 13 children with mental retardation, the association filed a class action suit in the U.S. District Court against the state of Pennsylvania for failing to provide publicly supported education for all students with mental retardation. The class action suit was a strategic move by the plaintiff's lawyer, Thomas Gilhool, because the court decision would affect all children with mental retardation in the state. His second strategic move was to base the case on the right of every American child to an education. Using expert witnesses before a panel of three judges, Gilhool elicited testimony establishing that individuals with mental retardation could profit from an education and contribute to society. After 2 days of hearings, the parties reached an agreement.

The court ordered the state to provide the necessary education and rejected the argument that a lack of funds, personnel, and facilities were legitimate reasons for substandard education. The court maintained that if, in fact, the state did not have the resources to educate all the children, the children with disabilities must take a share of the burden with other children but that they should not have to bear the entire load of the state's financial difficulties. As a postscript to the decision, which further substantiated the plaintiff's contention that there was a general absence of programs, a survey of all eligible children with mental retardation and not enrolled in school was conducted by the state of Pennsylvania. The survey indicated that 14,267 children had been denied access to the public schools (Gilhool, 1973).

The Pennsylvania case signaled the beginning of a succession of suits in other states for the following reasons:

1. It established that all children, both normal children and those with disabilities, have a right to an educational program appropriate to their ability.
2. It established the precedent that every state has the obligation to provide the personnel and resources to meet the instructional needs of the child.
3. It itemized a due process procedure whereby parents and students can approve or challenge the school system's action on a change of educational status to the extent that the final decision can be settled in the courts, if necessary.
4. It established the necessity of fulfilling an individual's present rights (i.e., those that must be immediately exercised and safeguarded).

The Pennsylvania case was a major breakthrough on behalf of individuals with disabilities' right to receive an appropriate education. A previous case, *Diana v. State Board of Education of California* (1970), and a related decision in *Mills v. Board of Education in the District of Columbia* (1972) helped this cause. The *Diana* decision led to modifications in state codes related to the testing, assessment, and assignment of individuals from minority groups to classes for students with disabilities. The *Mills* decision extended the results of the Pennsylvania case by affirming that all individuals with disabilities have the right to a public education. These cases also established a judicial foundation for organizations working on behalf of individuals with disabilities by encouraging state legislatures to enact further laws. If those laws were not forthcoming, the same groups had the option of turning to the courts. Both of these alternatives required time, effort, and money. Furthermore, states were inconsistent in supporting legislation for various groups of individuals with disabilities. What was needed? Simply, a form of legislation that would apply to all states and all forms of disability, with a funding basis to support the necessary education. That form of legislation was in its early states of development when the Pennsylvania case became prominent in the field of special education.

More recent cases of litigation were reported by S. Davis (1993). She noted the case of an 8-year-old boy with severe intellectual and communication disabilities whose school district felt his low level of intellectual functioning precluded him from participating in regular class and whose behavior would be too disruptive to the class. They felt he should be in a self-contained classroom located in an out-of-district school for children with multiple disabilities. The chief judge in this case ruled that "Inclusion is a right, not a privilege for a select few" and ordered a New Jersey school district to develop an inclusive education plan for the boy and concluded that, in regard to the education of children with severe disabilities:

• "Rafael and children like him may be harmed by being placed in segregated classes, away from friends and family, and surrounded by inappropriate role models."
• "Success in special schools and special classes is unlikely to lead to Rafael functioning successfully either in integrated education settings or in the community."

- "Rafael and all children with disabilities need access to integrated experiences where they can learn to function effectively. Correspondingly, nondisabled people need to learn to function with disabled people through such experiences" (*Oberti v. Board of Education of the Borough of Clementon School District*, 1992).

Inclusion, the opportunity for all students to participate in the totality of the school experience (S. Davis, 1993), is discussed later in this chapter.

Another case involving the right to an inclusive education and affirmed in court reported by S. Davis (1993) is that of Rachel Holland in California. The judge in this case ruled that this child had the right to be educated in the regular classroom and noted that "a placement in other than a regular class is a fallback choice made only after it is determined that placement in regular classes will be unsuccessful" *(Board of Education, Sacramento City Unified School District v. Rachel Holland)*

Legislation

The growing urgency of appropriate education for individuals with disabilities can be documented by the increased number of laws passed in the states. According to the Constitution, each state should assume the responsibility of establishing school law, districts, procedures, and in some instances, financial support. In effect, there are 50 state plans and definitions of state and local partnership in the conduct and funding of education for all children, youths, and adults. Thus, states differ in the extent of their support of education for individuals with disabilities, as well as medical facilities, research, and employment possibilities.

In 1961 President John F. Kennedy appointed a panel to prepare a "national plan to combat mental retardation." He recognized that the office of the president could be used to develop approaches to a problem that existed in every state when no state had the means to the solution. The panel's *Report* (The President's Panel on Mental Retardation, 1963) established long-term goals in the following areas:

- Research and scientific manpower
- Prevention
- Clinical and social services
- Education, vocational rehabilitation, and training
- Residential care
- The law
- Public awareness
- Planning and coordination of services

The Panel's findings and recommendations were applicable to other areas of disability and, more importantly, were placed into law by Congress. These laws have generated more equal-opportunity legislation guaranteeing the rights of individuals with disabilities to use public facilities, receive an education, or obtain employment.

After the groundwork and impetus established in the 1960s for persons with disabilities and disadvantages, significant landmark legislation was passed in the 1970s and 1980s. The laws that are particularly relevant can be divided into five categories: vocational rehabilitation, special education, vocational education, mental retardation/developmental disabilities, and employment service legislation. These are discussed in chronological order to give readers an appreciation of past efforts to improve education and other services to these individuals. The most recent significant legislation then is described.

 The first civil rights law for persons with disabilities: The Rehabilitation Act of 1973

Vocational Rehabilitation

The Rehabilitation Act of 1973, Public Law 93–112, has been referred to as the civil rights law for persons with disabilities. The greatest importance of PL 93-112 is that Section 504, pertaining to equal access or treatment, allows students and their parents to initiate a complaint against a school for discrimination. Federal funds could be withheld if the school is found to be discriminatory. In addition, postsecondary institutions are prohibited from discriminatory recruitment, testing, admissions, and services. Another important feature is Section 503, which requires employers to initiate "affirmative action" for all employment settings. It also covers such areas as upgrading, transfer, demotion, layoff, and termination. The significance of Section 503 to education is the importance of school programs to better prepare students for the workplace; students still must be qualified for these jobs to be given equal opportunity and to institute discriminatory objections, if justified. Other aspects of PL 93–112 that relate to the educational system are the greater focus on opportunities for persons with more severe disabilities and an Individualized Written Rehabilitation Plan (IWRP) between the rehabilitation counselor and client to ensure a more appropriate and agreeable plan.

The regulations of PL 93–112 were not actually passed until 1977, which reflects the controversy and opposition generated by this legislation. Amendments to the Act in 1983 included authorizations for demonstration projects relative to transition of students from school to work and in 1986 included state transition plans and financial support for training and placement of persons with disabilities into either supported and competitive employment. Thus, collaborative efforts with the educational system and its students were an important intent of this law and its amendments in the 1970s and 1980s.

 The Bill of Rights for children with disabilities: The Education for All Handicapped Children Act of 1975

Special Education

The Education for All Handicapped Children Act Amendments of 1975, Public Law 94–142, has been referred to as the Bill of Rights for children with disabilities. The term *children* is used, although it is intended for individuals between the ages of 3 and 21.

It is the purpose of this Act to assure that all children with handicaps have available to them, within the time periods specified . . . a free appropriate public education which emphasizes special education and related services designed to meet their unique needs, to assure that the rights of the children with handicaps and their parents or guardians are protected, to assist States and localities, to provide for the education of all children with handicaps, and to assess and assure the effectiveness of efforts to educate children with handicaps. (Section 601 (c) of Public Law 94–142)

Some of the important components mandated by PL 94–142 are Individualized Education Programs (IEPs), due process procedures, parent/guardian consultation, least restrictive environment (LRE), nondiscriminatory testing and evaluation, confidentiality of information, right to a free and appropriate education, assurance of a "full array of services" and detailed timetables, and incorporation of vocational education as an appropriate component of a secondary student's school program (Missouri LINC, 1992). The components most important to this book's focus are discussed in the following paragraphs.

Due process is a course of legal proceedings in accordance with established rules and principles for enforcing and protecting individual rights. The basic elements of due process procedures are listed in Figure 1.1.

* The child is represented by a parent surrogate when the parent or guardian is not known, the parents are unavailable, or the child is the ward of the state.
* The parents have the opportunity to participate in the evaluation and determination of the child's program.
* The parents receive written and oral notification in their native language before the child's status in the educational program becomes the subject of evaluation, hearings, or reviews.
* The educational agency establishes a specific period of time for the completion of each procedure.
* The parents receive written results of identified procedures and have the opportunity to respond to all notifications.
* Impartial hearings are conducted if parents disagree with decisions. In conjunction with hearings, parents can examine all relevant records, obtain independent educational evaluation, be represented by council, produce and examine witnesses, present evidence, receive records of hearings, and obtain written findings of fact and decision.
* Parents may appeal decisions to an appropriate civil court.
* The burden of proof for recommended action is on the educational agency.
* The educational agency conducts a periodic review of procedures.

FIGURE 1.1 Basic elements of due process procedures.

Public Law 94–142 specifically requires local educational agencies (LEAs) to establish a written IEP for each student who is receiving or is expected to receive special education. The law mandates that each state and LEA shall ensure policies and procedures for developing, implementing, reviewing, maintaining, and evaluating the IEP, regardless of which institution or agency provides special education for the student. The IEP should be developed, reviewed, and revised at the beginning of each school year. Although the program will contain references to services and goals to be obtained by the student, parents, and teachers, it should not be interpreted as a binding contract for the school system or agency. State and local educational agencies are responsible for establishing appropriate services so that the individual will achieve specified goals, but the agencies have not violated federal regulations if an individual falls short of the projected objectives.

The formulation of the IEP is the responsibility of the LEA. Each meeting for the purpose of writing, reviewing, or revising the IEP shall include the following participants:

- One or both of the student's parents
- The student, when appropriate
- Other individuals, at the discretion of the parent or agency

The list in Figure 1.2, derived from various state standards and federal regulations, describes several components of an IEP.

Although the number of services that can be required from a school district is limited, many of the basic components in the IEP process have been upheld in the Supreme Court case of *Hendrick Hudson School District v. Rowley.* The IEP is a compiled document outlining the present and projected status of the student. It has generated so much interest that numerous articles and materials have been published specifically relating to the effective design and execution of the IEP.

The IEP also provides numerous opportunities for professional personnel to improve educational measures in career development.

- The IEP can be a focal point for parent–teacher cooperation in meeting mutually defined objectives. These objectives will be the primary responsibility of the teacher and other professionals involved in educational services. However, the parents' assistance and areas of cooperation should be identified to continue basic themes and activities that were first introduced in the educational setting. The parents' role and efforts will be discussed separately in Chapter 4.
- The IEP requires that the teacher specify long-term goals and short-term instructional steps required to obtain the goals. The IEP functions as a broad-scale marker of the direction in teaching content and skills and can be used as a tool in the management of resources. These resources can be interpreted as services, personnel, and materials.
- The IEP provides other personnel with an overview of the student's educational program and career objectives. This total view would be valuable for curriculum coordinators, counselors, therapists, aides, substitute teachers, and cooperating

- A statement of the student's present levels of educational performance, including academic achievement, social adaptation, prevocational and vocational skills, psychomotor skills, and self-help skills.
- A statement of annual goals describing the educational performance to be achieved by the end of the school year, according to the IEP. These goals would correspond to the areas of performance as identified in the above component and could include other domains.
- A statement of short-term instructional objectives, which are measurable, intermediate steps between the present level of educational performance and the annual goals.
- A statement of specific educational services needed by the student includes all specific education and related services that are required to meet the unique needs of the student, including the type of physical education program in which he will participate, any special instructional media and materials that are needed, and the career education program in which the student may participate.
- The date when the above services will begin and end.
- A description of the extent to which the student will participate in regular education programs.
- A justification for the type of educational placement that the student will experience.
- A list of the individuals who are responsible for the implementation of the IEP.
- Objective criteria, evaluation procedures, and schedules for determining, on an annual basis, at least whether the short-term instructional objectives have been achieved.

FIGURE 1.2   Components of an Individualized Education Program.

instructors from such disciplines as physical education, home economics, and vocational education. The overview also defines the responsibilities of cooperating professionals who design curriculums aimed at intermediate objectives.

- The IEP contributes to the continuity of educational efforts as the student progresses through the system or moves from one system to another. Each step in the development of the plan and its subsequent evaluation and revision add an increased amount of information about the student's abilities and difficulties. This composite may decrease the amount of time and effort that instructors must expend in establishing baseline measures of competence. As a fundamental reference, the plan is extremely helpful for students who must change systems because of personal circumstances or because other services that meet their particular needs have become available.

- The IEP identifies the "who, what, when, and how" of educational services and evaluation. *Who* refers to the learner and professionals involved in the instructional process. *What* refers to the forms of instruction, assistance, or review that will be conducted within a given period of time. *When* refers to the period of time covered in the plan or the specific period when the student will receive designated services. *How* refers to the measures and means by which program planners will determine student achievement. Although these four questions have been simplified in this discussion, they are extremely important in meeting the multiple needs of the student with a disability.
- The IEP is another means through which the instructor can specify and obtain career development objectives. The sections dealing with statements of educational performance, objectives, and services should contain references to the student's progress in career development.

The 1983 amendments granted authority for projects on transition, as the vocational rehabilitation amendments of the same year, and also initiated parent-training project funds. The 1986 amendments, among other things, established new project grants for the development of transition, technology, educational media, and materials for students with special needs (Missouri LINC, 1992).

Vocational Education

The Education Amendments of 1976, Public Law 94–482, Vocational Education Section provisions, are built on the original Vocational Education Act of 1963 and its amendments of 1968. The 1968 amendments required that states spend at least 10% of the basic federal and state grant-in-aid funds on vocational programs that would meet the unique training needs of students with disabilities. This provision was continued in the 1976 amendments with the stipulation that half of the 10% set-aside money is provided by state and local funds. This prevented the practice of substituting federal monies for state funds in vocational education programs for students with disabilities to increase the total amount of fiscal support available for future efforts.

The law was also consistent with provisions of The Education of All Handicapped Children Act relative to vocational education and state plans.

The Carl D. Perkins Vocational Education Act of 1984, Public Law 98-524, which was also an amendment to the Vocational Education Act of 1963, was very important new legislation for students with disabilities and disadvantages to further their participation and success in vocational programs. Of particular importance was its mandate of appropriate assessment of students' interests, abilities, and special needs, that students and parents must be notified about opportunities and options available to them by ninth grade, and the inclusion of vocational services as a component of the IEP.

Developmental Disabilities and Mental Retardation

The Developmental Disabilities Assistance and Bill of Rights Act Amendments of 1987, Public Law 100–146, were amendments to the original act of 1963. Public Law 100–146 enables youth with severe disabilities to pursue competitive employment goals by authorizing grants to support the planning, coordination, and delivery of specialized services to persons with developmental disabilities. The law mandates the development of plans and programs for transition from school to adult life. Public Law 100-146 also mandates a federal interagency committee to plan for and coordinate activities and for states to set up protection and advocacy systems for these individuals (Horne, 1991).

Employment Services

The Comprehensive Employment and Training Act (CETA) of 1973, Public Law 93-203, was passed to provide job training and employment opportunities for economically disadvantaged, unemployed, and underemployed persons. It required coordination of services with other employment and training-related programs such as vocational education and vocational rehabilitation. The federal funds provided communities with grants to design and administer comprehensive employment and training programs that serve the needs in their areas. Amendments in 1978 provided mandates in giving more opportunities to individuals with disabilities, including the Job Corps. CETA was replaced by the Job Training and Partnership Act (JTPA) of 1982, Public Law 97–300, which is authorized to prepare unskilled adults and youth for productive employment. Provisions of PL 97–300 require a State Job Training Coordinating Council, service-delivery areas appointed by the governor to receive federal funds, and Private Industry Councils (PICs) appointed by local elected officials to plan job training and employment service programs at the service-delivery area levels. Students with disabilities and disadvantages may be eligible for these programs, although the law does not specify them as such.

It should now be obvious that many pieces of legislation were passed in the 1970s and 1980s in an attempt to address the needs of youth and adults with disabilities and disadvantages. These laws, and others not presented here, have benefited these individuals; many excellent programs were established; and some important changes and improvements did occur. As noted previously, however, much more remains to be accomplished if the majority of these individuals are to realize their potentials and lead satisfying, productive lives.

The next section presents current major legislation that has been enacted to further amend the various laws described above and to continue the attempt to better meet the needs of persons with disabilities and disadvantages.

TABLE 1.1   **Major Legislation Important to the Career Development of Persons with Special Learning—1990s**

Category	Legislation/Year
Civil rights	Americans with Disabilities Act (ADA), Public Law 101–336, 1990
Special education	Individuals with Disabilities Education Act (IDEA), Public Law 101–476, 1990
Vocational education	Carl D. Perkins Vocational Education and Applied Technology Amendments, Public Law 101–336, 1990
Vocational rehabilitation	Rehabilitation Act Amendments, Public Law 102–69, 1992
Employment	Job Training Reform Act Amendments, Public Law 102–367, 1992
	School-to-Work Opportunities Act, Public Law 103-239, 1994
Social services	Developmental Disabilities Assistance and Bill of Rights Act Amendments, Public Law 101–496, 1990, Public Law 103–230, 1994
Educational reform	Goals 2000: Educate America Act, Public Law 103–227, 1994

MAJOR LEGISLATION OF THE EARLY 1990s

The legislation of the early 1990s demonstrated a renewed commitment to better meeting the educational, vocational, social, accessibility, and other critical unmet needs of both children and adults with disabilities and those who are disadvantaged. These will be identified and described in this section.

Table 1.1 briefly illustrates the most current major legislation to enhance the transition of persons with disabilities to a successful community and vocational adjustment. Because the laws are constantly being amended and reauthorized, readers interested in any changes to these and other legislative acts passed on behalf of persons with special needs should write the U.S. Department of Education, Office of Special Education and Rehabilitative Services, 400 Maryland Ave., SW, Washington, DC 20202-2524, for further information.

The Americans with Disabilities Act of 1990

The Americans with Disabilities Act (ADA), Public Law 101–336, is a further extension of the earlier federal legislation enacted to ensure the civil rights of persons with disabilities. It is intended to guarantee these individuals equal opportunity in employment, public accommodations, transportation, state and local government services, and telecommunications relay services. The employment provisions apply to private employers, state and local governments, employment agencies, and labor unions. The

President Bush signing the ADA bill.

ADA prohibits discrimination in all employment practices, including job applications procedures, hiring, firing, advancement, compensation, training, and other terms, conditions, and privileges of employment. It applies to recruitment, advertising, tenure, layoff, leave, fringe benefits, and all other employment-related activities.

Employers are still able to select the most qualified applicant available if the decision is made on essential skills needed for successful performance on the job. For example, if a job justifiably requires a certain level of manipulative skills and speed of work, and the person with a disability fails to meet those levels, all other factors being about even, the other applicant should be selected for the job.

Employers must also provide reasonable accommodation for the job and work environment so that otherwise qualified applicants with a disability can perform its essential functions. The accommodation, however, must not pose an undue hardship on the employer. Examples of reasonable accommodations are making existing facilities accessible to and usable by the individual with a disability; restructuring a job; modifying work schedules; acquiring or modifying equipment; providing qualified readers or interpreters; or appropriately modifying examinations, training, or other programs. The individual with a disability requiring the accommodation must be otherwise qualified, and the disability must be known by the employer. In addition, an employer is not required to make an accommodation if it would impose an "undue hardship" on the operation of the employer's business.

Congress has enacted an ADA tax credit to assist small businesses in meeting the requirements of the law, that is, those with annual gross receipts less than $1 million who employ 30 or fewer full-time employees. An annual credit of up to $5,000 is available.

Persons interested in learning more about the ADA can readily obtain information from state agencies such as Vocational Rehabilitation and the Job Service. The employment provisions of the ADA are enforced under the same procedures applicable to race, sex, national origin, and religious discrimination under title VII of the Civil Rights Act of 1964. Complaints regarding actions that occur may be filed with the Equal Employment Opportunity Commission or designated state human rights agencies. Good reference sources are *The Americans with Disabilities Act at Work* (Arc, 1991) and an article written by Linthicum, Cole, and D'Alonzo (1991). Further discussion of the ADA is presented in Chapter 6.

The Individuals with Disabilities Education Act of 1990

The IDEA, Public Law 101–476, amended and changed the name of the education of All Handicapped Children Act of 1975 and changed the use of the term *handicapped* to *disabled*. The major purpose of this law is to ensure that all children with disabilities have available to them a "free appropriate public education" that includes special education and related services designed to meet their unique needs. The legislation also ensures that the rights of children and youth with disabilities and their parents are protected. It assists states and local educational agencies in providing for these students' needs and assesses the effectiveness of efforts to educate these children appropriately.

The new legislation requires that no single procedure can be used to determine an appropriate educational program for the child. Children must be assessed in all areas related to the suspected disability. If a child's parents disagree with the results of an evaluation, they have the right to obtain an independent evaluation. The school district then must consider the results of the evaluation when making any decisions about the educational program for the child.

IDEA added an important provision related to the focus of this book—it mandated transition services. IEPs are now required to include "a statement of the needed transition services for students beginning no later than age 16 and annually thereafter. When determined appropriate, transition services may begin at age 14 or even younger. In fact, the U.S. House of Representative Committee reporting on the law encouraged earlier services, stating

> age 16 may be too late for many students, particularly those at risk of dropping out of school and those with the most severe disabilities. Even for those students who stay in school until age 18, many will need more than two years of transitional services. Students with disabilities are now dropping out of school before age 16, feeling that the educational system has little to offer them. Initiating services at a younger age will be critical. (U.S. House of Representatives Report No. 101-544, 10, 1990)

Transition services are defined as:

a coordinated set of activities for a student, designed within an outcome-oriented process, which promotes movement from school to post-school activities, including post-secondary education, vocational training, integrated employment (including supported employment), continuing and adult education, adult services, independent living and community participation. The coordinated set of activities shall take into account the student's preferences and interests, and shall include instruction, community experiences, the development of employment and other post school adult living objectives, and when appropriate, acquisition of daily living skills and functional vocational evaluation.

The transition mandate focuses on *students' adult adjustment preparation needs* and requires the active participation of several cooperating agencies and services.

Unfortunately, at this time, not much is known about state and local agency implementation of the mandate or about changes in their policies, procedures, and practices to promote the effort (Ward & Halloran, 1993). One important federal initiative to support the career development of students with disabilities is monies that have been made available to states from the U.S. Office of Special Education Programs. These funds allow state vocational rehabilitation and special education agencies to develop more cooperative projects to develop, implement, and improve services for secondary youth, enabling them to make a more successful transition from school to employment and community adjustment. The results from states who have received these project grants is still unknown. More on transition is presented in several chapters throughout this book.

The Carl D. Perkins Vocational and Applied Technology Education Act of 1990

The Carl D. Perkins Vocational and Applied Technology Education Act of 1990 (Perkins II), Public Law 101–336, is purported to be very important vocational legislation for students with special learning needs. It is intended to assist in fulfilling the transition services provisions of the IDEA. A further extension of the earlier vocational education legislation described earlier, this version requires that each local agency receiving federal funds adhere to the following list of assurances:

- Equal access to a full range of vocational programs
- Provision of information no later than beginning of ninth grade
- Establishment of appeal procedures for parents, students, teachers, and area residents concerned with decisions affecting their interests
- Vocational education programs provided in the LRE
- Coordination among appropriate representatives from vocational education, special education, and vocational rehabilitation; progress toward vocational goals and objectives that will be monitored through the IEP for students with disabilities and the Individualized Vocational Education Plan (IVEP) for students who are disadvantaged

- Assistance in entering vocational programs and in receiving transitional services
- Assessment that ascertains students' potential to successfully complete vocational programs in the most integrated settings possible
- Provision of supplementary services (curriculum, equipment, classroom modifications, support personnel, and instructional aids and devices)
- Provision of guidance, counseling, and career development activities by professionally certified counselors and teachers
- Provision of counseling and instructional services to facilitate the transition from school to postschool employment and career opportunities (American Vocational Association, 1990)

The Perkins Act provides more federal funds to be expended for vocational education than previously. Students with disabilities and disadvantages fall under the category of "special populations" in this version of the law, which also includes individuals of limited English proficiency, those who participate in programs to eliminate sex bias, and those in correctional institutions. This version of the law constituted a major shift in the provision of vocational-technical education. Earlier provisions tended to separate and isolate vocational educators, students, and curriculum from the rest of the school community. This version now emphasizes academic as well as occupational skills preparation, is directed toward "all segments of the population," and emphasizes closer linkages between school and work. The Act's technical preparation provision attempts to make high school more relevant for at-risk students by linking it with 2-year community or technical college curriculums to produce skilled technicians. This reform effort focuses on the "average" students who make up the middle 50% of the high school population (Hull, 1992).

The Rehabilitation Act Amendments of 1992

The Rehabilitation Act Amendments of 1992, Public Law 102–69, the reauthorization of the Rehabilitation Act of 1973, contains a significant presumption of the potentials of persons with disabilities by noting that *a person with a disability, regardless of the severity of the disability, can achieve employment and other rehabilitation goals, if the appropriate services and supports are made available.* This is a significant change in a policy that previously required evidence that the person with a disability had potential for some type of gainful employment. With the passage of this legislation, rehabilitation agencies are responsible for working closely with other agencies and programs, including the local education agency, to better unify the service system. The amendments recognize that many students with disabilities will exit school in need of rehabilitation services. Thus, each state agency must develop a plan to ensure coordination of services with the state education agency so that students will be served immediately after exiting the school system. This will require IWRPs to be completed before the student leaves the school program (Revell, 1993).

As Revell (1993) noted, now there is a consistent set of public legislation through the ADA, IDEA, and Rehabilitation Act Amendments of 1992. These three laws are now very much synchronized regarding philosophy, policy direction, and expectation (Gloeckler, 1993). If the agencies responsible for carrying out these laws follow the directives, the transition from school to successful adult adjustment will be more greatly ensured for youth and adults with disabilities.

Job Training Reform Amendments of 1992

The Job Training Reform Amendments of 1992, Public Law 102–367, offers youth and adults with disabilities and who are economically disadvantaged a greater opportunity to participate in a variety of training and employment programs relating to the JTPA. The amendments support a variety of transition programs and services such as supported employment, job coaches, internships, community-based training combined with educational services, entry employment experiences, postsecondary education transition services, apprenticeship training, and many other related services. The law also promotes interagency coordination to deliver appropriate employment and training programs that will prepare youth for the transition from school to work and community living.

Educators should actively encourage JTPA program representatives to participate in interagency transition teams to pool resources so student needs can be most appropriately met. The State Job Training Office or local service-delivery area representative should be contacted for specific information.

School-to-Work Opportunities Act of 1994

The School-to-Work Opportunities Act of 1994 (P.L. 103–239), signed into law by April 1, 1994, represents a cooperative effort between the Departments of Education and Labor. This act establishes a national network within which all states can create statewide school-to-work opportunities systems that are a part of comprehensive educational reform. It is intended to be integrated under the Goals 2000: Educate America Act (P.L. 103–227), so that all students, including those with special learning needs, can participate in a performance-based education and training program to learn the skills needed for "high-wage" employment and/or continuing education.

 State and local applications for federal grants must show how programs will ensure the opportunity to participate is given to economically disadvantaged students, low achieving students, students with disabilities, and dropouts.

School-to-Work Opportunities Act of 1994

The School-to-Work Opportunities Act is intended to improve the knowledge and skills of youths by integrating academic and occupational learning, integrating school-based and work-based learning, and building effective linkages between secondary and postsecondary institutions. Every school-to-work program must include the following:

- Work-based learning that provides a planned program of job training or experiences, paid work experience, workplace mentoring, and instruction in general workplace competencies and in a broad array of elements of an industry
- School-based learning that provides career exploration and counseling, instruction in a career major (selected no later than the 11th grade), a program of study that is based on high academic and skill standards as proposed in the Goals 2000: Educate America Act and typically involves at least 1 year of postsecondary education, and periodic evaluations to identify students' academic strengths and weaknesses
- Connecting activities that coordinate involvement of employers, schools, and students; matching students and work-based learning opportunities, and training teachers, mentors, and counselors

Partnerships between elementary, middle, and secondary schools and local businesses are promoted so students can be exposed to a vast array of career opportunities to help them select a career that is consistent with their interests, goals, strengths, and abilities.

"When President Clinton placed his signature on the Goals 2000: Educate America Act on March 31, 1994, he did more than just sign into law this innovative and comprehensive program to improve education. It was the day that America got serious about education."

U.S. Department of Education informational flyer (April 1994)

Goals 2000: Educate America Act

The Goals 2000: Educate America Act is intended to present voluntary national standards describing what all students should know and be able to do at certain grade levels. The national standards will provide a focus, not a national curriculum or federal mandates, so students can leave school with the skills and knowledge needed to succeed.

The Educate America Act supports a "bottom-up" grass-roots approach to school reform, with the federal government assisting states and local communities in the development and implementation of their own comprehensive and innovative reform programs. A broad-based leadership team composed of policymakers, educators, business and civic leaders, parents, and others will help create each reform plan. Federal funds will be provided to support state and local improvement efforts. By the second year of funding, 90% of the money will flow to local schools and districts to support their own plans. Parent information and resource centers are also being encouraged to help parents learn the knowledge and skills they will need to be effective partner's in their child's education.

The Educate America Act establishes a National Skills Standards Board to promote the development of occupational skill standards that will define what workers will need to know and to ensure that American workers are better trained. It also encourages the development of innovative student performance assessments to gauge progress in the core subjects. The first appropriation of $105 million was released in fiscal year 1994, with significant increases projected thereafter.

The preceding and other legislative amendments, such as the Developmental Disabilities Assistance and Bill of Rights Act Amendments of 1990 and 1994 and other laws passed in the early 1990s, reflect the continued social consciousness of the United States to be responsive to the career development needs of its citizenry, including those who have special learning problems and needs.

INTEGRATING INSTRUCTIONAL SERVICES

In the 1960s, special classes for students with disabilities were the most prominent placement. However, much controversy reigned during this decade because of the watered-down curriculum many of the students received, the high rate of dropouts, self-esteem and social isolation problems, and the poor vocational/adult adjustment they experienced after leaving the school. A myriad of studies were conducted, which are not identified here because of their vintage. However, Dr. Loyd Dunn's (1968) famous article questioning the value of the special education approach during this period should be mentioned, because it seemed to strike the conscience of the field and to start the process of a more integrative approach for these students.

A major reason for the ineffectiveness of many special education classes during the late 1960s was the lack of qualified teachers. Special education teacher training programs were just getting underway during this decade, so trained personnel specialists were not prevalent. However, the entire country was becoming more concerned about integration in the late 1960s, spurred forth by such emerging concepts as the normalization principle (Wolfensberger, 1972). Thus, several other service-delivery model options emerged: regular classroom placement, consultant model in which the special educator works with the regular class teacher, itinerant teacher traveling to various schools to consult with regular class teachers, and the resource classroom where the student spends part of the time. In the past 20 years, three integrative and interrelated concepts or approaches surfaced with the goal of placing the student with learning difficulties into the regular programs and classes of the public schools: mainstreaming, regular education initiative, and inclusion. A fourth noteworthy approach, advocated by Reynolds, Zetlin, and Wang (1993), 20/20 Analysis, is also presented because of its potential application to the career education approach of this book. Each is discussed briefly in the following sections. More detailed explanations of these and other instructional delivery models and concepts are presented in several special education texts (e.g., Cronin & Patton, 1993; Langone, 1990; Mercer & Mercer, 1993; Polloway & Patton, 1993; Schloss, Smith, & Schloss, 1990; and others).

Mainstreaming

Although not specifically mentioned in The Education for All Handicapped Children Act (PL 94–142) in 1975, this legislation gave the impetus to the mainstreaming approach, which is basically the placement of the student in regular classes whenever and wherever possible. The concept of mainstreaming is that children have a right to, and can benefit from, participation in the least restrictive educational program (LRE) they can manage.

In April 1976 the delegate assembly at the 54th Annual International Convention of The Council for Exceptional Children (CEC) adopted the following definition of mainstreaming as a statement of policy.

Mainstreaming is a belief which involves an educational placement procedure and process for exceptional children, based on the conviction that each such child should be educated in the least restrictive environment in which his educational and related needs can be satisfactorily provided. This concept recognizes that exceptional children have a wide range of special education needs, varying greatly in intensity and duration; that there is a recognized continuum of education settings which may, at any given time, be appropriate for an individual child's needs; that to the maximum extent appropriate, exceptional children should be educated with non-exceptional children; and that special classes, separate schooling or other removal of an exceptional child from education with non-exceptional children should occur only when the intensity of the child's special education and related needs is such that they cannot be satisfied in an environment including non-exceptional children, even with the provision of supplementary aids and services. (The Council for Exceptional Children, 1976)

One major problem with the institution of this approach in the 1970s and 1980s was the lack of training provided to regular class teachers on how to provide effectively for these students needs. Thus, considerable resentment toward the concept and approach resulted. Only when the LRE principle, specified in the Act, was adhered to, did mainstreaming become successful.

Regular Education Initiative

The Regular Education Initiative (REI) evolved in the 1980s because of the belief by certain reformers that the special education delivery system was inadequate (W. E. Davis, 1989). The basic message of the REI was that classroom teachers should be responsible for the education of all students in their charge and that principals should be authorized to distribute resources for children who have learning problems. The basic assumption of the REI is that regular classroom teachers are charged with the following responsibilities: (a) Educate all students assigned to them. (b) Make and monitor major instructional decisions for all the students in their class. (c) Provide instruction that follows a normal developmental curriculum. (d) Manage instruction for diverse populations. (e) Seek, use, and coordinate assistance for students who require more intense services than those provided to their peers (Jenkins, Pious, & Jewell, 1990).

The REI, like other proposed changes, was not without controversy. Semmel, Abernathy, Butera, and Lesar (1991) surveyed 381 special and regular educators about their perceptions and opinions of the REI and found that both regular and special education teachers preferred the current special education delivery system. The teachers preferred pullout special education services rather than the consultant model in which students participate fully in the regular classroom and where the special education teacher has no direct instructional time with the students. Overall, the respondents felt the REI approach was not appropriate for most students.

Support for this survey was voiced by Banks (1992), a teacher who noted that her colleagues were very concerned about regular classroom placement of students who do not have the prerequisite skills and techniques to adjust in that setting. She noted that neither regular class nor special class teachers wanted students dumped into these classrooms without their having the requisite skills. Byrnes (1990), a school administrator, suggested not too quickly jumping on the bandwagon. Rather, she recommended that educators appreciate diversity and keep all options open, because no single delivery system can be considered best for all. As she noted, "the REI debate has been philosophical and theoretical. It needs to be augmented by practical and operational perspectives" (p. 345).

The plea for general education to become involved in special education concerns fell essentially on deaf ears, and now attention has turned to a new movement called *inclusive education* or *inclusive schools* (Fuchs & Fuchs, 1994).

Inclusion

Inclusive education is the most recent version for the thrust of integrating students with disabilities into regular classes or the mainstream. Inclusion is a controversial concept. As Fuchs and Fuchs noted, "Like the REI, the newer term seems to defy straightforward interpretation. And like the REI, this is partly because 'inclusion' means different things to people who wish different things from it" (1994, p. 299).

Many advocates of inclusion or full inclusion will state that it requires all students with disabilities to receive their total education within a regular classroom setting. Many professionals strongly believe this is the only alternative and are committed to this approach as the only option for these students. Others approach inclusion on an individual student basis—that this is another option for students depending on their needs and capabilities to benefit from such a placement.

According to Schrag and Burnette,

Inclusive schools do not just mainstream students—they include them. They maintain a continuum of educational options in order to provide choice and meet the needs of individual children. Inclusive schools forge strong ties with their communities, coordinating services with community agency personnel and embracing parents as equal partners. Students work in flexible learning environments, with flexible curricula and instruction that is accessible to all. All students work toward the same overall educational outcomes; what differs is the level at which these outcomes are achieved and the degree of emphasis placed on them. (1994, p. 64)

"The push to integrate all disabled kids in regular classes is destructive! Those demanding full inclusion are interested in only one thing—socialization . . . but it is only one value and not the only reason taxpayers support the schools."

Albert Shanker, President, American Federation of Teachers (1994)

The inclusion movement has stimulated considerable controversy and debate throughout the country and received a great deal of media attention. The American Federation of Teachers, for example, while noting the importance and right of all students to be in regular education, question the full inclusion being promoted by many special educators and parents. The federation noted that it is unreasonable to expect regular teachers to meet the needs of their nondisabled students if they are expected to teach anyone who is placed in their class; in January 1994, it called a halt to full inclusion. On the other hand, advocates of full inclusion believe that with proper supports and teacher aides, almost every child with a disability can and should be in regular classes so they experience a more normal environment with their age-appropriate peers. It remains to be seen as to whether this will happen pervasively throughout the country.

A more moderate position on inclusion is taken by John Heskett, a state education agency coordinator of special education services and former President of the National Association of Special Education Administrators:

the opportunity to be fully included in the regular classroom must be considered for any student with a disability. However, full inclusion may not be the required service for all students with disabilities. The process of individual determination must include, but not be limited to, the ability of the student to benefit from the integrative experience and the appropriateness of inclusive education relative to the goals, objectives, and services called for in the IEP. . . . Inclusion is a mechanism for achieving appropriate Least Restrictive Environment (LRE) decisions for individual students. (1993, pp. 2, 8)

The national special education association, the CEC, has taken a position that appears to be similar to Heskett's. Their policy on inclusion is presented in Figure 1.3.

The preceding discussion only touches on the major concepts and approaches to providing students with the most appropriate learning setting. As can be noted, each approach seems to advocate flexibility, options, and appropriate outcomes within the student's capabilities. However, Fuchs and Fuchs (1994) note that REI opts for a cooperative effort between special and general education but the full inclusionists opt for the elimination of special education. Their excellent article should be read for more detailed knowledge on this topic.

How well are students with disabilities being included in the mainstream of the school community? Although much is currently appearing in the newsprint noting the espousing of inclusion activities by many schools, a study by The Arc (S. Davis, 1992) found more than 75% of students with mental retardation were being educated in totally segregated settings with little interaction with their nondisabled peers, experience few opportunities for learning about career options and other postschool possibili-

CEC POLICY ON INCLUSIVE SCHOOLS AND COMMUNITY SETTINGS

The Council for Exceptional Children (CEC) believes all children, youth, and young adults with disabilities are entitled to a free and appropriate education and/or services that lead to an adult life characterized by satisfying relations with others, independent living, producing engagement in the community, and participation in society at large. To achieve such outcomes, there must exist for all children, youth, and young adults a rich variety of early intervention, educational, and vocational program options and experiences. Access to these programs and experiences should be based on individual educational need and desired outcomes. Furthermore, students and their families or guardians, as members of the planning team, may recommend the placement, curriculum option, and the exit document to be pursued.

CEC believes that a continuum of services must be available for all children, youth and young adults. CEC also believes that the concept of inclusion is a meaningful goal to be pursued in our schools and communities. In addition, CEC believes children, youth, and young adults with disabilities should be served whenever possible in general education classrooms in inclusive neighborhood schools and community settings. Such settings should be strengthened and supported by an infusion of specially trained personnel and other appropriate supportive practices according to the individual needs of the child.

POLICY IMPLICATIONS

Schools. In inclusive schools, the building administrator and staff with assistance from the special education administration should be primarily responsible for the education of children, youth, and young adults with disabilities. The administrator(s) and other school personnel must have available to them appropriate support and technical assistance to enable them to fulfill their responsibilities. Leaders in state/provincial and local governments must redefine rules and regulations as necessary, and grant school personnel greater authority to make decisions regarding curriculum, materials, instructional practice, and staffing patterns. In return for greater autonomy, the school administrator and staff should establish high standards for each child and youth and should be held accountable for his or her progress toward outcomes.

Communities. Inclusive schools must be located in inclusive communities; therefore, CEC invites all educators, other professionals, and family members to work together to create early intervention, educational, and vocational programs and experiences that are collegial, inclusive, and responsive to the diversity of children, youth, and young adults. Policy makers at the highest levels of state/provincial and local government, as well as school administration, also must support inclusion in the educational reforms they espouse. Further, the policy makers should fund programs in nutrition, early intervention, health care, parent education, and other social support programs that prepare all children, youth, and young adults to do well in school. There can be no meaningful school reform, nor inclusive schools, without funding of these key prerequisites. As important, there must be interagency agreements and collaboration with local governments and business to help prepare students to assume a constructive role in an inclusive community.

Professional Development. And finally, state/provincial departments of education, local educational districts, and colleges and universities must provide high-quality preservice and continuing professional development experiences that prepare all general educators to work effectively with children, youth, and young adults representing a wide range of abilities and disabilities, experiences, cultural and linguistic backgrounds, attitudes, and expectations. Moreover, special educators should be trained with an emphasis on their roles in inclusive schools and community settings. They also must learn the importance of establishing ambitious goals for their students and of using appropriate means of monitoring the progress of children, youth, and young adults.

FIGURE 1.3   CEC policy on inclusive schools and community settings.

Note. From *CEC Policy Manual, Section 3, Part 1* (p. 8) by The Council for Exceptional Children, 1994, Reston, VA: The Council for Exceptional Children. Originally approved by Delegate Assembly of the CEC in April 1993. Copyright 1994 by The Council for Exceptional Children. Reprinted by permission.

ties, and often receive no vocational training, functional living skills training, or motivation for living and working in the community (S. Davis, 1992). Although this is only one study, it appears that much remains to be accomplished for the inclusion concept to be implemented, at least in the case of students with mental retardation.

There is almost universal concurrence that students with special learning needs should be given the opportunity to learn in regular classes like everyone else—*if this setting is the LRE for meeting their learning needs.* One other major reservation by many educators, particularly those with the functional skills/career education orientation, is whether or not the educational program emphasis will include enough instruction in those areas to prepare each child to become a productive member of society.

20/20 Analysis

The 20/20 Analysis approach (Reynolds, Zetlin, & Wang, 1993) is an innovative noncategorical approach to providing special assistance to the top 20% (high-achieving) and lower 20% (low-achieving) students so that adaptations in the instructional program can be made to better meet their needs. Reynolds and co-workers note that most school districts conduct numerous categorical programs, namely, special education, Chapter 1 for students who are economically disadvantaged, migrant education, immigrant programs, limited English proficiency, and numerous others. They further noted,

> The burgeoning categorical programs present enormous problems of management, coordination, and efficiency. Each category tends to have its own special teachers, eligibility requirements, timeline, reporting and accountability system, and bureaucratic managers. (Reynolds et al., 1993, p. 295)

Although most of the students who fall into the lower 20% category are those who normally receive special education services, the approach does allow the de-labeling of the students and an integration with other students with special learning problems. Because very little research provides conclusive evidence that students with mild disabilities need qualitatively different forms of instruction than other students, the need of these individuals is more intensive assistance and time to learn (Bereiter, 1985; Brophy, 1986). According to Reynolds and his colleagues, the 20/20 Analysis approach provides a strategy by which such needs can be attained while discarding "the excessive disjointedness of current narrowly framed, input-oriented, categorical approaches to educating marginal students" (1993, p. 298).

The 20/20 Analysis approach should stimulate educators who are grappling with the integration challenge to study the approach and to consider its adoption to meet the needs of many students who have special learning needs.

FINAL COMMENTS

What should be the appropriate educational focus in American schools has been a topic of great concern in this country for several decades. In the opinion of many experts, the entire educational system needs restructuring. The stage finally has been set for significant change. The recently passed Goals 2000: Educate America Act is designed to support fundamental reform system-wide in all schools. Thus, it is an opportune time for professionals and advocates of all students, including those with special learning needs, to work closely with educational reformers in restructuring the educational system for all students. If this is not done, these individuals will suffer the consequences of trying to compete in this rapidly expanding global economy in which we now live.

The present developmental- and academic-oriented curriculum of most schools has not effectively prepared a large proportion of students for successful adult functioning. Most of these students simply do not respond positively or appropriately to a college-oriented delivery system that presents them with failure and embarrassment experiences. Many students with special learning needs come from such dire home and family situations that their learning and behaviors in the school situation need a different approach. Otherwise, the result is an increasing proportion of dropouts, school failure, school dissatisfaction, behavior problems, delinquency, and joblessness.

Many educational leaders would like to see one unified educational system rather than a number of separate categorical programs such as special education. Whether such an admirable goal can ever be achieved is yet to be seen. Some schools may claim to have accomplished such a goal. But, for the most part, too many schools continue to educate most of their special needs and disruptive students in a combination of regular classes, resource rooms, specialized programs, and/or special classes or alternative programs.

In spite of the enabling legislation, monies, increasing professional personnel, and the creation of new concepts, approaches, strategies, and models for "fixing the system," not enough has changed on a broad scale, because many personnel in the field do not want to change their policies, curriculum, and instructional methods. At the same time, many other professionals in the education system have worked diligently to continually improve their school systems. The dedication and effectiveness of numerous administrators, counselors, and teachers who provide their students with effective teaching and personal development opportunities is impressive. Many outstanding accomplishments have been made over the years; however, much remains to be done in most schools if the education of all students is to be satisfactory.

We must *quit reinventing the wheel* and instead face the arduous but meaningful task of restructuring and fine tuning our curricula and collaborative efforts so the educational efforts of the schools are effective for all students. In the following chapter, one effective solution that holds much promise for providing students with a more appropriate educational focus is presented.

ACTIVITIES

1. Based on the student outcome data presented in this chapter, write a philosophical statement that clearly explains what you now believe should be the major purpose of education in your school district. Then, identify the educational goals that you would establish for your students who have learning difficulties.

2. Given the present legislative mandates and the present climate of inclusion, what curriculum areas do you believe must become part of the total curricular effort for the Goals 2000: Educate America Act to be achieved for all students, including those with special learning needs?

Chapter 2

A Functional Skills Curriculum Approach

Preliminary Questions About the Topic

1. Explain what exactly is meant by the terms *functional curriculum* and a *functional curriculum approach.*
2. Who should be taught functional skills?
3. Identify and describe some of the major functional skills curriculums that are being advocated for students with special learning difficulties.
4. What is career education, and what is its relationship to the functional skills curriculum approach?
5. What is the difference between career education and vocational education?
6. What are the most compelling reasons for implementing the career education approach in the public schools?
7. What is outcome-based education?
8. When and by whom was the transition concept introduced?
9. What are three major components that are needed for effective transition?
10. What four areas of content must the Individualized Education Program (IEP) contain for transition services?

The need to provide a more functional curriculum for students with special learning needs and to address their transitional needs is not a new concept in American education. Special educators have recognized this need for decades, and there have been some notable efforts in many schools throughout the country. Terms such as *life skills, independent living skills, persisting life situations, occupational education, work–study, work experience, occupational adjustment, personal-social adjustment, social learning, vocational education, cooperative education, career education,* and *career development* are examples of descriptions from the past and present that have been used to reflect functional curricula for students with special learning needs.

The first section of the chapter begins with a discussion of functional skills and identifies some current functional skills curricula materials and guides. Two models of functional skills curricula that are excellent contributions to the field are identified and described. Next, the transition approach is reintroduced briefly and is followed by another current educational thrust—outcome-based education.

Finally, the career education approach is presented, including a historical account of the career education movement followed by an explanation of its basic concepts and approach. After reading this detailed section, the reader should understand career education's close relationship to the functional skills approach. An example of the well-conceived career education curriculum model developed by Gary Clark concludes the chapter.

FUNCTIONAL SKILLS CURRICULUM

It is being more widely recognized that most, if not all, students need an appropriate blend of academic and functional skills instruction, which should be taught not only in school but also in home and community settings. Functional skills are those that are academic and others that are critical for success in community/adult functioning. These include independent living, social, communication, leisure/recreation, and vocational skills.

 "Functional curriculum is instructional content that focuses on the concepts and skills needed by students in the areas of personal-social, daily living, and occupational adjustment."

Gary Clark (1991)

The Division on Career Development and Transition (DCDT) of The Council for Exceptional Children (CEC) has published an excellent position paper advocating the functional curriculum approach as an important component in the provision of an appropriate education (G. M. Clark, Field, Patton, Brolin, & Sitlington, 1994). Some of the major tenets expressed in this paper follow:

- A life skills instruction approach should be a part of every school curriculum (i.e., included within existing course work) or a recognized and approved option (i.e., alternative course work) for all students at all grade levels.
- The first consideration for life skills education settings should be general education and the community.
- Least restrictive instructional alternatives must always be considered after the decision is made that the instruction in life skills content is not feasible or is inadequate in a general education setting.
- It is the responsibility of general educators at the elementary and middle school levels to ensure the applicability of basic skills education to the functional demands of independent living for students at school, at home, and in the community.
- Special educators should provide specialized or direct instruction in functional skill areas at a level of such quality that there can be no question of commitment to meeting students' needs. (Council for Exceptional Children, DCDT, 1994).

The CEC noted that life career development and transition programming must begin in early childhood and continue throughout adulthood. As noted in that paper, a continually growing body of literature suggests that an appropriate education for students with special learning needs must be determined in terms of individual needs relative to the functional skills demands of adulthood.

The Board of Directors of the CEC Division on Mental Retardation and Developmental Disabilities (1994) approved a position paper on April 15, 1992, advocating a deemphasis of the regular education track for a greater functional skills approach. Although noting that the interaction of peers within the regular classroom should be a first consideration, the CEC cautions that the needs of students in general education sometimes differ from those with mental retardation. Thus, many of these students may need specialized programs such as community-based instruction and an emphasis on life skills and vocational training (T. E. C. Smith & Hilton, 1994).

Unfortunately, the intent of life skills instruction is sometimes misinterpreted. The December 13, 1993, issue of *U.S. News and World Report* contained the following criticism of special education:

> Special education classrooms become convenient places for teachers to send struggling students they don't want in their classrooms; academics, in such cases, takes a back seat. Indeed, special ed instructors often do as much social work—sometimes known as life skills—as teaching. In one special ed class in Ohio, students learned how to bake a frozen pizza in an oven. (Shapiro et al., 1993, p. 46)

Obviously, the writer of this article had little understanding of the many important benefits of such an activity to the students and jumped quickly to inappropriate conclusions without understanding the total situation and instructional goals established for these students.

Basic Concepts

In many respects, special education has been teaching functional skills to most of its students for a long time. As noted by G. M. Clark (1994)

> A functional curriculum approach is a way of delivering instructional content that focuses on the concepts and skills needed by all students with disabilities in the areas of personal-social, daily living, and occupational adjustment. What is considered a functional curriculum for any one student would be the content (concepts and skills) included in that student's curriculum or course of study that targets his or her current and future needs. These needs are (should be) based on a nondiscriminatory, functional assessment approach. (1994, p. 37)

 "A 'functional curriculum approach' has no restrictions regarding the type or location of instructional delivery."

Gary Clark (1994)

Functional skills curriculums are often associated with students with more severe learning difficulties. However, there is greater recognition today that this approach is also important for a wide variety of students, not only those with special learning needs but also those for whom the general curriculum holds limited value. As G. Clark noted, "Current functional curriculum models focus directly on knowledge and skills that need to be taught and leave the delivery procedures and instructional environment decisions to users" (1994, p. 37). Clark distinguishes between the terms *functional curriculum* and *a functional curriculum approach*. He describes the former as a document or written guide that is used for all students in a particular setting, whereas the latter has no restrictions regarding the type or location of instructional delivery. The functional curriculum approach places considerable responsibility on both general and special educators to make sure the functional content prescribed on the IEP is delivered effectively.

Many educators are currently examining ways that academic and functional skills can be offered together in integrated settings. With the current emphasis on inclusive education, instructional strategies such as individual planning, curriculum alignment, cooperative learning, and team teaching are being instituted to facilitate the successful integration of students with disabilities into general education settings (Field, LeRoy, & Rivera, 1994). Thus, functional skills really do not need to be taught in a separate curriculum, because they are important for all students to acquire.

A functional curriculum approach requires opportunities for community-based instructional experiences. As noted by J. Beck, Broers, Hogue, Shipstead, and Knowlton, commenting on the potential conflict between trying to both integrate students in regular classes and provide learning experiences in the community, the functional curriculum approach "can present conflicts of time and instructional priorities, or it can present a golden opportunity for collaborative planning between general and special education teachers as well as for inclusive education" (1994, p. 44). Chapters 11 and 13 refer to these authors' program of life skills instruction for kindergarten and other elementary students in inclusive settings.

Functional Curriculum Models and Materials

Educators can draw on several functional curriculum models and materials in adopting this approach. Table 2.1 lists some functional skills curricula and guides that are but a few of those available from various publishers and other sources. In Chapter 11, Teaching Personal–Social Skills, several social skills curricula are identified. The remainder of this section provides a brief description of two curriculum development models that are excellent efforts to provide functional curriculum programs.

A Top-Down Model for Curriculum Development

Cronin and Patton (1993) have conceptualized a four-stage model of curriculum development in the functional skills area. The four stages begin with: (a) an identification of the major adult domains and subdomains that students will need to function in as adults; (b) the identification of the major life demands or situations that most adults will encounter; (c) identification of specific life skills needed to meet each of the life demands; and (d) the organization of the instruction to successfully teach the functional life skills. Their model is presented in Figure 2.1. Each stage is briefly discussed next.

Stage 1: Adult Domains.   The six domains of the model are employment/education; home and family; leisure pursuits; community involvement; physical/emotional health; and personal responsibility and relationships. Each of the domains is broken down further into 23 subdomains to better organize the 147 life demands. For example, the domain of employment/education consists of the subdomains of general job skills, general education/training considerations, employment setting, and career refinement and reevaluation.

Stage 2: Major Life Demands.   The 147 life demands represent the events or activities encountered in everyday life by most persons. For example, the life demands for the subdomain of general job skills are seeking and securing a job, learning job skills, maintaining one's job, and understanding fundamental and legal issues.

Stage 3: Specific Life Skills.   Each of the life demands can be broken down into specific life skills. For example, for seeking and securing a job, specific life skills could include identifying marketable job skills and interests, identifying sources of job possibilities, and locating the site of the prospective job on the map. The skills identified in the author's guide represent only a sample of the many possibilities that may need to be considered for various students. These skills are the ones that will become the instructional objectives in the student's IEP or individualized transition plan (ITP).

Stage 4: Organize for Instruction.   Cronin and Patton (1993) recommend a continuum of options for teaching life skills. They note that life skills instruction can be delivered as a comprehensive grouping of specific life skills courses; in select topical life skills courses; in a single generic life skills course; as a portion of exiting courses dedicated to life skills topics; and/or infused into the established content of existing courses. In

TABLE 2.1   Examples of Functional Skills Curricula and Guides

Name	Publisher	Description
Adaptive Living Skills Curriculum (ALSC)	The Riverside Publishing Company	Used with the checklist of Adaptive Living Skills (ALS). 24 specific skill modules are organized into four domains: personal living skills, home living skills, community living skills, and employment skills.
The Life Skills Series I and II	PCI Educational Publishing	A fun-to-play board game format with blank draw cards, assessment booklets, and teacher's guide covering 16 areas such as eating skills, behavior skills, money skills, safety skills, survival skills, etc.
Functional Living Skills for Moderately and Severely Handicapped Individuals	Pro-Ed	Guidelines for teaching domestic skills, community mobility, social-interpersonal development leisure skills, and functional academics.
Independent Living Skills Curriculum	University of Oregon	Covers such topics as budgeting and bill paying, nutrition and menu planning, grocery shopping, personal hygiene, cooking, household management.
The Syracuse Community Referenced Curriculum Guide	Paul H. Brookes	Guide and manual for implementing the curriculum and teaching community living, academic, social, communication, and motor skills.
Tools for Transition	American Guidance Service	Comprehensive program including teacher's manual, student workbook, script booklets, blackline masters, videocassette.
Survival Skills System and Resource Guide for Transition Materials from School to Work	The Conover Company	Assessment and training programs for daily living covering such areas as vocational assessment, vocational exploration, career planning, social skills, and job seeking skills.
Top-Down Approach for Curriculum Development	Pro-Ed	See description in text.
Taxonomy of Community Living Skills	American Association on Mental Retardation	See description in text.

essence, the options become an infusion approach, an augmentation approach, or a course work approach. Their guide provides many excellent examples of how instructional delivery can be achieved in both the classroom and in community-based settings, conducting assessment activities, selecting appropriate materials, and implementing a life skills approach.

FIGURE 2.1   Top-down approach to curriculum development.
Note. From *Life Skills Instruction for All Students with Special Needs. A Practical Guide for Integrating Real-Life Content Into the Curriculum* (p. 10) by M. E. Cronin and J. R. Patton, 1993, Austin, TX: Pro-Ed. Copyright 1993 by Pro-Ed. Reprinted by permission.

Readers interested in learning more about this very well-conceived and organized approach are encouraged to refer to Cronin and Patton's publication entitled *Life Skills Instruction for All Students with Special Needs* (1993).

Taxonomy of Community Living Skills

Dever (1989) presents a list of all the things that people in the United States must be able to do to get through the day, the week, the month, the seasons, and the year. It lists every skill that people must perform in their daily lives, which range from obtaining a job to getting along with one's spouse to figuring out what to do when one is lost. It assumes that these are precisely the skills that people with mental retardation must acquire to take their places in the community. In other words, Dever's list is a taxonomy of the goals of instruction for persons with mental retardation, and its development constitutes the first step in the traditional concept of instruction: First, define the goals, and second, develop curricula leading to those goals. The taxonomy is most useful for those who develop curricula for persons with mental retardation (and perhaps for people with other disabilities as well).

Dever's taxonomy lists the skills in five domains: personal maintenance and development, homemaking and community life, vocational, leisure, and travel. These domains are shown in Figure 2.2, which depicts the individual in the center of the figure, with the community life domains surrounding the person. Connecting the person with the community is the travel domain.

The taxonomy is not a curriculum, but rather, a list of the end points for all curricula for persons with mental retardation. Traditionally, such curricula have included skills such as motor skills, communication skills, and academic skills. While these skills are important, they do not constitute end points for curricula, but rather, intermediate points that lie along the pathways to the ends. Therefore, these and other intermediate skills are not found in the taxonomy and must be derived by considering the goals and what a learner must do to attain them. This task must be carried out separately in each community because each community places unique performance demands on its residents. An example of the domain pertaining to homemaking and community life is illustrated in Figure 2.3.

Most of the goals listed in the taxonomy are not unique, because most have been available in instructional circles for a long time. However, they have never been together in one list, and in this respect, the taxonomy is unique.

Dever's taxonomy is also unique in the fact that it includes glitches as an instructional thrust within each domain. *Glitches* are the transient problems with which everyone must deal on a daily basis. For example, we all must deal with events like breaking our shoelaces in the morning and missing our transportation to work. Experience indicates that such problems pose major obstacles for persons with mental retardation, and if they do not learn to deal with them, they will not be able to live without assistance (personal communication, R. B. Dever, February 15, 1994).

FIGURE 2.2   Organization of the taxonomy of instruction goals for persons with mental retardation.

Note. From *Community Living Skills: A Taxonomy* by R. B. Dever, 1988, Washington, D.C.: American Association on Mental Retardation. Copyright 1988 by American Association on Mental Retardation. Reprinted by permission.

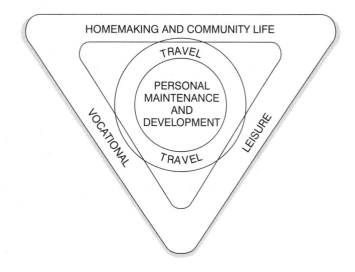

Domain H
Homemaking and Community Life

I. The learner will obtain living quarters

    A. Find appropriate living quarters

    B. Rent/buy living quarters

    C. Set up living quarters

II. The learner will follow community routines

    A. Keep living quarters neat and clean

    B. Keep fabrics neat and clean

    C. Maintain interior living quarters

    D. Maintain exterior of living quarters

    E. Respond to seasonal changes

    F. Follow home safety procedures

    G. Follows accident/emergency procedures

    H. Maintain foodstock

    I. Prepare and serve meals

    J. Budget money appropriately

    K. Pay bills

III. The learner will co-exist in a neighborhood and community

    A. Interact appropriately with community members

    B. Cope with inappropriate conduct of others

    C. Observe requirements of the law

    D. Carry out civic duties

IV. The learner will handle "glitches" in the home

    A. Cope with equipment breakdowns

    B. Cope with depletions of household supplies

    C. Cope with unexpected depletions of funds

    D. Cope with disruptions in routine

    E. Cope with sudden changes in the weather

FIGURE 2.3   Example of a domain from the taxonomy of instruction goals for persons with mental retardation.

Note. From *Community Living Skills: A Taxonomy* by R. B. Dever, 1988, Washington, D.C.: American Association on Mental Retardation. Copyright 1988 by American Association on Mental Retardation. Reprinted by permission.

TRANSITION EDUCATION

Several years ago, the Assistant Secretary of the U.S. Office of Special Education and Rehabilitative Services, Madeline Will, presented a keynote address, "Let Us Pause and Reflect—But Not Too Long," at the annual convention of the CEC. During her presentation, she recounted a speech she had heard from a state special education director, who proclaimed the need for a greater collaborative effort between special education, vocational education, and vocational rehabilitation. He highlighted in his speech a need for a greater focus on teaching students more substantial independent living skills, social and interpersonal skills, and vocational skills. He felt this was absolutely necessary if they were to have a chance to become productive adults.

 "Let us pause and reflect—but not too long!"

Madeline Will (1984a)

Ms. Will thought the special education director's speech was right on target with what needed to be done for the benefit of the students. The only problem was that the speech was given in 1969, and the needs he was talking about had still not been met in 1984, the year of Ms. Will's speech. As this is written in the mid-1990s, many schools have still not instituted a curriculum approach that will prepare students who have special learning needs to become productive, successful adults.

Ms. Will is given credit for introducing the transition movement. As noted previously, special education legislation in 1983, 1986, and 1990 established transition as an important component of the educational process for students with special learning needs. Much of what proponents of the "transition concept" advocate is not new. Rather, it is quite similar to much of what has been done by many special educators for years in work-study programs, life skills curriculums, vocational education, and the career education movement in the 1970s and thereafter. Indeed, as Halpern (1992) noted in his article entitled "Transition: Old Wine in New Bottles," we have been trying to design programs to prepare young people with disabilities for adult adjustment for over 30 years. We developed cooperative/work study programs in the 1960s, career education in the 1970s, and transition in the 1980s and 1990s. Halpern noted that "in the area of curriculum and instruction, we are still frequently deficient in what we teach, how we teach, and where we teach. Curriculum content still tends to focus too much on remedial academics and not enough on functional skills" (p. 206).

The Individuals with Disabilities Education Act (IDEA)—whose federal transition-related regulations became effective November 13, 1992—states that the IEP should contain statements of each public and participating agency's responsibilities or linkage before the student leaves school. A commitment by the participating agency regarding its financial commitment should also be included. The IEP must include a statement of the needed transition services in four areas of content: instruction, community involvement, work/vocational skills, and daily living skills and functional assessment if needed. Although originally the focus was on school-to-employment success, it soon changed to adult adjustment.

 "Transition planning requires a new way of looking at students and their educational programs. It demands that the IEP team create a vision of the student as an adult and plan for the adult environments the student will enter."

Arden Stephens (1992)

Transition education is not simply developing cooperative relationships with community agencies and recommending additional services for students and their families to contact. Transition requires three major components to be an effective effort by the schools: (a) a functional/career development curriculum; (b) a collaborative effort with employers, agencies, and parents; and (c) a postsecondary support and follow-up system until successful community/job adjustment occurs.

Thus, the transition approach requires the active participation of many educators working cooperatively, community-based instruction, collaboration with parents and agencies, follow-along and follow-up services, and a substantial functional curriculum beginning at the elementary level. The school must do as much as possible to prepare the student for employment and community living. If further services are necessary, community agencies will provide additional training and placement assistance if they believe the school has done its part. In most respects, the transition concept is remarkably similar to the career education concept—that is, a process that begins at the elementary level and continues into postschool services until the individual is successfully integrated into community life.

Readers interested in a greater knowledge base on all aspects of transition education are referred to two excellent textbooks: Rusch, Destefano, Chadsey-Rusch, Phelps, and Szymanski (1992), *Transition from School to Adult Life: Models, Linkages, and Policies*, and G. M. Clark and Kolstoe (1990), *Career Development and Transition Education for Adolescents with Disabilities*. More on the transition concept is presented in Chapter 8.

OUTCOME-BASED EDUCATION

Another school-restructuring effort that is presently being advocated for the educational system in general is that of outcome-based education (OBE). As with other innovations and proposals for change, there is considerable resistance to its tenets, not only from parts of the education sector but from many outspoken critics outside education.

"OBE is a philosophy which drives the way in which instruction is organized, delivered and evaluated in our schools. Its purposes are to equip all students with the knowledge, skills, and competencies needed for future success in school, in the workplace, and in advanced studies, and to establish conditions in schools which maximize achievement and success for all students."

Missouri Department of Elementary and Secondary Education (1992)

The OBE approach is designed so that student outcomes define the curriculum and the learning time depends on the needs of each student. Grades are based on the mastery of specified outcomes, and expectations are high for all students. Academic and vocational goals are interfaced. In the case of students with disabilities, adaptations and modifications can be addressed in the IEP process.

The OBE system has been developed so that learning happens by design not by accident. The system allows maximum freedom and flexibility to adapt instruction to

50

Point of View

Over the past 10 years, teachers and administrators, researchers, and state and federal policymakers have been concerned with transition practices. Yet, limited empirical research is available on what constitutes best transition practices. Thus, emerging practices are often labeled "best" without sufficient supporting research. The unfortunate consequence of this situation is the wholesale adoption of practices that may not be effective (Chadsey-Rusch & Rusch, in press).

In a series of investigations, the Transition Research Institute at Illinois has identified studies for which evidence is available to support the claim that the practices they describe are effective (Kohler, in preparation, 1993; Kohler, DeStefano, Wermuth, Grayson, & McGinty, in press; Rusch, Kohler, & Hughes, 1992). Based on an analysis of over 60 studies contributed by researchers in career, vocational, special, and rehabilitation education, and the Institute's research (Kohler, in preparation), five categories of transition practices appear to warrant the label "best practices." These practices include student-focused systematic transition planning, family involvement, interagency and interdisciplinary teaming and collaboration, program structure and attributes, and student involvement.

Student-Focused Systematic Transition Planning

Postschool outcomes will vary by students, but typical areas addressed in the transition plan include residential, employment, social and interpersonal, medical, recreational and leisure, mobility, community access, and overall well-being. Planning should determine the outcomes desired by the student (with family input), and a plan should be formulated to achieve those outcomes. Students must be provided an opportunity to assert and advocate for themselves, make their needs known, self-evaluate progress toward meeting their goals, and solve problems.

Family Involvement in Planning, Education, and Service Delivery

Families need help in identifying programs that will meet the needs and interests of their sons and daughters. Specifically, they need information about and access to the adult service system as well as other postschool options. They also need to be empowered to make decisions that enable them to facilitate their children's attainment of self-selected and valued outcomes after high school.

Interagency and Interdisciplinary Teaming, Collaboration, and Service Delivery

Because so many different people and agencies are often involved in facilitating the transition process, teaming and collaboration among the participants is critical. This includes interagency cooperation among state and local agencies. When personnel from different professions, advocacy groups, and agencies are collaborating in using a student- and family-centered approach, the result should be reduction of duplicative services, elimination of turf issues, and delivery of services that ensure desired outcomes. In addition to the student and family and educational personnel, the team may also include individuals associated with vocational and rehabilitation, employers, postsecondary representatives, friends, peers, and advocates.

Program Structure and Attributes

Practices that should be considered under the category of program structure and attributes include providing services within inclusive and integrated settings. Further, high schools should collect student follow-up data on which to base restructuring of existing practices to promote valued outcomes for all students.

Student Development

A critical component of the transition process involves teaching students skills and strategies that will enable them to reach their goals. Research conducted by Kohler (in preparation) identified six student development categories, including assessment, accommodation and support, career and vocational curricula, work experience, employment skills training, and life skills training. Within each category, a number of practices have been identified and rated for importance. Within each of the six categories, the following transition practices were rated highest and lowest.

Categories

1. Assessment
   Highest: Ongoing assessment
   Lowest: Traditional vocational assessment
2. Accommodation and support
   Highest: Identification and development of natural supports
   Lowest: Peer mentorship
3. Career and vocational curricula
   Highest: Career and vocational curricula infused throughout academic subject areas
   Lowest: Technical preparation curriculum options
4. Work experience
   Highest: Matching students to jobs
   Lowest: Job shadowing
5. Employment skills training
   Highest: Community-based vocational skills training
   Lowest: Longitudinal vocational training
6. Life skills training
   Highest: Self-determination skills training
   Lowest: Leisure skills training

The knowledge is now available to change the course of today's youths with disabilities in preparing for the challenges facing them tomorrow. If the practices that currently are validated by research could be introduced in every high school in the near future, drastic improvements in secondary special education effectiveness would be realized.

Clearly, a youth's high school experiences provide one of the cornerstones to ensuring success throughout life. Our failure to provide an effective high school experience results in personal shortcomings, including failure to attain additional education and training to help mold a career of personal choice.

Adapted in part from *Transition from School to Adulthood for Youths with Disabilities* by J. Chadsey-Rusch and F. R. Rusch, in press, New York: McGraw-Hill.

Frank R. Rusch is Professor of Special Education and Director, Transition Research Institute, at the University of Illinois, Urbana-Champaign.

Janis Chadsey-Rusch is Associate Professor of Special Education at the University of Illinois, Urbana-Champaign.

individual learning styles. Students can work at their own pace, and schools can develop their own approach to OBE because their is no state prescription. The OBE system offers teachers the opportunity to be more involved in local education planning and to decide how they will meet state standards (Minnesota Department of Education, 1990).

One of the first states to implement a statewide OBE approach was Minnesota, which adopted broad learner goals and program-level learner outcomes. School districts implementing the approach were required to conduct an assessment process that provided data to all decision makers regarding student progress. Some important assumptions in their approach follow: Content is prescribed in terms of learner outcomes (what is to be learned) rather than the course syllabus; criterion-referenced assessment rather than norm-referenced testing is used; and learning is the constant and time the variable, rather than the usual reverse. In this way, special education students should be able to function in general education if the stated outcomes are appropriate (Ysseldyke, Algozzine, & Thurlow, 1992).

It is difficult to conceive that there would be so much resistance to the intent of the OBE approach. But, as with other proposals for improving or fixing the system, detractors resist understanding the approach and considering its implementation. Several state and local educational agencies, such as this writer's own school district, have endorsed the approach and are working toward its implementation in their schools despite some opposition from traditionalists who want to retain the Carnegie Unit and its grading and competition orientation.

The preceding approaches for functional curriculum implementation have many common components and relate very closely to the career education approach, which was introduced in the 1970s, and the Life-Centered Career Education (LCCE) curriculum, presented in Chapter 3. The career education approach, the framework from which the LCCE curriculum was constructed, is presented next.

CAREER EDUCATION

This book advocates a career education curricular approach to meet the functional skills and transition needs of students with learning difficulties, as well as students in general. Thus, in this section, it is important to give the reader some background on the concept so that the close relationship of the career education approach to the functional skills, transition, and OBE movements can be understood.

What Is Career Education?

The term and concepts of career education were first introduced to the field as an educational reform by the U.S. Commissioner of Education Dr. Sidney Marland at a national educational convention to secondary school principals in Houston, Texas. Marland and other national leaders were extremely concerned about the high dropout rate in American schools and felt that one of the major reasons was the failure of the educational system to provide students with the knowledge and skills relevant to future adult functioning.

Career education can be conceived as

> an effort that begins no later than kindergarten and continues throughout the entire K–12 system for all pupils that aims to make *work—paid and/or unpaid,* a meaningful part of total lifestyle. Both its emphasis on beginning at the kindergarten level and its emphasis on using the concept of "work" as a basis for K–12 educational reform distinguish "career education" from other currently popular "schooling to employment" program proposals. (Hoyt, 1993, p. 36)

According to Hoyt, a major feature of career education is its emphasis on regarding the classroom as a workplace for both teachers and students. Thus, career development and the teaching–learning process are both emphasized.

 Career education—a lifelong process that infuses a careers emphasis in all subjects, grades K–12, including job training, apprenticeship programs, mentoring, career exploration, and the nonpaid work done as a family member, citizen, and leisure seeker.

Career education can be conceptualized as a progression of four interrelated stages: career awareness, career exploration, career preparation, and career assimilation.

* *Career awareness* begins at the elementary level and is intended to make students aware of the existence of work (paid and unpaid) and workers and how students will fit into the work-oriented society in the future. Career awareness relates to the self-awareness aspect of human development that is occurring during these years.
* *Career exploration,* the second stage, emphasized at the middle school/junior high level, is intended to help students explore their interests and abilities in relation to life-style and occupations. Students should learn to examine their own unique abilities and needs, be exposed to many hands-on experiences, and be given the opportunity to engage in several community-based experiences.
* *Career preparation,* emphasized at the high school level, is a period for career decision making and skills acquisition. Students should be able to identify their specific interests and aptitudes and the type of life-style that will meet these characteristics.
* *Career assimilation* is the transition of the student into postsecondary training and community-adjustment situations. The student should be able to engage in satisfying avocational, family, and civic/volunteer work activities as well as gaining paid employment. Continuing education and follow-up services will be needed by many students at this stage.

Hoyt (1987) identified these seven major goals of career education: (a) to help persons in career awareness/exploration/decision-making; (b) to equip persons with general employability/adaptability/promotability skills; (c) to promote and implement pri-

Career education involves learning appropriate behavior to get and keep a job.

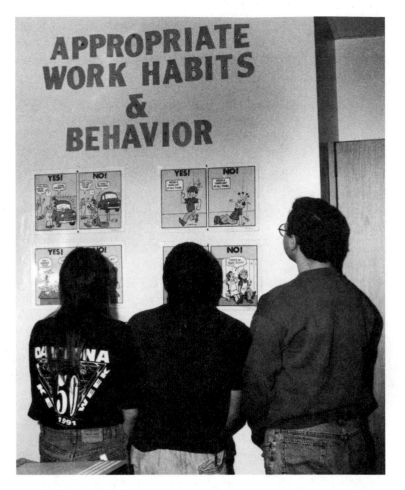

vate sector–education system partnerships; (d) to relate education and work so that better choices of both can be made; (e) to reform education by infusing a "careers" emphasis in classrooms; (f) to make work a meaningful part of the individual's total life-style; and (g) to reduce bias and stereotyping and thus protect freedom of choice. Some of these goals are similar to those advocated by the transition and school-to-work legislation.

 One's career consists of many roles—occupational, avocational, family, and civic.

Central to understanding the concept of career education is the concept of *career roles.* An individual's career is multifaceted; that is, it consists of several work roles that one engages in during one's lifetime. Persons who are in school are engaged in the primary career role of a student. When they leave school and become permanently

FIGURE 2.4 Illustration of the major work roles that comprise one's career.

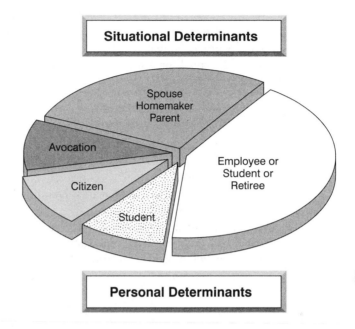

An illustration with "Situational Determinants" at the top and "Personal Determinants" at the bottom, with pie segments labeled: Spouse Homemaker Parent, Avocation, Citizen, Student, Employee or Student or Retiree.

employed, a job is a primary part of their career, but they will most likely also engage in the other career roles of family member (spouse, father/mother, etc.), community member who engages in volunteer work and other citizenship activities, and as a participant in productive leisure, recreational, and other avocational activities such as hobbies. Thus, *one's career is more than a job*, it is all the important work one does in a lifetime. Retirees no longer may receive compensation for the work they do, but they engage in many productive work activities in their later life that contribute to the benefit of themselves and others.

An illustration of the many career roles comprising one's career is presented in Figure 2.4. Note that a career is influenced by one's own personal determinants (e.g., intellectual and physical characteristics) and situational determinants (e.g., community, educational program). Thus, educators are an important determinant in the type of career and success their students will eventually experience.

A historical account of some major events that occurred to promote the adoption and implementation of career education throughout the country for both general and special education is presented below.

Historical Aspects

During the decade of the 1970s and into the 1980s, career education progressed rapidly in most states. When Dr. Marland returned to Houston in 1976 to keynote the first National Commissioner's Conference on Career Education, he reported that "probably never in our educational history has there been such enormous movement toward a central concept of reform over such a brief span of time" (Neil, 1977). At the Helen Keller Centennial Conference, Hoyt (1980) noted that the career education concept has survived for a full decade—three times as long as the typical educational reform movement.

Some of the major historical events having direct implications for individuals with learning difficulties follow:

- *In 1972 the federal Special Education Agency (then the Bureau of Education for the Handicapped) endorsed career education.* The bureau's director, Edwin Martin, declared career education a top priority and made funds available for a large number of curriculum and materials development projects, in-service and preservice training, and research studies.
- *In 1973 a National Topical Conference on Career Education for Exceptional Children and Youth was held.* This important conference, cosponsored by the CEC and the American Vocational Association (AVA), launched the concept of multidisciplinary career education, which received endorsement from professional teacher associations. The conference brought together legislators, lawyers, advocates, business and industry leaders, and an array of educators from various disciplines who presented service-delivery models, methods, and materials for providing career education.
- *In 1974 a U.S. Office of Career Education was officially established within the Office of Education.* Kenneth B. Hoyt was appointed the director of the U.S. Office of Career Education and established leadership for career education within the federal bureaucracy. The office wrote and disseminated important position papers and monographs, sponsored workshops and miniconferences with significant individuals and organizations, funded special projects, and promoted legislative and programmatic developments.
- *In 1975 the Bureau of Education for the Handicapped (BEH) sponsored a conference for nationally recognized leaders entitled "Research Needs Related to Career Education for the Handicapped."* After several days of intensive group interactions and problem solving, members of the conference established priorities that set BEH funding patterns. In St. Louis later that year, a small band of concerned educators organized a committee to establish a new division within the CEC that would focus on and promote implementation of career education. The new division was entitled the Division on Career Development (DCD). A similar group formed within the AVA became known as the National Association of Vocational Education Special Needs Personnel (NAVESNP).
- *In 1976 the Division on Career Development (DCD) was provisionally approved as the 12th division of the CEC by an overwhelming vote of its Board of Governors.* The division elected its officers and became a significant branch of CEC. Two other important events that occurred during 1976 were the first *National Commissioner's Conference on Career Education* and the passage of the *Vocational Education Amendments.* The Commissioner's Conference drew over 8,000 enthusiastic participants who exchanged ideas about providing career education to all age groups. The Vocational Amendments required that 10% of federal funds be allocated for students with disabilities as outlined in Public Law (PL) 94–142.

- *In 1977 the Career Education Implementation Incentive Act (PL 95–207) helped states infuse career education into school curricula so that it became part of ongoing local instruction and was not considered just vocational education.* Congress declared, "A major purpose of education is to prepare every individual for a career suitable to that individual's preference . . . career education should be an integral part of the Nation's education process which serves as preparation for work."

- *In 1978 the CEC issued a position paper supporting career education.* Career education was described as the "Totality of experiences through which one learns to live a meaningful, satisfying work life . . . provides the opportunity for children to learn, in the least restrictive environment possible, the academic, daily living, personal-social and occupational knowledges and specific vocational skills necessary for attaining their highest levels of economic, personal, and social fulfillment. The individual can obtain this fulfillment through work (both paid or unpaid) and in a variety of other social roles and personal life styles . . . student, citizen, volunteer, family member, and participant in meaningful leisure time activities."

- *In 1979 Special Institutes and the National Topical Conference on Career Education for Exceptional Individuals were held in conjunction with one another.* This conference, sponsored by the CEC and the institutes, brought together a wide variety of professional workers who demonstrated that career education could be infused and implemented into a variety of settings by numerous methods. Approximately 1,000 people weathered the blizzard of 1979 in St. Louis and expressed enthusiasm for continuing the conferences on a more frequent basis.

- *In 1980 the DCD started to form state DCD units.* The division's membership became the fastest growing in the CEC, and states began to organize at the grassroots level.

- *In 1981 the DCD conducted an International Conference on Career Development.* Despite severe nationwide financial constraints, the conference was highly successful and set into motion the planning of a similar conference that has been held every 2 years since. In addition, several states now conduct conferences at their state and local levels.

- *In 1982 the Career Education Incentive Act was repealed on October 1, and the Office of Career Education began the process of phasing out.* The Career Education Incentive Act was never intended to be renewed; instead, it was designed to provide federal incentive funds so that state and local districts could initiate career education and make it part of their educational effort. The Omnibus Budget Reconciliation Act of 1981 moved career education into the block grant program with the hope that most state departments of education and local school districts would make career education a priority and appropriate even more funds. Thus, the block grant approach could be a significant boon to the future of career education.

- *In 1983 two important career education national conferences were held.* The Second National Conference on Career Education was held June 13 to 16 in Louisville, Kentucky. Kenneth Hoyt, on leave from the federal government to serve as Distinguished Visiting Scholar at Embry-Riddle Aeronautical University, spearheaded its development. In polling career education proponents across the country, Hoyt found an overwhelming positive response to such a conference. The other important conference was sponsored by the CEC's DCD in cooperation with NAVESNP and the Special Needs Division of the AVA. It was held October 20 to 22 in Chicago. Both of these conferences demonstrated that interest and enthusiasm for career education were not waning but progressively growing (Brolin, 1983a, pp. 4–6).

Many other significant activities have had direct implications on the education of students and adults with disabilities. First, several early career education curriculum models were used successfully with special education students. These were the school-based model (G. M. Clark, 1979), experience-based model (Larson, 1981), career development model (Egelston-Dodd & DeCaro, 1982), and life-centered, competency-based model (Brolin, 1978). The reader is encouraged to review the models, curriculum, and in-service techniques discussed in these publications and other sources. Second, a substantial body of career education literature has become available in the form of journals, textbooks, monographs, curriculum guides, and teacher and student materials. Third, over 20 states have career education legislation, and most have career education coordinators and resource centers. The career education approach was endorsed by the Council of Chief State School Officers and many other influential groups (Hoyt, 1982).

In the decade of the 1990s, grass-roots support for career education continues. Wickwire noted that there are many career education-related

> programs and services in many schools, local and intermediate school districts, state departments of education, public and private community and state agencies, and by platforms and programs in professional and community associations such as the American Association for Career Education, National Career Education Leaders' Communication Network, National Association for Industry-Education Cooperation, California Career Education Association, Ohio Career Education Association, and Women's American ORT. (1993, p. 20)

Career education also continues to be a recognized need and viable approach for students with special learning problems and disabilities. The DCD, renamed the Division on Career Development and Transition (DCDT) in 1993, of the CEC conducts biannual international conferences that include many presentations on the topic, and the DCDT's journal, *Career Development for Exceptional Individuals*, contains many articles reporting on career education programs across the country. And, as noted earlier, much of what is being advocated today—namely, transition education, functional/life skills education, outcome-based education, and the like—closely approximate the basic tenets of career education.

Why Adopt the Career Education Approach?

There are many reasons why educators should seriously consider infusing the career education concept and curriculum approach in their classrooms and school district programs. Some of these were noted earlier in this chapter, for example, Hoyt's seven major goals. Listed next are some of the major benefits of a career education approach, such as the one described later in this chapter, for enhancing the future adult adjustment of students with special learning needs and problems.

- It emphasizes teaching students all the important skills they will need to function as a productive family and community member, participant in meaningful leisure and recreational pursuits, and for securing entry-level employment on a job that is satisfying to the person.
- It addresses each individual's total life-style and the quality of life that every individual is entitled to achieving.
- It provides a mechanism by which all students can be educated together so that more normal relationships can be experienced and where all ability levels can learn to appreciate each other.
- It requires all teachers and others to have a functional life skills focus and to learn more about the world of work, paid and unpaid.
- It opens the doors of the school to a wide variety of community representatives—employers, agencies, volunteers, and others.
- It encourages greater communications between school personnel and families and a more active partnership in teaching their children the skills they will need to become productive students, citizens, family members, and employees.
- It offers students a more interesting, motivating, and understandable purpose for their education because it directly relates the teaching–learning process to the real world and its requirements.
- It builds a greater sense of self-determination in the students by promoting each individual student's self-esteem and self-confidence.
- It enhances the learning of greater basic academic skills by infusing career education concepts into various general education subjects.
- It provides an overall framework for the total curriculum by virtue of its developmental, sequenced, and competency-based approach.

An additional benefit for special educators to consider is that career education is not specifically only a special education program; rather, it is an educational approach that many regular educators are implementing for general education students as well. Thus, career education is not just for students with special learning needs, it is for all students.

The preceding is not a complete list of the benefits that result from instituting a career education curriculum. More benefits, such as the requirement for a substantial community and family component, will become apparent throughout this book.

A School-Based Career Development and Transition Education Model for Adolescents with Disabilities (Clark's Model)

Career education is particularly important for persons with disabilities. Whether they are qualified for certain jobs or not, the evidence exists that *over half of the adults with disabilities will not be employed at any point in time.* Because most people need to work, these individuals could be productively engaged in *unpaid work activities* such as volunteer and other community work, important home responsibilities, and construc-

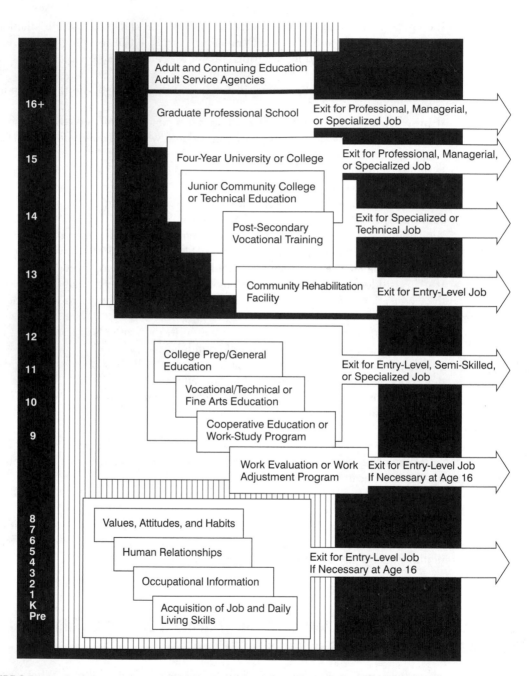

FIGURE 2.5   A school-based career development and transition education model for adolescents with handicaps.

Note. From *Career Development and Transition Education for Adolescents with Disabilities* by G. M. Clark & O. P. Kolstoe, 1990, Boston: Allyn & Bacon. Copyright 1990 by Allyn & Bacon. Reprinted with permission.

tive leisure and recreational activities that are of benefit to their general health and well-being. In this way, these individuals can experience and feel a sense of self-worth and dignity by contributing productively to their family, community, and themselves, even though they are unemployed. In the process, they can build further self-confidence, social, and functional skills that will enhance their chances for employment when the opportunity arises.

One career education curriculum model that has focused on students with disabilities has been a school-based conceptualization developed by G. M. Clark (1979). The focus of this model, as illustrated in Figure 2.5, is on life-career development beginning at the preschool level and continuing through adulthood. Four content elements comprise the model: (a) values, attitudes and habits; (b) human relationships; (c) occupational information; and (d) acquisition of job and daily living skills. Each of these is discussed briefly next.

The first component, values, attitudes, and habits, presents a major challenge in determining which should be taught. It is recommended that certain specific values that are known to be beneficial for individual and group success in life should be addressed. Examples are courage, honesty, cooperation, respect, courtesy, efficiency, reliability, and the like.

The second component, human relationships, focuses on purposeful instruction in the personal–social behaviors that are needed for acceptance by others, that is, friendliness and sociability. Thus, a deliberate effort must be made to teach students the skills that will help them to create and maintain positive human relationships.

The third component, occupational information, involves knowing about all those aspects of the world of work that are critical for individuals to know about. Topics in this area include occupational roles, occupational vocabulary, occupational alternatives, and basic information on the realities of the world of work.

The fourth component, acquisition of job and daily living skills, interfaces these two types of skills because of their close relationship to each other. For example, the basic skills needed for reading a recipe at home are similar to those needed by a cook in a restaurant. On the other hand, there are also many daily living skills one needs that are not directly related to job demands. Thus, these skills are very important to acquire for both personal usefulness and occupational functioning.

Interested readers can secure detailed information on this approach by obtaining the following publications: G. M. Clark (1979), *Career Education for the Handicapped Child in the Elementary Classroom* (Love Publishing, Denver) or G. M. Clark and Kolstoe (1990), *Career Development and Transition Education for Adolescents with Disabilities* (Allyn & Bacon).

FINAL COMMENTS

Students with special learning needs should receive an appropriate blend of academic and functional life skills content if they are to be prepared for a successful adult outcome. The career education approach presents a viable method for meeting the functional skills and transition needs of students with disabilities while helping to increase student motivation to learn the academic and enrichment subjects as well. The approach has evolved over a period of 25 years and is important for all students to receive as a part of their total educational program. For students with special learning needs, it lends itself very well to the current focus on inclusive education. A functional skills/career education approach holds the promise of generating much acceptance and adoption by regular class teachers because they realize that it is an excellent mechanism for stimulating all students to learn practical information and skills.

It is not easy for anyone to successfully compete in today's modern and complex society. Almost everyone is worried about finding a good job, making enough money, living on their own, having meaningful friendships, being able to engage in leisure and recreational pursuits of interest, and other areas of life that affect a satisfying life-style. To achieve success in life, one must be a competent person—to have the skills to compete and assimilate into the fiber of the community. We must give all students such an opportunity. To do this, schools must offer a curriculum that meets the contemporary needs of its community in regard to productive paid and unpaid work, living, and leisure pursuits.

With the career education approach, the emphasis is on the word *career*. Education focuses on what the student needs to learn to have a productive career as a family member, contributing citizen, employee, and as a participant in meaningful avocational activities such as hobbies, recreational endeavors, and other leisure-time activities. This is a "whole-person approach" to education.

In Chapter 3, a specific career education curriculum is presented and described. Although this curriculum was developed initially for students with special education needs, it was built on the general career education principles that have been developed for all students. Thus, its tenets and application are relevant for all students.

ACTIVITIES

1. In this chapter, four related curriculum approaches were presented. What is the possible contribution of each in helping you to conceptualize a curriculum effort that could result in preparing your students for a more successful adult adjustment?

2. Identify all the major skills or competencies you believe your students should be taught in a K–12 curricular effort so that by the time they leave the educational setting they will be well equipped to secure satisfying employment and function independently and interpersonally in their home and community activities.

Chapter 3

Life-Centered Career Education Curriculum

Preliminary Questions About the Topic

1. What important components or conditions are needed for an effective curriculum model?
2. Under what learning conditions can most students, especially those with special learning needs, be most effectively taught?
3. Besides the basic academic subjects, what curriculum areas or domains should be included in a schools curriculum?
4. What are the three major instructional settings where students need to be taught?
5. How long do the most implemented educational innovations generally last?
6. What is meant by the term *work personality,* and when should educators give attention to its development in their students?
7. What are the four stages of development or learning that need to be addressed in organizing and delivering instruction in a career education program?
8. What daily living skills are important for students to learn in their educational program?
9. What personal-social skills are critical for students to learn?
10. What occupational knowledge and skills should students learn before leaving the school program?

hapter 2 presented a strong case for infusing a substantial functional skills/career development component into the regular curriculum (K–12+) to better ensure that students make a successful transition from school to employment and community living. But we can't just theorize about the need, we must have an organized framework on which such a curriculum thrust can be instituted. Such a framework, or educational system, must be flexible so that various methods and materials can be integrated into its design to meet the needs of a diverse group of students.

This chapter presents and explains the *Life-Centered Career Education (LCCE) Curriculum*. The vast majority of educational innovations last only 3 to 5 years; the LCCE curriculum has evolved and expanded over a 20-year period. In fact, the LCCE curriculum is more widely used throughout the country today than ever. LCCE is one curriculum that embraces current, progressive educational thinking, looking beyond the long-term tradition of the Carnegie Units and the narrow core curriculum concepts that have prevailed for decades.

In the following sections, the LCCE curriculum model and its major components, its curriculum and training materials, and its rationale for adoption are presented.

THE LCCE CURRICULUM MODEL

Unlike the traditional educational approach in which students are taught knowledge for knowledge's sake through the academic and enrichment subjects of reading, spelling, mathematics, history, art, chemistry, economics, and others, the LCCE curriculum approach is to focus on *the skills that the individual must know to become a more effective person.* In other words, the skills needed to *function* as a productive worker and citizen in the home and community. LCCE is a direct result of the career education movement and models of the 1970s. Considerable research and demonstration efforts at numerous school districts have contributed to its development and refinement over more than 20 years, resulting in a widely adopted and implemented curricular effort that mirrors the recognized need for an outcome-based, functional skills emphasis for students in American schools.

For years it has been demonstrated that a large proportion of students, including those with special learning needs, learn best if the material presented is practical, familiar, hands-on, and meaningfully related to the real world. Esoteric, theoretical, and unpractical instruction is not very effective with these students. Most students who are given an appropriate blend of functional skills with general academic instruction will be more motivated to learn the academic and functional skills they need for living and working in their communities. At least, this is the LCCE philosophy.

The LCCE model incorporates the basic tenets of the career education approach, which were described in Chapter 2. In summary, these tenets are the broader view of the term *career*, the four stages of career development, the substantial involvement of the students' families and community resources, and 22 major life skill competencies that are deemed critical for students to learn by the time they leave school to succeed as adults. The LCCE curriculum/transition model is presented in Figure 3.1.

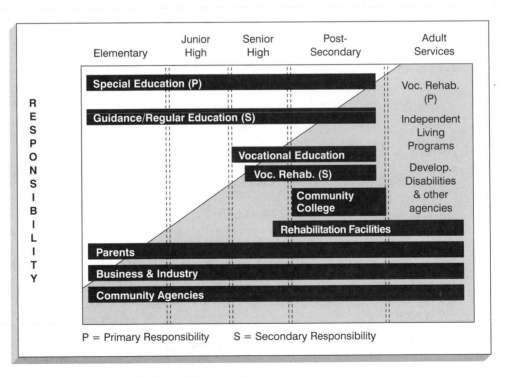

FIGURE 3.1   Curriculum/LCCE transition model.

Note. From *Life Centered Career Education: Professional Development Activity Book* (p. 43) by The Council for Exceptional Children, 1993. Reston, VA: The Council for Exceptional Children. Copyright 1993 by The Council for Exceptional Children. Reprinted by permission.

LCCE is a functional skills/transition curriculum built on the concepts of career development. Figure 3.1 illustrates how the LCCE competencies and the four stages of career development can be integrated into the scope and sequence of an academically based curriculum. The model promotes the concept of infusion—that is, teaching the competencies in regular class subjects whenever possible. As Figure 3.1 shows, the emphasis on the LCCE functional skills (the gray area) should increase at the higher grade levels, although many career awareness and exploration activities should be taught at the elementary levels. The lower half of the graphic illustrates when parents, employers, and agencies should be involved with educators throughout the curriculum effort. The collaboration among all these groups is a key element of the LCCE approach.

The LCCE functional skills curriculum approach recognizes the importance of academic skills as a basic foundation for the student's education. It also recognizes, as noted previously, the importance of infusing functional skill instruction in the areas of daily living, personal-social, and occupational guidance and preparation into the overall curriculum, K–12+, and into most academic subjects, to enhance the students' learning in all four areas. Figure 3.2 presents the three functional skills curriculum areas, 22 competencies, and the 97 subcompetencies comprising the LCCE curriculum.

As noted previously, the LCCE curriculum model consists of four major components: (1) a focus on three curriculum areas, consisting of 22 major competencies and 97 subcompetencies; (2) instruction that is provided in three settings—school, home, and community; (3) a K–12 scope and sequence consisting of four stages of career development or learning; and (4) a focus on teaching the student all the important work roles that constitute a career—employee, family member, citizen/volunteer, and productive use of recreational and leisure time activities such as hobbies. Each of the four components is next.

Component 1: The Competencies

All 22 competencies and the 97 subcompetencies of the LCCE have been subjected to rigorous review by hundreds of school personnel who have agreed that the competencies reflect major outcomes required for successful community living and working. The LCCE model has been described as an *adult adjustment approach* because it focuses on skills and competencies needed for a successful career (G. M. Clark & White, 1980). The following discussion briefly describes the three curriculum areas and the 22 competencies.

Daily Living Skills

The competencies under the daily living skills category include the following: (1) managing personal finances; (2) selecting and managing a household; (3) caring for personal needs; (4) raising children and meeting marriage responsibilities; (5) buying, preparing, and consuming food; (6) buying and caring for clothing; (7) exhibiting responsible citizenship; (8) using recreational facilities and managing leisure time; and (9) getting

Point of View

Public education continues to be thrust into the spotlight and scrutinized with regard to remediation and accountability. Often, as educators, we look beyond the immediate and grasp for new and well-intended solutions to redeem the perception of quality. Our mission, however, is to educate our youth with those qualities that lead to a successful, productive citizenry. Such concepts as applied education, academic integration, technical preparation, career awareness, and others give us some insight into the matrix of purposeful, functional skills. Therefore, any curricular attempt to focus functional academics, coupled with enhancing the opportunity for students to enter adulthood with certain basic competencies, becomes a candidate for the illuminating spotlight.

A survey conducted on a local level disclosed that 80% of students with disabilities are unemployed 2 years after leaving high school. The potential for correcting this grim situation is certainly within our grasp. A partial solution resides in providing our children with a curriculum that will introduce them to a systematic program that focuses on the realities and responsibilities they will encounter during their transition from school into the world of work. It is common knowledge among special educators that our graduates with disabilities tend to fail on the job primarily because they lack the skills related to job performance.

Exclusively addressing this single dimension will not, however, address the total student's needs. The nature of the problem is much broader and encompasses such areas as daily living skills, personal–social skills, as well as occupational guidance and preparation. If we are to truly provide our students an opportunity to gain meaningful employment and to attain meaningful levels of economic, social, and personal fulfillment, schools must incorporate career education programs. Such programs must involve the child's family, the school, and the community. For the program to be most effective, it must begin in elementary school and continue through middle school and high school. Such programs must have the total support of the staff, administration, and local board of education. Without this commitment, any career education effort will be fragmented, and results will fall short of the school's expectations.

The LCCE program has far surpassed our expectations. We have incorporated it successfully into our total curricular program and find that it has important applications for all students. Through the joint efforts of our professional staff, administration, board of education, families, and community, our students are experiencing higher levels of independence and enjoying life to its fullest.

Richard McMullin is the Superintendent in the North St. Francois County R-1 School District, Bonne Terre–Desloge, Missouri.

Edward Garrigan is the Assistant Superintendent in the North St. Francois County R-I School District, Bonne Terre–Desloge, Missouri and supervises the district's special education programs.

Curriculum Area	Competency	Subcompetency: The student will be able to:	
DAILY LIVING SKILLS	1. Managing Personal Finances	1. Count money & make correct change	2. Make responsible expenditures
	2. Selecting & Managing a Household	7. Maintain home exterior/interior	8. Use basic appliances and tools
	3. Caring for Personal Needs	12. Demonstrate knowledge of physical fitness, nutrition & weight	13. Exhibit proper grooming & hygiene
	4. Raising Children & Meeting Marriage Responsibilities	17. Demonstrate physical care for raising children	18. Know psychological aspects of raising children
	5. Buying, Preparing & Consuming Food	20. Purchase food	21. Clean food preparation areas
	6. Buying & Caring for Clothing	26. Wash/clean clothing	27. Purchase clothing
	7. Exhibiting Responsible Citizenship	29. Demonstrate knowledge of civil rights & responsibilities	30. Know nature of local, state & federal governments
	8. Utilizing Recreational Facilities & Engaging in Leisure	33. Demonstrate knowledge of available community resources	34. Choose & plan activities
	9. Getting Around the Community	38. Demonstrate knowledge of traffic rules & safety	39. Demonstrate knowledge & use of various means of transportation
PERSONAL-SOCIAL SKILLS	10. Achieving Self-Awareness	42. Identify physical & psychological needs	43. Identify interests & abilities
	11. Acquiring Self-Confidence	46. Express feelings of self-worth	47. Describe others' perception of self
	12. Achieving Socially Responsible Behavior—Community	51. Develop respect for the rights & properties of others	52. Recognize authority & follow instructions
	13. Maintaining Good Interpersonal Skills	56. Demonstrate listening & responding skills	57. Establish & maintain close relationships
	14. Achieving Independence	59. Strive toward self-actualization	60. Demonstrate self-organization
	15. Making Adequate Decisions	62. Locate & utilize sources of assistance	63. Anticipate consequences
	16. Communicating with Others	67. Recognize & respond to emergency situations	68. Communicate with understanding
OCCUPATIONAL GUIDANCE AND PREPARATION	17. Knowing & Exploring Occupational Possibilities	70. Identify remunerative aspects of work	71. Locate sources of occupational & training information
	18. Selecting & Planning Occupational Choices	76. Make realistic occupational choices	77. Identify requirements of appropriate & available jobs
	19. Exhibiting Appropriate Work Habits & Behaviors	81. Follow directions & observe regulations	82. Recognize importance of attendance & punctuality
	20. Seeking, Securing & Maintaining Employment	88. Search for a job	89. Apply for a job
	21. Exhibiting Sufficient Physical-Manual Skills	94. Demonstrate stamina & endurance	95. Demonstrate satisfactory balance & coordination
	22. Obtaining Specific Occupational Skills		

FIGURE 3.2 Life-centered career education competencies.

Note. From *Life Centered Career Education: A Competency-Based Approach* (4th ed., pp. 12–13) by D. E. Brolin, 1993. Reston, VA: The Council for Exceptional Children. Copyright 1993 by The Council for Exceptional Children. Reprinted by permission.

3. Keep basic financial records	4. Calculate & pay taxes	5. Use credit responsibly	6. Use banking services	
9. Select adequate housing	10. Set up household	11. Maintain home grounds		
14. Dress appropriately	15. Demonstrate knowledge of common illness, prevention & treatment	16. Practice personal safety		
19. Demonstrate marriage responsibilities				
22. Store food	23. Prepare meals	24. Demonstrate appropriate eating habits	25. Plan/eat balanced meals	
28. Iron, mend & store clothing				
31. Demonstrate knowledge of the law & ability to follow the law	32. Demonstrate knowledge of citizen rights & responsibilities			
35. Demonstrate knowledge of the value of recreation	36. Engage in group & individual activities	37. Plan vacation time		
40. Find way around the community	41. Drive a car			
44. Identify emotions	45. Demonstrate knowledge of physical self			
48. Accept and give praise	49. Accept & give criticism	50. Develop confidence in oneself		
53. Demonstrate appropriate behavior in public places	54. Know important character traits	55. Recognize personal roles		
58. Make & maintain friendships				
61. Demonstrate awareness of how one's behavior affects others				
64. Develop & evaluate alternatives	65. Recognize nature of a problem	66. Develop goal-seeking behavior		
69. Know subtleties of communication				
72. Identify personal values met through work	73. Identify societal values met through work	74. Classify jobs into occupational categories	75. Investigate local occupational & training opportunities	
78. Identify occupational aptitudes	79. Identify major occupational interests	80. Identify major occupaitonal needs		
83. Recognize importance of supervision	84. Demonstrate knowledge of occupational safety	85. Work with others	86. Meet demands for quality work	87. Work at a satisfactory rate
90. Interview for a job	91. Know know to maintain post-school occupational adjustment	92. Demonstrate knowledge of competitive standards	93. Know how to adjust to changes in employment	
96. Demonstrate manual dexterity	97. Demonstrate sensory discrimination			
There are no specific subcompetencies as they depend on skill being taught				

FIGURE 3.2 *continued*

around the community. These competencies are directly related to the avocational, family, and civic roles that were mentioned earlier in the chapter. But the attainment of daily living skills can lead to many occupational possibilities. The students must learn these competencies to survive in today's fast-moving society. Educators currently do not emphasize daily living skills enough, because they assume that these competencies will be learned incidentally in the home and elsewhere. For most students this typically does not happen. The school therefore must make a deliberate effort to provide this instruction.

 Daily living skills and interests lead to job possibilities such as clerk, stockperson, nursing aide, child-care worker, grocer, cook, maintenance worker, forklift operator, food service worker, housekeeper, press cleaner, laundry worker, furniture upholster, photographic finisher, and barber.

Personal–Social Skills

The competencies under the personal–social skills category include the following: (10) achieving self-awareness; (11) acquiring self-confidence; (12) achieving socially responsible behavior; (13) maintaining good interpersonal skills; (14) achieving independence; (15) achieving problem-solving skills: and (16) communicating with others. Lack of the personal–social skills contributes to the major downfall of all individuals in work and other settings—no matter how competent the individual may be in other skills. Curricular emphasis on these competencies is critical.

 Personal-social skills are critical for successful performance on most jobs. Skills in this area include getting along with others, taking criticism, accepting supervision, making vocational decisions, knowing proper behavior, respecting the rights of others, following directions, and being honest and loyal.

Occupational Skills

The competencies in occupational skills category include the following: (17) knowing and exploring occupational possibilities; (18) selecting and planning occupational choices; (19) exhibiting appropriate work habits and behaviors; (20) seeking, securing, and maintaining employment; (21) exhibiting physical and manual skills; and (22) obtaining a specific occupational skill. Occupational skills are most often associated with *career education*. They deserve major curricular emphasis; however, because the occupational skills are subsumed under daily living and personal-social skills, the three curriculum areas are inextricably linked. The first two occupational competencies, awareness of occupational possibilities and making appropriate occupational choices, should be taught within a broad context; educators should not pressure the student into making a premature occupational choice. Knowing and exploring occupational possibilities, exhibiting appropriate work habits and behavior, and developing physical and manual skills should be tackled almost immediately after the student enters school. The senior high school is the appropriate time for emphasizing the remaining three competencies.

Occupational skills development begins in the elementary school and depends on substantial career awareness and career exploration activities, experiences, instruction, and assessment.

In presenting this competency-based approach I do not intended to deemphasize the importance of basic academic instruction. Students should still be taught reading, mathematics, social studies, and science, but a specific purpose should underlie the traditional practice of bringing an individual to a certain grade level at the end of a year or teaching the student to master some kind of physical activity. In this instance, the specific purpose is the development of 22 important life-sustaining competencies, and every teacher at every grade level has a stake in each student's career development.

Component 2: School, Family, and Community Relationships

A competency-based curriculum involves changes in the roles of teacher and counselor and requires more involvement from family and community agencies, including the business and industrial sector. Students should also be allowed to express their opinions and must be given the opportunity to influence the direction of the curriculum.

School Personnel

All members of the school community should share responsibility for providing career education and competency development for students. Unfortunately, little is done to ensure that this responsibility is applied systematically. Many educators wish to hold on to the traditional mode of imparting knowledge. They concentrate on grade-level content and manipulate the classroom environment for that purpose (E. J. Moore & Gysbers, 1972). Career education responsibilities must be clearly delineated and assumed by various personnel. Many regular classroom teachers have opposed mainstreaming because they feel that students with disabilities will be pushed on them. These teachers must be shown that they have important roles in teaching knowledge, information, and *skills* that will result in a successful career for the student in later years. The school administration must provide special considerations for teachers and in-service personnel assuming who teach students with disabilities.

Regular class teachers are important in helping students develop feelings of self-worth and competence by providing situations where each student can learn and be accepted by other class members. Almost every regular class teacher can help the student develop at least one competency. Home economics and industrial arts teachers are particularly significant in helping students acquire daily living and occupational skills, while counselors are integral helpers in the personal–social and occupational guidance areas. Table 3.1 presents examples of the types of school personnel who could assist the student in learning various competencies at the elementary, middle school/junior high, and high school levels.

TABLE 3.1   Possible LCCE Competency Instructional Subject Areas

Competency	Elementary	Middle School/ Junior High	Senior High
Daily Living Skills			
1. Managing personal finances	Math, language, reading	Business, math	Home economics, math
2. Selecting & managing a household	Language, social studies	Home economics, vocational	Home economics
3. Caring for personal needs	Science, health	Home economics, health	Home economics
4. Raising children & meeting marriage responsibilities	Health	Home economics	Home economics
5. Buying, preparing & consuming food	Reading, language	Home economics	Home economics
6. Buying & caring for clothing	Reading, language	Home economics	Home economics
7. Exhibiting responsible citizenship	Social studies	Social studies, music	Social studies, music
8. Utilizing recreational facilities & engaging in leisure	Health, physical education	Physical education, art, music, counselors	Physical education, art, music, counselors
9. Getting around the community	Health, science	Home economics	Driver's education
Personal-Social Skills			
10. Achieving self-awareness	Language, social studies	Music, physical education, counselors	Art, music, counselors
11. Acquiring self-confidence	Health, science	Art, music, physical education, home economics, counselors	Physical education, counselors, social studies, art, vocational education, music

TABLE 3.1 *continued*

Competency	Elementary	Middle School/ Junior High	Senior High
Personal-Social Skills			
12. Achieving socially responsible behavior— community	Social studies, language	Physical education, counselors	Social studies, music
13. Maintaining good interpersonal skills	Language, social studies	Counselors	Music, counselors
14. Achieving independence	Social studies, language	Counselors	Counselors
15. Making adequate decisions	Language, social studies	Math, counselors	Science, counselors
16. Communicating with others	Language, reading	Language arts, music, speech, physical education	Language arts, speech, music, art
Occupational Skills			
17. Knowing and exploring occupational possibilities	Reading, social studies	Vocational education, home economics, counselors	Counselors
18. Selecting and planning occupational choices	Language, social studies	Business, vocational education, home economics	Counselors
19. Exhibiting appropriate work habits & behaviors	Science, art	Vocational education, math, home economics, art	Home economics, vocational education, music
20. Seeking, securing & maintaining employment	Language, social studies	Counselors	Counselors
21. Exhibiting sufficient physical–manual skills	Art, physical education	Vocational education, home economics	Vocational education, home economics
22. Obtaining specific occupational skills	Social studies, art, music	Vocational education, home economics	Vocational education, home economics

Special education teachers assume a different role within this competency-based career education curriculum. The special educator becomes more of a consultant or advisor to other school personnel, parents, and community agencies and industries by coordinating services and integrating the contributions that the school, community, and family can make in meeting each student's career development needs. They will become increasingly important as resource personnel to the regular classroom teachers who will need in-service assistance; methods and materials consultation; modification and materials development assistance; and relevant information on the students' basic academic skills, values, and attitudes. Special classroom instruction may still be needed for many students who cannot be appropriately educated in regular classes. The special educator should monitor each student's progress and should also direct the energies of the school staff to ensure that the student acquires these competencies in as inclusive setting as possible.

Family

The individual's family is extremely important in career development. The family can provide meaningful assistance to school efforts by providing the student with hands-on experiences, positive reinforcement for achievements, a secure psychological environment, community experiences and involvements, participation in family decision making, specific job tasks around the house, an atmosphere that encourages meaningful leisure and recreational pursuits, and other career development opportunities. The family must work closely with the school personnel to coordinate their efforts sequentially and consistently, must assist in the development of community resources, must assist as a volunteer or aide in school settings and functions, and must serve on advisory and action committees related to career education. Family members can help schools in public relations, fund-raising, resource development, and other efforts needed to enhance school operations. Chapter 4 is devoted to family involvement and pursues more information relevant to these ideas.

Community Involvement

A wide array of agencies and organizations can assist school personnel and families in helping the student acquire the 22 career education competencies. Agencies, organizations, and civic clubs such as YMCA, YWCA, Red Cross, League of Women Voters, Jaycees, Kiwanis, Rotary, Chamber of Commerce, Planned Parenthood, Parks and Recreation, Public Health, 4–H, Boy Scouts, churches, libraries, Girl Scouts, and Campfire, Inc., are all resources that can be used to help students acquire daily living skills and career education experiences. Groups that may help students to acquire personal–social skills include many of the preceding organizations as well as state employment services and mental health, counseling, and university organizations. Occupational skills can be developed by using a wide variety of agencies and organizations including vocational rehabilitation and state employment services, community action programs, Veterans Administration, rehabilitation workshops, and the Governor's Committee on Employment of the People with Disabilities. Business, industry, and labor also offer a wealth of assistance: banks, grocery stores, department stores, factories, insurance companies, repair shops, gas stations, loan companies, and many other businesses can be used effectively in planning daily living and occupational learning activities. Chapters 5 and 6 will provide more detailed information and guidance in this area.

The interaction and interface of these three curriculum areas to career development cannot be overemphasized. It will take considerable time and effort to develop these relationships, the benefits will be obvious, and the career education of students will be more fully realized.

Component 3: Stages of Career Development and Learning

Career education consists of several different stages or phases. As illustrated in Figure 3.3, the LCCE model includes four stages of career development: career *awareness*, career *exploration*, career *preparation*, and career *assimilation*. Because students with severe disabilities need more time to develop the skills required for successful career functioning, these stages will begin earlier and last longer for these individuals.

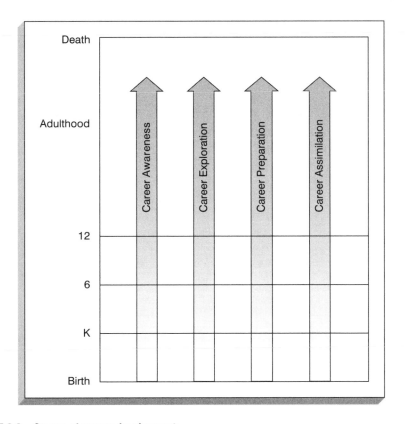

FIGURE 3.3   Stages of career development.

Career Awareness

During the elementary years, career awareness should be emphasized. When learning daily living skills, students must become aware of how to manage and use money appropriately, how to manage and maintain a home, how to take care of personal needs properly, how to assume responsibility for raising children and living as a family, how to purchase and prepare food, and how to select and care for clothing. In addition, students will learn how to assume civic responsibilities and roles, how to fulfill interests and needs by becoming aware of recreation and leisure activities, and how to achieve greater mobility in the community.

Personal–social skills will help students develop a sense of self-worth and confidence as well as help them become more aware of their feelings, values, and potentials. In addition, students will develop communication skills such as reading, writing, and speaking. They will become more aware of socially desirable behavior and learn how to interact appropriately with others. As students gain confidence, they will develop independent relationships. Finally, personal–social skills will enhance students' awareness of how to approach and solve problems and will teach them to think independently.

As they acquire occupational skills, students will begin to develop positive attitudes about work. They will begin seeing themselves as potential workers and will begin to explore different types of jobs and their requirements. As they become more aware of work habits and behaviors needed for success in work, they will develop a work personality based on a unique set of needs and physical and manual skills.

Attitude, information, and self-understanding are three main elements of career awareness. Attitudes are the foundation on which the career education structure is built. Young children must learn that people make many conscious efforts at producing some benefit for themselves and others, including working. They can learn that people work for many reasons: economic, psychological, and societal. They need to understand that work can provide a major source of personal identification and satisfaction. Information helps the student learn the variety of ways people earn a living and how they use their time in avocational, leisure, and other life pursuits. Self-understanding enhances the development of students' careers by making them more aware of their relationship to the world and by helping them identify their eventual adult roles (Kolstoe, 1976).

Career awareness is not that difficult to infuse into the elementary curriculum. To a limited extent, most teachers already discuss various careers such as police officer, fire fighter, mail carrier, doctor, nurse, and homemaker. But the career education concept requires purposeful discussion of careers so that students become aware of career aspects in relation to themselves. Like any other form of education, career education must be designed sequentially, so that whatever happens at each grade level is built on and leads toward competency attainment.

Career Exploration

Career exploration begins at the elementary level, but it should receive greater emphasis during the middle school/junior high school years. During this phase, students begin a more careful self-examination of their unique abilities and needs in relation to the world of work, avocational interests, leisure and recreational pursuits, and all other roles related to career development. It is important for school personnel to design curriculum and instructional experiences so that self-exploration can occur. This process should include the use of a variety of techniques, experiences, and settings relevant to each individual. The incorporation of community resources is crucial during this stage of career development.

Daily living skills instruction should encourage students to explore various methods of managing personal finances, selecting and managing a home, caring for various personal needs, child-rearing and family living methods, buying and preparing nutritious food, buying and caring for clothing, engaging in civic activities, pursuing recreation and leisure activities, and trying various modes of community transportation. These explorations can be personalized to each individual student's emerging set of attitudes, values, and needs by using various courses, field experiences, clubs and organizations, home activities, and community involvements such as part-time jobs, hobbies, reading, and conversation.

Personal–social skills exploration should help students begin to seriously question who they are and assist them in leaving the child status they assumed during the elementary years. Guidance and counseling help students identify unique abilities, needs, and interests as they relate to career development. Individual and group counseling activities such as role playing, modeling, values clarification, and other inter- and intrapersonal activities should be available to help students gain better understanding of themselves and others.

Occupational skills preparation helps students to examine carefully several occupational clusters and engage in a variety of hands-on experiences, both in and out of school. To fully understand characteristics of various occupational possibilities, students need to observe and analyze them firsthand, try them out in simulated situations, and talk to employers about various aspects of jobs and work. To select and begin planning tentative occupational choices, students will need assistance from guidance personnel so they can receive a thorough assessment of their vocational aptitudes, interests, and needs. At this time, occupational choices can be only generally related to any specific area, because the student's interest and needs will change during high school. Students should be encouraged to try various work samples, simulated job tasks, and community jobs, and should develop work habits and behaviors, physical and manual skills, and other competencies needed in the workplace. Prevocational classes such as industrial arts and home economics will be beneficial during the junior high school years.

Career exploration is the link between career awareness and career preparation. During this stage, young students begin to think seriously about their particular set of aptitudes, interests, and needs and how these can be directed toward meaningful and successful adult roles. Sequential exploration activities and experiences should be planned so that by the time students are ready for high school, a more highly individualized educational plan can be designed, and a more relevant career preparation program can be offered.

Career Preparation

Career preparation is not solely confined to one period of schooling. Like other stages of career development, it begins in the early grades and continues throughout life. But for most individuals, particularly for those who do not go on to postsecondary training, the high school years are critical for reaching the necessary level of competence in the three curriculum areas that compose the 22 life career development competencies.

Educators should monitor and promote a curriculum that will help students master the nine competencies involved in daily living skills. Home economics, math, business, health, driver's education, social studies, and physical education will help students attain these nine competencies.

If development of personal–social skills has been satisfactory at the elementary and junior high levels, students are ready to learn and practice those personal–social skills needed for community living and working. The professional should identify any specific difficulties that students may have in learning these seven competencies and design procedures for their remediation. This may be accomplished by consulting with classroom teachers on procedures for remediating the difficulty, by altering classroom instruction to fit the needs of students, or by using individual and group counseling. Counseling, role playing, modeling, values clarification, and other techniques are effective with most students. Professionals should perceive each student as an independent and nearly adult-functioning individual who is to be listened to and respected. Their job is to help students identify specific interests and aptitudes and help them find an effective life-style.

Development of occupational skills can be more specifically directed toward the student's tentative career choices. Students should be able to select from a variety of vocational courses and community job experiences that fit the aptitudes, interests, and abilities composing their work personality. If students have acquired work habits and behaviors, physical or manual skills, and work values and attitudes during the elementary and junior high years, they can begin to select an appropriate occupational area and develop specific occupational skills. However, this may be counterproductive if students are forced into making a premature career decision. Some students may choose to enter college or other postsecondary programs. In the process of learning a specific occupational skill, students also acquire a much more positive self-concept, gain confidence in their ability to learn a specific skill, and master other personal–social skills. Guidance and special education workers are responsible for teaching students how to seek, secure, and maintain employment. This competency should be emphasized throughout the high school program.

Because experience will be a major part of career preparation, students should be encouraged to use community resources. Intensive vocational assessment is also necessary to help students test the realism of their career choices and training needs. Finally, many students may need more than the traditional amount of time to prepare for a successful career and should be given additional time in either the high school or postsecondary setting.

Career Assimilation

Career assimilation can occur during the secondary or postsecondary years, depending on the student's readiness for this stage of career development. Work experience programs give students the opportunity to be placed in an actual job as if they were being employed as regular workers. Work programs may be either full- or part-time and may last longer than one semester, depending on each student's ability level and needs.

Although career assimilation is usually associated with job placement, students should also be given the opportunity to assume avocational, family, recreational, civic, and other nonpaying adult work roles so they can assess their abilities and needs in these areas, as well as in paid employment. School personnel should work closely with the family. For example, the student should be given specific household responsibilities, which include managing finances, managing a home, caring for personal needs, living as a member of a family unit, buying and preparing food, buying and caring for clothing, becoming involved in civic activities, engaging in self-planned recreation and leisure-time activities, getting around the community, and developing and maintaining satisfactory social relationships. Although school and family have probably worked on these competencies together before this stage, students should now practice these skills without assistance from the family.

Career assimilation pulls all previous stages together. During this stage, educators will identify whether the student still needs to refine any of the competency skills. It is the most realistic stage of the career education program and may extend intermittently over several years for many students. Therefore, community resources are crucial to life career development and success and should be included in this final stage. Most students will have important lifelong learning needs. Provisions must be made to account for these needs. Therefore, follow-up and supportive services are an important aspect of career assimilation.

Component 4: The Career Roles

Another unique feature of the LCCE curriculum design is its focus on not only future occupations but also those many unpaid work roles necessary to adult life: (1) the many work tasks associated with living in a family, being married, and perhaps raising a family, and/or living by oneself in the community; (2) being a good citizen, neighbor, and engaging in such civic activities as volunteer work, voting, helping friends and neighbors, and the like; and (3) engaging in avocational activities such as hobbies, vacations, games, spectator sports, and other leisure time activities that are of benefit to oneself and others.

The career education concept views people having careers throughout their lifetime. Thus, when children are in school, their primary career is their work as a student, but they also need to learn proper behaviors and skills to function adequately as a family member, citizen, and participant in appropriate leisure time pursuits.

Figure 3.4 presents a three-dimensional model illustrating the interaction of the first three components of the LCCE approach: (1) competencies; (2) school, family, and community experiences; (3) and stages of career development. Although the model is not intended to be factorially or mathematically pure, it demonstrates that one or more resources available in the school, family, or community can be used to teach any of the competencies at each career development stage. For example, competency 1 (managing personal finances) should be taught in a math class at the elementary, middle school/junior high, and senior high level. Before the competency is taught, the elementary teacher should provide the student with a sufficient awareness of the importance of this skill, including how people acquire the skill, what kinds of things are involved in learning the skill, and what people can do with this skill (e.g., family responsibilities, job possibilities). With this background, the student becomes more aware of the importance of this competency in the real world and therefore becomes more receptive to learning the necessary skills. The student begins by learning how to identify money and make correct change. As upper-level elementary or middle school students learn basic skills, they should be provided with exploration experiences in and out of the school so they can observe how other people make wise expenditures, obtain and use bank credit facilities, and so on. During late junior high and early senior high, students should crystalize their skills in this competency area (preparation) with further complementary community and family experiences. Finally, during the assimilation stage, students have the opportunity to independently display their skill for this competency. Students may use this competency for family living and may have the interest to get a job that requires this skill.

The preceding four components (the three curriculum areas with 22 competencies, three instructional settings, four stages of career development, and four major career/work roles) discussed in this section are the heart of the LCCE curriculum approach. Besides the conceptual framework, an extensive set of curriculum-based assessment and instructional materials has been developed with the assistance of hundreds of teachers and educational consultants. These are described in the next section, along with the recently developed staff development training materials for use by school district personnel.

LCCE CURRICULUM MATERIALS

Many models and many types of curriculum materials are available to assist educators in instituting functional skills efforts in their schools. Some of these were identified and described in Chapter 2. One problem, however, is that many who have conceptualized a model provide little or no curriculum materials, and many who have developed curriculum materials have no conceptualized model. Thus, it is up to the users to operationalize the model and/or materials the best they can. Some educators prefer this approach and are able to do it well; others want a more organized and extensive set of curriculum-based materials from which they can modify and expand their instructional efforts as needed.

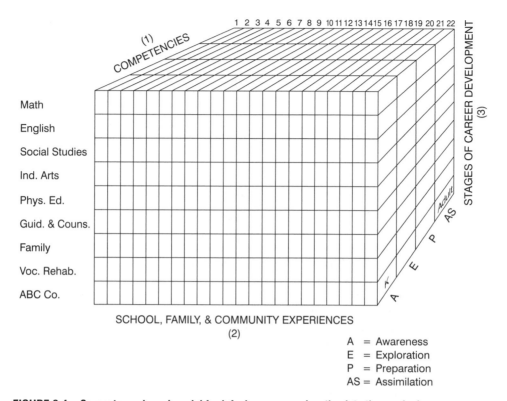

FIGURE 3.4   Competency-based model for infusing career education into the curriculum.

The LCCE curriculum model and its concepts are supported by both a variety of curriculum-based assessment measures and an extensive set of lesson plans that have been written to cover all 400 instructional objectives subsumed under the 22 competency/97 subcompetency matrix composing the system. In addition, an extensive staff training program with videotapes and other materials is available to school districts interested in learning the complete system and how it can be best implemented. Each of the LCCE curriculum and training materials is briefly described next.

Basic Curriculum Guide

The LCCE curriculum guide, *Life Centered Career Education: A Competency-Based Approach* (Brolin, 1978, 1983b, 1989, 1993a) provides the framework for building a comprehensive and systematic effort for infusing the 97 LCCE subcompetencies into academic subjects. The guide provides the background on career education concepts and the LCCE model and then presents a set of 97 subcompetency units with instructional objectives, suggested activities, and adult/peer instructional roles for supportive assistance. Teachers can develop their own specific lesson plans from the guidelines provided. The guide also contains a competency rating scale covering each of the 97 subcompetencies and a suggested Individualized Education Program (IEP) form with transition components (Brolin, 1993a).

Competency Assessment Batteries

The *LCCE Knowledge Battery* (Brolin, 1992a) is primarily a screening instrument. It assesses the career education knowledge of 7th- through 12th-grade special needs students, although it can be used with younger age regular class students as well. The knowledge battery consists of two forms, which comprise 200 multiple-choice questions covering the first 20 competencies of the LCCE curriculum. The last two competencies do not lend themselves to knowledge assessment.

The *LCCE Performance Battery* (Brolin, 1992a) covers all competency areas except competency 22, obtaining specific occupational skills, which depends on the skill being taught. Each competency test consists of five questions that require the student to demonstrate application of a subcompetency area or to respond in writing or verbally to questions that reflect such competence. Examiners are equipped with work sheets, score sheets, procedures, and specific guidelines for test administration.

The *LCCE Self-Determination Scale* (in preparation) is the most recent measure developed and assesses students on the concept of self-determination. This 40-item self-report instrument was developed by The Arc staff, based on a federal research project. The study project identified four LCCE competencies and 17 subcompetencies as most nearly approximating the concept of self-determination. Items were then devised and field-tested to finalize a reliable and valid measure.

More detail on these instruments is provided in Chapter 7.

Competency/Instructional Units

More than 1,000 lesson plans covering the daily living, personal–social, and occupational guidance and preparation domains of the LCCE curriculum have been developed and field-tested with the assistance of many school personnel and their students. The daily living skills area consists of 472 lesson plans; the personal–social area has 370 lesson plans, and the occupational area has 286 lesson plans.

The LCCE lesson plans address each of the 400 instructional objectives that comprise the 97 subcompetencies presented in the LCCE curriculum guide. The lesson plans are written to address the three levels of career education learning in the LCCE model (i.e., career awareness, career exploration, and career preparation); to provide instruction in the three major instructional settings (i.e., home, community, and school); and to span the four major career roles that students will need to participate in to be a productive adult (i.e., family member, citizen/volunteer, employee, and leisure seeker). Thus, the lesson plans cover the entire range of 400 instructional objectives contained

Pat Burch teaches her students the LCCE curriculum.

in the basic curriculum guide (Brolin, 1993a). Users can modify them, add to them, and otherwise use them in conjunction with the assessment measures, to provide a comprehensive career education program with a scope and sequence from the elementary through the high school or postsecondary years.

Detailed descriptions of the LCCE instructional units and their lesson plans are covered in Chapters 10 to 13.

Staff Training Materials

An extensive set of staff training materials has been developed so school districts can train their own personnel to implement the LCCE system. The training program consists of three major pieces: a trainer's manual, set of videotapes, and an activity book.

The *LCCE Trainer's Manual* (Brolin, 1993c) provides staff developers with step-by-step guidelines for organizing and conducting up to 30½ hours of in-service training.

The manual includes masters for trainees' handouts, transparencies, and support text for the trainer. The manual includes a 13-minute videocassette that presents an overview and discussion of the LCCE curriculum approach, which can also be presented to administrators, school boards, parents, and community groups. Guidelines for LCCE implementation and evaluation are also contained in this manual.

The second piece of the LCCE staff development package is a set of 10 videotapes that the trainer will intersperse throughout the training course (Brolin, 1993c). The tapes cover such topics as: the need to change and the law; the LCCE curriculum, assessing functional skills, teaching daily living skills, teaching personal–social skills, teaching occupational skills, instructional materials utilization, business and industry, parent involvement, interagency collaboration, curriculum modification and change, and individualized transition planning and implementation.

The third piece of the LCCE training package is the 458-page *Life Centered Career Education: Professional Development Activity Book* (Council for Exceptional Children, 1992), which is designed for use by all trainees along with the curriculum guide. The activity book, packaged in a three-ring notebook, is divided into 10 training sessions, corresponding with the videotapes described previously, and contains a series of activity sheets, resource materials, copies of all transparencies shown on the videotapes, and assignments to enhance the training effort.

The LCCE training program package can be used either in its entirety or in part, depending on the time constraints and needs of the school district. If school districts prefer to have outside consultants conduct the training, The Council for Exceptional Children (CEC) can provide trainers who are implementing the curriculum themselves.

RATIONALE FOR ADOPTING THE LCCE CURRICULUM

The LCCE curriculum offers educators a comprehensive framework for organizing an effective functional curriculum that will prepare students to be productive members of their community and the labor market. It has been built on many of the proven career education concepts presented in Chapter 2 and has been developed and field-tested in a large number of school districts throughout the country.

 Students need to develop a "work personality" beginning at the elementary level.

The LCCE model states that transitional programming must begin at the elementary level with purposeful and organized instruction directed at the development of a work personality and the important career/life skills needed for successful adult functioning (Brolin, 1993a). The *work personality* is an individual's work habits, work behaviors, work values, work motivation, and positive work ethic—all the important positive characteristics one needs to be successfully employed. A work personality type is illustrated in Figure 3.5.

FIGURE 3.5 **The work personality.**

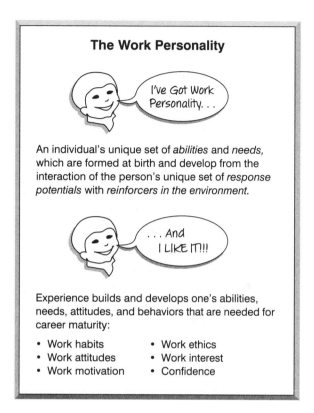

The North Dakota State Department of Instruction has advocated the use of the LCCE curriculum to educators throughout their state. In 1990, one of their guides provided a detailed explanation of how the curriculum could be used by school districts throughout the state. Figure 3.6 lists of some the major features of the curriculum from their perspective and the compelling reasons to use this approach.

According to Halpern, Benz, and Lindstrom (1991), four conditions are needed for a capacity-building curriculum model to work. Such a model must be (1) guided by a set of program standards, (2) implemented through a set of efficient and effective procedures, (3) supported by the provision of training and materials, and (4) documented with concise and effective materials.

The LCCE curriculum meets the four conditions needed for the capacity-building curriculum model. Figure 3.7 illustrates how each of these four conditions is addressed in the LCCE curriculum system. A brief explanation of each follows:

• *Set of Program Standards.* The LCCE Curriculum Guide, *Life Centered Career Education: A Competency-Based Approach* (Brolin, 1978, 1983b, 1989, 1993a) provides the conceptual model and set of standards for the curriculum.

The LCCE curriculum lends itself well to the core curriculum concept . . . and is recommended as a guide for local curriculum review and development.

The 22 competencies can serve as a framework for infusing life-centered skills into all aspects of the curriculum by applying appropriate skills and knowledge of academic and content area subjects to everyday real life situations.

Each subject area is a vehicle for teaching life skills. LCCE is a way of tying curriculum content to the real world.

Unlike other curriculums, life-centered competencies apply to all students.

The concept of least restrictive environment and the life centered competency concept are closely interrelated.

Practice of these skills must occur as much as possible in the natural environment with nonhandicapped peers and other members of society.

Attending to the 22 LCCE competencies can aid the IEP team more than any other assessment information.

The student's present level of functioning in the LCCE competencies is basic to establishing goals and objectives which will lead toward more successful overall functioning.

Core curriculum areas must be kept in the forefront during each IEP review . . . the 22 competencies may serve as a frame of reference in reestablishing priority areas.

FIGURE 3.6   Excerpts from the North Dakota State Department of Instruction guidebook.
Note. From *Special Education in North Dakota: Guide II. Educational Programming for Students with Mild to Moderate Mental Retardation,* 1990, Bismarck, ND: North Dakota Department of Public Instruction. Copyright 1990 by North Dakota Department of Public Instruction. Reprinted by permission.

- *Concise and Effective Materials.* An extensive set of curriculum-based assessment instruments and over 1,000 lesson plans have been developed and field-tested, covering all 400 instructional objectives contained in the LCCE curriculum guide.
- *Professional/Staff Development Methods.* The LCCE staff have developed a videotape staff development training program with an accompanying *Trainer's Manual* (Brolin, 1993c) and trainee activity book (Brolin, 1993b) for school district staff to train their own people. In addition, the CEC's Professional Development section conducts regional conferences on LCCE and training programs at schools requesting in-service training programs.
- *Set of Effective and Efficient Implementation Procedures.* An implementation process has been developed and field-tested and is outlined in detail in the *Trainer's Manual* (Brolin, 1993c) and other staff development materials.

The preceding materials and training programs are all available from the CEC at 1920 Association Drive, Reston, VA 22091.

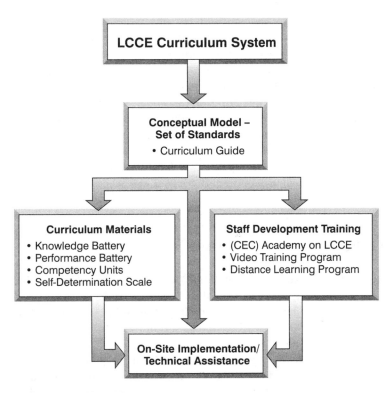

FIGURE 3.7 LCCE curriculum system.

Note. From *Life-Centered Career Education: Trainer's Manual* (3rd ed., p. 4) by D. E. Brolin, 1993, Reston, VA: The Council for Exceptional Children. Copyright 1993 by The Council for Exceptional Children. Reprinted by permission.

FINAL COMMENTS

Students with special learning needs and others should be taught an appropriate blend of academic and functional life skills content if they are to be prepared for a successful adult outcome. Although the term *career education* is not as prominently used today as it was before the introduction of the transition movement, it continues to be used by many proponents of the approach because it more specifically focuses on the purpose of the educational efforts that need to be emphasized for all students of all types—career development. Many school districts are presently touting a new discovery called "Partnerships with Industry" or something similar. Students at all levels are spending more time with employers, their parents, and others learning about the world of employment so they can begin developing their career interests (and work personality) earlier.

The LCCE competency-based approach does not advocate elimination of current courses or a significant change in the structure of education. Instead, it recommends that educators change the focus of instructional content to meet the career development needs of students and for the family and community resources to become an integral part of this educational process. Each instructor must decide how the competencies can be delivered and integrated into the existing courses. With the movement toward an inclusive education for all students, the LCCE approach provides a mechanism for making this important goal logical and successful.

Almost everyone wants to attain a satisfactory quality of life that includes satisfying employment, financial security, friendships, independence, leisure time, and for many, a family. All of these outcomes require individuals to learn to work productively in their home, community, and on a job. A substantial career education effort, incorporated into the ongoing curriculum of the school, can lead toward this end.

ACTIVITIES

1. Prepare a presentation to your school board to convince them that a more substantive career education/functional skills approach, more specifically, the LCCE curriculum, needs to be implemented in your district. Be prepared to explain the nature of the LCCE curriculum and to give a strong argument in favor of its adoption.
2. Review the 22 competency/97 subcompetency matrix of the LCCE curriculum presented in Figure 3.2, and conduct a curriculum analysis to determine in what general education subjects each of these functional skills could be taught to your students if your school has a full inclusion policy.

Part 2

Family and Community Resources

Chapter 4

Family Involvement

Chapter 5

Agencies, Organizations, and Informational Resources

Chapter 6

Business and Industry Involvement

Chapter 4

Family Involvement

Michael Wehmeyer and Sharon Davis

Preliminary Questions About the Topic

1. How and why has family involvement in education changed in recent years?
2. What are some compelling reasons for educators to involve families in a substantial and meaningful way in their educational efforts?
3. How do you believe parents view the educational and decision-making process that they experience with the professional educators?
4. What do you believe are the typical attitudes of the professional educator about parent involvement and child planning?
5. What is the dilemma that educators often find themselves in as they try to meet their responsibilities to the student and family while working within the constraints of their own system?
6. What are some of the major barriers that often preclude satisfactory school–parent relationships?
7. What strategies can be employed to encourage active and productive family involvement with the school?
8. How can families be advised to assist their child in preparing for the eventual transition from school to work and community living?
9. How would you advise families to become actively involved in the Life-Centered Career Education (LCCE) process?
10. As an educator, what would you do to encourage family involvement in LCCE and/or any other functional skills/transition curriculum effort?

The Individuals with Disabilities Education Act (IDEA) was written and structured to ensure parental and family involvement in the educational planning and decision-making process for their son, daughter, or family member. Cutler summarized IDEA as "a declaration of your child's educational rights and of your rights as a parent to *participate in the educational process*" (1993, p. 3, italics added) when describing the special education process to parents. According to IDEA, parents and professionals are equal partners in the Individualized Education Program (IEP) process. Although this does not mean that all participants hold equal knowledge of educational terms or procedures, it does mean that all are to share equal status in decision making.

IDEA assigns numerous responsibilities to family members by providing procedural safeguards that protect their rights in the planning and decision-making process. The act uses the term *parent* when referring to the student's biological parent, guardian, surrogate parent (when the child is a ward of the state), or a person acting as the parent of a child, such as a grandparent. The law requires that parents be provided access to educational records regarding their family member, be notified in advance of planning, evaluation, and placement meetings, and it provides due process procedures when decisions are reached that violate these requirements or that do not adequately solicit the involvement of parents.

These safeguards are in place to enable parents to become equal partners in the education process. They are typically viewed as a list of rights, but rights and responsibilities go hand in hand. Parents should prepare for meetings by reviewing their child's past education records, developing goals and objectives based on what they see as needed, and talking with teachers and other personnel about the meeting. Their participation in the meeting should be equally reciprocal, with all parties, professionals, family members, adult service providers, and the student working together to design and implement an educational program that best meets the unique learning needs of the student.

Unfortunately, the involvement of families in the educational planning process is too often limited by one or the other party, and the professional/parent relationship is often adversarial instead of collaborative, a problem instead of a partnership. This chapter discusses family involvement in educational planning, emphasizing the important role of families, particularly parents, to ensure a successful transition from adolescence to adulthood for youth experiencing disabilities and at risk for school failure. The discussion begins with a historical overview of family involvement in education, addresses barriers to and strategies for effective communication between families and professionals, and concludes with specific strategies for involving families through the LCCE process.

FAMILY INVOLVEMENT IN EDUCATION

For much of the first half of the 20th century, schools were responsible only for academic instruction, while families were responsible for emotional and social development and instruction (Flaxman & Inger, 1991). Social changes of the 1960s and 1970s, changes in the structure of the family and society, and changing demographics in America have significantly altered the role of schools in society and the role of parents regarding school responsibilities (Flaxman & Inger, 1991). Parents no longer accept a passive role in educational planning and demand a voice in issues ranging from school budgeting and personnel decisions, to curricular decisions and other areas that have traditionally been assigned to education professionals. Schools no longer teach only academics to a restricted population of students; now schools must address complex topics such as prevention of acquired immune deficiency syndrome (AIDS) and sex education or driver's education with students from diverse ethnic and socioeconomic backgrounds who possess widely different learning styles and abilities.

The contemporary notion of parental involvement dates back to the early 1960s, when the passage of federal legislation designed to address societal problems mandated parental involvement in planning and decision making about curriculum, instruction, and school improvement. The Head Start program was among the first to employ such a model, bringing educators and parents of young children together to address both child- and family-related issues (Flaxman & Inger, 1991). Similarly, the Education for All Handicapped Children Act of 1975 mandated such collaboration.

Such legislative intent typically emerges from an advocacy agenda targeting equal access and representation to ensure ongoing fairness and equality. This was the case, for example, for youth with disabilities. As early as the 1940s, parents of children with disabilities recognized that their sons and daughters were capable of much more than medical and educational professionals were attributing to them and, through grass-roots organizing, began to demonstrate this and to advocate for equal access to educational services. Once access to educational services was mandated by legislation, families advocated for appropriate services, expanded opportunities to participate in school life, access to vocational and rehabilitation services, and mainstreaming and integration.

Parental involvement into the next century will undoubtedly take on increased importance. One only has to examine today's headlines to realize that this is true. For example, school choice, where families are allowed to choose the educational setting for their son or daughter, will necessitate increased family involvement. By selecting which school their children attend, families will wield increased control in determining the educational settings, materials, and instructional methodologies used by professionals. As in most free market systems, those educational settings and personnel that best meet the needs of the consumer (families and students as well as business and industry) will prosper, while those designed to meet the needs of the educational system alone and that perpetuate outdated or irrelevant practices will decline. The concept of family empowerment is not unique to education. Many federally funded services, for example, vocational rehabilitation, are placing greater emphasis on family and consumer empowerment and are implementing procedures that enable families and people with disabilities to assume greater control in decision making and to choose services that more adequately meet their needs.

Several other factors suggest that family involvement in education will increase in the 21st century. Flaxman and Inger (1991) identified several basic ways that parents can be involved in schooling. Parents can be involved directly with decision making in the schools, as is the case for school choice. Recent trends in site-based management procedures in education essentially require that principals, teachers, and parents come

94

Point of View

As a parent of an adult daughter with a disability who has finally made a successful transition from school to employment and independent living in the community, and as a professional in a disability field, I have a dual perspective on issues faced by both parents and professionals as they consider the futures of individuals with disabilities. I am particularly concerned about the generally dismal employment picture for people with disabilities. We know that people with all levels of disability are capable of competitive employment when they obtain a job based on their abilities and are provided appropriate support to learn and maintain the job. Yet, the National Longitudinal Transition Study (Wagner et al., 1992) found that only 43% of youth with mental retardation were employed full-time 3 years after school. Few were earning wages sufficient to support themselves independently. Employment is the key to adults living fulfilling lives and being contributing citizens to their communities.

Professionals often blame parents for such high unemployment rates. Parents are said to have low expectations for their child's employment, to worry that if they go to work, their sons and daughters will lose government entitlements that provide subsistence and health coverage, and to prefer that their children work in a protected, sheltered environment. On the other hand, some professionals believe that parents have unrealistic views of what their son or daughter can accomplish in the workplace and expect them to be happy with whatever menial job is provided.

I believe that on the whole parents are simply facing reality. In too many instances, their children are not provided the functional skills necessary to live and work in the community, such as those provided by the comprehensive LCCE. Many students with disabilities do not participate in vocational education to learn specific job skills and do not have opportunities to work in real jobs during their school years, experiences that lead to higher employment rates for youth after leaving school.

Youth with disabilities leave school, and families learn there is no entitlement to services. There is no one to step in to guide them through

together to manage the school and solve problems unique to that school and community, illustrating a second situation in which parental involvement might be direct.

Another way that parents will be involved in schooling is through parenting training programs and initiatives. Head Start is a good example of educational services that must incorporate parent training and parenting training to be successful. Many early childhood education programs likewise use parent-training procedures that teach parents to assume responsibilities traditionally held by professionals. Parents may essentially become paraprofessionals by receiving training to conduct some activities that would otherwise be school directed, such as limited physical or occupational therapy procedures, or by providing repetition and practice in activities important to language, motor, or cognitive development.

the adult service system, as the school guided them through their child's education years. Parents may be totally unfamiliar with the vocational rehabilitation system. There may be no agency in their community to which they can turn to obtain help for their son or daughter in finding a job and to provide job support services. Parents are often left on their own. If the children manage to obtain the typical fast-food job, they find unpredictable, part-time hours, low wages, no benefits and no public transportation. Even the paratransit system may not accommodate erratic work schedules, night and weekend hours. Parents provide the transportation if they can. Often, parents end up with two choices: Their sons or daughters sit at home with no meaningful activities, or they get on the van and go to the sheltered employment settings.

Schools can have a major influence on changing this situation. In fact, I believe the younger generation of parents will demand more of the schools. Many are already requesting their children receive an inclusive education alongside children without disabilities. They need and want to be active partners with the school in planning and implementing their children's IEP. Educators need to help them create a vision for their children's future as citizens in their commu-

nity, living, working and participating in the community's leisure life. Schools must provide options for vocational education and real job experiences for students with disabilities before they leave school. Transition planning for each student should focus on the individual's interests, abilities, and life choices. Educators can play a major role in helping parents provide experiences to help their sons and daughters achieve independent lives in the future while being realistic in addressing barriers. The LCCE curriculum is a tool that can help schools reach this goal.

Sharon Davis is the Director of the Department of Research and Program Services at The Arc (a national organization on mental retardation). Dr. Davis received her doctorate in Educational Administration from Cornell University after teaching in public schools in New York State. She has worked in areas related to vocational education, students with disabilities, and prevention of mental retardation and is the author of The Arc's report cards on inclusion in education and employment (S. Davis, 1992, 1993).

Finally, as schools become more of a focal point for community-focused activities that have not previously been the domain of education, families, and schools will once again find themselves as partners. Although many educators disapprove of schools assuming broader responsibility in social issues, the reality is that many public schools have become providers of other direct services, including child care, health, counseling, and referral services. Once again, the face of education has had to change. Schools have undertaken such responsibility for a number of reasons, not the least of which is that research shows that they are educationally beneficial. Adequate support services enable families to provide their children a stable home environment that encourages development. As Flaxman and Inger pointed out, "children with fewer physical, emotional and social problems are easier to teach and deal with in the classroom" (1991, p. 5).

Rationale for Family Involvement

Families must be involved in the educational planning process and a parent–professional collaboration established for a number of reasons. Some of these are pragmatic, others more ideological. Sinclair and Christenson (1992), noting that collaboration is an attitude integral to the success of students, speak to the latter when outlining the theoretical underpinnings of a partnership approach in education. These authors propose the following:

- *Only through collaboration can real change occur.* As illustrated in the prior discussion, schools and professionals alone cannot meet the complex, multiple needs of children in America today. According to Sinclair and Christenson: "The sheer number of at-risk children, problem situations and changing demographics of American society dictate a collaborative stance" (1992, p. 12).
- *Child development and learning do not occur in a single environment and without influence from multiple sources.* "Children learn, grow and develop both at home and at school. There is no clear cut boundary between home and school experiences for children and youth. Rather, there is a mutually influencing quality between experiences in these two settings" (Sinclair & Christenson, 1992, p. 12).
- *The definition of education has expanded with advances in understanding about human learning and cognition.* Again, according to Sinclair and Christenson, "a learning environment is educative when it enables the individual to learn and develop specialized skills: it is miseducative when it fails to encourage positive human development. The educative community is produced when learning environments of the home and school are linked together and carefully coordinated to serve the developmental needs of the individuals" (1992, p. 12).

The theoretical validity of parent–professional collaborations is based on the recognition that learning and education occur each moment of the day and cannot be confined only to educational classrooms during school hours. The role of education is to prepare children and youth to succeed as adults. It is evident that to accomplish this professionals in education must actively involve families and collaborate with parents to ensure learning opportunities throughout the student's day. In this sense, there must be a positive collaboration between home and school and there must be active family involvement for educators to achieve their stated goals and to succeed in their chosen vocation. This theoretical stance has been substantiated by research that documents that parental participation in the educational process results in more positive educational outcomes for students, including better school attendance, reduced dropout rates, enhanced student self-esteem and confidence, and improved educational achievement scores (Flaxman & Inger, 1991). Sinclair and Christenson (1992) summarized the primary effects of family involvement as follows:

- "All forms of parent involvement strategies seem to be useful, however, those that are meaningful, well planned, comprehensive and long lasting offer more options for parents to be involved and appear to be more effective. Student achievement is greater with meaningful and high levels of involvement.

- "Parent involvement affects noncognitive behavior; student attendance, attitudes about school, maturation, self-concept, and behavior improve when parents are involved.
- "There are benefits for parents, teachers, communities and schools when parents are involved. In general, there are more successful educational programs and effective schools.
- "Student achievement gains are most significant and long lasting when parent involvement is begun at an early age" (Sinclair & Christenson, 1992, p. 13).

There are pragmatic reasons to create strong family involvement in educational planning and decision making for youth with disabilities. Among the foremost is that IDEA requires this involvement. However, numerous other reasons illustrate why educators who are committed to providing the best possible education for learners at risk for failure and students with disabilities involve families in a meaningful manner and would do so even if there was no legal mandate.

As described earlier, human development and learning cannot be compartmentalized as occurring only in restricted environments. Children learn across multiple environments, and learning in one domain has an impact on learning in all other domains. For teachers to succeed, home environments and families must be conducive to learning and development. This recognition has driven the changing role of schools in our society, and it should be this factor that compels educators to establish effective, truly collaborative partnerships with families.

For students with disabilities, there are other pragmatic reasons to involve families. Only two participants in any given IEP or transition planning meeting will be members of every meeting for the student: The student and the family member. Teachers, administrators, related service personnel, and adult service providers all will change from year to year and school to school. In our increasingly mobile society, parents can help maintain continuity by providing information about students' previous educational experiences and placements, their learning successes, and school failures. This is important even when educational records are available that document the same time span (which is frequently not the case). Examined alone, without the benefit of meeting with and talking to students and their families, educational documents such as diagnostic and placement information, family, medical and psychological histories, even past IEPs, become a litany of disability, disease, and disorder. They accentuate problems, focus on weaknesses, and set expectations for failure. Few educational records contain the hopes of the family or the dreams of the student. Few educational records capture the "other" side of the story: the family's struggle to secure adequate services, to be recognized as an equal partner.

Families are a repository of information about the student, her strengths and abilities, likes and dislikes, limitations, and idiosyncrasies. They can tell you how a student spends her spare time, her hobbies and interests, and whether she has ever maintained a checkbook or has access to a computer at home. The student's sister can tell you how many friends she has in the neighborhood. Parents can tell you if their son can cook a simple meal, has ever interviewed for a job, or reads the paper daily. There are not enough checklists available to encompass the amount of information to be gained from family members—information critical to educational, and more importantly, adult success.

This information becomes particularly important to the transition planning process. The 1990 amendments to Public Law (PL) 94–142 (IDEA) mandate that IEPs for students 16 and over contain transition-related goals and objectives. Transition services are defined in the act as *"a coordinated set of activities for a student, designed within an outcome-oriented process which promotes movement from school to post school activities"* [Sec. 602(a)(19)]. Postschool activities are broadly defined and include postsecondary education, vocational training, integrated and supported employment, continuing and adult education, adult services, independent living, or community participation. The law also requires that the *"coordinated set of activities shall be based upon the individual student's needs, taking into account the student's preferences and interests, and shall include instruction, community experiences, the development of employment and other post-school adult living objectives, and when appropriate, acquisition of daily living skills and functional vocational evaluation"* [Sec. 602(a)(19)].

These requirements take into account the critical importance of families and, when viewed in conjunction with language in the law mandating parental involvement, serve to broaden the focus on family involvement to include the student himself. To achieve outcome-oriented transition goals, educators need to tap resources available through families. Only the students and their families can, indeed have the right to, make decisions about where the students live and work as adults. Educators bring expertise on how to learn skills that lead to these outcomes. Adult service providers hold knowledge about systems that support these outcomes. It is, however, the right of all individuals in our society to make choices and decisions about their lives, and the presence of a disabling condition does not abrogate that right on an a priori basis.

Finally, families must be equal partners in decision making because, quite frankly, they have the most to gain or lose from the educational process. When youths leave school to unemployment or jobs that do not provide sufficient wages to support independent living, it is the family that typically provides a home. If youths leave school without a job and with no opportunity for postsecondary education, it is the family that finds them work. Several studies examining adult outcomes for youth with disabilities confirm that families become, in essence, the student's case manager. Sitlington, Frank, and Cooper (1989) found that of 648 graduates with learning disabilities who were out of school for 1 year and employed, 43% found their jobs themselves and 40% identified families as having found their job for them. Only 5% found jobs through a community agency, and 6% through school. Of 908 youth with learning disabilities out of school one year, 64% lived with their family. Sitlington, Frank, and Carson (1991) found that 3 years out of high school 46% of youth with mental retardation lived with a family member and 31% relied primarily on parents for financial assistance and support. Wehmeyer, Kelchner, and Richards (1993) found that of 408 adults with mental retardation (mean age, 36 years) 35% lived with a parent or relative.

It is apparent that, legal requirements aside, the involvement of families in the educational planning and decision-making process is more than a good idea, it is essential to adult success and, in reality, the success of the educational process. However, there are significant problems in establishing a collaborative relationship between school and home. Parents frequently feel alienated by the IEP planning process and rarely contribute as equal partners. Gilliam and Coleman (1981) asked IEP committee members to rank committee members on their relative influence during a meeting and their contribution to the meeting. Parents were ranked 8 in influence (after special education teachers, psychologists, special education directors, supervisors and consultants, regular education teachers, and guidance counselors) and 10th in actual contributions (behind all of the above as well as principals and speech therapists).

Likewise, educators are often frustrated by the seeming lack of interest from family members. There are a number of reasons for the present circumstances, which are addressed next. There are also solutions to these problems, and these are highlighted subsequently.

Barriers to Effective Family Involvement

Sonnenschein (1981) characterized the parent–professional partnership as an "uneasy relationship," an apt decision in many chases. A partnership is a two-way street, and to understand breakdowns in collaborations between home and school, one needs to examine the actions and beliefs of both parties.

Professionals' Mishandling of Parents

You don't have to speak to many parents of children with disabilities to understand that, when it comes to the educational planning and decision-making process, families feel powerless, pressured, and put-upon. Truth is, the educational planning and decision-making process, historically, has been one in which families are *not* equal partners in planning, and their participation has often been marginalized. Some factors leading to this outcome are examined next.

Professionals bring to the table biases that influence every decision they make. These biases are often manifested in beliefs about others involved in planning and decision making. Too often, processionals' conceptualizations of parents lead to unequal partnerships. Sonnenschein (1981) identified several such conceptualizations.

Many professionals perceive parents as "vulnerable clients" and view their role in the school–home interaction as one of a helper. Relationships built on these assumptions typically have the professional as the expert, someone who has the answers and, essentially, the power and control to change outcomes for the family. Such relationships do not lend themselves to equal partnerships or collaborative efforts. A related perception, according to Sonnenschein (1981), is that of parents as "patients." Historically, the birth of a child with a disability has been viewed as an event precipitating a grieving and acceptance process, much as that described when coping with the death of a loved one. Parents are labeled as being at one point or another in this acceptance continuum and often are seen as not coping well or experiencing stress or anxiety as a result of their inability to come to terms with their child's disability. This leads to perceptions that family members, themselves, need remediation and attention. Once again, a relationship based on these assumptions does not lend itself to effective collaboration. The truth of the matter, however, is that family coping with the birth of a child with a disability differs widely from family to family and is best described by the individual family's coping strategies and abilities than by some global strategy.

Singer and Powers (1993) summarized the problems with these first two types of relationships when describing the tenets of traditional models of caring for families. One such tenet has been that family support is oriented toward professional control and the fitting of families into programs. The assumption is that special expertise is required to assist troubled families and that families should turn over decision making to professionals and program administrators. A second tenet is that "families are necessarily pathological because of the burden imposed by raising a child with a disability" (Singer & Powers, 1993, p. 4). Accordingly:

> this orientation stresses family problems and uses language derived from medicine in which pathology, treatment, cure and prescription are common terms. It is assumed that parents require training, need assistance to learn how to raise their children and, invariably, are distressed. (Singer & Powers, 1993, p. 5)

Yet another common perception of families is one of blaming the family for the child's disabling condition. Turnbull and Turnbull experienced this, stating that professionals they were dealing with never "came right out and said, 'You caused it,' but everything they did was based on that premise" (1978, p. 42). Early theories regarding the cause of certain disabilities, most noticeably autism, explicitly blamed parents (usually mothers), for their child's condition. There is often an underlying assumption by professionals that the parent is somehow to blame for the disability. Whether this perception is grounded in fact, and is indeed true, or simply part of the mythology of disability professionals, its impact on creating partnerships is devastating.

The perception that the parent is responsible for the child's disability exists in part because many parents hold feelings of guilt and harbor questions about their own culpability in their child's developmental outcomes. If one is the birth mother of a child with fetal alcohol syndrome, this guilt is probably well founded. If one's child has Down syndrome, it is not. In either case, it is a short distance from parental feelings of guilt to professionals' assumptions of responsibility. In a similar manner, parents frequently are perceived as less observant, intelligent, and perceptive. Part of this emerges from inappropriate assumptions that, because the child has these characteristics, the family does also. Again, views of the parent as responsible or less able stigmatize parents and build barriers to collaboration and partnership. Myths about the family's inability to contribute to the planning and decision-making process are too widely accepted and often are misused to prevent effective collaboration and partnerships. Cutler (1993) lists several such myths:

- Parents are naive laypersons who cannot and should not teach.
- Parents are too emotionally involved to evaluate their children.

• Parents are still obedient school pupils who should be seen and not heard. (Cutler, 1993, p. 17)

The roots of the first myth lie in our stereotyped belief of the school's role in society. Many educators, indeed, many people in general society, continue to hold to the view that schools should only teach academics (the three R's) and that teaching should be done by experts. This belief, however, contradicts what we know about learning. As described previously, learning and development occur every minute of every day, and for education to be most effective, educators must capitalize on this fact. Parents spend the most time with their children and in the long run are their only consistent teacher. Teachers who can effectively involve parents as teachers (*not* parents as expert educators who replicate what occurs in the classroom) are effective and successful.

The second myth harkens back to perceptions about parents as victims, clients, or patients. The assumption is that until parents "work through" their grief and accept the child's disability (acceptance is implicitly defined as viewing the child as the professional does), then they cannot move past the emotional and mental barriers they have erected to contribute in a meaningful manner. This belief is inaccurate, yet pervasive.

The final myth springs as much from the system as from any particular bias individual educators may hold. School systems are complex bureaucracies that often require "insider" knowledge to navigate. Educators themselves come to accept this as fact in a very short time, but because they are in the system, they can at least somewhat work their way through the maze. Parents are viewed as outside the system, and many educators soon portray parents as naive about the "way things really work" and as such, believe that parents need to let them (the educator, administrator, etc.) work the system for them. Add to this the belief that professionals hold a key to teaching and learning, and it is obvious that the parent who tries to become active and demands equal treatment is seen as naive and in some ways incapable.

When parents or family members enter the system and attempt to overcome the various barriers to equal partnership, they acquire a reputation and are sometimes seen as a problem and labeled as aggressive or unrealistic, creating yet another barrier to partnerships. Some parents find that this occurs very early on in their interactions with schools and may adopt an equally strident position, digging in for trench warfare instead of trying to work with schools. The cycle repeats itself and the home–school relationship is confrontational and, ultimately, destroyed. Although families may eventually obtain at least some of what they want, it is at great cost to the family, educators, and the student. There are no winners in this situation. Many parents come to the conclusion that this process is more harmful than helpful for their child and decide not to fight the system. As a result, they are apt to not press for what they want for fear that the resulting environment will be more difficult for their child.

Not only do professional assumptions about parents and their role in education have an impact on family involvement, but beliefs about children with disabilities, about their capabilities, and ultimately, about disability in society have an impact on family involvement. Families are frequently typed as being unrealistic about their child's present or future capabilities based at least partially on professionals' beliefs about disability and children with disabilities. The well-known "self-fulfilling prophecy" is still alive and well. Cutler lists several myths about students with disabilities that impact family involvement:

- These children's disabilities are the source of all problems.
- These children can learn only by rote.
- These children can't handle a full day. (Cutler, 1993, p. 36)

This list could be expanded with little difficulty. Ultimately, what one expects of children with disabilities reflects what one believes about disability. Historically, people with disabilities have been viewed from either a medical model or an educational model. The medical model emphasizes disease and cure, placing the responsibility for treatment in the hands of highly skilled and trained professionals. The educational model places less emphasis on disease and treatment but replaces efforts to cure with efforts to fix disability. Both perspectives view disability as outside the norm. If the norm for society is walking on two legs, people who do not walk and instead use a wheelchair is atypical and seen as needing to be cured or fixed so that they can experience the joy of being normative. In both cases, we lose sight of the person and emphasize the disability. We attribute actions and behaviors to the disability and eventually expect less from people with disabilities. When our expectations are fulfilled, it reinforces our beliefs and compounds the problem.

Parents' Mishandling of Professionals

An equal number of barriers to collaboration are raised by parents or family members. Like educators, parents bring inaccurate perceptions and beliefs to the home–school relationship. Cutler identified three such false beliefs held by many parents:

- Educators are super experts in their field.
- Educators are totally objective.
- Educators are free agents. (1993, p. 29)

As Cutler notes, these myths are the mirror images of the myths about parents. They are, in many ways, as damaging to family involvement as beliefs about parents. Educators have skills and training that enable them to work with students with disabilities and to provide answers to difficult problems and situations. They also have a large number of students, limited time, and high demands on their time. Educators are as constrained by the system as parents are and often equally frustrated. However, the stereotype of the professional as the expert and holding all knowledge, perpetuated by schools and readily accepted by many parents, places undue burden on teachers and creates unrealistic expectations among parents. These unrealistic expectations are often played out in unreasonable demands on the teachers' time and unfair criticism if the teacher is unable to deliver.

If parents are viewed as too emotional or unobjective to be useful to the process, educators are viewed as too objective, or at least, educators feel the need to maintain this image. This has been reinforced by the fact that, during their training, almost all educators become familiar with the concept of "professional distance." Some professions, such as counseling, have emphasized distancing and the maintenance of absolute objectivity as necessary for success. In other cases, objectivity has been emphasized to prevent professional burnout or overinvolvement and internalization of the family's problems. In either case, it is unfair to characterize teachers as totally objective, just as it is to characterize parents as unobjective. Educators may strive to maintain credibility by distancing themselves from the family at least partially because it is expected of them. Needless to say, partnerships cannot be formed under these circumstances.

The final false belief about educators held by many parents is described by Cutler as the belief that educators are free agents. According to Cutler:

> Many parents ask why, if the school personnel know a program is needed, they don't just set it up. Since it is the school's job to educate all children, parents expect that school people will do what is necessary. (1993, pp. 35–36)

What these parents fail to take into account is that far from being a free agent, teachers and educators are bound to a system that is often slow and unresponsive and does not have unlimited time, budget, or personnel. Teachers are often caught between their empathy and agreement with the family member and the reality that advocating on behalf of the parent may be perceived as disloyal and, in some circumstances, lead to ostracism, limited career options, and job loss. Additionally, educators may find themselves with conflicts between what they see as their responsibility to the student and their responsibility to the family. When these various responsibilities conflict, it is little wonder teachers distance themselves from the process.

Parents and families contribute to barriers to effective collaboration in other ways as well. Many professionals feel thwarted in their attempts to work with families because the family member is searching for a professional who will tell them what they want to hear. Typically referred to as "shopping around" and associated with the diagnosis process, it is not unusual for family members (for both good and bad reasons) to disregard as valid one professional's advice or efforts to collaborate because they do not coincide with the family's expectations. If professionals are guilty of bringing biases and expectations to the table, so too then are parents and family members.

The experience of having a child with a disability is one that is frequently associated with perceptions and beliefs that are not conducive to effective partnerships. While we eschew the traditional perceptions of parents as detailed previously, we do not wish to dismiss as invalid the range of emotions and feelings that accompany the birth of a child with a disability and the impact of this experience on family stress and coping. The truth is, many children with disabilities require more time and energy on the part of parents than do many children without disabilities. There are truths imbedded in the older notions of the cycle of acceptance of disability. Parents feel disillusioned, disappointed, frightened, frustrated, alone, vulnerable, guilty, and as if they have been treated unfairly. They also feel committed, joyful, excited, hopeful, confident, and proud. It is unfair to represent one without the other.

For some parents, however, the experience of raising a child with a disability can become overly stressful. Likewise, some parents may cope with their child's disability by creating unrealistic expectations (both too positive or too negative) or by denying certain limitations. These scenarios, however, are not uncommon to parents of children without disabilities. Stress and unrealistic expectations may lead to parents not being honest with themselves or professionals about their feelings and expectations. Parents who are overwhelmed at home may find it difficult to admit to a professional that they do not want or are not, at that time, capable of taking on additional responsibilities such working with their child at home or participating in multidisciplinary team meetings (Cutler, 1993). Parents may feel that their authority or integrity is threatened by professional advice and adopt a "no one is going to tell me what to do" attitude. Finally, parents who experience a great deal of stress may become overreliant on professionals, resulting in unreasonable demands for attention and time.

One frequent barrier to family involvement is that, too often, parents and educators approach a problem or an issue from different temporal orientations. Educators tend to be future oriented, looking at what may happen 1, 5, or 10 years later. Parents, often by necessity, must take one day at a time and are not able or willing to look at what is in store for their child. Many of us procrastinate when having to consider what may be negative outcomes. Parents may be fearful of the future, misunderstand possibilities, and as such have little interest in long-term objectives. In far too many cases, medical professionals, and sometimes educational personnel as well, have painted negative outcomes as the only possibilities for their child. Even in the 1990s, parents are frequently told, at the time of the birth of their child with a disability, that institutionalization is the only option they can reasonably consider. This doom and gloom prophesy understandably contributes to parental unwillingness to focus on future outcomes.

Other barriers that contribute to ineffective family involvement are not erected by either the educators or families but instead are legitimate differences. Parents and educators alike may feel a certain competitiveness, probably unconsciously, in the collaborative process. Parents feel that, because they know the child best, they can be the most effective teachers. Professionals feel that their background and expertise make them the best teacher. Legitimate claims on both sides, which illustrates that there is little utility to placing blame in the breakdown of the home–school collaboration process. It should be evident that all parties contribute to their situation and that it will require efforts from all parties to remedy the situation.

STRATEGIES FOR PARENT–PROFESSIONAL PARTNERSHIPS

To overcome barriers to family involvement, professionals need to recognize that the role of the family in education has changed and will continue to change. As such, the role of the educator must change to accommodate for and take advantage of these shifts. McFadden and Burke (1991) identified a new paradigm for human services, including education for the next century. This paradigm "envisions a social order wherein most important decisions are made at the local level . . . and people are empowered to develop their own solutions to issues affecting their lives" (p. iii). Themes represented in this paradigm are empowerment, leadership, choice, and flexibility. Already, school reform proposals reflect these themes. Within this paradigm, it becomes the responsibility of the professional to increase the participation of family members in the decision-making process. McFadden and Burke stated:

> It is our belief that decisions that affect the quality of life experienced by people with developmental disabilities and their families are best made in consultation with and participation by the consumers themselves [people with disabilities and their families]. (1991, p. iv)

Educators rarely see students and their families as "consumers." The terms *teacher* and *student* connote a relationship far removed from that of a consumer, who dictates by his or her action what services are provided. The teacher–student relationship is more like a parent–child relationship. To move toward a truly collaborative relationship, educators need to incorporate into their multiple identities the role of enabler and to view as their responsibility the empowerment of families and students to assume greater control in educational planning and decision making. By so doing, they will set the stage for more positive adult outcomes for youth with disabilities and for greater success on their part.

Singer and Powers (1993) identified several basic principles of family support that can be applied to empower families to be involved in educational planning and decision making. Practices that empower seek to enhance a sense of community for families. Special education has and continues to be a process by which students and families become separated from the mainstream of the school community. We have set up a separate track for students with disabilities and in the process have removed families from the mainstream. For example, instead of becoming active with other parents through the Parent Teacher Associations, families of students with disabilities join the Special Education Parent Teachers Associations (SEPTA). To enhance a sense of community for families of youth with disabilities, educators need to emphasize the common needs of all families and work to improve the family's link with the broader community and wider ranges of support.

A second tenet of family involvement is to focus more broadly on the family's needs, not just on child-focused concerns. This recognizes that student success is linked directly to family success. Schools are increasingly becoming the location for community-based family services. Even if such services do not exist, the schools can provide a referral service. Third, educators must encourage shared responsibility and collaboration. Parents are equal partners by law and must be viewed as such by professionals. As Singer and Powers (1993) elaborated, all families have strengths and when problems are identified in a family, members can learn to solve these problems if given the opportunity and resources. Practitioners must put aside assumptions and biases and enable family members to experience meaningful control and choice.

Attempts to empower families must recognize and protect the integrity of the family unit. America is a pluralistic, diverse society, and educators must respect cultural beliefs and differences. Singer and Powers (1993) also pointed out that professionals must respect family boundaries and privacy to the greatest degree possible. Many special educators at least imply that the home environment should replicate the school environment. For example, a teacher may have families give their child a work sheet. Instead, activities in the home must be configured within the flow of the natural routine. Many developmentally and educationally valuable opportunities are in the home, and families can be guided to use these as learning experiences (some specific to the LCCE are provided later).

In addition to reevaluating how they perceive their role in the educational process, educators need to reexamine their perceptions about and expectations for people with disabilities.

We have suggested that the medical and educational models of disability have led to limited expectations for students with disabilities. There have been other, equally debilitating, perceptions of people with disabilities throughout history. In the late 1800s and early 1900s, people with disabilities were viewed as menaces and linked with crime, poverty, promiscuity, and the decline of civilization or construed as objects to be feared or dreaded. They were seen as subhuman (e.g., vegetable or animal-like) and were objects of ridicule. This was reflected in the language used about people with mental retardation. For example, labels describing levels of severity of mental retardation (idiot, imbecile, and moron) because used as insults.

As societal understanding of disability progressed, these negative stereotypes were replaced by less pejorative but no less damaging perceptions. People with disabilities were viewed as objects to be pitied, worthy of charity. Many people with disabilities were perceived as "holy innocents" (e.g., special messengers, children of God, etc.) and thus incapable of sin and not responsible for their own actions. This perception was slowly edged out by the perception of people with disabilities as "eternal children." Particularly for people with mental retardation, this perception was influenced by testing that deified "mental age," and adults with disability were excluded from adult roles because they had "the mind of a 3-year-old." Educational classifications of disability also created unfair stereotypes. Students with mental retardation are labeled as trainable or educable. One hardly expects a "trainable" student to hold adult roles such as spouse or employee.

Most professionals do not retain perceptions of disability that reflect beliefs held early in the century. However, vestiges of the latter perceptions remain and impact how people interact with individuals with disabilities, what is expected of them, and what opportunities are made available. Adults with "the mind of a 3-year-old" are not expected to hold a job. "Holy innocents" cannot learn about sexuality and relationships. Recipients of pity and charity are to be helped and not accepted as colleagues, friends, or neighbors. In a very real sense, perhaps the most important change that needs to occur is how educators specifically and the public in general view disability.

People with disabilities have emphasized one factor as critically important in changing attitudes and perceptions: People with disabilities are people first. By focusing on the person and not the condition, one can talk about hopes, dreams, abilities, and strengths. The 1992 amendments to the Rehabilitation Act and the 1993 amendments to the Developmental Disabilities Act both contain language that embodies the way in which people with disabilities must be perceived. Both acts state that

> disability is a natural part of human experience and in no way diminishes the rights of individuals to live independently, enjoy self-determination, make choices, contribute to society, pursue meaningful careers and enjoy full inclusion and integration in the economic, political, social, cultural and educational mainstream of American society. [Sec. 2(a)(3)(A - F)]

Disability is seen not as aberrant, outside the norm, or pathological, but as a part of being human. All human abilities and experiences exist on a continuum, and disability is a part of that continuum, not off of it.

Viewing people with disabilities inside this continuum allows us to apply new labels to people with disabilities: neighbor, colleague, home owner, card collector, baseball fan, parent, dancer, dog owner, spouse, leader, role model, and friend. Not all people with disabilities will, however, actually own a home; not all people without disabilities own homes. Some people with disabilities will not be good leaders; some people without disabilities are poor leaders. The key is that people with disabilities are people first, and they have the right to be valued and experience dignity and respect independent of any qualifier others might put on them.

If educators act on the premise that their efforts are to empower families and place value on individuals with disability as people first, it is likely that the battle is won. Such attitudes will manifest themselves in changes in behavior and action. Flaxman and Inger (1991) provided some pragmatic suggestions for school practices that encourage family involvement and reflect the orientation described:

- Increase the awareness and sensitivity of school staff to parents' time constraints: announce meetings long enough in advance to allow parents to arrange to attend.
- Give parents blanket permission to visit the school at all times—to visit the classroom, use the library, or talk to the teachers or administrators.
- Establish or support family learning centers in schools, storefronts, and churches and offer help to parents who want to help their children learn.
- Make the school facilities available to a variety of community activities.
- Facilitate teen-, single-, working- and custodial-parent peer support groups.
- Provide before-school child care so that working parents can see teachers before going to work.
- Conduct evening meetings, with child care, so that working parents can attend.
- Conduct evening assemblies to recognize students and parents for their contributions to the school.
- Establish bilingual hotlines for parents.
- Send messages in the family's language not only on routine notices but also on things parents can do at home to help educate their children.
- Do not make last-minute school cancellations.
- Print all signs in the languages spoken by school families. (Flaxman & Inger, 1991, p. 6)

Sonnenschein (1981) pointed out that if educators assume that all parents have strengths and view parents as partners, they will quickly build a relationship based on mutual trust and respect. She identifies the following visible indicators of such a relationship:

- Information, impressions, and evaluations are promptly and openly shared.
- Collaborators are able to communicate their feelings, needs, and priorities without worrying about being labeled in a derogatory way.
- Collaborators can ask each other for help without being made to feel weak or incompetent and are able to say "I don't know" or "I don't understand" without fearing the loss of respect or credibility.
- Efforts are made to avoid the use of jargon or any practice that tends to make the other feel like an outsider. Careful attention is given to the implementation of procedures that encourage dialogue and equal sense of control. (Sonnenschein, 1981, p. 65)

Sinclair and Christenson (1992) echo these indicators in identifying five key elements of effective and respectful parent–professional interactions: (1) mutual respect for skills and knowledge; (2) honest and clear communication; (3) two-way sharing of information; (4) mutually agreed upon goals; and (5) shared planning and decision making. Like many others, these authors emphasize communication as the first step in collaboration.

FAMILY CONCERNS IN TRANSITION PLANNING

We have already identified that the families of students at risk for school failure or of students with disabilities have (with the exception of the student) the most to gain and the most to lose from transition from school to adulthood. Although greater numbers of adult children are living at home with their parents than ever before, these rates for young adults with disabilities exceed national averages. Young adults with disabilities generally remain unemployed or underemployed, dependent on family members for living expenses and arrangements and are socially isolated. Most families share one primary concern in transition planning: that their child be enabled to live as independently as possible.

Many families may feel unsure about their role in transition planning. They are uncertain of the options available once their child leaves the public schools and, in many cases, have avoided thinking about this outcome. Previously, they had only educators to deal with in planning and decision making, now adult service providers, vocational rehabilitation counselors, and others are involved in the planning process. The "insider" knowledge about how to work the educational system does not transfer directly to these other systems, and parents feel as if they must start again. They are frequently surprised to learn that, on graduation, no entitlement programs guarantee work or independent living. For these and many other reasons, the transition period may be more stressful and anxiety provoking, not to mention confusing, than when the adolescent was a young child.

Educators can do much to ease these concerns and facilitate effective parental and family involvement in transition. They can explain the concept of transition and transition services to parents, make them aware of mandates in the law, and provide families the knowledge to move forward into the planning process without stumbling over gaps in communication. Teachers can make parents aware of the transition and community-based activities that their child is experiencing in school. By presenting positive options and the image of the student as a capable employee or community participant, teachers can create a framework that allows parents to move beyond previously held stereotypes or expectations. Transition-related goals and objectives should be a part of students' educational programs from elementary school onward, but during adolescence, these become particularly important (and mandated by law). Families who have had experience with transition goal setting throughout their child's educational program will be more willing and able to participate in transition planning during adolescence.

It is important to assist families to help their child develop positive work habits and behaviors, self-determination skills, and the self-confidence to succeed. Again, this is not something educators can do for families. Educators must be enablers and must provide families the support and information necessary to accomplish this on their own. S. Davis and Wehmeyer (1991) suggested the following 10 steps for families to promote independence and self-determination, and educators could provide information such as this to parents:

1. Walk the tightrope between protection and independence. Allow your child to explore her world.
2. Children need to learn that what they say or do is important and can influence others. This involves allowing risk taking and exploration.
3. Self-worth and self-confidence are critical factors in the development of self-determination. Model your own sense of positive self-esteem to your child.
4. Don't run away from questions from your child about differences related to her disability. That does not mean, however, focusing on the negative side of the condition. Stress that everyone is individual, encourage your child's unique abilities, and help her accept unavoidable limitations.
5. Recognize the process of reaching goals, don't just emphasize outcomes.
6. Schedule opportunities for interactions with children of different ages and backgrounds.
7. Set realistic but ambitions expectations.
8. Allow your child to take responsibility for his own actions—successes and failures.
9. Don't leave choice-making opportunities to chance.
10. Provide honest, positive feedback. Focus on the behavior or task that needs to be changed.

Mike Wehmeyer speaking to teachers and parents on the topic of self-determination for youth with disabilities at the Portland Hilton.

In some circumstances, it becomes difficult, if not impossible, for educators to provide information such as this without seeming judgmental or arrogant. In those circumstances, it is probably wise for the educator to serve as a referral agent and connect the family with support and advocacy groups. Most of these organizations consist of parents and family members who have experiences similar to that of the family and who can provide information without posing as an expert. The federal government funds Parent and Training Information Centers in every state that provide multiple information and support services. Disability-specific support and advocacy groups, such as The Arc, have state and local chapters around the country that run support groups and provide information and referral services. The transition period may consist of networking with other families, which provides valuable connections and information.

STRATEGIES FOR INVOLVING FAMILIES IN LCCE

The LCCE curriculum was conceptualized to include the family as an integral part of the educational planning and decision-making process, as well as to include families in activities that augment school- and community-based lessons and activities. One of the features of the LCCE is that it requires the school to work more closely with the family and community resources. The majority of learning occurs outside school. Career education promotes a partnership with parents and community resources whereby what is deemed important to learn about the world of work is taught beyond the confines of the school environment. In the process, parents and community members can become more aware and supportive of the school's program and objectives. (Brolin, 1993a, p. 5)

Because the LCCE focuses on career education and addresses the totality of the student's future and avocational needs, it is critically important that practitioners using LCCE secure active involvement from families based on a strong school–home partnership. Loyd and Brolin emphasized that:

The LCCE Curriculum Program should encourage parents to get involved in the career development of their sons and daughters. Parents/family members are role models and provide an awareness of the responsibilities related to work. They can be responsible for teaching basic life skills and attitudes through both modeling and actual home and community training. They play the initial role in the career development process through the establishment of the life skills and attitudes. The collaborative efforts of the school and parents/family members should be directed toward maximizing the students' career development in school, home and community. (1989, p. 1)

Many of the lesson plans in each of the LCCE competencies contain specific home activities that augment the school-based activity. These activities include detailed instructions and needed equipment to assist parents in their home-based actions. Additionally, however, the LCCE process is most effective if practitioners go beyond implementing just the home activities. The LCCE competencies and subcompetencies address specific behavioral and attitudinal areas involved in career education and critical for a successful transition from school to work. These skills and competencies can serve as the basis for establishing a dialogue between school and home. Families who understand that they are working on practical activities with their child have practical, beneficial outcomes will be more likely to participate. As discussed earlier, however, this must be a two-way dialogue.

When family members understand the applicability of the home-based activities and feel empowered as part of the decision-making team, they can initiate activities that meet needs identified in the LCCE but go beyond scripted lesson plans. Teachers could provide families ideas such as the following as a starting point for how they can become actively involved in the LCCE process:

1. With younger children, encourage the development of gross and fine motor activities by providing frequent opportunities for physical exercise or motor-oriented activities around the house. This should include fine motor activities involved with preferred leisure and spare-time activities.

2. Provide opportunities for students to engage in hands-on experiences with activities that give students a concept of certain work-related activities. This may include working with family members on household repair and maintenance activities that incorporate common tools. This also may include using a

computer at home and participating in financial planning and decision-making activities.

3. Assign specific jobs to the student. These duties should be completed to specifications and within a certain time frame. A second level of expectation is related to the student's development of a plan of action to complete the job. This plan may include following a routine, maintaining a schedule, and returning tools or utensils to specified locations.

4. Identify jobs performed by various workers in the community. Visit job sites and discuss them in detail at home. Actively involve the student in these discussions and observations. Such discussions help the student to express personal observations and ask questions about work. They also help build work values, interests, and long-term aspirations.

5. Discuss the work of family members, necessary training, difficulties, and rewards. If possible, arrange a visit to the parents' work site or facility. This will add to the student's knowledge and perception of the family's role in the community.

6. Provide a variety of family projects and activities, such as camping trips, sports events, travel, and church events so the student can build leisure, recreation, and social skills. These family projects and outings also provide students with disabilities with an opportunity to communicate ideas and feelings. These types of communications are important in helping students build positive concepts of themselves and their various roles in society.

7. Insist that students make their own decisions. Reinforce the process of making decisions, including investigating alternatives and consequences. Problem-solving and decision-making abilities are essential to the development of self-determination and autonomy and emerge from experiences with choice and decision making in the home.

8. Help students to feel psychologically secure by providing reinforcement for success and by providing the opportunities to contribute in family decision making. Evaluation should be honest but not focused on the student, instead on the task. If a student is unsuccessful, positive feedback regarding how to correct this and support to ensure success are effective learning tools.

9. Work closely with school personnel to achieve educational goals and objectives that are tied to adult outcomes. Several classroom activities are richly supported by the cooperation of the family. For example, teachers often use classroom activities to teach students about their parents' occupations. The activities may include role playing, child–parent interviews, and class field-trips to the parents' workplace. The class functions also support the family's attempt to build personal skills such as communication and problem solving.

10. Help school personnel develop community experiences that will expand curriculum opportunities, such as field trips, guest speakers, and work experience.

11. Encourage part-time work experiences, community projects, and hobbies that expose the student to various people and their careers.

12. Become involved in school advisory committees concerned with curriculum, development of resources, and other career education matters.

What many teachers realize is that parents and family members can effect change in the schools when teachers cannot. Family members can serve as the teacher's greatest advocate to implement functional, community-referenced programs such as the LCCE and to ensure that adequate resources are devoted to this effort. Likewise, home and school cooperation can make up for limitations in the teacher's activities. For example, because of financial constraints, schools may limit the number of field trips per year. However, under the direction of the classroom teacher, parents can include their child in family outings to centers of work activity.

The use of the competencies in the IEP and for transition planning provides a sound basis on which professionals and parents can meet to exchange opinions and form plans. Parents may not be able to initiate measures within the home that prepare their child in all of the 22 competencies, but they should be able to better understand the direction of the school program and identify competency areas that can be implemented immediately within the home. The student's attainment of the 22 competencies can be a reference point for teacher–parent interactions related to transition planning. This enables teachers and families to begin the planning process with a common understanding of what skills are necessary for transition and what it will take to complete this process. Kokaska and Brolin (1985) listed several suggestions related to conducting, planning, and evaluating activities around the LCCE competencies:

1. Evaluate the student's current status relative to the competencies to be achieved during the school year. This is standard practice in educational settings but is more difficult at home. Families cannot be expected to observe and record progress on activities in the same way teachers do. Families can provide feedback to teachers regarding their child's progress on home activities related to the competencies. This might be accomplished through written notes or a daily log that is passed from the school to the home.

2. Involve as many family members as possible in the planning and progress of activities designed to educate students in the competencies. Many of the student's experiences with competencies in the daily living skills and personal social skills can involve peers and siblings or other relatives. This procedure ensures the greatest number of "teachers" available in the educational program. One must be cautious, however, not to unfairly place siblings, cousins, or other relatives and peers in a structured, systematized role of "teacher" and taking away from the role of friend, playmate, and caretaker. Again, family involvement in instructional activities needs to follow the natural flow of the family's environment and not impose roles such as "teacher" on family members.

3. Emphasize the importance of career development as a process that extends from childhood through adult years. Parents of younger children will have difficulty visualizing further down the road, nor should they be forced to do so. Few families of toddlers without disabilities have plans for their adult years. However, by continuing to focus on career development with its stages of acquisitions, families can move through similar stages of awareness related to their child.

   4. Encourage parents to ask questions, make suggestions, voice opinions, and contribute goals. The greater the parental involvement in LCCE planning, the more the student will gain from the process.

   5. Be open and straightforward with families in the planning process. This does not mean being brutally honest or unfairly pessimistic. Educators need to recognize their biases and how they impact expectations for students within the LCCE. Collaborations are built on trust and mutual respect, and these are only built when communication is open ended.

   6. Develop a schedule of activities that parents can follow and that coincides with the classroom lessons. The schedule should be specific to the individual student and family situation. This does not mean that you have to send your lesson plans home with the student. The parents' schedule provides them with an estimation of those classroom lessons, daily assignments, or exercises that students should complete at home. It also allows families to plan ahead for home activities, identify resources, and prepare activities.

Finally, Loyd and Brolin (1989) provide a list of practical, day-to-day strategies teachers can use to encourage family involvement in LCCE:

   1. Schedule career development conferences to meet with parents about the educational program. These should be as frequent as necessary, separate from the IEP or transition planning meeting, and can occur outside the school facility if appropriate. This provides parents a forum for providing input to the process that does not include the baggage that mandated planning and placement meetings include.

   2. Visit the student's home and, if possible, provide instruction in that setting to ensure generalization. At the very least, make it known that you are willing to visit the home and consider it important. Do not push the issue if families are not comfortable.

   3. Encourage families to make classroom observations and visits when LCCE activities occur. Leave time following the observation to answer questions, explain teaching techniques, and reinforce the parents' efforts.

   4. Involve parents in district-wide discussions about transition and career development. Identify community discussions that focus on issues important to the transition process, and attend these with parents.

   5. Provide more structured workshops for families on the LCCE process and program so that parents can get a more comprehensive look at the LCCE. Remember that this should be optional, and parents should not be expected to acquire the same sophistication about the LCCE that teachers hold.

   6. Host dinners during which child care is provided so that parents can relax and talk informally about the LCCE program, career development, and the transition from school to work.

Loyd and Brolin (1989) also provided examples of parent–family contributions to the LCCE curriculum competencies. The following examples show how the LCCE curriculum competencies can be emphasized and practiced in the home.

Managing Personal Finances. One of the simplest ways the family can assist the student in this competency is to provide experience in identifying money correctly and to allow the student to make purchases and return with the correct change. Depending on the student's ability level, managing a weekly allowance is a possible ongoing activity. These skills and concepts coincide with the competency achieving independence.

Selecting and Managing a Household. Using basic appliances and tools is a subcompetence for which the family often provides direct instruction. Maintaining a home is usually a daily activity in which the student can participate. Modeling will be beneficial, but participation is helpful training for this competency and ultimately leads to the student's becoming self-sufficient.

Caring for Personal Needs. Dressing appropriately, a subcompetency of this competency, can be dealt with directly in the home. Teaching the child this skill does not mean picking out the clothes for him but rather assisting in clothing choices. This competency also encompasses basic hygiene and grooming, which can be fostered in a variety of ways in the home.

Raising Children and Meeting Marriage Responsibilities. These skills entail successfully modeling the responsibilities and life-style of marriage. Parents can emphasize the importance of carrying out these responsibilities.

Buying, Preparing, and Consuming Food. Because this competency encompasses the selection, purchase, and preparation of food, it can easily be demonstrated, explained, discussed, and practiced continually under direct parent supervision.

Engaging in Civic Activities. This competency includes informing the student of basic laws, rules, and regulations in the local community, taking the student to different organizations, and exposing her to a variety of activities in the community. Parental involvement can provide a strong motivation for the student to participate in civic activities.

Pursuing Recreation and Leisure. Parents can familiarize the student with recreational facilities and ways to spend leisure time, engage in recreational and leisure activities with the student, and encourage the student to choose recreation and leisure activities within her budget. Allowing the student to join in planning family vacations or outings can further develop the student's interest in recreation and leisure. (Loyd & Brolin, 1989)

These are only a few of the ways families can be involved in LCCE competencies and subcompetencies. The possibilities are limited only by the ability and willingness of educators and families to work together to achieve a common goal.

FINAL COMMENTS

In this chapter we have tried to emphasize the importance of family involvement in educational planning and decision making, transition planning, and the LCCE process for students at risk for failure and students with disabilities. The family involvement must reflect changes in education and understanding of learning in development that have occurred in the last few decades. Educators who want to succeed must empower families and students to take greater control in the educational process. They must work with families to develop collaborations in which family members are truly equal partners. In so doing, many educators will need to examine their beliefs about families and their role in education and about people with disabilities and their role in society. By adjusting their practices to meet these changes, educators can ensure greater educational success for their students as well as greater vocational satisfaction and success for themselves.

ACTIVITIES

1. Develop a Parent/Family Involvement Plan, outlining the steps you would undertake to meaningfully involve your students' families in your functional curriculum efforts. Compose a compelling set of reasons that will convince most of the parents to become a substantial partner in your educational activities.
2. Assume that your parents are ready and willing to participate in your curricular efforts and that you are implementing LCCE. Review the competencies in the personal–social or occupational domains, and develop a list of activities that the families could engage in to help their child to learn the competencies in the domain.

Chapter 5

Agencies, Organizations, and Informational Resources

Preliminary Questions About the Topic

1. Name three federal governmental agencies that are instrumental to promoting career development and transition services, and explain their particular contribution.
2. Identify six or more local community agencies and other resources that you would use to prepare your students for functional skills and transition services.
3. Explain the possible roles of the rehabilitation counselor in providing services to educators and students who are in school and those who have left.
4. How would you go about determining what agencies you need to be involved with your students, and how you would gain their cooperation?
5. What is a rehabilitation facility, and how can it be used by the educational program?
6. What is JTPA, and how can it help students with learning difficulties in their career development?
7. What postsecondary services are available to teach the functional life skills that these students will need to secure satisfactory employment and function independently in their community?
8. What local and professional organizations can help provide information, guidance, and/or direct services for career development needs?
9. Explain the composition of a Community Resource Directory and its use.
10. Identify three particularly useful national information systems or sources that will enhance your career development and transition efforts.

One of the major contributions of the career education concept has been the involvement of numerous community agencies and organizations in the career development efforts of the school. In addition to drawing on considerable expertise not readily available in the school setting, there are several particularly significant reasons for involving community agencies and organizations. First, these agencies and organizations have funds, equipment, contacts, and a constituency far beyond the resources of the school. Second, the agencies and organizations can assist in the improvement of the school's curriculum and courses. Third, the agencies and organizations sometimes lend financial support for pressing needs the school encounters in implementing career education. Fourth, the general public's negative attitudes and misconceptions toward individuals with disabilities and other learning difficulties will be counteracted as these agencies and organizations become partners in career development efforts.

Numerous civic, professional, and private nonprofit organizations and government agencies are located in most middle-sized and large communities. Besides the many local avenues for career development, there are several state and national resources that local personnel should use for additional information, literature, contacts, funding possibilities, and in some cases, direct services.

Educators in the schools cannot expect to teach all of their students all of the functional skills to the level that they will need for living and working successfully in their communities. In the previous chapter, the importance of the family involvement in the educational process was discussed. This chapter identifies and describes several important resources to assist educators in providing career development experiences and other services for their students. The first section identifies and explains the key federal, state, and local agencies that are available to help educators. This is followed by a section on suggestions on how to access the agencies that need to be involved for career development services. The next section identifies and explains some important national, state, and local organizations for career development assistance. The final section describes some of the major informational systems for obtaining materials and references on career education, functional skills, and transition programming.

GOVERNMENT AGENCIES

This section will identify and describe some of the major federal, state, and local government agencies that are responsible for the education and career development of persons with disabilities and those who are disadvantaged. The first agencies to be discussed are those at the federal level. Readers should refer to Table 5.1 to get an overall picture of the agencies to be discussed.

Point of View

When beginning transition planning, the teacher's first and best resource is the student. The student's interests, aptitudes, and needs, translated into adult life goals, provide a vision of the future environment for the student. An understanding of the student and the future environment demands are the basis for determining the resources needed to obtain the goal. In transition planning, parents are the next best resource. When student and parent goals coincide, all involved in planning are working together for the same outcome. It is at this point that the transition planning team can identify the agencies, organizations, and instructional resources necessary for the student to become successful in her chosen future environment. Instructional resources include the entire community, of which the school is a part.

Teachers frequently do not have time to develop collaborative relationships with all the agencies and organizations available to students. Most often, these relationships are initiated through the needs of one student. The transition team creates the path to the future environment, and team members (including the student and parents) take responsibility for exploring the needed resources. As teachers make contact with agencies and organizations to meet the needs of one student, they build a directory of resources to use in the future. The resources are most often local, including local offices of state agencies such as Vocational Rehabilitation and Mental Health/Developmental Disabilities. As teachers search for resources, they also develop relation-ships with individuals in agencies and organizations. These relationships are essential to collaborative planning. Once developed, acquisition of the resource for the next student becomes easier. Some school districts publish their own local resource directory. This is helpful to teachers when explaining to students and parents what resources are available. However, to gain access to the service for a student, the relationship between teacher and individual in the agency or organization is instrumental in obtaining timely service.

Transition planning calls for an interdependence of schools, the home, the community, and local agencies and organizations. The search for appropriate services may include national data bases, state or national organizations, and networking with experts in various fields. These searches are especially helpful when the transition planning team ia unsure of what local resources exist to meet the student's needs. For most students, the transition plan will lead to relationships and a balanced interdependence with individuals in local businesses, agencies, and organizations.

Arden Stephens is Coordinator for students with special learning needs in the Columbia, Missouri, Public Schools and former director of Missouri Linc.

TABLE 5.1   Federal Agencies Important to the Career Development of Individuals with Disabilities and Other Learning Difficulties

Agency	U.S. Department/Branch
Office of Special Education and Rehabilitative Services	Education
Office of Special Education Programs	
Rehabilitation Service Administration	
National Institute of Rehabilitation Research	
Office of Adult and Vocational Education	Education
Administration for Children and Families	Heath & Human Services
Administration on Developmental Disabilities	
President's Committee on Mental Retardation	
National Council on Disability	Independent Agency
Veterans Administration	Veterans Administration

Federal Agencies

The primary agencies in the U.S. Department of Education that are responsible for the delivery of education and rehabilitative services for persons with disabilities are the U.S. Office of Special Education Programs (OSEP) and the Rehabilitation Services Administration (RSA). Both agencies are divisions of the larger Office of Special Education and Rehabilitative Services (OSERS), which also includes the National Institute for Disability and Rehabilitation Research (NIDRR), which stimulates technology efforts and funds research and demonstration projects.

OSERS and its divisions are responsible for implementing the IDEA and Rehabilitation Act to ensure that special education programs and services are expressly designed to meet the needs and develop the full potentials of students with disabilities and that comprehensive rehabilitation service programs reduce human dependency, increase self-reliance, and fully use the productive capabilities of all persons with disabilities. Programs include support to universities for training of teachers, rehabilitation counselors, and other professional personnel; grants for research; financial aid to help state agencies initiate, expand, and improve their resources; and media services such as captioned films for hearing impaired persons. RSA funds regional offices and state agencies on an established formula to carry out their program of services. One other Department of Education unit, the Office of Vocational and Adult Education (OVAE), administers the vocational education monies that are given to their respective state agencies to conduct programs for students, including those with disabilities and those who are disadvantaged.

The Administration on Developmental Disabilities (ADD), under the Administration for Children and Families of the U.S. Department of Health and Human Services, administers formula grants to states for use with individuals who incurred developmental disabilities before the age of 22. This includes about 3 million people with mental retardation, cerebral palsy, epilepsy, and autism. The agency awards grants to university-affiliated programs and to programs of national significance. It has also established state protection and advocacy services for these individuals. According to a report from the Committee on Energy and Commerce (U.S. House of Representatives, 1993), a substantial portion of individuals with developmental disabilities and their families do not have access to appropriate support and services from generic and specialized service systems and remain unserved or underserved. Another division of this agency is the President's Committee on Mental Retardation, which compiles information, conducts studies, promotes research, advises the Administration, and acts as a liaison among federal, state, local, and private agencies concerned with mental retardation.

 The National Council on Disability spearheaded the development of the Americans with Disabilities Act (ADA) of 1990

The National Council on Disability (NCD) is an independent federal agency composed of 15 members appointed by the president of the United States and confirmed by the U.S. Senate (Robert Muller, who wrote the foreword to this book, was a member for 6 years). It was established in 1978 as an advisory board within the Department of Education. The Rehabilitation Act Amendments of 1984 transformed the Council into an independent agency. The mission of the NCD is to provide leadership in the identification of emerging issues affecting people with disabilities and in the development and recommendation of disability policy to the president and Congress. Although many government agencies address issues and programs affecting people with disabilities, the NCD is the only federal agency charged with addressing, analyzing, and making recommendations on issues of public policy that affect people with disabilities regardless of age, disability type, perceived employment potential, economic need, specific functional ability, status as a veteran, or other individual circumstance.

Some recent examples of the NCD's activities are conducting hearings, forums, and conferences on such topics as assistive technology, ADA research, rural and Native American issues, health insurance, personal assistance services, minorities; testifying before Congress on various disability issues; providing guidance to the President's Committee on Employment of People with Disabilities; and disseminating information to person's with disabilities, their families, the administration, the Congress, and the public.

One final but important federal agency is the Veteran's Administration (VA), which offers a broad range of programs, including medical care, rehabilitation, education and training, income support, and other benefits for eligible veterans with disabilities and their dependents. Their vocational rehabilitation service provides evaluation, counseling, training, employment, and other rehabilitation services to veterans with disabilities and many services to surviving dependents, including those with disabilities. Veterans Administration regional offices and hospitals are situated throughout the country.

State Agencies

It is very important for educators to know about and use the various state agency resources that are available to most communities. A knowledge of these resources must be viewed as a major responsibility so that educators can better ensure the best possible preparation of their students for a successful transition from school to employment, community living, and participation. Because states have different bureaucratic organizational structures, it is impossible to illustrate exactly where and how these agencies are located and administered. This is something that will have to be discovered by the practitioners themselves.

In this section, several agencies that are felt to be the most important ones for educators to interface with while their students are still in school are identified and described. The agencies are Vocational Rehabilitation, including its Supported Employment component; the Bureau for the Blind; Developmental Disabilities; State Employment Services; and Job Training Partnership Act (JTPA) Programs. Although it takes some time to learn about and successfully involve the agencies and other organizations that are responsible for providing services to these individuals, the final result will be well worth the effort. Each of these is discussed next.

Vocational Rehabilitation

State vocational rehabilitation (VR) programs are a partnership between the federal and state governments. Approximately 80% of the funding for these programs comes from federal dollars. The state VR program's function is to provide a planned sequence of individualized services designed to assist persons with disabilities to reach a vocational goal. To be eligible for these services, the individual (1) must have a physical and/or mental impairment that constitutes or results in a substantial impediment to employment, and (2) must be able to benefit from an employment outcome from vocational rehabilitation services. A list of services available through the VR program is presented in Figure 5.1

Some of the services listed in Figure 5.1 are at no charge, whereas others depend on the needs and resources of the individual and the agency's policies. Educators need to become familiar with this agencies' resources and policies to use them appropriately and to advise their students and parents.

An important change in the 1992 Rehabilitation Act Amendments is that an individual with a disability is presumed to be capable of benefitting from VR services unless the state agency can demonstrate by "clear and convincing evidence" that the individual cannot. The state VR agency can no longer find individuals ineligible for their services without an extended evaluation proving the person is not employable. In addition, the phrase "assessment for determining eligibility and VR needs" replaced "evaluation of rehabilitation potential."

 With the passage of the Individuals with Disabilities Education Act (IDEA), state VR agencies have an increased role in the transition of students from school to employment.

Vocational counseling and guidance

Vocational assessment

Vocational and other training services

Maintenance for additional costs incurred while participating in rehabilitation

Transportation in connection with the rendering of any vocational rehabilitation service

Services to family members of individuals with disabilities if necessary to the adjustment and rehabilitation of the individual

Interpreter services and note-taking services for individuals who are deaf, and tactile interpreting for individuals who are deaf-blind

Reader services, rehabilitation teaching services, note-taking services, and orientation and mobility services for individuals who are blind

Telecommunications, sensory, and other technological aids and devices

Work-related placement services including job search assistance, placement assistance, job-retention services, and personal assistance services

Follow-up, follow-along, and specific postemployment services necessary to maintain services

Occupational licenses, tools, equipment, initial stocks and supplies

Transition services that promote or facilitate the accomplishment of long-term rehabilitation goals and intermediate rehabilitation objectives

On-the-job or other related personal assistance services provided while an individual with a disability is receiving vocational rehabilitation services

Referral and other services designed to assist individuals with disabilities in securing needed services from other agencies through cooperative agreements

Supported employment services for individuals with severe disabilities and for whom competitive employment has not traditionally occurred

Rehabilitation technology services

Other goods and services necessary to render an individual with a disability employable

FIGURE 5.1   Services available from state vocational rehabilitation agencies.

The need for better coordinated and collaborative services among agencies has been recognized as important to institute for decades. In 1977, a historic "memorandum of understanding" between the federal agency for VR and the then U.S. Office of Education was released as a commitment of the two agencies to pursue methods by which the two delivery systems could achieve greater cooperation and provide complementary services. The commissioners of the two agencies transmitted memorandums to their state directors, requesting them to seek a coordinated service delivery for persons with disabilities.

In the years after the historic memorandum, some progress has been made in achieving a more cooperative effort. In some states, much closer working relationships evolved, and rehabilitation counselors have become important collaborators while the students are still in the educational program. Unfortunately, many state and/or local rehabilitation agencies, for various reasons, opted to wait to provide services at the time of graduation or thereafter, depending on the students' needs.

 Rehabilitation counseling is now a related special education service.

The importance of rehabilitation counseling to the special education effort was enhanced in 1990 with the passage of the IDEA legislation, which included it as a related service for students with disabilities, particularly in relation to transition services. The importance of this legislation is that it permits schools to hire rehabilitation counselors for their transition programs.

Rehabilitation counselors should be involved early in the students' program, as early as the elementary years, in those states where the agency is willing to become involved earlier. These professionals possess a wealth of knowledge about the labor market and the vocational potentials of persons with various disabilities. They can advise parents and educators on various skills and behaviors that should be emphasized during the early years so these children are prepared to benefit from higher-level functional skills and vocational instruction at the secondary level. The counselors are a valuable source of information about community training opportunities and can help unlock closed doors because of their many contacts with employers and other agencies and organizations such as the employment service and rehabilitation facilities. However, as one study in Alabama has uncovered in surveying rehabilitation counselors (Browning & Brechin, 1993), improved coordination, understanding, and cooperation between special education and rehabilitation are needed for students to receive better transition services.

 "Supported employment" programs are a boon to the vocational preparation and employment of persons with severe disabilities.

Created in the 1986 Amendments to the Rehabilitation Act, supported employment has become an important thrust for school transition programs. The 1992 Amendments state that those eligible for services are individuals with the most severe disabilities and who, because of the nature and severity of their disability, need intensive supported employment services to enter or retain competitive employment.

Supported employment services include "time-limited" ongoing support services and other appropriate services the individual needs, such as the following:

• Placement in jobs in an integrated setting for the maximum number of hours possible for the individual

- Intensive on-site job skills training and other training provided by skilled job train-ers, co-workers, and other qualified individuals
- Follow-up services including regular contact with employers, trainees, parents, guardians, or other representatives of trainees to reinforce and stabilize the job placement

No specific number of hours per week is required for a successful supported employ-ment placement, but rather, placements should be for the maximum number of hours possible based on the unique strengths, resources, interests, concerns, abilities, and capabilities of the individual.

Bureaus or Commissions for the Blind

The bureaus or commissions for the blind are VR agencies that are either a unit of the larger state VR agency or a separate commission, as is the case in 25 states. The reha-bilitation counselors are trained to assist their clients to learn daily living skills, mobil-ity, complete job application forms, and to meet other needs. The agency also funds reader services for college students who are visually impaired.

Developmental Disabilities

Many students in special education can be classified as having developmental disabili-ties. The federal government has provided funds to cover medical assistance, job train-ing, and social and other services, which are administered by a special state agency. In Missouri, for example, that agency is located in the Developmental Disabilities section of the Department of Mental Health. The state agency's role has changed dramatically over the years and now may include the coordination of Medicaid funding for institu-tions and community-based waivers and the coordination of state funds earmarked for persons with developmental disabilities including adult day programs, group home ser-vices, sheltered work programs, and the provision of advocacy services. The services provided vary greatly from state to state and community to community. In North Dakota, for example, caseworkers from the agency have worked closely with school personnel from age 14 on to help long-range transition services.

The 1990 Amendments to the Developmental Disabilities Assistance and Bill of Rights Act defines *developmental disability* as a severe, chronic disability of a person 5 years of age or older with the following characteristics:

- Is attributable to a mental or physical impairment or combination of mental and physical impairments
- Is manifested before the person attains age 22
- Is likely to continue indefinitely
- Results in substantial functional limitations in three or more of the following areas: self-care, receptive and expressive language, learning, mobility, self-direction, capacity for independent living, and economic self-sufficiency
- Reflects the person's need for individualized and coordinated special services

Infants from birth to age 5 who have substantial developmental delay or specific congenital or acquired conditions also qualify if there is a high probability of developmental disabilities resulting if services are not provided.

Each state has a Developmental Disabilities Council, which is mandated to promote, through systematic change, capacity building, and advocacy, a consumer- and family-centered comprehensive system and a coordinated array of services, supports, and other assistance for individuals with developmental disabilities and their families. This council is often the leading edge in promoting the delivery and coordination of services between education, state agencies, private agencies, and communities.

 The state employment service employs a specialist to work specifically with persons who have disabilities.

State Employment Services (Job Services)

There are more than 2000 local employment service offices throughout the country to help employers find workers and to help workers find jobs. Each office is mandated by law to employ a specialist trained to work with persons with disabilities. The state employment services agency can serve as a valuable information resource for students with disabilities and also for those who are disadvantaged. The agency can provide school personnel with a wealth of information regarding the community's labor market needs and the skills their students will need to be considered for employment. Other services that the agency can offer many students are the following:

* Assessment to determine vocational aptitudes and interests
* Job search assistance workshops to develop job-seeking skills
* Youth program to enhance students in transition
* Vocational guidance and counseling

The agency can assist employers who hire and train persons with disabilities and certain others to obtain the Targeted Jobs Tax Credit (TJTC) for giving these individuals the opportunity to become stable employees.

An often overlooked service of the employment service is its research program. One of the information data bases available to students is the State Training Inventory (STI), a computerized inventory of state and local training resources that assists users in identifying local schools, colleges, training programs, and the training programs they offer. Each state publishes an STI through their Department of Labor or Manpower or State Occupational Information Coordinating Committee (SOICC). The 1992 STI data base includes 17,500 schools and 200,000 training programs. This information is available at little or no cost and is constantly being expanded and updated.

Each state also conducts an Occupational Employment Statistics survey on an ongoing basis, which is collected for over 750 occupations. This survey is conducted in every county in the state and includes:

* The typical or average staffing pattern of each industry in terms of occupational employment in each industry to total industry employment
* The industries in which people work and their employment
* Occupational employment projections

 The Dictionary of Occupational Titles, Occupational Outlook Handbook, *and* Occupational Outlook Quarterly *are important tools for career education programs.*

The U.S. Department of Labor integrates data from all states into national labor statistics and projections. The U.S. Government Printing Office publishes manuals that are very helpful to persons planning for the future. The *Dictionary of Occupational Titles* was developed in response to the demand for standardized occupational information to support job placement activities. The use of this information has expanded from job-matching applications to various uses for employment counseling, occupational and career guidance, and labor market information services. The *Occupational Outlook Handbook* is updated every 2 years and describes about 250 occupations in detail. It covers approximately 87% of all jobs in the nation and is used as a reference book describing not only occupations but also what the work is like, what education and training are needed, advancement possibilities, earnings, job outlook, and employment projections. The *Occupational Outlook Quarterly* provides career updates every 3 months.

Educators' expectations about the future influence the decisions they make concerning the curriculum, their students' Individualized Education Program (IEP), and their transition programs. Because work is such a vital part of each student's life, the information provided by the state and U.S. Department of Labor can be a very important part in making decisions.

Job Training Partnership Act Program

The JTPA program was created to prepare youth and unskilled adults for entry into the labor force and to afford job training to economically disadvantaged individuals and others facing serious barriers to employment who are in special need of training to obtain productive employment. Six primary services provided by JTPA are the following:

* Assessment of the individual's strengths and abilities
* Preemployment training for job-seeking and -keeping skills
* Try-out employment by paying the wages for first 125 hours for employers who provide the training and permanent employment
* On-the-job training where employers are reimbursed for 50% percent of the wages while the worker is being trained
* Institutional skills training at vocational technical schools and community colleges
* Summer youth employment and training program so youth can get paid experience and develop work maturity (Steele, Burrows, Kiburz, & Sitlington, 1990)

Many individuals are eligible for JTPA services, and several school programs across the country are involving their students in JTPA programs. Interested readers should contact their local state employment service agency or the mayor's office to obtain specific information for programs in their area.

In addition to the preceding agencies, which offer services at the local level, the departments or divisions of special education and vocational special needs also play extremely important roles in funding services in the schools. The state special education agency administrates the state agency for the education of exceptional children; offers technical assistance to school districts and programs; conducts seminars and workshops; disseminates information; conducts student identification and needs studies; promotes the development of professional services; and promotes, writes, and enforces legislation.

The vocational education/special needs program administers the federal/state legislation that relates to vocational education for disadvantaged individuals and those with disabilities (called *special needs*); promotes the development and funds programs in secondary and postsecondary educational settings; and works closely with universities in developing personnel training programs, conducting special projects, developing and disseminating materials, and other activities of career development.

 The IDEA legislation states the IEP should contain statements of each public and participating agency's responsibilities or linkage (or both) before the student finishes school— including the agency's commitment.

Local Agencies and Programs

Each of the state agencies described provides services at the local level. Regional and local offices are located in many cities throughout the state. People from rural areas will need to find out where the nearest office is located. In addition to these agencies, some other important programs and services are available. Figure 5.2 shows the variety of community resources available in many communities. A description of some of these programs follows.

Community Rehabilitation Programs (Rehabilitation Facilities)

The 1992 Rehabilitation Act Amendments changed the previous term of "rehabilitation facility" to "community rehabilitation program." Each state VR agency is required to maintain a State Plan for community rehabilitation programs, which includes an inventory of those available in the state, a description of the use of each, a determination of needs for such programs, and a list of the projects they are conducting to achieve state goals.

Most community rehabilitation programs or rehabilitation facilities are private, nonprofit agencies that offer clients the opportunity to receive a comprehensive vocational assessment, work habits and work skills training, vocational guidance, independent liv-

Business-Labor-Industry
Chamber of Commerce
Banks
Credit unions
Insurance companies
Utility companies
Department stores
Restaurants
Grocery stores

Service Organizations
League of Women Voters
4-H clubs
Boy Scouts
YMCA, YWCA
Optimist clubs
Church groups
Youth groups
Lions
Kiwanis
Rotary
American Legion

Private Agencies
Rehabilitation facilities
Sheltered workshops
Lutheran Family & Children
  Services
Catholic Social Services
Jewish Services
Group homes
Independent Living Centers

**Community
Resources**

Schools
Vocational-technical schools
Community colleges
Trade/proprietary schools

Federal & State Agencies
Vocational Rehabilitation
Employment Service
JTPA programs
Mental Health
Public Health
Developmental Disabilities
VA Services
Protection & Advocacy

**National, State, & Local
  Organizations**
State & Local Council for
  Exceptional Children
State Rehabilitation Association
Disabled American Veterans
United Cerebral Palsy
State & Local Association for
  Retarded Citizens (Arc)

FIGURE 5.2   Some community resources important to career development of individuals with disabilities and who are disadvantaged.

ing skills training, and job placement services. Progressive facilities use a considerable amount of community-based experiences rather than segregate their clients in one building, although the amount of this depends on the nature of the person being served.

Community rehabilitation programs and facilities employ evaluation specialists, instructors, work supervisors and job trainers, counselors, case managers, job placement specialists, and other professionals, depending on the size and nature of the agency. These facilities are largely financed by the referrals they receive from the state vocational rehabilitation agency and others who pay for various services that lead to the employment of the individual. The final job placement may be in supported employment for those individuals who are deemed in need of this type of supervised working arrangement.

Educators should involve rehabilitation facilities in providing career development services to students who will need a more concentrated and specialized emphasis in functional skills. This involvement should begin at least during the junior year if not before. Facility personnel can be of substantial assistance in planning the career development activities and services for these students. Few rural areas will have ready access to such a service; however, near the end of the students' educational program or shortly thereafter, arrangements for postschool services may be financed by the vocational rehabilitation agency if it is deemed a feasible goal by that agency. This is another reason that the involvement of the vocational rehabilitation agency is so important while the students are still in school.

Vocational–Technical Education Schools and Community Colleges

In many states, postsecondary community colleges and vocational–technical schools provide selected opportunities for students with disabilities and those who are considered disadvantaged to learn job and daily living skills. This is an area that has never developed to meet the needs of the majority of students with special needs because of resistances by some and lack of adequate skills by others who work in these settings. Admission to these schools has always been a controversial issue despite the pressing needs of so many of these individuals when they are not prepared for community living and employment considerations after leaving the secondary school; and most of them are not prepared.

Some vocational schools and community colleges have accepted the responsibility for providing meaningful and quality postschool programs for students with special needs. They have established vocational assessment and job placement services in order to ensure the student's success. Specific instruction is provided in regular on-campus facilities and resources, in specially designed settings, or in community-based training settings with employers and others. Vocational education instructors are a very important resource because of their specific skill areas expertise and their contacts within the business community. Funding for these programs is generally contributed by the vocational education/special needs division and/or special education state agencies.

Other Agencies and Community Services

In each state, a protection and advocacy agency is available for people with developmental disabilities or their parents if they are having difficulty finding help in their communities. In some communities, private social service agencies such as Lutheran Family and Children Services, Catholic Family Services, and Jewish Services are available to help families and individuals resolve personal adjustment problems, interpersonal conflicts, and social and emotional difficulties. Trained social workers, using individual and group methods, help the student to find ways of fulfilling personal–social needs. Group homes and residential programs, with funding from state agencies, are another excellent resource in some communities. These facilities provide supervision while the residents receive vocational training and other career development services. Some provide substantial training in daily living skills and personal–social development, particularly if they are not affiliated with another rehabilitation program. These agencies generally also provide a limited staff for individual and group counseling. Independent living centers/programs, funded in part from VR funds, are another resource in some communities. These facilities provide a wide array of services—such as advocacy and awareness, attendant care, counseling, information services, and referral—to people with physical and other disabilities.

The number and type of agencies serving people with disabilities in various communities in each state are substantial. Although most of these services are not located in small rural towns, they are available to residents if they are willing to be transported to them. Professional workers from agencies such as VR can be contacted to make appropriate arrangements. With the current emphasis on planning for the transition of students from school to postsecondary services and eventual employment, cooperative planning among agencies is essential to ensure there are no gaps in services. More will be presented on interagency collaboration later.

ACCESSING THE AGENCIES

Many parents, advocate groups, professionals, and politicians have worked hard to achieve the legislation, funding, and personnel that are needed to provide important services to people with disabilities and other disadvantages. Thus, it is the responsibility of professionals who are working with these individuals to learn about these resources and how to access them for the benefit of their students or clients. In this section, some suggestions on approaching this challenge are presented.

Steps to Accessing Agencies

1. Develop or secure a Community Resource Directory that identifies all possible sources of assistance in meeting student needs. Besides reviewing information contained in this book on such resources and sending for more specific information relative to your state, a good source of information is the local telephone directory. In the Columbia, Missouri, directory, for example, are three pages of resources listed under the category *human services.* The resources are divided into various categories, e.g., abuse–adult, abuse–child, alcohol and drug abuse/addition, child youth services, counseling services, crisis intervention, disabled, services, employment services, health services, legal assistance, and volunteer services and opportunities. Telephone calls and/or correspondence to these agencies should result in relevant information on their services and appropriate contact persons. A sample community resource data form and work sheet used by schools implementing the LCCE curriculum are presented in Figure 5.3.

Education Level: _____

LCCE Community Resource: _____

Related to LCCE Curriculum Domain(s):

_____ Daily Living Skills

_____ Personal–Social Skills

_____ Occupational Guidance and Preparation

Name of Resource Person: _____

Address: _____

_____

_____

Telephone: (   ) _____

Related Career Education Stage(s):

_____ Awareness

_____ Exploration

_____ Preparation

_____ Assimilation (Placement/Follow-up)

Type of Resource:

_____ Field Trip   _____ Speaker

_____ Classroom Consultant   _____ Student Tutor

_____ Instructional Materials   _____ Work Experience

_____ Training Site   _____ Other (Please List)

_____

_____

_____

Detailed Description of Resource: _____

_____

_____

_____

_____

_____

_____

_____

_____

_____

_____

FIGURE 5.3   Community resource data form and work sheet.

COMMUNITY RESOURCES WORKSHEET

Page _____ of _____

LCCE COMPETENCY	COMMUNITY RESOURCE	METHODOLOGY	NOTES

FIGURE 5.3 *continued*

2.   *Determine what needs of your students cannot be fully met by the school.* Examples of such needs might be vocational assessment, work adjustment training, vocational counseling and guidance, personal counseling, behavior modification, medical services, daily living skills training, social skills training, community work experience, family counseling/services, financial services, advocacy, interpreter, reader services, transportation, supported employment, special equipment, and job placement. The individual student's needs should be specified in the IEP and/or transition plan for that year. A rationale for why each of the identified needs cannot be met by the school program should be written so the agencies contacted will have clear justification for their involvement.

3.   *Contact representatives from agencies that information from your resource directory indicates can provide for these needs.* In deciding which agencies to contact, be sure you have reviewed the eligibility requirements relative to disabilities and ages served, financial needs tests, and the like. The more familiar you are with the agencies' requirements and services, the greater the chance for success. It is suggested that you invite the agency caseworkers to the school to meet you and the students and to become familiar with your needs. As you may recall, the IDEA regulations now require a transition plan that involves agencies, and most of them are also mandated to collaborate with schools in transition planning. Remember, these agencies are charged by law to serve these individuals; thus, they will have to justify their reasons for denying any services that you believe are warranted. Obviously, you do not want to develop a threatening, aversive relationship with the agencies but rather, a cooperative, partnership in serving the students and their families.

4.   *Additional suggestions.* Some further suggestions or cautions in developing a collaborative relationship with community agencies are probably warranted. First, remember, they are serving a wide array of persons with disabilities and problems, not only school-age children. Second, they do have limited funds, as you do, and must use their money judiciously and not duplicate what others can do. Third, most caseworkers are not always familiar with all the disabilities, characteristics, and learning problems associated with special education students. Thus, they need to become more knowledgeable and appreciative of these students needs. Fourth, professional jealousies and rivalries do exist and, unfortunately, protecting one's turf is almost a normal occurrence in the field of human services. Thus, considerable time may be needed to establish an atmosphere of trust and respect for each other's efforts. And, fifth, there will always be some hard-headed caseworkers who are unresponsive to the educator's needs. In these instances, the educator should contact the supervisor to achieve the needed assistance.

Interagency Agreements

Local interagency agreements initiated by the local educational agency provide one way to enhance the cooperation of community agencies to participate more actively in the career development/transition efforts of the school district. Written agreements are preferred, although they do not guarantee the expected collaborative effort from the agencies.

Several states, including Iowa, Kansas, and Minnesota, have instituted impressive interagency ventures to get various agencies to work more closely together to provide relevant transition services. As noted by Everson and McNulty (1992), the focus of interagency teams is to identify, create, and maintain services and supports needed by the students rather than matching them to existing slots or placements.

Minnesota has been a leader in initiating interagency cooperative agreements. In 1982, special education, vocational education, and vocational rehabilitation agencies developed their agreement. Shortly thereafter, a State Transition Interagency Committee was established and then an Interagency Office on Transition Services. This latter agency provides information and technical assistance to local education agencies, assisting communities in establishing interagency agreements and conducting workshops on interagency planning for transition (Minnesota Department of Education, no date).

Persons interested in developing more formalized interagency agreements at the local level should investigate what state-level agreements have been written between agencies at that level to gain some direction and leverage for their situation. An example of one state-level interagency/cooperative agreement is provided in Appendix A.

ORGANIZATIONS

Numerous private, nonprofit, volunteer, professional, and other organizations that are dedicated to providing persons with disabilities and other problems are also available in many small-to-large communities. Many of these were started by parent groups and other concerned citizens who felt that specific areas of need required special attention. Some cities will have local affiliates of the state and national organization, for example, The Arc (a national organization on mental retardation—formerly known as the Association for Retarded Citizens), United Cerebral Palsy, and the National Easter Seal Society. These parent/volunteer organizations receive considerable guidance and support from the state and national organizations to carry out their policies and objectives. They often support or operate day-care facilities, sheltered workshops, group homes, or other direct service programs at the local level.

The number of organizations that are committed to serving and enhancing the quality of life of persons with disabilities is impressive. One cannot help but wonder how anyone with a disability can be unserved or underserved with the vast amount of money and array of services that have been created over the past decades. Professional workers do have resources at their disposal if the effort is made to identify and use them. A list of some particularly important organizations for career development services is provided for the reader's reference in Appendix B.

 The Division of Career Development and Transition is an important professional organization for those involved in conducting career education and transition services.

Sandra Squires, past president of DCD (now DCDT), presents an award to Kenneth Hoyt for his leadership in the career education movement. Fred Weintraub, assistant director of CEC, looks on.

Professional organizations are also very important resources and instigators of improving services to people with disabilities and those who are disadvantaged. One organization that is particularly important to the career development effort is The Council for Exceptional Children's (CEC) Division on Career Development and Transition (DCDT). Several position papers prepared by the division were alluded to in earlier chapters. This organization, existing since 1976, conducts an international convention every 2 years, conducts numerous sessions on career education at the annual CEC convention, sponsors regional and state conferences, and keeps members informed of major legislative developments. The organization produces a professional journal (*Career Development for Exceptional Individuals*) to inform its members of the latest research activities, model programs, and issues in career development and transition planning. It also produces a newsletter with the latest information on legislation, projects, resources materials, and implementation strategies.

Another related organization that promotes career development for persons with disabilities, disadvantages, and limited English proficiency is the National Association of Vocational Education Special Needs Personnel (NAVESNP), affiliated with the Special Needs Division of the American Vocational Association (AVA). NAVESP publishes *The Journal for Vocational Special Needs Education* and a newsletter, holds conferences and workshops, and promotes legislation.

Two other organizations that focus on career education for all students and have demonstrated commitment to persons with disabilities and the disadvantaged are the American Association for Career Education (AACE) and the National Career Development Association (NCDA). Both of these professional groups also hold conferences, publish newsletters, and keep members informed of important developments in the field. These organizations have collaborated with DCDT in conducting important national conferences.

As indicated previously in Figure 5.2, many service organizations can and have helped develop viable career education programs.

As indicated in Chapter 6, where those resources are described, industry, labor, and business resources can provide students with community work experiences and observations; help develop career-oriented curricula; assist in job placement efforts; provide volunteers for the school; and elicit support for career education throughout the community. Many community resources such as banks, credit unions, insurance companies, utility companies, department stores, restaurants, and grocery stores can give students information and experiences in the daily living skills areas. These sources are also a powerful influence for obtaining additional and needed funds from the government and private sectors.

Service organizations and other civic groups can help to develop viable career education programs. The League of Women Voters, church groups, youth groups, Lions International, and others generally look for projects that will benefit the community. These organizations can also provide schools and agencies with the talents of their members. *Rotary International Magazine* has featured a special section on the relationship between education and work. The American Legion adopted career education as a priority and has continued to emphasize ways in which members can assist school efforts in career development.

The list of community, state, and national resources for carrying out career development efforts is almost endless. Space does not permit identifying all the important resources. Persons interested in obtaining more detailed information on these and other national, state, and local organizations and services for persons with disabilities have several excellent resources at their disposal. These include the HEATH Resource Center, the National Center for Research in Vocational Education/TASPP, and the CEC Information Services, which will be described in the next section.

INFORMATION RESOURCES

Several national information centers are identified and described in this section so that educators can obtain additional information that will enhance their efforts with students who have disabilities or specific learning difficulties. Once again, only a selected list of resources is presented because space restrictions. Each of these is listed in Table 5.2 for quick reference and is described in the following paragraphs.

National Clearinghouses

The first important resource presented is five clearinghouses that provide specialized information to teachers, students, counselors, policymakers, parents, disability advocates, and people with disabilities.

ERIC Clearinghouse on Disabilities and Gifted Education

The Clearing house on Disabilities and Gifted Education is one of the federally sponsored Educational Resources Information Centers (ERIC), and is operated by CEC (1920 Association Drive, Reston, VA 22091). CEC produces the Exceptional Child Education Resources (ECER) data base of more than 80,000 abstracts from the profes-

TABLE 5.2   Information Systems for Materials on Career Development for Individuals with Special Learning Needs

Organization	Location
ERIC Clearinghouse on Disabilities and Gifted Education	CEC, Reston, VA
ERIC Clearinghouse on Adult, Career, and Vocational Education	Ohio State University
Health Resource Center (National Clearinghouse on Postsecondary Education for Persons with Disabilities)	Washington, D.C.
National Clearinghouse of Rehabilitation Training Materials (NCHRTM)	Oklahoma State University
The Council for Exceptional Children Information Services	CEC, Reston, VA
National Center to Improve Practice (NCIP)	Newton, MA
National Center for Youth with Disabilities	University of Minnesota
The Center for Education and Work	University of Wisconsin–Madison
Technical Assistance for Special Populations, The National Center for Research in Vocational Education, University of California	University of Illinois
Transition Institute	University of Illinois
President's Committee on Employment of People with Disabilities	Washington, D.C.

sional literature. Its quarterly journal, *Exceptional Child Education Resources,* provides abstracts and indexes of the most recent additions to the ECER data base. The ECER's unique contribution is the inclusion of books, dissertations, and many journal articles not included in the ERIC collection. CEC can provide either an ERIC–CEC product or a data base search. Products include publications such as books, monographs, or reports; brief products such as summaries of current topics, digests, research briefs, and minibibliographies; and directories of research projects. Custom computer searches are complete CD-ROM or on-line searches of the ERIC, ECER, or related data bases customized to meet specific user needs. Interested persons should call 1-800-328-0272.

ERIC/ACVE: Clearinghouse of Adult, Career, and Vocational Education

The ERIC/ACVE Clearinghouse is located at Center for Education and Training for Employment, The Ohio State University, 1900 Kenny Road, Columbus, OH 43210-1090 (1-800-848-4815). The focus of the ERIC Clearinghouse is formal and informal career education at all levels that encompasses attitudes, self-knowledge, decision-making skills, general and occupational knowledge, and specific vocational and occupational skills; formal and informal adult and continuing education relating to occupational, family, leisure, citizen, organizational, and retirement roles; vocational and technical education that includes new subprofessional fields, industrial arts, and vocational rehabilitation for individuals with disabilities. The center has several bibliographies and information analysis papers on career development.

HEATH Resource Center: National Clearinghouse on Postsecondary Education for Individuals with Disabilities

The HEATH Resource Center, a program of the American Council on Education, is located at One Dupont Circle, Suite 800, Washington, DC 20036-1193 (1-800-544-3284). It operates under a congressional mandate to collect and disseminate information nationally about disability issues in postsecondary education. The center is funded by the U.S. Department of Education and is intended to increase the flow of information about educational support services, policies, and procedures related to educating or training people with disabilities after they leave high school. More specifically, the HEATH Resource Center has the following functions:

* Identify and describe educational and training opportunities.
* Promote accommodations that enable full participation by people with disabilities in regular, as well as specialized, postsecondary programs.
* Recommend strategies that encourage participation in the least restrictive and most productive environments possible for each individual.

HEATH publishes a newsletter three times a year, free of charge to members. The newsletter provides information on campus programs and legislation and reviews new publications and media products. The center produces fact sheets, resource papers, guides, and directories related to disability issues as they occur on college campuses, vocational technical training schools, adult education programs, independent living centers, and other community-based training programs. The toll-free telephone number is 1-800-544-3284 (in the Washington, DC, area, it is 202-939-9320).

National Clearinghouse of Rehabilitation Training Materials

The National Clearinghouse of Rehabilitation Training Materials (NCHRTM) resources is funded by the Rehabilitation Services Administration and is located at Oklahoma State University, 816 West Sixth Street, Stillwater, OK 74078 (800-223-5219). NCHRTM disseminates information on vocational rehabilitation with primary concentration on in-service training of personnel. Materials from special education are included, however, to respond to the transition needs of students in the period between the education and employment. Resources include print and media not found in traditional sources. An *NCHRTM Memorandum* is published quarterly, listing available materials and their cost.

Centers for Educational Information/Services

Several additional sources of information to the field that are not considered clearinghouses but provide valuable resource information that can be used for career development programs are presented next.

The Council for Exceptional Children Information Services

As the major professional organization in the education of exceptional individuals, CEC publishes materials in both print and nonprint formats that facilitate continued improvement in services. A list of the products includes the following:

- *Exceptional Child Education Resources (ECER)*. This resource contains more than 80,000 abstracts of the published professional literature covering the education and development of individuals who have disabilities or who are gifted. ECER is available in print and CD-ROM formats.
- Topical bibliographies based on the references in ECER.
- Professional books and nonprint media on instructional methods and materials, administrative procedures and programs, training of personnel, legislation and legal procedures, and projected changes in education and training of individuals with disabilities or those who are gifted.
- Journals and newsletters published by CEC and its divisions. The two prominent journals are *Exceptional Children* and *TEACHING Exceptional Children.*
- Custom computer search of the ERIC and ECER data bases on request.

Information can be obtained by writing CEC, 1920 Association Drive, Reston, VA 22091.

The National Center to Improve Practice

The National Center to Improve Practice (NCIP) is a relatively new center located at the Education Development Center (EDC), Inc., 55 Chapel Street, Newton, MA 02158-1060 (800-225-44276). The NCIP is a joint endeavor between both EDC and WGBH Educational Foundation, Boston's public television station, to improve outcomes of students with disabilities by helping practitioners to effectively use technology, media, and materials to enhance instruction. Because knowledge alone does not promote change, the NCIP has designed a process for knowledge use called the *Dynamic Approach to Change.* Through this approach, the NCIP seeks to support change agents—those individuals in schools or districts who provide administrators, practitioners, and parents with the knowledge, resources, and training they need to embrace and implement innovative uses of technology, media and materials. The NCIP's approach is dynamic because it integrates a variety of media including newsletter packets, an electronic resource library and bulletin board, and video conferences; provides technical assistance to change agents through written guidelines, network support, and training institutes; encourages communication and sharing through electronic network conversations and video conferences; and expands the knowledge base through action research.

National Center for Youth with Disabilities

The National Center for Youth with Disabilities is a project located at the University of Minnesota, Adolescent Health Program, D-124 Mayo Memorial Building, Box 721, Harvard Street at East River Road, Minneapolis, MN 55455 (800-333-NCYD). The center focuses on adolescents with chronic illness and disability and the issues surrounding their transition to adult life. Its goal is to foster coordination and collaboration among agencies, professionals, families, and youth in the planning and provision of services, and to promote awareness of and responsiveness to the student's health and social needs. The center offers a National Resource Library, which maintains a data base containing separate bibliographic, program, training/education, and technical assistance files; it offers workshops and conferences at state and national levels supporting the design and implementation of state and community programs for youth and their families; it offers publications of monographs, bibliographies, and newsletters on vital issues regarding adolescence and disability; and it offers technical assistance.

The Center for Education and Work

The Center for Education and Work is located at the University of Wisconsin-Madison, 964 Educational Sciences Building, 1025 West Johnson Street, Madison, WI 53706-1796 (800-446-0399). The center is supported by national, state, and local contracts and grants. Staff conduct research, develop instructional and in-service materials, provide technical assistance, and disseminate products worldwide. The center's expertise lies in vocational and technical education, education for employment, vocational equity, business and industry training needs, labor market information, career development, students with disabilities and students at risk, program evaluation, corrections, and administration. Several products are available from the center on the following topics: curriculum development, exemplary secondary and postsecondary programs, best practices for the rehabilitation of learning disabled students, interagency linkages, technical preparation, ADA implementation, and replicating jobs with business and industry for persons with disabilities.

Technical Assistance for Special Populations Program

The Technical Assistance for Special Populations Program (TASPP) is a resource affiliated with the National Center for Research in Vocational Education at the University of California, Berkeley. It is located at the University of Illinois, Department of Vocational and Technical Education, 345 Education Building, 1310 S. Sixth Street, Champaign, IL 61820 (217-333-0807). The TASPP is a resource and referral source for practitioners, researchers, and policymakers working in vocational education with special needs populations at the secondary and postsecondary level. Other objectives are to initiate and support networks of professionals serving special needs students and to provide technical assistance on selected topics or problems crucial to improving the quality of vocational education programs provided to special populations. TASPP conducts workshops, publishes a quarterly newsletter on critical issues and policy options, and develops materials for national distribution.

Secondary Transition Intervention Effectiveness Institute

The Secondary Transition Intervention Effectiveness Institute is located at the University of Illinois, College of Education, 110 Education Building, 1310 S. Sixth Street, Champaign, IL 61820 (217-333-2325). The purpose of the institute is to operationalize a research model that will effect improvements in transition services. The institute addresses both the theoretical and practical problems associated with the transition needs of youth with disabilities with the goal of seeking solutions through interventions, evaluation, technical assistance, and the development and implementation of more appropriate policy. An impressive array of research and technical reports has been published by the institute's staff since its inception in 1985.

President's Committee on Employment of People with Disabilities (PCEPD)

The President's Committee on Employment of People with Disabilities (PCEPD) is a resource located at 1111 20th Street, N.W., Suite 636, Washington, DC 20036 (202-653-5044). It serves as a national source of information and assistance on employment issues for persons with disabilities. It conducts an annual conference on the employment of people with disabilities, seminars, and workshops on a range of issues centered around employment. It publishes various publications and sponsors the Job Accommodation Network, an information system, developed by employers for employers, to exchange ideas about practical steps they have taken to accommodate persons with disabilities, located at the West Virginia University Rehabilitation Research and Training Center, Morgantown, WV. Each state has a Governor's Committee on Employment of People with Disabilities and is also another excellent information source.

Some other important sources that will not be described but should be mentioned are the Apple Office of Special Education Programs at Apple Computer, the IBM National Support Center for Persons with Disabilities, and The National Rural Development Institute's Resource Center at Western Washington University. Again, the sources provided in the previous section should be contacted if further information is desired.

FINAL COMMENTS

After reading this chapter, readers should be encouraged by the vast number of agencies, organizations, and informational sources that are available to help schools to provide a substantial career development, functional skills component to their curricular efforts.

Community interest and involvement in career education is not new. As Hoyt stated many years ago,

> it seems more legitimate to ask whether the education system will work with the broader community in career education than to ask whether the community is willing to work with the formal education system. (1976 p. 25)

Those who have professed that career education lacks resources and community support are mistaken. The resources are there if the time and attention are given to developing the necessary contacts, relationships, and methodologies for using them appropriately.

In communities with limited resources, state and national organizations may become more important. These organizations should be available to assist if they are contacted for relevant purposes. The amount of free technical assistance, materials, and referrals to other helpful sources by these associations and organizations is often overwhelming. A substantial number of different organizations serve as advocates for individuals with special needs and are extremely receptive to assisting community personnel.

Career education requires school personnel to collaborate with those outside their internal structure. It requires certain individuals to assume a coordinating role if all the necessary resources are to be appropriately orchestrated. Although this is no easy task, it is indeed necessary if we are to offer the comprehensive and relevant curriculum that these learners deserve.

It is encouraging to see the numerous articles, projects, books, reports, guides, and instructional materials that are available. Those of you who become familiar with the resources printed in this chapter and the appendixes should be able to identify and secure useful information and tools for your work.

ACTIVITIES

1. Conduct a community job survey of those agencies, organizations, and other resources in your community that could be important collaborators for a career education/transition program of services in your school. Secure names of appropriate contact persons, the contribution they could make, and the address and telephone number of the resource.

2. Refer to the LCCE curriculum matrix in Figure 3.2 and determine which of the resources you have identified can contribute to the instructional effort needed for each of the 97 subcompetencies.

Chapter 6

Business and Industry Involvement

Preliminary Questions About the Topic

1. Why is this the best time in U.S. history for instituting more substantial vocational training and placement services for students with special needs?

2. What are some of the key provisions of the Americans with Disabilities Act (ADA) that will help educators to expand employment opportunities for their students?

3. Identify ways in which employers can contribute to the career education curriculum of the school.

4. What are some of the commonly used sources of job leads?

5. What are some of the underused sources of job leads?

6. What considerations should go into providing students with a work experience component in their educational program?

7. What are some meaningful ways that educational programs can involve business and industry personnel in their career education program?

8. Identify some of the large corporations that have developed outstanding policies and procedures for providing persons with special needs training and employment opportunities.

9. What large corporation has been a leader in developing computer and other technology and special training programs to enhance the employment and daily living skills potential of persons with disabilities and the disadvantaged?

10. What important considerations should be adhered to in conducting job placement efforts for persons with more severe disabilities?

The American labor market has been changing quickly and dramatically in the 1990s. Large companies and corporations are downsizing their work forces to survive and become more efficient and productive. Large numbers of previously employed Americans are out of work, looking for new jobs or retraining, and settling for positions that often pay less than what they previously made. Although new federal employment legislation to provide training and employment opportunities for unemployed Americans has just been passed as this text is being completed, well-paying jobs continue to be difficult to secure for those who lack the experience and technical skills needed in the workplace.

What are the implications of employment possibilities for individuals with disabilities, for the disadvantaged, and for others with special learning needs and who may have been one of the many school dropouts? Will they again be shunted further into dead-end, low-paying, unstimulating jobs, which comprise the so-called "secondary labor market?" Will there be more unemployment among this group of citizens? Once again, only time will tell, but in the meantime, educators and rehabilitation personnel must rise to the occasion, dig in, and meet this next formidable challenge. This will require a much closer interface with business and industry than ever before. Otherwise, special education needs will not be addressed, and these individuals will be left out in the cold.

The career education approach, with its focus on teaching productive work behaviors and other functional skills, provides a mechanism for bridging the gap between the schools and employers. A career education curriculum makes sense to employers because of its emphasis on basic academic skills, general employability skills, work attitudes and behaviors, and personal–social areas such as building self-confidence and interpersonal skills. In fact, there is evidence that employers believe that an employee's self-confidence is perhaps the most important of a wide variety of skills that are needed for successful job functioning (O'Leary, 1989).

This chapter begins with a further discussion of the ADA, which was introduced in Chapter 1. This legislation is a good indicator that business and industry recognize the importance of using the potentials of persons with disabilities and that they will become more responsive to their employment needs from now on. The chapter then presents sections on education–industry partnerships, discusses specific contributions of business and industry to educational programs; suggests ways in which educators can contact and involve members of the business and industrial community; and identifies some resources that both employers and educators can use to enhance the individual's employability. Guidelines for interviewing persons are given. The final section relates to important considerations in placing students with severe disabilities in the workplace.

THE AMERICANS WITH DISABILITIES ACT

The United States Congress enacted numerous bills during the 1970s and 1980s to help protect persons with disabilities against discrimination and other types of unjust practices. Most present-day educational reform proposals call for closer working rela-

Point of View

As our nation moves toward becoming an information-oriented high-technology occupational society, it will become increasingly necessary for all persons entering and participating in that society to acquire a number of kinds of occupational skills. For too long, many youth have left the secondary school with few or no marketable occupational skills and have, as a result, spent up to 10–12 years in the secondary labor market, where more positive career development experiences are next to impossible to obtain.

It is now clear that, for almost all youth, the question on leaving high school is no longer "Should I go to college or should I seek employment?" Rather, the question today must be "Should I go to a four-year college, or should I attend some other type of postsecondary institution to acquire the skills necessary for participation in the emerging occupational society?"

If youth acquire these skills, it will be important to find employers willing to allow them to enter into the primary labor market in spite of their youth. Employer discrimination among youth in hiring practices has been very widespread for far too many years. It is hoped that

this can be overcome. A second major responsibility of employers is continuing education of their employees. America has a lot of catching up to do to be in the same important position occupied by employers in other advanced industrial nations.

The Life-Centered Career Education (LCCE) approach is a natural and effective way of building the proper kinds of employer/education relationships. We must continue to develop these relationships and implement such an approach if we are to enhance the employability potential of all students, including those who have special learning needs. All students have the right to earn a decent living and achieve job satisfaction as a result of our educational system's efforts.

Kenneth B. Hoyt is University Distinguished Professor at Kansas State University and is the former and only director of the U.S. Office of Career Education. He is the nation's foremost expert and leader in the area of career education.

tionships between education and the business and industry sector. The Carl D. Perkins Vocational and Applied Technology Education Act of 1990 (Public Law 101–392), for example, encourages but does not mandate the formation of business and education partnerships as a means to infuse more resources into schools and to enhance education programs.

The ADA of 1990 was enacted to pull everything together so that a truly comprehensive act of equality became a reality for persons with disabilities throughout the country. In regard to employment, Title I of the Act deals with discriminatory employment practices and specifies that *no covered entity shall discriminate against a qualified person with a disability relative to application procedures, hiring, advancement, discharge, employee compensation, job training, or other terms, conditions of employment.* "Qualified individuals with a disability" are defined as:

> an individual with a disability who, with or without reasonable accommodation, can perform the essential functions of the employment position.

The ADA definition of *an individual with a disability* is someone who has a physical or mental impairment that substantially limits one or more major life activities. *Life activities* include walking, speaking, breathing, working, performing manual tasks, seeing, hearing, learning, and caring for oneself. The definition of a *mental impairment* is any mental or psychological disorder, such as mental retardation, organic brain syndrome, emotional or mental illness, and specific learning disabilities. *Physical impairments* cover a range of physical and medical conditions and diseases.

It is necessary to identify the essential functions of a job to know whether the individual with a disability is qualified to do the job.

ADA regulations list several types of evidence to be considered in determining whether or not a function is essential:

* Employer's judgment
* Written job descriptions prepared before advertising or interviewing applicants for a job
* The amount of time spent performing the function
* The consequence of not requiring a person in this job to perform a function
* Work experience of people who have performed a job in the past and work experiences of people who currently perform similar jobs

The employer's judgment is an important consideration regarding a job's essential functions.

Other major terms to know about in addressing your client's job placement needs are "reasonable accommodation" and "undue hardship." An employer must provide a reasonable accommodation for the qualified applicant or employee with a disability unless it can be shown that the accommodation would impose an undue hardship. A *reasonable accommodation* may include making existing facilities more readily accessible to and usable for these individuals by installing ramps and widening doorways and aisles to accommodate a wheelchair. It may also include restructuring a job, modifying work schedules, reassigning persons to vacant positions, purchasing special equipment or devices, or modifying existing equipment. The obligation to provide a reasonable accommodation applies to all aspects of employment and applies whenever a person's disability or job changes.

An employer cannot deny employment to qualified applicants or employees because of the need to provide reasonable accommodation, unless it would cause undue hardship. *Undue hardship* includes such factors as the nature and cost of the proposed accommodation, the overall financial resources of the organization, and the type of operation of the covered entity (U.S. Department of Education, Office of Special Education and Rehabilitative Services, 1992).

 Organize an ADA Implementation Task Force like Herman Miller Corporation did.

The May/June 1992 and November/December 1993 issues of *Facility Management Journal* describe how one corporation, Herman Miller, a furniture manufacturer, put the ADA into action by going beyond the letter of the law to meet its spirit and provide equal access and equal opportunity for people with disabilities. It organized an ADA Implementation Task Force of 12 people representing the marketing, people services, research, corporate relations, operations, and facility management departments. One of its subcommittees revised job descriptions to include only essential functions and to use more inclusive language. For example, a job description might state that a person have the ability to move rather than lift a box. They also established a formal and informal procedure for employees to request accommodations; the request is then processed through a rehabilitation services team leader and a disability management team if needed. A transitional work center is available to help employees get back to work. The subcommittee also educates work team leaders to look at an applicant's ability, not the disability. They refer to the nondisabled person as temporarily able-bodied (TAB). The company also formed groups to address making their facilities and products accessible and to develop a variety of communication tools, such as newsletter articles, video presentations, and resources persons, to educate their employees and others aware of the ADA and its requirements. The program has been highly successful in raising the awareness level and truly meeting the spirit of the ADA legislation (Hauser, 1993).

Another corporation that has been in the forefront of accommodating and employing persons with disabilities for many years, thanks in large part to the efforts of Bob Muller (see Foreword), is Steelcase, Inc., of Grand Rapids, MI. In their first edition of *Workwell Magazine,* they note

> Since the passage of the Americans with Disabilities Act, reams of information have been published on ways to accommodate people with disabilities. Unfortunately, much of it doesn't get past the front door. (Steelcase, no date, p. 28)

They note that many office modifications for persons with disabilities are inexpensive, for example, a footrest, a lowered telephone, or an adjustable-height work surface. Two related approaches to provide work stations that truly enable people with disabilities to do their job are presented in the article, which also notes that "businesses that embrace the spirit of the law gain access to needed human resources, while ensuring that millions of qualified individuals fully participate in the workforce" (Steelcase, no date, p. 29). Steelcase has become a leader in promoting the civil rights and employment of persons with disabilities. Their *Employee Handbook* provides information and direc-

REASONABLE ACCOMMODATION

That which can be adapted without undue hardship. If an individual with a disability is *qualified* to perform the essential functions of a job, you need to decide if accommodation is necessary for the individual to perform them.

Example	Accommodation
Making facilities accessible	Revising workspaces and restrooms; revising entry/doors to staff meeting rooms; rearranging employee lounge/lunch room; revising emergency procedures
Job restructuring	Reassigning non-essential job duties to another employee
Part-time or modified work schedule	Flexible or adjusted work schedules to allow for medical treatments, transportation schedule, and break periods
Reassignment to a vacant position	An employee who can no longer perform essential job functions (and another reasonable accommodation will not enable the employee to perform the job) should be offered an opportunity to move to a vacant position for which the individual can perform the essential job functions
Acquisition or modification of equipment or devices	Electronic visual aids; braille materials; talking calculators; high contrast computer screens; magnifiers; audio recording; telephone handset amplifier; telecommunications devices for deaf persons; mechanical page turner; raised or lowered furniture
Modifications of examinations, training materials or policies	Removing the driver's license requirement for a job in which the essential job functions do not include driving; closed captioned video training materials
Qualified readers or interpreters	Allowing for readers, interpreters or attendants on a part-time basis in cases where it does not cause undue hardship

COMMON ADA TERMINOLOGY

Term	ADA Definition
Accessible	A facility that can be approached, entered and used by individuals with disabilities easily and conveniently.

FIGURE 6.1   Reasonable accommodation.

Note. From *Employee Handbook* (p. 4) by Steelcase, Inc. Reprinted by permission.

tion to their employees relative to the ADA legislation. Figure 6.1 presents an example of some guidelines they provide their personnel in making reasonable accommodations for employees and potential employees.

 "Together we have begun shifting disability policy in America from exclusion to inclusion; from dependence to independence; from paternalism to empowerment. . . . we do not have a single person to waste."

President Clinton (October 6, 1993, White House PressRelease)

Qualified individual	An individual with a disability who satisfies the requisite skills, experience, education and other job-related requirements of the employment positions such individual holds or desires, and who, with or without reasonable accommodation, can perform the essential functions of such a position.
Disability	Having any physical or mental impairment that substantially limits one or more major life activities; having a record of any such impairment; or being regarded by others as having such an impairment.
	The ADA specifically excludes as disabilities: homosexuality, bisexuality, transvestism, transsexualism, pedophilia, exhibitionism, voyeurism, gender identity disorders not resulting from physical impairment, and other sexual behavior disorder; compulsive gambling, kleptomania or pyromania; and psychoactive substance use disorders resulting from *current* illegal use of drugs.
Essential job functions	Fundamental and not marginal job duties. Job descriptions should specify and can serve as evidence of the essential functions of a particular job.
Readily achievable	Easily accomplished without much difficulty or expense considering: (1) the nature and costs involved in the action; (2) the resources of the facility or facilities involved (i.e., the bank), the number of persons employed at such facility, the effect on expenses and resources or impact of the action on the operation of the facility; (3) the overall financial resources of the entity (i.e., the holding company), overall size of the business with respect to the number of employees, the number, type and location of its facilities; and (4) types of operation(s) of the covered entity.
Reasonable accommodation	One that can be adapted without undue hardship.
Undue hardship	Action requiring difficulty or expense.

FIGURE 6.1 *continued*

President Clinton stated

Our Nation can ill afford to waste this vast and only partially tapped source of knowledge, skills, and talent . . . this waste of human ability cannot be reconciled with our tradition of individual dignity, self-reliance, and empowerment. I congratulate the small business and industry leaders, labor leaders, and community leaders from all walks of life who are working together to implement the ADA and the Rehabilitation Act. Our ongoing progress attests to the fundamental vitality and openness of our free enterprise system and to our abiding commitment to civil rights for all. (October 6, 1993, White House press release)

Bob Muller and former Chairman Robert Pew of Steelcase, Inc., who both have championed the employment rights of persons with disabilities.

It is obvious that the ADA has been a substantial force in stimulating even greater responsiveness to the employment needs of our citizens with disabilities. It has helped open the doors of business and industry even further to educators who are willing and able to develop effective partnership programs that will aid in the educational reform that most believe is badly needed in our schools.

PARTNERSHIPS WITH EDUCATION

Shortly after the introduction of Partnerships with Education, in the early 1970s, the U.S. Chamber of Commerce, the National Alliance of Businessmen, General Motors Corporation, the Industry Education Council of California, General Electric Company, New York Life Insurance Company, the Bell System, and many other large national companies and associations developed career education efforts to collaborate with school systems. Since those early efforts, many others have instituted collaborative partnerships with their school districts as their attempt to provide needed assistance to their communities and its young people.

Despite the early efforts at partnerships between education and business and industry, graduates still are not prepared to meet employers' needs, and the discrepancy between the students' skills and the demands of the available jobs is growing (Tindall, 1992). As Tindall has noted, with the current movement to provide business and industry with more qualified workers,

> Special educators need to be aware that school restructuring and reform are inevitable . . . and that we must ensure that special education students are part of the planned revisions. . . . it is imperative that plans include special education students. (1992, p. 333)

As Hoyt (1993) has noted, at a recent national conference, "Youth Apprenticeship—American Style" co-sponsored by 36 organizations, not one special education or vocational rehabilitation organization was represented. In addition, the conference publication lacked any references to special education students.

"Our nation's 43 million people with disabilities want to participate and contribute like everyone else. I'm calling on CEO's of businesses, large and small, to join this dedicated group. It's good for America. It's good for business."
James Brady, Vice Chairman, National Organization on Disability ("The National Organization on Disability," 1993)

The U.S. Department of Education's *America 2000: An Education Strategy* (1991) calls for each American business to become involved in reforming the schools in their communities (Phelps & Maddy-Bernstein, 1992). As noted by James Brady, the former Press Secretary for President Reagan who was disabled in an assassination attempt on the President, business and industry are being organized and becoming more committed to the national goal of expanding employment opportunities for people with disabilities. Several hundred companies have joined the Disability 2000-CEO Council, pledging their support to this important national goal.

The opportunity for education and business and industry to form even more meaningful and substantial partnerships has never been greater. The seeds have been planted for schools to initiate greater and more substantive collaborative partnerships to involve business and industry personnel in its curriculum efforts. As noted by Phelps and Maddy-Bernstein, "most of the current calls for reform speak eloquently and directly to the charge of uniting the education and business communities in such an endeavor" (1992, p. 33). They cite several effective partnerships that have become model business–education collaborative efforts for at-risk students. These include the California Peninsula Academies—where teachers work together to implement a coordinated curriculum in which academic and technical learning is integrated with mentors, summer employment, job shadowing, and the like—and the Portland Investment—using a multiagency planning team including representatives from business, schools, city government, and the Urban League.

It should also be noted that the National Alliance of Businessmen has promoted the development of effective school–business partnerships and has found it essential to building an effective coalition of many committed organizations and sectors. They have also found it important to establish an intermediary organization to manage day-to-day efforts and to manage progress (Phelps & Maddy-Bernstein, 1992).

Another example of meeting the needs of students with special needs has been reported by D. H. Clark (1993) at the Center for High-Tech Training for the Disabled, Valencia Community College, in Orlando, FL. The programs offered by the center in computer programming and computer-assisted design are directed by a Business Advisory Council, comprising leaders from industry and representatives of collaborating agencies. This ensures training that is responsive to the needs of Central Florida businesses while meeting the training needs of the trainees with disabilities.

It should be apparent that mechanisms for building partnerships are being instituted across the country. Educators generally must take the initiative, and if they do, the business community will probably be quite responsive.

CONTRIBUTIONS OF EMPLOYERS

The resources and personnel within the sectors of business and industry are so extensive that educators must understand the objectives and means of collaboration. They should identify objectives and possible joint efforts before approaching members of business and industry. At the same time, they should be open to suggestions presented by these same members. In other words, educators should approach business and industry with an opening statement such as

> I have an idea on ways that we can work together in the career development for individuals with disabilities. Do you have additional suggestions?

This is contrasted with the question: "What should we do?" which may only serve to alert businesspersons to the fact that the educator has not done her "homework."

This section includes discussions of several ways in which business and industry can assist educational programs. The following list provides suggestions for building a collaborative effort between major sectors in career development.

Identify trends in the economy
Further contacts with business and industry
Become advocates
Serve as a classroom resource
Provide program consultation
Provide work experiences
Participate in conferences and workshops
Provide instructional and resource materials

Trends in the Economy

Educators are always interested in trends that determine enrollments for years to come. Educators must be attentive to the overall condition of supply and demand in the labor market, as well as specific shortages within particular categories of employment that offer opportunities for their students. Reports on employment by categories, age groups, and industries are available through several government agencies, although the Department of Labor is principally responsible for providing the public with continual assessment of the labor situation. For example, the Department of Labor projected a 32% growth in service-work jobs during the 1980s and 1990s. Job prospects for clerical workers, who are the largest part of the workforce in America, were projected to grow by 27%. Demand for craftsmen and skilled laborers such as carpenter, auto mechanic, and tool and die worker also increased. Sales jobs in retail stores, manufacturing, and wholesale firms grew by 28%. Categories that experienced slow growth or no growth include production workers (those on assembly lines), unskilled laborers (e.g., freight and stock handlers) and farm workers. This type of information constantly appears in such government publications as the *Monthly Labor Review* and *Occupational Outlook Quarterly*. Special reports and reprints can be obtained from the regional office of the Department of Labor, Bureau of Labor Statistics.

Community members of business and industry can translate major trends in the economy and labor force into the potential affects of such movements on job development and training for individuals with special needs. Businesspersons are often able to identify surges in demands for workers with particular skills, changes in job classifications, modifications of skill requirements that are due to the introduction of new machines or work routines, and growth or recession of the local economy. All of these factors affect the training, placement, and projected employment of various types of workers.

Teachers, counselors, placement personnel, and other educators associated with the several aspects of career development may not be expected to be familiar with every machine and routine in the electronics or fast food industry. However, their familiarity with labor force data, general requirements for jobs within industries, and current conditions within the marketplace will improve communication between educators and local lenders in business and industry. This familiarity also provides a basic foundation for understanding the observations and recommendations from businesspeople relative to changes in procedures and practices within the educational community.

Contacts with Business and Industry

Self-reliance is a major part of the collective American personality. Most Americans believe that a person's efforts account for her success or failure, whether she falls into the white- or blue-collar categories. Such terms as *clout, influence* and *pull,* to name a few, are used in a derogatory fashion to identify individuals who have advanced in the organization or achieved an objective based on means apart from their work skills.[*]

[*] These terms, as well as the expression "It's who you know that counts," are not confined to the world of work.

Educators would be fooling themselves if they did not imagine that meeting people in business and industry for the purpose of securing contacts was a necessary function associated with developing jobs for their students. American workers would like to believe that their success on a job is due to their own efforts and ability, but individuals with special needs have stated that they would first like to have a chance at a job.

Individuals from one walk of life or profession (education and rehabilitation) need an entree to another sector (business and industry), simply because the normal training and pursuit of professional goals does not bring members of one sector into frequent contact with those from the other. Bankers are more acquainted with other bankers than they are with teachers because most of the working day and, very often, their social life includes other bankers. Thus, it is a question of how an educator can meet individuals in business and industry who can help train or employ their students. One answer is to use all possible leads and contacts within business and industry.

Educators can use the resources of vocational rehabilitation, employment services, rehabilitation facilities, youth training programs, and just about any organization that has contacts with business and industry. Such contacts are important because they

1. Economize on the educator's time and energy, which are needed to complete other responsibilities, and
2. Provide an element of support for the employer interview.

An educator can approach an employer independently and achieve favorable benefits for the program. However, the chances for success are enhanced if the placement personnel are recommended or endorsed by another businessperson.

In their extensive review of rehabilitation and job placement of individuals with disabilities, Zadny and James (1976) distinguish between formal and informal sources of job leads. Contacts with members of business and industry (employers) fall in the category of informal sources and are also characterized by Zadny and James as "underused." These underused channels may provide better results simply because the commonly used sources support greater numbers of job seekers. The two categories of sources appear in Table 6.1.

Professionals can use the information in Table 6.1 to place clients, students, or just plain job seekers. Underused sources of information can be categorized as personal contacts between professionals, workers, and businesspersons with prospective employers. As program personnel develop greater contacts with community organizations, advisory groups, and members of the business and industrial sector, they take advantage of underused channels of information and avoid excessive competition from other applicants for jobs.

Advocates for Persons with Disabilities

Many large corporations have enthusiastically publicized their belief of the capability of persons with disabilities to become outstanding and productive employees. Examples of some statements in various publications follow:

TABLE 6.1   Used and Underused Sources of Job Leads

Commonly Cited Sources	Underused Sources
Newspaper want ads	Past employer
State employment service	Past clients
Private employment agencies	Counselor's acquaintances
Help wanted signs	Employers cited by employers who have hired clients
Yellow pages	
Trade publications	Counselor's co-workers
Unions	Service persons
Civil service bulletins	Client family and friends
Business pages of newspaper	Workers at business hiring clients
Employers who have hired clients	

Note. From "Another View on Placement: State of the At 1976," *Studies in Placement Monograph No. 1* (p. 29) by J. J. Zadney and L. F. James, 1976, Portland: Portland Oregon School of Social Work, Portland State University. Copyright 1976 by Portland State University. Reprinted by permission.

Our experience with persons who have disabilities has been outstanding. (Bruce Carswell, Sr. Vice-President, GTE Corporation)

Hiring and training men and women who are disabled is clearly a plus—for companies, for those eager to help themselves, and for our economy. (Colby H. Chandler, Chairman and CEO, Eastman Kodak Company)

Success can only be attained by the full utilization of all resources, the most important being people. (J. J. Albenze, Administrator, Westinghouse Corporation)

These and many other similar statements in support of employing persons with disabilities are contained in the 1987 publication *Disabled Americans at Work* (The President's Committee on Employment of Person's with Disabilities, 1987), which is available from the U.S. Government Printing Office and developed by several corporations in cooperation with the Dole Foundation and the President's Committee on Employment of People with Disabilities. A list of the corporations that provided information about some of their employees with disabilities in that publication is presented in Table 6.2. It should be emphasized that this list of companies in Table 6.2 is just an example of some of the many large and small companies that have become strong advocates and employers of persons with disabilities and other disadvantages.

The momentum for employing persons with disabilities continues to grow in the 1990s, thanks in part to the ADA legislation. But many American businesses and industries have had a long history of being advocates for these individuals. No doubt, a survey of resources in one's own community would result in a larger number of businesses and industries who are engaged in many important advocacy activities on behalf of these individuals.

TABLE 6.2   Examples of Corporations and Companies with Special Concern About Employing People with Disabilities

Sector	Company
Chemical industry	Dow Chemical
	Stauffer Chemical Company
	W. R. Grace & Co.
Communications industry	GTE
	AT&T
	IT&T
	New England Telephone
Computers and electronics	Honeywell
	Sperry
Consumer goods and services	Phillip Morris
	Miller Brewing Company
	Eastman Kodak Company
	Sears
	Continental Can
	Motion Designs
	Proctor & Gamble
	United Airlines
	General Mills
Energy and utilities	Washington Water Power
	Baltimore Gas & Electric
	Pennsylvania Power and Light Company
	Montana Power Company
	Texaco
	Duke Power Company
	Edison Electric Institute

Note. From *Disabled Americans at Work* by the President's Committee on Employment of People with Disabilities, 1987, Washington, DC: U.S. Government Printing Office.

Classroom Resource

Business and industry are providing schools with a myriad of teaching programs and materials to help teachers learn more about such important topics as ecology. In fact, some businesses even train teachers to use their programs. And because most teachers don't have the time to look for information they could use to put corporate material in perspective for their students, many corporations will assist teachers further in obtaining relevant information.

Members of business and industry can also help teachers to select materials, training manuals, or instructional guides. For example, placement personnel may review appli-

TABLE 6.2 *continued*

Sector	Company
Finance, banking, and insurance	Aetna Life and Casualty Allstate American Express Blue Cross, Blue Shield Mutual of Omaha The Prudential Insurance Company
Health and medical	Abbott Laboratories Merck & Co. Hospital Corporation of America
Heavy manufacturing	Westinghouse Rockwell International General Dynamics E.I.L. Instruments General Motors Corporation Innovative Concepts Phifer Wire Products, Inc. American Can Decc Company Steelcase Raytheon Company
Restaurant/hospitality	Burger King Corporation Valentino's Restaurant Refuge Restaurant The Marquette and the Northstar Hotels Marriott Corporation McDonald's

cation forms or provide suggestions on training students for interviews. Plant supervisors can suggest training procedures that teachers can use in school or workshop environment to prepare students for the world of work. Although vocational educators are usually familiar with changes and modifications in selected industries, personnel from various companies should continue to advise them on changes in materials, machines, or routines that should be reflected in the training program.

Prepare your resource person is one rule that educators should keep in mind whenever they ask a representative from business or industry to act as a speaker, consultant, or tour guide to groups of students, faculty, or parents. Preparation should include an interview with program personnel and presentation of printed or visual information about the resource person's role and importance in the development of the exceptional person's career. Preparation will give resource people an idea of what is expected of them and how they can use their time and resources more efficiently. This information will influence the resource person's decision regarding continued involvement with the school system.

Program Consultation

The scope of a career development program, including vocational training and placement, requires several skills on the part of educators. These skills are essential to such program components as student evaluation, program evaluation, management of resources, and cost analysis. In addition, these skills may be used to resolve specific problems relative to minimum wage laws and work-study assignments, cooperative agreements between the school system and other agencies, and placement evaluation of former students and their employers.

Opinions from members of the business and industrial sector may help educators to find solutions to mutual problems.

Representatives from business and industry can also advise program directors about the competencies required by teachers or other personnel to prepare students for the job market. Jobs, skills, and work roles are in constant change, and those people who prepare students to enter such a fluid market must also command certain competencies.

Work Experience

If there is one ingredient that stands out as the prominent link between business and industry and the education system across the country, it is their cooperation in work experience or work-study programs for students. Business and industry have been active in collaborative efforts to develop field experience, student internships, summer employment, and on-the-job training. These programs provide students with hands-on experiences that test their interests in particular jobs; provide a source of evaluation for supervisory personnel; train students to use tools and complete tasks; and reward them for the amount of energy that they have invested in the experience. Although it may be a cliché to say "experience is the best teacher," almost every significant program for students normally involves work experience.

Program personnel should consider two significant points in establishing a series of work experiences for their students.

First, a sequence of experiences should be available so that individuals from elementary school through adult education can be involved in appropriate work positions, meeting their level of maturity, interest, and ability. Work experience is not the final stage of a training program. Ideally, work experience should be an integrated element of the training program and should be available at various points in the student's career development. Such a series of experiences provides the individual and program personnel with several forms of evaluation relative to intended occupational roles. It also allows the student to experiment with work roles that may benefit him at later stages of development, as in the instance of a change of occupations.

 Work experience is not *the final stage of a training program.*

Second, work experience is a training device. If program personnel permanently place a student in a work–study position, then they have lost that position as a training experience for other students. We are well aware of the temptation to place students in employment when the same firms indicate that there are openings. But the real value of work experience is that a number of students can be cycled through a series of work tasks that have been identified and evaluated by supervisors and educators. This knowledge becomes a standard by which other students can be measured and trained. Eliminating a training site or series of experiences forces educators to repeat the laborious effort of locating another cooperative businessperson, establishing communication with supervisors, and investing additional time that could have been used to help more students find employment.

One variation on work experience is the involvement of faculty members in similar on-the-job routines. For example, Kern High School District, Bakersfield, CA, financed the placement of its vocational instructors in a work–study position in community businesses. Because these instructors were to train students before placing them in the community, the district made sure that the teachers knew about the work routines and tasks that would be required of the students. The in-service training of the faculty allowed them to work on jobs that they would later teach to their students.

Most students find employment during their high school years. These jobs are generally found by the student's family, friends, or the student. Whether or not students with disabilities are getting much educational benefit and adequate exposure to the real world of work, other than compensation, is something educators should be concerned about if they want to prepare these students for meaningful careers. Halpern, Dorenz, and Benz (1993) suggest that educators consider encouraging students to decline or shorten some types of high school employment if it is not adequate vocational learning. Schools need to improve their linkages to the business world so employers can contribute to a more substantive career development experience for the students. They note that new vocational training options should be considered such as apprenticeship programs that are so prevalent in Europe. These options are beginning in the United States now as youth apprenticeship programs and work-based learning programs become more prominent for regular class students in our high schools. Hopefully, students in special needs programs will also be given the same opportunity.

Conferences and Workshops

Conferences and workshops bring people together to discuss themes, problems, issues, or actions related to career development for individuals with special needs. These events can be used to explore such concerns as

- Partnership of business/industry and education
- Preparation to meet the changing job market
- Education's role in retaining the employee who is disabled while on the job
- Requirements imposed by legislation

Various organizations within the business world, as well as individual companies, have sponsored conferences and workshops in the broad area of career education for American youth and workers. As long ago as 1977, the White House Conference on Handicapped Individuals made recommendations pertinent to extended cooperation by business and industry with education in career development of these individuals. Some of the delegates' recommendations also provided additional themes for joint conferences and workshops. The President's Committee on Employment of the Handicapped (now renamed The President's Committee on Employment of People with Disabilities) (1977) recommended:

- A national public awareness program should be developed to recognize employers who hire disabled people.
- Training for supervisors should emphasize the use of workers with disabilities.
- Transitional employment programs should be developed (e.g., psychosocial centers for mentally restored people and occupational training centers for individuals with intellectual deficiencies).
- Vocational schools, sheltered workshops, and other places of training should teach the skills that really meet the needs of local employers.

Instructional and Resource Materials

Business and industry and education have cooperated for several years in the preparation of students for work roles.

An elaboration of the kinds of materials related to career education provided by organizations and companies is unnecessary; any description would soon be outdated as materials are changed or exhausted. The important thing to remember is that these materials will exist as long as business/industry is involved in the career development of the American worker.

INVOLVING BUSINESS AND INDUSTRY

The previous section identified the potential contributions of members of business and industry to a career development program. This section suggests how educators can contact and involve members of business and industry in career development programs that benefit the entire community. The following list provides suggestions:

- Invite business and industry to serve on a Community Advisory Committee.
- Give presentations to civic organizations
- Issue publications about program (e.g., brochures, reports, news release items).
- Advertise in business publications.
- Conduct job fairs, workshops, and institutes.

Community Advisory Committee

The role of a Community Advisory Committee, such as the one described earlier by D. H. Clark (1993) can be a significant factor in the success of the career development program. If school personnel anticipate that the community will accept the individual with special needs and support school programs, then the Advisory Committee must be more than a perfunctory group whose members' names enhance the program director's stationery. Campbell, Todd, and O'Rourke (1971) and Phelps (1976) state that the committee can provide valuable service by

1. Reviewing program components, such as instructional materials, facilities, equipment, and cooperative training agreements
2. Identifying community contributions, resources, and effective measures of public relations
3. Developing evaluation designs that will be included in the program

There is no hard and fast rule as to how many members should be on the committee or for what length of time they should serve. Members of the committee would most likely include representatives from major industries that may employ graduates of the program. School personnel, however, should not assume or convey the impression that the members of the committee are obligated to find jobs for students or hire a certain number of graduates. The members' principal role is to assist the program and function as advocates for the students in the community. The following list of suggested members of the committee represents a cross section of the major groups of individuals who are interested in student success or who can directly influence training procedures:

1. Personnel or employment managers who would be able to advise educators about application forms, interview procedures, and employment trends
2. Supervisors who are in direct contact with employees with special needs and can identify potential difficulties they may have in the work setting
3. Directors or managers of a firm that employs a number of workers with disabilities and who would speak to businesspersons about the company's successful experiences in employment or accommodation
4. Members of parent organizations who are strongly interested in career development efforts and could support school programs by forming coalitions of parents and workers with disabilities and other special needs

5. Members of community agencies involved in the training and placement activities who could provide information on the challenges faced by the adult individual with special needs

6. Member of an insurance firm acquainted with the practices and rates for industries that employ workers with special needs

7. Individuals with disabilities who have succeeded in the work world and can provide unique insights into the program's training and placement components.

Even though committee members may have expertise in particular areas, educators should not assume that these members are familiar with the issues and problems involved in the career development of individuals with special needs. The members should attend a series of information sessions, informing them about the school program, community efforts, and the national scene. At times, members of the committee may conduct these sessions. But school personnel must initially plan the overall direction until the committee members have had time to identify their interests and request information on specific areas.

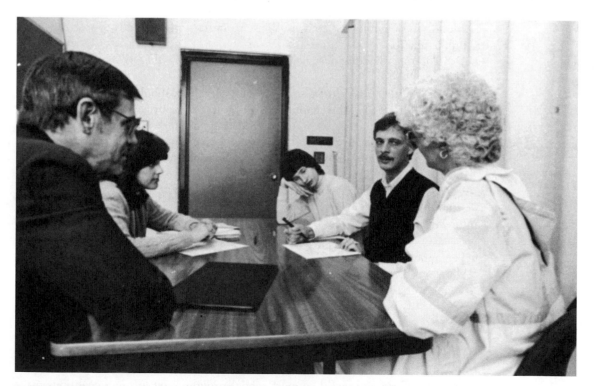

Participation in Community Advisory Committees is one of the many ways in which business and industry can contribute to the planning and implementation of career education programs.

Civic Organizations

The term *civic organizations* is used broadly to include all groups interested in improving the well-being of members of the community. The organizations serve as fertile ground for contacts with members of the business community, simply because both the educator and businessperson share a desire to improve conditions for members of the community. This mutual respect provides educators with an opportunity to present the benefits of the training and placement program and pursue possible leads for further involvement with business and industry. Several program directors have said that some of their strongest supporters or employment leads have been discovered when a businessperson approached the educator after a presentation to a civic group.

Educators should regard presentations to civic organizations as a major public relations project. The speaker should use any form of audiovisual technique or publication that would involve the audience.

1. The presentation should emphasize major points so that the audience will not get "lost" in too many figures and details.
2. The speaker should involve the audience by eliciting questions about career development, training, placement, or job success.
3. Materials should be available to members of the audience who wish to read at their leisure or contact other sources of information.
4. Former or current students of the program should be included in the presentation to dispel the audience's possible misconceptions about the abilities of individuals with special needs.

Program Publications

The educator should always try to focus the community's attention on the students' goals and achievements. This can be accomplished through personal presentations, as described in the previous section, meetings with civic leaders, and interviews with business and parents. However, publications can be used as a ready reference when the educator is unavailable and can also be distributed to the public as well as to members of business and industry. The educator can use several kinds of publications to advertise career development and to involve members of business and industry. These publications would include the following:

1. An attractive brochure that provides an overview of the program, its intents, and the *advantages* that the program can offer to the reader: The brochure can help educators to make contacts and obtain interviews with employers. Brochures may include pictures of students at work to convey the impression that one of the goals and accomplishments of career development is successful employment.
2. Several types of reports that provide "hard data" about the program: This information is necessary to justify expenditures and is valuable to administra-

tors, teachers, members of the Community Advisory Committee, and members of the community who wish to know how their tax dollars are spent. The most frequent topics for these reports include successful placements by work titles; identification of business firms that have hired students; the amount of money that former students have earned over a period of time; and the amount of tax dollars these students returned to the community.

3. News release items that can be used by the local media in direct reprints or broadcasts or that can provide the basis for a feature story. The news release can advertise the availability of qualified workers, such as a "work wanted" advertisement. The advertisement may include the unique accomplishments of the student, such as the completion of a training program for mechanics or computer operators.

Business publications can also be used to publicize career development and to involve business and industry. Several industries and companies publish their own materials. Anyone who has ever sat in a doctor's or dentist's office may have spent a long period of time paging through what are termed the *trade journals*. Articles about workers with disabilities have appeared in many of these publications. Educators at the local and state level should be aware that such journals can help to advertise and inform potential employers about career development.

Job Fairs, Workshops, and Institutes

Several organizations (parent groups, associations formed by individuals with special needs, government agencies) have attempted to educate employers and other personnel in business and industry about the positive qualities of workers with special needs. These organizations have combined their talents, contacts, and efforts to achieve the following:

1. Inform employers about ways they can meet recent changes in affirmative action laws.
2. Display the achievements of other employers who have hired these workers.
3. Provide a meeting place where employers can interview prospective employees.
4. Provide a forum to discuss common problems experienced by both employers and employees.
5. Discuss local or regional job openings and projected changes in the supply and demand of labor.
6. Increase employers' knowledge about the abilities and skills of an untapped segment of the labor force.

These efforts may be presented over local or educational television and could be organized into the traditional conference or the increasingly popular job fair. The job fair is a central location at which representatives from business and industry interview applicants. It benefits individuals by providing several interview possibilities within one location.

This section has focused on ways in which educators can contact and involve representatives of business and industry in career development activities. The following are some important considerations permeating the numerous attempts:

- *Involve members of business and industry as soon as possible in your educational programs.* There are several reasons for this recommendation. First, the active cooperation and commitment of members of business and industry may be stronger if they are approached in the formative stages of a program or project rather than serving as symbolic representatives. Second, they may be able to suggest important changes or ways of getting support while the program or project is in the developmental stages. This is especially crucial if the project includes provisions for cooperation with business and industry. Some educators have spent considerable time planning a project, preparing staff and students, identifying training experiences and appropriate industries, and then approaching business and industry with the expectation that employers, supervisors, managers, and businesspersons would just fit right into their plan. This course of action is not recommended.
- *Maintain a continuity in communications with members of business and industry.* Business executives are accustomed to a certain degree of punctuality, and supervisors want precision. Both are especially discouraged when they are approached by several representatives of the same program or project. Just imagine what your response might be if three of four salespersons for the same project called you on the telephone during your office hours. The continuity of communication is also important once individuals are involved in the program, as emphasized in the discussion of the Community Advisory Committee.
- *Publicize the link between business and industry and education as much as possible.* Of course, any efforts at publicity should be approved by the principal agents involved in the program or project. Once publicity has been approved, educators should use as many resources as possible within the community, area, state, region, and nation. Successive stages of information contain a corresponding vehicle for communication with the public. For example, the community may have a small, neighborhood or local newspaper and radio station. A larger area may be covered by a large-city newspaper, television station, and several AM–FM radio channels. A state would be covered by official publications written by members of the legislature or speeches entered into the official proceedings. The region may be covered through professional publications that pertain to the particular industry. And the nation may release information through federal agencies that are concerned with education and employment of individuals with special needs. Publication of an existing collaboration between business and industry and education can help to expand programs, as well as improve employment possibilities for these individuals, as discussed in the following section.
- *Encourage the involvement of business and industry by using as many resources as possible.* The previous discussions of publications and committees includes references to the many agents within a community who can become advocates for train-

ing programs. These advocates, whether civic groups, parents' organizations, or influential citizens, will need the information and encouragement of educators. Furthermore, educators must be aware of the potentials for the involvement of the entire community and should coordinate activities with the goals of the career education program.

EMPLOYER RESOURCES

Many employers may be reluctant to consider hiring persons with special learning needs because of their lack of knowledge or experience, misconceptions, fears, reservations, a poor previous experience, or for a myriad of other reasons that can be resolved by the professional willing to work closely with them. The potential employer needs to know that educators and rehabilitation personnel are available to help both the trainee and employer in the transition phase with on-site training, counseling, and other services that will be required for the placement to succeed. One of the major ways the professionals can help employers is to provide them with information on available resources that may assist them in their efforts to accommodate their workers with disabilities. Some of these are identified and described briefly below:

* *ABLEDATA* is a consumer referral service that contains more than 18,000 listings of adaptive devices for all disabilities. It responds to requests for information from persons with disabilities and from employers. Address: 8455 Colesville Road, #935, Silver Springs, MD 20910-3319. Phone: (800) 227-0216, voice and Telecommunication Device for the Deaf (V/TDD).
* *Disabled Access Credit* (Section 44 of the IRS Code) encourages small business to comply with the ADA by providing a tax credit of up to $5,000 per year. The employer or small business can deduct 50% of "eligible access expenditures" between $250 and $10,000. More information is available from the local IRS office.
* *The Targeted Jobs Tax Credit* (TJTC, Section 51 of the IRS Code) provides a tax credit of 40% of the first $6,000 earned per employee, provided the individual is employed at least 90 days or 120 hours. An employer may not claim TJTC and on-the-job training for the same wages. More information is available from IRS Publication 907 or from the State Job Service or Vocational Rehabilitation office.
* *Architectural and Transportation Barrier Removal Tax Reduction* (Section 190 of the IRS Code) provides a tax deduction to employers for up to $15,000 for making facilities and public transportation vehicles accessible to employees and customers. All alterations must meet the Department of Treasury Standards.
* *Job Accommodation Network* (JAN) is an information network for employers. Operated by the President's Committee on Employment of People with Disabilities, it is a data base containing specific information about how individual tasks can be done by persons with limitations. It provides free consulting service on the ADA and pro-

vides information on aids, devices, and methods for accommodating workers with disabilities. JAN enables employers to discuss with other employers accommodations that have proved successful. Phone: (800) ADA-WORD (V/TDD).

- *Arc National on-the-Job Training* has been in operation for several decades. The program is funded by the U.S. Department of Labor. Funds are available for training persons with mental retardation in business and industry; the employer will be reimbursed for training and employing the person for a specified length of time. Persons interested in more specific information should contact the project at The Arc's national headquarters, 500 E. Border Street, Suite 300, Arlington, TX 76010. Phone: (817) 277-3491.

- *The Industry-Labor Council's National Center on Employment and Disability,* which acts as a consultant and technical assistant on employment of persons with disabilities, provides a clearinghouse for information on topics such as accessibility, outreach and recruiting, reasonable accommodation, legislation, and disability management. The center offers various forms of training to industry and maintains an extensive array of informational materials relative to employment of persons with disabilities. Address: The Human Resources Center, 201 I.U. Willets Rd, W., Albertson, NY 11507-1599. Phone: (516) 747-6323.

- *Projects with Industry* is a program administered by private industry and rehabilitation agencies. The focus of the program is job placement, work adjustment, skills training, and/or linkage with business and industry so that rehabilitation services become more responsive to the needs of employers. Interested persons should contact their nearest vocational rehabilitation agency office.

A vast array of associations and other organizations can be of assistance to employers seeking information and advice on employing persons who are disabled and disadvantaged. A good resource for this information is the *Encyclopedia of Associations* (1992).

 IBM makes many important contributions to the improved quality of life for persons with disabilities.

IBM has been a leader in enhancing the quality of life and the employability of persons with disabilities through the use of their technology for many decades. In 1985, they established their Special Needs Information and Referral Center (SNIRC). The Center maintains a sizable data base of available products, suppliers, and agencies. IBM supports a demonstration facility and conducts awareness seminars for executives inside and outside of IBM. The seminars increase awareness and knowledge about the employability of people with disabilities and current assistive technology.

In addition, IBM offers several other services to enhance the career development of persons with disabilities and those who are disadvantaged. Through its Disabilities Assistance Network, IBM loans computers and software at no charge to federally funded disabilities support centers across the United States. IBM has helped establish

53 centers nationwide that train people with disabilities for careers in information processing industries. In addition, IBM sponsors over 100 job training centers for the economically disadvantaged, primarily in word processing, and a Basic Skills/Literacy Support Program for those who do not have the skills to enroll in job training. In 1993, IBM opened its Job Training and Competency Center in Arlington, VA, to demonstrate how the private sector can participate in successful partnerships with community-based organizations serving persons with disabilities and the disadvantaged and to provide management and staff development and training.

The center also exhibits the IBM Independence Series, which is a group of products designed to help people with visual, physical, and speech and hearing disabilities to achieve greater personal and professional independence through technology. Eight products are currently available, five of them to increase accessibility to everyday activities:

- *Screen Reader*, for individuals with vision impairments, is a screen text-to-speech conversion tool that provides equal access to computer information.
- *Phone Communicator,* for persons who are hearing and/or speech impaired, provides telephone communications with another person via a touch-tone telephone and communicates with both Baudot and ASCII TDDs, displaying a full-screen view of the dialogue from both parties. Any telephone conversation can be saved and printed.
- *VoiceType*, for people with physical impairments, is a flexible speech-recognition program that provides an affordable keyboard alternative by speaking.
- *AccessDOS* is a utility to enhance keyboard access for IBM DOS users for each of the programs described previously.
- *KeyGuard*, is a molded template to enhance keying accuracy so the keyboard can be positioned at any angle; the person with a mobility impairment can use it with a minimum of effort.

IBM has also developed a variety of input devices, readers, speech synthesizers, a braille printer, and screen-enlargement software that interface with the previously mentioned systems. In addition, IBM has produced a program entitled *SpeechViewer* to increase the efficiency of speech therapy, *SpeechViewer II*, and *THINKable* for helping clients practice thinking skills in four focus areas relating to communication and daily living skills. Information about IBM products can be obtained by calling 800-IBM-3333 for the number of the nearest branch office.

The preceding discussion reflects the considerably improving receptivity of business and industry about the employment of persons with disabilities and other learning difficulties. The President's Committee on Employment of People with Disabilities (1993) published, for employers, the following guidelines for conducting a job interview with these individuals:

- Make sure your company's employment offices and your interview location are accessible to applicants with mobility impairments, visual, hearing, or cognitive disabilities.
- Be willing to make appropriate and reasonable accommodations to enable job applicants with a disability to present themselves in the best possible light. For example, offer assistance to applicants who are blind or have limited use of their hands in completing their job application forms; provide an interpreter for an applicant who is deaf; and offer detailed or specific instructions to persons with cognitive disabilities.
- Don't let a rehabilitation counselor, social worker, or other third party take an active part in or sit in on an interview unless the applicant requests it.
- Make sure you have in-depth knowledge of the essential job functions regarding the position for which the applicant is applying, as well as the details of why, how, where, when, and by whom each task or operation is performed. This will enable you to structure the interview better and ensure that all questions are job related.
- Relax and make the applicant feel relaxed. Don't be afraid of making mistakes. At the same time, remember that candidates (particularly those applying for professional positions) must be expected to assume an equal share of the responsibility for making your interaction with them comfortable.
- Don't speculate or try to imagine how you would perform a specific job if you had the applicant's disability. The person with a disability has mastered alternate techniques and skills of living and working with her particular disability. You should ask an applicant to describe how she would perform a certain job function if it is an essential part of the position.
- Concentrate on the applicant's technical and professional knowledge, skills, abilities, experiences, and interests, not on the disability. Remember, you can't interview a disability, hire a disability, or supervise a disability. You can interview a person, hire a person, and supervise a person.
- If the applicant is not technically or professionally qualified for the position in question, end the interview. If the applicant is qualified, feel free to discuss in an open, honest, and straightforward manner how he plans to perform specific on-the-job duties and what he will need to get the job done. Remember, all questions should be job related and asked in an open-ended format.

Another set of guidelines is presented in Figure 6.2. These have been written by Steelcase, Inc., and portray the perspective of an employer.

The preceding guidelines and those in Figure 6.2 also have implications for those placing students in work experience placements during their high school years. These guidelines should help the educator or transition specialist in preparing prospective employers for interviewing students and integrating them into the work setting.

GUIDELINES FOR INTERVIEWING AND HIRING INDIVIDUALS WITH DISABILITIES

Recruiting	Review the job description or any other documentation that delineates the essential job functions. If using an employment agency, be sure their recruiting and screening practices do not discriminate against a qualified individual with a disability. Look at alternative ways of advertising that will reach individuals with disabilities.
Pre-Interview	Be sure your tests, physical examinations, application procedures, do not screen out people with disabilities who may, with reasonable accommodation, be able to perform the job.
	Make accommodations, if necessary, to testing procedures to allow for the person's disability.
	Review your selection criteria for screening candidates.
Interview	Treat the job candidate with a disability the same as any other job candidate.
	Make the person comfortable.
	Maintain eye contact.
	If the person requires any special assistance, offer to help.
	Maintain a professional environment.
	Focus on the job tasks and the candidate's ability to perform each of them.
Discussing the individual's disability	Provide opportunity for *individual* to initiate discussion on the effect their disability has on their capacity to perform job duties.
	Once the individual has *initiated* the discussion about his or her job duty limitations, maintain focus on performance of job duties.
	Pinpoint any barriers—physical or psychological.
	Decide which barriers can be overcome through reasonable accommodations.
	Look at reassigning non-essential job duties to another employee.
Integrating the individual with disability into the work force	Prepare co-workers to work with the disabled individual.
	Provide training, if necessary.
	Discuss openly any anxieties co-workers may have.
	Brainstorm ideas for overcoming barriers.
	Use a proactive approach to solving problems that might arise.
	Assign a partner to work closely with individual for the first few weeks.
Working with the new hire with disability	Welcome the new hire with disability as you would any new hire.
	Provide orientation.
	Make sure the new hire feels comfortable letting co-workers, as well as you, know about problems that arise.
	Focus on the person's abilities—the reason you hired the individual in the first place.

FIGURE 6.2   Guidelines for interviewing and hiring individuals with disabilities.
Note. From *Employee Handbook* (p. 6) by Steelcase, Inc. Reprinted by permission.

STUDENTS WITH SEVERE DISABILITIES

Unlike many individuals with mild disabilities, most individuals with substantial developmental disabilities will need the assistance of a job developer or placement person who contacts employers on behalf of the individual (Hagner & Daning, 1993). The supported employment program has been a boon to this effort in more recent years.

How can job developers and others involved in the placement process most appropriately approach employers? Hagner and Daning (1993) attempted to answer that question by interviewing 49 job developers from 26 organizations in one state. The investigators found that a considerable variety of techniques and methods were used but that they were generally quite successful after four or five employer contacts. Most important to create jobs employers needed were personal contacts and a trusting relationship and the ability to work with employers, rather than responding to want-ads openings. Another important finding was the caution about mentioning the person's disability during the early stage of discussions.

Students with severe disabilities usually require considerably more accommodations than those with mild disabilities. Employers will need to know that these individuals, once successfully placed and accommodated, will make loyal and dependable workers. Some of them will be content to work on tasks that other employees find aversive or boring, although many others will be able to perform highly challenging and complex tasks, overcoming the imposition of a physical, sensory, or learning disability.

Educators working to place their students in business and industry will need to follow several important principles. These include:

1. *Placing students who are ready for such an experience.* This requires adequate assessment of the student's vocational interests, abilities, and needs and matching them carefully to the community's resources. The student must be a willing participant in the placement decision.

2. *Assuring the employer that the student has the essential basic work habits, behaviors, interest, and ability for the placement.* This requires the educational program to provide its students with general employability skills training and adequate orientation to the world of work before placement, although further training in this area will also be a major objective of the experience.

3. *Providing a job coach or support person who can orient employees to the student and be available to provide whatever training and supervision is needed.* This will be especially critical during the initial period of training and will gradually fade in its intensity as the student becomes acclimated and able to function appropriately. The job coach or trainer will need to be available to return more frequently at various times in the training period when the student needs more extensive training, supervision, or problem resolution.

4. *Keeping in frequent contact with the student's supervisor and employees regarding progress and needs.* It is important for the student to get as many work and interpersonal experiences as possible. The educator should ensure that the student is treated as much as possible as any new employee would be and is expected to perform duties that the job coach/trainer deems reasonable and an important training objective.

A job performance rating form and a job task sheet should be used to gain frequent input from the supervisor and co-workers to determine the student's work performance and behavioral functioning and needs.

Many businesses and industries are providing persons with more severe disabilities with the opportunity for vocational training and employment. Two Minneapolis hotels, The Marquette and The Northstar, have been recognized internationally for their pioneering program of hiring and training persons with disabilities—particularly those with cognitive disabilities. In their stewarding department, more than 100 of their 120 employees have disabilities, and they have reduced their annual turnover from an industry-wide average of 150% percent to 11%.

Marriott Corporation is another major employer of persons with disabilities, who account for about 5% of Marriott's work force nationwide. Marriott provides on-the-job training at many of its locations and works closely with many school systems and professional organizations to hire these individuals, including many with developmental disabilities. Much joy and satisfaction can result, not only for the employee but also for the employer who provides these individuals with the opportunity to prove their ability to be productive and loyal workers.

"A diverse culture is our reality and our future."
McDonald's Corporation

McDonald's Corporation continues to be particularly responsive to the abilities of persons with disabilities. McDonalds's has developed a comprehensive field training program to provide sensitivity training, including dispelling common myths and presenting facts about disabilities, and exercises for its employees to heighten their appreciation of the inconvenience that a disability presents. McDonald's has been a pioneer in the employment of people with disabilities for over 30 years and is an outstanding example of a major company that is giving persons with mild-to-severe disabilities a chance to become a productive citizen and employee.

FINAL COMMENTS

The opportunity for educators to form even more meaningful and substantial partnerships has never been greater. The ADA has been a positive force in promoting this opportunity, and for the most part, business and industry have been responsive to the mandate to provide the accommodations necessary for these individuals to be successful and productive employees. Now, it is up to the educational system to respond accordingly by not only forming meaningful partnerships but working together with community agencies in preparing their students more adequately for the world of work and community living.

The methods and materials for providing an educational program that meets the contemporary and complex needs of its community and its students have been developed. School districts now need to restructure their overall curriculums so these methods and materials are adequately incorporated. The preparation of students with special learning needs for successful adult adjustment is a formidable task. The curriculum must institute a scope and sequence (K–12) that inculcates in these students a self-awareness, self-esteem, and work personality that will lead to the successful attainment of those life skills that are needed for a productive life in their community.

If the educational system does not prepare its students with all of the important basic functional skills needed for training and placement in the labor market (i.e., academic, daily living, personal–social, and occupational), the result will be failure and continued rejection of these individuals as worthy and productive citizens. Now that much of business and industry have accepted the challenge and responsibility to be educators, it is up to the schools to become even more proactive in designing community-based experiences that will truly result in their students' successful career development.

ACTIVITIES

1. Conduct a survey of those businesses and industries in your community that could be potential work experience sites and future employers of your students. Secure the names of appropriate contact persons, and interview some of these individuals to discern the level of awareness and receptivity toward working with the school in your career education/transition program.

2. Refer to the LCCE Curriculum Matrix in Figure 3.2 and determine which of the resources you have identified can contribute to the training needs of your students relative to the 97 LCCE subcompetencies/skills.

Part 3

Instructional Planning

Chapter 7

Functional/Career Assessment

Chapter 8

Individualized Educational and

Transition Planning

Chapter 9

Instructional Materials and Resources

Chapter 7

Functional/Career Assessment

Donn E. Brolin and Stephen W. Thomas

Preliminary Questions About the Topic

1. What is the difference between norm-referenced and criterion-referenced tests?
2. What is meant by the term *functional assessment*?
3. What legal mandates presently exist that require educators to use functional assessment measures?
4. What are some important advantages and disadvantages of using a functional assessment approach?
5. What is a functional job analysis?
6. Identify several particularly useful functional assessment instruments for career development and transition planning.
7. What is curriculum-based vocational assessment (CBVA)?
8. Explain what is meant by the term *career assessment*.
9. Identify and describe the four Life-Centered Career Education (LCCE) curriculum-based instruments that have been developed for instructional planning.
10. List some of the organizations that can be contacted to obtain information about various functional/career assessment measures.

Assessment is a necessary and important component of the educational process that provides educators with information from numerous sources so informed decisions can be made on the behalf of their students. In the case of career education and transition planning, a functional assessment approach is particularly critical in helping the student to identify strengths, weaknesses, and instructional needs in those skills areas needed for successful personal development and employment.

Functional assessment involves two primary methods of measurement: norm-referenced testing and criterion-referenced testing. Norm-referenced tests compare an individual's performance on academics, dexterity, aptitude, interest, intelligence, and so on to those of other individuals. Criterion-referenced tests evaluate the individual's performance at some absolute standard that is independent of the performance of others. This type of assessment focuses on what the person knows and can do so that specific strengths and weaknesses can be discerned.

Although both assessment approaches are important in conducting functional/career assessments with individuals who have disabilities or are disadvantaged, many professionals believe the criterion-referenced approach will yield the most relevant data for instructional planning, particularly in transition planning for students with disabilities (e.g., Brown, Browning, & Dunn, 1992; Halpern, Lehmann, Irvin, & Heiry, 1982). As noted by Browning, Dunn, and Brown,

> assessments need to be conducted throughout the entire transition period rather than serving as a data-based resource for only a single point in time. The kinds of assessment information needed will vary at different stages of the transition process. (1993, p. 197)

There is no lack of tools in conducting vocational assessments. A study by DeStefano, Linn, and Markward (1987) found 144 different assessment instruments being used in various transition programs. This prompted Browning and Brechin (1993) to recommend that educators need to define functional assessment so they can use appropriate assessment measures. Those authors note that ecological functional assessments in community-based settings are also very important assessments to conduct during the secondary years, when students are provided more training experiences in community settings. Browning and Brechin also suggest that assessment endeavors be a cooperatively developed program developed by and approved by the students, their parents, and all significant service providers involved in the transition process.

This chapter begins with a discussion of the functional assessment approach. Next, more specific functional assessment measures, both norm-referenced and criterion-referenced, are identified and described. The next sections discuss career assessment and then explain and illustrate the four LCCE instruments that have been developed for this purpose. A case study is presented to depict the use of two LCCE instruments.

FUNCTIONAL ASSESSMENT

Education and rehabilitation professionals have always sought efficient, comprehensive, and accurate ways to assess the strengths and needs of the persons they serve.

However, because of widely differing settings, populations, and goals, practitioners have been hard pressed to find sound, standardized instruments that are quick and easy to use and can be broadly applied. Standardized tests and work samples associated with vocational evaluation and assessment are not always available, and when in the hands of inexperienced users may not always yield valid results. Curriculum-based assessments are often too time-consuming for some teachers, and the lack of standardization limits their accuracy.

As a result, numerous functional assessment inventories and rating forms have been developed for the purposes of initial screening and planning. The concept of "functional" assessment has grown from a desire for practical, concrete information on how well individuals learn and perform in a variety of situations and environments. The development of supported employment and community-based service-delivery models, transition mandates in education and rehabilitation, and the Americans with Disabilities Act (ADA) have placed a growing emphasis on the "functional" aspects of independent (and interdependent) living and working.

Defining Functional Assessment

Two key definitions of functional assessment that have value in career assessment models are presented in this section. The first definition is from the *Functional Assessment Inventory Manual*.

> In simplest terms, functional assessment is a systematic enumeration of vocationally relevant strengths and limitations. (Crewe, Athelstan, & University of Minnesota, 1984, p. 3)

This definition contains several key elements. The first is the reference to "systematic enumeration." To improve efficiency in administration and ensure thorough coverage of all functional areas, a systematic, well-organized process should be incorporated. This includes a systematic and uniform procedure for determining how each functional area can be reliably and validly rated. Once all functional areas have been assessed and rated, a functional profile of strengths and needs (weaknesses) can be established that will enumerate the various functional deficits that require attention. Resulting functional profiles can then be systematically matched to the functional requirements of courses, training, jobs, and transition environments so that accommodation and successful placement can be planned and achieved.

The second important element in this definition, "vocationally relevant," defines the setting where the functional skills are to be assessed and applied. Although this definition stresses the vocational factors, Crewe et al. (1984) also refer to the "personal" aspects to be covered in functional assessment that are needed beyond vocational situations. The Functional Assessment Inventory was designed primarily to assess vocationally relevant functional skills in vocational rehabilitation clientele, but the functional areas included in the instrument relate to a broader range of functioning.

The third and final element, "strengths and limitations," provides the basis for determining functional ability. Again, functional ability profiles specify the types of services

Point of View

All effective education and transition planning requires a thorough assessment of student abilities, needs, and potential in relation to career and life goals. The development of these individual functional profiles involves the collection of performance-based information regarding abilities and limitations as well as the accommodations and services needed to overcome the identified limitations in a variety of settings. Accommodations are a key element not only for improved performance in the classroom but for ensuring successful employment under the Americans with Disabilities Act.

Profile information can be collected using a variety of instruments and techniques including but not limited to norm-referenced and criterion-referenced tests, functional assessment inventories, work samples, vocational evaluation systems, curriculum-based assessments, situational assessments, and community-based assessments. Depending on the severity of the disability, any

number of assessment instruments and techniques can be used in conjunction with staffing, file review, interviewing, and behavioral observation. Although one student might profit from the use of standardized tests and work samples, another would be more appropriately assessed through situational and community-based techniques. Differing abilities and goals require versatility in the assessment process.

In recent years, work samples have fallen out of favor in some education and rehabilitation settings. However, this has often resulted from a misunderstanding and misuse of the instruments. When creatively used, work samples can reduce bias (frequently associated with standardized tests), enhance career exploration and decision making, and provide opportunities to try out various accommodation methods that can improve learning and performance. When community-based strategies are unavailable, work samples can serve as excellent "hands-on" tasks to

or accommodations needed to minimize or overcome limitations. Profiles can also be used to match individual functional abilities to the functional requirements in a variety of settings.

The second definition to be examined was developed by Halpern and Fuhrer:

Functional assessment is the measurement of purposeful behavior in interaction with the environment, which is interpreted according to the assessment's intended uses. (1984, p. 3)

This definition emphasizes the importance of environment and its influence on behavior and is not specific to any one setting or purpose. "It speaks to the diversity of information often sought through the administration of functional assessment proceobserve and address behavior and performance issues. This calls for flexibility in their use and in interpretation of results for consumers and practitioners.

The vocational assessment process is no longer limited to evaluating potential for vocational training and placement. It has been expanded to include a broader range of personal, social, and independent living factors that have an impact on inclusion and quality of life outcomes. Generating useful transition information has challenged the creative talents of vocational evaluators and vocational assessment specialists. It has also provided opportunities for students and consumers to become involved in collecting assessment information and making decisions about planning directions. This process of involvement ensures ownership and provides the student with the information needed to make informed choices. The assessment of decision-making skills and the ability to learn how to make appropriate decisions (essential for self-determination) are becoming a more critical part of the assessment process.

The need for better planning to achieve transition goals requires the kind of information that can be collected through a versatile vocational evaluation and assessment process. Without thorough assessments, the accuracy of planning information will be reduced, students will not have the information necessary to make meaningful education and life decisions, and the sense of ownership required to optimize involvement will be diminished. Information collected through evaluation and assessment is empowering not only to rehabilitation and education professionals but to students who live with the outcomes of transition plans.

Stephen W. Thomas is professor and director of the Graduate Program in Vocational Evaluation, Department of Rehabilitation Studies, East Carolina University, Greenville, North Carolina.

dures" (Thomas, 1992, pp. 4–5). Ecological assessment, often associated with supported and community-based employment, requires sensitivity to how individuals function in every environment they encounter (including the classroom).

Advantages and Disadvantages of Functional Assessment

Several key advantages have promoted the increased use of functional assessment.

1. Functional assessment provides a quick yet thorough overview to individual functioning. It is often easy and inexpensive to administer and can be used by anyone, including the person being rated (i.e., self-rating process).

2. Functional profiles can be developed to direct planning for service delivery. Profiles serve as a baseline of performance and behavior for comparison to the functional goals associated with a specified environment. Differences in the functional levels will help tailor planning and service delivery to achieve success in the targeted environment.

3. Standardized inventories, rating instruments, and tests can provide pre- and postassessment opportunities to evaluate the degree and effectiveness of service delivery in achieving the functional goal.

4. Functional assessments are easy to interpret, and because they relate to basic functional activities, they are easy to explain to participants and their families and convert into plans.

5. Resulting profiles can be readily matched to settings where the functional requirements are known.

Several key disadvantages have limited the effective use of functional assessment.

1. Many inventories have not been standardized, so little is known about their utility and accuracy (i.e., reliability and validity).

2. Rating bias or error may occur with untrained raters or with subjective rating processes.

3. Possessing functional skills differs from the ability to perform a complex task or set of tasks composed of a combination or series of functions. Functional profiles only indicate an individual's potential abilities and do not ensure success in the classroom, the job site, or the community.

4. When functions are assessed individually, there is limited understanding of how they can be applied when used in more complex and unrestricted situations where numerous functions are required.

5. There is a lack of uniformity in the content, categories, and use of functional assessment instruments. Guidelines do not exist for the development, standardization, or use of such instruments. Because of the varied settings, populations, and goals, standardization will be difficult.

6. It is difficult to determine on the continuum of functioning the precise cutoff between a strength and a limitation. This is often dictated by environmental requirements.

In spite of their shortcomings, functional assessment instruments serve an important purpose. They direct the systematic collection of information that can help determine if more comprehensive evaluations are needed or if planning can proceed. Although they provide a quick method of screening, they should not be considered the final word in assessment.

Mandates and Uses of Functional Assessment

Some of the early legislative mandates for functional assessment appeared in vocational rehabilitation. Many rehabilitation state agencies based eligibility on the number and degree of functional limitations (e.g., walking, standing, speaking, memory). The severity of a disability was often based on the documentation of two or more functional limitations. With the advent of supported employment and community-based service-delivery models, functional assessment inventories have rapidly grown in popularity.

Within the medical rehabilitation model, functional assessment—generally referred to as *functional capacity evaluation*—focuses on physical functioning activities such as strength, endurance, mobility, and range of motion. Occupational and physical therapists in rehabilitation hospitals and work-hardening centers usually provide these types of assessments to industrially injured workers to determine their potential to return to previous employment. This is a much more specialized application of functional assessment than is found in vocational rehabilitation, community-based, education, or transition settings.

With the emphasis on transition in the Individuals with Disabilities Education Act (IDEA), school personnel need a comprehensive and systematic way to assess functioning in the wide variety of transition environments available to students in and out of school. Transitional areas such as work, independent living, personal/social/family, and recreation involve combinations of functional skills that call for an in-depth assessment (often referred to in the legislation as a "functional vocational evaluation"). The movement toward outcome-based education has focused on the functional skills students need to successfully enter and master specific content domains and competencies. Many state offices of education have developed competency guides that target specific functional requirements in all classes and provide a blueprint for developing functional assessment strategies.

The most recent and significant legislation mandating the assessment of functional skills is the ADA (Equal Employment Opportunity Commission, 1991). The employment provisions under Title I of the act define disability as "A physical or mental impairment that substantially limits one or more of the major life activities of such individual." Two important terms in this definition, "substantially limits" and "major life activities," have a direct relationship to the functional assessment process. *Major life activities* mean "*functions* such as caring for oneself, performing manual tasks, walking, seeing, hearing, speaking, breathing, learning, and working." The term *substantially limits* means:

1. Unable to perform a major life activity that the average person in the general population can perform or
2. Significantly restricted as to the condition, manner, or duration under which an individual can perform a particular major life activity as compared to the condition, manner, or duration under which the average person in the general population can perform that same major life activity

With regard to the major life activities of working, "the term *substantially limits* means significantly restricted in the ability to perform either a class of jobs or a broad range of jobs in various classes as compared to the average person having comparable training, skills and abilities."

For individuals to qualify for employment under the ADA, they must possess a significant functional limitation to living or working. Reasonable accommodations must be provided to enable individuals with disabilities to perform the "essential functions" of a job. If vocational training is designed to prepare students to successfully perform the essential functions of targeted jobs, then schools will also be required to make similar accommodations in the classroom. The key to a successful ADA-based vocational assessment is the accurate identification of functional strengths and limitations and the determination of reasonable accommodations that can minimize or eliminate the identified limitations (Thomas, 1992).

An interesting provision in the ADA employment regulations is the requirement that applicants be able to explain to potential employers how they would perform the essential functions of the job. It spells out a process whereby an employer can discuss accommodation needs with the prospective employee. The regulations state:

> To determine the appropriate reasonable accommodation it may be necessary for the covered entity to initiate an informal, interactive process with the qualified individual with a disability in need of the accommodation. The process should identify the precise limitations resulting from the disability and potential reasonable accommodations that could overcome those limitations.

Results of the functional assessment must be shared with consumers so they can effectively participate in this interview process. Information is empowering, and only when participants are provided with understandable assessment results will they be able to make well-informed decisions and become fully participating team members in planning their own transition objectives. One of the most beneficial skills we can teach the people we serve is how to successfully describe to employers their functional abilities and accommodations that can be used to competitively perform the essential functions of a particular job. Assessing this potential in students will help determine if they possess sufficient decision-making skills to understand and verbalize the results clearly. Students who can articulate approaches to, and accommodations for, specific tasks may not require as much assistance as individuals who cannot understand or explain their functional strengths and needs. In this situation, someone will need to be empowered to represent the student. This process of empowerment involves sharing functional strengths and limitations profiles with students and discussing their understanding of and agreement with their profiles (Thomas, 1992).

Although functional assessment evolved from the need for a quick and easy technique to collect a broad range of information on an individual's strengths and limitations, the influence of legislation on its recognition and continued acceptance cannot be ignored. With increasing legal mandates for its use, there is greater importance for the standardization of functional assessment instruments.

Instrumentation in Functional Assessment

Functional assessment instruments have taken many forms, including rating scales, inventories, standardized tests, and test batteries. Rating scales and inventories are the most common functional assessment instruments. Such inventories can be purchased commercially or developed locally or may result from the modification of a commercially available scale. Information is collected through file review, staffing, interviewing, observation, test and work sample administration, situational assessment, and curriculum-based assessment, and is used to respond to the questions on the scale. These types of inventories are composed of a series of functional items (e.g., learning ability, vision, use of hands) that represent a comprehensive range of functional categories (e.g., physical, cognitive, personal, social). Each item contains a series of descriptive statements used to rate functional competence. For example, regarding the item of "making change," a rater could be asked to choose one of the following statements that best describes functional competence:

a. Can make change up to and above $20.00
b. Can make change up to $10.00
c. Can make change up to $5.00
d. Can make change up to $1.00
e. Cannot make change

These forms by themselves are not assessment tools in the strictest sense of the word, but simply provide the means for systematically recording, rating, and profiling functional information as it is collected. The accuracy of the ratings depends on the accuracy of the instruments and techniques used to collect the required information and to code it on the form.

Rating Scales/Inventories

The first example of a rating form is the Functional Assessment Inventory (Crewe et al., 1984). It is composed of two rating forms with 30 functional items, each containing four descriptive choices. Examples of the functional items are learning ability, memory, hearing, use of hands, and speed. Items are also included that address support issues such as stability of condition, interest in working, financial incentives, and support from family and friends. Ten items that provide assessment in areas considered to be employment strengths (e.g., looks, personality, skill, motivation) conclude the Functional Assessment Inventory.

The first form, the Functional Assessment Inventory, is completed by the professional; while the second form, the Personal Capacities Questionnaire, is completed by the consumer. Responses on the two forms can be compared and discussed with the participant and the participant's family, thus enhancing their involvement in the process. The Functional Assessment Inventory was originally designed for use with vocational rehabilitation clientele, and the manual contains reliability and validity studies based on this population.

The second example of a rating form is the Consumer Employment Screening Form (CESF) (Moon, Goodall, Barcus, & Brooke, 1986). Although somewhat similar in its rating procedure to the Functional Assessment Inventory, the items on the CESF tend to be more basic (e.g., independent work rate, independent sequencing of job duties, adapting to change, time awareness, and independent street-crossing skills). The CESF does not have a form that can be completed by the consumer, but it does include a second form that can be used to conduct a functional job analysis. This enables the professional to match the functional requirements of a job or a specific vocational class. Like the Functional Assessment Inventory, the CESF contains rating areas that address support issues such as supervision needs, financial incentives, benefits needed, and family involvement. Space is provided after each item for comments. The inventory was designed for use in supported employment and is a part of a comprehensive training manual for supported employment service delivery. No standardization studies are reported in the manual containing the CESF.

The Supported Employment Technical Assistance Project (1989) modified the CESF for persons with traumatic brain injury. Items were added or revised to address functional issues common to head injury. The most noteworthy changes to the form were the inclusion of expanded items and space to document and describe the effects of attempted accommodations on functioning.

The Brigance® System offers two instruments that are particularly useful for assessing important functional academic skills and life skills. The Inventory of Essential Skills (1987) covers the academic areas of reading/language arts, math, and study skills. Life skill assessments are available in the areas of food and clothing, money and finance, travel and transportation, and communication and telephone skills. Rating scales measure the applied skills of health and attitude, responsibility and self-discipline, job interview preparation, communication, and auto safety. Student record books indicate competency levels and define instructional goals. The more recent Life Skills Inventory (1994), a criterion-referenced assessment tool, has been designed to assess listening, speaking, reading, writing, comprehending, and computing skills in nine life-skills sections: speaking and listening skills, functional writing skills, words on common signs and warning labels, telephone skills, money and finance, food, clothing, health, and travel and transportation. The instrument is also intended to serve as a curriculum guide by providing teaching sequences for functional life skills.

Standardized Rating Scales

A number of standardized behavior rating scales assess various functional skills. Examples include the Prevocational Assessment and Curriculum Guide, the Vocational Assessment and Curriculum Guide, the Vineland Adaptive Behavior Scales, and the AAMD Adaptive Behavior Scale. These instruments report reliability and validity studies and are norm-referenced.

The Prevocational Assessment and Curriculum Guide (PACG) (Mithaug, Mar, & Stewart, 1978) covers 46 specific school and workshop expectations arranged in 9 areas: attendance/endurance, independence, production, learning, behavior communications skills, social skills, grooming/eating skills, and toileting skills. The inventory is supplemented by a curriculum guide to assist in setting instructional goals.

An extension of the PACG is the Vocational Assessment and Curriculum Guide (VACG) (Rusch, Schutz, Mithaug, Stewart, & Mar, 1982). Similar in its structure and use to the PACG, it was normed on service and industrial employees and geared to entry-level employment in light industry, food service, janitorial, and other service occupations. The VACG inventory and curriculum guide were designed primarily to address functioning in vocational settings.

The Vineland Adaptive Behavior Scales (Sparrow, Balla, & Cicchetti, 1985) is available in three editions: the Interview Edition, Survey Form (297 items); the more comprehensive Interview Edition, Expanded Form (577 items); and the Classroom Edition (a 244-item questionnaire). The interviews are administered to parents and care givers, and the Classroom Edition is completed by a teacher. The Vineland contains 11 subdomains organized into the four domains of communication, daily living skills, socialization, and motor skills.

Other standardized inventories such as the AAMD Adaptive Behavior Scale (School Edition) (Nihira, Foster, Shellhaas, & Leland, 1981) provide software for scoring and profiling and provide an instructional planning manual. Whatever type of standardized inventory is chosen, it should be comprehensive in its coverage of functional skills and behaviorally descriptive in the rating and interpretation process.

Basic Skills Assessment Through Standardized Testing

Because a number of functional assessment inventories lack standardization and objectivity, some professionals prefer to rely on standardized tests of functional skills. As with most untimed standardized tests, the participant is asked to answer specific questions from knowledge domains, in this case, functional skills. Some of the shorter tests focus more on basic or adaptive skills such as the Adaptive Behavior: The Street Survival Skills Questionnaire, the Social and Prevocational Inventory Battery (forms R & T), and the Tests for Everyday Living. Longer and more expensive performance-based assessment systems such as the Pre-Vocational Readiness Battery (VALPAR 17) provide opportunities for behavior observation, evaluation of learning styles, and exploration of accommodations.

The Adaptive Behavior: The Street Survival Skills Questionnaire (SSSQ) (Linkenhoker & McCarron, 1983) is an untimed, individually administered test containing nine subtests: basic concepts, functional signs, tools, domestics, health and safety, public services, time, monetary, and measurements. The administrator asks a question, and the respondent chooses the correct answer from a series of four pictures, by pointing to the picture or saying the corresponding letter (A, B, C, or D). All nine scales do not need to be administered; however, a total functional score cannot be obtained from a prorated administration. Subtests from many of the functional assessment instruments reviewed can be administered and interpreted individually, but this practice limits the development of a complete profile. Each SSSQ subtest has 24 questions, and the results can be scored and profiled by hand or on a computer, and deficiencies can be matched to a curriculum guide.

The Social and Prevocational Information Battery (SPIB) (Halpern, Raffeld, Irvin, Link, & Munkres, 1985) is available in two forms: form "R" for students with mild intellectual deficiencies and form "T" for students with moderate intellectual deficiencies. This untimed, paper-and-pencil test can be orally administered to individuals or groups. It provides an assessment in nine areas: job search skills, job-related behavior, banking, budgeting, purchasing, home management, physical health care, hygiene and grooming, and functional signs. A learning activities resource kit is available with the SPIB to address identified limitations.

Vocational Assessment Measures

Vocational assessment or evaluation has been an important component to the career education effort for many years and is another functional assessment approach. Many commercial evaluation systems have been developed over the past 20 or more years and have been used by several school systems. Some of the most noteworthy are the McCarron-Dial Work Evaluation System (P.O. Box 45628, Dallas, TX 75245); the Vocational Research Institute (VRI) assessment (Suite 1502, 1528 Walnut St., Philadelphia, PA 19102), particularly the APTICOM and Vocational Transit; and the TAP System and related instruments produced by Talent Assessment, Inc. (P.O. Box 5087, Jacksonville, FL 32207). Each of these systems offers computerized components to expedite and expand capacities to relate assessment findings to specific training and/or jobs that may be within the capabilities of the individual.

The TAP System, for example, is a "hands-on" assessment of several work samples or tasks that measure such functional skills as gross and fine motor dexterity, color and finger discrimination, spatial aptitude, and other aptitudes that are important on various jobs. The assessments can be given in just a few hours. Computer management reports to relate results to specific job possibilities are available for Apple or IBM personal computers. The TAP System is supported by several other assessment measures: the PIC, which assesses vocational interests; the VIP, which assesses learning and personality styles, and the M.DOT, which is a job-matching system that provides information on jobs that match qualifications and interests.

The University of Arkansas Research and Training Center in Vocational Rehabilitation (P.O. Box 1328 Hot Springs Rehabilitation Center, Hot Springs, AR 71902) has developed its Employability Assessment Materials, a series of functional assessment measures that are being used successfully in many schools and rehabilitation settings. The Work Personality Profile (WPP) is a work behavior rating instrument that assesses 58 items that are essential to achieve and maintain suitable employment. The WPP takes 5 to 10 minutes to complete after an observation period of 1 week. A parallel self-report instrument, WPP-SR, is also available. The Work Performance Assessment (WPA) is a work-simulation procedure designed to assess an individual's response to typical on-the-job supervisory behaviors. The Employability Maturity Interview (EMI) is a 15-minute structured interview of 10 questions that measure individuals' readiness for vocational planning by focusing on their levels of self-knowledge and occupational information. The Job Seeking Skills Assessment (JSSA) assesses the individual's ability to complete job application forms and present oneself in an employment interview. These instruments, and others developed at the center, were extensively field tested, statistically analyzed, and well validated.

One example of a well-designed and standardized measure of vocational aptitudes and interests is the Occupational Aptitude Survey and Interest Schedule-2 (OASIS-2), developed by Professor Randy Parker (1991a, 1991b) of The University of Texas-Austin. This instrument is used to assist young adults to help them in their vocational self-exploration so they better achieve vocational self-understanding, decision making, and goal setting, and eventually attain a satisfying career. The OASIS-2 consists of two tests: the Aptitude Survey and the Interest Schedule, both of which are normed on a national sample of 1,505 8th- to 12th-grade students. The instrument can be administered by teachers, counselors, and other professionals to assist in the career development of all students, including those with disabilities or who are disadvantaged. The Aptitude Survey consists of five subtests, which measure six aptitudes that are directly related to skills and abilities required in over 20,000 jobs listed in the *Dictionary of Occupational Titles* (1977) general ability, verbal, numerical, spatial, perceptual, and manual dexterity. The Interest Schedule measures 12 interest factors directly related to the occupations listed in the *Guide to Occupational Exploration* (Harrington & O'Shea, 1984). Excellent reliability and validity data have been collected.

Another more recent development in this area is the concept of curriculum-based vocational assessment (CBVA), which is an ongoing process of collecting data while the student is engaged in vocational education programs (Stodden, Ianacone, Boone, & Bisconer, 1987). Stodden and Ianacone are noteworthy leaders in developing this approach, which can be instituted at the middle school/junior high school level as well as later.

One example of a CBVA program has been described by Swisher and Clark (1991), who integrated the career education concepts of career awareness and exploration into the basic concepts of CBVA. They contend that if students are exposed to sufficient middle school/junior high school awareness and exploration experiences that are monitored through a CBVA approach, then more appropriate vocational recommendations can be developed at the ninth-grade level and beyond. To develop their exemplary curriculum-based assessment and exploration program, Swisher and Clark analyzed the nature of the business, home economics, and industrial arts classes with the instructors to identify their generalizable and vocational skills. They then devised a series of 150 work sample activities that could be provided to the students over up to a 90-hour period. The result of this effort was a Practical Arts Evaluation System (PAES), which has become "an invaluable tool in the education and transition planning for students with special needs" (Swisher & Clark, 1991, p. 14).

The preceding examples of functional assessment approaches and materials are only a sample of what is available. Although basic skills tests, such as the ones cited, can assess transition skills, recent developments in the standardized testing of functional skills have focused on the information needs specific to transition planning. One major functional skills assessment package that falls into this category is the Life Centered Career Education (LCCE) Assessment System (Brolin, 1992a). When the LCCE Assessment Batteries are used as a component of the LCCE curriculum, continuity in transitional assessment, planning, and instruction can be optimized. The closer the relationship between the content of functional assessment and educational competencies, the greater the accuracy in targeting student needs and achieving instructional outcomes. A detailed description of the LCCE Assessment System is presented in the next section.

CAREER ASSESSMENT AND THE LCCE INSTRUMENTS

Career Assessment

Career education is a broader concept than vocational education. Therefore, career assessment is also more encompassing because it focuses on the individual's interests, needs, aptitudes, and abilities that relate to all types of productive work activity that one does in the home and community—avocational and vocational activities.

Career assessment is a developmental process beginning at the elementary school level and continuing through adulthood. In a position paper on the topic, The Council for Exceptional Children's Division on Career Development and Transition (DCDT) described the process as

> related to all aspects of career education, including not only preparation for employment, but also preparation for the productive roles of a family member, citizen, and participant in leisure, recreational, and avocational activities. The career assessment process should be a foundation for individualized program planning and transition planning from kindergarten through adulthood. The goals of this process should be specifically geared to providing the information needed to make decisions in all areas of career education programming; these decisions may be related to developing an individualized program or determining what assistance the learner needs to succeed in an ongoing program. (Sitlington, Brolin, Clark, & Vacanti, 1985)

The career assessment approach inherent in the LCCE curriculum is a curriculum-based assessment approach—that is, using the material to be learned (or similar material) as the basis for assessing the degree to which it has been learned or mastered. Within the field of career education, the field of vocational education has a parallel term (introduced in the previous section), CBVA, to discern vocational instruction needs. Sitlington notes that, "to obtain maximum applicability of the two assessment concepts to the field of career education, we must do two things: 1) define the curriculum as all experiences in which the learner is involved, including community-based experiences and 2) define the career education curriculum" (1991, p. 2).

Sitlington believes the LCCE curriculum meets the second criterion in that it

> provides a series of competencies which can form the basis for an individual's career education program, and which can be adapted to meet individual program and/or learner needs. The newly developed LCCE Knowledge Battery and the accompanying LCCE Performance Battery provide the tools which professionals can use to apply the concepts of curriculum-based assessment and curriculum-based vocational assessment . . . should not be used alone to determine the learner's strengths, interests, and instructional needs, but they will provide a strong framework upon which an effective career/vocational assessment can be built. They will also allow professionals to broaden the application of curriculum-based assessment and curriculum-based vocational assessment to include career education content. (1991, p. 2)

The LCCE Assessment System

Four LCCE assessment measures are available to assess the career education competencies contained in the LCCE curriculum. Each of these measures provides a different approach so educators can select from a range of measures depending on their own situation and needs. In addition, educators are encouraged to use other measures such as those described earlier to provide the most comprehensive and appropriate career assessment for transition planning.

The four LCCE instruments, published by the Council for Exceptional Children (CEC), are described briefly next. Examples from each are provided.

The LCCE Competency Rating Scale

The LCCE Competency Rating Scale (CRS) is built around the 22 competencies and 97 subcompetencies composing the LCCE curriculum. The subcompetencies serve as the actual CRS items. A manual, contained in the appendix of the LCCE Curriculum Guide (Life Centered Career Education: A Competency Based Approach, Brolin, 1993a), presents specific behavioral criteria on which to judge student mastery level for each subcompetency. These criteria approximate the behavioral/instructional objectives that are subsumed under each subcompetency unit in the Curriculum Guide.

The CRS was developed with the philosophy that teachers who work closely with the students can fairly accurately assess their competency levels, given helpful and appropriate guidelines. The CRS Manual provides these guidelines; identifies who should do the ratings and when they should be done; and provides criteria for the ratings, a rating key defining numerical rating values, a CRS Record Form for recording and summarizing ratings, and demographic information.

CRS users rate their students on a 3-point scale on each of the subcompetencies as either not competent, partially competent, or competent. Younger students will be too young for rating of some of the subcompetencies; thus, a "Not Rated" (NR) response should be given. Ratings are recorded and summarized on a CRS Record Form so that a profile of the student's strengths and weaknesses in the 97 subcompetency areas can be discerned and a domain score obtained for each of the three curriculum areas: daily living, personal–social, and occupational guidance and preparation.

The CRS provides a quick and inexpensive method of curriculum-based assessment. It can be used at any grade level and with any type of student. It is particularly useful at the elementary level, where a limited number of functional skills instruments related to the transition effort are available. An example of one page from the CRS is presented in Figure 7.1.

The LCCE Knowledge Battery

The second instrument, LCCE Knowledge Battery (KB), was developed to provide LCCE users with a more objective instrument for assessing students on their level of competency attainment. The KB is a criterion-referenced assessment that contains 200

LIFE CENTERED CAREER EDUCATION
Competency Rating Scale
Record Form
DAILY LIVING SKILLS

Student Name ___Susan___ Date of Birth ___1–10___ Sex ___F___

School ___Progressive___ City ___Columbia___ State ___MO___

Directions: Please rate the student according to his/her mastery of *each* item using the rating key below. Indicate the ratings in the column below the date for the rating period. Use the NR rating for items which cannot be rated. For subcompetencies rated 0 or 1 at the time of the final rating, place a check (✓) in the appropriate space in the *yes/no* column to indicate his/her ability to perform the subcompetency with assistance from the community. Please refer to the CRS manual for explanation of the rating key, description of the behavioral criteria for each subcompetency, and explanation of the *yes/no* column.

Rating Key: 0 = Not Competent   1 = Partially Competent   2 = Competent   NR = Not Rated

To what extent has the student mastered the following subcompetencies:

Subcompetencies	Rater(s)	JR	JR							Yes	No
	Grade Level	7	8								
	Date(s)	5/25/93	5/6/94								
DAILY LIVING SKILLS DOMAIN											
1. Managing Personal Finances											
1. Identify Money and Make Correct Change		2	2								
2. Make Responsible Expenditures		1	1								
3. Keep Basic Financial Records		0	*1								
4. Calculate and Pay Taxes		0	0								
5. Use Credit Responsibly		0	*1								
6. Use Banking Services		0	*2								
2. Selecting and Managing a Household											
7. Maintain Home Exterior/Interior		1	1								
8. Use Basic Appliances and Tools		1	1								
9. Select Adequate Housing		0	1								
10. Set Up Household		0	1								
11. Maintain Home Grounds		1	1								
3. Caring for Personal Needs											
12. Demonstrate Knowledge of Physical Fitness, Nutrition, and Weight		1	1								
13. Exhibit Proper Grooming and Hygiene		1	2								
14. Dress Appropriately		1	2								
15. Demonstrate Knowledge of Common Illness, Prevention, and Treatment		0	0								
16. Practice Personal Safety		0	1								

FIGURE 7.1   Curriculum-based assessment for career education: A one-page sample from the CRS.

Note. From *Life Centered Career Education: A Competency-Based Approach* (4th ed., p. 140) by D. E. Brolin, 1993, Reston, VA: The Council for Exceptional Children. Copyright 1993 by The Council for Exceptional Children. Reprinted by permission.

multiple-choice questions covering the three LCCE domains. Ten questions cover the first 20 competencies of the LCCE Curriculum. The last two competencies, covering physical-manual skills and specific occupational skills, do not lend themselves to knowledge assessment.

The instructional objectives of the LCCE curriculum were, like the CRS, used as the basis for developing KB test items because they define the important content areas of the curriculum. Questions for each competency were divided among the subcompetencies composing the competency and their instructional objectives. The KB comprises two forms (A and B) and takes from 2 to 4 hours to administer, depending on the students.

The KB was developed over a period of several years with the assistance of several school personnel. A number of experienced educators were involved in writing appropriate items, which were revised several times after field testing of different versions with hundreds of students across the country. A detailed technical report is available to describe the extensive development and validation of the instrument.

Although the KB was developed originally for 7th- through 12th- grade students with mild intellectual and specific learning disabilities, many users find the instrument useful with a variety of students. However, caution is advised in too quickly interpreting its results without keeping its development and validation in mind. It is important to remember that the LCCE KB, like any other assessment, is just a sample of basic knowledge. No measure should be considered to reveal every student's actual level of competency. Rather, such instruments are useful screening devices to assist educators in instructional planning efforts.

An example of one page from one of the KB forms is presented in Figure 7.2.

The LCCE Performance Battery

The third instrument, the LCCE Performance Battery (PB), was developed to provide a more functional, real-life measure of the competencies in the LCCE Curriculum. The first 21 LCCE competencies are addressed in the instrument. Competency 22 is not assessed, because its assessment depends on the specific occupational training area in which each student is being instructed.

The PB is a nonstandardized criterion-referenced instrument. It contains a combination of open-ended questions, role-playing scenarios, card sorts, and several hands-on activities that require the student, for example, to make a meal, use a telephone directory, and fill out a credit application. Because of the length of time required to assess actual performance in some of the LCCE competency areas, many advanced knowledge or cognitive items were used for some of the competency assessments. Three types of items make up the battery: performance, simulated performance, and performance-related knowledge.

As with the CRS and KB, the subcompetencies and instructional objectives from Life Centered Career Education: A Competency-Based Approach (Brolin, 1993a) were used in determining and developing test items. The PB presents a more realistic approach to assessing students' actual abilities and behaviors beyond what is gained from the more objective KB. Students must demonstrate an activity reflecting adequate

---

PERSONAL-SOCIAL SKILLS QUESTIONS

Practice Multiple-Choice Item

When people are nice to you, it makes you

   a. angry.

   b. disappointed.

   c. happy.

   d. sad.

---

*Circle the LETTER of the **BEST** Answer*

91. Which physical need does your body require the MOST of to stay alive?

   a. clothing

   b. oxygen

   c. shelter

   d. sleep

92. An important part of feeling good about yourself is

   a. being happy with what you are doing.

   b. making money.

   c. telling others how good you are.

   d. wishing you were someone else.

93. Which of the following requires the MOST ability?

   a. playing a tape

   b. talking on the telephone

   c. typing a letter

   d. watching television

94. Your interests should be

   a. like other people's.

   b. like your friends'.

   c. like your parents'.

   d. what you like.

FIGURE 7.2   Objective assessment of competency in career education: A one-page sample of the LCCE Knowledge Battery.

Note. From *Life Centered Career Education* (p. 56) by D. E. Brolin, 1992, Reston, VA: The Council for Exceptional Children. Copyright 1992 by The Council for Exceptional Children. Reprinted by permission.

command of the LCCE competencies and their subcompetencies. All subcompetencies are addressed in the PB tests. Each competency test has five questions. A manual provides detailed directions for administering, scoring, and reporting the results. A special feature of the PB approach is its flexibility in scoring, which allows examiners to use their discretion in deviating from the suggested correct responses based on regional and cultural differences.

The PB has two forms, A and B. Because it would take more than 30 hours to administer the battery to small groups of students, users generally select one or more PB tests to administer at a time based on the results of the CRS and/or KB assessments. Often these tests are administered before and after students are instructed in one of the LCCE competency areas. Many teachers like the PB because it is the most natural and realistic measure of their students' functional/transitional skills.

The first two pages of one LCCE PB test (competency 17) are presented in Figure 7.3. The entire test for this competency—which includes the other questions, score sheet, and work sheets—is provided in Appendix C for readers interested in the entire nature of test construction.

The LCCE Self-Determination Scale

The most recent addition to the LCCE Assessment System was developed by The Arc (a national organization on mental retardation) from federal funding in cooperation with the author. The instrument will be published by The Council for Exceptional Children in spring 1995. The LCCE Self-Determination Scale (SDS) is a 40-item self-report instrument in which students choose from one of three response (no, maybe, yes) to their perceptions and beliefs relating to the concept of self-determination.

The Arc staff determined that four LCCE personal–social competencies closely approximate what experts believe to be inherent in the concept of self-determination: competency 10, self-awareness; 11, self-confidence; 14, independence; and 15, making adequate decisions. These competencies and their 17 subcompetencies were deemed representative of what The Arc considered to be the four domains of self-determination: self-awareness, self-confidence, choice and decision-making skills, and goal attainment behaviors.

The SDS was developed to augment the LCCE KB and PB assessments. Unlike the KB and PB, the SDS is a self-report measure. In addition, the scales differ: The KB provides information about the knowledge the students possess about the competency areas related to self-determination, whereas the PB assesses students' abilities to transfer that knowledge to practice, and the SDS assesses students' beliefs about themselves and their skills in this area. Thus, a complete picture of the student's abilities and attitudes related to self-determination can result.

An example of several items contained in the SDS instrument is illustrated in Figure 7.4.

LCCE PERFORMANCE TEST 17
Form A

**KNOWING AND EXPLORING OCCUPATIONAL POSSIBILITIES
(OCCUPATIONAL GUIDANCE AND PREPARATION)**

MATERIALS FOR DUPLICATION

Test Question 1: Occupational Remuneration
Test Question 2: Job Information
Test Question 3: Values from a Job
Test Question 4: Job Categories
Test Question 5: Investigate Job Opportunities
Want Ads Sheet
Score Sheet

MATERIALS NEEDED

Telephone directories

DIRECTIONS

This test can be given in approximately one class period. Answers may be written or given orally, but care must be taken so other students do not overhear responses. Some directions and vocabulary used in this test may be too advanced for some students and may require further explanation. This test assesses the students' ability to:

1. identify remunerative aspects of work

2. locate sources of occupational and training information

3. identify personal values met through work

4. classify jobs into occupational categories

5. investigate local occupational and training opportunities

SCORING PROCEDURES

If the test has previously been administered to the student, circle the number of times on the score sheet.

Examples of appropriate responses are provided on the score sheet for items that may have several acceptable answers. Some questions may have only one acceptable response. For questions requiring demonstrations or role-playing, the examiner must make a judgement about scoring. Further guidelines are presented below.

Written Responses—On the score sheet, circle the example(s) the student has identified. If the student gives an example that seems appropriate but is not listed on the score sheet, record that response on the line provided. Then record the student's score.

FIGURE 7.3   Sample pages from the LCCE Performance Battery, competency 17.

Note. From *Life Centered Career Education* (pp. 531–532) by D. E. Brolin, 1992, Reston, VA: The Council for Exceptional Children. Copyright 1992 by The Council for Exceptional Children. Reprinted by permission.

Performance Test 17—Form A (cont.)

Oral Responses—For test questions to which the student responded orally rather than in writing, record the student's response on the score sheet and score the response.

Observed Responses—For test questions requiring the student to perform by demonstrating or role-playing, record the response immediately after the response is made. If the task is not performed appropriately, note the reason for the point loss on the line provided.

Each question, including subquestions, is worth up to 2 points. A student must obtain a total score of 8–10 for mastery. Record the final score on the Student Competency Assessment Record (SCAR).

Allow students to respond to each request before reading the next task.

Question 1: Occupational Remuneration (Group Administration)

To the Examiner: Students are to provide explanations for differences in occupational remuneration and why people take lower paying jobs. Also, students are to answer a question concerning types of reductions to paychecks. Distribute Test Question 1.

Read to Students: Look at Test Question 1 and read along with me. People get paid different amounts of money depending on the kind of job they have. Lawyers and doctors make more money that dishwashers and food servers. (a) Give one reason why this is so. (b) Explain why people take lower paying jobs when others pay so much better. (c) When thinking of how much money you're going to make at a job, you must also consider what reductions will be made to your paycheck before you get it. An example of reduction is money taken out for your retirement plan. List two other possible reductions there may be to a person's paycheck.

Question 2: Job Information (Group Administration)

To the Examiner: Students are to use telephone directories to list four local sources (other than school) of occupational information. Distribute Test Question 2 and telephone directories.

Read to Students: Look at Test Question 2 and read along with me. There are many different places you can go to get information about jobs. Using the phone book, find four places in your town or area, other than school, where you could go to find information about jobs or careers and write the four places on the lines provided.

Question 3: Values from a Job (Group Administration)

To the Examiner; Students are to identify personal values met through work. Distribute Test Question 3.

Read to Students: Look at Test Question 3 and read along with me. There are many personal values, or rewards, that a person can get from a job. Why do you think bus drivers work as bus drivers? Besides money, what is another reward each of the following employees get from his or her work?

FIGURE 7.3 *continued*

Name _____

Circle the answer that best describes you. There are no right or wrong answers. Answer each question according to what you think is the best answer for you.

1.   I know I can do good work.   no   maybe   yes
2.   I am an important person.   no   maybe   yes
3.   I speak up for my own self.   no   maybe   yes
4.   I make decisions based on how I feel at the time.   no   maybe   yes
5.   I do the leisure activities I want.   no   maybe   yes

FIGURE 7.4   Five items from the LCCE Self-Determination Scale.
Note. From M. L. Wehmeyer in *Self-Determination Scale* (p. 1) by D. E. Brolin, in press. Available 1995. Reston, VA: The Council for Exceptional Children. Reprinted by permission.

The four LCCE instruments, coupled with other measures and ecological assessments that provide other valuable assessment data for career/transition planning, can provide educators with a comprehensive armamentarium of instruments from which to make good, solid instructional decisions throughout each student's educational program. The next section presents a case study to illustrate the use of the LCCE instruments.

Case Study

Sam is almost ready to begin his senior year in high school. Sam's LCCE KB and PB results, which are recorded on the Student Competency Assessment Record (SCAR), are presented in Figure 7.5. The scores are Sam's test results on these measures before 9th- and 12th-grade admission. The CRS was completed when Sam was in the fourth and seventh grades.

Inspection of Sam's KB results before beginning ninth grade reveal that Sam's knowledge base in three daily living skills areas, no personal-social skills areas, and one occupational area were at the mastery level (a score of 8 or above). He was administered PB tests in these four competency areas to further determine his ability to perform in these areas. Note that he scored at the mastery level in two of the four areas. Thus, with the cautions noted previously about tests in general, the LCCE measures projected a basically satisfactory level of functioning in Sam's ability to take care of his personal needs and to engage in meaningful leisure and recreational pursuits. Thus, total mastery was checked in the far column on the right. Note that the SCAR ratings in this column include those for 12th grade as well; normally, a student completes several SCAR forms over time. Other measures may be used to confirm Sam's level of ability in these areas if needed.

STUDENT COMPETENCY ASSESSMENT RECORD (SCAR)
LCCE INVENTORY

Student's Name __SAM__   Age __18__   Grade __12__

School __ANYTOWN__   Examiner __Smith__

LCCE COMPETENCY	# ITEMS	KNOWLEDGE BATTERY FORM A SCORE	FORM B SCORE	# ITEMS	PERFORMANCE BATTERY FORM A SCORE	FORM B SCORE	MASTERY TOTAL	PARTIAL	NONE
I. DAILY LIVING SKILLS		DATE 4/92	DATE 4/95		DATE	DATE			
1. Personal Finances	10	3	(9)	10	/	6 4/95		✓	
2. Home Management	10	6	(8)	10	/	(8) 4/95	✓		
3. Personal Needs	10	(8)	(9)	10	(8) 5/92	/	✓		
4. Family Living	10	4	(8)	10	/	7 5/95		✓	
5. Foods	10	(9)	7	10	6 5/92	/			✓
6. Clothing	10	5	7	10	/	/			✓
7. Citizenship	10	7	(10)	10	/	5 5/95		✓	
8. Recreational/Leisure	10	(8)	(10)	10	(8) 5/92	7 5/95		✓	
9. Mobility in Community	10	6	(8)	10	/	(8) 5/95	✓		
TOTALS	90	56/62 %	76/84 %				3	4	2
II. PERSONAL-SOCIAL SKILLS		DATE 4/92	DATE 4/95		DATE	DATE			
10. Self-Awareness	10	7	(9)	10	/	(8) 4/95	✓		
11. Self-Confidence	10	6	1	10	/	/			✓
12. Responsible Behavior	10	6	5	10	/	/			✓
13. Interpersonal Skills	10	5	6	10	/	/			✓
14. Independence	10	7	6	10	/	/			✓
15. Decision Making	10	4	7	10	/	/			✓
16. Communicating	10	1	(8)	10	/	(8) 5/95	✓		
TOTALS	70	36/51 %	42/60 %				2	0	5
III. OCCUPATIONAL SKILLS		DATE 4/92	DATE 4/95		DATE	DATE			
17. Occ. Possibilities	10	7	(9)	10	/	6 4/95		✓	
18. Occ. Choices	10	(8)	(9)	10	5 5/92	(9) 5/95	✓		
19. Work Behavior	10	6	5	10	/	/			✓
20. Securing Employment	10	2	2	10	/	/			✓
21. Physical / Manual	10	—		10	2 5/92	(9) 5/95	✓		
22. Occ. Skills	10	—		10	/	/		✓	(CRS)
TOTALS	90	23/58 %	25/63 %				2	2	2
GRAND TOTAL	200	115/58 %	143/72 %				7	6	9

*Note: In the last column (Mastery), check *Total* for each competency the student has met or exceeded the criterion level of 8 (Knowledge Battery) and 8 (Performance Battery); check *Partial* if the criteria was met for only one Battery; check *None* if none were met.

FIGURE 7.5   Sam's Student Competency Assessment Record (SCAR), which records his results on the LCCE Knowledge Battery and Performance Battery.

Note. From *LCCE Professional Development Activity Book* (p. 398) by D. E. Brolin, 1993, Reston, VA: The Council for Exceptional Children. Copyright 1993 by The Council for Exceptional Children. Reprinted by permission.

Based on the assessment results, Sam's characteristics, the functional skill instructional effort instituted previously, and the available resources, the instructional team decided to focus on the following LCCE competencies during the ninth grade so appropriate career planning could be initiated by the 10th grade: personal finances (1), family living (4), interpersonal skills (13), decision making (15), communication skills (16), and occupational possibilities (17). Based on these results, other competencies needing to be learned better would be covered during 10th and 11th grade. During the 10th and 11th grades, the CRS was used to obtain teacher ratings of Sam's progress in the competency areas. (Note: More frequent KB administrations could be conducted if necessary.)

Before beginning his senior year, Sam was reassessed on the KB (Form B), and PB tests were administered and/or readministered in competency areas in which KB scores indicated a possible mastery level of knowledge. Inspection of his SCAR Profile reveals considerable progress in the competency areas of the daily living skills domain but not particularly significant gains in the other two domains. Sam achieved mastery scores on only two of seven personal–social competencies on the KB. He also scored at the mastery level on both PB tests, so the instructional focus on learning communication skills was apparently quite successful. However, a serious drop in the self-confidence (11) competency resulted, as well as relatively low scores in the other personal–social competencies.

Sam's scores in the occupational domain reveal he gained knowledge partially well about the world of work (17) and that he learned even better the process of making occupational choices (18), scoring at a mastery level on both the KB and PB. In addition, his physical-manual skills (21) were assessed at a mastery level on the PB. His development of a specific occupational skill (22) was rated at a partially mastered level on the CRS (this competency is not assessed by the KB and PB). However, work habits and behaviors (19) and the ability to seek, secure, and maintain employment (20) were poor.

It can be noted from Sam's profile that he has some serious deficiencies in several competency areas going into his final year of school. If a greater emphasis on some of these competency areas had begun earlier, perhaps Sam would not have so many deficiencies. The instructional team must make some hard decisions and focus on those competency areas in which Sam has good potential for learning in his last year. One other important assessment information should be noted. Recall that Sam's score on the self-confidence competency (11) dropped dramatically on retest. He was administered the LCCE SDS, which further confirmed this area to be a real problem area for Sam. His self-report profile indicated a definite lack of self-confidence; thus, a special effort of counseling and success experiences will be important for him in instructional planning. In one study of LCCE, self-confidence (O'Leary, 1989) was found to be the most desired competency by employers who reviewed the LCCE competency matrix.

The LCCE assessment measures can be of important assistance to educators, along with other academic and functional skills instruments, in focusing instruction on the greatest areas of need and avoiding unnecessary efforts. This chapter can only introduce its readers to the topic. For additional information and a more extensive review of the entire range of assessment measures and methods, the reader is referred to G. M. Clark and Kolstoe's text *Career Development and Transition Education for Adolescents with Disabilities* (1990) and Cronin and Patton's publication on *Life Skills Instruction for All Students with Special Needs* (1993). Persons interested in more information or in reviewing the LCCE instruments should contact The Council for Exceptional Children, 1920 Association Drive, Reston, VA 22091. In addition, a list of organizations that can be contacted regarding other functional assessment measures is presented in Appendix D.

FINAL COMMENTS

Assessment is more than testing. It is a systematic process of using information from a wide array of sources so educators and significant others can make informed decisions about their students. It has become generally recognized in the field that there is a need to focus more instructional and assessment activities on the critical skills that students will need in order to compete in today and tomorrow's rapidly changing and demanding society.

Criterion-referenced assessment is recommended over norm-referenced approaches because it is more useful in discerning students' proficiency level and in writing Individualized Education Programs (IEPs) and Individualized Written Rehabilitation Plans (IWRPs). Although there are a myriad of standardized and nonstandardized assessment measures to choose from, most do not relate directly to the curriculum of the students. The adoption of criterion- and domain-referenced measures, such as the LCCE instruments, will provide a more specific focus on the students' needs so that instructional needs for transition planning can be identified and tracked. These can be supplemented with other formal and informal assessment measures that the professional believes are also important.

In Chapter 8, some further reference to the use of assessment in the development of student IEPs and individualized transition plans is presented by Iva Dean Cook, Carol Opperman, and Melody Thurman-Urbanic.

ACTIVITIES

1. Discuss how you would establish and conduct a functional career assessment program in your district from elementary through the secondary years. When would these assessments begin, what kind of assessment measures would you use, and when and how would they be administered?
2. Refer back to the case of Sam. Given his SCAR profile, what would you recommend as the focus of his instructional program for the senior year? What other assessment measures would you use to verify and establish his major instructional needs? What are some important considerations that would go into your instructional decision making?

Chapter 8

Individualized Educational and Transition Planning

Iva Dean Cook, Carol Opperman, and Melody Thurman-Urbanic

Preliminary Questions About the Topic

1. How has the Individuals with Disabilities Education Act (IDEA) resulted in a major policy shift relative to providing students with transition curricula and services?
2. What are some of the key components that are essential for transition to be successfully conducted?
3. What barriers often impede the successful implementation of transition services and programs?
4. What exactly is the difference between the intent of the Individualized Education Program (IEP) and the Individualized Transition Plan (ITP)?
5. Identify the categories of student needs that should be contained in the ITP.
6. What is meant by *interagency agreements,* and who is required to implement them?
7. What roles and responsibilities do you believe agencies, parents, and others must assume in the transition planning and preparation process?
8. What assessments should be conducted to provide direction for transition planning?
9. Why do the Life-Centered Career Education (LCCE) developers believe it qualifies as a comprehensive transition model?
10. What changes do you believe need to be undertaken in most school districts to respond adequately to the transition needs of students?

E ducators of students with special learning needs have become increasingly more aware in the past few years of the need to provide their students with career education and career information to facilitate successful transition from school to the adult environment. The IDEA of 1990, originally enacted as the Education for All Handicapped Children Act of 1975, mandated that transition services be made available to all students age 16 or younger. This has prompted school districts throughout the country to become even more responsive to the career development needs of their students than was accomplished during the career education movement of the 1970s and early 1980s, which preceded the newer federal mandate called transition.

It is both unfortunate and fortunate that it has taken a federal mandate for the career development and functional skills needs of our students with special learning needs to be more adequately addressed. Although it is still too early to determine the impact of the recent legislative mandates that give more attention to students' career development needs, it is significant that what was promulgated 20 to 30 years ago is finally being given the opportunity to be infused into the educational system. As noted by Halloran,

> the IDEA provisions represent a major policy shift from permissive to prescriptive, required services. This policy shift differentiates transition services from the movements of the 1960s, 1970s, and 1980s which encouraged improved services to achieve educational outcomes without a clear statement of entitlement for all youth with disabilities. (1993, p. 12)

This chapter focuses on individualized student planning. We discuss the transition concept, the IEP, and the ITP. We then attempt to describe how the LCCE curriculum and its IEP form can be used to address the transition needs of students with special learning needs.

THE TRANSITION CONCEPT

Although the idea of carefully planning for the successful movement from school to work has been evident in the literature for many decades, it is only in the last few years that service providers have been required to seriously examine, expand, and develop collaborative efforts to facilitate the process called *transition* (Wehman, et al., 1989; Will, 1984b; Gemmel & Peterson, 1989).

Transition is an outcome-oriented process encompassing a broad array of quality services and experiences that lead to employment (and other life roles). The original conceptualization of transition in 1984 by Assistant Secretary of the U.S. Office of Special Education and Rehabilitative Services, Madelyn Will, and her colleagues focuses on the movement of students from high school to employment, as depicted in Figure 8.1.

Since the introduction of the transition concept by Will and colleagues, the concept has expanded to include many other adult-outcome objectives in addition to many community living outcomes. An expanded view of transition (Brolin, 1993a) that repre-

FIGURE 8.1   Major components of the transition process (OSERS model).

Note. From *OSERS Programming for Transition of Youth with Disabilities: Bridges from School to Working Life* by M. Will, 1984, Washington, DC: Office of Special Education and Rehabilitative Services, U.S. Department of Education, Office of Information for the Handicapped.

sents the thinking of many professionals in the field in using the familiar bridge model is presented in Figure 8.2. The model acknowledges elementary as well as secondary programs for transition efforts. And, as can be seen, the three bridges link elementary and secondary students not only to employment but also to community living, integration, and socialization.

Successful transition requires a number of key components to be successfully conducted:

- Interagency cooperation
- Individualized Transition Plans
- Employer incentives
- Supported employment (for some individuals)
- A functional career curriculum
- Collaborative efforts with employers, agencies, and parents
- A postsecondary support and follow-up system to ensure community and job adjustment

FIGURE 8.2   Expanded view of transition.

Note. From *LCCE Professional Development Activity Book* (p. 399) by D. E. Brolin, 1993, Reston, VA: The Council for Exceptional Children. Copyright 1993 by The Council for Exceptional Children. Reprinted by permission.

Point of View

According to the mandates of the Individuals with Disabilities Education Act (IDEA), every student with a disability must have an Individualized Education Program (IEP) that includes a transition plan to help students prepare for the demands of life beyond the school setting. Determining the skills most needed by individual students and then selecting an appropriate curriculum for teaching those skills are challenging tasks, indeed. Fortunately, help is available in the LCCE curriculum package and assessment batteries (Brolin, 1992a, 1992b) available from The Council for Exceptional Children (CEC). For over 15 years, teachers have been using Brolin's Life Centered Career Education: A Competency Based Approach to provide the framework for selecting the daily living skills, personal social skills, and occupational skills needed by individual students. The expanded curriculum, published in 1992, offers teachers over 1,100 lesson plans, tested in the classroom and known to be effective in developing the functional skills identified in a student's IEP.

Although the Life-Centered Career Education (LCCE) curriculum addresses 97 competency areas, individual students will always need special skills not included in the curriculum. The beauty of the LCCE approach is that it is very easy for a teacher to add new competencies using the LCCE lesson format. For example, each lesson plan includes an LCCE objective, which identifies the specific competency that is being addressed; a lesson objective, which clearly states the student outcome; and a list of instructional resources needed to conduct the lesson. This is followed by a few lines introducing the lesson; a statement of where the lesson will take place (e.g., school, home, etc.); and the number of sessions it will take to complete the lesson. The steps involved in the actual instructional task are then presented; and finally, a lesson plan evaluation is available that describes an activity and

Transition seeks to maximize the productivity, community participation, and independence of students with special education needs and to ensure that students receive the opportunities and services needed for adult adjustment (Cook & Thurman-Urbanic, 1990).

Facilitators of Transition

Research has found consensus on several major facilitating factors in a successful transition effort (e.g., Halpern, 1985; Higgins, Fowler, & Chandler, 1988; D. Johnson, Bruininks, & Thurlow, 1987). These investigations seem to agree that the following are critical requirements for successful transition services:

performance criteria. Having a clear and simple framework for preparing instructional material is more than half the battle.

Teachers who need to develop lessons for competencies not presently covered in the LCCE curriculum can look to other publishers or to the Educational Resources Information Center (ERIC) data base for additional ideas. ERIC is a federally funded information system that has been stockpiling educational information for almost 30 years. It contains more than 440,000 journal annotations and over 340,000 education related document abstracts. The ERIC data base may be accessed on CD-ROM in many libraries or on-line using your personal computer. On-line services are available through a number of data base vendors including DIALOG (1-800-3DIALOG), Maxwell On-line (1-800-955-0906), and the Internet system. The ERIC data base is easy to search, and it contains many excellent ideas for constructing lesson plans in a variety of skill areas. Many ERIC documents are research based, and the strategies described have been tested and analyzed for their effectiveness. For a fee, custom computer searches are available

through the ERIC Clearinghouse on Disabilities and Gifted Education. To initiate a search, call ERIC-CEC at 1-800-328-0727.

To get a really good understanding of how to use the LCCE system to serve students with disabilities, teachers and other members of the school-based team can attend one of the regional training workshops offered by CEC. Also available is a complete training package that includes 10 hours of videotapes, a Trainer's Manual, and Professional Development Activity Books for each trainee. To learn more about these materials, contact The Council for Exceptional Children, 703-620-3660.

Jean N. Boston is Director of Publications for The Council for Exceptional Children in Reston, Virginia.

- Team members explore all possible solutions to meet student needs
- Commitment
- Expanded interagency linkages
- The sharing of ideas and strategies between the agencies
- Favorable community atmosphere toward the students and their employment
- Decrease in duplicated and overlapping services
- A referral system that sends students to the most appropriate agencies

One study comparing successful and unsuccessful placement of secondary students with disabilities found that more than 50% of the total influence in the training and placement process was due to the nature of the education program itself (Heal, Copher, DeStephano, & Rusch, 1989). The investigation found that many individuals with disabilities are not encouraged to contribute to their own economic independence or to fulfill societal expectations for employment. The authors cite the 50% employment rate they found for special education graduates as a good indicator that better transition services are needed. An important finding from the study was that the most important elements in the success of students are a strong transition team effort, employer support, employment supervision, and community acceptance.

Benefits of Transition

The benefits of providing early transition planning and gainful employment for students before they leave school have been reported by Wehman and his colleagues (1989). They cite the following benefits to students in early transition programs:

- Institution of the necessary curricular changes (instructional and programmatic) to better facilitate the process
- Teachers who actually go into the community with their students and learn the specific needs and demands of various employers
- Teachers who can provide support and assistance to transitioning students while they are still in school
- Better continuity of service with agencies, employers, and parents
- Better case management from school to adult services
- Parent support

Wehman and colleagues advocate job placement before graduation to reduce the risk of not receiving services after graduation; to reduce the possibility of being put on long waiting lists for services; and to help offset the negative effect on high unemployment of special education students by securing the job while they are still in high school.

Barriers to Successful Transition

Many barriers that impede the progress of transitional planning have been identified (Beck, 1988: Bellamy, 1985; Didley, 1987; Halpern, 1985; Naylor, 1985; Ward & Halloran, 1989). Those cited most often follow:

- Duplication of services by the education agency and service providers
- Lack of social integration of special education students into regular classes
- Inaccessibility to vocational education
- Poor planning linkages and lack of adequate adult services
- Poor data management and transfer between schools and agencies
- Lack of parental involvement
- Community prejudice and discrimination

One of the greatest barriers to transition seems to be the need for students to be better prepared to exhibit more appropriate social skills (Beck, 1988; Neubert & Tilson,

1987; Rose, Friend, & Farnum, 1988; Wehman, 1981; Wehman & Hill, 1985). This research also has indicated that the majority of problems experienced by on-the-job transition participants relate to inappropriate work and social behaviors rather than the task-related difficulty of the job.

Developing the social skills necessary for success in the world of work is one of the more challenging tasks of educational programs. Educators will need to give more emphasis to this area if community-based training and placement efforts are to succeed (Wehman & Hill, 1985).

Summary

All of the discussed recommendations for transition are readily accepted ideologically; in practice, however, their adoption is not expected to take place overnight. Unfortunately, while administrators and policymakers struggle to make decisions on the future of transition in this country, many students, parents, educators, and employers will become frustrated with the inadequacy of program-delivery systems. A position statement by the Council for Exceptional Children's (CEC's) Division on Career Development (CEC/DCDT) entitled "Career Development for Students with Disabilities in Elementary Schools," states the following:

> The Division of Career Development is comprised of professionals who are committed to the aim that all children with disabilities have access to an instructional program which focuses on life/career development and transitional demands. (G. M. Clark, Carlson, Fisher, Cook, & D'Alonzo, 1991, p. 117)

"Transitions occur throughout one's lifetime and include both paid work and the work roles of students, homemakers, family members, volunteers, and retirees, as well as productive recreational, avocational and leisure activities. Many people encounter problems when making various transitions. Adults in transition, especially many of those with disabilities, sometimes become confused and need special assistance to help them solve their problems and make wise decisions. The 'transition from school-to-work' concept is inextricably related to the career development concept that has been theorized and implemented in various education and agency settings for many years."
(Brolin & Schatzman, 1989, pp. 22–23)

INDIVIDUALIZED EDUCATION AND TRANSITION PLANS

The IEP

The IEP is a written document that summarizes the educational program for the student. The IEP may be developed as early as elementary school. The contents of the stated goals are derived from an analysis of the student's strengths and weaknesses. The

IEP not only establishes the goals it also determines the services the local educational agency (LEA) must provide to assist in meeting those goals. The IEP also enhances the communication needed among parents and school personnel (Palloway, Patton, Payne, & Payne, 1989).

Traditionally, special educators have had the responsibility for those persons needing special education services as mandated by PL 94–142 (Education for All Handicapped Children's Act of 1975). Figure 8.3 shows the general process used for identification and placement. The law mandates that the IEP be written for all students and contain the following components:

- Present level of performance
- Annual goals
- Short-term objectives
- Special education and related services
- Extent and participation in regular education programs
- Dates and initiation of services and duration of services
- Objective criteria, evaluation procedures, and schedule for assessing short-term objectives

FIGURE 8.3   Process for identification and placement.

Note. From *Transition Manual: TRIAD Telecommunications Project* (p. 39) by I. D. Cook and M. Thurman-Urbanic, 1990, Institute, WV: West Virginia Graduate College. Copyright 1990 by West Virginia Graduate College. Reprinted by permission.

These required services were expanded with the passage of the IDEA of 1990. As noted previously, the IDEA requires that the IEP incorporate a new provision: A statement of the needed transition services must be included, and a statement of interagency responsibilities or linkages must be included if these services are the responsibility of a state or local agency other than the school responsible for the student's education.

The IDEA expands the IEP team membership. In addition to the student, the student's teacher, parents, the LEA representative, and professionals from any other agency responsible for providing or paying for transition services must be present at the IEP meeting. Related legislation, for example, the Americans with Disabilities Act (ADA), Rehabilitation Act, and Carl Perkins Vocational Education Act, provide support and services for students in transition from school to the community and the world of work.

The IEP has traditionally been used as the foundation for each identified special education student's educational program. The heart of this foundation has been primarily academic; however, time and research have revealed a greater need—career education. Therefore, more effective transitional services, as now mandated by federal law, are made available to the student. Legislative mandates have also introduced a partner component to the IEP—the ITP.

The ITP Component

The ITP component is a written record of the student's long-range goals and needs for employment and other community living objectives that also specifies how they will be achieved. The ITP should outline programming needs and future opportunities; should contain precise objectives and activities; should have input from parents, students, educators, and adult service providers; and should be longitudinal (Didley, 1987). Generally, the ITP is a component of the IEP, although some school districts have opted to have a separate document for this purpose.

As noted by Polloway and Patton (1993), the intent of the ITP differs from that of the IEP. The ITP is a plan for services, whereas the IEP is a plan for skill or knowledge acquisition. Like IEPs, ITPs have no set format, but unlike IEPs, ITPs have no required elements. School districts generally organize ITPs around transition areas that they have determined to be important.

The IEP/ITP is the educational map for students, kindergarten through the 12th grade. The components include a profile of the student's current level of performance, the curriculum options, needed support services, and ongoing assessment. During the last few years of secondary education, plans are made to assist the student in achieving functional mastery of the major competencies needed for successful adult outcomes.

It is important to involve all persons in transition planning who may be able to give valuable input into decision making regarding transition-related activities for the student. Participants may differ at the secondary and postsecondary levels. Regardless of the student's age and/or grade level, the student and the parent/guardian/primary care giver must always be at the center of the planning process. Someone such as a transition coordinator should coordinate the transition planning to ensure that information flows smoothly among agencies. Figure 8.4 provides an example of possible participants for transition planning at the secondary and postsecondary levels (Cook & Thurman-Urbanic, 1990).

The IEP/ITP should include a statement of the interagency responsibilities or linkages before the student leaves school. Thus, although it is the responsibility of the local educational agency to initiate transition planning, it must be done in cooperation with local adult service providers.

As the student enters the final years of schooling, the ITP can provide the framework for planning the student's transition from school to the community and employment. The ITP will reflect the student's changing needs and will delineate major goals, including vocational/educational, residential options, community service, health services, and financial support services. The IEP/ITP should include specific steps and activities for goal attainment, time frame for steps and activities, the identity of the person responsible, a time frame for completion, and finally, the date when accomplished. It should outline logical steps that the family, school, and agencies can take in planning

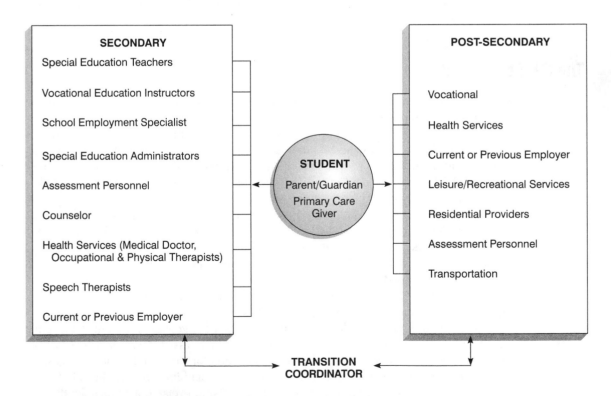

FIGURE 8.4   Participants in transition planning.

Note. From *Transition Manual: TRIAD Telecommunications Project* (p. 76) by I. D. Cook and M. Thurman-Urbanic, 1990, Institute, WV: West Virginia Graduate College. Copyright 1990 by West Virginia Graduate College. Reprinted by permission.

Melody Urbanic planning transition services with one of her students.

the student's transition to achieve appropriate access to adult services and/or employment. Figure 8.5 presents a services referral checklist that can be used as a guide for selecting specific services for individual students.

The IDEA reemphasizes the individualized nature of planning. It is important to note that "the services the student receives should be based on individual 'preferences and needs,' *not* currently available programs or services. This wording encourages the development of new, restructured human service delivery models" (Whetstone, 1993).

Interagency Agreements

Formal, written interagency agreements are needed for effective transition programs. Individual states are required, by law, to have cooperative agreements between the State Departments of Education and Vocational Rehabilitation. These agreements provide a focus for the LEAs to ensure that each student with a disability is identified and provided with the appropriate services, including transition. Some cooperative agreements clearly delineate when each agency becomes responsible for education and vocational training by student age. As noted in Chapter 5, an example of a state-level (West Virginia) interagency agreement is presented in Appendix A.

A service responsibility chart may also be included with an interagency agreement to specify the activities provided. An example of such a chart is presented in Figure 8.6, developed by the West Virginia Department of Education and Division of Rehabilitation Services. The chart delineates responsibilities by preschool services, special education, vocational education, and the state rehabilitation agency.

Service Item	Date to Be Completed	Person Responsible	Date Completed
Referral to vocational rehabilitation			
Referral to MR/DD			
Referral to			
Referral to			
Social Security Card			
Medicaid application			
Medicare application			
SSI			
SSDI			
Guardianship			
Welfare			
Food Stamps			
Medical exam			
Psychological exam			
Social history			
Educational summary			
Special transportation			
Residential services			
Group home			
Family support			
Foster Care			
Respite services			
Counseling			
Waiver for minimum competency test			

FIGURE 8.5   Services referral checklist.

Note. From *Transition from School to Work* (p. 94) by P. Wehman, S. Moon, J. M. Everson, & J. M. Barcus, 1988, Baltimore, MD: Paul H. Brookes. Copyright 1988 by Paul H. Brookes. Reprinted by permission.

Didley (1987) suggests that interagency agreements work only if the models developed for local school districts are based on local needs and services. He further suggests that these local school districts develop resource guides for transitional services facilitating collaboration and allowing the community, at large, to ensure quality transitional services. Didley perceives as a goal of the collaborative transition model the advocacy for public acceptance of and involvement with employing persons with special learning needs in the community. Parental involvement is also viewed as an integral part of collaboration (Cook & Thurman-Urbanic, 1990).

The identification of case managers or transition coordinators is an important consideration in transition planning and in implementing interagency agreements. In Figure 8.7, we present our suggestions for the responsibilities of case managers from elementary to the postsecondary levels.

School administrators must recognize the need for staff flexibility to deliver appropriate curriculum and services in terms of timing and location. Research has shown that off-campus jobs are far more valuable to the transition of students than simulated work activities in the classroom (Cook & Thurman-Urbanic, 1990).

Career/Vocational Assessment

Before an IEP and its ITP component are developed, a comprehensive career/vocational assessment should be completed as part of the total process of assessment and evaluation. As noted in Chapter 7, the CEC Division on Career Development and Transition (DCDT) describes career assessment as embracing not only vocational but also the avocational and daily living skills areas as a necessary foundation for individualized program planning and transition planning from kindergarten through adulthood.

The components of a comprehensive career/vocational assessment, from our perspective, are presented in Figure 8.8. Individuals who may be responsible for contributing to these data are also found in the graphic. The results of these assessments will provide the data from which the IEP/ITP can be developed (Cook & Thurman-Urbanic, 1990).

Summary

Four key elements of transition that must be addressed in transitional planning follow:

1. Systematic career/vocational training throughout the early, middle and secondary school years
2. Effective work by cooperative and interagency teams
3. Parent, consumer, and employer involvement in the transition planning process
4. Community and professional awareness and support of multiple employment options

Services must be available and accessible to all students/clients with disabilities. The activities below can generally be provided by the specified agency. Where there is an overlapping or duplication of services, the question of WHO INITIATES SERVICES and WHO IMPLEMENTS SERVICES will be resolved at the local educational agency, preferably at the PAC/IEP conference.

Continuum of Services	Provided by Preschool	Provided by Spec. Ed. 5–21	Provided by Vocational Ed.	Provided by Rehabilitation Services
A. Referral	Awareness Child find Screening Referral to assessment	Awareness Child find Screening Referral to assessment	Awareness Referral to assessment Referral to assessment (intake process)	Awareness (case finding) Screening (referral development)
B. Assessment	(Formal/informal) Developmental data Psychological/behavioral	(Formal/informal) Educational data Psychological/behavioral	(Formal/informal) Prevocational exploration program Vocational and career development/special needs	(Formal) Current general health status and special examination Evaluation of vocational (Elig.) a. Preliminary diagnostic study (Elig.) b. Thorough diagnostic study to determine nature and scope of services (Vocational goals/strengths, functional limitations) Eligible students, ages 14 and above, in or out of school
C. Individualized program	Individualized education program (IEP)	Individualized educational program (IEP) (Ages 5–21)	Instructional vocational plan (VIP) (secondary students only) 4-year education plan	Individualized written rehabilitation Plan (IWRP) for all eligible students/clients. Developed jointly by client and counselor and if appropriate by guardian with participation in PAC and joint staffing with appropriate school personnel (The services, objectives, and goals included in

D. Program planning and implementation activities	Family consultation	Career education Prevocational education Formal vocational assessment Special (separate) vocational education College preparation curriculum	Career/prevocational education Regular vocational education Modified regular vocational education Special vocational education Adult programs	the IWRP and IEP should be complimentary.) IEP/IWRP Individualized written rehabilitation program Regular vocational education/work adjustment (O.J.T., selective training experiences, co-op and related programs). Adaptive regular (specially designed vocational education/work adjustment) Work experience Vocational assessment services as specified in Section B Special (separate) vocational education/work adjustment Vocational and other training including personal and vocational adj., books, tools and other training materials. All on individual needs basis to eligible clients (client owned)
E. Service delivery system including related services	Special tools, devices, equipment, (student loaned) Instructional modification Special support staff (aides, tutors and paraprofessionals)	Interpreter/notetaker Reader services for the blind Special tools, devices, equipment (student loaned) Instructional modifications	Interpreter/notetaker Reader services for the blind Special tools, devices, equipment (student loaned) Instructional modifications	Interpreter/notetaker Reader services for the blind Tools and/or materials for planned job placement (client owned) Special tools, devices, equipment (client owned) Technical assistance re: modifications or supportive services

FIGURE 8.6 Service responsibility chart.

Note. From Cooperative Agreement by West Virginia Department of Education and the Division of Rehabilitation Services in Transition Manual: TRIAD Telecommunications Project by I. D. Cook and M. Thurman-Urbanic, 1990, Institute, WV: West Virginia Graduate College. p. 39. Copyright 1990 by West Virginia Graduate College. Reprinted by permission.

Continuum of Services	Provided by Preschool	Provided by Spec. Ed. 5-21	Provided by Vocational Ed.	Provided by Rehabilitation Services
E. Service delivery system including related services (cont.)	Related services (OT, PT and speech therapy) Curriculum modification and development Special transportation needs Monitoring services and student progress Parent training	Special support staff (aides, tutors and paraprofessionals) Related services (OT, PT and speech therapy) Curriculum modification and development Special transportation needs Monitoring services and student progress Vocational guidance and counseling Family consultation Work experience/work study Formal vocational assessment Job development and placement Supportive employment Sheltered workshop	Special education instructor Special support staff (aides, tutors and paraprofessionals) Related services Curriculum modification and development Monitoring services and student progress Vocational guidance and counseling Cooperative education programs (OJT) Prevocational exploration programs Job development and placement Work experience Supportive employment (task analysis)	Monitoring of services and client progress Vocational guidance and counseling General medical-coordination of services if needed to vocationally prepare for job placement or supported employment a. Assist in location training stations b. Modify work environment c. Adaptive appliances d. Reimburse employers Physical and mental restoration Formal vocational assessment (work evaluation and functional assessment) Additional services provided as appropriate Supported employment Job placement
F. Access	Center-based accommodations	Public school accommodations Job training site accommodations	Vocational school accommodations Job training site accommodations	Individual/home accommodations Job training site accommodations
G. Exit	Transition	Transition	Transition	Transition

FIGURE 8.6 *continued*

Level 1: Elementary (K–8)

Transition Coordinator: Special Education Teacher

Responsibilities

- Conduct an ongoing evaluation of students' achievement performance in academics and career development.

- Use assessment date in program development, and implementation.

- Write IEPs for students with a futuristic perspective.

- Develop basic academic skills with personal-social, daily living, and occupational guidance and preparation skills infused.

- Encourage parents to participate in planning and developing career education competencies.

- Keep an up-to-date profile on individual students.

- Form partnerships with regular educators, parents, adult service providers, and representatives of business and industry.

- Share student profiles (strengths, weaknesses, interests, etc.) with receiving environment (e.g., secondary education staff).

Level 2: Secondary (8–12)

Transition Coordinator: Secondary Special Education Teacher

Responsibilities

- Identify students for transition planning at the beginning of the school year.

- Collect and analyze assessment data and update student profiles.

- Coordinate the assessment and modification of curriculum as needed to prepare students for successful transition into adult life.

- Identify and become familiar with available postschool options, including vocational/educational, residential, community, health and financial support services.

- Form partnerships with adult and representatives of business and industry.

- Organize and implement individual transitional planning meetings.

- Provide leadership in and for the development of the ITPs.

- Ensure that input is provided from students, teachers, parents, and as appropriate, adult service agencies and former or current employers.

FIGURE 8.7 Transition preparation responsibilities for transition coordinators/case managers.

Note. From *Transition Manual: TRIAD Telecommunications Project* (pp. 99—101) by I. D. Cook and M. Thurman-Urbanic, 1990, Institute, WV: West Virginia Graduate College. Copyright 1990 by West Virginia Graduate College. Reprinted by permission.

- Advocate as needed, with administrators, for changes needed in the delivery from a classroom-based model to a community-based delivery system.
- Coordinate the implementation of transition plans.

Level 3: (Final Year)

Transition Coordinator/Case Managers(s):
Secondary Special Education Teacher/Vocational Education

Responsibilities

Special Educator (Same as in Level 2)/Vocational Education.

- Attend ITP meeting and provide information on appropriate vocational goals.
- Ensure equal access into vocational education for students with disabilities.
- Provide students and parents information on vocational education by the beginning of the ninth grade.
- Collect and analyze vocational evaluation data.
- Identify community cooperative agencies for job training and placement.
- Assist with job placement, job-site training or postsecondary vocational preparation for students during their last year in school.

Level 4: Postschool to Adulthood

Transition Coordinator(s):
Case Manager: Vocational Rehabilitation/Community Agency/Parents or Guardian

Responsibilities

- Continue to monitor and evaluate the progress of job training and placement activities.
- Ensure that support services (e.g. medical, psychological, therapeutic, financial management and residential options) are provided.
- Ensure the highest level of independence in job placement (e.g., movement from an enclave work site to supported or competitive employment).
- Address the needs for high quality of life (e.g., the rights and responsibilities of citizenship are ensured through full participation in the broad spectrum of leisure and community activities).

FIGURE 8.7   *continued*

FIGURE 8.8 Components of a comprehensive career/vocational assessment.

Note. From *Transition Manual: TRIAD Telecommunications Project* (p. 45) by I. D. Cook and M. Thurman-Urbanic, 1990, Institute, WV: West Virginia Graduate College. Copyright 1990 by West Virginia Graduate College. Reprinted by permission.

COMPREHENSIVE CAREER/ VOCATIONAL ASSESSMENT

Elementary Level:
- Health
- Psychological
- Social
- Daily Living
- Occupational Guidance & Preparation

Secondary Level:
- Cognitive Skills
- Manual Skills
- Interpersonal Skills
- Perceptual Skills
- Work Aptitudes
- Interests
- Previous Experience
- Job Exploration
- Social Adjustment

- Special Education Teacher/Specialist
- Vocational Education Teacher/Evaluator
- Vocational Rehabilitation Evaluator
- Parents
- Social Workers
- Psychologists/Guidance Counselors
- Speech/Hearing Clinicians
- Physical/Occupational Therapists

Education for those with disabilities should address these elements and prepare them for competitive or supported employment. Thus, school systems cannot focus on transition alone and ignore the quality and content of foundation services, including elementary and secondary preparation, as well as vocational opportunities offered by community agencies.

Our major goal in the education and training of persons with special learning needs should be to prepare these individuals for independence as adults. Obviously, career/vocational education and training provide the important foundation for transitioning students from school to the community and the world of work. The most compelling support for transitional services and the concept of service delivery through an interagency cooperative model may be drawn from the major pieces of federal legislation.

 "Collaboration is a key element in the transition process. Through collaboration, youths can receive planned, appropriate, and nonduplicated services. Many individuals are likely to participate in the transition process, including individuals charged with identifying persons in need of transition assistance, educators, clients, families, and service providers."

(Chadsey-Rusch, Rusch, & Phelps, 1989, p. 232)

THE LCCE IEP AND ITP

The transition concept is inextricably related to the career development concept that has been theorized and implemented in various education and agency settings for many years (Brolin & Schatzman, 1989). As noted by the CEC's DCDT position paper entitled "Career Development for Students with Disabilities in the Elementary Schools" (G. M. Clark et al., 1991), successful transition will not take place without the adoption of a functional curriculum.

The LCCE curriculum and its functional skills lend themselves nicely to providing a comprehensive instructional program (kindergarten to postsecondary) that will prepare students with special learning needs for a successful transition from school to productive living and working in their communities. An illustration of how LCCE can be used as a transition model was presented in Chapter 3. Figure 8.9 demonstrates how curriculum planning can be instituted in each of the three LCCE curriculum/instructional domains (daily living, personal-social, and occupational skills) for the first three stages of career development/learning so a developmental and logical sequence of activities can be provided in each of the 22 competency areas.

An LCCE IEP with an integrated ITP component has been constructed for educators who are using the LCCE curriculum approach. The LCCE IEP form contains 10 sections to meet the legislative requirements of PL 94–142 and IDEA. Because most school districts are bound by their own local or state IEP forms, the LCCE IEP may be used either as is or as an addendum to the district's mandated forms. The LCCE IEP form with its integrated ITP component is presented in Figure 8.10 with a hypothetical eighth-grade student named Susan as an example.

 "In adopting a specific career model for developing the foundation for transition, it is helpful in carrying out the continuous curriculum-based assessment if instruments such as those contained in the LCCE model do accompany the curriculum materials."

(Cook & Thurman-Urbanic, 1990)

The curriculum-based instruments described in Chapter 7—LCCE Competency Rating Scale (CRS), the LCCE Knowledge Battery, the LCCE Performance Battery, and the LCCE Self-Determination Scale—are available to provide the necessary data for developing and evaluating the content of the IEP. Other measures may also be used, depending on the orientation and needs of the assessment team.

The LCCE IEP form provides a document with functional skills and transition components that can be constructed from the LCCE competencies and can be evaluated at least in part by the LCCE assessment instruments. In developing the LCCE IEP form, it is suggested that annual goals be selected from the 22 competency areas of the curriculum and that short-term objectives be selected from their 97 subcompetencies. Thus, the educator will be able to establish goals, success criteria, and a method of recording the necessary individualized plans and then evaluating their outcomes. Although they are designed to be used separately, the combination of the LCCE IEP,

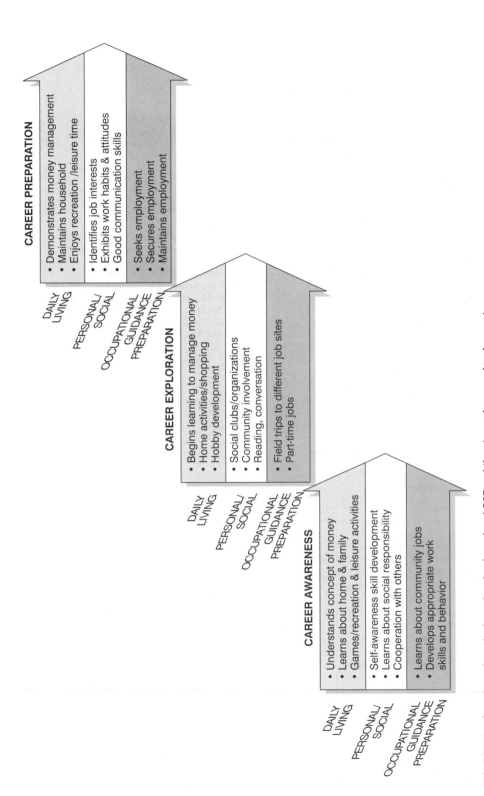

FIGURE 8.9 Overview of curriculum planning based on LCCE and the stage of career development.

Note. From *Transition Manual: TRIAD Telecommunications Project* (p. 49) by I. D. Cook and M. Thurman–Urbanic, 1990, Institute, WV: West Virginia Graduate College. Copyright 1990 by West Virginia Graduate College. Reprinted by permission. Originally adapted from *Life Centered Career Education* (3rd ed., pp. 10–12) by D. E. Brolin, 1989, Reston, VA: The Council for Exceptional Children.

LIFE CENTERED CAREER EDUCATION
INDIVIDUALIZED EDUCATION PROGRAM FORM
(Use attachments as needed for each student)

Student's Name: ___Susan___ School: ___Progressive___ Grade: _8_ Grade: _6/3/95_

SECTION I: Present Level of Educational Performance

Reading Level:	3.3 (CAT)	Math Level:	2.0 (CAT)
CRS Scores:	DLS (.59) PSS (.61)	OGP (.21)	(Maximum = 2.0)
KB Scores:	DLS (40%) PSS (43%)	OGP (25%)	TOT (38%)
PB Scores:	Mastery (Comp. 8)	No Mastery (Comps. 3, 5, 18, 21)	

SECTION II: Annual Goals

A. Academic Goals (see attachment)

B. LCCE Functional Skills for Transition Preparation (check those that apply)

This student will progress toward acquiring functional behaviors in the following competency areas. (Check the appropriate annual goals.)

X 1. Managing Personal Finances
__ 2. Selecting and Managing a Household
__ 3. Caring for Personal Needs
X 4. Raising Children and Meeting Marriage Responsibilities
__ 5. Buying, Preparing, and Consuming Food
__ 6. Buying and Caring for Clothing
__ 7. Exhibiting Responsible Citizenship
__ 8. Utilizing Recreational Facilities and Engaging in Leisure
__ 9. Getting Around the Community
__ 10. Achieving Self-Awareness
__ 11. Acquiring Self-Confidence

__ 12. Achieving Socially Responsible Behavior
__ 13. Maintaining Good Interpersonal Skills
__ 14. Achieving Independence
__ 15. Making Adequate Decisions
X 16. Communicating with Others
X 17. Knowing and Exploring Occupational Possibilities
__ 18. Selecting and Planning Occupational Choices
__ 19. Exhibiting Appropriate Work Habits and Behaviors
__ 20. Seeking, Securing, and Maintaining Employment
__ 21. Exhibiting Sufficient Physical–Manual Skills
__ 22. Obtaining Specific Occupational Skills

C. Other Transitional/Support Services Goals (check those that apply)

__ 1. Financial Assistance/Income Support
__ 2. Advocacy Legal Services
__ 3. Medical
__ 4. Insurance

__ 5. Transportation
__ 6. Other _____
__ 7. Other _____
__ 8. Other _____

SECTION III: Specific Educational Services Needed

Goal & Subcomp. Numbers	Special Services Needed	Special Media/Materials and Equipment	Individual Implementors
A	(See attachment)		
B 1 (3, 5, 6)	Job shadowing experience (banks, credit agencies), simulated business activities, speakers, home assignments	Credit banking, & other forms, LCCE lesson plans, materials for setting up a model bank & store, transportation	Special education/math/business ed. teachers, bank & credit company employees, parents, peers.
B 4 (17, 18)	Visits to public health department and day care centers, student role-play activities, community imput	Varous health charts, thermometers, tub for bathing, medicine bottles, transportation	Special education/health teachers, school nurse, parents, public health nurse, nursery school personnel, child guidance center staff
B 16 (68, 69)	Group activities, role-playing (e.g., TV show)	Videotapes & films, telephones, audio recorders	Special education/speech/ language arts teachers, parents, peers, TV or radio interviewer
B 17 (71, 72, 73)	Field trips, role-play activities/ simulations, community input, home assignments	Bulletin boards, occupational literature, magazines, newspapers	Special education/work-study teachers, career counselors, employers, Chamber of Commerce, VR counselor

FIGURE 8.10 Form for preparing student's LCCE IEP.

Note. From *Life Centered Career Education: A Competency Based Approach* (4th ed., pp. 146–149) by D. E. Brolin, 1993, Reston, VA: The Council for Exceptional Children. Copyright 1993 by The Council for Exceptional Children. Reprinted by permission. The attachments mentioned in Sections IIA, III, IVA, and IVC are not included here; they can be found in Brolin's (1993) text.

INDIVIDUALIZED EDUCATION PROGRAM FORM

SECTION IV: Short-Term Individual Objectives

A. **Academic Goals (see attachment)**

B. **LCCE Functional Skills for Transition Preparation (check those that apply)**

___ 1. Identify Money and Make Correct Change (1)

___ 2. Make Responsible Expenditures (1)

_X_ 3. Keep Basic Financial Records (1)

___ 4. Calculate and Pay Taxes (1)

_X_ 5. Use Credit Responsibly (1)

_X_ 6. Use Banking Services (1)

___ 7. Maintain Home Exterior/Interior (2)

___ 8. Use Basic Appliances and Tools (2)

___ 9. Select Adequate Housing (2)

___ 10. Set Up Household (2)

___ 11. Maintain Home Grounds (2)

___ 12. Demonstrate Knowledge of Physical Fitness, Nutrition, and Weight (3)

___ 13. Exhibit Proper Grooming and Hygiene (3)

___ 14. Dress Appropriately (3)

___ 15. Demonstrate Knowledge of Common Illness, Prevention, and Treatment (3)

___ 16. Practice Personal Safety (3)

_X_ 17. Demonstrate Physical Care for Raising Chidren (4)

_X_ 18. Know Psychological Aspects of Raising Children (4)

___ 19. Demonstrate Marriage Responsibilities (4)

___ 20. Purchase Food (5)

___ 21. Clean Food Preparation Areas (5)

___ 22. Store Food (5)

___ 23. Prepare Meals (5)

___ 24. Demonstrate Appropriate Eating Habits (5)

___ 25. Plan and Eat Balanced Meals (5)

___ 26. Wash/Clean Clothing (6)

___ 27. Purchase Clothing (6)

___ 28. Iron, Mend, and Store Clothing (6)

___ 29. Demonstrate Knowledge of Civil Rights and Responsibilities (7)

___ 30. Know Nature of Local, State, and Federal Governments (7)

___ 31. Demonstrate Knowledge of the Law and Ability to Follow the Law (7)

___ 32. Demonstrate Knowledge of Citizen Rights and Responsibilities (7)

___ 33. Demonstrte Knowledge of Available Community Resources (8)

___ 34. Choose and Plan Activities (8)

___ 35. Demonstrate Knowledge of the Value of Recreation (8)

___ 36. Engage in Group and Individual Activities (8)

___ 37. Plan Vacation Time (8)

___ 38. Demonstrate Knowledge of Traffic Rules and Safety (9)

___ 39. Demonstrate Knowledge and Use of Various Means of Transportation (9)

___ 40. Find Way Around the Community (9)

___ 41. Drive a Car (9)

___ 42. Identify Physical and Psychological Needs (10)

___ 43. Identify Interests and Abilities (10)

___ 44. Identify Emotions (10)

___ 45. Demonstrate Knowledge of Physical Self (10)

___ 46. Express Feelings of Self-Worth (11)

___ 47. Describe Others' Perception of Self (11)

___ 48. Accept and Give Praise (11)

___ 49. Accept and Give Criticism (11)

___ 50. Develop Confidence in Oneself (11)

___ 51. Demonstrate Respect for the Rights and Properties of Others (12)

___ 52. Recognize Authority and Follow Instructions (12)

___ 53. Demonstrate Appropriate Behavior in Public Places (12)

___ 54. Know Important Character Traits (12)

___ 55. Recognize Personal Roles (12)

___ 56. Demonstrate Listening and Responding Skills (13)

___ 57. Establish and Maintain Close Relationships (13)

___ 58. Make and Maintain Friendships (13)

___ 59. Strive Toward Self-Actualization (14)

___ 60. Demonstrate Self-Orgainization (14)

___ 61. Demonstrate Awareness of How One's Behavior Affects Others (14)

___ 62. Locate and Utilize Sources of Assistance (15)

___ 63. Anticipate Consequences (15)

___ 64. Develop and Evaluate Alternatives (15)

___ 65. Recognize Nature of a Problem (15)

___ 66. Develop Goal-Seeking Behavior (15)

___ 67. Recognize and Respond to Emergency Situations (16)

_X_ 68. Communicate with Understanding (16)

_X_ 69. Know Subtleties of Communication (16)

___ 70. Identify Remunerative Aspects of Work (17)]

_X_ 71. Locate Sources of Occupational and Training Information (17)

_X_ 72. Identify Personal Values Met Through Work (17)

_X_ 73. Identify Societal Values Met Through Work (17)

___ 74. Classify Jobs into Occupational Categories (17)

FIGURE 8.10 *continued*

INDIVIDUALIZED EDUCATION PROGRAM FORM

___ 75. Investigate Local Occupational and Training Opportunities (17)
___ 76. Make Realistic Occupational Choices (18)
___ 77. Identify Requirements of Appropriate and Available Jobs (18)
___ 78. Identify Occupational Aptitudes (18)
___ 79. Identify Major Occupational Interests (18)
___ 80. Identify Major Occupational Needs (18)
___ 81. Follow Directions and Observe Regulations (19)
___ 82. Recognize Importance of Attendance and Punctuality (19)
___ 83. Recognize Importance of Supervision (19)
___ 84. Demonstrate Knowledge of Occupational Safety (19)
___ 85. Work with Others (19)
___ 86. Meet Demands for Quality Work (19)

___ 87. Work at a Satisfactory Rate (19)
___ 88. Search for a Job (20)
      89. Apply for a Job (20)
___ 90. Interview for a Job (20)
      91. Know How to Maintain Post-School Occupational Adjustment (20)
___ 92. Demonstrate Knowledge of Competitive Standards (20)
      93. Know How to Adjust to Changes in Employment (20)
___ 94. Demonstrate Stamina and Endurance (21)
      95. Demonstrate Satisfactory Balance and Coordination (21)
      96. Demonstrate Manual Dexterity (21)
      97. Demonstrate Sensory Discrimination (21)

C.   Other Transitional/Support Services Objectives (see attachment)

SECTION V: Data and Length of Time relative to specific educational services needed for this student

Goal Number	Beginning Date	Ending Date	Goal Number	Beginning Date	Ending Date
B 1 (3, 5, 6)	9-1-95	12-15-95			
B 4 (17, 18)	9-1-95	12-15-95			
B 16 (68, 69)	1-10-96	5-20-96			
B 17 (71, 72, 73)	1-10-96	5-20-96			

SECTION VI: Description of Extent to which this student will participate in the regular educational program

	Percentage of Time	Narrative Description/Reaction
Language arts	15 %	Build greater communication skills
Math	10 %	Use practical, everyday situations and materials
Science	___ %	
Social science	___ %	
Vocational (Bus.) & Work Study	15 %	Limited typing & clerical skills—resource room needed
Physical education	5 %	No physical limitation
(other) __Health__	10 %	Provide supports and some coteaching lessons
(other) __Speech__	5 %	Has problems expressing self; shy

FIGURE 8.10   *continued*

INDIVIDUALIZED EDUCATION PROGRAM FORM

SECTION VII: Justification for type of educational placement of this student

Narrative Description/Reaction

LCCE SCAR/KB/PB measures indicate these as primary needs and relate to student's interests and preferences at this time. Not enough instruction has been provided in these areas and it is felt she can benefit from this focus.

SECTION VIII: Individual Responsible for implementing the individualized education program and transitional services

Name	*Role/Responsibility*
Special education, vocational education, math, health, work-study, and language arts teachers	Participating in assisting Susan to learn the subcompetencies noted in Section IV B
Bank, credit company, nursery school, TV & radio interviewers, career counselors, Chamber of Commerce personnel, vocational rehabilitation, guidance center, & public health workers	
Parents/families, peers	

SECTION IX: Objective Criteria, Evaluation Procedures, and Schedule for assessing short-term objectives

Objective Criteria can be found in the LCCE Competency Rating Scale (CRS), and the LCCE Knowledge Battery (KB), and the LCCE Performance Battery (PB). Criteria listed reflect the short-term individual objectives checked in Section IV, Part B, of this form.

Evaluation Procedures can be determined by the IEP Committee reviewing the manuals for the Competency Rating Scale, Knowledge Battery, and Performance Battery.

Schedule for Assessment should include time, date, frequency, place, etc.

PB pretests to be administered prior to instruction and posttests upon completion. KB to be readministered in 1 year.

SECTION X: Estimated Date, Location, and Time for the next IEP Committee Review Conference

11/1/95   10: A.M.   Junior High School   Room 100

FIGURE 8.10 *continued*

competency units (lesson plans), the CRS, the Knowledge and Performance Batteries, and the Self-Determination Scale can be considered a complete planning, instructional, and evaluation package (Brolin, 1992a, 1992b, 1993a, in preparation).

Muskegon (Michigan) Intermediate School District has developed a transition planning guide sheet using the first 21 competencies of the LCCE Curriculum to identify planning options and agencies that can support their efforts in each of the competency areas. The occupational guidance and preparation component of the guide sheet is presented in Figure 8.11 to illustrate how one school district is organizing resources that can be involved in the total career development of its students. In addition, the first page of Muskegon's individual transition service plan, again using the LCCE curriculum areas, competencies, and subcompetencies, is presented in Figure 8.12 to illustrate how they record transition planning activities.

Summary

The LCCE approach provides educators with a method and the materials for implementing a transition component to the IEP that will meet students' functional skills needs as well as the requirements of federal legislation for an appropriate educational program and transition planning. The LCCE assessment instruments presented in Chapter 7, the IEP form presented in Figure 8.10, and the LCCE instructional unit lesson plans provide educators with a comprehensive evaluation, planning, and instructional system.

"Since the end product of transition in special education is successful community adjustment as experienced by former special education students, adult adjustment may be viewed as a general measure of the effectiveness of special education programs."

(Weisenstein & Elrod, 1987, p. 39)

FINAL COMMENTS

With the movement toward inclusive schools whereby students will be served to the maximum extent possible in general education classrooms in inclusive neighborhood schools and in community settings, community support becomes even more critical for successful transition endeavors. The CEC policy paper on inclusion (1994) notes that "there must be interagency agreements and collaboration with local governments and business to help prepare students to assume a constructive role in an inclusive community." Thus, systematic planning is essential for successful inclusive efforts and must include the support of the community.

The LCCE transition model presented in Chapter 3 is the most comprehensive model to date. The model's three dimensions integrating 22 competencies, the three instructional settings (school, home, community), and four stages of career develop-

TRANSITION PLANNING GUIDE SHEET
(Occupational Guidance and Preparation)

Annual Goals	Objectives/Competencies	Planning Options	Agency Support
		Prevocational Training	
17. Knowing and Exploring Occupational Possibilities	70. Identify Remunerative Aspects of Work 71. Locate Sources of Occupational and Training Information 72. Identify Personal Values Met Through Work 73. Identify Societal Values Met Through Work 74. Classify Jobs into Occupational Categories 75. Investigate Local Occupational and Training Opportunities	Classroom Programs Local School Programs Community-based Sites	JTPA Skills Center MRS MEGA
		Assessment	
18. Selecting and Planning Occupational Choices	76. Make Realistic Occupational Choices 77. Identify Requirements of Appropriate and Available Jobs 78. Identify Occupational Aptitudes 79. Identify Major Occupational Interests	Local Curriculum-based Assessment MAISD Assessment	Goodwill MEGA
		Vocational Training	
19. Exhibiting Appropriate Work Habits and Behavior	80. Identify Major Occupational Needs 81. Follow Directions and Observe Regulations 82. Recognize Importance of Attendance 83. Recognize Importance of Supervision 84. Demonstrate Knowledge of Occupational Safety 85. Work with Others 86. Meet Demands for Quality Work 87. Work at a Satisfactory Rate	Regular Vocational Training Muskegon Consortium Newaygo Voc. Tech. Center Modified Vocational Training/Support Community-based sites/MAISD Community-based sites/LOCAL Individual Vocational Training (IVT) Work Study	MRS JTPA MEGA MOKA
21. Exhibiting Sufficient Physical/ Manual Skills	94. Demonstrate Stamina & Endurance 95. Demonstrate Satisfactory Balance and Coordination 96. Demonstrate Manual Dexterity 97. Demonstrate Sensory Discrimination		
		Employment	
20. Seeking, Securing, and Maintaining Employment	88. Search for a Job 89. Apply for a Job 90. Interview for a Job 91. Know How to Maintain Post-School Occupational Adjustment 92. Demonstrate Knowledge of Competitive Standards 93. Know How to Adjust to Changes in Employment	Competitive Competitive/Support Supported Employment Enclave Sheltered Volunteer	Michigan Rehab. Services (MRS) Competitive Competitive Support Supported Employment Goodwill Enclave Sheltered HGA JTPA

FIGURE 8.11   A sample guide sheet for transition planning.

Note. From Muskegon, Michigan Area Intermediate School District.

INDIVIDUAL TRANSITION SERVICE PLAN
(PAGE _____ OF ____)

NAME: _____ DATE: _____ SCHOOL: _____ TRANSITION PLAN #: (CIRCLE ONE) (INITIAL) (2) (3) (4) (5)

(1) OUTCOMES

Check (√) "Transition Areas" that need to be addressed: (Attach additional pages if necessary)

( ) DAILY LIVING SKILLS
OUTCOME: _____

( ) OCCUPATIONAL GUIDANCE AND/OR PREPARATION
OUTCOME: _____

( ) PERSONAL/SOCIAL SKILLS
OUTCOME: _____

( ) POST-SECONDARY EDUCATIONAL/TRAINING OPTIONS
OUTCOME: _____

(2) GOALS/OBJECTIVES

(Attach additional pages if necessary)

ANNUAL GOALS	ANNUAL OBJECTIVES/COMPETENCIES	ACTIONS TO MEET GOALS	PERSON(S) RESPONSIBLE	EVALUATION PROCESS TIMELINE

(3) AGENCIES

(NEEDED ASSISTANCE/INVOLVEMENT)

AGENCY	PURPOSE	PERSON RESPONSIBLE/CONTACT	DATE CONTACT COMPLETED
( ) MRS ( ) CMH ( ) OTHER ____			

(4) SIGNATURES

STUDENT: _____ DATE: _____ TEACHER/TRANSITION COORDINATOR: _____ DATE: _____ OTHER: _____ DATE: _____

PARENT: _____ DATE: _____ AGENCY REPRESENTATIVE: _____ DATE: _____ OTHER: _____ DATE: _____

FIGURE 8.12 A sample form for developing an individual transition service plan.
Note. From Muskegon, Michigan Area Intermediate School District.

ment, provide educators with a total scope and sequence approach from kindergarten through the postsecondary years. This approach provides an excellent framework for ensuring students and their families of a total approach to meeting all the instructional needs required for successful transition and adult adjustment.

ACTIVITIES

1. What transition areas would you include in the ITP component of your IEP? What differences would there be, if any, at the various grade levels?
2. Review the LCCE IEP form presented in Figure 8.10 and complete one of the following:
   a. Write a statement defending the appropriateness of this form by your local education agency (LEA) for IEP/ITP planning.
   b. Write a statement to explain changes you would need to make for your LEA.
   c. Submit another format and defend its appropriateness for IEP/ITP planning.

Chapter 9

Instructional Materials and Resources

Iva Dean Cook, Carol Opperman, and Melody Thurman-Urbanic

Preliminary Questions About the Topic

1. What options should be considered in using materials to teach the Life-Centered Career Education (LCCE) competencies/subcompetencies to individual students?

2. Examine a model and steps for matching instructional materials to the characteristics of the learner, and discuss implications for its use.

3. Why is it important to adopt a format such as the one presented in Figure 9.2 for correlating materials to the LCCE curriculum?

4. How would you apply the instructional materials model in Figure 9.1 to completing a student profile sheet in planning instruction for individual students in diverse settings?

5. If you were asked to share a brief, written description of your teacher-made materials with your colleagues, what would you include in your guidelines?

6. What information about individual students would be helpful to you in selecting appropriate materials to meet individual learner needs?

7. What sources would you access when searching for appropriate materials related to the LCCE curriculum?

8. What steps would you take to facilitate lesson planning for all students with disabilities regardless of whether they are served in inclusive schools or special classes?

9. What are the educational implications for selecting materials and resources for students with various special learning needs?

10. How do the LCCE curriculum objectives apply to each category of students with special learning needs?

236

During the 1980s, teachers and administrators alike identified a lack of appropriate instructional materials available for use in transition from school-to-work programs as one of the most significant barriers to program implementation. Although a shortage of transitional instructional materials was commonly reported as a major cause preventing transition implementation, in fact, some very comprehensive transitional instructional materials were available to school district personnel. The concern may have been a residual effect of the excellence movement, which resulted in a strong push to increase academic standards. Teachers were very much involved in meeting this reform initiative and may not have had the time or administrative encouragement to search for transitional instructional materials, although most teachers were concerned with their students' transition from school to work and community living instructional needs. This concern is once again surfacing as teachers and administrators address the transition mandate of the Individuals with Disabilities Education Act (IDEA) by searching for instructional materials needed to address both the district's transition program and their students' individualized transitional needs. This time the result is different. Teachers and administrators are finding that many transitional instructional materials are available for use in developing their functional curriculum.

As a teacher trainer, I have found that teachers (prospective and practicing) want transitional instructional materials that are teacher friendly. They want instructional materials and resources that can be used immediately to address their students' individualized transitional needs. Teachers also want comprehensive transitional instructional materials and resources. These materials must be able to address the diverse needs of their students and to provide a wide scope of career skills for the purpose of preparing their students to function in their current and future ecological environments. Finally, teachers want materials that can be used with other students and that can be easily incorporated or infused into the existing inclusionary programs. The Life-Centered Career Education (LCCE) curriculum program addresses all of these teacher requirements and has been available for over 20 years.

Teachers also need to be aware that other transitional instructional materials meet these criteria are available for developing their functional programs. These materials can be used as either separate programs or to supplement other existing materials such as the LCCE materials. No matter what transitional instructional materials are selected, the most critical factor is selecting materials that meets students' individualized needs in the transition from school to work and community living.

Dr. Robert J. Loyd was an Assistant Professor of Special Education at the University of Missouri-St. Louis and is a Council for Exceptional Children (CEC) Academy Trainer for the LCCE Curriculum. He is presently a Clinical Assistant Professor at the University of Missouri–Columbia.

A t one time, career education was defined as "the totality of experience through which one learns about and prepares to engage in work as part of her or his way of living" (Hoyt, 1975, p. 4). Currently, career education is viewed as a life experience program that teaches the skills that prepare students to transition from school to the community and the world of work. This concept of career education implies that many professionals, representing various agencies, are responsible for teaching career education concepts and that these competencies should be integrated into the school's total curriculum. As stated by Luftig:

> A quick glance at the LCCE curriculum reveals that all of the curriculum components are not directly related to school. That is, while many of the competencies deal directly with school-related subjects, other competencies are best taught under the auspices of other institutions and groups such as family or the community. Thus, a well-rounded career education curriculum should contain material found in the child's school, family, and community environment. (1987, p. 367)

The LCCE curriculum provides the teacher with a clear idea of the functional skills needed to prepare the student for the many stages of transition. The LCCE Knowledge and Performance Batteries, (Brolin, 1992a, 1992b) which are curriculum referenced, provide information that helps the teacher select which of the competencies/subcompetencies to teach the individual student. Knowledge of student characteristics, gleaned from other assessment data, can be used to help make process decisions. The teacher must analyze the data and create the instructional goals and objectives for writing the Individualized Education Program and Individualized Transition Plan (IEP/ITP). The LCCE competencies may be written as goals, and the subcompetencies as objectives. The goals and objectives lend themselves to a sequential selection and placement of materials and resources in the instructional process, beginning in the elementary grades and extending into adulthood. Materials needed to convey the curriculum goals and objectives to the student may be found in diverse environments.

The instructional units, which are part of the LCCE curriculum materials, include lesson plans that contain suggestions for materials and resources found throughout the student's environment. A variety of commercial materials may be used to supplement those suggested in the LCCE units. This chapter presents a model for matching instructional materials and resources to the characteristics of the learner. Each step in the model is described. Exceptional people are defined, and their characteristics and implications for materials/resources are discussed.

MATCHING MATERIALS TO THE CHARACTERISTICS OF THE LEARNER: A MODEL

As demonstrated in Figure 9.1 (Cook 1974), several major steps should be considered when matching materials to the characteristics of the learner. This section deals with knowledge of instructional materials beginning with location.

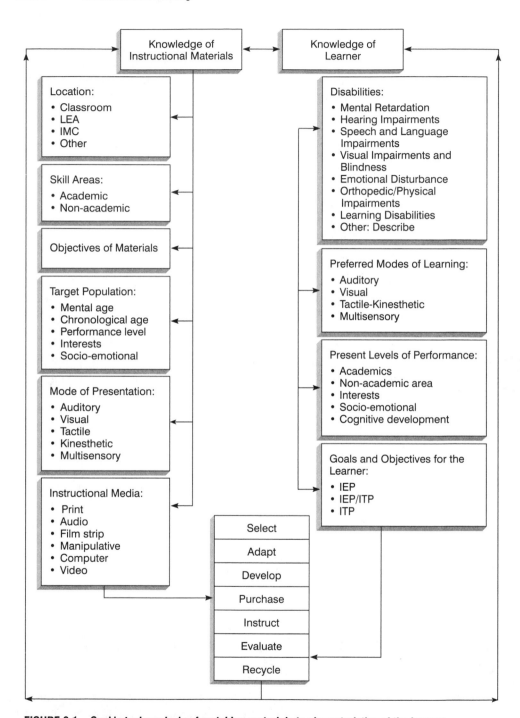

FIGURE 9.1   Cook's task analysis of matching materials to characteristics of the learner.

Note. From *Materials Handbook* (p. 8) by I. D. Cook, 1974, Institute, WV: West Virginia College of Graduate Studies. Copyright 1974 by West Virginia College of Graduate Studies. Reprinted by permission.

Locating Materials

The first step in the model is to locate the materials that can be correlated to the LCCE goals and objectives. Materials may be found in the school, the community, and/or an Instructional Materials Center (IMC).

Until the early 1960s there was a scarcity of appropriate materials for students with special learning needs. Those available were developed for teaching basic skills and were not relevant to the needs and characteristics of all learners. Because of President John F. Kennedy's concern for the education of persons with mental retardation, a committee was appointed to study the problem. An outgrowth of the committee's efforts and recommendations was the funding of two model IMCs, which were followed by similar centers established at regional and local levels throughout the country. Over the last 20 years, these materials have proliferated, and school systems have increased funding for purchasing materials. Thus, teachers are faced with the difficulty of accessing appropriate materials from this array of sometimes inappropriate collections.

In reviewing these materials, the model in Figure 9.1 suggests that several factors be analyzed:

1. Skill areas
2. Objectives of the materials
3. Target population
4. Mode of presentation
5. Instructional media

Skill Areas

In-depth analysis of materials is carried out to determine whether the academic and nonacademic needs of students will be addressed. The competency-based approach of the LCCE curriculum is not intended to deemphasize the importance of basic academics and nonacademic instruction and training but is meant to be infused into other content/skill areas. The question to be answered is, For which skill area are the materials designed? For example, are the materials intended to teach mathematical concepts?

Objectives of the Materials

The next step is to determine whether the materials objectives correlate with the competencies/subcompetencies of the LCCE curriculum. If the skill area is math, can the materials be used to teach some or all of the subcompetencies under competency 1, managing personal finances?

Target Population

A major consideration in selecting materials is to determine the target population for whom the materials would be suited. Attention should be directed to whether the materials are age appropriate and/or appropriate for the developmental levels of the students for which they are being reviewed.

Schloss et al. (1990) cite two types of problems with materials available to secondary teachers and students. First, the instructional materials may have been intended for elementary students with special needs. Second, some material may have been originally designed for regular secondary students (p. 14). As stated by Langone, "teachers should review many possible approaches and programs, deciding which individual programs or combination of them is the best match with each students' needs." (1990, p. 233)

Mode of Presentation

Central to learning and instruction is the idea that materials must be based on the learning styles of students. "Because of their strengths and weaknesses in auditory, visual, and kinesthetic modalities, different students may require programs that meet specific learning styles" (Langone, 1990, p. 233). G. M. Clark and Kolstoe expanded this concept by citing the need to "consider logical and analogical styles as related to left- or right-brain functions" (1990, p. 199).

Instructional Media

As noted, for some students, the modality emphasized is important. This raises some important questions about media. Is the material primarily print? Is it primarily auditory? Is the print supported by audiotapes, or are other stimulus–response combinations used?

A materials correlations chart, as presented in Figure 9.2, is a way of organizing information as materials are reviewed and correlated to the competencies and subcompetencies of the LCCE curriculum (Cook, 1993, p. 207). The first column allows the teacher to select and record in the subject area in which the competencies and subcompetencies are to be infused. Additional columns provide a record of competencies/subcompetencies to be taught, correlation of materials to the competencies, and the levels and modes of presentation.

Once a general collection of materials has been identified and recorded, the second major step in instructional decision making is a thorough assessment of the learner characteristics.

KNOWLEDGE OF THE LEARNER

Knowledge of the characteristics of individual students, their learning styles and performance levels, and the IEP/ITP goals and objectives will provide a basis for making decisions regarding instructional methods and materials. In this section, we will integrate the four steps comprising this component as we present several examples of students with different disabilities.

Within the term *individuals with disabilities*, Public Law 101–476 includes those with mental retardation, hearing impairments including deafness, speech and language

			Levels			
Subject	LCCE Competency/ Subcompetency	Commercial Materials	K–4	5–8	9–12	Mode of Presentation

LCCE DOMAIN: _____

FIGURE 9.2 Materials correlation chart.

Note. From Task Analysis of Matching Materials to Characteristics of the Learner by I.D. Cook in *Life Centered Career Education: Professional Development Activity Book* (p. 267) by D. E. Brolin, 1993, Reston, VA: The Council for Exceptional Children. Copyright 1993 by The Council for Exceptional Children. Reprinted by permission.

impairments, visual impairments including blindness, serious emotional disturbance, orthopedic impairments, autism, traumatic brain injury, and other health impairments, or specific learning disabilities. The educational needs of individuals may be met through many placement options including regular and special education. In 1993, The Council for Exceptional Children (CEC) released an inclusion policy, which broadened the placement options and states:

> CEC believes the concept of inclusion is a meaningful goal to be pursued in our schools and communities. In addition, CEC believes children, youth, and young adults with disabilities should be served whenever possible in general education classrooms in inclusive neighborhood schools and community settings. Such settings should be strengthened and supported by an infusion of specially trained personnel and other appropriate supportive practices according to the individual needs of the child. (CEC, 1993)

The concepts espoused in the policy have implications for making decisions regarding curriculum and materials as well as staffing patterns. The nature of personnel preparation programs limits the effectiveness of cooperative instructional planning between regular and special educators. The policy states that students with disabilities should be served whenever possible in general education classrooms and in neighborhood schools and community settings and should be supported by an infusion of specially trained personnel. This implies that, in addition to placements in special education, separate classes, special schools, out of school environments, and in regular school part-time, all individuals with disabilities have the option of full inclusion in general education classrooms. Such policy changes require that general educators and special educators be prepared to work together effectively in making decisions regarding curriculum, materials, and instructional delivery.

Preparing simple learning characteristics profiles for each student early in the school year and keeping an up-to-date LCCE materials correlations chart will facilitate lesson planning for all students with disabilities regardless of whether they're served in inclusive schools or special classes. Curriculum and instructional tools, such as textbooks, media, materials, and technology must be carefully selected to assist those with disabilities to learn to their maximum ability and make the transition from school to the community and the world of work.

Cook (1993) provides a series of profile sheets for developing learner characteristics profiles. These formats, as illustrated in Figures 9.3 and 9.4, may be used to guide the selection and adaptation of materials to teach a diversity of students of all ages in a variety of environments. As the variation in students' abilities and disabilities are reviewed, implications for materials decisions will likely emerge. What are the characteristics of those with disabilities and implications of decisions regarding selection of material and resources?

The following sections contain case studies of students illustrating the principles described earlier in this chapter and in the preceding chapters.

Student's Name: _____		Date: _____	

*Learning Characteristics	*Implications for for Materials/Resources	**LCCE Competencies	*Materials
e.g., memory deficit	Materials should provide for short incremental steps and overlearning		

*   To be completed by special education teacher

** To be completed by regular education/special education teacher

FIGURE 9.3 Student profile sheet (for mainstreamed student).

Note. From Task Analysis of Matching Materials to Characteristics of the Learner by I.D. Cook in *Life Centered Career Education: Professional Development Activity Book* (p. 271) by D. E. Brolin, 1993, Reston, VA: The Council for Exceptional Children. Copyright 1993 by The Council for Exceptional Children. Reprinted by permission.

*Learning Characteristics	*Implications for for Materials/Resources	*LCCE Competencies	*Materials
e.g., memory deficit	Materials should provide for short incremental steps and overlearning		

Student's Name: _____   Date: _____

*   To be completed by special education teacher

FIGURE 9.4   Student profile sheet (self-contained classroom placement).

Note. From Task Analysis of Matching Materials to Characteristics of the Learner by I.D. Cook in *Life Centered Career Education: Professional Development Activity Book* (p. 273) by D. E. Brolin, 1993, Reston, VA: The Council for Exceptional Children. Copyright 1993 by The Council for Exceptional Children. Reprinted by permission.

AMOS

Amos, a 12-year-old boy, is very quiet and insecure. He constantly needs to have directions repeated. He is easily distracted and darts from one activity to another. Amos's mother was 17 when he was born. Oxygen was cut off for a period of time during Amos's birth, resulting in some brain damage. He has two siblings, an older brother and a younger sister. Tests demonstrate that both siblings have normal intelligence. Adam has good health; other than the usual childhood illnesses, there is nothing unusual in his health history.

Amos has a low socioeconomic background. He lives in a rural area, and his family receives Aid to Dependent Children from Human Services. In spite of this background, he is generally clean and dressed in clean clothes.

Amos is classified as mildly mentally impaired. He is programmed with the regular classroom for physical education, health, music, art, homeroom, recess, and lunch. Amos goes to a resource room for reading, language arts, mathematics, science, and social studies. In the classroom, he is best in visual-motor functioning. He has acceptable handwriting, and his completed work is usually neat. His weaknesses include inadequate short-term memory and reading skills and extreme lack of confidence. Amos was retained in first grade. He has received speech therapy in the past. He is not now receiving speech therapy.

Mental Retardation

Students who have mental impairments are those who evidence significantly subaverage general intellectual functions resulting in or associated with impairments in adaptive behavior and manifested during the developmental periods. The term *mildly impaired* refers to those students who require specially designed instruction and basic academic and practical skills to develop adequate social, personal, and vocational competence sufficient for self-maintenance. The term *moderately mentally impaired* refers to those students who require special instruction in basic communication, sensory motor, self-help and independent living skills, and vocational training to function in employment/supportive employment and community living/supervised community living. The term *severely mentally impaired* refers to those students who require systematic instruction in self-help skills and routines to function in society with assistance in all areas, including the possibility of functioning in specially designed work settings. Problems among these students are medical problems and dysfunctional behaviors. The term *profoundly mentally retarded* refers to those students who have limited capabilities in all areas of development and who are totally dependent on others.

Educational Implications

The main goal of teachers of students who are mentally impaired is to foster independent behaviors that allow these students to assume adult roles and responsibilities as they transition from the school setting to the community and to the world of work. Programs for the mildly mentally impaired generally include academic, communication, vocational, social, emotional, and community living skills. Programs for the moderately mentally impaired include functional academic, basic communication, sensory motor, community vocational skills. For students who are severely mentally impaired, programs generally include self-help, leisure, behavior management plans, communication/augmentative communication skills, social and vocational skills, daily routine, and personal care training. Programs for profoundly mentally impaired students include basic development in self-help, communication/augmentative, sensory motor training, and social responsiveness.

The student who is mentally impaired faces more problems in the area of adaptive behavior (street behavior) than in the area of low intellectual functioning.

LCCE Applications

The LCCE curriculum provides ample opportunities to develop adaptive behavior. The competencies/subcompetencies contained in the three domains (daily living, personal-social, occupational guidance, and preparation) are the thrust of all programs for students with mental impairments. These competencies and subcompetencies may be infused into the regular curriculum. Firsthand observation shows us that adults who are mentally impaired struggle daily with these three domains. If we begin to earlier identify the needs of students with mental impairment and develop and implement functional curricula, then we better prepare them for the transition from school to work. Whether the impairment is mild to moderate to severe, within the LCCE, competencies and subcompetencies address the needs of students on their level. Again, as with most other exceptionalities, the emphasis is on hands-on, real-life learning activities and experiences, rather than the academic approach that has so dismally failed these students in the past.

Implications for Materials and Resources

Numerous studies (Denny, 1966; Ellis, 1970; Fisher & Zeaman, 1973; Spitz, 1973; Zeaman & House, 1963; Zigler, 1966), have delineated specific characteristics of individuals with mental retardation and teaching implications. Some major conclusions from these studies were that persons with mental retardation have a deficiency in short-term memory that is due to inadequate rehearsal strategies, have a deficiency in input organization, have difficulty in selecting and attending to relevant dimensions, and are poor in incidental learning. The teaching implications follow (Mercer & Snell, 1977):

- Verbal or imagery rehearsal activities should be encouraged.
- Material should be grouped at input (e.g., redundancy, spacing).
- The number of irrelevant concepts should be reduced.

Individuals who have intellectual deficiencies have difficulty handling abstract concepts. Such concepts must either be avoided or presented in a manipulative, hands-on way (Luftig, 1987). Learning must be sequential and provide for overlearning. Because the mental age of individuals with retardation is below their chronological age, materials for teaching must be of high interest and low vocabulary content. Concepts taught must be relevant and also age appropriate. When needed, print material should be accompanied by audiovisual support. For those students who have difficulty completing tasks, small chunks of learning and distributed practice rather than mass practice should be provided.

Because of the limitations of students with mild retardation, concepts should be introduced in a number of settings, using a variety of materials. The materials should be kept within the interest and performance range of the student. Therefore, the teacher may choose a basic text and still provide the student with many supplementary books, teacher-prepared materials, films, filmstrips, and records. Resource persons and field trips are necessary to supplement classroom activities. Do not have the students repeat activities to the point of boredom. Refer, instead to the wealth of suggested auxiliary material.

(Cook, 1987)

STEPHANIE

Stephanie is a 12-year-old girl. She has a hearing loss of 72 db, which puts her within the deaf range. She is four grades behind her peers in academic subjects, although she is of average intelligence. She is socially immature because of limited communication ability. She is currently placed in a self-contained classroom.

Hearing Impairments

Students who are deaf or hearing impaired/hard of hearing are those whose auditory acuity delays or inhibits the development of speech and/or language skills and adversely affects developmental and educational performance. The deaf student is one with profound or total loss of hearing sensitivity to the extent that processing linguistic information with or without amplification is impaired and requires specially designed instruction. The student with a hearing impairment is one whose sense of hearing is functional but whose hearing loss, whether permanent or fluctuating, causes a speech and/or language deficit to the extent that specifically designed instruction is required.

Educational Implications

As with other students with disabilities, those with hearing impairments also require the same functional curriculum as their peers. The main goal of teachers of students with hearing impairments is to teach language and the means to communicate. The only adaptations a teacher needs to make for students with hearing impairments is in delivery and presentation. Teachers must be knowledgeable of signing, of assistive technology, of needed speech and pathology services, and of strategies for effectively communicating with students with hearing impairments. For instance, students should be seated in direct view of the teacher, and the teacher should face students with hearing impairments to allow for lip reading. Audiovisual presentations should always be preceded by a written outline or notes specific to the audiovisual materials. A functional curriculum addresses a key problem for students with impairments—motivation.

LCCE Applications

The LCCE provides motivational considerations to the student with a hearing impairment by bypassing limited reading ability and involving the student in hands-on life-centered learning activities. As with many other students with special needs, students with hearing impairments need to work hands-on, or they become bored or begin to lose motivation. The competencies and subcompetencies under daily living skills, personal-social skills, and occupational guidance and preparation are a wealth of hands-on, real-life learning activities that are not impeded by the generally low reading ability of students with hearing impairments.

Implications for Materials and Resources

"The most common adaptation for students with hearing impairments are amplification devices including auditory training units and hearing aids" (Bigge, 1988, p. 117). An augmentation such as manual signing by interpreters may also be provided for many students, but the pictorial format is another option. This approach requires that teachers adapt materials so that concepts are conveyed through signs, graphics, or other means of visual form.

Postschool opportunities are greater than ever for individuals with hearing impairments. Thus, it is critical that the public school programs teach the content outlined in the LCCE curriculum. The focus here is to select materials appropriate for the language levels. It is important to develop or adapt materials to supplement or replace commercially available materials. Examples of teacher-made materials include pictures, diagrams, and drawings. Technology applications for individuals with hearing impairments are increasing with a primary focus on both communication and educational difficulties caused by the sensory handicap.

Think It Through (Nugent & Stone, 1981), one example of a level-III videodisc-based program, was developed by staff of the Media Development Project for the Hearing Impaired (MDPHI). This program helps individuals with hearing impairments develop independent thinking skills. Students are presented with problematic situations by the videodisc and must define the problem and choose a solution (p. 98). This program addresses Competency 15 in the social skills domain and is one example of the emerging technology designed to assist educators in providing students with hearing impairments with the same opportunities for functional skills development as their peers.

"Many of the problems facing deaf adults in our society are job related. Limited English skills, poor educational and vocational training, and employer prejudice make finding appropriate jobs very difficult. The underemployment and low-level employment of deaf adults give them a financial handicap in addition to their physical disability."
(Kirk & Gallagher, 1989, p. 342)

TRAVIS

Travis is a 14-year-old boy who has a moderate articulation-phonology disorder as well as a language deficit. He performs below grade level in subjects where language mediation is required. When he speaks, it is obvious that he has a speech disorder. This sets him apart from his peers at an age when peer acceptance is important.

Speech and Language Impairments

Students with communication disorders are those who evidence language, articulation, fluency or voice disorders that adversely affect educational performance, including communication skills and social and emotional development within the school environment. Students with language disorders may exhibit deviant or delayed development or loss following development. Disorders may include difficulties with the form of language (semantics) or the function of language (pragmatics). Students with articulation disorders may exhibit the substitution of one phoneme (class of speech sounds) for another, distortion of phonemes or addition of phonemes, errors of syllable structure, or the presence of phonological process disorder. Students with fluency disorders may exhibit disruptions in the normal flow of speech that occur frequently or are markedly noticeable and are characterized by behaviors such as repetitions or prolongations of sound or symbols, blocks, hesitations, revisions, incomplete phrases, and avoidance behaviors or ancillary movements indicative of stress or struggle; their voice is characterized by inappropriate voice or vocal quality, pitch, or loudness resulting from pathological conditions, psychogenic factors, or inappropriate use of the vocal mechanism.

Educational Implications

All too often, language disorders is given less attention than other categories of impairment. However, it is imperative that educators recognize these deficiencies as early as possible in the student's education. Early intervention of difficulties with speech and language will better facilitate the student's success and acceptance, not only by peers but also by the community. A large part of the career education curriculum consists of going into the community and meeting potential employers. Individuals who have communication problems are generally deemed less intelligent or less capable than peers without communication problems. Therefore, a program of activities that address deficiencies in language, articulation, and fluency or voice disorders should be implemented as early as possible. As with all populations with special needs, children who have difficulties with communication suffer from personal–social adjustment problems. Early screening and regular therapy by speech/language pathologists for these students will help them deal more effectively with social and personal–social adjustment.

LCCE Applications

The LCCE again addresses the domain of personal–social skills in a way that is beneficial to students with communication disorders. The entire curriculum containing daily living skills, personal–social sills, and occupational guidance and preparation is appropriate for these students. The competency of communicating with others, which is under personal–social skills, addresses knowing subtleties of communication (subcompetency 69), which is a very important skill for students who have speech and language deficits. They rely on subtleties of communication daily, and the subcompetency that addresses this and recognizes it as a life skill is highly beneficial. Competency 11— acquiring self-confidence—also addresses the needs of these students. For instance, subcompetency 46 states the student will be able to express feelings of self-worth; subcompetency 47, describe others' perception of self; subcompetency 48, accept and give praise; subcompetency 49, accept and give criticism; and subcompetency 50, develop confidence in one's self. Again, this area or domain is probably the most important for special education students in general and is highly effective for students with communication disorders.

Implications for Materials and Resources

Language and communication are basic to learning and to personal–social skills development (LCCE competencies 10 to 16). Students may have a range of deficits in language ability that necessitate intensive training in language and/or communication skills as well as modifications in materials and resources to meet the student-response needs. "The preliminary challenge for the special education teacher, before considering modifications, is to identify student response methods or access activities" (Bigge, 1988, p. 67).

 "Children with primary speech disorders typically respond to the regular education program with some additional help for their special communication needs."

(Kirk & Gallagher, 1989, p. 284)

ALLEGRA

Allegra is a 16-year-old girl who, as the result of a medical problem, lost her sight at the age of 1 year. She is very alert and intelligent. Allegra is one of seven children and attended a school for students who are blind until age 12, after which she was enrolled in regular education. During the last 4 years, she has been provided an itinerant teacher as well as orientation and mobility training. Allegra aspires to become a writer.

Visual Impairments and Blindness

Blind and partially sighted students are defined as those with a physical disability in a limited visual field such that even with the use of lenses or corrective devices, the child requires modification of instructional methods and materials or supplementary assistance to function and learn. Students identified as blind and partial sighted include those with organic impairments resulting in no vision or visual limitations that after best correction result in educational handicaps requiring special services and/or materials. Blind students have central vision acuity of 20/200 or less in the better eye with correction, or a visual field that subtends an angle of 20 degrees or less. Partially sighted students have visual acuity greater than 20/200 but less than 20/70 with correction.

Educational Implications

The acquisition of knowledge and skills of students with visual impairment, probably more than any other population, relies on the teacher's ability to obtain the needed assistive technology, be flexible in using aids, and exhibit overall ingenuity in presenting the materials in a meaningful way. Students with visual impairments need the same curriculum as their sighted peers. The only adaptation cited is the one that conveys the curricular concepts, which are otherwise inaccessible to these students. Written information on the chalkboard or other written material is an example. A teacher of a student with visual impairments must be sure that all written material is presented either orally or by the use of one of several sensory aids or assistive technology.

LCCE Applications

Because the area of daily living skills is always a large part of training a student with visual impairments, the LCCE curriculum fits in quite appropriately to the training and educational needs of students with visual impairments. Also, because students with visual impairments, as with other handicapping conditions, have problems with personal–social adjustment, the domain of personal–social skills also addresses their needs quite adequately. For instance, competency 10 (achieving self-awareness), 11 (acquiring self-confidence), and 14 (achieving independence) all offer the teacher and the student a good starting point in dealing with personal–social needs. The domain of occupational guidance and preparation offers a framework to assist students with visual impairments with one of the more challenging life choices they will ever have to make: finding a job that they can do and for which others will acknowledge their ability. Competency 17—knowing and exploring occupational possibilities—has six subcompetencies with lesson plans to address the competency. Competency 20—seeking, securing, and maintaining employment—offers many critical life skills training opportunities. Competency 21—exhibiting sufficient physical-manual skills—is especially useful to a student with visual impairments. The subcompetencies deal with (94) stamina and endurance; (95) satisfactory balance and coordination; (96) the demonstration of manual dexterity; and (97) the demonstration of sensory discrimination. The entire LCCE curriculum is useful and beneficial to a student with visual impairments, as it is for students with all other exceptionalities, and can be presented orally or transcribed into braille or otherwise accessed through the use of assistive technology.

Implications for Materials and Resources

Individuals with visual impairments or blindness cannot participate fully in the curriculum, either in special or regular education, unless the teacher adapts the presentation and response methods. Examples of presentation alternatives include braille, auditory aids, computer programs with voice output, readers, and transcribers.

For low-vision children and youth, large print is necessary. Standard print may be enlarged photographically or by using computer software. A dark felt pen may be used to darken a graph or a diagram. When introducing vocabulary, words may be written in large print on the chalkboard or the overhead projector rather than relying on regular printed text.

Children and youth who are blind rely on tactual and auditory aids. Braille is the primary tactile system used by blind persons. Hard-copy braille provides a permanent record, while paperless braille allows immediate feedback for editing purposes. A slate and stylus may be used for note taking, for personal use, and in class.

A technological advancement for accessing print is the Optacon, which "translates visual text into a raised, vibrating, tactile print that is not braille but a tactile counterpart of visible symbols" (Lindsey, 1993, p. 186). Anna L. Hunt, in an interview response to a question about the developments in technology, stated:

> Other means of meeting communication needs of learners with visual impairments are auditory aids, such as recorded books, cassette tape recorders for taking notes and recording assignments, and the Language Master Special Edition. The Language Master, which is a speaking device, contains spellcheck, dictionary, thesaurus, grammar guide and word games. The word games are an activity related to the LCCE competency #8—Engaging in Leisure Time. The Kurzweil Reading Machine from Kurzweil Computer Products orally reads in synthesized speech, any available printed material. (A. L. Hunt in an interview with I. D. Cook, October 1993)

Tactile Graphics Display, an electronic, low-cost, assistive aid, produces textured lines and shapes that are important to learning history, geography, mathematics, and map study. The ability to read maps facilitates both communication and mobility (LCCE competencies 6 and 16). Speech synthesizers, a resource that may be used by regular or special educators, allow individuals with visual impairments to have access to much of the available computer software.

Four commonly needed skill areas for visually impaired students are typing, listening, daily living, and orientation and travel skills. The IEP/ITP can reflect these priority needs of persons with visual impairments. A functional curriculum, daily living skills, personal–social skills, and occupational guidance and preparation should be mandatory skill areas.

 "All too frequently, even in recent years, otherwise capable, intelligent people with impaired vision have assumed dependent lives, remaining unemployed or returning to their parents' homes following graduation from high school or college because they have received no training in specific employment skills."

(N. G. Haring, 1982, p. 286)

STEPHEN

Stephen is a 16-year-old boy. He has difficulty building and maintaining satisfactory relationships with his peers and teachers. He also has difficulty completing class assignments, and this has affected his academic progress. He functions at the eighth grade academically. Sometimes Stephen appears to be depressed and unhappy. He often behaves inappropriately.

Emotional Disturbance

A student identified with a behavior disorder is one whose condition adversely affects educational performance and is manifested by one or more of the following characteristics over a long period of time and to a marked degree:

* An inability to learn that cannot be explained by intellectual, sensory, or health factors
* An inability to build or maintain satisfactory interpersonal relationships with peers and teachers
* Inappropriate types of behavior or feelings under normal circumstances
* A general pervasive mood of unhappiness, depression, or an emotional problem manifested by withdrawal
* A tendency to develop physical symptoms or fears associated with personal or school problems
* Or a schizophrenic condition

Behavior disorders do not include students who are socially maladjusted unless it is determined that they also meet the preceding definition.

Educational Implications

The implications for special educators are the facts that students who have behavior disorders need assistance and guidance in developing and exhibiting acceptable behaviors that allow them to develop positive interpersonal relationships as well as to continue effective learning in a classroom setting. Effective teacher strategies for assisting students with behavior disorders to attain their goals are the use of behavior management, affective education that address the emotional and social needs of the child, and career education that heightens that child's leisure skill development. The overall goal is to provide an environment that will modify or help the student control the behavior problem, that will enhance the student's feeling of self-worth, and that will help the student's self-control so that appropriate learning can occur.

LCCE Applications

The LCCE competencies and subcompetencies under personal–social skills address the needs of students with behavior disorders very effectively. For instance, competencies 10 to 16 deal with achieving self-awareness, acquiring self-confidence, achieving socially responsible behavior, making adequate decisions, and communicating with others. Under each of these competencies are several subcompetencies that provide the teacher and student with lesson plans to address the level of development appropriate for the student. Under competency 12 (achieving socially responsible behavior), the first subcompetency states that the student will be able to develop respect for the rights and properties of others (51). As the student develops this respect and understanding, he will naturally sequentially move to the next subcompetency (52), which is that the student will recognize authority and follow instructions. Competency 53 states that the student will be able to demonstrate appropriate behavior in public places. The next is a little more introspective and requires a higher level of socially responsible behavior of the student. Competency 54 states that the student will be able to know important character traits. The last subcompetency is 55, the student will be able to recognize personal roles.

The LCCE succinctly addresses the crucial area for students with behavior disorders within the personal–social domains. Under the daily living skills domain are nine competencies, several of which directly address common problems of children with behavior disorders. Competency 7 (exhibiting responsible citizenship) and 8 (using recreational facilities and engaging in leisure) generally address problems with this population of students.

Under occupational guidance and preparation, competency 19 (exhibiting appropriate work habits and behavior) is a very critical competency for students with behavior disorders. Under this competency, the student is guided through subcompetencies 81 (following directions and observing regulations); 82 (recognizing importance of attendance and punctuality); 83 (recognize importance of supervision); 84 (demonstrate knowledge of occupational safety); 85 (work with others); 86 (meet demands for quality work); and 87 (work at a satisfactory rate).

Unlike the general academic curriculum, which sometimes falls short in holding the attention of a student with behavior disorders, the LCCE curriculum does hold the attention of a student with these needs because it is real-life, it is situational, and it elicits hands-on participation. The teacher must provide a focus and directly assist emotionally disturbed students in acquiring the personal–social skills, competencies 1 to 16, in the LCCE curriculum.

Implications for Materials and Resources

To the casual observer, students in a class for the emotionally disturbed may appear to be working with the same or similar materials in use in regular classrooms in the same building. This is usually true, but a closer inspection will reveal that these materials have been selected and slightly or greatly modified to consider the learning and social-emotional characteristics of these children. (Meyen, 1990, p. 242)

Meyen (1990) presents selection principles for use by the special education teacher suggested by Wood (1986). These include selecting materials that have qualities for catching and holding student's attention, that address several objectives simultaneously, that elicit active participation, that are adaptable to the developmental levels of individual students, and that provide for a successful outcome.

A priority for those with an emotional disturbance is personal–social adjustment as their behavior interferes with school functioning. Their characteristics include lowered academic performance, inability to build or maintain satisfactory interpersonal relationships, and pervasive moods of unhappiness or depression. They often exhibit a short attention span, lack of motivation, low frustration levels, poor self-concept, and often are easily distracted. Materials selected must be relevant and interesting and at the appropriate instructional level. Materials should be highly structured and elicit the student's participation. The LCCE competencies listed in the personal–social domain (competencies 10 to 16) are especially critical and should be directly taught because of the characteristics of this population.

 "One way for the school to increase the probability that students will misbehave or be truant is to offer instruction for which pupils have no real or imagined use. Not only will such 'education' fail to engage the attention of pupils, it will also hinder their social adaptation by wasting their time and substituting trivial information for knowledge that would allow them to pursue rewarding activities."

(Kaufman, 1985, pp. 159–160)

"Appropriate curriculum content can be a major vehicle for working with youths who have behavior disorders. Proper placement and appropriate curriculum materials can help eliminate many incipient behavior problems. The number of responses in a child's behavioral repertoire can be widened considerably through the medium of curriculum."

(Graubard, 1973, p. 271)

BEA

Bea is a 6-year-old girl with a mental age of 3-11 and a chronological age of 6-3. Bea was born without use of her right arm and leg. No effective corrective measures were found until she was age 5, when her leg and hip were operated on at a Shriner's Hospital. After numerous trips to the hospital and three admissions, one of several months' duration, Bea can now walk with a slight limp. She is due for a follow-up this month. Her right arm is presently immobilized by a cast, and she has almost no control of her right hand.

Bea's mother says that her daughter had several convulsions right after birth and was given sleeping drops until the age of 2 weeks. She has not taken anticonvulsive medication or suffered convulsions since then.

Bea's overall health is described as good. She has about one cold per winter and sometimes suffers from earaches with the colds. She sleeps well but has a poor appetite and poor teeth. Bea never learned to walk until after surgery at age 5. Her mother says that discipline is not a problem, because Bea is "a really good kid." She notes that Bea does not want to share toys and has a bad temper at times. She was vague about methods of discipline used but did mention the withholding of privileges.

The Stanford-Binet test revealed Bea's strength on those items requiring purely visual performance. She clearly had difficulty on items requiring fine motor performance, and she failed the picture vocabulary item at age IV level, although she passed it at age III level. The present testing shows her functioning at a mental age of 3 years 11 months, with a consequent IQ in the range of mild intellectual disabilities.

Raw score on the Vineland Social Maturity Scale was 2, which yields an age equivalent of 3–0. Her human figure drawings consist solely of faces with distinct eyes, noses, and mouths.

Cognitive factors observed include Bea's academic potential as measured by Stanford-Binet, which is presently in the lowest 1% of all children her age. It is not known, however, whether this is the result of mental deficiency or developmental lag coincident to her physical handicap. In either case, she will be at a severe disadvantage if placed with a group of ordinary first graders. Bea's vision and hearing are apparently average, but it is expected that they will be checked in routine screening during the first month of school.

Bea seems to be a happy, cheerful child, although she seems accustomed to having her own way. There seems to be no reason why she cannot socialize with her peers—provided that she is not put into a position where her physical handicaps will show to her disadvantage. Teachers should cooperate with her parents on enforcing a firm but gentle discipline—stressing her competence to do things for herself and to persist at challenging activities.

Orthopedic/Physical Impairments

Students with orthopedic/physical impairments have physical disabilities, which may be congenital or caused by accident or disease, resulting in permanent, temporary, or intermittent medical disabilities. These disabilities require modification of curriculum, instructional strategies, and/or related services. The type, extent, and/or duration of services are determined by the nature of the individual's disability. The term *physical disabilities* includes orthopedically impaired, which consists of the following:

- Disabilities caused by congenital anomaly (e.g., spina bifida, congenital amputation, osteogenesis imperfecti)
- Disabilities from other causes (amputation, cerebral palsy, dystrophies and atrophies, and conditions that cause contractures)
- And other health impairments causing limited strength, vitality, or alertness as a result of chronic or acute health problems such as heart condition, rheumatic fever, asthma, sickle cell anemia, hemophilia, epilepsy, cystic fibrosis, cancer, or diabetes

Educational Implications

Because of the uniqueness of each student with a physical impairment, the curriculum involves a variety of philosophies, instructional strategies, or procedures, environmental arrangements, equipment, materials, learning activities, skill sequences, and/or criteria for successful educational performance. Some areas of consideration are physical, psychological, emotional adjustment to the physical disability including treatment, care and maintenance, death and dying, use of prosthetic or orthotic devices, eating, dressing, toileting, physical mobility, personal hygiene, and basic communication. Specialized curricular areas need to address the particular disability. The special educator's concern is not the origin of the disability but rather how the disability impedes a child's learning. Unless the type and degree of severity of a disability interfere with or impede learning in a regular classroom, there is no need to specify special instruction or strategies for the student in this category.

LCCE Applications

The LCCE curriculum in its three domains addresses the basic needs of students who are physically disabled. The nature of this disability calls for a physical approach to learning. Students need to learn how to get around in the community, how to care for their personal needs, and how to acquire community-needed resources. The personal–social skill domain addresses many of the problems generally associated with a student who has a physical disability, especially competencies 10 (achieving self-awareness), 11 (acquiring self-confidence), and 14 (achieving independence). These competencies, along with those in the occupational guidance and preparation domain, help these students attain their full right to citizenship, the right to work.

Implications for Materials and Resources

Clark and Kolstoe stated "we have no substantial indication that persons with impaired physique or health differ as a group from other disabled or nondisabled group in their general or overall adjustment" (1990, p. 68). Unless a disability interferes with a student's ability to work in a regular classroom, she is not identified as having a disability and served elsewhere.

As stated by Reynolds and Birch (1982), part of the school administrator's and teacher's daily work includes organizing educational programs in terms of pupils' educational needs by matching instructional designs to cognitive rates, learning styles, and their present and projected educational achievements and making technology the servant of pupils and teachers.

One way that individuals with physical impairments may be helped, if they have difficulty engaging in appropriate motor activity, is through the use of computer technology:

> Three important factors must be considered when designing programming using computer technology: method of access to be used, chronological age of the individual, and educational or life functioning area(s) to be enhanced. (Lindsey, 1993, pp. 172–173)

Computers may be used for educational purposes, at home for leisure games and budgeting, and in the community (e.g., at work, at the bank) (Lindsey, 1993). Computer games allow persons with physical impairments to engage independently in recreation leisure skills. With adaptive devices, students can move about.

When it's necessary to adapt or develop materials for a person with a physical disability, the materials should approximate, as closely as possible, those used by students without disabilities.

...children and youth with physical impairments tend to experience problems related to environmental control, mobility, energy level, and access that make early and consistent career and occupational guidance, encouragement, and training especially necessary.

(Reynolds & Birch, 1982, p. 298)

SEBASTIAN

Sebastian is an eighth grader with a learning disability. He is above average in intelligence and learns some things easily and quickly. He is verbal but has difficulty with the basic skills of reading, handwriting, spelling, and written expression. Sebastian can read on the fifth-grade level with adequate word recognition and comprehension. He performs at the fourth-grade level in spelling.

Learning Disabilities

Students with learning disabilities have a disorder in one or more of the basic psychological processes involved in understanding or in using language, spoken or written, which may manifest itself in an imperfect ability to listen, think, speak, read, write, spell, or to do mathematical calculations. The term does not include a learning problem that is primarily the result of a visual or motor handicap, mental retardation, emotional disturbance, or environmental or cultural differences, or economic disadvantage.

Educational Implications

The major goal of a program that addresses learning disabilities is to enable the student to achieve goals in an integrated, sequential, and developmental manner. Strategies that work effectively for students with learning disabilities generally focus on four major curricular components:

1. Academic instruction
2. Social/emotional skills
3. Organized study skills
4. Career education

Special educators need to be especially organized in working with these students. A successful teacher generally tries the simplest presentation of a flexible approach with students who have learning disabilities. Teachers of these students also need to be familiar with, and be able to use, the predominant mode of learning for each child (i.e., visual, auditory, tactile, kinesthetic). Finally, early intervention is one of the best strategies in assisting students with learning disabilities to begin to cope with and effectively manage their learning difficulties.

Students with learning disabilities generally make up the largest group of students identified as needing special education. They generally lack interpersonal skills (work habits and attitudes, social communication skills), job-related academic skills, and specific vocational skills to learn more than entry-level personal service jobs. This places them in a particularly difficult position: They have high-to-normal intellectual functioning, yet because of those areas in which they lack skill, they are often perceived as less capable than students with mental impairments. Students with learning disabilities are also often at more of a disadvantage regarding interpersonal skills than are students with mental retardation. Generally, students with learning disabilities have difficulty with accepting and giving constructive criticism and with explaining their difficulties.

LCCE Applications

Under the LCCE domain of occupational guidance and preparation, competency 19 (exhibiting appropriate work habits and behaviors) and its seven subcompetencies deal specifically with developing and maintaining the type of skills and behaviors necessary to be a productive member of society. The practicality of this approach is appreciated by students with learning disabilities because they see it as a real-life skill and it provides them with enough physical activity and movement to satisfy their physical needs. It provides them an opportunity to excel in areas of everyday life, which fills emotional needs. Students with learning disabilities generally have lived with a lot of failure in academic areas. Therefore, LCCE is a better alternative in meeting their needs. As a curricular approach, it is a better alternative than merely adhering to an academic curriculum.

Mercer (1983) emphasized the need to provide career and vocational options for students with learning disabilities and to make the necessary adaptations to accommodate their needs.

Implications for Materials and Resources

As with other exceptional students, the diverse learning needs of those with learning disabilities imply that materials need to be modified to meet individual needs. Polloway et al. (1989) provided several recommendations that briefly summarize the implications of learning research on significant deficiencies common to individuals with handicapping conditions. First, concrete, meaningful content should be emphasized in initial instruction. "Concrete concepts depend on direct observation (hence the term concrete) and often involve objects, but observable actions and events are also included" (Carpignano & Bigge, 1983, p. 223).

The second recommendation of Polloway et al. (1989) is to "ensure mastery of new material through overlearning and repetition." Gearheart also suggests that "repetition of items maintains information in a person's consciousness, whereas stimulus enrichment and elaboration are needed for deeper encoding" (1985, p. 122). To prevent boredom, a variety of materials must be used when it is necessary to repeat concepts.

Third, Polloway et al. (1989) recommend that learners be provided with methods of verbal mediation and strategies for learning, recalling, and problem solving. Understanding and learning what is needed to get around the community (LCCE competency 9) and applying these concepts independent of others provide an example of problem-solving.

Fourth, Polloway et al. (1989) note the need to increase attention. Several methods for increasing attention were discussed. "Using novel and varied stimuli properties in instructional materials and increasing motivation through reinforcement are two other logical and effective ways to increase attention and thus capitalize on students' learning abilities" (p. 28).

Fifth, ensuring success was recommended. One way to ensure success is to select, modify, and/or adapt materials and resources to the student's ability. The student profile sheets, Figures 9.3 and 9.4, are formats used to indicate the student characteristics and major competencies and serve as a major approach to planning for successful task completion for the student.

Further recommendations by Polloway et al. (1989) were to provide incentives, to sequence instructions from easy to difficult, and to use a variety of methods and materials.

Certainly the types of employment possibilities available to individuals with mild mental handicaps, learning disabilities, and behavior disorders in a highly technological society should be directly related to the quality of programs designed to instruct them. As professionals become effective at providing meaningful instruction and long-term services, the status of jobs available to these individuals should rise.

(Langone, 1990, pp. 374–375)

Summary

The goal is to reduce barriers and make the LCCE curriculum accessible to all students regardless of their ages. For this to occur, teachers must be knowledgeable of available materials and learning characteristics. After materials have been correlated to the LCCE competencies, the second step in instructional decision making is a thorough assessment of the learner characteristics, which is then used for IEP/ITP development. Having knowledge of specific disabilities, students' learning styles, performance levels, and goals and objectives for the learner (IEP/ITP) will provide a basis for making decisions regarding methods and materials for instructing learners with special needs.

LEARNER–MATERIAL MATCH

Finally, the learner–material match is made. Materials may be selected, adapted, or when necessary, new ones may be developed or purchased if needed to convey the curriculum to the student. The process follows:

1. Review the LCCE materials correlation chart. Are there materials listed that correlate with the objectives on the student's IEP/ITP?
2. Are the materials appropriate as they are, or do they need to be adapted for use with the student based on specific learning characteristics?
3. Is there a need to develop materials?

The learning task stays the same. The LCCE curriculum is appropriate for all students, those in regular and special education. However, if a student has difficulty acquiring skills and information through the available materials and resources, the first type of modification to try is adaptation of instructional materials and activities. Characteristics associated with different exceptionalities may necessitate minor and sometimes major modifications of available materials. The student profile formats presented in Figures 9.3 and 9.4 may be used to guide the adaptation/modification of materials.

Materials Development

A final option in the learner–material matching process is to develop materials. As teachers face the problem of individualizing instruction in the philosophy of mainstreaming or full inclusion, teacher-constructed materials are more important than ever.

Too often, suitable materials are not available; the steps in commercial materials may be too great for a student to understand and master, and intermediate levels may need to be inserted. When it is necessary to substitute for or supplement commercially available materials, the skills to be taught, developmental levels of students, and cost should be the focus of materials development. Some possible formats include learning centers, learning packets, games, simulations, projects (art, etc.), media, charts, posters, bulletin boards, and more. A format for describing teacher-made materials is presented in Figure 9.5 (Cook, 1993).

FINAL COMMENTS

It is obvious that the market is full of materials that address concepts covered in the LCCE curriculum. The problem is not a lack of materials; it is ensuring that the materials succeed in facilitating learning. As we customize instruction for individual students, it may be necessary to use the options discussed in this chapter: selection, adaptation,

Producer:

Title:

Focus Area:

Mode of Learning:

Description:

Objectives:

Content:

Procedure for Use:

Cost:

Equipment Needs:

Comments:

FIGURE 9.5   Outline for describing teacher-developed materials.

Note. From Outline for Describing Teacher Developed Materials by I. D. Cook in *Life Centered Career Education: Professional Development Activity Book* (p. 279) by D. E. Brolin, 1993, Reston, VA: The Council for Exceptional Children. Copyright 1993 by The Council for Exceptional Children. Reprinted by permission.

and development of materials. After instruction, if a student doesn't reach criterion or demonstrate attainment of the LCCE curriculum competencies/subcompetencies, recycling of the stages as outlined in the model in Figure 9.1 should occur. A sampling of instructional materials, correlated to the competencies and subcompetencies of the LCCE curriculum, is presented in Appendix F. This list is limited, and the materials included should not be regarded as an endorsement to their quality; further, it is not an exclusive list. Many of the subcompetencies may be cross-referenced on the materials correlation list. For instance, materials listed under one competency may also be found under another if the materials are appropriate to both.

The materials in the list range from kindergarten to adulthood and address all competencies of the LCCE curriculum. A variety of modalities are addressed. The title, author, publisher, content description, reading, and/or interest levels are also included. A listing of publishers follows the materials list. In addition to these materials listed, the LCCE curriculum also provides instructional units/lesson plans, which include easily accessible, noncommercial materials and functional activities.

ACTIVITIES

1. For each individual student described in this chapter, summarize, in a short narrative, the provisions you would make to ensure that appropriate materials and resources are available to assist these students in learning the concepts outlined in the LCCE curriculum.

   Amos
      Provisions:

   Stephanie
      Provisions:

   Travis
      Provisions:

Allegra
    Provisions:

Stephen
    Provisions:

Sebastian
    Provisions:

2. In the following matrix, sketch out for one semester, in any subject matter you teach, the career education content you want to infuse and what you would recommend to be taught in separate programming. Address each of the components across the top of the matrix. Include the activities and materials to be used for teaching the unit. The materials may be selected from the list contained in Appendix F and/or other sources.

Component / Subject	Daily Living	Personal Social	Occupational
Reading			
Language Arts			
Math			
Social Studies			
Other			

Note. From *Curriculum Methods and Materials for the Handicapped in Career/Vocational Education, Part 4, Developing Learning Activities* by I. D. Cook, 1979, Institute, WV: West Virginia Graduate College. Copyright 1979 by West Virginia Graduate College. Reprinted by permission.

Part 4

Instructional Delivery

Chapter 10

Daily Living Skills

Chapter 11

Personal–Social Skills

Chapter 12

Occupational Guidance and Preparation

Chapter 10

Daily Living Skills

Preliminary Questions About the Topic

1. Develop a list of all the daily living skills you believe students should learn before they leave the educational system.
2. What regular class and special class subjects would be appropriate for teaching these skills?
3. List what you consider to be particularly important instructional strategies to use in teaching these skills.
4. How would you involve parents in the instructional effort needed for their children to learn these skills?
5. How would you convince reluctant parents to become involved in this area?
6. Why would community-based instruction be an important component of your instructional program?
7. Which of the daily living skills that you have identified would need to have a community-based component?
8. How would you capitalize on the interests and aptitudes some of your students would have in certain daily skills areas for vocational planning and placement?
9. What would be some convincing reasons you could use to get regular class educators to teach daily living skills?
10. Who should assume the major responsibility in ensuring that the students are being taught sufficient daily living skills at the various levels?

Only 40% of former students with disabilities can perform such basic daily living and functional mental skills as looking up telephone numbers, using the telephone, counting change, telling time, and reading common signs. This was the finding of SRI International from their National Longitudinal Transition Study of individuals who were followed for a 5-year period in the late 1980s (U.S. Department of Education, Office of Special Education Programs, 1992). This national study concluded that daily living skills are an extremely critical instructional need for students with special learning needs and that schools need to give considerably more attention to this area of the curriculum if these individuals are to attain the level of competence needed for independent functioning.

Although considerable recognition to the importance of teaching daily living skills has been professed by many writers in the field (e.g., G. M. Clark & Kolstoe, 1990; Cronin & Patton, 1993; Mercer & Mercer, 1993), these skills usually are not taught enough; consequently, there is considerable need to increase instructional efforts in this area. The evidence clearly reveals that most students do not learn these skills incidently, rather, direct instruction must be provided so they acquire them at a satisfactory level of competence.

This chapter first presents an introductory discussion of some considerations and techniques for teaching daily living skills. The next section describes each of the 9 daily living skills competencies and 41 subcompetencies contained within the Life-Centered Career Education (LCCE) curriculum. Instructional objectives and activities are suggested. Several activity tips and sample lesson plans are interspersed to illustrate how career education concepts and materials can be infused into various subjects. In the next section, teachers who have implemented the LCCE approach into their classes at the elementary level and high school level provide their explanations of how they are doing it. Next the implications of daily living skill instruction for occupational preparation are explained. An example of how LCCE infusion into a leisure-science curriculum is also presented. The chapter concludes, like previous chapters, with some final comments and suggested activities for the readers.

TEACHING DAILY LIVING SKILLS

Daily living skills, sometimes referred to as *independent living skills*, are those required to function independently or within a family environment. Some examples of daily living skills are budgeting, banking, personal care, cleaning, purchasing necessities, cooking, driving a car, using public transportation, engaging in meaningful leisure-time activities. These skills are those needed to become responsible adults within the home, school, community, and the job. Responsibility for teaching these skills rests jointly with special and regular educators, parents, and peers (West et al., 1992).

Throughout this book, the importance of family and community involvement and partnerships has been stressed. Successful career education in this curriculum area is extremely dependent on the involvement of these resources. In the case of family members willing to participate in helping to meet their child's instructional needs, much of the teacher's focus in this curriculum area can be reinforced and further expanded in the home setting. In addition, community resources such as grocery stores, clothing stores, banks, recreational centers, transportation companies, governmental agencies, and many others can provide valuable assistance. Suggestions for the involvement of these resources has been addressed in previous chapters and so is not be repeated here. Rather, attention is directed primarily to the teacher's role in this curriculum area.

Daily living skills are necessary for successful independent living and working in modern society. Acquisition of these skills can also lead to vocational possibilities for students, depending on their particular abilities, interests, and needs. These skills must be systematically included in daily lessons rather than taught haphazardly or overlooked entirely. Teachers will need to consider the individual's particular learning characteristics before they plan objectives and methods and evaluate the student's progress. These efforts will help teachers and learners to notice improvements in such daily living skills functions as maintaining personal appearance, managing finances, and getting around in the community.

Daily living skills can and should be taught in various course subjects, community-based activities, and in home assignments. In addition to the many obvious benefits for teaching these skills substantially to students with special learning needs, this instructional focus "can provide exciting and realistic activities for reaching academic, general cognitive, and language and communication, as well as social skills" (Langone, 1990).

Daily living skills can be infused into a wide range of academic subjects, for example, reading, English, math, government, social studies, science, and such courses as home economics, physical education, and health. Through a process such as curriculum mapping (i.e., determining what subjects and levels to teach each of the agreed-on life skills), a curriculum committee and/or other educators in the school can identify how these skills can be infused into the school's curriculum.

Some of the instructional approaches or strategies that are particularly important to provide students in this curriculum area follow:

- Numerous hands-on experiences with real materials such as tools and appliances
- School resources such as the cafeteria, nurse, clerical, transportation, and housekeeping services to reinforce the importance of these skills for not only personal functioning but also for employment
- Community-based experiences such as tours, shadowing, mentoring, and instructional opportunities
- Volunteers such as parents and community members to provide classroom demonstrations and activities for students in these skill areas
- Games, simulations of community resources, role-playing, computers, and videotapes to provide interesting and challenging activities and demonstrations for skills development
- Peer tutors who have particular expertise and enthusiasm for tutoring the students in areas of special need
- The cooperative learning approach

Point of View

Career education is an area of concern to all persons involved with exceptional children, youth, and adults today in our work-related society. The main problem I address here is beginning career education early enough in a student's life, through the cooperative efforts of students, parents, teachers, and the community.

Elements of career education, such as daily living skills, self-awareness, attitudes toward work, decision-making skills, and employability skills, must be dealt with early in each student's life. This training will provide a valuable beginning that will shape each student's attitudes and behavior toward the working world.

The school has an obligation of continuing the career education process that should begin at home. Daily living skills fit nicely into this plan, when guidance and counseling runs concurrently with career-related academic instruction and survival skill development. Young students can begin preparation, not only for work but also for day-to-day survival skills.

Parents, teachers, guidance counselors, occupational specialists, work experience teachers, the business community, and the students all play a vital role in formulating and carrying out this aspect of career education.

Teachers can use the classroom as a learning facility that can help students learn daily living skills. For instance, in teaching employability skills, the teacher becomes the employer and the student becomes the employee. Grades and, in some instances, token money may become the wages. A classroom store can be set up where students can purchase school supplies with token money they have earned from working in the classroom. The idea of incorporating a money system leads the way to setting up a classroom banking system, savings accounts, and loans. In this way, the students learn not only the expected

The cooperative learning approach has gained considerable attention and use by many educators over the past two decades and is an excellent technique to integrate students with special learning needs with regular class students. Cooperative learning is a mainstream alternative to ability grouping, remediation, or special education pull-out programs. It provides both special education and at-risk students with the opportunity to develop significant relationships with other students in class. The teacher must carefully structure the learning situation so all students have an important contribution to the successful completion of the task. Group members can help each other learn various material, but everyone has her own responsibility for achieving the goal. For students with special learning needs, a cooperative rather than a competitive or individual approach is particularly appropriate. Teaching daily living skills lends itself very well to a cooperative learning endeavor.

curriculum, but also survival skills such as budgeting money.

Hardly a subject within the school curriculum does not have some relationship to daily living skills. Math (e.g., time, money, measurement), English (e.g., reading), language arts (e.g., writing skills), and Social studies (e.g., map skills) include teaching career concepts.

The special education teacher should assume the leadership role in helping other professionals apply the best of their knowledge and skills on behalf of the students. Without the leadership of the special educator, little will be accomplished; it is the special educator who knows the students best and must acquaint other educational personnel with the nature of each student's disability and its potential effect on future accomplishments.

Career education brings meaning to the learning and practice of basic academic skills, by demonstrating to students the multitude of ways in which these skills are applied in work and daily living. It answers the frequently asked question, "What am I learning this for?"

Methods of instruction vary widely, but the basic principle is to show students how their studies relate to jobs, and to teach them employability skills such as good work habits, decision-making capabilities, and basic economic education.

If you are a teacher who wants to increase the relevancy of education, stimulate students' interest, increase the use of community resources, and create an awareness of the world of work, then try to infuse career education and its daily living skills component into your curriculum.

Carol Ellington-Pinske is an ESE Middle School teacher at Hillsborough School in Plant City, Florida.

Team teaching is another effective approach for providing students with special learning needs access to regular classes. LCCE instruction is being provided in many schools, with a special education teacher teaming with a regular class teacher to teach many of the daily living skills. One example is the teaming with home economics teachers for the skill areas of cooking, clothing, home management, and personal care. One cannot help but be impressed, when witnessing such a collaborative atmosphere, by the effectiveness of the instructional effort that usually results from carefully designed team teaching efforts that have a specified and important outcome for the students.

Community-based instruction (CBI) is becoming more common in many school districts throughout the country. This instructional approach generally involves individualized or small group experiences that occur routinely or more than once as contrasted to field trips. CBI provides students with the opportunity to draw on their skills and use problem-solving strategies with guidance as needed from the teacher. As noted by J. Beck et al., "the general education curriculum divides information into subject areas, but in the real world, students must combine skills and knowledge, and use them in functional ways" (1994, p. 45). Thus, a community-based component is very important to instructional success with students, especially those with special learning needs. In the section on the LCCE competencies, suggestions for incorporating CBI are presented.

Peer tutoring, which has been used for years, is gaining greater recognition today as an effective technique for engaging all students in the learning of daily living and other skills. Basically, it is an interchange between two students in which the tutor helps the tutee in learning content material. Tutors may be of the same age or older than the tutee. Tutoring can take place within the classroom with all students participating, or it can occur outside the classroom or with only one or a few students off to the side of the classroom. The tutor can be the expert, or there can be reverse-role tutoring where the student who is having difficulty serves as tutor to the more able tutee. Teachers who use this approach are generally quite positive about it. To be successful, however, it is important to provide positive feedback to the students, supervise the students adequately, train the tutors, and make regular use of the technique to keep the students familiar with the system (Warger, 1991).

A wide variety of instructional strategies and approaches can be used in teaching daily living skills. In this section, only some have been discussed. Good teachers will be creative, flexible, and collaborative in designing instructional experiences and effective strategies to meet the needs of their students.

LCCE COMPETENCIES

The Division on Career Development and Transition's (DCDT's) publication *Integrating Transition Planning Into the IEP Process* identifies the LCCE curriculum as "a good example of a comprehensive functional curriculum" (West et al., 1992, p. 24) because it includes life skills in the three major environments or domains of adjustment identified by Halpern for the postschool years: personal–social networks, daily living, and employment (1985, p. 24).

In addition to general life skills development, the daily living skills curriculum area of LCCE focuses on three of the four major career roles composing the concept of career development advocated in this book: the work of a family member, citizen/volunteer, and productive avocational activities such as hobbies and other leisure pursuits. Daily living skills instruction also promotes, to a somewhat lesser extent, occupational development and future possibilities. This area is addressed later in the chapter.

In this section, the 9 LCCE daily living skills competencies and their 41 subcompetencies are presented. The competencies and subcompetencies are illustrated in Figure 10.1. As each of these is presented in the following discussion, several activity tips and sample lesson plans—including those taken from the more extensively written LCCE competency unit curriculum materials published by the Council for Exceptional Children (CEC) (Brolin, 1992b)—are interspersed to illustrate how instructional activities could be organized within such a framework.

1 Managing Personal Finances

The ability to regulate finances is a crucial determinant of adult success for everyone. Therefore, teachers must provide numerous activities that prepare students for their roles as spenders, savers, and managers of their money. This should include the following subcompetencies:

1.1 Count Money and Make Correct Change

The beginning skill for this subcompetency is the successful identification of several forms of currency. Students with visual disability may accomplish this skill by becoming familiar with the size of metal coins and by folding paper money of various denominations at different corners. Arithmetic exercises or play stores can be used to teach primary-grade students how to count and manipulate coins and bills.

Numerous teaching aids and commercial workbooks are available to help teachers initiate activities that would require students to make correct change and use money in various situations. Parents can provide students with money to buy lunch or spend on field trips. Other objectives related to this subcompetency should include demonstrating the ability to make change and identifying uses of money in society.

1.2 Make Reasonable Expenditures

The ability to select goods and services is valuable in a society that experiences inflation, economic stagnation, and prosperity. This subcompetency focuses on the student as a consumer who can use tags and labels to evaluate merchandise, who considers the advantages and disadvantages of discount stores, and who develops strategies for buying during bargain sales. These skills are especially helpful to those with low incomes. Teachers can acquire commercial materials that include specific exercises in consumer education. However, in general, the instructor should conduct classroom activities that require students to compare products sold at different stores or markets, itemize their family's purchases during a given period of time, or construct a shopping list and record prices of items at a given store. These assignments can begin at the primary level, and experience has taught us that students use these skills repeatedly through the adult years. These practices also sharpen the student's ability to make decisions regarding which products and services to use.

A final consideration for all consumers is an awareness of common advertising gimmicks and traps. Local consumer protection agencies and groups can provide the class with materials and demonstrations that will further supplement this part of the curriculum. Other objectives should include distinguishing essential items from luxuries and engaging in comparative shopping.

Curriculum Area	Competency	Subcompetency: The student will be able to:	
	1. Managing Personal Finances	1. Count money & make correct change	2. Make responsible expenditures
	2. Selecting & Managing a Household	7. Maintain home exterior/interior	8. Use basic appliances and tools
	3. Caring for Personal Needs	12. Demonstrate knowledge of physical fitness, nutrition & weight	13. Exhibit proper grooming & hygiene
	4. Raising Children & Meeting Marriage Responsibilities	17. Demonstrate physical care for raising children	18. Know psychological aspects of raising children
DAILY LIVING SKILLS	5. Buying, Preparing & Consuming Food	20. Purchase food	21. Clean food preparation areas
	6. Buying & Caring for Clothing	26. Wash/clean clothing	27. Purchase clothing
	7. Exhibiting Responsible Citizenship	29. Demonstrate knowledge of civil rights & responsibilities	30. Know nature of local, state & federal governments
	8. Utilizing Recreational Facilities & Engaging in Leisure	33. Demonstrate knowledge of available community resources	34. Choose & plan activities
	9. Getting Around the Community	38. Demonstrate knowledge of traffic rules & safety	39. Demonstrate knowledge & use of various means of transportation

FIGURE 10.1   Life-centered education competencies: Daily living skills curriculum area.

Note. From *Life Centered Career Education: A Competency-Based Approach* (4th ed., pp. 12–13) by D. E. Brolin, 1993, Reston, VA: The Council for Exceptional Children. Copyright 1993 by The Council for Exceptional Children. Reprinted by permission.

◆ **Activity Tip**

Students can keep a record and calculate their parents' expenditures for a week or their own expenses for a longer period. The student should pace budget headings on the left-hand side of a ruled sheet of paper. The days of the week or months of the year are placed at the top of the page. Dollar amounts are entered for the following budget headings: rent, utilities, food, transportation, clothing, medical expenses, insurance, taxes, entertainment, savings, others. Advanced students can calculate the percentage of expenditures per budget heading. ◆

1.3   Keep Basic Financial Records

Successful adults can maintain a minimum number of records. However, they must be able to identify those receipts, bank statements, or contracts that should be preserved to plan a budget, meet bills, and file tax returns. The goal of these activities is to help the student develop a personal system of record keeping and filing. Children are introduced to logical systems when they develop hobbies that involve organizing events or

3. Keep basic financial records	4. Calculate & pay taxes	5. Use credit responsibly	6. Use banking services
9. Select adequate housing	10. Set up household	11. Maintain home grounds	
14. Dress appropriately	15. Demonstrate knowledge of common illness, prevention & treatment	16. Practice personal safety	
19. Demonstrate marriage responsibilities			
22. Store food	23. Prepare meals	24. Demonstrate appropriate eating habits	25. Plan/eat balanced meals
28. Iron, mend & store clothing			
31. Demonstrate knowledge of the law & ability to follow the law	32. Demonstrate knowledge of citizen rights & responsibilities		
35. Demonstrate knowledge of the value of recreation	36. Engage in group & individual activities	37. Plan vacation time	
40. Find way around the community	41. Drive a car		

FIGURE 10.1 *continued*

materials, such as collecting stamps, pictures, or bubble gum cards. Several commercial publishers provide instructional materials explaining banking procedures and how to maintain records and calculate taxes. The crucial concern for the teacher is whether the student has practiced and uses a record-keeping system. Once students incorporate a system into their daily activities, they have acquired the necessary skills for the development of this subcompetency. Other objectives should include constructing a personal budget for a given length of time and recording income and expenses and balance over time.

1.4 Calculate and Pay Taxes

Students will not need to calculate and pay taxes in authentic situations until they have earned incomes subject to local, state, and federal taxes. However, the instructor should prepare the student by conducting classroom activities examining the several kinds of taxes (sales, luxury, gas) that affect the student's earnings and savings. These activities can help students identify which items are taxed, how much tax they should pay, and how taxes are collected and used. Secondary school programs should include exercises that will familiarize students with income tax forms, procedures for filing returns, and agencies that provide tax assistance. Other objectives should include demonstrating the ability to complete a tax form.

1.5   Use Credit Responsibly

This subcompetency covers loans and credit cards. Initial familiarity with banks, passbooks, checks, deposits, and the like can begin in the elementary grades. Teachers can establish classroom banks and accounts in conjunction with exercises on the use of money. Shopping trips, as discussed in subcompetency 1.2, can be financed by checking, savings, or charge accounts maintained through the classroom deposits. All of these exercises depend on an actual acquaintance with the community's financial establishments. Although teachers have an opportunity to visit banks, savings and loan facilities, and credit unions, the family has access to these establishments over a longer period of time. Teachers should encourage parents to explain how to use these facilities when they take their children with them to make deposits or withdrawals. Teachers can supplement these activities by asking representatives from these establishments to show the class how to use these services. Other objectives should include the proper care of credit cards, which could present a major problem to students if they are not used wisely.

1.6   Use Banking Services

Students must learn how to manage checking and savings accounts so they can pay their bills and manage other financial manners. Thus, it is important for students to learn—to the extent possible—instructional objectives that focus on writing checks, making deposits, recording transactions, using the ATM, making deposits and withdrawals, and recording savings transactions. The following lesson plan is an example of how one of the objectives comprising this subcompetency area can be taught to an elementary or middle school class at the career awareness level. The instructional resources included in the lesson plan (i.e., checks, fact sheet about checks and checking accounts, bank statement, and work sheet) are not included in the sample. The lesson plan was taken from the daily living skills competency unit manual published by the CEC (Brolin, 1992c).

Lesson Plan 1   1.6.1A:1

LCCE Objective 1.6.1   Open a checking account

Lesson Objective: Student will learn what a checking account is and will be able to identify basic vocabulary associated with opening a checking account

Instructional Resources: Fact Sheet **Checks and Checking Accounts**, Worksheet **Checks and Checking Accounts**, Sample Sheet **Checks, Bank Statement**.

Lesson Introduction: How many of you have received and cashed a check? Today you will learn about checks and checking accounts. You will learn what a check is, why we use checks and what a checking account is.

School Activity: **Time: 1 session**

Task:

1. **Advance Preparation:** Use Sample Sheet **Checks** to write a check for each student. (Checks are also used in Lesson Plans 8, 9, and 10.)
2. Distribute checks to students. Ask students why they might not be able to cash their checks. Be sure to include ideas such as the check writer has not opened a checking account and does not have a balance.
3. Distribute Fact Sheet **Checks and Checking Accounts**. Use the students' checks to facilitate the fact sheet discussion.
4. Distribute and discuss Sample Sheet **Bank Statement**. Use the students checks and the fact sheet to facilitate discussion.
5. Distribute and explain Worksheet **Checks and Checking Accounts**. Students work with a partner and discuss responses with the class after completing.
6. Have students identify times when they may write checks or use a checking account as a family member/homemaker, citizen/volunteer, employee or for avocational activities.

Lesson Plan Evaluation:

Activity: Students will complete Worksheet **Checks and Checking Accounts**.

Criteria: Student will complete the worksheet with 80% accuracy.

Career Role: Family Member/Homemaker, Employee, Citizen/Volunteer, Avocational

Career Stage: Awareness

Note. From *Life Centered Career Education: Competency Units for Daily Living Skills* (Vol. 1., p. 203) by D. E. Brolin, 1992, Reston, VA: The Council for Exceptional Children. Copyright 1992 by The Council for Exceptional Children. Reprinted by permission.

2   Select and Manage Household

A major portion of the average person's salary is spent on housing. In certain parts of the country, the monthly rent for an apartment or house may exceed the costs for food. Housing costs that exceed the average worker's salary place increased stress on his ability to maintain independence. The young person may have to reside with the family for a longer period of time or seek peers who will share costs. These situations require individuals to be alert for ways to minimize expenses for maintaining a home.

2.7   Maintain Home Exterior/Interior

Although the majority of young adults will live in apartments, they should understand and practice skills that contribute to the preservation of both the exterior and interior of the dwelling. Students should learn the common tools, products and equipment used in both inside and outside for home maintenance work. Students should review owner's manuals, observe demonstrations, learn safety procedures, and then learn to use the various materials required for satisfactory interior and exterior home maintenance.

◆ **Activity Tip**

Students and parents cooperate in constructing a large diagram of their house or apartment. Symbols that represent various tools required to maintain and clean the dwelling and that the student can use successfully should be entered at the bottom of the diagram. Students can create their own symbols for such functions as sweeping and dusting. A chart can be added indicating the functions and the days of the week. The chart can help parents and teachers keep track of the student's progress. Both the diagram and chart can be expanded to fit the student's abilities. ◆

2.8   Use Basic Appliances and Tools

Appliances can be used to clean or repair the home. The latter include such tools as a hammer, saw, screwdriver, or wrench. The teacher's goal is to develop student competencies with appliances and tools that would be used in the home to maintain cleanliness and ensure that doors, windows, and locks are in working order. This means that students would be able to make basic home repairs and improvements such as replacing screens or light bulbs, tightening screws or bolts, and painting doors or walls. The special education teacher should plan these activities with the assistance of home economics and industrial arts teachers. Other objectives should include using safety procedures in working with tools and appliances. A sample lesson plan written by a teacher using her own format for teaching this subcompetency is presented next.

Sample Lesson Plan

Author: Lynn S. Miller
Level: Elementary   **Situation:** Students with multiple disabilities
Period: Language arts   **Time Span:** One week

Objective: Subcompetency 2.2: Students will identify and demonstrate the use of basic appliances and tools found in the home.

Activity Title: *Field Trip to an Appliance Store*
Goal of Activity: Students will participate in a field trip to a local appliance store and will identify a variety of home appliances and tools.

Activity: Students will take a field trip to an appliance store in the community. While touring the store, each student will compile a list of as many appliances and tools as possible. Students may need assistance from the teacher to develop a list. The students should ask a store employee for any catalogs or advertising material concerning home appliances and tools that are available. Students should also collect a business card that they can put into their field trip file.

Activity Title: *My Home Appliances and Tools Notebook*

Goal of Activity: Students will compile a booklet picturing basic home appliances and tools.

Activity: Students will look for pictures of a variety of home appliances and tools found in magazines, newspapers, catalogs, and brochures that they have received from an appliance store. After pasting their pictures onto a piece of construction paper, students will label each tool and appliance. These pages will be placed in a booklet form and titled *My Home Appliance and Tools Notebook*. The students will also discuss the function of each appliance and tool.

Activity Title: *Are You Using Your Appliances and Tools Correctly?*

Goal of Activity: Students will become familiar with safety procedures involved in using various home appliances and tools.

Activity: The teacher will bring several home appliances and tools to the classroom and will discuss and demonstrate procedures for using these materials safely. While showing students how to use each device, the teacher should explain what the appliance or tool is used for. Before each student has the opportunity to operate the appliance or tool, the student should be aware of the safety procedures involved in operating the device. A photograph will be taken as the student demonstration is taking place. Students wil construct a bulletin board using these photos. They will label each appliance and tool and make a list of safety procedures that will accompany each photo.

Evaluation: After discussing their field trip to the appliance store, students will illustrate and write a sentence or a short story about their experience. Students will also share *My Home Appliance and Tools Notebook* with their parents and should list the appliances and tools found in their homes. Finally students will discuss the function and safety procedures of a variety of home appliances and tools.

Related Subcompetencies: 3.16   Practice personal safety
                             12.53 Demonstrate proper behavior in public places
                             16.68 Communicate with understanding

2.9   Select Adequate Housing

Awareness of a family's needs for living space and facilities begins in the primary grades. Students can draw their homes or apartments, collect pictures of various rooms, and identify family functions in each part of the dwelling. This general inquiry leads to expanded knowledge of various types of housing available in the community. The teacher should stress the advantages and disadvantages of each dwelling. This includes discussions about space, costs, utilities, and location. Students in the intermediate grades can gather information by interviewing realty agents, family members, and newspaper advertisers. Secondary students should continue with specific exercises related to renting a home or apartment, deposits, leases, tenant rights and responsibilities, and community agencies that can assist the individual with more complicated decisions involving the purchase of property. Another objective should be identifying important considerations in renting an apartment or buying a house.

2.10   Set Up Household

Setting up a household requires students to learn how to obtain utility services, basic household items, and furniture and appliances. Parent and community-based field trip experiences are important activities to include in these lessons. For example, parents can discuss with their child the utilities used in the home, show records of bills and installation agreements, and take them to visit stores that sell basic household items, furniture, and major appliances. The use of telephone directories and newspapers is also important in gaining an adequate understanding of the use of services and the purchase of basic household items.

2.11   Maintain Home Grounds

The subcompetency called maintain home grounds is an extension of 2.7 and requires the student to perform home maintenance and repairs such as grass cutting, painting, bush trimming, and the like. Parents and persons employed in this type of business are to be involved in the students' career development.

3   Caring for Personal Needs

Adequate hygiene, physical condition, and health care are of special importance to those individuals who are susceptible to injury, illness, or irritation associated with their impairment. Relatives will probably try to help these individuals learn how to take care of personal needs, but the teacher's objectivity can help to balance the emotional involvement of relatives who identify with the individual.

3.12   Demonstrate Knowledge of Physical Fitness, Nutrition, and Weight

Development of the Special Olympics was motivated by the fact that individuals with mental retardation had received little or no instruction in physical education or recreation in public schools and institutions. The Special Olympics help to dramatize that all individuals possess physical competence. Proper care and development of the body are vital to meet the physical demands of everyday life. Students should demonstrate knowledge of major body parts and perform exercises or activities that benefit development. As students develop fundamental knowledge of basic food groups, nutrition, and weight control, teachers should enlist cooperation of physical education, recreation, and home economics professionals. Students can maintain their own health charts by recording maturation, eating habits, or games and exercises. Other objectives include performing activities that maintain appropriate physical fitness and demonstrating eating practices that contribute to proper nutrition.

3.13 Exhibit Proper Grooming and Hygiene

Students should demonstrate ability to brush their teeth, wash their hands and face, use handkerchiefs, towels, and napkins, and maintain a clean appearance. Teachers from intermediate grades through adult education should continue to help students develop these abilities and expand their awareness of personal hygiene and grooming habits that are appropriate for males and females. This is one of the most vital subcompetencies because acceptance of an individual by peers, adults, and employers is usually based on personal appearance. Another objective should include demonstrating the use of appropriate health and grooming aids.

◆ Activity Tip

Each student constructs a grooming card that he can carry in a wallet or purse. The grooming card is similar to an identification card but contains reminders of grooming appropriate to the student's concern (i.e., hair style, make-up, and clean glasses). Teachers, counselors, and parents periodically check the grooming card for proper identification! ◆

3.14 Dress Appropriately

Social standards concerning acceptable attire for both men and women have become less rigorous. The broad range of acceptable attire presents a new burden to teachers who must instruct students on the types of clothing that are appropriate for different weather conditions, social settings, and work situations. Elementary school students could construct bulletin boards containing displays that illustrate the major forms of dress. When planning activities related to this skill, teachers should focus on the relationship between health and appropriate attire. Teachers can also use role-playing techniques to help adolescents become more aware of the social ramifications involved in dressing to meet the occasion. Students can use the feedback provided by role playing to evaluate the appropriateness of their attire. Another objective should include demonstrating competence in selecting appropriate leisure and work attire.

3.15 Demonstrate Knowledge of Common Illness Prevention and Treatment

Demonstrating knowledge of illness prevention and treatment methods is one of the most complex subcompetencies. This area includes information about illnesses and basic symptoms, hazards to health that occur in the home, basic first-aid techniques, and obtaining assistance for various medical problems. The lessons on illness will be significant to individuals who must guard against dangers in the environment that can complicate a primary disability, for example, respiratory infections for the physically disabled, or an inflamed eyelid for the deaf. Students in the primary grades should begin learning basic health measures that will prevent illnesses or injury. The students' experiences will provide ample subject matter, and the instructor should provide numerous practice sessions requiring students to contact emergency facilities in the event of illness or injury. The range of subject matter increases as instruction includes first aid, safety considerations, health facilities, and professionals. Local public health facilities or agents can provide demonstrations and audiovisual aids to assist instruction in these competencies.

Sample Lesson Plan

Author: Lynda Glascoe

Level: Junior high school   **Situation:** Resource specialist program

Period: Four (home activity included)   **Time Span:** One week

Objective: Subcompetency 3.15: The student will differentiate between healthful and unhealthful products advertised in magazines and on television. These activities should be used after basic instruction on nutrition and chemical abuse.

Activity Title: *Do Magazines Advertise Healthful Products?*

Goal of Activity: Students rate products advertised in magazines according to their appropriateness to good health.

Activity: The teacher leads a discussion on how advertising affects eating habits and how this could influence health. Provide different types of magazines (women's, teens', and sports). The student cuts out advertisements of products that can be eaten or are related to health (e.g. food, drinks, medicine, and cigarettes). The student glues each advertisement on a separate piece of paper and answers the following questions about each product (this can be done in questionnaire form or written in a paragraph).

1. Is this product good for you?
     Yes   No   Don't know
2. Do you like it?
     Yes   No   Don't know
3. Would you use it?
   Yes, a lot
   Yes, sometimes
   Yes, but only when an adult says it's okay
   No

Activity Title: *Does Television Advertise Healthful Products?*

Goal of Activity: Students rate the appropriateness of products advertised on television to good health.

Activity: Students will watch television during *normal* viewing hours and will record the time and the program they watched. Since this activity will probably be conducted almost entirely at home (unless a television is available for classroom use), parent involvement is important. Teachers should contact parents to explain the objectives of this activity and encourage their assistance. After students have listed all commercials that advertise products to eat or drink (including medicines), students will answer the questions given in the previous activity. These activities will be included in a folder with the previous cutouts.

Evaluation: Students will list five healthful and five unhealthful products that are frequently advertised in magazines or on television. Given five advertisements, the student will state reasons why the product is healthful or unhealthful.

Related Subcompetencies: 15.64   Look at alternatives

15.63   Anticipate consequence

3.16   Practice Personal Safety

Objectives for the subcompetency of practicing personal safety focus on home security, personal assault, and self-defense techniques. This skill area has become extremely important with the rising violence and crime in our society. The involvement of parents, law enforcement officials, self-defense specialists, and community services such as gas and electric companies can help students learn safety precautions and potential hazards. Role-play activities will enhance this instruction, which should begin at the elementary level.

4   Raising Children—Family Living

Learning to raise a family begins with the individual's experiences as a family member. Teachers should help students observe child-rearing practices of their families, relatives, or neighbors. Many of the skills required in mastering the subcompetencies will be based on students' observations and reporting skills. Students' observations can help teachers prepare lessons on successful child–parent interactions. Experience is the best teacher, but when room for experimentation is limited, observation of others' experiences also avoids needless trial and error. Teachers in secondary and adult programs can also provide students with ample opportunity to ask questions about raising children and can provide them with enough sources of information so that students may obtain in-depth answers.

4.1   Demonstrate Physical Care for Raising Children

Children have various needs at successive developmental stages. Infant care and feeding, inoculation for diseases, appropriate diet, clothing, exercise, and protection are important throughout all stages of development. The intensity of these needs may vary depending on all particular characteristics of the individual. Students can use their own life experiences with each topic area to develop appropriate methods of working with their future children. This is one way the teacher can emphasize child-rearing procedures when, in actuality, the main topic of consideration is projected to some time in the future. Other objectives should include demonstrating proper care of a child and demonstrating basic protection measures for a child.

◆ **Activity Tip**

Each student is given an egg and a shoe box. The egg represents a new baby, and each shoe box is a bed or home. The student is to provide and care for the child. The student must plan a schedule that includes bathing, feeding, changing, and so on. Classroom discussions can include the difficulties and fun aspects of the assignment. ◆

4.2   Know Psychological Aspects of Raising Children

In preparing the student to meet the psychological responsibilities of marriage and child rearing, the teacher must develop the student's awareness of some basic emotional needs. Discussions of love, support, and acceptance probe the structure of the student's sense of self and identify the conceptions and attitudes that are basic to the individual's behavior. These encounters may include identification of the student's needs as a child or at various stages of development, reflections on behaviors that meet these needs, and the parent's role in providing for this aspect of the child. In understanding their emotional needs as children, students can approach the problem of building a psychological environment that fosters personal growth. Other objectives should include identifying potential family problems and identifying community agencies that provide assistance with family problems.

◆ **Activity Tip**

The teacher or counselor arranges the class into a "family circle." All students are members of the same family. Each session focuses on an incident or problem that confronts a family (i.e., planning a vacation or sending a child to summer camp). Teachers should select problem areas that have particular importance to the class. The students can question the professional for more details but must present alternative solutions, writing, and other creative endeavors that reflect individual and group solutions. ◆

4.2   Demonstrate Marriage Responsibilities

The focus of the teacher's lessons should be on the personal adjustments that each partner must make during marriage. Students can certainly observe the give and take in decision-making processes that occur in their families: They may also have some experience adjusting to brothers and sisters, playmates, club members, or peers. Of course, these situations hedge around the actual experiences accompanying marriage. Nevertheless, these experiences test students' abilities to plan cooperatively with others, express their opinions, and develop other basic skills that contribute to a successful marriage. The teacher may discuss various aspects of marriage that require careful decision making. Mutual concern and respect, shared responsibilities in the home, earning a living, managing the household, visiting relatives, and planning a family are just a few issues for discussion. Other objectives should include identifying personal and joint adjustments in life-style necessary in marriage.

5 Buying and Preparing Food

Competency 5 relates to the purchase, preparation, and consumption of food. It also involves an area of life that functions as a reward; thus, food is used frequently as a reinforcer for student performance in the classroom. The role of food as both a necessary substance for life and reward for behavior places an additional responsibility on teachers who must develop student abilities in distinguishing between the two. The following subcompetencies are by no means the last word in planning, purchasing, and preparing food, so teachers should expand this area to meet the particular needs and abilities of their students.

5.20 Purchase Food

Purchasing food is related to the subcompetency on making responsible expenditures (1.2) and provides ample opportunity for teachers to train students in the use of measuring units of food and calculating costs. Unfortunately, students are often immersed in a world of advertisements for foods. Buying goodies can become the subject matter for daily assignments in purchasing meals at the school cafeteria, calculating the cost of a bag lunch, or projecting future expenses for after-school snacks. In later years, with the recommended assistance of home economics instructors or representatives from community consumer organizations, students should be exposed to lessons that will help them recognize differences in the quality of foods, various types and cuts of meat and fish, and the advantages of sales and specials. Other objectives should include identifying community sources of information about food prices and constructing a shopping list within a budget.

◆ **Activity Tip**

The teacher provides the class with a list of basic food items. Students price each item at their local store or supermarket. These prices form the basis for activities requiring students to compare prices of food items, compute costs for a given number of items, and select items based on fixed amount of money. The complexity of the activity can be adjusted to the ability of the individual student. ◆

5.21 Clean Food Preparation Areas

Teachers should stress that the cleaning process is just as important as preparation of food. After all, food disappears, but dirty dishes remain for the next meal. This subcom-

Students from Grand Rapids, Michigan, Central High School learning grocery shopping skills.

petency includes skills involved in the use of various cleaning measures and materials, disposal and removal of waste products, and storage of utensils. Cleaning up is also an appropriate area for lessons emphasizing safety factors and measures involved in the entire preparation and clean-up process.

The lesson plan presented next is an example of how two of the LCCE objectives that are contained in this subcompetency area can be taught in conjunction with a community-based field experience. Note that this is a career exploration lesson plan and that it addresses two of the career roles composing the LCCE model: family member/homemaker and employee.

Lesson Plan 3   5.21.1E:3
                                                                     5.21.2E:3

LCCE Objective 5.21.1   Identify importance of personal hygiene in food preparation areas.

LCCE Objective 5.21.2   List reasons for cleaning work area and materials after food preparation.

Lesson Objective: Student will learn the importance of cleanliness practices when working with food.

Instructional Resources: Field trip to fast-food restaurant.

Lesson Introduction: Recent studies in the health field have found that disease is spread more quickly by touching than by any other way. Consider a person who has a slight cold and coughs into his hand. If he then makes a sandwich for someone and shakes hands with someone else, those two people are exposed to the cold. The cold germ is passed on to other people through touch. No wonder hospitals are placing such importance on simple hand washing carefully and often as a way to stop the spread of disease.

Community/School Activity: **Time: 2 sessions**

Task:

1. Take a field trip to a fast-food restaurant. Ask the manager to explain clean work area procedures to the students and the importance of personal hygiene, empahasizing washing hands properly. Direct the students to each notice two cleanliness practices they think are important to report to the class the next day.
2. In the second session, have students discuss their experiences on the field trip and report the two practices they observed.
3. Have students break into small groups.
   - Each student is asked to think of one example of when or where it is important to wash hands afterwards or before.
   - See which group can come up with more examples. Have them share their lists.
   - Also have them discuss why washing hands is important as a family member and as an employee.

Lesson Plan Evaluation:

Activity: Students will participate in the field trip.

Criteria: Student will report to the class two cleanliness practices observed on the field trip.

Career Role: Family Member/Homemaker, Employee
Career Stage: Exploration

Note. From *Life Centered Career Education, Competency Units for Daily Living Skills* (Vol. 2, p. 745) by D. E. Brolin, 1992, Reston, VA: The Council for Exceptional Children. Copyright 1992 by The Council for Exceptional Children. Reprinted by permission.

5.22   Store Food

Proper food storage is useful in the overall management of financial resources and family health. This process requires that students learn how to store food and identify when food is spoiled. Teachers can use numerous instructional aids available from consumer organizations or companies that manufacture storage devices. Another objective should be demonstrating techniques for storing food.

5.23   Prepare Meals

To prepare an entire meal, the student will need to know how to use utensils, follow directions, identify various forms of measures, clean, cut, and prepare food, and use devices for cooking and baking. Every school curriculum should train the student in the skills involved in managing the preparation of a meal, either by direct manipulation or instruction. Teachers can certainly include parents in the instruction of buying and preparing food. Other objectives should include preparing a meal according to directions and demonstrating kitchen safety measures.

5.24   Demonstrating Appropriate Eating Habits

Society has developed standards of behavior pertaining to eating in the company of other individuals, whether in family or public situations. These standards of etiquette are bent only slightly for some students with disabilities. Individuals who are blind must eat peas with the same skill as their companions who can watch peas rolling around on the dinner plate. An inability to conform to these standards even with some slight modification to accommodate the disability places these individuals in situations that elicit disapproval and rejection by other members of society. Therefore, the student should be made aware of the standards and should demonstrate the ability to use necessary eating utensils and the accessories available to people with physical limitations. These skills should be taught in the primary grades, reinforced in the home, and practiced in specifically designed field trips in the community. Another objective should be demonstrating abilities in restaurants or other public eating places.

5.25   Plan and Eat Balanced Meals

It is quite a step from eating properly to planning appropriate foods for breakfast, lunch, and dinner. Planning does not need to include actual preparation of a meal. Even if students cannot or do not choose to prepare foods, they should know the nutritional value and relationships between food, health, and growth so that they can choose meals that provide the greatest benefits. Many individuals eat "junk foods" that are high in sugar content but low in protein. This is the type of situation that the individual with disabilities must avoid. Second, adequate meals are important for those individuals who receive supplementary ingredients to their diets, such as calcium for bone development, medications of various sorts, and injections. These supplements balance and interact with other nutrients. If a student is careless about her diet, her mental and physical performance will be lowered and her health endangered. Teachers should note that this subcompetency is also related to the one on physical fitness, nutrition, and weight (3.12). Other objectives should include developing a list of foods that are beneficial to health and planning meals within a specified budget.

6   Buying and Caring for Clothes

The old expression that "clothes make the man" has undergone some alterations, but it still signifies a cultural standard that serves as a powerful tool in the classroom. Whether blue jeans or formal dress, sport shoes or high heels, fashions, styles, and the latest "in thing" interest students from elementary through adult education classes, because clothes are related to identity and social acceptance. Proper choice or modification of clothing can improve the appearance of individuals with disabilities and minimize physical deficiencies.

6.26   Wash/Clean Clothing

The principal objective in subcompetency 6.26 is to teach students how to care for clothing. This skill will enhance the student's appearance and use of financial resources. Primary-grade students can become familiar with the effects of various laundry detergents and water temperatures by washing dust cloths, handkerchiefs, and towels. When students begin to wash their clothes, they will need instruction about the various laundry products and about operating washers and dryers. These steps require cooperation from parents, who are in a better position to evaluate these skills.

6.27   Purchase Clothing

Some students will have experience with or influence over the purchase of clothing and food products before they have learned other basics of consumer buying (i.e., shelter, health, transportation, and leisure). The observant teacher will recall the numerous children who accompany their mothers on shopping ventures in the supermarket and clothing stores. These same teachers may face a bitter battle in attempting to counteract students' impulse buying habits. If successful, the teacher will have impressed the student with such considerations as how to select appropriate clothing for different occasions, balance clothing needs with available funds, identify well-made versus poorly made garments, and coordinate purchases relative to the student's needs and finances. Other objectives should include recording one's measurements, identifying clothing for a basic wardrobe, and planning a wardrobe based on a specific budget.

6.28   Iron and Store Clothing

Home economics teachers can help students acquire skills involved in preparing and ironing various types of clothing. Teachers should provide instruction about the why, when, how, and where of storing seasonal clothing. Once again, every attempt should be made to coordinate classroom and home instruction. Skills for this subcompetency include matching thread color and learning the mechanics of preliminary planning and basting, simple hand sewing, machine sewing, and appropriate stitches for different types of tears.

◆ Activity Tip

Each student should have access to a clothing repair kit either at school or home. The classroom or home economics teacher should assign specific repairs to be completed at home, or the student may bring items from home to repair sessions at school. Teachers and parents can monitor materials for the kit, its location, and use according to the abilities and attitude of the student. ◆

7   Exhibiting Responsible Citizenship

Over the past decade, the community participation of people with disabilities has steadily increased. This participation has been encouraged by the success of other groups of individuals who have demonstrated and lobbied for legislation to ensure equality in housing, education, and employment. Once significant laws have been passed at the local, state, and federal levels, these citizens must be prepared to continue their roles as advocates to translate legislation and regulations into daily social practice.

7.29   Demonstrate Knowledge of Civil Rights and Responsibilities

Subcompetency 7.29 includes knowledge of the individuals' rights when being questioned by officers of the law and knowledge of sources of legal assistance that can be used to help individuals answer the questions. Teachers cannot help students develop this combination of skills very easily. Students should role play situations in which they are confronted by officers. Law enforcement officials or members of legal aid associations may also give classroom presentations that concern violations and citizen responses during interrogation. Students should register for selective service classification at age 18. In some instances, the military may be a possible occupational choice. Another objective should be identifying information required for registration with the selective service.

7.30   Know Nature of Local, State, and Federal Governments

The teacher should help each student understand fundamental reasons for the existence of laws, government, and the various roles and duties of government officials. Instead of emphasizing the consequences of violating a law, the teachers should explain how officials and citizens within the community affect changes in the law and how already existing laws benefit them. The teacher may approach the larger federal structure from the same vantage point as in the previous subcompetency. Local and federal structures contain three major administrative, legislative, and judicial areas, as well as a set of statutes, regulations, and agencies. The student should be aware of the instances in which federal law takes precedence over local and state laws. Another objective should be identifying appropriate elements of the Constitution and Declaration of Independence.

7.31 Demonstrate Knowledge of the Law and the Ability to Follow the Law

Citizenship rights and responsibilities are a major element in the entire competency. Subcompetency 7.31 involves identification of laws enacted to assist citizens including those with disabilities. But each right contains a responsibility of citizenship, and students should be aware of obligations that include obeying laws, paying taxes, and being informed on problems and issues within the society. Another objective should focus on an adequate understanding of the basic court system and its procedures.

7.32 Demonstrate Knowledge of Citizen Rights and Responsibilities

The reasons for voting should be emphasized throughout the elementary years. Many secondary students who have the opportunity to register and vote will enroll in training programs. This situation provides teachers with a chance to use practical lesson plans based on student experiences with the process of registering and voting. Other objectives should be identifying the dates, issues, and offices to be decided in coming elections, and soliciting sources of information to speak to the class.

◆ Activity Tip

Students collect an "Advocacy Notebook" of pictures, articles, and information pertaining to the rights of individuals with disabilities. The material should reflect the expanding role of individuals in civic and social functions. It can be gathered from newspapers, magazines, or brochures collected on field trips or distributed by classroom speakers. Teachers should enlist the cooperation of individuals who have been active in community affairs. ◆

8   Utilizing Recreation and Leisure

A steady decrease in the number of hours in the average work week has resulted in an increase in the amount of time, energy, and attention that workers can devote to recreation and leisure. Various professional and parent organizations have placed great emphasis on physical education, leisure, recreation, and art. Expanded programs, special events, and conferences will contribute to the development of physical abilities, as well as public acceptance of the individual's participation in society. The activities involved in this competency prepare them for yet another area of integration and, therefore, must be considered a distinct and valuable part of the overall curriculum. The career cluster of hospitality and recreation occupations also provides opportunities for future employment if the individual demonstrates particular interest and skill in these competencies.

8.33   Demonstrate Knowledge of Available Community Resources

Teachers can begin to teach elementary school students about functions, events, and facilities available in community agencies, schools, or churches. The next step includes cooperative efforts between teachers, parents, and recreation leaders to encourage and include the students as participants, as well as observers. Based on this encouragement, students can develop an awareness of the range of recreational activities in which they can participate, as well as the resources and facilities accessible to them in the community. An important objective is to strongly promote participation in recreational activities outside the home as soon as possible.

8.34   Choose and Plan Activities

Many subcompetencies related to the use of recreation and leisure require actual field experiences. These experiences enable the student to plan leisure activities. Planning should include factors such as cost, location, travel, physical requirements, use of equipment, and number of participants. The planning and decision making will incorporate the students' experience with prior activities and test their self-awareness (refer to competency 10 in Chapter 11). An important objective is to have each student develop an individual plan of leisure activities.

8.35   Demonstrate Knowledge of the Value of Recreation

Understanding recreational values is closely linked to development of self-awareness. It includes students' understanding of the role of recreation in the overall development of life and can function as a balance to everyday pressures that they may confront in striving toward independence. But students can only internalize this understanding by using leisure time effectively and by becoming involved in activities, clubs, or hobbies. This requires coordinated effort between parent, teacher, and recreational personnel.

◆ **Activity Tip**

Teachers, recreation and physical education personnel, parents, and students should contribute to the construction of a leisure grid. The grid lists the skills required of students as (1) participants, (2) observers, and (3) employees in each leisure area. Each sport, activity, or hobby provides students with opportunities to record their observations about recreation and employment possibilities. The grid can be supplemented by pictures, newspaper or magazine articles, and student essays. ◆

8.36 Engage in Group and Individual Activities

Adequate participation in group activities depends, in part, on the individual's physical fitness and ability to interact with other members of the group. Therefore, the teacher should design or adapt games and group activities that contribute to both goals. The student's physical characteristics are a consideration, but we have enough examples—from blind skiers to basketball players in wheelchairs—to know that physical constraints do not always prevent an individual from engaging in particular activities. Other objectives should include demonstrating proper care of equipment used in an activity, learning safety rules, and sportsmanship.

8.37 Plan Vacation Time

Adults initiate vacations, but children can be included in some of the planning. Children can wrestle with such major questions as, "When should the family take a vacation? Where should we go? Why should we go there? What will we do when we get there? How much will it cost? Do we have enough money for a vacation?" Throughout the questioning process, teachers and parents should present several considerations so children can understand that the final plan comprises several decisions involving family needs and resources. Other objectives should include identifying available sources of information that assist in planning and constructing a vacation plan.

9 Getting Around the Community (Mobility)

In a society that encourages mobility and places importance on such things as cars, campers, ski trips, and coast-to-coast air flights, it is no wonder that teenagers and adults value their ability to move at will. This ability is even more important for those who struggle to commute between home and places of employment, recreation, or health services. Diligent training can prepare individuals who have visual, physical, and mental disabilities to move freely within the community. These individuals should receive training on how to use guide dogs or canes, drive cars, use wheelchairs or carts, and use other forms of transportation. The following subcompetencies are based on the assumption that individuals can move within the community with or without the assistance of devices such as artificial limbs, mechanical devices, or sonic sensory aids.

9.38 Demonstrate Knowledge of Traffic Rules and Safety

The basics of traffic rules, signs, symbols, and sounds should be taught in the elementary grades. Their importance is based on safety for all members of the community. Teachers should use posters, field trips, and numerous audiovisual aids to emphasize the responsibilities of both pedestrians and motorists.

9.39   Demonstrate Knowledge and Use of Various Means of Transportation

Students should be acquainted with the specific forms of transportation available within the community. Teachers should construct lessons that emphasize advantages and disadvantages, costs, schedules, availability, and convenience of various forms of transportation. The lessons should include information on how students can use aids such as tickets or tokens, route maps, and illustrations provided by various carriers. A second important area of instruction would include the student's ability to interpret maps and locate addresses within the community. Finally, students use appropriate forms of transportation to reach school, work, or recreational destinations.

◆ Activity Tip

The treasure hunt game can be used to test students' mobility skills. Parents, friends, and other teachers can assist on hunts that expand from the classroom or home, to the neighborhood, and to the larger community. The hunt should emphasize all aids that students may use to reach their final destinations and should help them understand the roles of various community workers who can provide assistance. ◆

9.40   Find Way Around the Community

Subcompetency 9.40 focuses on teaching students how to find specific addresses so they can locate not only friends but places of business and recreation or leisure. Students will learn how to use city and state maps with the help of family members who should expose them to actual community-based experiences. Another objective is to help students become knowledgeable of community resources and to become familiar with everyday symbols and signs encountered in community mobility.

9.41   Drive a Car

One of the major goals of most high school students is to sit behind the wheel of a car. Teachers can use this to help students develop several other subcompetencies, as well as academic skills. The teacher should work with other instructors to coordinate driver's education lessons. This is especially important if driver educators are responsible for instruction in the driver's manual, state examination, and behind-the-wheel training. Classroom teachers could also be of assistance in teaching aspects of the manual. Teachers can construct layouts of highways and streets (from posterboard or plywood) that contain numerous traffic signals and signs. Other objectives should include identifying appropriate procedures for a driver after being involved in an auto accident and demonstrating ability to make minor repairs on a vehicle.

The final lesson plan for presented for daily living skills instruction relates to this final subcompetency. The lesson plan is a career preparation level of instruction and involves learning road signs, reviewing state driver's manuals, and taking a relevant

Students from Grand Rapids, Michigan, Central High School learning transportation skills.

vehicle safety sign test. The lesson plan spans all career roles as noted at the bottom of the sheet. The lesson may need to be taught over more than the one session indicated. More detailed and specific instructional objectives and lesson plan activities can be obtained by obtaining the LCCE competency unit manuals (Brolin, 1992a to 1992d; Roessler & Brolin, 1992) described in Appendix E.

Lesson Plan 11   9.38.3P:11

LCCE Objective 9.38.3   Identify vehicle safety signs of the driver's education sign test.

Lesson Objective: Student will successfully identify vehicle safety signs from a practice driver's test.

Instructional Resources: Fact Sheet **Road Signs**, colored pencils or markers, state driver's manuals, Worksheet **Vehicle Safety Sign Test**.

Lesson Introduction: Today we are going to take a practice test that is very nearly like the vehicle safety sign test which you must pass to get a driver's license. When you have finished, we will evaluate how well you did.

School Activity: **Time: 1 session**

Task:

1. Distribute copies of Fact Sheet **Road Signs** and colored pencils or markers.
   - Have students color the signs to make them more realistic.
   - Students may refer to the fact sheet and to driver's manuals as needed.
2. Divide class into pairs, and have students drill each other on identification and meanings of signs.
3. When students are satisfied that they know the signs and meanings, distribute and administer Worksheet **Vehicle Safety Sign Test**.
   - Students are to refer to the Fact Sheet **Road Signs** while completing the test.
   - It is suggested that the class be allowed the same amount of time to complete the test as is permitted in your state for the actual test.
4. When students are finished, read correct responses to items, and allow students to correct their own tests. Discuss any incorrect answers.

Lesson Plan Evaluation:

Activity: Students will complete Worksheet **Vehicle Safety Sign Test**.
Criteria: Student will complete the test with 12 of 15 accurate responses.

Career Role: Family Member/Homemaker, Employee, Citizen/Volunteer, Avocational
Career Stage: Preparation

Note. From *Life Centered Career Education: Competency Units for Daily Living Skills* (Vol. 3, p. 1430) by D. E. Brolin, 1992, Reston, VA: The Council for Exceptional Children. Copyright 1992 by The Council for Exceptional Children. Reprinted by permission.

EXAMPLES OF LCCE INFUSION

Elementary Level

One example of the use of the LCCE approach at the elementary level has been reported by J. Beck et al. (1994), who developed and implemented a life skills program oriented to adult outcomes for children in inclusive settings beginning at age 5. These educators note that

> an examination of the functional skills outlined by Brolin reveals a number of areas that also are taught in the elementary general education curriculum for students without disabilities; examples are time, money, seasons (appropriate clothing), and health (body care). When general education and special education teachers collaborate to plan age-appropriate lessons, these functional skills can be incorporated into lessons and units. (J. Beck et al., 1994, p. 47)

The authors note that the objectives they incorporated into their students' Individualized Education Programs (IEPs) were based on the LCCE competencies/subcompetencies for both classroom and CBI.

An elementary teacher in Grand Rapids, Michigan, Diane Wisniewski, provides the following account of her use of the LCCE curriculum at Thornapple Elementary School:

I teach in a categorical learning disabled classroom. My students are third and fourth graders who range in ability from first- to fourth-grade level. I service children with learning disabilities, emotional impairments, and speech and language impairments. I have found that all of my students have benefited from the use of the LCCE tasks and objectives. Some examples of objectives that I have incorporated in my room follow:

Competency 1. Managing personal finances: Subcompetency 1. Count money and make correct change. At class centers in my room, the students start by identifying different coins and bills by name and value. Then as they progress, I give them work sheets saying "Show me $34.16," "Show me 46 cents or $.46 or 46¢." The students then count out the different amounts. When they are finished, they are checked by a peer or staff. This also promotes cooperative learning.

We take this one step further, opening a school store, where the students run it exclusively. They make posters, for advertising, they set up the shop, name the shop, fill the jars with the sale items, count out the items for a sale, and calculate the costs to the buyers. Additionally, they make change with staff assistance and cooperatively count out the profit. This objective addresses many areas across the regular curriculum and LCCE objectives. In this store operation, we incorporate all of our special needs students in our building. We are working for a group outing and also to put some of the profit back into the community. This entire project also relates to other LCCE competencies and subcompetencies, mainly, competency 5, subcompetencies 20 and 21, and competency 19, and subcompetencies 81 and 85.

Competency 9. Getting Around the Community: Subcompetency 38. Demonstrates knowledge of traffic rules and safety. In this lesson, I incorporate a social studies lesson, which is called "communities." In each lesson, I displayed one or two new directional signs from our community. We have open discussions on each, talk about their importance, where we would see and use these, and then draw and display them. At the end of each unit, the students sketch their community and incorporate the signs in the appropriate places. This activity can be used across the curriculum as well as reinforced on outings in the community.

Wisniewski and her colleagues have conducted curriculum mapping to categorize the LCCE skills (competencies and subcompetencies) so they can be incorporated into a K–12 scope and sequence. They have broken down the skills into even smaller units to meet the needs of all of their students.

Diane Wisniewski, special education teacher, teaching her elementary students how to count money and make correct change (Thornapple Elementary School, Grand Rapids, Michigan).

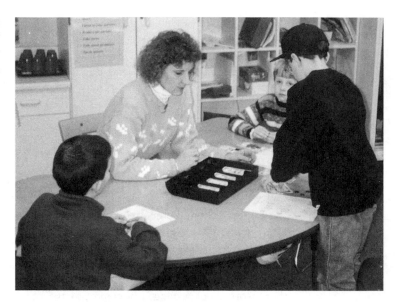

Secondary Level

Pat Burch, Special Education Teacher/Transition Coordinator from North St. Francois County R-1 Public Schools in Bonne Terre–Desloge, Missouri, has used the LCCE Curriculum with her students for many years. She provides this example of how she teaches one of the daily living skills competencies to her students.

I would like to share a few unique approaches and teaching strategies that we have implemented while teaching daily living skills competency 4, raising children and meeting marriage responsibilities. This area is a most valuable life skill and should not be regarded as something our students will acquire on their own. Many of our students develop relationships, marry, and raise a family after graduation. A successful marriage and the knowledge, skills, and ability necessary to make this commitment are critical for them to be happy and well adjusted. It is important to teach our students to show love, concern, understanding, support, and to share responsibilities in a marriage. The demands of raising a family and working in today's society can be extremely stressful, especially for students with special needs. Learning to cope with these stresses in a positive way is provided through unit 4 LCCE lesson plans. Along with independence comes responsibility. For our students to develop successful relationships and raise their children in safe, loving, satisfying homes is critical. The children of our students also deserve the opportunity to grow and mature in safe, happy homes. Teaching LCCE competency 4, raising children and meeting marriage responsibilities, helps to ensure that this happens.

The following strategies and activities that we have successfully implemented in teaching LCCE unit 4 have helped to bring the unit alive and have made teaching the various subcompetencies an enjoyable, positive learning experience for students, parents, and their teachers.

The LCCE approach stresses community and agency involvement. In teaching unit 4, as well as other units, I believe experiences with and obtaining assistance from various agencies are critical. We have established a working relationship with our County Health Department. Their staff has graciously provided us with informative pamphlets, materials, videos, samples, and packets pertaining to a number of LCCE lessons dealing with stress, prenatal care, immunizations, safety, child care, diseases, and so on. We have also opened our classroom doors to various health department personnel, who have shared valuable knowledge and expertise with our students, thus enhancing our LCCE curriculum.

Our students, as well as other community members, have the opportunity to receive valuable help and assistance through this agency for numerous services, such as child care, nutrition, immunizations. Unfortunately, many of our students in the past did not follow through and seek this assistance, although it was stressed within the classroom. I believe the primary barrier to students' acquiring needed services was a fear of the unknown. Students were not sure where specific agencies were located or what to expect from personnel once they were contacted. We have helped alleviate this barrier, not only by having the agency visit our classroom, but by also expanding the classroom into the community to include visits to the agency. We have found that once given the opportunity to experience an actual visit to the agency in a controlled setting, our students' fears are relieved. They now not only know and understand where the County Health Department is located but also have become familiar with personnel and services provided. The County Health Department becomes a valuable source of assistance to our students in raising children and meeting marriage responsibilities.

Parents, family members, and former graduates of our program also provide information and shared experiences as guest speakers within our classroom. This not only provides and brings meaningful life experiences into the classroom, but it elevates the self-esteem of our students, their parents, and former students. They feel a valuable sense of respect and accomplishment. Out students are proud of their accomplishments, and they can see hope for a positive, productive future for themselves.

We always strive to make our LCCE lessons as realistic as possible. Our students definitely relate to and learn more from real materials and people than just reading about or discussing written information in the classroom. We obtain and use real materials when possible, whether comparing one baby formula to another, the proper way to feed a baby, or taking a budget-making field trip to the baby department of a local store to choose necessary and appropriate clothing and items for an infant. Former students have also visited our classrooms with their own new infants, allowing us to experience these lessons with a real baby. All of these opportunities provide meaningful experiences in a controlled setting. (Burch, 1994, personal communication)

Pat Burch, Special Education Teacher/Transition Coordinator, and class members learning about raising children and meeting marriage responsibilities (North St. Francois County R-1 Public Schools, Bonne Terre–Desloge, Missouri).

Burch's strong support for the LCCE curriculum has been contagious in her school district, which is moving toward implementing the approach in a K–12 scope and sequence. In addition, Burch has been called on to give several presentations on her work throughout the state and has become one of the trainer's employed by the CEC to conduct LCCE Academies throughout the country.

OCCUPATIONAL POSSIBILITIES

Teaching daily living skills not only enhances students' abilities to function independently in their home and community, but results in students' developing occupational interests and abilities. In Table 10.1, the nine LCCE daily living skills competencies and their subcompetencies are listed with examples of occupational possibilities that relate to each competency. These are just a few examples of the large number of potential jobs that students who become interested and competent in one or more of these areas may qualify for, with further training, in later life.

TABLE 10.1   The Daily Living Skills with Occupational Possibilities

Competencies and Subcompetencies	Occupational Possibilities
1. Managing personal finances	
Manage money	Clerk
Keeping financial records	Ticket seller
Banking and credit	Checker at supermarket
Buying wisely	Bookkeeper
Taxes	
Keep bills paid	
2. Selecting and managing a household	
Care for a home	Maintenance worker
Repair appliances	Plumber's assistant
Repair broken furniture	Electrician's assistant
Repair electrical items and plumbing	Groundskeeper
Renting or buying	Painter
Maintenance of lawn and grounds	Bricklayer's assistant
3. Caring for personal needs	
Grooming and hygiene methods	Cosmetologist
Sex education	Nurse's aid
Physical fitness	Dental assistant
	Personal care attendant
4. Raising children and meeting marriage responsibilities	
Setting goals	Day-care attendant
Making decisions	Nursery attendant
Choosing life-styles	
Managing available resources	
Expanding and controlling family size	
Providing for the needs of children and adults	
Ensuring the safety and health of all family members	

TABLE 10.1   *continued*

Competencies and Subcompetencies	Occupational Possibilities
5. Buying, preparing, and consuming food Planning meals Purchasing, caring for, and storing food Preparing proper meals Work safety in the kitchen Proper use and care of kitchen equipment, e.g., stove, blender, knives, etc.	Waiter/waitress Food preparation Bus girl/boy Restaurant custodian
6. Buying and caring for clothing Purchase appropriate clothing Clean, press, and repair clothing Construct garments Construct drapes, wall hangings, etc.	Clothing alterations Laundry facility attendant Dry cleaner Clothing sales Interior design worker Textiles factory worker
7. Exhibiting responsible citizenship Know about laws of this country Know about one's rights Know how to register and vote Know about local laws Know about other pertinent citizenship matters	Nightwatchman Security guard Dispatcher County/city clerical worker
8. Using recreational facilities and leisure Know and engage in leisure activities Know and use leisure resources Engage in avocational interests/hobbies	Park attendant Pool attendant City facility upkeep Sports equipment repair
9. Getting around the community (mobility) Use of intercity and intracity travel resources Drive a car Obey traffic laws Know agencies that can increase mobility In general, know how to get around efficiently	Taxi driver Bus driver Forklift operator Tractor operator

Note. From *Life Centered Career Education: Professional Development Activity Book* (pp. 161–163) by D. E. Brolin, 1993, Reston, VA: The Council for Exceptional Children. Copyright 1993 by The Council for Exceptional Children. Reprinted by permission.

One additional effort to illustrate the application of the LCCE curriculum approach to career development has been reported by Elrod and Gilliland (1991–1992). They note that career education concepts can be infused into a blended leisure–science curriculum using a functional application so that students with mild disabilities and disadvantaged environments can gain an expanded view of career options. Elrod and Gilliland have developed instructional units using the subcompetencies of competency 8, utilizing recreation and leisure, to demonstrate a neoprogressive curricular example of what they call "eclectic functionalism," that is, where "traditional subject areas are blended and taught in non-traditional ways, emphasizing experiential learning where possible" (1991–1992, p. 21). Interested readers should refer to their article in the *National Forum of Special Education Journal* for specific information on their work.

FINAL COMMENTS

All of the competencies presented in this chapter are important for individuals with special learning needs and disabilities to learn so they can function successfully as adults. The great challenge of teaching daily living skills is to translate educational goals into manageable components of instruction for individual students, given the circumstances that teachers encounter during the "average" day. It is important to consider the teacher's circumstances as well as the unique learning styles of the students in his class. The increased emphasis on inclusion places even greater demands on all educators to handle the complexities of meeting all of their student's needs.

Teachers should identify areas of the curriculum that already contain lessons relative to the daily living skills competencies. Ideally, lesson plans should be developed for each LCCE subcompetency to meet the multiple learning characteristics of the students. Because such a task would take years to accomplish, an extensive set of LCCE lesson plans is available for this curriculum area, as well the personal–social and occupational area (Brolin, 1992b).

Daily living skills should be the easiest group of competencies to integrate and teach to students, with the assistance of family and community resource persons. Although much of this area is already being taught, in many cases, it is not done extensively enough. This chapter is intended to provide enough information and examples to help educators and parents provide a comprehensive approach to this important curriculum area.

ACTIVITIES

1. Review the daily living skills matrix in Figure 10.1, and then determine what regular education and special education courses would be most appropriate for teaching each of the LCCE subcompetencies to your students. Then, identify those subcompetencies/skills in which you would attempt to involve the parents.

Finally, identify the subcompetencies for which you would include CBI and what community resources you would use to help you teach the subcompetencies.

2. Develop an instructional objective around one of the subcompetencies, and then write a lesson plan for your students, using the LCCE lesson plan format, addressing one of the career stages, instructional settings, and career roles. An LCCE lesson plan outline is provided in Appendix G. The three lesson plans presented in this chapter also can be used for reference purposes. Note the code number in the upper right-hand corner of the lesson plans appearing in the chapter. This coding system is a method to identify exactly what LCCE competency, subcompetency, objective, career education stage, and lesson plan number is to be taught. For example, for competency 1, managing personal finances, the first lesson plan in the daily living skills domain is 1.1.1A:1, where 1 = competency number, 1 = subcompetency number, 1 = objective (identify coins and bills less than or equal to $100 in value), A = career awareness stage or level, and 1 = lesson plan 1. You may want to use this coding system in writing your lesson plan.

Chapter 11

Personal–Social Skills

Preliminary Questions About the Topic

1. Why should personal–social skills be emphasized in the curriculum of every school?
2. What are the important personal–social skills that should be taught in the schools?
3. Identify as many instructional strategies as possible that are useful for teaching personal–social skills.
4. What are the major environments in which personal–social skills should be taught?
5. What are the seven Life-Centered Career Education (LCCE) competencies comprising the personal–social curriculum area?
6. Give an example of an activity tip that would be useful in teaching the LCCE subcompetency "identifying emotions."
7. Explain how you would use the community to provide appropriate instruction and experiences in an LCCE subcompetency area.
8. Define self-determination, and explain its importance and relationship to the personal–social skills area.
9. Identify a conceptual model for developing and providing self-determination instruction to your students.
10. Explain how LCCE can be used to provide self-determination instruction to your students.

Violence and crime have become increasingly critical problems in American schools. Numerous students bring weapons to school, thousands of violent crimes occur in and around school, many teachers and students fear for their lives everyday, and the incidence of criminal behavior continues to rise dramatically in young people, who now account for over 40% of the reported crimes despite representing only 20% of the population (Walker & Sylvester, 1991). Other problems related to social skill deficits include racial and ethnic discrimination, gang wars, school dropouts, post-high school unemployment, teenage pregnancy, teenage suicide, drug and alcoholic abuse, and general social maladaption (Iannacone, Wienke, & Cosden, 1992).

Seventeen State Boards of Education that had developed lists of outcomes or specific competencies they expected their students to achieve identified personal–social adjustment as one of the most critical areas to provide their students (National Center on Educational Outcomes, 1993). Only academic and functional literacy were rated higher. However, this curriculum area is probably the most neglected and perhaps the most difficult for educators to address; consequently, in most schools, students do not receive an organized, systematic, comprehensive, and continuous instructional program of personal–social skills development. Thus, social skills instruction is typically not considered an important component of the school's curriculum.

Who will teach students appropriate personal–social behaviors and skills? Many critics believe that schools should not assume a social work function, that their responsibility is to teach academic skills. However, because academic, interpersonal, and occupational success depends so much on social competence, and because many families are themselves incapable or unwilling to provide this guidance and instruction, schools must give more emphasis to incorporating this curriculum area into their programs.

This chapter focuses on the seven personal social skills competencies in the LCCE curriculum. The first section presents a discussion of suggested techniques and strategies for teaching the personal–social skills. This section refers to the extensive work by Joni Alberg and her colleagues at the Research Triangle Institute in North Carolina. Some of the many social skills curricula in use are also identified in this section. The next section provides a detailed description of each of the 7 LCCE competencies and their 28 subcompetencies with suggested instructional objectives and activities, activity tips and several sample lesson plans to illustrate the infusion of career education concepts and materials. The following section discusses the topic of self-determination and some recent work and concepts by leaders in the field. This section also explains how several LCCE personal–social competencies have been incorporated into a self-determination curriculum developed by The Arc.

TEACHING THE PERSONAL–SOCIAL SKILLS

As in the case of the daily living skills, personal–social skills instruction can and should be taught in a variety of courses, community-based activities, and home assignments. It

Point of View

The concepts of self-determination and quality of life have recently taken on increased importance in the disability-related fields, including special education. The focus on self-determination is occurring as persons with disabilities, their families, educators, and service providers are questioning the passive stereotypes and roles often assigned to individuals with disabilities. These stereotypes are in direct conflict with typical expectations of adults. According to Ward, "self-determination, which includes self-actualization, assertiveness, creativity, pride and self-advocacy, must be part of the career development process that begins in early childhood and continues throughout adult life" (1992, p. 389).

In addition to the emphasis on self-determination, there is an increasing focus in special education on preparation that is rooted in a quality of life focus. The quality of life orientation requires that we consider the wide range of variables that contribute to the student's quality of life rather than taking a more narrow view that focuses only on more traditional outcomes, such as academics and work preparation.

Personal–social skills, as defined by LCCE, have a great influence on one's ability to be self-determined and on the quality of life one experiences. Personal–social skills development therefore is valuable in and of itself. However, the degree to which these skills are mastered also affect the development of academics and employment skills. Generalization research supports the importance of teaching critical skills in all environments in which we expect students to be able to use the skills. The importance of personal–social skills and the need to promote generalization make it imperative that personal–social skills be taught and reinforced in the home *and* the school. These skills are far too important to be delegated to an isolated setting, and they are integral to preparing students for satisfying and successful lives.

Sharon Field is an Associate Professor (Research), Wayne State University, Detroit, Michigan, and a former President of the Division on Career Development and Transition (DCDT).

is astonishing that personal–social skills instruction receives such limited attention in our schools. With the wide recognition of its importance and the large number of commercial and teacher-made materials developed to implement it, one would expect a greater effort to teach these skills. Reasons for this problem can only be left to conjecture: for example, they are too difficult to teach, there is too little time with other requirements to meet, they are not deemed that important, or teachers feel others should do it. Yet, as noted previously, the evidence is clear that a large proportion of students are not being equipped with appropriate personal–social skills and behaviors.

Teachers use numerous techniques to teach personal–social skills. Many of the strategies and approaches identified in Chapter 10 for daily living skills (e.g., community-based experiences, volunteers, games, role playing, videotapes, and cooperative learning) are also appropriate for personal–social skills. Other techniques relevant to this curriculum area include the following:

Various small-group activities incorporated into the lesson plans

Positive reinforcement for certain activities

Brainstorming and consensus-forming activities

Organizing debates or panels of students and/or guests to discuss topics and appropriate behaviors given various scenarios

Bibliotherapy to expose the students to works of literature in which characters with limitations successfully confront life's challenges

Individualized learning centers in which students work at specific tasks at their own rate

Regular classroom discussions covering topics within this area

Coaching and modeling

According to Iannacone et al. (1992), teachers generally prefer integrating social skills instruction within other academic content areas to addressing it in a discrete content area.

Values clarification is a process that focuses on the student's particular mode of reaching decisions and the special importance of his actions and goals. One of the strengths of this approach is that it does not advocate a special set of values that supersede those of the student. The approach concentrates on the process so that the student becomes aware of the value, its relationship to other values, and fundamental aspects of change that the student could use if he decided to modify his beliefs.

A strength of values clarification rests on the numerous activities that have been suggested by advocates. Activities are applicable to classes for adolescent and adult groups and have been used with elementary-grade students. It is recommended that teachers and counselors review the activities carefully if they attempt to engage certain individuals with disabilities, because mental ability and emotional factors are variables in the anticipated results.

◆ **Activity Tip**

The following game can help students clarify values related to employment and personal goals: A former student has a comfortable job at Company A. She learns about an attractive job opening at a new Company B. The position at Company B pays more and provides training that the company will finance. But if she decided to accept the position at Company B, she would have to travel a greater distance to work. The former student could cut the travel time by moving from her current dwelling, but her boyfriend would then be farther away. Her relatives encourage her to explore the possible job. Some of her pals at Company A tell her to forget it, because Company B may fold and besides they need her for their sports team. What should she do? ◆

Alberg, Petry, and Eller (1994) reviewed the literature and identified the strategies listed in Table 11.1 as well-demonstrated strategies for teaching social skills. As the authors note, these strategies can be used alone or in combination and should be adapted to meet your learning style, those of your students, and their developmental age. Because the goal of this instruction, and all functional skill instruction, is for the students to apply what they learn in the many settings of the real world, it is important not only to integrate the instruction throughout the curriculum, but to provide many community-based experiences so generalization and maintenance will occur.

Carter and Sugai (1989) have also studied the social skills curriculum area relative to training techniques and available curricula. They note that "selection of a given strategy or curriculum rests on the teacher's ability to assess the individual's learning difficulties, identify and implement the most viable strategy, and measure its effects on the student's performance" (Carter & Sugai, 1989, p. 36). They note that teachers have many strategies at their disposal that can be used individually or in combination. In Table 11.2, Carter and Sugai provide a list of instructional strategies for teaching social skills and identify some of the advantages and disadvantages of each strategy. This information should be helpful to teachers contemplating a social skills curricular effort.

TABLE 11.1 Instructional Strategies for Teaching Social Skills

Instructional Strategy	Description
Modeling	Exposing target student(s) to live or film/tape models who perform the desired skill. Stories and books can also be used.
Practice/rehearsal	Practicing a specific skill or sequence of behavior, in a structured setting; this is similar to role playing the desired response.
Role playing/taking	Assuming various roles in interpersonal situations.
Incidental teaching	Making use of "teachable moments" to provide instruction as opportunities arise in natural contexts throughout the day.
Positive reinforcement	Rewarding the use of socially appropriate behaviors (e.g., approval, special privileges, tokens or points that can be exchanged for rewards). Reinforcement should occur frequently when the student is first learning a skill.
Prompting	Giving a student cues which help evoke the desired behavior.
Coaching	Prompting a student to use a skill by (1) giving clear instructions for what to do, (2) allowing the student to practice the skill, and (3) providing feedback on the correct aspects of the response.

Note. From *The Social Skills Planning Guide* (pp. 2–13) by J. Alberg, C. Petry, & S. Eller, 1994, Longmont, CO: Sopris West. (Permission to reproduce must be obtained from Sopris West.)

TABLE 11.2   Descriptions, Advantages, and Disadvantages of Instructional Tactics for Teaching Social Skills

Instructional Strategy	Description	Advantages	Disadvantages
Modeling	Exposing target student to display of prosocial behavior.	Easy to implement.	Not sufficient if used alone.
Strategic placement	Placing target student in situations with other students who display prosocial behaviors.	Employs peers as change agents. Facilitates generalization. Is cost effective.	Research data inconclusive when used alone.
Instruction	Telling students how and why they should behave a certain way, and/or giving rules for behavior.	Overemphasizes norms/expectations.	Not sufficient if used alone.
Correspondence training	Students are positively reinforced for accurate reports regarding their behavior.	Facilitates maintenance and generalization of training. Is cost effective.	Very little documentation of effectiveness.
Rehearsal and practice	Structured practice of specific prosocial behavior.	Enhances skill acquisition.	Not sufficient to change behavior if used alone.
Positive reinforcement or shaping	Prosocial behaviors or approximations are followed by a reward or favorable event.	Strong research support for effectiveness.	Maintenance after treatment termination is not predictable.
Prompting and coaching	Providing students with additional stimuli/prompts which elicit the prosocial behavior.	Particularly effective after acquisition to enhance transfer to natural settings.	Maintenance after treatment termination is not predictable.
Positive practice	A consequence strategy in which student repeatedly practices correct behavior.	May produce immediate increases in prosocial behavior.	Long-term effectiveness not documented. Less restrictive approaches should be used first.
Multimethod training packages	Multicomponent instructional package which incorporates several behavioral techniques.	Greater treatment strength and durability. Applicable to a wide range of children and settings.	

Note. From "Social Skills Curriculum Analysis" by J. Carter & G. Sugai, 1989, *Teaching Exceptional Children, 22*(1), p. 38. Copyright 1989 by The Council for Exceptional Children. Reprinted by permission.

How can educators find the time and space to integrate sufficient social skills instruction into their curriculum? Alberg and her colleagues (1993) interviewed many educational practitioners who, although they stated finding time to teach social skills was very difficult, found the time because of their strong belief in its importance for the students' total education. In their visits to many programs, Alberg et al. noted that many teachers were integrating the instruction into existing curricula and into other aspects of the school day. They also found that the involvement of a variety of school personnel greatly enhances the generalization and maintenance of the skills learned to different settings and events. Readers interested in a more in-depth presentation of social skills instruction and program selection are encouraged to obtain the publication *The Social Skills Planning Guide* (1994) by Alberg et al., published by Sopris West, Inc., Longmont, CO.

Numerous social skills curriculums and programs have been developed and are commercially available for educators. Alberg and associates (1993) conducted an extensive review of available social skills programs and selected eight for field study of their use by educators. The authors selected two curriculums each for preschool, elementary, middle/junior high, and high school/adult levels:

Preschool	*My Friends and Me* (Davis, 1988) American Guidance Service *Play Time/Social Time* (Vanderbilt/Minnesota Social Interaction Project, 1993) Communication Skills Builders
Elementary	*Skillstreaming the Elementary School Child* (McGinnis, Goldstein, Sprafkin, & Gershaw, 1984) Research Press *TRIBES: A Process for Social Development and Cooperative Learning* (Gibbs, 1987) Center Source Publications
Middle/Junior High	*The Walker Social Skills Curriculum* (Walker, Todis, Holmes, & Horton, 1988) Pro-Ed *The Prepare Curriculum* (Goldstein, 1988) Research Press
Senior High/ Postsecondary	*Learning to Get Along: Social Effectiveness Training for People with Developmental Disabilities* (Jackson, Jackson, Bennett, Bynum, & Faryna, 1991) Research Press *Life Centered Career Education* (Brolin 1992a, 1992b, 1993a, 1993b) The Council for Exceptional Children

Further information on these and other social skills curriculums can be obtained by securing the publication noted earlier, *The Social Skills Planning Guide* (Alberg et al., 1994).

 Students needs to learn adequate social skills so they can function adequately in the four major career roles.

Elksnin and Elksnin (1991) reviewed eight commercial social skills programs designed for adolescent populations:

1. *ACCESS* by Walker, Todis, Holmes, and Horton (1988, Pro-Ed)
2. *ASSET* by Hazel, Schumacher, Sherman, and Sheldon-Wildgen (1981, Research Press)
3. *Getting Along with Others* by Jackson, Jackson, and Monroe (1983, Research Press)
4. *The Prepare Curriculum* by Goldstein (1988, Research Press)
5. *Skillstreaming the Adolescent* by Goldstein, Sprafkin, Gershaw, and Klein (1980, Research Press)
6. *Social Skills for Daily Living* by Schumacher, Haze, and Pederson (1988, American Guidance Service)
7. *Social Skills in the Classroom* by Stephens (1978, Cedars Press)
8. *Waksman Social Skills Curriculum* by Waksman and Messmer (1985, AIEP Education)

Elksnin and Elksnin studied these programs to determine whether their content contained instruction in the 20 interpersonal skills areas identified by Greenan (1986) as important generalizable skills necessary for success in vocational training programs and jobs. Elksnin and Elksnin found that only 15% to 70% of these generalizable interpersonal skills were contained in the various programs. The authors called for more job-related social skills instruction to be instituted for students with special needs. This recommendation is very important for educators. In providing social skills training to their students, educators must keep in mind the ultimate purpose of the effort, that is, to teach students how to function in the various career roles—family member, citizen, employee, and as a contributing and acceptable participant in social and recreational activities.

So many social skills curricula are on the market that deciding what to use is often overwhelming to educators. Carter and Sugai (1989) have developed a Social Skills Analysis Checklist, which seems to hold promise for educators seeking some guidance on this matter. They propose several "yes" or "no" questions for the potential user to ask that relate to the instructional strategies presented in Table 11.2.

> Does the curriculum use: 1) modeling, 2) strategic placement, 3) instruction, 4) correspondence training, 5) rehearsal/practice, 6) prompting/coaching, 7) positive reinforcement shaping, or 8) positive practice? Then, six programming questions are posed: 1) are assessment procedures/instruments included, 2) is the curriculum adaptable to individual needs, 3) can the curriculum be used with small groups, 4) can personnel implement the curriculum without specialized training beyond that described in the curriculum, 5) is the cost of implementation reasonable and manageable, and 6) are strategies included that will promote maintenance and generalization of skills. (Carter & Sugai, 1989 p. 38)

Based on the answers to these questions, the educator should be able to make a more informed decision.

If students can better understand that the purpose of the educational program is to help them to acquire the proper behaviors and skills they will need to become successfully and happily employed, to attain satisfactory friendships and acceptance by others, and to become an independent and productive member of the community, a greater reduction in the socially maladaptive behaviors of many students should result in schools that embrace this life-centered, student-focused approach.

"Career education at the elementary level consists primarily of an evolvement of social skills necessary in job, family, and societal adjustment; an understanding of oneself; a development of basic communication skills; an introduction to the general idea of the world of work; and an exploration of a variety of meaningful careers."

(Gillet, 1980)

LCCE COMPETENCIES

As mentioned, the personal–social skills curriculum area involves those abilities that are necessary for personal achievement and satisfactory interpersonal relationships. While the daily living skills form the structure of the individual's abilities, the personal–social skills are the muscle and blood that propel the individual toward fulfillment. One's sense of achievement and fulfillment determines quality of life. The individual's ideas about his present status, potentials, and interactions with other people should also be considered. Today, the term *self-determination* is the common reference for this concept and is presented in the following section.

An individual's potentials for successful, independent living cannot be judged merely on the basis of academic performance or competency assessments.

In this section, the 7 LCCE personal–social skills competencies and their 28 sub-competencies appearing in Figure 11.1 are presented. Instructional objectives and activities for each are suggested. Several activity tips and some sample lesson plans from the three LCCE personal–social skills competency unit curriculum manuals (Brolin, 1992d), published by The Council for Exceptional Children (CEC), are interspersed throughout the section to illustrate teaching ideas.

10 Achieving Self-Awareness

Individuals with disabilities are part of the new sense of freedom in America. They have been the subjects of an increased number of television documentaries, magazine articles, and newspaper reports. Legislation now guarantees these individuals equal rights to transportation, education, housing, and employment. Individuals with disabilities are entering the mainstream of society more than ever before. Being able to know oneself (self-awareness) therefore has much to do with becoming a contributing and productive member of society. Critical subcompetencies that make up this important competency area are discussed next.

Curriculum Area	Competency	Subcompetency: The student will be able to:	
	10. Achieving Self-Awareness	42. Identify physical & psychological needs	43. Identify interests & abilities
	11. Acquiring Self-Confidence	46. Express feelings of self-worth	47. Describe others' perception of self
	12. Achieving Socially Responsible Behavior— Community	51. Develop respect for the rights & properties of others	52. Recognize authority & follow instructions
PERSONAL-SOCIAL SKILLS	13. Maintaining Good Interpersonal Skills	56. Demonstrate listening & responding skills	57. Establish & maintain close relationships
	14. Achieving Independence	59. Strive toward self-actualization	60. Demonstrate self-organization
	15. Making Adequate Decisions	62. Locate & utilize sources of assistance	63. Anticipate consequences
	16. Communicating with Others	67. Recognize & respond to emergency situations	68. Communicate with understanding

FIGURE 11.1   Life Centered Career Education competencies: Personal–social curriculum area.

Note. From *Life Centered Career Education: A Competency-Based Approach* (4th ed., pp. 12–13) by D. E. Brolin, 1993, Reston, VA: The Council for Exceptional Children. Copyright 1993 by The Council for Exceptional Children.

10.42   Identify Physical and Psychological Needs

The skills involved in identifying needs enter into the physical, psychological, and social domains. There are some minimal needs for physical existence, but it is much harder to describe basic requirements in the social and psychological realms. How do we measure quantities of security, self-worth, esteem, and love? One way to determine the answer to that question is for students to identify their needs, talk about them, draw them, collect examples of them, and examine the ways in which other persons attempt to meet their needs. Varied classroom activities concerning the necessities of life will lead students to a realization about those things that they regard as essential to their lives.

◆ **Activity Tip**

The want ads of the local newspaper can provide a rich resource of ideas that can help students identify personal needs. People advertise so they can gain employment, sell home furniture, or join a car pool. Students can cut, paste, and place ads in various categories of interest. ◆

10.43   Identifying Interests and Abilities

Individuals with disabilities discover their abilities through their interests. How can a child try or attempt to accomplish anything if his interest cannot be aroused? Aren't

44. Identify emotions	45. Demonstrate knowledge of physical self	
48. Accept and give praise	49. Accept & give criticism	50. Develop confidence in oneself
53. Demonstrate appropriate behavior in public places	54. Know important character traits	55. Recognize personal roles
58. Make & maintain friendships		
61. Demonstrate awareness of how one's behavior affects others		
64. Develop & evaluate alternatives	65. Recognize nature of a problem	66. Develop goal-seeking behavior
69. Know subtleties of communication		

FIGURE 11.1 *continued*

childhood hobbies a means of building confidence through interest? If individuals are to achieve independence through competent behavior, then they must have numerous experiences with those things they like to do, can do, and would attempt to do if given adequate support. With support, trial and error can help the individual build an awareness of physical and spiritual capabilities. This is especially important for able-bodied persons who, through accident, injury, or operation, enter the category of disabled. For these individuals, the rehabilitative process involves supportive efforts that help them identify interests that correspond to their altered abilities. Teachers should plan activities that require students to identify interests and abilities that are common to most people. They should engage their students in activities that will help them identify their own interests and abilities, set future goals, and devise strategies for implementing and reaching these goals.

10.44   Identifying Emotions

Teachers can begin classroom activities that deal with emotions by creating a nonjudgmental climate in which students (whether children or adults) feel free to talk about feelings. Primary-grade students should identify such emotions as happiness, sadness, and anger and should have had exposure to these emotions long before entering school. Older children should begin to work with the problem of recognizing the various ways in which emotions can be expressed. Students should be involved in role-playing situations or should report observations that emphasize various indices of emotions, for example, body language, facial expressions, and tone of voice. A second major objective should be for teachers to develop students' ability to distinguish the consequences of the emotion for others, but particularly, for the self. For example, an expression of anger by an employer may have different consequences from a similar demonstration by an employee. The employer is allowed to let off steam, but the employee may lose his job. Finally, teachers should identify means through which students can release emotions constructively. An appropriate expression of emotion is unique to each individual. Teachers and parents should exert a great deal of time and effort in establishing a foundation of trust that will encourage students to explore feelings and find adequate ways of expressing them. Another objective should be identifying ways in which emotions affect behavior.

◆ Activity Tip

The Emotions Bulletin Board is a sure hit. Students can photograph each other in "typical" expressions, cut photos from newspapers and magazines, superimpose one photo on another, and add their own zany captions and quotes. ◆

The following lesson plan is an example of how one of the objectives of this subcompetency area can be taught to an elementary or middle school class of students at the career awareness level. The work sheet is not included. The lesson plan was taken from the Personal–Social Skills competency unit manual published by the CEC (Brolin, 1992d).

Lesson Plan 17   10.44.4A:17

LCCE Objective 10.44.4.   Differentiate particular emotions in self and others.

Lesson Objective: Student will become aware of how particular emotions appear in self and others.

Instructional Resources: Worksheet **Identifying Emotions,** panel (three or four actors or dramatic readers from community drama troupe, performing arts company or school drama class).

Lesson Introduction: Today we have several guests with us from _____. Their names are _____. They are going to show us what emotions *look* like when actors are on stage. They have agreed to play characters who are going through various feelings and emotions. Watch for the emotions they show us and we'll discuss them later.

School Activity: **Time: 1 session**

Task:

    1. Define the following terms:
- "verbal cues"—what an actor *says* to indicate emotions
- "nonverbal cues"—what an actor *does* to indicate emotions

2. Instruct the class to watch for emotions demonstrated by the actors. Possibilities include: anger, sadness, fear, joy, happiness, surprise.

3. The actors perform short role-plays, demonstrating a variety of human emotions. Their demonstrations convey situations in various career roles, including examples from home, work and community life and from leisure activities as well.

4. Four role-plays (or dramatic readings) will be performed. Use the first two as examples. After each of them, record class input on the board:

   • The students look for a variety of emotions in the person who is acting (or reading) *and* in the people who are observing (students).

   • The class members classify cues of various emotions as verbal or nonverbal.

   • The students identify the career roles the actors portray, and relate the emotions to those career roles.

5. Distribute and explain Worksheet **Identifying Emotions**

   • After the third role-play, the students work individually to record on their worksheet the emotions they observe, including verbal and nonverbal cues of each emotion.

   • The fourth role-play is handled in the same fashion.

6. The students share their worksheet responses with the class, and panel members affirm their responses whenever possible.

Lesson Plan Evaluation:

Activity: Students will complete Worksheet **Identifying Emotions.**

Criteria: Student will record at least six emotions observed, identifying the cues as verbal or nonverbal.

Career Role: Family Member/Homemaker, Employee, Citizen/Volunteer, Avocational

Career Stage: Awareness

Note. From *Life Centered Career Education Competency Units for Personal–Social Skills* (Vol. 1, pp. 134–135) by D. E. Brolin, 1992, Reston, VA: The Council for Exceptional Children. Copyright 1992 by The Council for Exceptional Children. Reprinted by permission.

10.45 Demonstrate Knowledge of Physical Self

Understanding the physical self contains objectives that are specific to the sexual role of the individual. The activities should enable students to develop an awareness of the similarities and differences in the anatomy and functioning of the male and female. This subject material has received increased attention among researchers, parents, consumer groups, and publishing firms primarily because of the long absence of discussion on the sexual role of individuals who are mentally retarded or physically disabled. Teachers should be aware that if they encourage classroom or small-group discussion and questions, they must be prepared to provide information. Objectives involves identifying general systems of the body, listing and describing physical characteristics, and identifying major parts of the body.

11   Acquiring Self-Confidence

Individuals with disabilities have been confronted for centuries with stories, fairy tales, works of art, and popular expressions depicting them as incapable. In some instances, they were not even regarded as human beings but as the embodiment of evil spirits. These ideas and stereotypes linger to this day, and most individuals with disabilities have had experience with abuse or pity by peers or elders. Despite these opinions and attitudes, the students with disabilities must build self-concepts as capable human beings so that they can reach personal objectives and attain dreams. Subcompetencies and some of their respective objectives are described next.

11.46   Express Feelings of Worth

Individuals begin to feel worthy when they experience expressions of value from parents, teachers, and friends. These declarations of worth may be difficult for the person with a disability to formulate. In our society, an individual's perceived worth is based on comparison to other people. Comparative statements are common in a culture that rewards individuals who demonstrate the drive to excel. The problem is that "doing better" is often determined in comparison to someone else. Individuals with disabilities can find themselves at a serious disadvantage if their abilities are always placed in some type of "better than the other person" derby. If the individual loses the race, he might perceive himself as being inferior to others which, in turn, may cause him to lose his sense of self-worth. The parent's and teacher's ability to work with the assets an individual has at his disposal is the key to this potential dilemma. They must move away from "you versus them" situations to "I can do" experiences. By emphasizing the "I can," the parent and teacher opinions change, with a corresponding influence on the attitudes and values of the individual. "I can" is a positive statement of value and worth in this society. How many times have we heard stories about individuals who were told they would never walk, run, or dance only to accomplish that very thing and more? The emergence and success of such events as the Special Olympics and Wheelchair Games illustrate that individuals with disabilities have a strong desire to demonstrate their worth through physical accomplishments regardless of how long it may take them to run a certain distance. Teachers and parents should provide opportunities in which students express how they feel about themselves in relationship to their accomplishments, successes, and failures. What experiences cause students to feel good, worthy, or pleased with their accomplishments? What experiences frustrate them? These expressions provide professionals with an opportunity to plan subsequent activities that will increase the quality and quantity of success experiences. Another objective should be identifying ways in which other people affect an individual's feelings of worth.

11.47   Describe Others' Perception of Self

Students should be able to describe overt expressions and subtle hints made by other people. Because most people are more sensitive to communications relative to themselves, they are more apt to interject their own interpretations onto the behavior of

Vocational rehabilitation counselors can help students build their self-confidence in preparation for their job-seeking activities.

another person. The individual with a disability encounters a particularly puzzling situation when she wonders whether a person is reacting to her personality or to the particular disability. If someone does not invite her to another party, was it because she did not conduct herself properly, or was it due to her artificial limb? She may never get the answer, and repeated instances of these nebulous situations damage the individual's self-confidence. What others think of us influences our attitudes toward the self. These attitudes are used as a basis for further judgments. Parents and teachers cannot control the attitudes of other people—in some cases, their own attitudes may be enough of a challenge. But they can instruct the student to observe another person's overt and subtle responses that reflect either positive or negative attitudes. Many of the lessons on communication (refer to competency 16) should include such reactions that convey attitudes of pity, disgust, condescension, and the like. The lessons should, however, emphasize positive reactions that reflect the individual's self-respect. She must guard against reactions that would be interpreted by other members of society as justification for their folly. Another objective should be constructing personal views of others toward her.

◆ Activity Tip

An effective exercise requires all students to say positive things about an individual. The class may be seated in a circle or at their desks, but the student under discussion should be facing the class. Each student has 15 to 20 seconds during which time other students say such things as, "He helped our team win the game. He came to school on time every day of the week. He knew the right answer to the weekly quiz." This activity helps build class unity, as well as individual confidence. ◆

11.48   Accept and Give Praise

Individual with disabilities need legitimate experiences in which other confirm and show respect for their behavior. Legitimate experiences include those daily activities in home, school, or other environments that involve students as contributing members. Students may receive respect and validation for their contributions from family, peers, teachers, or others. Students not only should receive recognition for their accomplishments but should also be supported for behaviors that will eventually result in accomplishment. Otherwise, students are only rewarded for one achievement, and this may be disproportionate to their total effort at home, in school, or on a team. It is easier to know how to accept praise after having experienced various forms of reward. Other objectives should include listing effects of praise on the self and others and demonstrating ability to offer praise to others.

Sample Lesson Plan

Author: Lynda Glascoe

Level: High school through community college   **Situation:** Resource setting or group meetings

Time Span: One class period

Objective: The student will be able to act out appropriate responses after he has received praise or criticism.

Activity This is a role-playing activity that can simulate actual employment situations. Each situation is described on 3-by-5-inch cards. Each card should contain enough detail to allow the student to understand the situation yet still encourage him to use his creativity. Second, two or more students are chosen for each activity. After the students have read the situation and chosen their roles, they will decide what they will do and say during the play. Third, the class discusses the situation, responses, and possible alternatives.

Examples: (1) Your best friend quit his job and you are hired to take his place. After one week, your boss praises your work and begins to tell you about your friend's problems on the job. (2) You don't feel like working today and your boss notices it. He says "Unless you shape-up, you won't have this job much longer." (3) You worked late last night on the job and your supervisor tells you "Pretty good. But, you could have done better."

Evaluation: Students will be able to identify appropriate responses to each situation.

Related Subcompetencies: 11.48   Accepting praise

11.49   Accepting criticism

19.81   Accepting supervision

11.49   Accept and Give Criticism

Criticism can have a positive effect when it refers to astute judgments relative to standards. However, it is more often taken in the negative vein of fault finding. Unfortunately, criticism causes individuals to feel less than adequate about themselves. This is one reason why students in secondary or college classes hate to receive a critical analysis of their assignments. Fearing a potentially harsh review, they produce less than they can. In a sense, they are already protecting themselves from devaluation. Is it any wonder, then, that when teachers begin to criticize, students become disinterested? Teachers have the arduous task of first convincing students to be open to criticism, and second, helping them recognize situations in which critical statements are of little value in changing or improving on a mistake. The teacher can accomplish these goals by providing respect for students while their work is being analyzed. Respect with criticism builds self-confidence. An attitude of respect says to the student, "You are someone." The critical element conveys the message, "You are someone who can improve on this mistake." The improvement reinforces the previous steps in the process. Another objective should be identifying positive and negative effects of criticism on self and others.

◆ Activity Tip

The teacher leads the class in a role-playing activity in which the classroom is the "work setting," half of the class are "employees," and the other half of the class are "employers." For one day, the "employers" note the characteristics such as promptness, response to instructions, attitude, proper attire, and quality of work. The "employers" share their reviews at the end of the day only to become "employees" on the next day. ◆

11.50   Develop Confidence in Oneself

Students should be aware of their innate dignity. At times, they may have to assert their rights to protect that dignity. These actions are founded on a trust in their ability to accomplish objectives. Trust begins with the first completed task in infancy and is subsequently nurtured by the individual's efforts to accomplish more difficult objectives. Often, the act of attempting a task strengthens one's trust in oneself. After developing faith in oneself, the individual can begin to form objectives and seek the means, appropriate to his ability, of accomplishing his goals.

For example, the movie *A Matter of Inconvenience* (Stanfield House, 1974) is based on individuals who, without sight or a leg, attempt to ski. The war veterans without a limb use one ski and two poles fashioned with small runners at the ends. The three skis function as supports to balance the transfer of weight at each turn. The women who are blind are followed by experienced skiers who provide instructions on turning, plowing, and breaking. These individuals experience skiing and enjoy themselves. Their accomplishments are judged by themselves and not in comparison to Olympic competitors. The experience is of value because it accomplishes an objective through a means that is appropriate to the individual. We are sure that these individuals' self-confidence is extended and that they will attempt other tasks because their trust in their abilities has been reinforced. They are, in a sense, developing faith in themselves.

Another objective should be evaluating the self in a variety of activities.

12   Achieving Socially Responsible Behavior

Society is held together by laws and understandings relative to the conduct of individuals toward each other. These laws have been gradually increased to extend protection to people with disabilities. But acceptance of the individual depends more on her ability to demonstrate responsible behavior in various kinds of social situations.

12.51   Developing Respect for the Rights and Properties of Others

Developing respect for the rights and properties of others involves one of the fundamental concerns on which the country was founded. It is a continuous subject of interest in television, radio, and newspaper reports and, therefore, offers ample opportunity for teachers and parents to pinpoint the reasons for respecting the rights of others and their possessions. Parents are the initial vital link in this competency. They are the ones who have to teach children to differentiate between what belongs to them and what belongs to someone else. Teachers reinforce these basic lessons as instances of ownership that will, no doubt, occur in the classroom. Respecting the rights of others becomes more complicated as individuals grow older and begin to exert their own opinions and power in taking command of possessions. This requires teachers to initiate lessons and draw on the student's experiences that emphasize the relationships of laws, ownership, and the protection of the community.

◆ Activity Tip

"Who Owns This?" is an activity that focuses on situations and decisions related to ownership of property. School situations, newspaper articles, and student experiences provide the teacher with material for discussions and students' essays. The teacher constructs the situation and possible questions to consider. For example, a boy brings a pair of goggles to a swimming pool. He lays them on a deck chair and goes for a drink. He returns to put them on, and another swimmer says that the goggles are his. There is one pair of goggles and two swimmers. What should the boys do? ◆

12.52   Recognize Authority and Follow Instructions

Just about everything students do in school is preceded by directions. The routine and even monotony of the school situation makes it difficult for teachers to impress on students that things are different in the employment world. If students don't pay attention or forget an instruction, they may have to do the assignment again, visit the principal, or lose points. The results become commonplace if they are experienced often enough. But if these lapses occur in an employment situation, students must face the consequences (i.e., "You're fired!"). An equally difficult task is for teachers to determine whether students can accomplish an objective or if whether they lack the skills to follow directions. Teachers often infer that students cannot follow instructions because the assignment has not been completed.

For example, a student is instructed to clean a room in the home economics model house. He is to dust, sweep, and operate a vacuum cleaner. If he did not receive prior instructions on how to operate a vacuum cleaner, he may be unable to fulfill the assignment. One possible teacher response is "Didn't you hear what I said?" This is one reason why students must be encouraged to ask questions or identify those things they do not know how to do before attempting a task. Employers have often said that employees with mental retardation are easier to work with because they will tell the employer about those things they don't understand. Another person may try to fake his way through the job.

12.53 Demonstrate Appropriate Behavior in Public Places

Students should be able to identify behaviors that are appropriate and expected in such places as restaurants, transportation facilities, churches, recreational settings, and public meetings. Students acquire this behavior by imitating other members of the family or peer group. If it is necessary for the teacher to modify these behaviors, the student, teacher, and family should agree on common objectives.

There are common denominators to acceptable behavior across all public places. Teachers should examine these similarities in classroom role-playing encounters, where students report on experiences with family or friends, field trips, or critical reviews of televised events. Like a seasoned athlete before the "big game," the student needs practice that should be supervised by teachers or parents. Another objective should be identifying reasons for appropriate behavior in public places.

Sample Lesson Plan 12.53

Author: Paul Perencevic
Level: High school
Time Span: Over one semester

Situation: Self-contained class composed of students with behavior disorders

Objective: The student will be able to demonstrate proper behavior in public places and learn to follow instructions.

Activity: This is a field trip activity in which members of the class visit a local mall. Teachers should identify target behaviors for the class as well as for individual students. They should give students instructions for following certain procedures, selecting items, standing in line, and responding to questions or comments by sales personnel.

Examples: (1) Students are told to stand in line with the selected items and wait their turns at the cash register; (2) students are provided with written instructions on how to purchase certain items. They follow the instructions from entrance to exit of the mall.

Evaluation: Teachers or aides should observe the target behaviors that they identified before the activity. The teacher can make immediate evaluations and should reinforce acceptable behavior while the students are in a community setting.

Related Activities: Prior practice of the expected behaviors can be accomplished through role-playing exercises in the classroom

12.54   Know Character Traits

Students should be familiar with those personality factors that generally allow them to participate in a group situation that result in a positive attitude of others. What are some of these positive traits? Cooperation, cheerfulness, and dependability form a solid foundation and are also considered necessary in employment situations. There are other traits, but each individual must discover them. This is where experience and observation of others are important factors in helping individuals to change. The ability to look at oneself with a critical eye is not reserved for those with advanced degrees; it comes from practice, with encouragement, at home and in the classroom. Teachers can help students build their observational skills by assigning projects in which students interview or consider someone of their choice and list outstanding characteristics. Once the characteristics are defined, teachers can translate them into behaviors students should attempt. Together, students and teachers should work on a plan of practicing and reporting the behaviors. For students who experience problems in performing acceptable behaviors, the teacher may structure a system in which there is a conscious effort to modify the behavior toward prearranged objectives. Another objective should be identifying character traits that inhibit acceptance.

12.55   Recognize Personal Roles

Several roles are identified across competency areas. Some of these roles are employee, citizen, parent, relative, and friend. Students should be able to describe and demonstrate responsible behavior to individuals (employer, parent, child) as well as groups (union, passengers, clubs) identified with a specific role. This subcompetency requires students to be actively involved in each role so they can realize its full meaning. For example, a student may be a member of a family by birth but not in practice. Parents should involve their children in as many family activities and decisions as possible, especially if the student has chosen a future role as parent and spouse. Teachers should place students in situations that provide understanding of the expectations of others for a particular role. For example, community personnel such as police officers, fire fighters, and employers should discuss their expectations of student behaviors and responsibilities in the roles of citizen and employee. Another objective should be identifying all possible future roles.

It is no accident that the 7 personal–social competencies appear in the middle of the 22 competencies. Acquisition of these skills is essential to the fulfillment of individuals with disabilities; moreover, once these individuals have command over personal–social skills, it is easier for them to learn and incorporate the daily living and occupational competencies in their lives.

The growth of self-esteem is woven into the personal–social competencies. Self-understanding (i.e., abilities, interests, needs, wants) and learning to interact constructively, appropriately, and responsibly lead to heightened positive attitudes about self-worth.

We must provide an environment in which self-esteem can be nurtured with the systematic infusion of the personal–social skills into a structured, continuous program. Isolated lessons and career education classes are fragmented efforts that yield fragmented results. This chapter provides educators with a focal point for weaving the competencies into a program that will raise the esteem of students with special learning needs.[*]

13   Maintaining Good Interpersonal Skills

Competency 13 explores the skills needed to establish and maintain successful forms of interpersonal relationships. It does not include all skills or offer a cookbook approach to an area that has received enough attention in books, magazines, and newspapers to fill a lifetime. It is a skill that interacts with the individual's feelings of confidence and independence and is a key to successful career functioning. Practice is the most crucial element of these competencies for teachers, parents, and students. Students with disabilities need the opportunity to role play expected behaviors and responses for such everyday events as listening to another person, asking questions, providing information, telling a story, and expressing emotions. Subcompetencies and the sense of the objective relation to this competency follow.

13.56   Demonstrate Listening and Responding Skills

Communication depends on the correct interchange of ideas or objects between people. Computers can be programmed to exchange information, but people depend on the meaning and implications of the message. They accomplish this by attending to the source of the message as well as to other nonverbal clues that may accompany it (refer to competency 16). The teacher should develop several abilities so students can complete this competency. Students should be able to attend to the message by using all available senses; develop adequate means of response, such as speaking, signing, or typing; determine the appropriate meaning of the message (verbal or nonverbal); and determine the correct manner of response. Another objective should be identifying negative aspects of listening and responding inappropriately.

[*] Paul Joseph Perencevic, special educator, quoted in Kokaska and Brolin (1985, p. 107).

Students need to practice behaviors that will help them exhibit socially appropriate behaviors in diverse community situations.

13.57   Establish and Maintain Close Relationships

Students should understand the process of dating, various customs relative to the relationship of individuals in the dating situation, and the responsibilities of each role. Parents and teachers face many difficult questions when they counsel young people. "When do I start dating? Should I date this type of person? How do I act on a date? Where do I go on a date?" These few questions provide enough fuel for years of classroom discussions, heart-to-heart talks, and personal growth. Other objectives should include identifying activities in the community that are appropriate for dating relationships and identifying ways to demonstrate that one is pleased on a date.

Families can nurture the skills for developing close relationships. Children learn about personal relations and respect by observing their parents and by interacting with brothers, sisters, or relatives. Before the primary grades, students may have already developed relationships of varying intensities with family members, neighbors, playmates, and therapists. The teacher can begin with exercises that help students identify the different types of relationships that already exist or can be observed in the family's community. Students should formulate answers to such questions as "What are the characteristics of a close relationship? In what manner do people respond to one another in a close relationship? What is its function?" By trying to find answers to questions like these, students develop an awareness of those individual needs that leads to the development of close relationships. Another objective should be identifying persons with whom the student could establish a close relationship.

The following lesson plan combines two LCCE objectives for this subcompetency area. The work sheet is not illustrated. This is a career exploration lesson plan that has application for all four career roles.

Lesson Plan 11

13.57.4E:11
13.57.5E:11

LCCE Objective 13.57.4   Identify characteristics of close relationships.

LCCE Objective 13.57.5   List different types of close relationships.

Lesson Objective: Student will explore the nature of different types of close relationships.

Instructional Resources: Worksheet **Who Am I Close To?**

Lesson Introduction: Close relationships are not always the same. You may feel close to different people now than you did last year. We are always meeting new people and, unfortunately, sometimes we lose track of people we were close to before. Today we will talk more about close relationships, and look more closely at some of the people you are close to now.

School Activity: **Time: 1 session**

Task:

1. Point out that close relationships are not always the same. The people we are close to now may not be the same people we were close to last year. Ask students to think about why this happens.
2. Distribute and explain Worksheet **Who Am I Close To?** for students to complete individually.
3. Lead class discussion of worksheet responses.
   - Ask students to share those characteristics they value the most in close relationships.
   - How have students' close relationships changed over the last year? (more of them, fewer of them, relationships with different people)?
4. Students take turns telling the class about one close relationship they have.
   - What characteristics does the person have with whom they share the relationship?
   - How long have they shared this relationship?
   - Does the student have good communication with the person?
5. Lead a class discussion about the students' relationship choices and why they feel close to those persons.

Lesson Plan Evaluation:

Activity: Students will explore the nature of one close relationship they have.
Criteria: Student will answer the three questions in Task 4 about his or her relationship.

Career Role: Family Member/Homemaker, Employee, Citizen/Volunteer, Avocational
Career Stage: Exploration

13.58   Make and Maintain Friendships

"Dear Abby" columns in newspapers and magazines are filled with the laments of people without friends. "What is a friend? What do students want in a friendship? What can they offer as a friend to someone else? How can they meet people who may become friends? What happens when a friend leaves? Do friends change as one becomes older?" These are just a few of the topic questions that can be used in individual and group activities throughout the year. Students can identify what they want in a friendship, various ways of meeting people and sharing interests, and responsibilities involved in being a friend. Teachers should help students form personal solutions to problems, because in the final analysis, the formula for "how to make friends and keep them" is unique to each person. Another objective should be identifying activities that can be shared with friends.

◆ **Activity Tip**

The teacher should use a coming event in students' lives to help them practice interpersonal skills. For example, a class member has been invited to a party given by a relative. All students can rehearse appropriate questions and responses by taking on the various roles of participants at the party. These rehearsals are applicable from elementary school through the adult years and can be applied to a variety of social situations. ◆

14   Achieving Independence

There is no magic in the term *independence,* and yet it looms as an ever present goal in the lives of almost everyone. Our lives involve a mixture of relationships, from dependence, through independence, to interdependence. Writers have debated whether an individual can ever be truly independent. Writers, who already have a measure of freedom, can debate concepts; but persons with disabilities, who only recently have been acknowledged as first-class citizens, would just like to experience the feeling.

Independent persons can assume responsibility for their jobs and other daily affairs in a competent manner.

14.59   Striving Toward Self-Actualization

Self-actualization is the point at which an individual is producing as near to her potential as possible, is aware of these accomplishments, and feels a sense of fulfillment in them. The emphasis is on current talents and abilities and the individual's feeling that she is doing her best. This competency may remind parents, counselors, teachers, and therapists of the part that self-actualization plays in their own lives. Teachers can create an atmosphere that is conducive to self-actualization by emphasizing students' positive qualities and by teaching them that what they can do is more important than what they cannot do. Self-actualization is not a final end-all goal but a realization that results from many incidents that cause individuals to achieve and feel satisfaction.

During the first 20 years of life, children and adolescents become aware of physical changes in their bodies and become too concerned about whether they measure up to standards. The psychological aspects of physical change are realized in later years, but their beginnings are established during those days when children have so little time for them. It is the responsibility of parents and professionals to plant those seeds of discovery. Other objectives should include identifying elements necessary for a satisfactory day and identifying important characteristics of personal growth.

14.60 Demonstrate Self-Organization

Numerous proverbs and sayings in our culture convey the idea that larger goals are accomplished by taking one step at a time. Self-organization is the process of arranging these steps into a pattern. The importance of self-organization is found in the fact that a task, like getting dressed in the morning, has to be repeated daily and is subject to a pattern of behavior that facilitates its accomplishment. Among other things, children's puzzles convey the idea that an organization—a pattern—is involved in solving the problem. After children learn to piece the puzzle together, they may use the same steps to complete the task again—because the method was efficient or just because they enjoy solving the problem in that particular way. Once students have developed the fundamental ability of creating and replicating patterns of behavior to solve problems, teachers can present an overview of a problem and ask the students to choose the best course of action. In other words, students learn to make current decisions. Completing mazes and the yearly income tax forms are examples of such a whole–part–whole approach. Commuting, dating, and shopping are other subjects for further review, analysis, and organization. Another objective should be demonstrating ability to organize daily activities.

◆ Activity Tip

Teachers and parents can cooperate effectively on the familiar "Things to Do" lists that students make for weekly projects or tasks. The lists provide students with an opportunity to identify goals and can serve as reminders of resources for accomplishing the objectives. They can also be used as sources for classroom discussions related to daily events and accomplishments. Some students may organize such a list for each subject in the curriculum. ◆

14.60 Demonstrate Awareness of How One's Behavior Affects Others

The goal of personal independence involves students' awareness of those behaviors that promote acceptance or rejection within society. This anticipation influences interaction within a family, social, or employment setting. Teachers and parents want students to understand and to foresee the effect of their conduct on others. Teachers at the primary level can begin with simple exercises in which students identify the way one person's behavior produces another's response. This is not a difficult task because the basic "cat and mouse" cartoons on television and in the comics depict these cause-and-effect relationships. The attraction of these stories is contained in the viewer's anticipation. Children know what is going to happen, and it does. The teacher can apply this principle to lessons in the classroom. Given a specific behavior, what will be the response? Of course, the subtleties of behavior and communication become more complicated at successive levels of development, but understanding consequences should be emphasized throughout education. Another objective should be identifying several aspects of behavior (i.e., appearance, manner, speech) and their effect on others.

15   Making Adequate Decisions

The process of making adequate decisions and problem solving is intrinsic to education. Reading, writing, and calculating and other basic skills prepare students to make appropriate decisions. Problem solving is usually identified with the previous curriculum areas and the sciences. But several facets of methodology can be applied to the broad area of personal–social skills to help students examine and improve their relationships with other individuals.

15.62   Locate and Utilize Sources of Assistance

Throughout the discussions on subcompetencies, teachers and parents have been reminded that students should identify the resources in their communities that can provide assistance in personal and family decision making. These resources should be experts in their given subject area, have experience in advising members of the community, and should be able to subdivide the decision-making process for their given subject area into sequential parts. Students should learn under what circumstances resources should be used and what potential outcomes will result.

15.63   Anticipating Consequences

Anticipating the consequences of a decision is the most difficult component to examine in the problem-solving process and the most neglected component of the process. How can students examine what is only anticipated? At this point, observation and inquiry will be of greatest assistance to students. Although students may have had little, if any, experience with potential consequences of a course of action, they may ask others how they handled a similar problem and what the consequences were. Everyone makes everyday decisions, and the consequences can be used as guides for those who are first examining similar problems and alternatives.

15.64 Develop and Evaluate Alternatives

At first glance, a problem may appear to have only one or two possible solutions. Students obviously limit the range of alternatives if they accept the visible solutions. Exercises related to differentiation of bipolar concepts expose students to the possibility that other solutions or positions can be used to solve problems, and that they must search for alternatives. The deep attraction of fictional mysteries, whether Sherlock Holmes or Nancy Drew, is that the characters refuse to accept answers that are easily available and seek other solutions to the puzzle. This principle should be applied to human relationships. Students should demonstrate ability to seek information and examine alternatives involved in individual and group relationships.

The following LCCE lesson plan addresses subcompetency 15.64 relative to developing alternatives for personal goal planning. The lesson plan is a career preparation level of instruction and spans all career roles. Family involvement in the lesson is encouraged. The work sheets are not included for the illustration.

Lesson Plan 6   15.64.2P:6

LCCE Objective 15.64.2. List possible alternatives with respect to a personal goal.

Lesson Objective: Student will develop alternatives to personal goals in different areas of life.

Instructional Resources: Worksheets **Personal Goal Alternatives, Goals Flowchart,** Home Worksheet **Personal Goals at Home,** Worksheet **Your Goal Flowchart.**

Lesson Introduction: How many of you would start off on a trip without knowing what your goal is—where you're headed? It's the same in your personal life. With a goal you know where you're headed. But you may find that you can't reach your goal. Maybe you need more time—or maybe it's no longer important to you. Sometimes you need to develop a "Plan B" alternative goal.

School Activity: **Time: 1 session**

Task:
1. Suggest these six areas in which people may have personal goals:
   - money (financial)
   - people (social)
   - body (physical)
   - school (educational)
   - worship (spiritual)
   - job (vocational)
2. Clarify concept of "Plan B" alternatives—a backup plan, in case the original plan is not attainable.
   - What might make a plan unattainable? Examples include: not enough time; goal might not be appropriate to the individual: circumstances change.

- Distribute and complete Worksheet **Personal Goal Alternatives** together as a class exercise.

3. Divide the class into small groups of three to four students and distribute Worksheet **Goals Flowchart.**

- Students complete the worksheet including Plan B alternatives for both Barry and Alice.
- "Plan B" alternatives can include any other choices within the designated career roles.
- Emphasize that it's O.K. to change goals; this does not imply failure, only growth.
- Discuss the worksheet with class, reviewing each group's "Plan B" alternatives for Barry and Alice.

4. Distribute and explain Home Worksheet **Personal Goals at Home.**

Home/School Activity: **Time: 1 session**

Task:

1. Each student asks a parent or another adult to assist him or her in completing **Personal Goals at Home,** identifying "Plan B" alternatives.

2. Lead a class discussion of each student's goals and alternatives as they are listed on the home worksheet.

- Emphasize that some decisions give more options or flexibility than others. They could lead in two or more ways—for example, deciding to graduate from high school could allow you to get a good job or go to college. Dropping out would limit your possible options. Relate to students' personal goals.
- Explain the fact that not to make a choice is really to decide—for example, if you don't decide to have anything for lunch, you really are deciding to eat nothing. Relate to students' choices.

3. Illustrate goal attainment with flowchart. Distribute Worksheet **Your Goal Flowchart** and explain example.

- Students create their own goal flow chart, identifying a personal goal and "Plan B" alternatives in any career role.
- Students who finish quickly may help those who have difficulty with this.

Lesson Plan Evaluation:

Activity: Students complete Worksheet **Your Goal Flowchart.**

Criteria: Student will complete worksheet with six out of eight appropriate steps.

Career Role: Family Member/Homemaker, Employee, Citizen/Volunteer, Avocational

Career Stage: Preparation

Note. From *Life Centered Career Education Competency Units for Personal–Social Skills* (pp. 1015–1016) by D. E. Brolin, 1992, Reston, VA: The Council for Exceptional Children. Copyright 1992 by The Council for Exceptional Children. Reprinted by permission.

15.65   Recognize the Nature of a Problem

Bipolar concepts include such examples as good and evil, positive and negative, pro and con. These terms are often used in reference to issues and relationships. However, more often than not, problems and relationships do not fall into such a neat dichotomy.

There may be several solutions to a problem or positions on an issue. The favored solutions are of greatest advantage to the individual and her set of values. Students should demonstrate ability to identify the extreme positions within a problem area, search for many solutions, and place each alternative on a progression. In using a methodology that includes this ordering of possible solutions, alternatives, or approaches, students can identify several ingredients that are intrinsic to the problem. Another objective should be examining various positions relative to a group's interpretation of ideas, feelings, and behaviors.

15.66 Developing Goal-Seeking Behavior

Behavior leading to the accomplishment of a goal is one of the most powerful ingredients to the success of persons with disabilities. Indeed, the successful individual who obtains a goal despite an inconvenience is often used as a role model for others who have disabilities. To replicate those successes, students should be able to identify goals and execute the appropriate behavior that will help them reach defined objectives. Teachers should discriminate between short- and long-term, realistic and unrealistic goals. Students should practice the organization of goals, outline behaviors they will need to reach those goals, practice the behaviors, and evaluate the results. Other objectives should include identifying potential barriers to goals and identifying resources that can help students to achieve their goals.

◆ Activity Tip

Goal of the Week activity sheets require students to identify successive steps to accomplish objectives. The objective should include activities outside the classroom such as fixing a bike, shopping for clothes, or attending a school event. The reports provide a weekly record of accomplishments that reinforce goal-seeking behaviors. ◆

16 Communicating Adequately with Others

Without adequate communication, individuals with disabilities are isolated. No person, disabled or not, is an island. Individuals who cannot convey their thoughts and feelings to others will have difficulty reaching fulfillment. In the final analysis, educators should focus on helping students develop communication skills. With these skills, students can gain protection, companionship, and understanding.

16.67 Recognize and Respond to Emergency Situations

Darley and Latane (1968) developed The Decision Tree to describe people's reactions in emergency situations. For a person to assist another who is in need, the bystander must (1) recognize that something is happening; (2) interpret the occurrence as an

Students practice skills on how to communicate with understanding.

emergency; (3) assume some personal responsibility in relationship to the situation or person; and (4) intervene. If any of these steps is not completed, then the needed assistance will not be provided. This progression gives teachers a structure for planning training activities. Students must first be able to attend to instances within the environment that either are direct signs of an emergency (fire, earthquake) or that could be interpreted as a danger signal (screeching car brakes followed by a loud "thud," or an individual collapsing in a restaurant). Assuming that students do take personal responsibility for action (which is a test of their values), they should be able to provide the appropriate form of communication with participants ("Can I help you?" or "What do you need?") and emergency personnel ("I wish to report an accident" or "I observed the following things"). These skills can be practiced in conjunction with subcompetencies 3.4 and 4.4. Another objective should be preparing a list of emergency information to be carried by the student.

16.68   Communicate with Understanding

In a society that places value on verbal skills (singing, acting, political oratory, salesmanship), the individual who has speech disabilities or problems speaking fluently is at a disadvantage. Individuals with speech problems experience many frustrations in their everyday dealings with other members of society. Even competent persons have occasional bad days when they mispronounce the boss's name, flounder among sentences in an interview, or are tongue-tied when meeting a prospective date. Teachers, parents, counselors, and therapists have a formidable task in preparing students to demonstrate proficiency in basic language skills, skill in regulating the loudness of voice according to the social setting, ability to participate in conversation, and verbal expression of emotion, information, and inquiry.

Sample Lesson Plan

Author: Christine Hughes

Period: Second   **Situation:** A resource room or special day class setting

Time Span: Six weeks

Activity Title: *Using the Telephone*

Objective: Competency 16.2: Students will be able to communicate adequately with others and will use the telephone as a means of obtaining information.

Goal of Activity: Students will role play and practice various telephone skills using a classroom telephone learning center.

Activity: Upon written request, local telephone companies are usually willing to provide used, gutted telephones that are no longer in use. Obtain a set of phones and organize a telephone learning center in your classroom in which students can practice various telephone skills. On separate pieces of posterboard, creatively describe and illustrate situations for students to role play and practice. Include the following sample student responses or invent your own.

Situation 1   Call a friend to talk for a while.

What to Say: "How did your day go today?"
                      "What did you do last weekend?"
                      "What do you plan to do this weekend?"

Situation 2   Call a friend to make plans to go somewhere.

What to Say: "Where would you like to go this weekend?"
                      "I would like to go to _____."
                      "I agree. We should go to _____."

Situation 3   Place an emergency phone call to the police department, fire department, or family doctor.

What to Say: "I want to report a prowler at _____." (Give address)
                      "I want to report an accident at the corner of _____ and _____."
                      "I want to report a fire at _____." (Give address)

Situation 4   Call a business establishment to determine job openings.

What to Say: "Does your company have any job openings at this time?"
                      "What positions are available?"
                      "What is the application procedure?"
                      "Could I schedule an interview at this time?"

Situation 5   Practice taking messages.

What to Say: "May I ask who is calling, please?"
                      "May I take a message?"
                      "What is your phone number?"

Situation 6   Call to schedule an appointment with your doctor, dentist, etc.

What to Say: "My name is _____, and I'd like to make an appointment with Dr. _____ on _____ for _____."

Evaluation: Let students choose partners and act out the situation of the week. Students will take turns being the caller and receiver of the call. Inform parents of your classroom activities. Encourage them to allow students to make these types of calls at home.

Activity Title: *Dialing for Information*

Objective: Competency 16.4: The student will be able to communicate adequately with others and will use the telephone as a means of obtaining information.
Goal of Activity: Under teacher supervision, students will use school telephones to obtain simple information.
Activity: Let students use school telephones under your supervision to make simple phone calls. Listed below are some suggested calls to make.

1. Call to order a pizza for the class.
2. Call to find out bus routes and schedules for a class field trip.
3. Call to find out the business hours of a field trip destination.
4. Call to find out the business hours of a local bank or store.
5. Call to find out the cost of bowling for a class field trip.
6. Call to find out the admission price to the local zoo, museum, or amusement park.
7. Call to find out what movie is playing and the admission price at a local theater.

Help students write a script to use while calling. Allow them to practice several times before making the call. This could be done individually or as a group. Have the student making the call look the phone number up in the telephone directory. If the number is unlisted, have the student call directory assistance. Provide students with a checklist of skills to keep in mind while making the call. This checklist could include such items as speaks clearly, speaks with expression, requests correct information, and accurately records information received.

Evaluation: Allow a different student to place calls for you or the class whenever necessary. Use the checklist as a means of evaluation. Inform parents of your classroom activities. Encourage them to allow students to make these types of calls.

16.69   Know Subtleties of Communication

Teachers should explore the area of what is meant in communication in contrast to what is said, signed, or written. In other words, we live in a world if intention. Students should realize that sometimes people disguise their messages to protect themselves. They may say or imply things so they cannot be held accountable. Schoolchildren soon learn that they can only be held accountable for what they say (or do). They realize that communication can occur through many channels and can operate at both the overt and covert levels. Commercials can be, perhaps, the biggest and most accessible source of lessons. Numerous advertisements on radio and television and in print use nonverbal components—the subtleties—of communication to convey messages other than what is stated or pictured. Students should be able to distinguish between the verbal and nonverbal messages so that they can improve their communication skills. They should be aware of those instances when they are producing dual messages (i.e., one level of acknowledged symbols and another one of intended meaning). Another objective should be practicing verbal and nonverbal forms of communication that are congruent with an individual's feelings.

SELF-DETERMINATION

The concept of *self-determination* has recently gained considerable recognition as an important instructional need for persons with disabilities. In this section, the concept is further discussed in relation to the personal–social skills area and the LCCE competencies.

Basic Concepts

An individual's opinion of her ability and her subsequent efforts to obtain goals are crucial to career education. The student's self-concept is an extremely important factor to successful learning and functioning. Self-concept or image is a learned phenomenon and can change based on new learning and experiences. One's self-concept influences what one will learn from experience. It is influenced by significant others such as parents, teachers, and those who foster change. Thus, the educational program and its curriculum focus provide an important influence on each student's self-concept development. The recent attention on the need for a more substantial self-determination focus in our educational programs relates directly to addressing the positive self-concept needs of the many students with special learning needs.

"Clearly, our state's youth in transition need to increasingly discover the right to self-determination, for it is through this self-empowerment that their level of human decency, pride, and sense of self-worth will be heightened and their quality of life enhanced."

(Browning, 1994)

Self-determination is rapidly gaining attention and acceptance as an important instructional focus that educators need to emphasize much more if students are to successfully make the transition from school to adulthood (Field & Hoffman, 1994). Field and Hoffman describe the concept as

the ability to define and achieve goals based on a foundation of knowing and valuing oneself. It is promoted, or discouraged, by both internal factors (e.g., values, knowledge and skills) and external factors (e.g., opportunities for choice-making, attitudes of others, etc.).

They have developed a model that focuses on the internal factors that are to be used as a guide for developing strategies and materials that promote the knowledge, skills, and values that lead to self-determination. Their model contains five major components: know yourself, value yourself, plan, act, and experience outcomes and learn. The model is illustrated in Figure 11.2. Persons interested in gaining further information should contact the authors at the College of Education, Wayne State University, Detroit, Michigan.

ENVIRONMENT

Know Yourself
- Dream
- Know your strengths, weaknesses, needs and preferences
- Know the options
- Decide what is important to you

Value Yourself
- Accept and value yourself
- Admire strengths that come from uniqueness
- Recognize and respect rights and responsibilities
- Take care of yourself

Plan
- Set goals
- Plan actions to meet goals
- Anticipate results
- Be creative
- Visually rehearse

Act
- Take risks
- Communicate
- Access resources and support
- Negotiate
- Deal with conflict and criticism
- Be persistent

Experience Outcomes & Learn
- Compare outcome to expected outcome
- Compare performance to expected performance
- Realize success
- Make adjustments

ENVIRONMENT

FIGURE 11.2   Model for self-determination.

Note. From "Development of a Model for Self-Determination" by S. Field and A. Hoffman, 1994, *Career Development for Exceptional Individuals, 17*(2), p. 165. Copyright 1994 by the Division on Career Development and Transition, The Council for Exceptional Children. Reprinted by permission.

Persons who are self-determined control their own lives and make their own decisions without the undue influence of others.

Another conceptualization of self-determination has been presented by Wehmeyer, who refers to it as "the attitudes and abilities necessary to act as the primary causal agent in one's life and to make choices and decisions regarding one's quality of life, free from undue external influence or interference" (1992). He notes that to be self-determined, students with disabilities must believe they can control their outcomes, be effective persons, know their strengths and needs, and build a positive self-concept and self-esteem. If this happens, they can become adults who can assume their own responsibility for choices and decisions, find their own jobs, and advocate for themselves.

According to Wehmeyer (1992), educational programs need to institute appropriate functional curricula, environments that encourage student choice and preferences, interactions with peers without disabilities, access to role models, experiences with success, and control in decision making. He notes that the limited research available on the subject has found that in most instances students with disabilities are given too little opportunity to express preferences and make choices or take responsibility for their actions in the classroom. In addition, appropriate involvement of the student's family and community is critical. These components are similar to those that have been noted in this book as important for providing a comprehensive career education, functional skills effort.

 "Self-determination leads to enhanced motivation and performance. Also, others note that a substantial number of experiments show that the opportunity to make direct decisions and therefore exercise control has been associated with an increased perception of psychological and emotional well-being.

(Browning, 1994, p. 94)

Students with special learning needs must learn the behaviors and skills needed to work and live independently in their communities. Thus, a curriculum must embody self-directed decision-making skills that include three important cognitive-behavioral, decision-making skills: goal setting, social problem solving, and requesting assistance (Browning, 1994). According to Browning

> our transitional programs fall short of instilling in their students enabling self-directing skills with which to choose, decide, and express interests and preferences regarding their own destiny. Such skills are sorely needed to enhance their ability to plan, manage, and direct their own lives and thus exert greater control over their own future. (1994, p. 102)

The importance of giving more attention to the self-determination instructional needs of students should be more apparent by now. This area of need falls clearly within the personal–social curriculum area. An example of one curricular effort using LCCE curriculum components to meet this need is described next.

Self-Determination and the LCCE Curriculum

Drs. Sharon Davis and Michael Wehmeyer of The Arc (formerly, Association for Retarded Citizens, National Headquarters) have developed a comprehensive self-determination curriculum based on several competencies and lesson plans from the personal–social curriculum area of the LCCE curriculum. Based on federal funding for the period 1990 to 1993, The Arc conducted an extensive literature review and discussions with and surveys of adults with mild cognitive disabilities to discern how well these individuals were able to make choices and decisions relative to their quality of life. The results were as expected; these individuals were quite limited in their ability to make such choices and decisions (Wehmeyer, 1992).

Based on the results of their study, The Arc staff reviewed various curriculums that held promise for teaching self-determination skills to students with disabilities. They then devised a core curriculum that would result in a framework for promoting self-determination. This core curriculum consists of four major domains:

1. Self-awareness
2. Self-confidence
3. Choice and autonomy
4. Goal attainment

For each domain area, a list of attitudes and abilities related to this outcome (self-determination) was identified. Project staff then selected the LCCE curriculum as being most applicable to their framework and identified 4 LCCE competencies and 17 subcompetencies that matched the structure of the model. Table 11.3 presents the structure of the resulting model.

The approximately 350 LCCE lesson plans composing the 17 subcompetency areas were field tested by project staff with over 500 students (ages 14 to 20) labeled as having mental retardation or learning disabilities. The lesson plans were organized sequentially, beginning with instruction in the self-awareness area (competency 10), then moving to self-confidence instruction (competency 11), and then to the choice and decision making and goal setting later (competencies 14 and 15). The Arc staff found the LCCE materials to be a comprehensive treatment of self-determination and recommended students begin instruction by at least ages 12 to 14 in regular classrooms with same-age peers without disabilities whenever possible.

The self-determination curriculum is now available from the CEC as part of its total LCCE curriculum package, including the Self-Determination Scale, described in Chapter 7.

FINAL COMMENTS

It is widely recognized that possessing adequate social skills is extremely important for all students in American schools, including those with special needs. Yet, as Iannacone

TABLE 11.3   LCCE Competency and Subcompetency Areas Used to Promote Self-Determination

Model Domain	LCCE Competency	LCCE Subcompetency
Self-awareness	10. Achieving self-awareness	42. Identify physical and psychological needs
		43. Identify interests and abilities
		44. Identify emotions
		45. Demonstrate knowledge of physical self
		61. Awareness of how behavior affects others
Self-confidence	11. Acquiring self-confidence	46. Express feelings of self-worth
		47. Describe others' perception of self
		48. Accept and give praise
		49. Accept and give criticism
		50. Develop confidence in oneself
Choice and decision making	15. Making adequate decisions	62. Locate and use sources of assistance
		63. Anticipate consequences
		64. Develop and evaluate alternatives
Goal attainment	14. Achieving independence	59. Strive toward self-actualization
		60. Demonstrate self-organization
		65. Recognize nature of a problem
		66. Develop goal-seeking behavior

Note. From *Administration Manual for Self-Determination Scale* by D. E. Brolin, in preparation. Available in 1995. Reston, VA: The Council for Exceptional Children.

et al. note, "there is little evidence to suggest that comprehensive and continuous social skills curriculum and instruction have a definite presence" (1992, p. 111).

With drug abuse as the number one problem in our schools, the immediate need to restructure curricula to provide more and better social skills training and to address career development issues becomes more obvious and critical. Despite this obvious need, social skills instruction is not considered a vital component of the school curriculum, and we appear to have lost sight of one of the most fundamental goals of our educational system; that is, to foster the development of human relationships and to help students to live and work cooperatively with others in their communities (National Education Association, 1938, 1952).

Teaching the competencies in the personal–social skills domain will increase the probability that students will function more adequately in interpersonal relationships and problem-solving situations. These skills are needed for home, community, recreational, and employment settings. People who have a successful quality of life and satisfactory adult adjustment can acquire the seven LCCE personal–social competencies: adequate self-awareness, self-confidence, socially responsible behavior, good interpersonal skills, independence, decision-making, and communication skills.

An individual's opinion of his ability and his subsequent efforts to obtain goals are crucial to successful career development. Educators must provide the opportunity for students to learn and demonstrate all of the important social skills, including those that build the important skills relating to self-determination, that will be needed for adult functioning. More career-oriented social skills instruction is critically needed in most schools. Educators cannot do this by themselves; they must involve not only the entire school community but family and community resources. As regular and special education services are integrated into a more unified educational system, the opportunity becomes even greater for students with special learning needs to be better integrated and embraced into the entire school program by other students and teachers. Integrated social skills instruction, such as that being promoted in this chapter, can help enhance this process.

ACTIVITIES

1. Review the personal–social skills matrix in Figure 11.1, and then determine what regular education and special education courses would be most appropriate for teaching each of the LCCE subcompetencies for your particular students. Then identify those subcompetencies/skills in which you would attempt to involve the parents. Finally, identify the subcompetencies for which you would include community-based instruction and what community resources you would use to help you teach the subcompetencies.
2. Develop an instructional objective around one of the subcompetencies, and then write a lesson plan for your students, using the LCCE lesson plan format, that addresses one of the career stages, instructional settings, and career roles, as well as the concept of self-determination. The LCCE lesson plan outline is contained in Appendix G.

Chapter 12

Occupational Guidance and Preparation

Preliminary Questions About the Topic

1. Identify what occupational knowledge and skills you believe students with special learning needs should acquire before leaving the secondary program.
2. Who should be involved in the occupational guidance and preparation of these students?
3. When should instruction in the occupational skills area begin, and what should be the focus at the beginning stages?
4. What contributions can the school counselor make toward the career development of students who have special learning needs?
5. What occupational information systems are available to help students identify realistic occupational goals?
6. What community resources are available to provide additional training for students who need postsecondary vocational training?
7. How can educators avoid violating the Fair Labor Standards Act (FLSA) relative to child labor and compensation requirements?
8. What are the various employability enhancement strategies materials available to assess and instruct students with special learning needs in important occupational areas and behaviors?
9. What responsibilities should educators at each of the levels assume in providing occupational guidance and instruction to their students?
10. What percentage of students with disabilities could be competitively employed if they were provided with sufficient guidance and training?

The workplace is changing dramatically in American society. Changes are occurring relative to the characteristics of the work force itself (age, sex, and ethnic composition), legislative mandates requiring adaptations in the work environments for persons with disabilities, and in the nature of jobs available as a result of the high-tech explosion and movement into the Information Age. Because three fourths of high school students will not complete college, considerable concern exists at all levels of government and industry to address the question of how this majority of individuals will be prepared for satisfying and well-paying employment.

As this is being written, plans are being made by federal government to implement a comprehensive school-to-work system in the United States. The School-to-Work Opportunities Act is being promoted to encourage schools to enrich and expand their existing school-to-work programs, including those of vocational education, youth apprenticeship, tech-prep education, cooperative education, career academics, and school-to-apprenticeship programs. The bill will help states develop work-based learning so students can work in chosen fields their last 2 years of high school and school-based learning opportunities so they can explore career opportunities with counselors and receive instruction in a career major. Postsecondary education will also be available.

Where do students with disabilities and other learning difficulties fit into the future plans? The answer remains to be seen. But it should be obvious to professionals and parents that these students will need to learn as early as possible the basic academic, daily living, personal–social, prevocational, and occupational skills that will be required to qualify for and benefit from the new programmatic efforts.

This chapter begins with a section on occupational guidance and includes a description of the Missouri Comprehensive Guidance System, developed by Professor Norman C. Gysbers, which is being implemented in numerous school districts throughout the country and beyond. This is followed by a section on occupational preparation techniques. The next section focuses on the six occupational competencies in the Life-Centered Career Education (LCCE) curriculum, which covers the major knowledge and skills students need to learn for occupational success. Each competency and subcompetency is described, sample lesson plans are presented, and a teacher using the LCCE approach and materials explains her use of them.

OCCUPATIONAL GUIDANCE

In a survey taken by the National Alliance of Business (NAB) of 4,170 high school principals and 2,675 small businesses, 95% of the principals said they would be willing to alter their school's curriculum to include courses that relate to specific careers, 74% of the employers said they would be willing to spend time and money working with a school and part-time workers to have better-trained employees, and 86% of the principals said they would be willing to spend time and money working with a local business to help students prepare for careers (National Association for Industry-Education, 1993).

Point of View

Instructing students with disabilities in the occupational skills—which focus on choosing a job (guidance) and preparing for a job (preparation)—is an extremely important, but often overlooked, aspect of American education. Although occupational guidance and preparation are important for all students, they are particularly significant for young people who are coping with the impact of disabilities on their lives. They need the foundation provided by occupational skill training throughout their vocational lives. Think of how such instruction might have made a difference in these three scenarios:

A high school junior with developmental disabilities that affect both her cognitive and mobility functions has no work experience, has never discussed employment with a counselor or her parents, and has never heard of the Division of Vocational Rehabilitation.

A second-semester college senior with a hearing impairment is 1 month from graduation and has no idea what jobs are possible within his major field of study.

A young employee with multiple sclerosis is having difficulty remembering, standing during the work day, and lifting heavy order catalogs; but she is unfamiliar with Title I of the Americans with Disabilities Act and the concept of job accommodation.

With instruction in occupational skills during their K–12 years, each of these individuals would be much better prepared to solve the problems associated with disability, job acquisition, and job retention. Hence, the occupational skills curriculum described in this chapter is a curriculum for all seasons of one's career development. It helps young people with disabilities understand their abilities and interests and relate them to a wide range of occupational roles. It involves students in practical work experiences in the home, school, and community that broaden their knowledge of the types of jobs people hold to make a living and the skills needed to retain employment. It prepares students for the challenges of job seeking such as organizing a job search, completing job applications, and conducting a job interview. And, finally, it introduces students to the many employment resources in their communities such as the Division of Vocational Rehabilitation, employment counselors, and facilities that specialize in vocational training and placement.

Choosing a job is, of course, only the first step. Students must learn how to get and keep a job. The occupational skills curriculum addresses each of those three important steps—choose, get, and keep. In fact, Chapter 11 brings to mind a popular country song with a slightly amended title, "Take this job and keep it."

Richard T. Roessler is a professor of rehabilitation, Department of Rehabilitation, University of Arkansas-Fayetteville. He is the co-author of the LCCE Competency Units for Occupational Guidance and Preparation (1992) published by The Council for Exceptional Children.

With greater recognition by school administrators that more career development components need to be instituted and a greater willingness to make changes that lead in this direction, the opportunity for improving the occupational guidance for students with special learning needs appears brighter than in the past. Many people have the capability to assist students in this area: School counselors, rehabilitation counselors, employment counselors, employers, teachers, family members, peers, and others are all critically important in helping self-determined students to learn more about their job potentials and the possibilities related to their own unique set of interests and abilities.

What kind of occupational guidance services can be instituted? Occupational guidance does not need to be only a professional counseling endeavor; rather, it should also consist of a variety of classroom and community-based experiences. The remainder of this section presents some of the important services or techniques that can be employed for students. It also provides one example of a comprehensive guidance program that is being implemented in many states to meet the needs of all students in a school system: the Missouri Comprehensive Guidance Program.

Counseling

Ironically, most of the counseling and advice that students receive, including those with special learning needs, is not from persons trained to do professional counseling. Rather, it comes mainly from family members, friends, peers, and some teachers. Professional counselors complain of heavy caseloads and too many noncounseling responsibilities to be able to do what they have been trained and hired to do. Thus, the counseling many students receive is not always based on what professionals believe to constitute a more scientific and knowledgeable helping relationship. Yet, if the three fourths or more of students with disabilities and other special learning needs are to reach their employment potential and become competitively employed, school counselors and others who are well-trained in occupational guidance must become more engaged in the guidance and counseling of these individuals.

Decision-making skills are the cornerstone of career education. If individuals can be provided with appropriate educational experiences, they should be able to make more effective decisions. Counseling may help individuals learn how to take risks, solve problems, select from alternatives, and explore their potentials in relationship to the occupational possibilities available in the real world. Counseling should be the responsibility of a variety of helping professionals who should use the same techniques in counseling individuals with disabilities or who are disadvantaged as they would use in counseling anyone else. Some basic principles for successfully providing this important service follow:

- Trust is one of the most important elements in the counseling process.
- People can learn to make logical career choices and decisions.
- To build trust, helpers must be able to genuinely respect, accept, and empathize with the individual.

- Self-concept is one of the most important determinants of career and personal development.
- Individuals can learn new behaviors and extinguish inappropriate ones.
- Significant others influence an individual's behavior and decisions.
- An individual's psychological needs, beliefs, goals, and values are inextricably related to occupational decision making and satisfaction.
- Helpers should use a personalized, humanistic, systematic, and flexible approach in responding to the individual's various characteristics and needs.
- A reciprocal relationship between counselor and client is necessary.
- Each person is a unique individual and may need a different counseling approach.

Major goals of vocational counseling are to help individuals learn about the world of work; identify appropriate experiences, courses, and persons who can assist in occupational awareness and exploration activities; choose more specific vocational aptitudes, interests, and needs; determine occupational training areas; and obtain job seeking and securing skills. Counselors should listen to what clients say about their interests, needs, and abilities. However, counselors should also consider the following:

1. Most individuals with special needs generally have fewer work experiences than other persons, and, therefore, their concept of the world of work may be narrower.
2. Many individuals with special learning needs have a long history of failure and rejection and, therefore, may underestimate their potentials and aspirations.
3. Some individuals may have difficulty understanding more complex verbal interchanges and may try to mask the fact that they do not comprehend what is being discussed.
4. Many individuals with cognitive limitations can benefit from shorter but more frequent interactions in which specific assignments are given.
5. Audiovisual equipment, blackboards, role playing, and other nondidactic techniques enhance counseling efforts.

Effective occupational guidance and counseling will provide individuals with more than occupational information, testing, and field experience. Occupational guidance and counseling should be a learning-oriented experience that involves an open, personal relationship between a well-trained counselor or special educator and an individual. Counselors should encourage individuals to explore their interests, needs, and abilities by actively listening to and empathizing with their feelings and thoughts. Clients should emerge from this experience with greater self-awareness and confidence in their ability to take responsibility for themselves. Counselors or educators should help clients to learn self-determination skills so that they can make realistic occupational choices and training decisions. Counseling is a process that must be purposely built into the educational program so that it evolves over a period of time and is open to change as students gain new information and experience.

Job Analysis

Job analysis and task analysis for occupational guidance may not seem necessary, but they are effective methods of learning about work, specific jobs, and interest areas. A job analysis is a systematic way of observing jobs to determine what the worker does, how she does it, why she does it, and the skill involved in its performance. Jobs should be analyzed precisely as they presently exist, excluding temporarily assigned tasks. A detailed job description should include all tasks and requirements that contribute to successful performance. Task analysis is the process of breaking a task into smaller steps or skills that are required to complete the task.

Job analysis can become a powerful career awareness and exploration tool for students. When students take field trips to various work sites, they should fill out a simple job analysis form, such as the one depicted in Figure 12.1, so that they can become aware of major characteristics and requirements of various jobs. The class and teacher should review each job analysis before students include it in their job information notebook. Students should be encouraged to ask each other questions relative to their separate analysis. Peers or teachers may need to help lower-ability students gather and report the proper information. When students become interested in a specific job, they can begin a task analysis. Once again, students become intimately involved in the task and learn a great deal about the nature of work by themselves and from other class members. In group counseling sessions, the analysis can become a focus of discussion and lively action. Once students have become more conscious and efficient in analyzing jobs, they should be able to use and understand occupational literature and other media. Job and task analysis is an important component of an occupational guidance program and should be part of elementary as well as secondary programs. It complements other career awareness and exploration techniques and, is a necessary and worthwhile endeavor for all students.

Simulations of Business and Industry

Establishing a simulated business in or out of school can be a realistic, hands-on experience that can add considerable relevance to both occupational guidance and preparation efforts. Students can assume roles with varying degrees of responsibility so they can get a better perspective of what the job entails.

Career City, developed by the Quincy Public Schools in Illinois, is an innovative example of a simulation. Career City consists of seven small buildings, which are located in the Resource Center of the elementary school. A greenhouse, grocery store, bank, bakery, photography shop, barber and beauty shop, and residential house are depicted in five-by-five-foot structures painted, decorated, and transported by special education students from the senior high school program. The major objective of Career City is to supplement the classroom curriculum by providing realistic, hands-on career experiences. This learning activity provides elementary school students with an array of career awareness experiences. Students learn to deposit checks in the bank, grow flowers and vegetables in the greenhouse, and use cameras and viewers in the photography

Job Title _____ DOT Title _____

Name of Firm _____ Code Number _____

Date of Analysis _____ Name of Analyst _____

A. Description of Work Performed _____

_____

_____

B. Job Requirements. Circle number of those required and comment if needed.

1. Adding _____   11. Use telephone _____
2. Subtracting _____   12. Life, carry, push, pull _____
3. Multiplying _____   13. Walk, run, climb, balance _____
4. Dividing _____   14. Stoop, kneel, crouch, crawl _____
5. Make change _____   15. Stand or sit _____
6. Use measuring devices _____ 16. Use hand tools _____
7. Read _____   17. Operate machines _____
8. Write _____   18. Other _____
9. Talk _____   19. Other _____
10. Follow instructions _____   20. Other _____

C. Working Conditions. Circle number that describes the job and comment if
   needed.

1. Extremely hot _____   8. Good lighting _____
2. Extremely cold _____ 9. Good ventilation _____
3. Humid _____   10. Tension and pressure _____
4. We _____   11. Distracting conditions _____
5. Dry _____   12. Hazardous _____
6. Dusty and dirty _____ 13. Work with others _____
7. Noisy _____   14. Other _____

D. Training Required _____

E. Salary _____

F. Hours Worked _____

G. Good features of the Job _____

_____

H. Poor features of the Job _____

_____

_____

FIGURE 12.1   Example of a job analysis form.

lab. Each career has a packet with all the necessary information and equipment that students may need to participate in the many learning activities. Many nonspecial education students also take advantage of this career awareness opportunity. All students seem to have a better understanding of each career after they have participated in the career awareness activities of Career City (Bocke & Price, 1976).

Simulation of an assembly line operation is another example of an activity that can help early elementary students develop career awareness. Students can be provided with information about industry and manufacturing occupations while they experience the importance of cooperation among workers in production efforts and friendly competition and pride in doing quality work. Assembly line workers can visit the class, and field trips can be arranged to certain industries.

At an elementary school in Plainview, Minnesota, students in grades 4 through 6 manage a school store. Their first step in organizing the venture is to gain approval and suggestions from their Career Education Citizen's Advisory Board. The board suggested that students approach local businesses about their plan for a school store, which was wholeheartedly supported. One sixth-grade class was responsible for ordering basic supplies—pencils, crayons, notebook paper, and erasers. A board of directors was elected to set up guidelines for operating the store. The board elected a store manager and personnel director, who developed job assignments and duties; sales people, stock people, and an advertising department. The advertising department consisted of several classes who competed against one another to see who could invent the best advertising gimmicks and promotions. A second venture by the school was a record shop. The school asked several radio stations to save records that were no longer in use. Students made purchases in cash from the record shop or traded used paperback books. A bookstore and travel bureau were other ventures that the school developed (J. Johnson, 1976).

D. Haring (1978) described a successful teacher-designed career education program in an economics class at Scottsdale High School in Arizona. Two hundred seventy-five students formed their own business enterprises that became part of a career education program called Project Work. The students created 89 companies that produced, advertised, and marketed products and provided services for fellow students or community members. Once operation was completed, the company divided the profits in various ways. Some business enterprises were corporations and paid their stockholders. Others were partnerships and sole proprietorships. Students paid appropriate taxes and licensing fees to the student government. Project Work was also conducted at a less sophisticated level in the lower grades. Students felt the project made them more aware of their interests and abilities and improved their attitudes and interest toward school and the teachers.

Business simulations are extremely effective in motivating students to learn academic material, become more knowledgeable about the world of work, and develop occupational interests and skills. School personnel can use simulations to integrate their students into business operations and activities with regular class students. The potentials of this technique are limited only by creativity, time, and financial constraints.

Field Trips and Speakers

Students should visit a variety of workplaces because direct experience increases the student's comprehension and motivation. Teachers should make field trips part of the curriculum. Field trips should be planned carefully to represent various business establishments in the community. Prior planning with the company should permit the time for students to observe and record pertinent job analysis information and to speak with some of the people who perform various jobs. The jobs to be viewed should generally be those the group would most likely be able to assume themselves. Classroom discussions should cover the importance, characteristics, and opportunities associated with each job.

Class speakers are a valuable adjunct to field trips. In some cases, it may be advantageous to have someone from the business speak to the class before a tour. She may distribute information, show films, answer questions, identify points of interest, and explain what the students are going to see. In other instances, it may be more beneficial to invite the speaker into the classroom after the trip. Workers should also be invited to such presentations. Former students can also be effective in eliciting the student's interest in and understanding of the industry and its jobs.

Career Information Center and Systems

Career information systems are an important development in occupational resources in recent years. The National Occupational Information Coordinating Committee (NOICC) is a federal interagency committee that promotes the development and use of educational, occupational, and labor market information. NOICC works with a network of state occupational information coordinating committees (SOICCs) who represent state producers and users of occupational information, for example, vocational rehabilitation, employment agencies, job training councils and economic development agencies. NOICC and the SOICCs have developed and made available occupational information systems, computerized data bases of occupational and educational data, and career information delivery systems (CIDSs), computerized information about occupations and training opportunities. CIDSs are available in about 45 states (McDaniels & Gysbers, 1992). Information on NOICC and SOICC activities can be obtained by contacting NOICC in Washington, DC.

Several commercial career information software systems are presently available for schools. Some of the systems that should be considered for use in working with students with special learning difficulties follows:

- Career Information System (CIS), developed by National CIS, University of Oregon, Eugene, OR 97403
- Coordinate Occupational Information Network (COIN), COIN Career Guidance Products, 3361 Executive Parkway, Suite 302, Toledo, OH 43606

- Guidance Information System (GIS), Houghton-Mifflin Company, Educational Software Division, P.O. Box 683, Hanover, NH 03755
- Kansas Careers, College of Education, Kansas State University, Bluemont Hall, Manhattan, KS 66506

Readers interested in an excellent evaluation of computer-assisted career guidance systems should obtain a copy of the *Journal of Career Development* (Winter 1990 issue).

A career information center can be integral to an occupational guidance delivery system. The center can provide students with a place to gather information about occupations and plan their occupational future with a counselor. This learning and planning should relate to what the student is receiving in classroom career-related activities. The center should also be a place where students can talk with other students about occupations. It should have a sufficient supply of materials so that students can find answers to career-related activities. Career information centers can be established at a fairly reasonable cost. Free materials are available from businesses, industries, and various organizations.

The center could provide the following services: career counseling on an individual basis, career seminars, career information to classes; career guidance material; administration and interpretation of aptitude, achievement, and interest tests; financial aid information; military information; information on employment trends, qualifications, and compensation; curriculum planning; resource center for faculty, staff, and parents; and liaison between the school and community, business, and other groups.

Some essential materials are *Occupational Outlook Handbook, Dictionary of Occupational Titles, Guide for Occupational Exploration,* subscriptions to career-related publications. *Encyclopedia of Careers,* a file of brochures on jobs, several regional newspapers, career-related library books, employment opportunity information, and audiovisual materials on interviewing and job-seeking skills. Furniture and equipment should include copying equipment, bulletin boards, overhead projectors, projection screens, a microfiche viewer, conference and work tables, furniture for conversational settings, display racks, bookcases, files, and desks and chairs.

One caution from Patterson and Curl (1992) regarding individuals with disabilities is that the career/occupational guidance systems and publications may not adequately reflect the opportunities available with, for example, the modifications or accommodations that can be made for these individuals. With this caution in mind, these materials may be used to expand the options for people with disabilities rather than limiting them.

A computerized job replication computer program developed at the Center on Education and Work, University of Wisconsin–Madison, is one example of an excellent effort to address this need. Their software program helps persons with disabilities explore jobs and identify potential employers by industry and job settings. A five-volume job replication series is also available through the center.

The Missouri Comprehensive Guidance Program

One example of how a comprehensive guidance program can be organized to meet the needs of all students in a school system is the Missouri Comprehensive Guidance Program model, which has undergone many years of developmental work and field testing in Missouri schools and beyond. The program is counselor driven with the assistance of a steering committee and various work groups. As illustrated in Figure 12.2, the model is organized around three major elements: content, organizational framework, and resources.

The first element of this guidance program, *content*, focuses on student competencies categorized into three areas: knowledge of self and others, career planning and exploration, and educational and vocational development. A valuable resource for this component is a resource kit consisting of a wide range of lesson plan type activities that can be used for student instruction in the three areas. The second element, organizational framework, provides the structural framework, programmatic activities, and suggested distribution of counselor time. A program manual is available to provide detailed instructions on program development. The third element, resources, addresses the persons and politics that are needed to support the program. Guidelines for this element are also provided in detail (Starr & Gysbers, 1993).

With the movement toward a greater integration of special education and general education, the Missouri Comprehensive Guidance Program Model provides an excellent vehicle by which students with disabilities and other learning problems can be assimilated into the ongoing guidance services of their schools. Persons interested in obtaining further information on the details of the Missouri model should contact Dr. Norman Gysbers, 310 Noyes Hall, University of Missouri-Columbia, Columbia, MO 65211 or Mr. Marion Starr, Assistant Director, Guidance/Special Needs, Missouri Department of Elementary and Secondary Education, P.O. Box 480, Jefferson City, MO 65101.

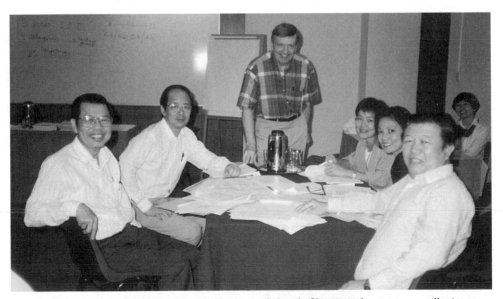

Norman C. Gysbers conducting a career guidance workshop in Singapore for career coordinators.

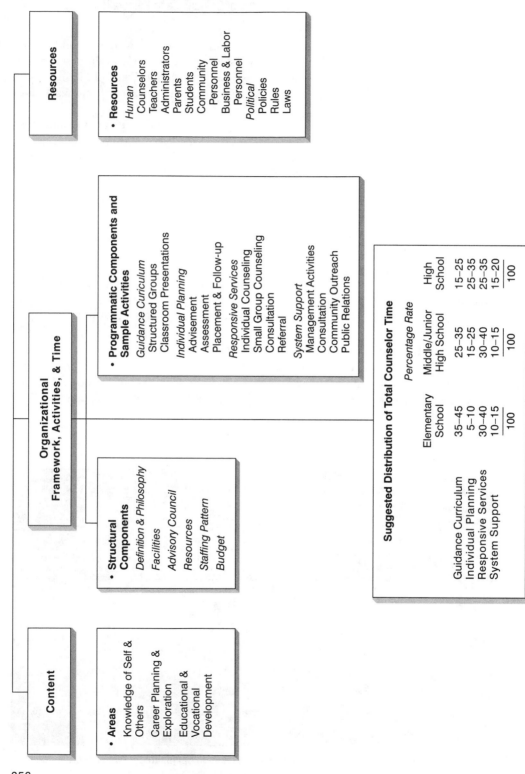

FIGURE 12.2 Missouri Comprehensive Guidance Program elements.

Note. From *Missouri Comprehensive Guidance: A Model for Program Development Implementation and Evaluation* (p. 6) by M. Starr and N. Gysbers, 1993, Jefferson City, MO: Missouri Department of Elementary and Secondary Education. Copyright 1993 by Norm Gysbers. Reprinted by permission.

Some recommended resources for more extensive information and ideas on counseling and guidance activities for students and program development are the following publications:

- G. M. Clark and Kolstoe (1990), *Career Development and Transition Education*
- McDaniels and Gysbers (1992), *Counseling for Career Development*
- Gysbers and Henderson (1994), *Developing and Managing Your School Guidance Program*

OCCUPATIONAL PREPARATION TECHNIQUES

For too many years, with some exceptions, too many students, including persons with disabilities and other disadvantages have been excluded from the mainstream of substantive vocational education. As Benz and Halpern (1993) found in their extensive in-depth follow-up study of former students with disabilities in Nevada and Oregon,

> the disadvantaged situations that certain subgroups of young adults with disabilities find themselves in after leaving school may have their roots in the discrepancies that occur in high school between the vocational and transitional services they reportedly need and actually receive. (1993, p. 209)

Meaningful vocational education opportunities must become available in all schools for all students who need and want them. Many different approaches and options have been developed over the years so each student can be adequately trained in the vocational area. This section provides some further suggestions and techniques for providing this instruction to students at the various grade levels.

Elementary/Middle School Students

Occupational preparation must begin early, at the elementary level, with appropriate career awareness, exploration, and prevocational activities and experiences that will provide the foundation for the more demanding vocational education programs at the secondary level. However, this is not prevalently implemented. S. C. Moore, Agran, and McSweyn (1990), in their survey of 100 elementary, middle school, and high school special education teachers in Utah, found that very little vocational or related training and experiences, such as learning a basic employment vocabulary or viewing different occupations, were provided younger children, although these were identified as important needs by educational leaders.

The elementary level is an important time to begin the career education process of career awareness and exploration so students begin acquiring the work personality described in Chapter 3.

Beginning at the elementary level, occupational activities should be designed in a systematic skill-building manner that combines a variety of methods for occupational preparation.

Work Tasks and Projects

Teachers can begin in the occupational preparation aspect of career development by assigning elementary students to a variety of work tasks that include keeping the erasers and blackboards clean, posting and keeping bulletin boards in order, cleaning up and putting away materials, organizing chairs for various classroom activities, cutting out posters and classroom materials, and a host of other prevocational tasks. In addition, students can become involved in various work projects during the year such as making collages, Christmas cards, and decorations; making presents for people in nursing homes; working with wood and learning other crafts; growing, collecting, and identifying plants; preparing stage sets and rehearsing for a class play; decorating Easter eggs; and building model stores and making products out of blocks to sell. Painting is also a particularly effective prevocational activity that helps students build physical-manual skills, work habits and behaviors, and personal–social competencies.

Most of these activities are generally conducted in elementary and middle school programs for all students and should be emphasized even more for students with disabilities in a purposeful manner. If the teacher emphasizes the relationship between these activities and the world of work, students will be able to judge how they feel about working at various jobs in the community. In this way, educators can plan a purposeful sequence of activities that are related to career education goals and objectives.

The family needs to be closely informed and involved in each series of prevocational activities for their children and can supplement the school's efforts with work activities in the home. Teachers should encourage parents to work with their children on school projects, both at school and at home, and help students to pursue specific interests and aptitudes when the school no longer can. Cooperation will help school personnel and family members to become closer and appreciate one another and, in the long run, will enhance the student's career development.

Simulations of Business and Industry

The simulated business approach mentioned in the occupational guidance section is also a specific occupational preparation technique. The students' experiences with Career City and the job analyses they have conducted should help them develop a relatively accurate idea of the job or jobs that they would be suited for within a simulated business. Thus, students can be "hired" to assume various employee roles within Career City. Creation of Career City or a simulated business will take considerable creativity, thought, time, cooperation among disciplines, and probably, money. However, these activities attract and benefit students and involve the school and community in an innovative and effective educational technique. Business and industry can offer technical assistance and materials, and parents and school personnel can use their expertise to help students develop the skills they need to succeed at various jobs within Career City.

On-Campus Training

The school cafeteria, library, gym, district warehouse, and housekeeping, clerical, and groundskeeping departments of schools are all resources that teachers can use in preparing their students for various occupations. Students are generally placed on a work site according to their interest and ability. In many cases, the job functions as a prevocational or career exploration experience. But if enough supervision and objectivity can be provided at the workplace, these placements are also valuable in helping to identify student interests and training potentials. Care must be taken that students are exposed to all aspects of the job and is not used primarily to do work that no one else wants to do.

In addition, job shadowing, where students observe and follow along behind an employee to learn about a job, and home assignments, which relate to specific occupational tasks, are two other occupational preparation techniques for use at this level. It is never too early to begin helping the student build a work personality.

Secondary-Level Students

In recent years, community-based vocational instruction and supported work placements have become more prominent, particularly for students with more severe disabilities. This section discusses several occupational preparation techniques that warrant consideration for use by school personnel at the secondary level for students with both mild and more severe learning disabilities and needs.

Experience-Based Career Education

Experience-based career education (EBCE) is a prominent model of the 1980s that is not particularly visible today. However, its approach to providing students with meaningful career exploration experiences is worthy of adoption with the necessary modifications. In the EBCE community-based approach, students explore a number of job sites in their community that are developed by a learning coordinator. Students receive hands-on exposure to the world of work but are not paid. These experiences are their first contacts with the world of work before they enter the skill-preparation stage. At the work site, students complete math, English, or other assignments that show how the worker uses each subject to complete a specific task. The program has been successful in helping students develop a positive self-concept, explore several occupations at no risk, develop positive work habits and behaviors, develop interests, and help relate academics to the job world.

The state of Iowa has implemented the approach extensively in many schools. Job shadowing is a form of EBCE, although the process is not as thorough and structured as the EBCE approach.

Job-Site Career/Vocational Training Programs

Job-site career/vocational training programs provide students with work experience and training in various community businesses and industries. A special educator or vocational educator generally supervises the overall preparation, placement, and supervision of students. Wisniewski, Alper, and Schloss (1991) note there are two major approaches to the on-site training approach: the train-and-place and the place-and-train models. Both models require some degree of preparation for the placement, but in the train-and-place model, the student is expected to have most of the competencies necessary for eventual success. In the place-and-train model, the student is trained on the job, based on a task analysis of the work assignment. Work study and work experience programs could be classified as this type of career/vocational training program. Another term for similar programs is community-based vocational education (CBVE).

Community-based vocational training should begin as early as possible and will depend on the individual student and her level and needs. Based on the student's vocational assessment and educational background, reasonable decisions should be made regarding appropriate work sites and jobs. Vocational plans should be systematic and must meet the student's needs. Teachers or counselors must carefully review the work site and have a clear understanding with those individuals for whom the student will interact. Career development and the work site must be ensured; therefore, expectations for the student and procedures for reaching these goals must be outlined with the work supervisors.

Many placement personnel believe that the students should receive pay for the work they do on off-campus jobs. Although this is perhaps desirable, students may think that the primary purpose of their working experience is to earn money. They may select certain work experiences primarily because of the money they can receive rather than the intrinsic exploration and preparation values. If money becomes more important than the value of this experience, the students will eventually suffer. It might be better to conduct these placements as if the students were taking a vocational education skill-building course. Then if they become proficient and productive after a period of time, monetary benefits can be made available. Teachers should consider this controversial issue when designing a program.

 "It is important for educators to know that as long as students with disabilities are engaged in vocational exploration, assessment, and training they are considered not *employees of the businesses and thus schools and businesses are not violating the provisions of the Fair Labor Standards Act (FLSA) relative to minimum wages, overtime pay, recordkeeping and child labor. Thus, schools should not hesitate to set up or expand their community-based transition programs."*

(Simon, Bourexis, & Norman, 1993)

Supported Employment

Supported employment is another training option for secondary and postsecondary programs. It is generally an approach that is used with adults with severe disabilities. An important component of this approach is the ongoing support at the work site by a job coach or employment training specialist, who ensures that the student learns the tasks and receives other services necessary for gaining as much independence as possible. Several models have evolved:

- Individualized Placement Model: On-site training and supports are provided.
- Enclave Model: Six to eight persons receive training and continuous supervision so they can work within a host company, which receives guaranteed productivity at a fixed cost.
- Mobile Crew Model: A group of persons is a member of a business such as a janitorial service that provides contractual services. Training and supervision are provided by a specialist.
- Benchwork Model: Contract work is secured, and the individuals are taught assembly-like tasks.

In all models, the ultimate goal is training that will lead to competitive employment and an integrated life-style as much as possible (Wisniewski et al., 1991). Supported employment was authorized as an appropriate vocational outcome in the Rehabilitation Act Amendments in 1986 and again in 1992.

The supported employment approach is an integrated community-based approach that has been shown to be more effective than a traditional rehabilitation facility or sheltered workshop service, although both of these agencies now generally have a supported employment component as well. Supported employment lends itself well to the current thrust of inclusion, because its focus is on an integrated provision of training and employment for individuals rather than a segregated one.

Rehabilitation Facilities (Community Rehabilitation Centers)

The traditional rehabilitation facility or workshop model has been changing over the years to meet the movement to provide assessment and training in the natural setting rather than a more restrictive, protected environment. For some individuals, however, such an in-house service may be a first step in the person's training outside school. Facilities and workshops of this nature are usually well-staffed with professionals with vocational evaluation, counseling, vocational education, and job placement training and certification. The facilities are set up as industrial enterprises, either offering subcontract work and/or manufacturing their own products. Thus, the rehabilitation-oriented facility can offer an important option for the vocational training of some students with disabilities and should be considered an important contributor to their eventual personal, social, and occupational success.

 "Imagine schools where the curriculum is so relevant to students future goals that discipline problems decrease dramatically, teenagers who were never successful in traditional classrooms become focused and excited about learning, and teachers find that their job can, indeed be fun and rewarding—the way they envisioned it when they chose their profession!"

(Williamson, 1994, p. 11)

Vocational Education

Williamson's (1994) statement, appearing in the March/April issue of *Missouri Schools*, exemplifies what proponents of both career education and the newly authorized tech prep program believe will result if their programs are implemented throughout the country. With the introduction of the tech prep program, a new vocational education option became available to some students who can benefit from a 2-year college. Tech prep expands vocational education to "combine applied academics with technology training in a way that makes sense to students. It links work experience with career choice and offers students early exposure to potential employers" (Williamson, 1994, p. 12).

The tech prep concept was introduced originally by Dr. Dale Parnell—a former superintendent, college president, and president of the American Association of Community and Junior Colleges (also a strong spokesperson for the career education movement since the 1970s). Tech prep is intended to address the needs of the "neglected majority," the vast groups of students in the middle quartiles of the secondary school population who fail to develop saleable skills by the time they graduate or leave the high school program. The tech prep program is so similar to the career education concept that it fits perfectly in addressing the occupational career role composing the concept. As one vocational technical school tech prep coordinator has professed, "If Tech Prep is to be really effective in high school, we must start in the upper elementary grades and middle schools to do lots of career awareness so that faculty, parents and students will understand the changes occurring in the workplace" (Kirkpatrick, quoted in Williamson, 1994, p. 13).

All tech prep programs must provide equal access to the full range of technical preparation programs to individuals who are members of special populations, including the development of services appropriate to the needs of such individuals. The impact of tech prep remains to be seen in regard to providing sufficient vocational training opportunities for a significant proportion of students with disabilities and other special learning needs. However, it seems to hold considerable promise for providing an important mechanism for implementing the intent of the recent school-to-work legislation and the career education approach advocated in this book.

One final program that should be mentioned under the Carl D. Perkins Act of 1990 is the provision for Vocational Education Lighthouse Schools. Secondary schools and area vocational schools can apply for grants to establish and operate high-quality, model vocational programs. Funds may be used to develop and disseminate model approaches for meeting the training needs and career counseling needs of minority, disadvantaged, disabled, and limited English proficiency students. This is just another example of the many mechanisms for educators to use in instituting quality occupational preparation programs for their students.

Postsecondary-Level Students

Many of the services available at the secondary level apply and extend into postsecondary services. The tech prep programs at vocational-technical schools, some community colleges, rehabilitation facilities, and Job Training Partnership Act (JTPA) programs are some of the most prominent services. Special educators need to establish relationships with these agencies so appropriate transitional efforts and follow-along efforts can be provided to ensure the individual's ultimate success.

Examples of Some Vocational Training Materials

Many commercially available materials have been developed to provide educators with useful occupational guidance and skills development tools. A few of these are presented next.

The Employability Enhancement Strategies

The Arkansas Research and Training Center in Vocational Rehabilitation at the University of Arkansas-Fayetteville, has developed assessment and instructional materials that can help educators to better address social/interpersonal skills, vocational choice-making skills, vocational coping skills, and job-seeking skills. Each of their materials is described briefly:

Social/Interpersonal Skills. The Conversion Rating Forms (CRF) measures the student's ability to use specific conversation skills in a role-play situation. Conversion Skills Training (CST) teaches techniques such as the greeting, the opening question, and showing interest.

Vocational Choice-Making Skills. Administered in a structured interview format, the Employability Maturity Interview (EMI) provides a measure of readiness for vocational planning. Individuals with lower readiness scores are involved in the Occupational Choice Strategy (OCS), which teaches problem-solving and decision-making skills in a vocational choice context.

Vocational Coping Skills. Products in the assessment/curriculum tandem that deal with job maintenance include the WPP (Work Personality Profile) (a 58-item behavior rating form), Behavior Management in Work Settings (BMWS), the Work Performance Assessment (WPA) (a 1-hour work simulation measuring student response to common supervisory demands), and Vocational Coping Training (VCT).

Job-Seeking Skills. The Job-Seeking Skills Assessment (JSSA) measures a student's ability to complete a job application and an interview successfully. Skills for each of these tasks are taught in two training packages: Job Application Training (JAT) and Getting Employment Through Interview Training (GET-IT!). These materials can be integrated easily into an occupational curriculum area such as LCCE and are valuable tools to help educators implement effective strategies that will prepare students for successful occupational functioning.

Talent Assessment, Inc.

As noted in Chapter 7, Talent Assessment, Inc., has specialized primarily in functional/career assessment materials. However, some of their products also provide important vocational training aspects. The Practical Assessment Exploration System (PAES) places students in simulated work environment in the classroom, where they engage in a progression of sequential activities comprising three major areas: business, consumer/home economics, and industrial technology. The components of PAES consist of complete curriculum materials, business activities unit, consumer/home economics unit, manipulatory unit, all data collection forms, computer scoring forms and software, and on-site training. Another product, the Expanding Horizons program, is a satirical program that takes students through the real job world starting with the first job interview to resigning from a job. Seven individual units allow for flexibility by the instructor, who can use the materials for individuals or large groups.

A Day in the Life Program

One particularly interesting and cutting edge computerized software effort to build integrated job skills into secondary programs has been developed at Pennsylvania State University (1993) and is published by Curriculum Associates, Inc. The program, A Day in the Life, is, according to its publisher, "a sophisticated departure from traditional instruction" by building basic skills, life skills, critical thinking, and problem-solving capabilities into five job areas: food services, health, maintenance, retail, and clerical. Learners develop, practice, and apply a variety of literacy skills critical for employability and job success through job-related problem-solving activities.

The A Day in the Life program presents realistic situations illustrating how entry-level employees integrate reading, writing, computation, and critical thinking skills to solve problems and solve goals. Computerized tutorial lessons help relate directly to the problem at hand. While the course ware provides literacy instruction, learners also perform actual projects encountered in a day in the life of a worker. The goal is to help the students acquire the basic skills needed for job success.

Many excellent vocational training materials have been developed recently and can be easily identified from the many catalogs and advertisements received by educators. In addition, some of the textbooks that can provide readers with more detailed information on occupational preparation techniques and approaches follow: Rusch (1986), *Competitive Employment Issues and Strategies;* Rusch, Destefano, et al. (1992), *Transition From School to Adult Life: Models, Linkages, and Policies;* Gaylord-Ross (1988), *Vocational Education for Persons with Handicaps* (1988), and the Clark and Kolstoe (1990) text that has been referred to frequently. In addition, two excellent rehabilitation counseling texts for reference on both occupational guidance and preparation techniques are Parker and Szymanski (1992) *Rehabilitation Counseling: Basics and Beyond* and Roessler and Rubin (1992), *Case Management and Rehabilitation Counseling.*

LCCE COMPETENCIES

The preceding two chapters focused on many skills critical to independent living. Daily living and personal–social skills are also important for occupational success. In fact, all the competencies of the LCCE curriculum relate to occupational functioning as well as satisfactory community living, whether in the areas of personal hygiene, communication, independence, or getting around one's community.

In this section, the 6 LCCE occupational skills and their 28 subcompetencies are presented. The competencies and subcompetencies are illustrated in Figure 12.3. The first three competencies involve occupational guidance activities, and the last three relate specifically to occupational preparation. Note that competency 22 does not have specific subcompetencies, because the occupational skill being taught will vary from student to student. Thus, users can write in the subcompetencies for this area when the specific training area has been determined. Activity tips and sample lesson plans from the LCCE competency unit curriculum materials published by The Council for Exceptional Children (Roessler & Brolin, 1992) illustrate the material.

17 Knowing and Exploring Occupational Possibilities

Individuals must have a broad perspective of the world of work before they can make satisfying and realistic occupational choices. This competency is closely allied to the career awareness and exploration stages of career education. Students should begin exploring the world of work and specific occupations almost immediately after beginning school. The more that students are aware of the reinforcing values of various jobs, the more likely it is that they will develop motivation and appreciation of the dignity of work and will identify with the occupational world. In conjunction with family and community resources, school personnel must provide an array of awareness and exploration opportunities (i.e., field trips, speakers, literature, summer work, and role playing) so that occupational possibilities are presented for the student's knowledge and exploration.

A variety of individuals should participate in making students aware of occupational possibilities. The elementary teacher can relate various subject matter to job information. She can also elicit the assistance of the student's parents, employers, and employees who work in various settings throughout the community. Many pamphlets and other media can be used. As students progress in their awareness of occupational possibilities, actual exploration of jobs of interest can be offered in school, family, and community settings. Most persons who participate in awareness activities should ideally be involved in helping students explore hands-on experiences and special interest areas. Figure 12.4 illustrates school, family, and community experiences that might be provided to help the student acquire various subcompetencies involved in competency 17, knowing and exploring occupational possibilities. The state employment services (job service), vocational rehabilitation agencies, community colleges, vocational schools, and newspaper ads can be important resources to adult learners.

17.70 Identify Remunerative Aspects of Work

In general, elementary students seldom consider the differences among jobs in regard to pay. As students get older and their needs become more clearly defined, this subcompetency takes on added significance. Inherent in this process is the understanding that remuneration often depends on such factors as the demand and supply of workers for the job, community needs for the services or goods provided by the worker, and the skill from training or formal education that students may need to perform the job. Students need to understand why people are paid to work and why there are different pay

Curriculum Area | Competency | Subcompetency: The student will be able to:

Competency	Subcompetency: The student will be able to:	
17. Knowing & Exploring Occupational Possibilities	70. Identify remunerative aspects of work	71. Locate sources of occupational & training information
18. Selecting & Planning Occupational Choices	76. Make realistic occupational choices	77. Identify requirements of appropriate & available jobs
19. Exhibiting Appropriate Work Habits & Behaviors	81. Follow directions & observe regulations	82. Recognize importance of attendance & punctuality
20. Seeking, Securing & Maintaining Employment	88. Search for a job	89. Apply for a job
21. Exhibiting Sufficient Physical-Manual Skills	94. Demonstrate stamina & endurance	95. Demonstrate satisfactory balance & coordination
22. Obtaining Specific Occupational Skills		

OCCUPATIONAL GUIDANCE AND PREPARATION

FIGURE 12.3   Life Centered Career Education competencies: Occupational guidance and preparation curriculum area.

rates for different jobs. This understanding relates to several of the subcompetencies associated with competency 1, managing personal finances, and can help students to calculate the amount of money they would receive from engaging in an occupation that interests them and to relate this information to making wise and necessary expenditures and paying taxes. Other objectives should include identifying the different kinds of wages (e.g., piece rate or hourly, weekly, or monthly wage) and what personal needs can be met with a salary expected from jobs that interest them.

◆ **Activity Tip**

Require each student to secure information on one job of interest per week for several weeks each semester. Students should develop and keep a job information sheet. On the left side of a sheet of paper, students should record the name of each job they investigate. The following information is recorded for each job: company, salary, training required, hours worked, and job duties. (This information might be taken from the Job Analysis Form presented in Figure 12.1 if it is used.) Parents can help the student investigate the jobs and complete the sheet. Weekly class discussions cover the jobs that the students have investigated and possible reasons for their salary level. A master list of community jobs can be developed to depict pertinent information relative to remunerative aspects. ◆

17.71   Locate Sources of Occupational and Training Information

Identifying sources of occupational information is closely allied to the previous subcompetency. In addition to the community sources, students should become familiar

72. Identify personal values met through work	73. Identify societal values met through work	74. Classify jobs into occupational categories	75. Investigate local occupational & training opportunities	
78. Identify occupational aptitudes	79. Identify major occupational interests	80. Identify major occupaitonal needs		
83. Recognize importance of supervision	84. Demonstrate knowledge of occupational safety	85. Work with others	86. Meet demands for quality work	87. Work at a satisfactory rate
90. Interview for a job	91. Know know to maintain post-school occupation-al adjustment	92. Demonstrate know-ledge of competitive standards	93. Know how to adjust to changes in employment	
96. Demonstrate manual dexterity	97. Demonstrate sensory discrimination			
There are no specific subcompetencies as they depend on skill being taught				

FIGURE 12.3 *continued*

Note. From *Life Centered Career Education: A Competency Based Approach* (4th ed., pp. 12–13) by D. E. Brolin, 1993, Reston, VA: The Council for Exceptional Children. Copyright 1993 by The Council for Exceptional Children. Reprinted by permission.

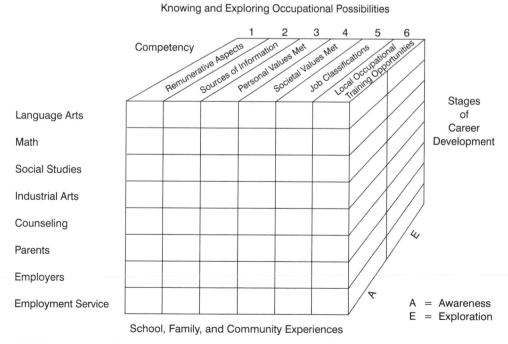

FIGURE 12.4   Examples of experiences related to knowing and exploring occupational possibilities (competency 17).

with such printed information as the *Dictionary of Occupational Titles, Occupational Outlook Handbook,* pamphlets from various businesses and industries, and government announcements. These materials provide a wealth of information that teachers can periodically review, discuss, and make available in the school counselor's office. Another excellent service is provided by commercial publishers who have developed a host of materials in the form of filmstrips, games, records, cassettes, and guides that require students to identify the kinds of information available from each source and how they can use these sources to obtain specific information about a particular job.

17.72   Identify Personal Values Met Through Work

Students should learn very early that many personal needs and values can be met by work and that work can become a personally meaningful part of their lives. At the same time, they must also learn that some personal needs and values may have to be gratified through leisure activities and other pursuits. One of the teacher's major goals should be to help students identify and choose a personally meaningful set of work values that foster their desire to become productive members of society. Values such as a sense of fulfillment, self-sufficiency, personal worth, positive self-concept, success, self-support, acceptance by others, satisfying social relationships, independence, and monetary gratification are examples of needs that students can meet through working. Field trips and classroom visits can give elementary students an opportunity to interact with various types of employed people and can expose them to ways in which these workers meet personal needs and develop values. Students can begin to identify the kind of personal values they presently possess and can visualize how to meet their needs through work.

Group discussions can give students an opportunity to hear how others arrive at their decisions. Parents can discuss the positive aspects of their jobs as well as ways in which they would like to change their jobs (e.g., more responsibility, variety, physical activity). They should explain how they meet these missing values and needs in their nonoccupational time. Secondary-level students who are on job sites and former students who are employed can also discuss many features of their jobs. Adult learners can identify what personal values they met and didn't meet while working at various jobs. Other objectives related to this subcompetency are helping students recognize the importance of work for economic functioning and building self-esteem.

17.73   Identify Societal Values Met Through Work

Students should be introduced to the ways workers affect society. Teaching activities can focus on specific ways individuals from various occupational categories contribute to the betterment of society (e.g., police officers, fire fighters, food service workers, janitors, farmers, computer operators, assembly line workers, clerks, and nurses). Teachers should cover an array of jobs that require various amounts of skill and training. In this way, students can learn that everyone, no matter what he does, contributes meaningfully to society. Weekly field trips, speakers, or class discussions can highlight the social contributions of one or more jobs. Representatives from unions and industries, government, the Chamber of Commerce, and small businesses as well as parents should be extensively involved. Other objectives related to this subcompetency are exploring the ways that employees who have different jobs work interdependently and identifying the rewards of different occupations.

17.74 Classify Jobs into Occupational Categories

During the elementary years, students should be able to identify the rudiments of major categories of jobs, particularly those that are relevant to their specific interests. At first, jobs can be classified primarily as white or blue collar, skilled or unskilled, and according to type of work, training, or required education. Students in secondary and adult programs can use information about job and occupational clusters contained in the *Dictionary of Occupational Titles, Occupational Outlook Handbook, Guide for Occupational Exploration,* and other guides that can add more specifically to learning activities. Teachers should request a representative from the local employment service to explain how students may use major job categories and major criteria. Students should be involved in organizing and participating with employers in a careers day program. Teachers can use bulletin boards, newspapers, and other media to illustrate different occupational systems. An objective associated with this subcompetency is to identify education, training, and reimbursement related to various occupational categories.

17.75 Investigate Local Occupational and Training Opportunities

Students should learn about various jobs in their community. After identifying community sources of occupational information, they should secure information from one source for a period of time, write it down, post it on a bulletin board, and present it to the class. Newspaper advertisements, radio announcements, flyers, and community job surveys are examples of such sources. This exercise enables students to understand and use all community sources of occupational information while learning about jobs and their availability. Students could learn this subcompetency early in the school years. For example, students who are involved in a speech therapy program can conceptualize various community occupations while they learn respective speech sounds. The therapist and teacher can provide a variety of interesting games, role-playing exercises, and other activities that will increase the student's motivation and learning. Close inspection of available jobs can help students learn more about the world of work, job differences, and requirements. Other objectives associated with this subcompetency are for students to identify appropriate sources of occupational information and determine appropriate methods of securing and using such information.

The following lesson plan is an example of how three LCCE instructional objectives for subcompetency 17.75 can be combined to teach a career awareness lesson. A home/school activity is also included in the lesson plan and addresses the career role of employee.

Lesson Plan 1

17.75.1A:1
17.75.3A:1
17.75.4A:1

LCCE Objective 17.75.1   Select an occupational area and find local employers in the Yellow Pages.

LCCE Objective 17.75.3   Utilize sources of employment information.

LCCE Objective 17.75.4   Locate sources of employment information.

Lesson Objective: Student will identify readily accessible sources of job openings in the local community.

Instructional Resources: Newspaper want ads, local shoppers' newspapers, other sources of local job leads.

Lesson Introduction: Keeping informed of job openings in the community is important. You must know where to get the information you need.

School Activity: **Time: 1 session**

Task:
1. **Advance Preparation:** Collect current sources of information on job leads in the community.
2. Students discuss sources of information about job openings in the community. List their sources on the chalkboard.
3. Present current examples of sources of job lead information, for example, newspaper want ads, openings listed in shoppers' newspapers, company literature, trade magazines, announcements in the business section of the newspaper and listings on laundromat or restaurant bulletin boards. Pass samples of each source around the class.
4. Small groups review the different sources of information on local job openings. Each group develops a list of five job openings in the community and uses the Yellow Pages to add address and telephone numbers to the job openings listed.
5. Explain the home activity to the students. Have them copy on a sheet of paper the job information sources listed on the chalkboard.

Home/School Activity: **Time: 1 session**

Task:
1. Students share job lead sources with their adult friends and ask them if they know of any other ways to learn of job leads. At the beginning of the next class, students add new job lead sources to the paper they prepared in class.
2. Students share new job lead sources with the class.
3. Volunteers offer to collect examples of the new sources of job lead information and bring them back to the class.
4. Students share new materials with the class when appropriate.

Lesson Plan Evaluation:

Activity: Students will collect information on local job opportunities and interview their adult friends regarding prospects for work.

Criteria: Student will list three ways to learn about local job openings and will list three jobs currently available in the community.

Career Role: Employee

Career Stage: Awareness

Note. From *Life Centered Career Education Competency Units for Occupational Guidance and Preparation* (Vol. 1, p. 145) by R. T. Roessler and D. E. Brolin, 1992, Reston, VA: The Council for Exceptional Children. Copyright 1992 by The Council for Exceptional Children. Reprinted by permission.

18 Selecting and Planning Occupational Choices

With a broad perspective of the world of work and the development of a positive set of work values, the student can begin to make preliminary and tentative occupational choices. Although elementary children may promulgate occupational aspirations as part of their career development, teachers should begin serious attempts to identify and direct secondary students toward relevant occupational choices. Many professionals become concerned about encouraging students to make occupational choices too early, believing that these students will be pigeonholed by selecting inappropriate work roles. However, young adolescents who have explored occupational possibilities and have developed personal–social skills are ready to think seriously about their future at about the ninth-grade level. Choices at this stage must be considered subject to change as students mature from further experiences. Making occupational choices gives the student's educational program more significance by revealing that the individual can contribute to society and function as an adult. In the case of adult learners, a considerable period of unemployment or failure may have occurred. Thus, a substantial period of time may pass before students can make an occupational decision.

18.76 Make Realistic Occupational Choices

Experiences from the previous subcompetency will help students discover many jobs that really do not meet their occupational needs, interests, or aptitudes. For those jobs that do, a second level of decisions needs to be made relative to jobs of highest preference. The demand for the occupation, required education and training, and other factors are significant at this level. Students should learn the career ladder that the occupation offers and occupations for which they might qualify. These tentative occupational choices should be based on an analysis of the whole person and should be systematically determined by students, parents, employers, and school personnel. Professional guidance and counseling are important for this subcompetency. Another objective that should be attempted is for the individual to be able to identify specific work sites where the job of choice is available and to try out the job.

18.77   Identify Requirements of Appropriate and Available Jobs

With a knowledge of sources of occupational information (subcompetency 17.2) and their major occupational needs, interests, and aptitudes, students should be ready to review the specific requirements and characteristics of appropriate and available jobs. Publications such as the *Dictionary of Occupational Titles* should be useful for individual and group sessions. The *Dictionary*, published by the Department of Labor, is a compendium of over 20,000 occupations representing the majority of jobs in the country. These activities can begin seriously during the 10th grade and can become a stimulus for independent job searching and decision making. Vocational assessment adds an important dimension to realistic decision making and planning, as do community resource personnel, who can give an in-depth personal analysis of the job's characteristics. A wide range of commercial games, materials, and packages are available for students. Another objective that should be attempted is to help students identify alternate, related occupations for which they are best qualified.

18.78   Identify Occupational Aptitudes

Use of extensive vocational assessment techniques can help students understand their vocational potentials and specific aptitudes. Before formalized vocational assessment, students will have had some indication of job areas that they are able to learn and perform successfully. Aptitudes or abilities in the following areas should be ascertained: verbal, numerical, spatial, form perception, clerical, motor coordination, finger dexterity, manual dexterity, and mechanical. The General Aptitude Test Battery (GATB) of the U.S. Employment Service is one instrument for identifying the strengths and weaknesses of some students. For others, work sample batteries can be particularly beneficial and provide a better indication of aptitudes than standardized test batteries such as the GATB, which some claim to be discriminating toward minorities relative to its cutoff scores. A substantial number of vocational assessment systems are new on the market and will be discussed in greater detail in the occupational guidance techniques section. Another objective associated with this subcompetency should be to help the student identify ways of developing needed aptitudes for occupational interests.

18.79   Identify Major Occupational Interests

By 9th or 10th grade, most students should have a basic idea of occupational areas that would interest them. These decisions are related more to what they think they would like to do, for example, "help people by working in a hospital as an aide or orderly," regardless of whether the job meets all or most occupational needs and aptitudes. If the jobs that the student identifies are not within her capability or need structure, she can explore related but more appropriate ones later. What is important is that each individual is beginning to focus on specific occupational areas or jobs based on her knowledge of occupations and self. In some situations, interest inventories can be valuable, but for the most part, interests evolve from experiences and explorations in the workplace. Although occupational interests are unique to each individual, students can learn how others arrived at such decisions by engaging in group interactions. Other objectives that relate to this subcompetency are to help students identify occupations that permit the pursuit of personal interests and the occupational needs that can be met from these jobs.

18.80   Identify Major Occupational Needs

As students acquire personal–social skills of self-awareness, self-confidence, socially responsible behavior, interpersonal skills, independence, and problem-solving, they should be ready to identify those major occupational needs that are presently part of their work personality. They should be able to determine whether needs such as high pay, independence, achievement, praise, responsibility, authority, use of talents and abilities, advancement, security, social service, variety, and social status are of major importance in their future work life. Group discussions on the topic, supplemented with presentations given by persons working in various occupations, should be provided so that students can make these decisions and other choices related to an appropriate work environment (e.g., outdoor vs. indoor work, sedentary vs. active, urban vs. rural settings). These discussions can serve as a basis for lively and soul-searching inquiry. Teachers can also attempt to have students identify the occupational needs that persons in occupations they are interested in tend to have.

◆ Activity Tip

Have the class construct a list of occupational needs. Ask various members of the class to define and discuss each need. After the students have identified all possible needs, teachers should construct an occupational needs inventory and hand it out to the students. Each students should check which needs he feels are high or low. Each need should be explained again before it is rated. The students should then identify their six most important occupational needs. Students will use this list later when they begin to examine their occupational interests and aptitudes. (The Minnesota Importance Questionnaire is a good instrument to obtain for this activity. Information about it can be obtained from the Department of Psychology at the University of Minnesota.) ◆

19   Exhibiting Appropriate Work Habits and Behaviors

Competency 19, exhibiting appropriate work habits and behaviors, transcends the entire educational chain from the early elementary years through adulthood and can be taught by everyone responsible for the individual's career development. Work habits are more than study habits, although both have many similar features. School personnel should emphasize the necessity of developing the work habits and behaviors that all students will need when they begin responsible jobs. At certain times, teachers may simulate working environments in the school setting to illustrate the kinds of expectations employers have of competent workers. Field trips, class speakers, and parents can also play an important role in helping students to develop this subcompetency.

19.81   Follow Directions and Observe Regulations

Employers expect their employees to follow directions accurately. These may be given verbally or in writing and will range from very simple one-step directions to those that are complex and require several steps that employees must remember and complete. Gaming and role-playing techniques can be particularly effective in helping students develop these skills. Exercises will need to begin early and be repeated intermittently throughout the grade levels so that all students, especially those who have a lower ability in this area, can learn and retain these skills. After students have learned the lower-order steps, they should gradually learn how to follow more complicated directions. Another objective should be for the student to be able to perform a series of tasks in the home requiring simple-to-complex written instructions.

19.82   Recognize the Importance of Attendance and Punctuality

The classroom situation can be organized to emphasize the importance of attendance and punctuality in the workplace. A classroom time clock is one method that can be used to promote this concept. The student should learn why attendance and punctuality are important to the employer (e.g., loss of production time, business income, and meeting deadlines). Students should learn acceptable and unacceptable reasons for lateness and absenteeism, and what the consequences are in both situations. Once again, employers and workers from various businesses and industries can be effective in presenting their own cases and company policies. Another objective that students should be required to meet is to identify appropriate actions to take if they need to be late or absent from work.

19.83   Recognize the Importance of Supervision

Although accepting supervision is related to previous subcompetencies, it is specific to various methods of supervision that are found in the workplace. Supervision can range from being infrequent and indirect to very frequent and direct. Supervision can be constructive, critical, or unfair. It is important for the student to understand the various forms of supervision and how they should react to supervision under different conditions. Role playing is a viable method of presenting students with various situations and types of supervision so they can learn appropriate ways of responding. Role-playing activities can be followed by group discussions that focus on different responses that can help students develop other methods of handling the situation. The teacher can also use various methods of supervising class members and then get reactions to the method. Other objectives that can be attempted for students are for them to observe and discuss supervisory policies in several workplaces and identify various responses that can be used for various types of supervisory practices.

19.84   Demonstrate Knowledge of Occupational Safety

Many employers are afraid to employ people with disabilities because they believe that these individuals will have more accidents. Thus, teachers should emphasize occupational safety skills to minimize the number of potential accidents that could occur and result in the individual's dismissal. Films, field trips, role playing, and class discussions are particularly important in helping students understand potential safety hazards and the necessary precautions they may need to take to avoid unnecessary accidents. Before placement on a community job site, students should be thoroughly prepared to handle all conceivable accidents that could occur at the workplace. This subcompetency should be taught at all levels of the school program so that by the time the students leave school, they are well versed in safety practices. Other objectives associated with this subcompetency should require the student to identify major reasons for practicing safety on the job and potential safety hazards that exist in various types of occupations.

19.85   Work with Others

The inability to get along with co-workers and supervisors is one of the most common reasons people fail on their jobs. Students must learn work expectations, and the school can become a fertile ground for teaching these interactive and cooperative skills. Teachers should create an environment that promotes development of these work skills by encouraging students to practice interacting and cooperating with others. Field trips, role playing, and group discussions can also be used to illustrate and stimulate discussion on reasons for working with others and the individual's importance in cooperative efforts and to help students identify positive and negative aspects of working together. Another objective might be to simulate actual work environments by developing projects that require students to interact and cooperate with others before they can complete a specific task.

◆ Activity Tip

Set up an assembly line operation with the assistance of industrial workers from the community. The assembly line operation should be as realistic as possible. Have the workers explain their jobs, particularly as they relate to this competency area. Initiate the work and assess the students on their ability to work with others, accept supervision, and master other subcompetencies related to this competency. Some students may be supervisors or assume other roles associated with this type of work. At the end of the day, the class should discuss the group's performance and future efforts. Rate each student on work habits and behaviors, and provide individual feedback that will increase the students' awareness of strong points and areas where they need to improve. (Further discussion and ideas related to this type of activity are provided later in the chapter.) ◆

19.86   Meet Demands for Quality Work

Students will need to know about quality standards for various types of jobs, particularly those that interest them. They should meet such standards on their work assignments, understand when and why such standards are not achieved, and work until they have met standards or until teachers have asserted whether students can perform at that level. Elementary students should strive for quality while they are engaged in projects. Students can be assigned as checkers to ascertain whether work has met the job requirements and can participate in discussions conducted to point out problems. The secondary students' job explorations and try-outs establish the expected criteria that will be used to evaluate their performance. Another objective of this subcompetency should be to have the student perform simulated work tasks at minimum quality standards.

19.87   Work at a Satisfactory Rate

It is important for students to learn that people are employed to make money for the employer. This requires that students learn how to do work correctly and at a sufficient speed. Teachers should require students to complete certain work activities within a specific period of time so that they form the habit as well as learn the concept. Time standards can be established for various work tasks in and out of the school, and teachers should chart the student's progress until she meets the criterion. Students should participate in establishing reasonable time standards so they can understand how and why time or piece rates are determined. Employers and workers can be useful in conveying the importance of this subcompetency, especially if these skills will help students earn more money. Other objectives associated with this subcompetency should be to help the student identify satisfactory rates required for various jobs of interest and reasons jobs must be performed at certain rates of speed.

The following is a description by Terri Chasteen, a special education teacher in Nixa, Missouri, of how she and her associates are implementing the LCCE approach and using its lesson plans to teach subcompetency 19.87 to her students.

I teach a work–study class consisting of six students who have mild intellectual disabilities, learning disabilities, or behavior disorders. Administrative support in this district has enabled the special education teachers to design two classrooms to meet the curricular needs of these students. One classroom consists of a life skills area with a complete kitchen including a washer and dryer and a living area. Another section of this classroom contains built-in study carrels and a lecture area. The other classroom is a more traditional classroom that includes several work stations such as office skills (filing, binding books, collation, and mailing) and woodworking (gluing, assembling, painting, finishing).

The class is currently working on the Occupational Guidance LCCE Instructional Unit 81, "Following Directions and Observing Regulations." At the beginning of each LCCE unit, the goals and objectives are shared with the students. This enables the students to know what they are expected to gain from the completion of each unit. These objectives are reviewed at the beginning of each lesson. Students are asked to follow directions every day in a variety of different ways. This unit allows them to explore methods to improve their skills in following directions. It also introduces them to the idea that following directions is an important skill not only in their daily routine but also in any of the careers they may choose.

The first lesson was a reflective time when students realized ways they had followed directions in the past. Each student was asked to relate a personal situation. (These students love to talk. The problem was getting them to stop.) Each student was asked to describe a time when she was asked to follow directions and the outcome. Independently, students were asked to write a paragraph describing an experience in following directions, including the outcome and how directions helped them.

The next lesson involved following verbal directions. Problems were discussed in following verbal directions that are vague, lengthy, complex, or hard to understand. Students developed a list of hints that would improve their skills at following verbal directions. A completed list was recorded on the work sheet "Responding to Verbal Instructions" and then placed in their life skills notebooks.

One adaptation I have included while working with the LCCE curriculum was to have the students make a life skills notebook. This notebook consists of information they might need in their future. For example: a resume, lists of information (names, addresses, phone numbers of persons to use as references), and copies of the fact sheets from the LCCE lessons.

The next lesson gave the students an opportunity to practice responding to verbal directions. As a class, the students wrote a dialogue with vague, unclear directions and the listener's appropriate response (i.e., write down directions, ask for clarification, etc.). A videotape was made as the students role played the dialogue. For additional practice students played the Directions Game.

This game is teacher directed. Each student is asked to complete a list of simple tasks given verbally. The game is continued by adding one task at a time until a mistake is made. The winner of the game is the student who can remember and perform the most tasks without making a mistake. This game not only allows the students practice using the strategies for following directions but also improves short-term memory skills.

The next lesson introduces the second half of the unit, which focuses on following written directions. This was a popular lesson because it allowed the students a chance to practice the skills outside the confines of the classroom. The lesson involved students' writing instructions for finding a location on the school grounds, without naming the location. The instructions were then exchanged, and the fun began.

Terri Chasteen, special education teacher, and her class working on the LCCE subcompetency unit relating to following directions and observing regulations (Nixa, Missouri, Public Schools).

We went beyond the lesson plan and actually took the written instructions and tried to find the location. It was interesting for the students to see for themselves the problems that can occur if the directions are not clear, logical, or in sequential steps. Back in the classroom, students discussed ways to improve writing instructions and the positive aspects of being able to follow well-written directions.

The last objective took several sessions to complete. Students were asked to perform a series of tasks in response to written directions. It was important to overlearn this skill. It was also important to show students the many times in their lives that they are asked to follow directions accurately. The students were asked to collect examples of written directions that would be used in their daily lives in the home, the workplace, and in leisure time. The class then practiced following directions in each of these areas: following a recipe, following written directions to complete an order form, following diagram directions to complete string hand games, and watching a demonstration to make balloon animals. An evaluation of this unit included following three oral and three written directions along with the completion of the work sheet "Comparing Types of Directions."

These students enjoy the learning experiences provided in the LCCE curriculum. The suggested lesson plans are easy to follow and give a variety of activities and ideas that are helpful in planning. It is written in a way that allows the teacher freedom to adapt the lessons to the instructional level of his students. This reduces the students' frustration. The students also respond well to the many hands-on activities, field trips, and guest speakers.

20   Seeking, Securing, and Maintaining Employment

After leaving the formal education system, many students have difficulty seeking, securing, and maintaining employment. Apparently, efforts at teaching this competency have failed to help many students retain this knowledge and ability over time. This is a major downfall of these individuals in the community and is especially unfortunate for those who have been through an extensive educational program. Educators should begin teaching this competency in the 10th grade and should continue instructing their students in this area each semester thereafter. Many commercial materials are available for teaching this competency, although professionals may want to develop their own.

20.88 Search for a Job

The ability to develop a logical step-by-step method of searching for a job is a crucial subcompetency. Knowing how to explore sources of information about possible jobs is a beginning. Teachers can help students develop this subcompetency by using bulletin boards to depict the steps that students can take to search for a job and explore various sources of information. Field trips to agencies that help people find jobs, role playing, games, and guest speakers can also help students to gain new perspectives in this area. Job descriptions and announcements, advertisements, and commercial materials on job-seeking skills are also available. Other objectives related to this subcompetency include identifying steps involved in searching for a job, researching a specific job, and following through on a job lead.

The following lesson plan from the LCCE competency unit manual on occupational guidance and preparation illustrates how subcompetency 20.88 could be addressed at the career exploration stage within the classroom situation. The work sheet accompanying the lesson plan is not included.

Lesson Plan 9   20.88.3E:9

LCCE Objective 20.88.3.   Arrange a real or simulated job interview.

Lesson Objective: Student will learn how to contact an employer using appropriate telephone skills.

Instructional Resources: Worksheet Checklist: **Telephoning a Potential Employer**, want ads, "Learner sets" of telephones from telephone company.

Lesson Introduction: Employer contacts about job leads may be made by telephone, letter or personal visit. Today's lesson focuses on the telephone contact.

School Activity: Time: 2 sessions

Task:
1. Discuss types of employer contacts suggested in want ads, for example, writing or telephoning the employer.
2. Students form pairs and identify three jobs for which they would like more information. Students record the jobs in their Job lead File for use in Lesson Plan 10.
3. The pairs present their leads and how they would contact the employers to the class.

4. Identify the telephone contact as one way to gather job lead information from an employer. Describe the behaviors for the telephone contact listed on Worksheet Checklist: **Telephoning a Potential Employer.**

5. Demonstrate the worksheet behaviors by playing the role of a job seeker. Ask a student to volunteer to play the role of an employer.

   • Select a job title and employer name.

   • Ask the student to assume the name of the employer and to imagine that he or she has an opening for the selected job title.

   • Ask the student to answer questions as he or she expects the employer would.

   • Role play the 12 worksheet behaviors.

6. Students rate the instructor's performance using the checklist on the worksheet (instructor demonstration).

7. Following the demonstration, stress the following points about how to telephone an employer:

   • Use a telephone in a private, quiet place.

   • Know the information to seek and give.

   • Have pencil and paper ready to record the employer's comments.

   • Use a pleasant tone of voice, be polite in responding and listen carefully.

8. In the second session, groups of four role-play the employer contact, taking turns playing the role of job seeker, employer and observers. The observers should use the worksheet to evaluate the job seeker's performance.

9. Record information on each student's performance as a job seeker as evaluated by the two observers.

Lesson Plan Evaluation:

Activity: Students will paractice the employer contact.

Criteria: Student will demonstrate 10 of 12 behaviors required to contact an employer based on information from the observers.

Career Role: Employee
Career Stage: Exploration

Note. From *Life Centered Career Education Competency Units for Occupational Guidance and Preparation* (Vol. 1, pp. 229–230) by R. T. Roessler and D. E. Brolin, 1992, Reston, VA: The Council for Exceptional Children. Copyright 1992 by The Council for Exceptional Children. Reprinted by permission.

20.89   Apply for a Job

An important objective in vocational programming should be to prepare students to apply for a job. Mastery of this subcompetency is another indicator of the student's ability and independence for vocational functioning. To demonstrate this, the student must become familiar with job application forms and procedures involved in applying for jobs. Beginning in at least the 10th grade, students should learn words that are typically used on application forms and interviews. Students should spend a great deal of time reviewing and completing application forms, learning job vocabulary, role playing, and collecting personal data needed for job applications. Another objective that students should be required to meet is to identify those factors they consider important to them in applying for jobs.

20.90   Interview for a Job

Interviewing skills are inextricably related to the other subcompetencies and should receive careful attention from educators. Employers, workers, and other community resources can help to prepare the student for an interview. Students must understand and learn steps involved in securing an interview, what to do and say when requesting an interview on the phone or in person, and how to handle themselves in the actual situation. Role playing, group discussions, films, speakers and demonstrations, games and commercial materials, videotapes, and other techniques are highly recommended. Other objectives for students should be to complete a simulated job interview in an actual business establishment and practice dressing for and transporting self to job interviews.

20.91   Know How to Maintain Postschool Occupational Adjustment

Occupational adjustment skills are concerned with how former students can resolve potential problems that they may encounter after they have obtained a job. Former students are a fertile source of information who can describe the most significant adjustments that students may need to make in a work environment. Role play depicting problem areas is a recommended technique that teachers can use to illustrate effective behaviors. Students should keep a notebook of techniques for future use. This subcompetency should be given considerable emphasis during the latter part of the high school program. Another objective for the student would be to identify sources of assistance for programs that students cannot personally resolve.

◆ **Activity Tip**

The students should invite former students back to school to discuss their jobs (or lack of them) and should develop a set of questions relating to postschool adjustment. Discussions should include problems that former students encounter, how they handle those problems, what they feel the students need to do to be successful, and influences that affect their present career functioning. Later, students should have the opportunity to observe former students working at their actual jobs. The former students should be encouraged to bring in people who helped them adjust. Some former students may not cooperate in this activity because of their desire to no longer be identified with their past. ◆

Vocational rehabilitation counselors can provide valuable assistance in helping students interview and search for jobs.

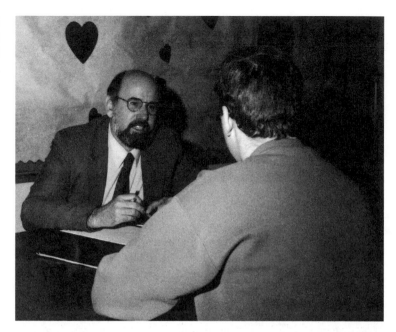

20.92   Demonstrate Knowledge of Competitive Standards

After students have secured a job, they must perform at the standard expected of other workers. If skills in adjusting to competitive standards are overlooked, former students may lose their jobs because of a misunderstanding of what is expected of workers and how they can advance their position and pay. Employers and workers present this kind of information and conduct on-site visits to various job locations so that students can observe what employers expect of workers at various jobs and how this can be best achieved. Other objectives for students should be to identify jobs of interest and their expected standards and how improvements can be achieved by the individual.

20.93   Know How to Adjust to Changes in Employment

Most people change jobs several times during their working career. Some people lose their jobs for various reasons. Others are promoted or find better positions. Students need to learn the factors that determine successful and unsuccessful job adjustment and how to deal with them. Another important objective of this unit of study is to know how to recognize and apply for promotional opportunities. The career preparation lesson plan on the next page is designed to help students know how to appropriately resign from a job.

Lesson Plan 5   20.93.4P:5

LCCE Objective 20.93.4.   Identify factors that lead to termination of employment.

Lesson Objective: Student will demonstrate the procedures to follow when leaving a job.

Instructional Resources: Worksheet **Quitting a Job,** Home Worksheet **Letter of Resignation,** Fact Sheet **Writing an Appropriate Letter.**

Lesson Introduction: Something happens on the job that upsets you. You say to yourself, "That's it. I quit." Have you just given yourself a bigger problem? Today we will talk about what is involved in leaving a job.

School Activity: **Time: 2 sessions**

Task:

1. Students discuss reasons for quitting a job, for example:
   - found a better job (economic reasons)
   - family/spouse relocation
   - career interest changes
   - same work all the time
   - poor working conditions
   - disagreeable supervisor
2. Small groups develop acceptable procedures (guidelines) to follow when quitting a job. Have the groups list their guidelines on the board.
3. Students review the rules on Worksheet **Quitting a Job** and answer the questions. Have them discuss responses when finished.
4. Students study Fact Sheet **Writing an Appropriate Letter** and identify the parts of a letter of resignation.
5. Explain the home activity to the students. Have them take Home Worksheet **Writing a Letter of Resignation** with them.

Home/School Activity: **Time: 1 session**

Task:

1. Students complete the worksheet at home. Have them select an employer and job for the letter.
2. Students ask a parent and/or friends about procedures they followed when resigning from a job.
3. Students discuss in pairs their letters of resignation. Students discuss in class what their parents and/or friends said about leaving a job.

Lesson Plan Evaluation:

Activity: Students will complete Worksheet **Quitting a Job** and Home Worksheet **Letter of Resignation.**

Criteria: Students will complete Worsheet **Quitting a Job** with 80% accuracy and write a letter of resignation.

Career Role: Employee

Career Stage: Preparation

Note. From *Life Centered Career Education Competency Units for Occupational Guidance and Preparation* (Vol. 2, pp. 580–581) by R. T. Roessler and D. E. Brolin, 1992, Reston, VA: The Council for Exceptional Children. Copyright 1992 by The Council for Exceptional Children. Reprinted by permission.

21 Exhibiting Sufficient Physical-Manual Skills

Occupations that the majority of individuals with disabilities obtain require physical stamina, endurance, coordination, strength, and dexterity. The jobs available to the many students with disabilities require considerable fine or gross motor dexterity, standing, pulling, pushing, lifting, and carrying abilities. Development of adequate physical-manual skills should begin shortly after they enter school. Teachers can design class activities to promote the use and development of skills that will help students to experience a great deal of personal success, pride, and satisfaction. Thus, a concerted focus needs to be made in this area.

21.94 Demonstrate Stamina and Endurance

Most jobs require a given amount of physical and mental stamina and endurance. The physical education instructor can assume a significant role in designing special programs to develop the student's skills in this area. Students should chart their progress toward attainment of criterion levels of performance. This type of program can be used at home, where purposeful tasks and responsibilities that relate to other subcompetencies can be designed. Several commercial programs are available for this subcompetency, but these would be unnecessary if the school personnel could develop the resources and activities within and outside of the schools that promote development of these skills. Other objectives that should be incorporated for this subcompetency are to require the student to identify jobs where stamina and endurance are absolutely critical and ways of building these skills to meet individual needs.

21.95 Demonstrate Balance and Coordination

The physical education instructor could assume a major responsibility in evaluating and designing specific individual activities that can improve each student's physical capacities. Teachers may need to consult a registered occupational therapist who can design specific tasks that measure and develop balance and coordination skills in a student with an orthopedic disability. Students should keep a cumulative record of their performance in various activities. This can document progress in terms of functioning level and can help them target new goals. Competitive games and charts may motivate students by drawing attention to the importance of these skills. Other objectives that should be met are to have students identify the relationship between balance and coordination to the world of work and to job performance and requirements of various jobs.

21.96 Demonstrate Manual Dexterity

A number of manual dexterity tests may assist people who direct the development of the student's manual dexterity. The Purdue Pegboard (Purdue Research Foundation, 1968), Minnesota Rate of Manipulation Test (Minnesota Employment Stabilization Research Institute, 1969), Wide Range Employment Sample Test (Jastak & Jastak, 1973), and Pennsylvania Bi-Manual Dexterity Test (Roberts, 1945) are examples of standardized instruments for evaluating and developing the student's manual dexterity. Evaluation of students should begin early and continue to serve as a basis for determining what work tasks are within the students' physical capabilities. Other objectives are to help students identify interests in occupations that require a fair degree of manual dexterity and reasons for developing a sufficient degree of dexterity for occupational and community life.

◆ Activity Tip

Use the Purdue Pegboard with another dexterity test to evaluate and motivate students to develop their manual dexterity skills. Individual and group charts can illustrate the students' progress at each testing session. Administer the test in a nonthreatening, gamelike manner and try to challenge students in an encouraging way. Give students three trials to improve and let them keep the test sheet after you have recorded their right hand, left hand, both hands, and assembly scores. The test should be administered monthly and can be used to plan physical activities that may enhance students' physical-manual skills. (Work samples and other tests may be used in a similar manner.) ◆

21.97 Demonstrate Sensory Discrimination

Many jobs require ability to distinguish sounds, shapes, sizes, and colors. The Talent Assessment Program (TAP; Talent Assessment, no date) is a work sample/task battery that relates sensory discrimination skills to vocational potential. Many teachers have also devised their own methods by using everyday objects. Evaluation of those skills should occur early in the school program. Other objectives are for students to be able to identify the need for sensory discrimination on jobs and the sensory discrimination they many need for jobs that they are interested in.

22   Obtaining a Specific Occupation Skill

Many professionals strongly believe that students do not need to leave the formal educational system with a saleable, entry-level occupational skill. Their arguments are that training can be best provided later, that too many other types of learning are necessary, and that secondary students are too young for specific occupational training. Although these arguments may be valid, individuals with disabilities and other learning difficulties need to acquire a skill before they leave the secondary school for the following reasons:

1. Most training facilities beyond the secondary level do not have enough specialists who can effectively meet their needs.
2. Many postsecondary programs are unattractive and dehumanizing or too long. Requirements for these programs are often stringent and unnecessary.
3. If the student can acquire a specific occupational skill before leaving the secondary school, the student, parents, instructors, employers, and significant others will have more confidence in his ability to learn a saleable skill.
4. Training in a specific occupational skill results in development and improvement of other competency areas (e.g., self-confidence, socially responsible behavior, interpersonal skills, independence, problem solving, communication skills, occupational awareness, work habits and behaviors, and physical-manual skills).
5. Some individuals may need more intensive training in skills than others.
6. Training results in a meaningful curriculum emphasis and makes other instruction relevant and reality based.
7. Training provides students with disabilities with an extra advantage over other individuals against whom they will be competing for similar jobs.
8. Attainment of an occupational skill can reveal higher-order potentials that students can pursue after the secondary program.
9. Training helps eliminate unrealistic occupational choices early enough so students receive training that is more appropriate to their individual needs and abilities.

Although some students may receive training in postsecondary programs, they should try to obtain a specific occupational skill during the high school years. In addition to the other daily living, personal–social, and occupational skills that are important to the growth of a work personality, students should select a training area that fosters awareness of personal and occupational interests. Selection should be a carefully designed process of career development that student, parents, instructors, and significant others can agree on.

Instruction in daily living curriculum areas may reveal special interests and aptitude for occupations in the clerical, maintenance, personal care, food service, computer, service, recreation and leisure, or transportation fields. Personal–social curriculum areas should reveal the most suitable work environment for the individual (i.e., noisy, calm, pressured, interactive, flexible, restrictive, closely supervised, routine, reinforcing, and impersonal). The occupational curriculum area should also reflect the student's work values, needs, interests, choices, work habits and behaviors, and physical capacities. Thus, in the process of becoming, a work personality emerges and forms to the extent that reasonable training choices can be determined.

FINAL COMMENTS

Most former students who become employed are in the secondary labor market, which comprises the low-paying, service-oriented jobs with little or no job promotion opportunities. Is this the most to expect from the educational system and the ability level of these students? We can expect a much better outcome for most of these students if they are better prepared for the demanding requirements of the real world.

Students must have substantial career education and transition services throughout their education program if they are to compete in today's high-tech occupational society. Occupational training models, materials, and techniques have been developed over the years to meet this need. But the school systems and their personnel must adopt them. The business community seems ready to provide more assistance than ever before, perhaps because they are in even greater need of qualified employees than previously. The Americans with Disabilities Act and School-to-Work Opportunities Act, which instituted work-based learning and tech-prep programs are good indicators of the window of opportunity that could be available to individuals with disabilities and other learning difficulties. A change in curriculum and lesson plans at every grade level is being required so children can learn more about different careers and to link their skills to the world of work.

Teaching the competencies in the occupational guidance and preparation curriculum area will increase the probability that students will select jobs that they can and want to do. People who have successful careers typically can perform the six competencies presented in this chapter. If the instruction begins early enough and the competencies are taught in their entirety, the final result will be employment success for the individual.

ACTIVITIES

1. Review the occupational guidance and preparation matrix in Figure 12.3 and then determine what general, vocational, and special education courses would be most appropriate for teaching each of the LCCE subcompetencies for your particular students. Then, identify those subcompetencies/skills in which you would

attempt to involve parents. Finally, identify the subcompetencies for which you would include community-based instruction and what community resources you would use to help you teach the subcompetencies.

2. Develop an instructional objective around one of the subcompetencies, and then write a lesson plan, using the LCCE format, for your students that addresses one of the career stages, instructional settings, and career roles.

Part 5

Implementation

Chapter 13

Career Education Programs

Chapter 14

Issues and Future Directions

Chapter 13

Career Education Programs

Preliminary Questions About the Topic

1. What are some of the major factors that affect the substantial implementation of educational innovations such as functional skills/transition approaches?
2. What significant challenges to educational change can you expect to receive from administrators, teachers, parents, agencies, employers, and students?
3. What 10 major barriers would constitute your "Hit Parade"—barriers that you believe hinder the implementation of educational innovations?
4. What are some of the ways of dealing with these challenges and the barriers that the various groups present to curriculum change?
5. What is the difference between program development and curriculum development? Which one is most typically done?
6. What is an Action Plan proposal, and how does it contribute to implementing educational innovations?
7. Why is career education instruction so important for elementary students, and what should be the focus at this level?
8. How do the goals of secondary education differ from those for elementary and middle school students?
9. How well does the Life Centered Career Education (LCCE) curriculum cover the 14 adult dimensions identified by Missouri LINC as important for transition planning and services?
10. In what type of educational settings, with what type of students, and at what educational levels is LCCE being implemented?

The overall goals of education and rehabilitation are to prepare the individual to live and work in society. If individuals with disabilities are to meet these goals, they must develop and integrate the necessary daily living, personal-social, and occupational skills into a rewarding and satisfying life-style. This includes learning about personal interests, needs, abilities, potentials, and the realities of a modern world. These understandings can help individuals make appropriate decisions about their careers. The implementation of the career education concept should be infused throughout the entire curriculum. Thus, if career education is to become a reality for individuals with special learning needs, professionals will need to make changes to implement a meaningful and purposeful career development program.

Until recently, most school systems have provided students with a content-oriented curriculum in which students learn a specific body of knowledge. This approach may not directly suit the individual's needs. Educators should adopt a process-oriented educational philosophy. Process education emphasizes the acquisition of specific skills that are necessary for community living and working and requires professionals to decide on desired outcomes that can be defined in precise, measurable terms. This does not negate the importance of or need for general education. Rather, the program must include both general and career education to maximize the student's career development.

If significant and positive changes in curriculum are to occur, the program should be carefully planned. It is not easy to convince people to substantially change the teaching, counseling, or services that they provide to students. They will need to believe in the need to change, be involved in making changes, and be recognized and rewarded for their efforts. Normalizing the educational and rehabilitation process is an important concept that will need administrative support.

A career development program will most likely succeed if education for all students is directed toward similar goals. This may not always be the case, however, because the curriculum focus for students' special needs sometimes differs from the programs planned for their peers. When this occurs, fewer school personnel are involved in the student's education program than if the entire student body was receiving inclusion-oriented career development. I strongly recommend a career development program that encompasses all students within the school system.

"The preparation for transition must be built upon the foundation of career education" (Began, 1990, p. 1). This statement by an educator in a Kansas school reflects the opinion of many school personnel and others throughout this country who are concerned about the future life of individuals with disabilities and those with other special learning needs.

This chapter begins by focusing on the process of curriculum change and the many challenges that influence successful change. The follow section identifies and discusses several important curriculum considerations for instituting a career education approach at the elementary/middle school, secondary, and postsecondary levels. The final section consists of descriptions of several school districts and others who are implementing the LCCE curriculum. Some of the program descriptions in this chapter were written by personnel from the schools implementing the LCCE approach.

Point of View

All students deserve high-quality educational programs provided through curriculum and learning experiences designed to prepare them for future education, community participation, independent living, meaningful employment, and active citizenship. While the debate about the transformation needed in general and special education continues, national agendas, federal initiatives, state school reform, and statewide testing programs are forcefully directing the curriculum and the focus of instruction. As efforts are made to uniformly apply the same standards to all students, a balance must be struck between the demand for tough, clear standards of academic excellence and the need for functional life skills instruction and integrated educational opportunities.

For students with disabilities of all ages, the acquisition of academic skills must be deliberately infused throughout the educational program with substantive Life-Centered Career Education (LCCE) concepts, materials, and experiences. Career education should permeate the entire curriculum and requires competency and subcompetency instruction at all levels in a variety of natural environments. The emphasis on and the direct instruction of these skills (daily living skills, personal–social skills, and occupational skills), all supported by academic skills, will greatly enhance the growth and development essential for students to participate within our rapidly changing and demanding society.

Today we have high expectations for quality individualized programs that will prepare students with disabilities for adult living. No longer acceptable are situation-specific learning, class-room-confined instruction, or totally segregated service delivery. Efforts must be rechanneled to create programs that meet functional curriculum needs of individual students in integrated educational environments within both school and non-school settings (home, community, employment, and recreational) to facilitate their transition from school to adult life.

Founded on 22 research-based competencies needed for adult living, the LCCE model offers an excellent framework for organizing an effective functional curriculum. In the three curricular content domains, the model addresses the major critical skills all students need for productive living. The model also promotes the concept of infusion into the general curriculum collaboration and partnership, hands-on experiential learning, instruction in varied integrated environments, informal and formal career/vocational assessment, and the formation of Individualized Education Program (IEP) goals and objectives for appropriate transition planning. The process described in this chapter provides many ideas for those who will be developing or improving on a comprehensive, ongoing career educational approach.

Mabrey Whetstone is Program Support Coordinator in the Division of Special Education Services of the Alabama State Department of Education.

THE PROCESS OF CURRICULUM CHANGE

Career education requires the active participation of the entire school community, parents, and various segments of the community. Interestingly, the current plea for educational reforms, including transition services, calls for cooperative effort and collaboration between these three educative forces. Although education of our young people is everyone's responsibility, collaboration simply has not taken place in this country. Perhaps the message has finally gotten across to the American people.

Change does not come easily. As the saying goes, "Everyone's for change, unless they have to do it!" In their 2-year federal project, Promoting Collaborative Planning of Career Education for Disabled Students, the Technical Education Research Centers (1980) identified several barriers that prevent collaboration from succeeding: time constraints, red tape, communication difficulties, turfdom and ego barriers, reluctance to share "power," disparate organizational goals, and coordination of efforts where typical line authority management techniques cannot be exerted.

Hoyt (1983) points out that before school and community interaction can truly take place and succeed, educators, parents, and other members of the community must agree on the purpose of education. They will need to clarify the basic purpose, goals, and objectives of the school if students are to have an organized and acceptable system of learning. The question of who the schools are for must also be answered. Changing curriculum will not occur unless educators pay considerable attention to these and many other issues. Two major problems are getting the community to accept responsibility and for the schools to loosen their hold. For members of the community to become involved, they must believe that they will get something in return. The proposal for involvement must make conceptual sense, and educators should be confident that what they propose will work. Otherwise, they will probably never be able to involve the community again.

Significant implementation of any functional curriculum/transition effort depends on several important factors:

- Increased administrative support
- Teacher involvement
- Coordination of school and agency activities
- Parent involvement
- Community opportunities

Roessler (1991a) notes that administrators must be convinced of the utility of the program. Thus, those promoting implementation must emphasize such positive outcomes as the large number of students who could be served, the fact that current students do not possess necessary life skills, and the instructional materials available. In the case of teachers, functional skills implementation depends on such factors as

- District commitment to the effort
- Staff development opportunities
- Incentives for program adoption
- The availability of effective student evaluation and instructional materials

In addition, the curriculum should be able to link its instructional units to Individualized Education Program (IEP) objectives, goals in the core curriculum, and graduation requirements.

Solutions to better coordination of school and agency services include getting mandates at the state level by agency and educational leadership so local programs are instituted. Career nights, social events, discussion groups at school and in homes, and home visits are suggested to enhance parent involvement. Increased community-based opportunities solutions can be instituted by restructuring the use of existing personnel and giving more emphasis to community living objectives (Roessler, 1991a).

In one state, Missouri, the Excellence in Education Act of 1985 prompted the state to identify learner outcomes for specific subject areas for grades 2 to 10. The resulting core competencies and key skills are used to guide curriculum development in Missouri's school districts. In its publication *Implementing Career Education at the Elementary School Level* (Stephens, 1990), Missouri LINC and the state education agency note that many LCCE competencies relate directly to the Missouri Comprehensive Guidance Program objectives and Key Skills for Missouri Schools. Their publication provides specific examples of how LCCE competencies and subcompetencies can be infused into various subject matter to meet their guidelines. This publication is available from the Instructional Materials Laboratory, 10 London Hall, University of Missouri-Columbia, MO 65211.

There are a multitude of reasons why curriculum change will present a challenge to those who bravely attempt it. Reformers should be aware of the many challenges that exist from the structure of the educational system, the educators, parents, agency personnel, employers, and the students themselves. Figure 13.1 contains a list of challenges that each one of these presents.

Studies of the barriers affecting the implementation of the LCCE curriculum have been conducted by Roessler and colleagues (Roessler, 1991a; Roessler, Brolin, & Johnson, 1992; Roessler, Loyd, & Brolin, 1990). The studies were conducted with several school district teachers involved in implementing the LCCE curriculum as part of the development and field testing of the assessment and instructional materials being designed by LCCE staff. This research effort led to the identification of 10 major barriers to LCCE implementation, which Roessler labeled so aptly "Your Hit Parade." The barriers are presented in Figure 13.2.

Curriculum changers must be ready to address the resistances and barriers to educational change if they expect to succeed. LCCE staff developed a strategic and operational planning model for contextual barrier interviews during the early stages of their research to systematically deal with major barriers to implementing career education efforts. Then, they developed an instrument called the Barriers Implementation Questionnaire (BIQ), in which staff identify the top barriers and their suggested solutions to each of the major barriers. Through a process of consensus, solutions can be finalized to deal with each one. For example, the following solutions were posed for the perceived barrier of involving parents in teaching and reinforcing LCCE instruction at home and in the community:

• Increase the number of occasions that bring parents and the school together, such as career nights, social events, home visits, and parent information packets.

Educational System
- Resistance to change
- Institutionalized/bureaucratic nature
- Inflexible, rigid policies/acculturation
- Standard programs
- Limited time for staff development
- Many priorities and pressures
- Schedule
- Graduation requirements
- Transportation costs
- Lack of release time for teachers
- Money for staff and other resources
- Time to do everything needed
- Hiring policies
- School philosophy/purpose of education
- Curriculum emphasis (content) and effectiveness
- Scope and sequencing

Educators
- Their professional orientation
- Resistance to change
- Lack of appropriate training and information
- Attitude
- Trying to meet the needs of diverse students
- Overworked
- Little reward or recognition for extra effort
- Lack of trust
- Lack of support
- Fear of appearing incompetent
- Turfsmanship
- Past failures

Parents
- Limited time to participate
- Inability to carry out activities
- Broken homes
- Mistrust of professionals
- Feel education is school's responsibility
- Too many other responsibilities and problems

- Lack training
- Disinterest
- Hopelessness of future
- Overprotective
- Unrealistic about their child's abilities
- Want their child to be educated like everyone else

Agencies
- Professional rivalries
- Turfsmanship
- Theoretical differences
- Administrative barriers
- Too many clients
- Lack of knowledge and training
- Unclear roles and responsibilities
- Past failures
- Unwillingness to change
- Unwillingness to share
- Fear schools/parents will expect impossible
- Limited funds
- Expect schools to do more

Employers
- Misconceptions
- Difference of opinions
- Learning their language
- Understanding the world of work
- Unclear of their contribution

Students
- Fear of failure and rejection
- Overprotected
- Pressures from parents and others
- Lack of normal experiences
- Learning characteristics
- Unrealistic expectations
- Decision-making problems
- Limited work experience
- Low expectations
- Academic rather than functional skills orientation

FIGURE 13.1   Challenges for curriculum change.

Note. From *Life Centered Career Education: Professional Development Activity Book* (pp. 364–366) by D. E. Brolin, 1993, Reston, VA: The Council for Exceptional Children. Copyright 1993 by The Council for Exceptional Children. Reprinted by permission.

1. Some parents view education of their children as the responsibility of the schools.

2. Some teachers are reluctant to change existing materials.

3. Schools lack specialized personnel (job developers, job coaches)

4. Community work sites are limited.

5. School and agency personnel are unaware of each others' contributions.

6. No money, personnel, and time for school/agency collaboration.

7. An overemphasis on basic education at the expense of career education.

8. Little time to develop and coordinate LCCE parent involvement.

9. Administrators lack knowledge of LCCE.

10. Teachers and parents are unaware of agency services.

FIGURE 13.2   Your Hit Parade: Top 10 barriers to LCCE implementation.

Note. From "Your Hit Parade" in *LCCE/Employability Enhancement Project* by R. Roessler, 1991, Columbia: University of Missouri-Columbia. Copyright 1991 by D. E. Brolin. Reprinted by permission.

- Develop a board-approved parent-compliance contract specifying the type and amount of parental participation required in the student's program.
- Have groups of parents meet at regularly scheduled intervals to discuss student progress.
- Conduct training programs that teach parents how to contribute to the school's LCCE efforts (Roessler, 1991a).

"Effective educational programs don't just happen. A sound philosophical base and an effective planning process are necessary."

(Gysbers quoted in Kokaska & Brolin, 1985, p. 253)

There is no simple recipe as to how career education can be structured in a kindergarten-to-postsecondary program. But the important point is that educators swing into action and start by developing an Action Plan. One example of such a plan is presented in Figure 13.3, which illustrates the preliminary plan developed by a Curriculum Committee of the Grand Rapids, Michigan, Public Schools for one of their schools interested in implementing LCCE. The reader should keep in mind that every school situation is different and that what works in one community will not necessarily succeed in another.

In the next section, more specific curriculum considerations are discussed in relation to elementary, secondary, and postsecondary programs and within the four curriculum areas of academic, daily living, personal–social, and occupational skills.

SPECIAL EDUCATION PROGRAMS AND SERVICES

West Middle School
615 Turner N.W.
Grand Rapids, MI 49504
(616) 771-3300

Classroom Services
Psychological Services
Social Work Services
Teacher Consultant Services
Speech and Language Services

LCCE ACTION PLAN PROPOSAL

Name(s):   LCCE Curriculum Committee   School: Central

A. INTRODUCTION

1. We believe the major objectives of the educational program for students with special needs are:
   a. personal/social skills
   b. independent living skills
   c. occupational skills

2. We believe our school/district needs to change its focus for these students because:
   a. students are unprepared to function in society
   b. students are dropping out of school
   c. current curriculum does not meet needs
   d. need to teach students to cope with a changing society

3. We propose the adoption of the Life-Centered Career Education (LCCE) Curriculum:
   a. to provide a "road map" to adult life (transition)
   b. to build self concept
   c. to keep students motivated and in school

4. LCCE is a curriculum approach that (explanation of LCCE):
   a. identifies "real life" needs for our students
   b. offers a vehicle to transition a student to adult life
   c. allows for the infusion of these competencies into current curriculum
   d. provides consistent programming between all schools
   e. allows students to become aware of their community
   f. students can see an end to a means (scope and sequence)

B. CHANGES NEEDED FOR IMPLEMENTATION

1. Curriculum Changes
   a. Review 225 credit requirement toward graduation
   b. Consistent course descriptions with competencies and objectives across the city
   c. Test all incoming 8th, 9th and 10th graders with knowledge batteries (all students)
   d. Competencies and objectives—as part of IEPC

FIGURE 13.3   Special education programs and services in Grand Rapids, Michigan.
Note. From Grand Rapids, Michigan, Public Schools, West Middle School.

2. Administrative Changes
   a. Building Principals knowledgeable about development of LCCE Curriculum
   b. Counselors will be knowledgeable about curriculum and implications

3. Staff Changes (e.g., how can LCCE be used when special education teachers are being used as tutors?)
   a. Grand Rapids Public Schools Special Education Teachers will be designated as LCCE or Grand Rapids

4. Parent Involvement
   a. Transition Planning
   b. Orientation (parent)

5. Community Involvement
   a. Partnerships
   b. Community Agencies
   c. Universities

6. Possible barriers and how they can be overcome
   a. Acceptance by Special Education Teachers/Inservice
   b. Acceptance by Regular Education Teachers/Inservice
   c. Acceptance by Special Education students/pairing up of peers

C. STEPS TO IMPLEMENT LCCE AND TIMELINES

Steps	*Timeline*
1. Identify Special Education courses in Objective Based Curriculum toward an Endorsed Diploma	11/30/92
2. Finalize Comp/Sub Comp/Objectives within courses	1/27/93
3. Administer knowledge batteries to Special Education students	1/30/93
4. Organize course objectives to be part of IEPC process	4/30/93
5. Calendar of meetings for remainder of year	11/14/93
6. *Plan* to inservice Administrators, Counselors	12/93
7. Review curriculum materials and needs	3/01/93

D. FINAL COMMENTS/RECOMMENDATIONS—Support for Staff!!!

Date: _____

By: _____   _____

_____   _____

_____   _____

FIGURE 13.3 *continued*

CURRICULUM CONSIDERATIONS

Much has been written about curriculum change and development. As Dever (1989) has pointed out, however, most instructional development efforts in the last 20 years have been program development for individuals rather than curriculum development per se. The difference between the two is that a program is what is taught to a specific learner over a specific period of time, whereas a curriculum is a statement of what anyone would have to learn to reach a goal. Dever noted that there is widespread confusion on this matter and that most program development guides have been labeled as curricula, which may account for the lack of curriculum development in recent years (1989, p. 395). He identified the LCCE curriculum as one of the few that meets this criterion.

Roger and David Johnson of the University of Minnesota have promoted and studied application of a cooperative learning approach (R. T. Johnson & Johnson, 1982; R. T. Johnson & Johnson 1983; R. T. Johnson, Johnson, & Rynders, 1981: Nevin, Johnson, & Johnson, 1982). For several years, they have investigated procedures that regular classroom teachers can use to ensure successful mainstreaming. Educators should maintain the following three assumptions:

1. It is unnecessary and unrealistic to ask regular classroom teachers to become experts in special education because expertise on special education is already in the school.
2. Any teaching strategy implemented in the regular classroom to facilitate the integration of students with disabilities should benefit the education of all students, not just those with special learning needs.
3. The first priority of mainstreaming is to build positive relationships between students.

Johnson and Johnson believe that when students are liked, accepted, and chosen as friends, mainstreaming has a positive influence on the lives of all students. They state that placing a student in the corner of a classroom and providing her with individualistic learning experiences is not effective mainstreaming. Their studies have revealed that students who have been placed in a cooperative learning environment have a higher self-esteem, interact more, feel accepted by teachers and other students, achieve more, and behave more appropriately in the classroom than those students who have been placed in competitive and individualistic conditions. The career education approach lends itself nicely to the cooperative learning model.

Through the process of conducting in-service workshops and developing a career education action plan for the school, the partnership between all possible school personnel, in addition to family and community representatives, can become established. An example of an action plan written by one school district is presented in Figure 13.3.

As indicated in earlier chapters, career education transcends the entire curriculum and requires competency and subcompetency instruction at all levels. Curriculum emphasis will vary from school to school and student to student, depending on the school's resources, philosophy, and preparedness. Based on our experience, career education instruction in academic, daily living, occupational, and personal–social skills follows the breakdown over the kindergarten-to-adult curriculum period, as depicted in Figure 13.4.

Each if these curriculum areas is next discussed in relation to elementary, secondary, and postsecondary programming.

Elementary/Middle School Programming

It is essential that career education be instituted substantially at the elementary level. Functional skills, self-knowledge, and knowledge of the world of work need to be taught at this level so the students can function at a much higher degree in the secondary grades. What is taught in a career education program is compatible with the skills required for transition services; thus, it is a vital component of the entire transition process. At the elementary level, the foundation for growth can be built by infusing career awareness and exploration activities into the variety of existing subjects being taught. Thus, students acquire basic daily living, personal–social, and occupational skills at a rudimentary level.

The importance of a career education emphasis beginning at the elementary level has been outlined in the position paper of the Council for Exceptional Children (CEC) Division on Career Development alluded to in an earlier chapter (G. M. Clark et al., 1991), which offered five critical principles relative to this need:

FIGURE 13.4 Suggested curriculum for career development at various grade levels.

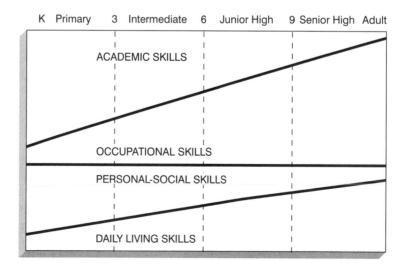

Diane Wisniewski teaching her elementary students LCCE skills (Thornapple Elementary School, Grand Rapids, Michigan).

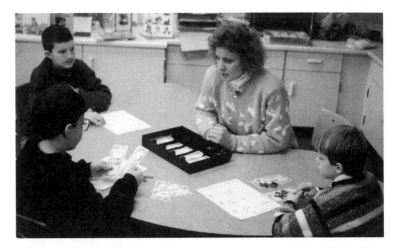

1. Education for career development and transition is for individuals with disabilities at all ages.
2. Career development is a process begun at birth that continues throughout life.
3. Early career development is essential for making satisfactory choices later.
4. Significant gaps or periods of neglect in any area of basic human development affects career development and the transition from one stage of life to another.
5. Career development is responsive to intervention and programming, when the programming involves direct instruction for individual needs.

G. M. Clark et al. noted that "it is unrealistic to expect satisfactory career development and transition education outcomes when intervention is delayed until students reach high school" and that "each student's IEP should go beyond basic academic skills to provide for instruction and guidance as needed for:

• Developing age appropriate functioning in independent daily living tasks, including knowledge and skills needed at home, at school, and in the community;
• Developing positive values and attitudes and age-appropriate behaviors for participating confidently in the home, at school, and in the community;
• Establishing and maintaining positive, age-appropriate interpersonal relationships in the home, at school and in the community; and
• Developing awareness of occupational alternatives, orientation to the realities of the work world, and achieving age-appropriate, gross and fine motor skills" (1991, pp. 117–118).

This strong position taken by national leaders reflects the pressing need for educators at the elementary and middle school levels to make the necessary modifications for a more substantial career education approach. Some guidelines for each of the four major curriculum areas constituting the approach described in this book are presented next.

Academic Skills Instruction

During the elementary years, students must learn functional academic skills, such as reading, writing, and arithmetic. This must be the primary emphasis during these years because academic skills lay the foundation for subsequent learning of the daily living and occupational skills needed for community living and working.

Daily Living Skills Instruction

Several subcompetencies can be taught during the elementary years in addition to basic academic skills. Daily living skills include identifying money and making correct change; making wise expenditures; dressing appropriately; developing grooming and hygiene skills; developing eating skills; understanding local laws and government; participating in basic leisure and recreational group activities; and understanding traffic laws and safety practices, which are subcompetencies that these students can learn or can begin to learn.

Personal–Social Skills Instruction

The elementary years are particularly important for developing adequate personal–social skills. The first few years of life are vital to personality development. Children with disabilities in particular are vulnerable to the attitudes and behaviors of others toward them, which, in many instances, may be manifested by ridicule, hostility, rejection, or physical abuse. Thus, they must learn how to handle these negative behaviors and should discover enough about themselves so that they feel they are worthwhile persons. This area needs much more attention if these students are going to benefit from educational efforts and attain optimal career development. All seven competencies and their subcompetencies should become part of the instructional program at the elementary level. All school personnel teaching these students should include personal–social development as part of instruction.

Occupational Skills

Career education highlights the need for elementary programs to provide much more attention to the student's occupational development at this level. Young children are interested in the world of work and actively seek to find out what their parents and significant others do to make a living. Educators should emphasize many of the following "work personality" building subcompetencies in this curriculum area during the student's elementary years: work attitudes and values; remunerative aspects of working; work habits (ability to follow directions, work with others, accept supervision, maintain good attendance and punctuality; achieve quality and quantity performance, follow safety procedures); and physical-manual skills (balance, coordination, dexterity, stamina).

Secondary Programming

Until recently, educators have perceived the secondary level as the point at which transitional efforts should begin. As noted earlier in this book, however, these perceptions are changing, and it is now generally accepted that substantial efforts at the elementary level are needed if the students are to gain the necessary functional skills by the time they leave the secondary program. At the secondary level, educators can concentrate on more extensive career exploration and preparation (skill-building) experiences if the elementary and middle school programs have done their part in providing substantive career awareness and exploration opportunities. The position paper by the Division on Career Development and Transition noted:

> The goals of secondary education are not the same as for elementary and middle school education. Basic skills are assumed for a majority of secondary students and the goal is to move them to higher levels of performance to prepare them for postsecondary education demands or for advanced levels of skills needed for employment. (G. M. Clark et al., 1994)

Some guidelines for instruction in the four major curriculum areas are presented next.

Academic Skills

At the junior high school level, a decrease in teaching academic skills should begin, although much of this instruction can be directed to teaching specific daily living and occupational skills. Of course, this will vary with the student and his potential and need for academic skills instruction. At this age, however, students begin questioning the relative value of what they are learning compared to what they will do later in life.

Daily Living Skills

At the junior high level, a much greater emphasis on daily living skills should occur. Learning about bank and credit facilities, home maintenance, adequate housing, use of basic appliances and tools, physical fitness, nutrition and weight control practices, marriage and child care practices, meal planning, preparation and purchasing, traffic rules, and use of various means of transportation are subcompetencies that can begin to be learned and perhaps acquired by the time students enter high school.

At the senior high school level, the student should have learned the subcompetencies that were taught earlier and also those that have not yet been taught or emphasized. Learning how to keep financial records, calculate and pay taxes, maintain a home interior, prevent and treat common illnesses, respond to questioning by the law, plan vacations, and drive a car are higher-order subcompetencies that some students may never learn adequately. Students unable to learn certain competencies or subcompetencies will need to know how they can receive assistance.

Personal–Social Skills

If educators attempt to help students develop personal–social skills during the elementary years, emphasis on these subcompetencies may be decreased during the secondary programs. This is not meant to de-emphasize the importance of personal–social skills. Rather, we mean to imply that if educators help students learn enough about themselves, develop self-confidence, and display socially responsible behavior, the need to learn other personal–social skills may be reduced. On the other hand, certain students who have not acquired these skills will need to spend a substantial amount of time in this area. All school personnel and guidance and counseling persons should use their special expertise to help students overcome unusually deficient behaviors. Rehabilitation counselors can also offer work adjustment services in a rehabilitation setting to help adult students acquire the personal–social skills needed for career development.

Occupational Skills

As the student progresses through the educational system, the occupational emphasis needs to become even greater. At the junior high school level, students should be exposed to industrial arts, home economics, and other vocational subjects so they can develop prevocational skills and motivations. Career exploration experiences in the community become important, and the opportunity to try out various jobs in the classroom and community (besides in the home) will enhance the student's self-concept as a productive member of society. Educators should initiate occupational guidance activities such as those discussed in Chapter 12 to assist students in career development and decision-making skills.

Secondary students learning communication skills.

During the high school years, occupational skills should form at least half of the curriculum for most students. A career Information and Assessment Center will help students learn more about jobs, specific vocational aptitudes and interests, and job-seeking skills and procedures. Such a center should be open at any time for the student, teacher, parent, and community representative and should be integral to students' weekly program. Vocational subjects, work or job samples, on-the-job work experiences in the community, and other activities of this nature should be provided. The entire school faculty should work toward the goal of helping students prepare for community living and working requirements, and economic, social, and personal fulfillment.

Postsecondary Level

Many students will not acquire a sufficient level of competence in functional skills to make the successful transition from the secondary program to work, community living, and participation. Thus, further opportunities to acquire the competencies needed for adult adjustment must be provided. Vocational-technical school, community colleges, rehabilitation programs, Job Training and Partnership Act (JTPA) programs, and other specialized centers are important contributors in the transition process and in the ultimate success or failure of individuals with special learning needs. Each of these agencies could adopt a functional skills focus, such as LCCE, and work closely with the secondary programs to provide a consistent continuum of services for students who need further training.

Academic Skills

Adult programs need to assess the extent to which the individual has acquired the academic skills needed for community living and working. For the latter, the emphasis should be on those academic skills needed for job goals. Variance in the number of academic skills that the student learns depends on the quality of public school services.

Daily Living Skills

Adult programs should provide training for students who have not acquired these subcompetencies but have the potential to acquire these skills. This needs to be carefully and systematically discerned.

Personal–Social Skills

Individual and group counseling services are generally an important service provided by adult programs. Thus, students who have deficiencies in this area will be given ample opportunity to learn the necessary personal–social skills for personal and vocational functioning.

Occupational Skills

The major emphasis of most postsecondary programs is vocational training. These agencies are well equipped to help students acquire all five competencies comprising the occupational guidance and preparation of the LCCE curriculum. Most of these agencies have more extensive vocational assessment and training materials and work closely with community employers for on-site vocational training and eventual placement.

The purpose of transition planning is not only for eventual employment but also for all other major aspects of adult functioning. Missouri LINC (Stephens, 1992) identified 14 important adult dimensions that must be addressed in transition planning if students are to become independent and successful: career planning, employment options, postsecondary education, financial assistance/income support, community participation, advocacy/legal services, transportation, recreation/leisure, self-advocacy, insurance, socialization/friends, personal management, living arrangements, and medical services. The LCCE curriculum covers most of these areas, which can provide a good foundation for the Individualized Transition Plan (ITP), as illustrated in Figure 13.5.

In summary, functional curriculums such as LCCE provide educators with a comprehensive scope and sequence approach from elementary to postsecondary programs. Such an approach defines the major goals of the educational program; discerns what should be taught at each level; provides a checks and balances system so students are continually assessed for their learning needs relative to functional skills; and results in a common language and understanding among educators at all levels as to the purpose of the entire educational process for their students. In the process, the students, their parents, and the community will also understand the focus and purpose of the entire program and the expected final result.

LIFE-CENTERED CAREER EDUCATION PROGRAMS

In the previous edition of this book, several school districts that had implemented LCCE were described. These included Pine Plains Central School District No. 1, Pine Plains, New York; Holly Hill Junior High School, Holly Hill, Florida; Oakland County Schools, Pontiac, Michigan; Leavenworth Special Education Cooperative, Leavenworth, Kansas; Huron Residential Services for Youth, Inc., Ann Arbor, Michigan; and Gault Junior High School, Tacoma, Washington, which is now a middle school. For this edition, only Gault was contacted regarding its status in providing students with the LCCE approach. JoAnn Balmer, the teacher, now retired, who provided the previous information, reported that although her school may not be following the LCCE approach to the letter, the district has as a whole adopted an integrated career curriculum approach in all school levels of special and regular education. Thus, the information about Gault Middle School has been retained.

The LCCE curriculum is being implemented in hundreds of school districts as well as countries such as Taiwan. In states such as Alabama and North Dakota, the state

Adult Role Dimensions

(Missouri LINC)	LCCE Competencies																					
	Daily Living										Personal–Social						Occupational					
	1	2	3	4	5	6	7	8	9	10	11	12	13	14	15	16	17	18	19	20	21	22
Career Planning Options										●							●	●				
Employment Options																	●	●				
Postsecondary Training																			●		●	●
Financial Assistance/Income Support	●																					
Community Participation							●	●	●													
Advocacy/Legal Services																						
Leisure/Recreation								●														
Transportation									●													
Self-Advocacy											●	●	●	●	●	●				●		
Socialization/Friends												●	●									
Personal Management	●	●	●	●	●	●																
Living Arrangements		●																				
Medical																						
Insurance																						
Other																						

FIGURE 13.5   Correlation of LCCE competencies to Missouri LINC's transition dimension.

agency has been particularly supportive of the curriculum and has strongly recommended its implementation. Mabrey Whetstone, the Point of View author for this chapter, has been instrumental in designating LCCE as a relevant functional skills curriculum for Alabama and has secured the LCCE curriculum materials and provided training for all districts receptive to its implementation. Chapter 3 mentioned the incorporation of the LCCE curriculum in one of the North Dakota curriculum guides.

Following is a description of some of the efforts to implement LCCE in some school districts throughout the country. Some of this information has been provided directly to the author by school personnel; the remainder has been extracted from materials published by the schools themselves.

Gault Middle School, Tacoma, Washington[*]

Junior high students can be the worst in the world and the best in the universe. The students at Gault are earthy, sometimes rude, and socially unskilled; however, once they have established a trusting relationship, they are caring, thoughtful, and accepting of their teachers and peers.

Gault is a school with a declining enrollment; most of the students are underachievers who have obtained the lowest CTBS scores in the district. The general staff is skilled and makes every effort to work effectively under difficult circumstances. They expressed a need for support personnel and alternatives so they could cope with the unique population at Gault. Resource students were especially in need of alternatives that would defeat the failure syndrome. The low self-concept among students blocked the achievement of their potentials.

When the staff decided that "the way it has always been" was not enough and that changes were necessary, they sought alternative methods that would resolve the problems. They scrutinized traditional instruction-drill-homework models in search of the answer. A closer look at the situation revealed the following ideas:

1.   Traditionally, resource students have been overindividualized. Every student worked in a corner on her own level, memorizing and completing extensive homework assignments without behavioral incidents; but none of the students could get along in a group setting. Anger in the form of verbal and physical abuse toward peers and supervisors and inability to share or work together on a project was the rule rather than the exception. This environment was not conducive to optimal learning, so the structure of the classroom was changed to a group process format.

2.   Students could not apply their knowledge. Every student had been drilled on fractions and decimals, but none of them could double a recipe or make correct change. Every student was able to add, subtract, multiply, and divide, but if

[*] Information was provided by JoAnn N. Balmer, who was a teacher at Gault Junior High School, Tacoma School District, Tacoma, Washington. (Gault Junior High School is now Gault Middle School.)

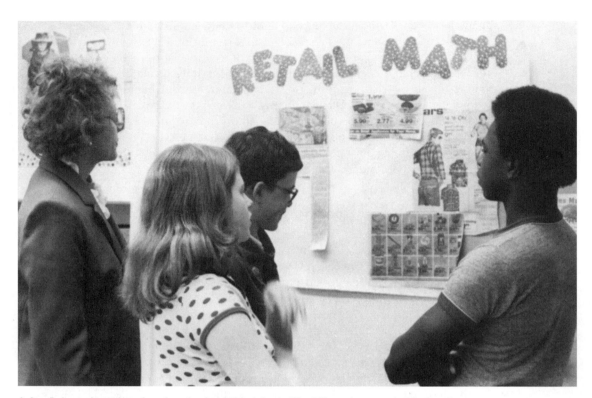

JoAnn Balmer shows her class how basic math relates to life skills and career development.

they were required to apply this information, most students drew a complete blank. Using math and English to solve problems in life was impossible. Memorizing facts in social studies and science was confusing because most students could not remember what they learned.

3.   Students had difficulty understanding cause-and-effect relationships. The use of reason by the teacher in the form of communication, values clarification, and positive reinforcement was the key toward building desired student self-control. Skill building was necessary in dealing with peer–adult conflict, if self-defeating behavior was to be erased from the student's repertoire. The students responded positively to a "soft glove" over a "hard-nosed" approach. Such an approach helped them move in the direction of a trusting relationship with the supervisor. At the onset of the semester, the students were informed that there would be no E's or "hacks," their performance in the class would be reviewed bimonthly, and their behavior would be discussed with the class group when necessary. They were told that we all care about each other because each individual is important (1) as a person, (2) for his contribution to the learning environment, and (3) to the group as a whole. Individual conferences and parent–student conferences were held as needed for the IEP process and when general goal evalua-

tion seemed appropriate. The teacher's behavior was also open for discussion. The class had a democratic structure.

4. The learning resource center atmosphere should be a supportive, trusting, and interesting environment where students can find themselves and be themselves. At Gault, pencils, paper, and emotional support were available to each student at all times through the day. A snack was in the cupboard if the student was hungry (better attention and work comes from a full stomach).

5. School is the job of the student. Most of the students lacked work skills, realistic employment goals, and employed role models in their community. Attendance, punctuality, task completion, appropriate behavior toward supervisors and peers, good grooming, acceptance of constructive criticism, and willingness to attempt all assigned jobs were used to help students develop work skills.

Students set three types of employment goals: (1) overshoot ("I want to be an attorney, and if I can't read or write, my secretary will do all that stuff for me"); (2) middle hugger ("Who needs a job? I have welfare"); and (3) undershoot ("I don't know what I will do because I can't do anything anyway"). Self-awareness and self-analysis had to be a major force in the curriculum. It was never expected that junior high students would know exactly what they wanted to do, but the students needed to set some goals if they were to start thinking about work and make the association between school and future work. Exploration of the job clusters and the academic, physical, and personality strengths needed in each area were infused into the program.

After 2 months of on-the-job study and a teacher who had a career/vocational background, career infusion was the logical model to follow. The major categories of the LCCE competencies and their incorporation into the general and resource curriculum are outlined in Table 13.1.

North St. Francois County R-I, Bonne Terre–Desloge, Missouri[*]

The LCCE curriculum has proven to be a valuable instrument that has enabled our School to Employment Transition Program to flourish and most importantly our students to succeed.

For years, our parents of special education students have been concerned about their children. One of their major concerns was whether or not their sons or daughters were going to make it on their own and become productive members of society. Unfortunately, we in education have discussed our students weaknesses and limitations with their parents, told them how far behind their children were to their peers, and that they were having difficulty in their classes. This made parents feel even more concerned.

[*] This information was provided by Pat Burch, Special Education Teacher/Transition Coordinator, North St. Francois County R-1 Public Schools in Bonne Terre–Desloge, Missouri, who has used the LCCE Curriculum with her students for many years.

TABLE 13.1 Life-Centered Career Education Competencies and Instructional Areas at Gault Junior High School

Competency Category	Instructional Area
1. Managing personal finances	*Math* Identifying coins and making change Verifying a bargain Writing and keeping a budget Writing checks: keeping and balancing a checkbook Understanding payroll deductions, income tax, social security Recognizing a bargain: reading and verifying advertisements
2. Selecting and managing a home	*Basic skills* (contact) *health* Decorating and maintaining the classroom Making basic home repairs Cooking and planning balanced meals Eating proper foods and controlling weight Understanding vitamins and minerals for basic health
3. Caring for personal needs	*Basic skills* (contact) *health, physical education* (contact) Developing hygiene and grooming skills Understanding the need for physical activity (health and weight control) Learning rules for common games as a participator and spectator Learning first-aid skills Obtaining knowledge of common illness and when to seek medical attention Obtaining knowledge of over-the-counter and prescribed medication
4. Raising children and meeting marriage responsibilities	*Health* Babysitting Learning home and school safety practices Identifying marriage responsibilities and appropriate dating behavior
5. Buying, preparing, and consuming food	*Math, basic skills* (contact) Developing table manners Planning and preparing nutritious meals on a budget Obtaining knowledge of the supermarket (sales, impulse buying, selection of a market, advertising) Storing food and using leftovers Recognizing the importance of kitchen cleanliness
6. Buying and caring for clothing	*Basic skills* (contact) *English, math* Reading and following label directions Using a washer and dryer (using settings, soap, bleach, fabric softener) Ironing

TABLE 13.1 *continued*

Competency Category	Instructional Area
6. (continued)	Selecting clothes (choosing colors, styles, and bargains) Mending Sorting clothing for laundry
7. Exhibiting responsible citizenship	*Social studies* Understanding school government (student, administrative structure, school board function) Registering to vote and fulfilling responsibilities Understanding city, county, state, national government function, and responsibility and service to constituents Understanding personal rights as a citizen Developing awareness of world problems and issues (malnutrition, conflict, nuclear proliferation) Gaining knowledge of the political process Mapping, charting, and reading graphs Developing basic knowledge of U.S. history (events, people)
8. Utilizing recreational facilities and engaging in leisure	*Physical education* (contact), *health* Developing knowledge of community recreational facilities (contact person, eligibility requirements, cost) Understanding need for recreation Understanding spectator sports
9. Getting around the community	*Math, English* Reading transportation schedules Developing awareness of requirements and responsibilities of being a licensed driver of a car, motorcycle Obtaining knowledge of insurance Reading maps Understanding the function of the police traffic division Planning a trip (cost of ticket, gas, miles per gallon) Developing awareness of bicycle safety practices
10. Achieving self-awareness	*Health, physical education* (contact), *English, social studies* Identifying values and emotions Identifying conflict and coping with stress Expressing feelings (anger, joy) Understanding and experiencing group interaction Developing awareness of body and its interaction in space
11. Acquiring self-confidence	*Health, social studies, English, math* Analyzing levels of competency performance and engaging in self-analysis Understanding potential level(s) of performance Developing awareness of strengths and weaknesses

TABLE 13.1 *continued*

Competency Category	Instructional Area
11. (continued)	Developing awareness and understanding of personal behaviors Coping and identifying with conflict and ability to identify owner- ship of the problem Accepting praise and criticism Accepting teasing Listening actively to others Analyzing and providing feedback to others Recognizing stress and when to seek assistance

12. Achieving socially
responsible behavior
	All contact and resource classes
	Developing acceptable field trip, assembly, and speaker behavior
	Knowing strengths and weaknesses and developing an active
	    plan to build on strengths and correct or accept weaknesses
	Understanding behavior in various situations (school, home, job)
	Recognizing the rights of self and others, the evils of assault, van-
	    dalism, abuse
	Recognizing a feeling of self in the world of school, family and
	    future employment
	Expressing realistic ambitions and hopes for the near and far
	    future
	Understanding school as his or her job

13. Maintaining adequate
interpersonal skills
	All contact and resource classes
	Developing ability to define, acquire, and maintain friendship
	Identifying different levels of friendship and acquaintanceship
	Understanding dating behavior
	Clarifying personal values in heterosexual relationships
	Establishing and maintaining close relationships
	Developing awareness of strengths and weaknesses in self-
	    organization on a variety of tasks (class, social, family)
	Developing ability to listen, ask questions, and respond
	    appropriately
	Gathering facts and setting realistic goals

14. Achieving independence	*All contact and resource behavior* Completing assigned responsibilities (see 13)
15. Making adequate decisions	*All contact and resource classes* Gathering facts, discussing alternatives, and reaching conclusions Understanding the need for goals in a variety of situations Becoming aware of the concept of cause and effect Accepting consequences for personal actions Seeking out the assistance of advisor, counselor etc., when a need for problem solving arises

TABLE 13.1 *continued*

Competency Category	Instructional Area
16. Communicating adequately with others	*All contact and resource classes* Recognizing and appropriately responding to emergency situations Realizing the need for academic abilities (reading, writing) to fulfill future goals Understanding the need for commercial types of communication in our daily lives (newspapers, TV, magazines) Developing knowledge of the psychology of advertising Completing forms
17. Knowing and exploring occupational possibilities	*All resource classes* Understanding the need for value such as self-concept, acceptance of others, independence, self-sufficiency Realizing and meeting the responsibility of completing assignments, making up assignments after an absence Realizing the advantages of work Obtaining knowledge on career clusters and the requirements of each Developing knowledge of unions, community industries Developing knowledge of steps in seeking employment and/or training
18. Selecting and planning occupational choices	*All resource classes* Obtaining knowledge of various types of jobs Identifying job categories Identifying appropriate types of work (outdoor vs. indoor) Identifying strengths and abilities (verbal, numerical, coordination, mechanical) Identifying possibilities for entry level jobs (first part-time job)
19. Exhibiting appropriate work habits and behaviors	*All contact and resource classes* Following written and verbal instructions Understanding the team concept (following and leading) Developing ability to take turns Developing ability to agree or disagree appropriately Developing awareness of the importance of attendance, punctuality, quality of work, and productivity
20. Exhibiting sufficient physical-manual skills	*Physical education* (contact) *health* Realizing the importance of exercise and diet to physical well-being Understanding and fulfilling a need for physical activity for optimal success toward future work and community living

Numerous times, parents have said to me, "When I am gone, what is going to happen to my son or daughter?"

Now, with the LCCE curriculum, parents can see that we are helping our students to learn skills to become independent and lead productive lives.

It means so much more to our parents to tell them that their sons and daughters can do things such as write checks, fill out job applications, buy and care for their clothing, and get along well with others, than it does to tell them that the student's math is on the fourth-grade level or reading is on the third-grade level.

Our parents feel relieved and happy. Someone is addressing the real needs of their child so that they can become independent and successful.

I believe that the LCCE program has helped to bring our families closer together. Parents and students are working on LCCE competencies at home. My students often share positive learning experiences they have at home with LCCE projects or lessons. Students' and parents' self-esteem has also been elevated. Family members are often asked to be guest speakers or helpers for our LCCE lessons. This has helped our parents to feel respected, as well as proud of their accomplishments. Our students are also proud of their parents, brothers, sisters, or other relatives for teaching and sharing with our class.

Because of these positive experiences, I believe our parents are now taking a more active role in the development and participation of IEPs.

Our students are excited about LCCE, because most of them for the first time in their lives can see that what they are learning directly helps them in their daily lives and in the future. Classes are meaningful. They no longer feel compared with their peers but now perceive the ability to acquire a skill to be used in life.

When our students can perform many of the LCCE skills they need to function day to day, they develop confidence, and when they have control of their environment rather than the environment controlling them, they feel more confident and better about themselves.

Searching for a job is always somewhat frightening, but can you imagine how much more difficult it would be if you did not have the skills necessary to communicate on a job interview? Some of our students thought it was so frightening they wouldn't even attempt to find a job; but as with many things in life, many students found, when given a chance to practice and to experience the situation in a controlled setting, the actual situation isn't that frightening. What our students were afraid of was the unknown, and once it is known, their fears are alleviated. LCCE provides our students these opportunities.

Teachers at North County are excited about the LCCE program. Nationwide, there is often a high turnover rate of teachers in special education because, given the traditional educational model, special teachers aren't always quite sure how much they are helping the student. Grade levels may have increased somewhat, but what difference did that make in the students' life? With LCCE, the teacher can see exactly how the students' level of independence is increased. They know students are being prepared for the future and know exactly what students need to focus on to prepare for living on their own.

Our teachers feel good about students' successes and what they are doing to get their students ready for the world.

Regular faculty members of our school respect our LCCE program. They can see the practical aspects that are offered through LCCE and can easily understand that a program is needed to prepare our students for the future. They see that the effort and time spent are very productive. Regular classroom teachers are incorporating LCCE objectives into their regular classrooms for our mainstream students. LCCE goals and objectives are clear to everyone; our special education program has more credibility because success can be measured. LCCE has helped to bring respect to special education staff and students.

The community also benefits from our LCCE program. Formerly, students were leaving special classes unprepared for the world and subsequently had to rely on their families for support. These students are now being employed and living independently. They hold jobs, provide services in the community, pay taxes, and do not rely on tax-supported programs for their livelihood.

Pat Burch teaching her students LCCE competency 3, relating to raising children.

Businesses in our community are providing employment opportunities for our students. Community people are opening their doors for field trips and as guest speakers.

Administrators and staff are proud of our students. They often take an active role in our LCCE activities and share our accomplishments with others in the community.

LCCE definitely enables parents, students, the community, and teachers to work together for a common goal, to ensure a successful transition from student to independent adult, family member, citizen, and employee.

Birmingham, Alabama[*]

The LCCE functional curriculum has been used exclusively in the Supported Vocational Training Program within the Jefferson County School System in Birmingham, Alabama, since 1987. The Supported Vocational Training Program (SVT) is a community-based work experience model based on the principles of supported employment within a vocational education setting. Supported Vocational Training has as its foundation a required functional curriculum taught primarily by special education teachers.

Students served by the Supported Vocational Training Program are in grades 9 to 12. Some are in comprehensive high school settings. Others are in area vocational centers. All students who participate in SVT and the LCCE curriculum are students with disabilities. The majority of these students have mild-to-moderate disabilities in the area of limited intellectual functioning paired with secondary disabling conditions. Exclusively, all students receive certificates of completion rather than high school diplomas on graduation from high school.

Simultaneously, students receive classroom instruction in the LCCE domains of daily living skills, personal social skills, and occupational guidance and preparation skills, as well as employability skills training by the SVT training staff. Students were given Form A of the LCCE Knowledge Assessment Battery in the fall of 1993. Performance Assessment Batteries are given on individual competencies as these units are taught throughout the school year, SVT staff use all domains of the LCCE, especially the occupational guidance and preparation domain as an infused curriculum resource for their employability skills classes. SVT staff, which consist of a special education-funded work instructor and a vocational education-funded transition coordinator/job developer/job coach, provide situational work assessments (in lieu of traditional vocational evaluation methods), unpaid work instruction/experience, part-time paid work experience and long-term career job placement services.

The LCCE functional curriculum has been officially adopted by Jefferson County Schools as our functional curriculum for students with disabilities. Within

---

[*] This information was provided by Beverly Lavender, Transition Coordinator, Jefferson County Schools, Birmingham, Alabama.

the Vocational Education Department, the home economics teachers are using the LCCE instructional units to provide alternative activities/instruction for students with disabilities within their home economics course of study. All facets of the LCCE infuse beautifully into our home economics curriculum. All regular education home economics teachers have access to the LCCE instructional units through our transition coordinator in the Vocational Education Department. A very high percentage of our students with disabilities elect home economics in the sixth, seventh and eighth grades.

At Minor High School, the Supported Vocational Training Program has been merged with a consultive special education model. Regular education academic instructors provide English, math, science and social studies instruction to students with disabilities. These instructors are using the LCCE instructional units as a resource/supplement to their traditional academic curriculum. Courses are also being offered on the master schedule with titles including LCCE math, LCCE English, LCCE science, LCCE social studies, and LCCE health at Minor High School and Gardendale High School.

As more regular education vocational education instructors become familiar with the LCCE instructional units, more of our trades and industrial education instructors may use the LCCE units to boost their required employability skills modules.

Community-based work experience program, Jefferson County Schools, Birmingham, Alabama.

Wayne and Kent Counties, Michigan (The Wayne State University Project)*

In Michigan, LCCE has been the focus of a large number of school districts, particularly in Utica, Muskegon, the metropolitan Detroit–Wayne County and the Grand Rapids–Kent County areas. A major project directed by Dr. Sharon Field at Wayne State University was conducted from 1991 to 1994 to build culturally relevant, community-referenced curriculum in Michigan using the LCCE Curriculum. Eight school districts worked closely with the Wayne State University staff. In Kent County, the school districts were Grand Rapids, Lowell, Rockford, and Wyoming. In Wayne County they were Dearborn, Inkster, River Rouge, and Wyandotte. Staff from each of these schools worked extensively with project staff to field test and modify the LCCE framework, lesson plans, and assessments for the culturally diverse students in their settings. This required sensitizing both the curriculum and the people using it to the cultural, ethnic, religious, and racial diversity represented in each school district. The result has been a substantive implementation of LCCE in most of these districts.

In the Inkster School District, which has predominantly black students, the LCCE curriculum is being used with the high school's special education students. Teachers have noted that LCCE "has helped make a difference. Teachers have definitely seen a change in student behavior, attendance, and overall attitude toward learning" (*The Sounding Board*, 1994, p. 12). Some of the students involved in the curriculum the Kent County school districts have expressed these opinions:

Nina (age 16): It's interesting. It teaches you different things you need to know for your life. . . . Now, we are going to Burger King on Monday, Tuesday, and Wednesday. We work and learn how Burger King works. It teaches us how to get along with others.
Todd (age 19): We work as a team. Before, I didn't get out in the community.
Michele (age 17): I think its made a difference. It's really easier to understand. Like how to clean—it's really doing it. We clean sinks, sweep and mop the floor, and wipe off the tables. When we learned about what tools to use, it was mostly paper work, but [we need] real activities, later.
Matt (age 17): I think it is excellent. We are learning to wash clothes, and what to clean with. When I get my own house, I'll know what to do with my money—how to budget. (Martinez, 1993, p. 11).

As an offshoot of the Wayne State Project, the Kent Transition Center (KTC) in Grand Rapids, in cooperation with the local school districts in the Kent Intermediate School District, has developed a transition implementation model using the LCCE curriculum as a central focus. Figure 13.6 illustrates how the LCCE competencies span the range of all seven program outcomes that have been determined as critical for transitioning their students as responsible citizens and competitive employees.

---

* This information was provided by Linda Ortman, transition specialist, Grand Rapids, Michigan.

Linda Ortman, transition specialist, providing on-site instruction at a community-based location in Grand Rapids, Michigan.

Other Schools and Districts

In Colorado, two particularly noteworthy efforts should be mentioned. The Aurora Public Schools, Aurora, Colorado, Department of Special Education modified their district-adopted regular education curriculum by developing their adjusted curriculum for moderate needs students to serve as a functional scope and sequence for their elementary students. Staff identified 25 LCCE subcompetencies they believed should be taught at this level and then specified the courses each should be taught, the materials needed, suggested time allotment, and several learning experiences to consider in delivering the instruction. The Colorado School for the Blind and Deaf has also adopted the LCCE curriculum and has made several presentations around the country describing their implementation efforts.

The use of the LCCE model for elementary students at Cordley Elementary School in Lawrence, Kansas, was reported in a recent issue of *Teaching Exceptional Children* by J. Beck et al. (1994), who established a set of functional skills and student objectives based on the LCCE competencies and subcompetencies. They note that many of the functional skills contained in the LCCE curriculum are taught in the general education curriculum for students without disabilities. Thus, when general education and special education teachers collaborate to plan age-appropriate lessons, the LCCE functional skills are incorporated into the lessons and units. A strong community-based instruction and inclusion focus has been instituted for the elementary students, which includes those with mental retardation.

FIGURE 13.6   Kent transition implementation model.

Note. From Kent County transition implementation model. Copyright by Kent Transition Center, Grand Rapids, Michigan. Reprinted by permission.

Competitive Employee
A person who can develop and apply occupational skills required for competitive employment in the workplace of the future.

STUDENT TRANSITION PROCESS

INDEPENDENT LIVING/ LIFE MANAGEMENT

- Apartment Living
- Interpersonal Relationships
- Social Recreation
- Job Readiness
- Financial Planning

- Managing personal finances
- Selecting and managing household
- Raising children and meeting marriage responsibilities
- Caring for personal needs
- Buying, preparing, and consuming food
- Buying and caring for clothing
- Exhibiting responsible citizenship
- Utilizing recreational facilities
- Getting around the community

COMPETITIVE EMPLOYMENT

- Supportive Employment
- Regular Employment

- Utilize competitive occupational skills to industry standards

ONGOING FOLLOW-UP

- Employment
- Life Management

- Ongoing feedback competitive employment readiness
- Revisiit Life Skills Competencies

Agency Collaboration
- Michigan Rehab. Servs.
- Community Mental Health
- Kent Client Services
- Goodwill

MICHIGAN REHABILITATION SERVICES

* Competenccies taken from: Life Center Career Education Curriculum, by Dr. Donn Brolin, Ph.D.

In Missouri, several school districts have implemented the LCCE approach. The Nixa R-II School District in Nixa, Missouri, is using LCCE as their functional curriculum for students with special needs to provide an organized and coordinated method of curricular presentation. The curriculum is currently being used in four special education classes at the secondary level and also in a regular class in consumer math. This class, designed as a-class-within-a class format, focuses on providing students with a more realistic experience of consumer. The rationale for the development of this class was concern about the students' retaining consumer math skills for later use. To meet these needs, the course was designed for students who may have difficulty succeeding in the more traditional consumer math class. Students apply for jobs in the microsociety of the classroom, use a time clock, are paid based on hours worked, and are responsible for maintaining a checking account. Students can select to be employed as a judge, reporter, insurance adjustor, bank teller, maintenance worker, and others. Many of the LCCE competencies fit naturally into the course outline. (Information provided by Terri Chasteen, Special Education Teacher, Nixa, Missouri.)

The Aurora R-VIII Schools, in Aurora, Missouri, Special Education Department, decided to use LCCE goals as a format for writing transition objectives. Their staff wrote more specific measurable objectives for each competency area so each could be taught in the primary grades. The staff adopted LCCE because of its flexibility and because its framework helps staff ensure that each student is given the opportunity to develop skills that will lead to successful adult living. They note that the LCCE curriculum aids them in determining if there are gaps in the students' transition program or if duplications are occurring as the students move from one level to another. In the implementation process, the specific objectives for each LCCE subcompetency are infused into many areas (i.e., math, reading, language arts, social skills, speech/language, daily living skills). A star is noted beside each IEP objective that is part of the student's transition program. The LCCE matrix or grid illustrating the 22 competencies and 97 subcompetencies is placed in the student's ITP folder as reference for needed instructional efforts.

The Grundy County R-IX Schools, in Trenton, Missouri, have instituted a substantial LCCE implementation effort in their schools. For example, at their Adams Middle School, LCCE competencies have been infused in both regular and special education classrooms. Regular class teachers have found LCCE to add variety and enrich the standard curriculum. Many key skills (mentioned in an earlier section) are taught through enrichment objectives that are found in LCCE. Special educators have found their students to be more motivated because they can see how the instruction is related to life outside the classroom. For example, a unit entitled "We're Growing a Future" used many of the LCCE objectives for this Earth Week activity. The personal–social domain is viewed as particularly important for these students and their many needs in this area. LCCE is considered to provide a format for providing direction to their students. Parents are receptive to this approach because they can understand the need to teach these competencies to their children. IEPs are more meaningful to all concerned. (Information supplied by Dorothy Hanes and Louise Reasoner, regular and special education class teachers, Trenton, Missouri).

The Missouri School for the Blind in St. Louis has adapted the LCCE curriculum for their students with visual impairments and blindness. They found that the curriculum needed only minimal modifications. They matched LCCE objectives to their existing courses to make the infusion process easier to track when implemented. They also added some additional objectives to meet the needs of their students.

Many other school districts in Missouri (e.g., Booneville, Marshall, Higginsville, Joplin, North Kansas City, Camdenton, Chillicothe, St. Charles, St. Louis, Hermann) have various degrees of LCCE in operation. In Minnesota, numerous school districts in both urban and rural areas have implemented LCCE at various levels and degrees. Some of these are located in Albany, Brainerd, Crookston, Paynesville, St. Cloud, St. Paul, and many other districts throughout the state.

Taiwan: An International Perspective

Several years ago, I spent considerable time with two Taiwanese professors from the National Changhua University of Education, Dr. Tian-way Sheu and Dr. Tair-Jye Chou, who came to the University of Missouri in Columbia to learn the intricacies of the LCCE system. Afterward, Drs. Sheu and Chou returned to their country to translate much of the LCCE curriculum materials into Chinese in preparation of a substantial implementation effort. The curriculum has become quite popular in the special schools of Taiwan, and presently the professors are re-editing the materials to implement the program for students with cognitive disabilities from 1st to 12th grade. Considerable research activity has also built into their efforts to assess the impact of the approach with Chinese students (Sheu & Chou, personal communication, 1994).

Drs. Tian-way Sheu and Tair-Jye Chou planning LCCE implementation activities in Taiwanese schools.

FINAL COMMENTS

As the examples presented in the preceding section indicate, the LCCE curriculum is being used at all levels and in many different educational settings. A particular strength of its curriculum model is its applicability for inclusive settings and general education students. This and other curriculums such as those identified in Chapter 2 are available to assist school districts conceptualize and institute the necessary functional skills efforts needed for students in their communities.

Functional skills curricula to enhance the career development and transition success for all students, including those requiring special education services, must begin at the elementary level. This is the conclusion reached by most experts in the field. It is not difficult to integrate career education concepts and materials into the ongoing developmental curriculum if educators are trained to do it. In fact, most will endorse this approach at this level. If an appropriate scope and sequence of career education instruction and experiences are implemented into the K–12+ programs of a school district, students will leave the educational system either prepared to function independently and obtain satisfactory employment or prepared to benefit from various postsecondary services opportunities.

The career education approach does not denigrate the need for a solid basic academic and enrichment skills focus to our educational efforts. Rather, it holds the promise for enriching it even more and providing a more realistic and practical component that will motivate students to see the importance of all subject matter, to attain higher levels of academic achievement, to stay in school, and to attain a successful adult outcome. Educators should be sanguine about the potential that combining conventional methods with a substantive functional skills/career development holds for delivering a complete and relevant educational program for their students.

ACTIVITIES

1. Based on your understanding of the career development process and important functional skills needing to be learned, identify the career education objectives/changes that you believe must be instituted at the elementary, middle school/junior high, senior high, and postsecondary levels for your students to develop an adequate work personality so they have the attitudes, behaviors, and skills needed to succeed after school.
2. Identify how you would counteract the resistances that you would most likely encounter from various groups that are needed to support these efforts.

Chapter 14

Issues and Future Directions

Preliminary Questions About the Topic

1. What are some of the major issues related to implementing a career development/functional skills approach for students with special learning needs?

2. What is meant by "old wine in new bottles" relative to new educational concepts or terms?

3. What are some of the problems and needs that impede implementing the career education approach?

4. Why is the educational establishment so difficult to change?

5. Explain the terms *machine bureaucracy, professional bureaucracy,* and *adhocracy* and how they relate to educational change.

6. What is meant by the saying, "The more things change, the more they stay the same!"?

7. What has research uncovered regarding the practice of Individualized Education Program (IEP) development?

8. How can all students be accommodated into the mainstream when it has so many problems handling the diversity it already has?

9. What solutions would you recommend to overcome the many barriers to educational change?

10. What do we know about best practices and the postschool outcome of students undertaking transition programs?

Throughout this text I have referred to the fact that important curricular changes are difficult to implement because of the numerous forces that can impede all efforts to improve the educational system—the bureaucracy, boards of education, and some administrators, teachers, other school personnel, families, agencies, employers, and even some students themselves.

Ten years have elapsed since the last edition of this textbook. In that edition, major issues and future directions relative to the career education concept were identified and discussed. What has been the response to what is being advocated in this book—a career education approach? Are students now acquiring the functional skills needed to make a successful transition from school to community living and working? Has any significant change actually occurred in the past 10 years to improve the educational outcome and quality of life of students in the thousands of school districts throughout this country who present special learning needs?

In this chapter, some of the same issues discussed in the previous edition are again posed. The chapter does not intend to cover all issues pertaining to the educational needs of students with special learning needs. Rather, it focuses on those related to the topic of this book and assesses the progress made in the last decade. After the discussion of major issues, some problems and possible solutions to the major issues and problems are presented. The contributions to this final chapter by close colleagues and friends, Drs. Gary Clark and Oliver Kolstoe, who have made significant contributions to the development of the career education concept for many decades, are greatly appreciated and valued.

MAJOR ISSUES

Many issues inextricably have an impact on any changes and implementation efforts in a school district. Funding, scheduling, grading, providing sufficient community-based instruction, the awarding of diplomas, and reassignment of personnel are examples. Although these are important issues, this section focuses on those that are particularly relevant to the career education approach advocated in this book. Some of these have been identified and discussed by G. M. Clark and Kolstoe (1990).

Issues Identified by Clark and Kolstoe

In their excellent text entitled, *Career Development and Transition Education for Adolescents With Disabilities* (1990), G. M. Clark and Kolstoe pose four important issues they believe should be addressed in planning for the successful implementation of career development and transitional programming for students needing special education services. Each of these is identified next with Clark and Kolstoe's opinion of each issue.

- Are high school classes as well suited to assimilating students with disabilities as the elementary school? At the upper grade levels, the discrepancy between students in

Point of View

Issues lead to challenges. A major issue in the notion of life skills education of students with disabilities today is instructional delivery. The two most obvious challenges in instructional delivery are what to teach and how/where to teach it. Even among those who want to teach life skills, these two challenges are not simple. First, life skills instruction is usually new territory because instructional content and teachers depend on curriculum developers to provide appropriate instructional materials. Second, instructional delivery involves presenting occupational and life skills content to a heterogeneous group of students, all of whom need some of the content, but only a few of whom need all of it. Third, students receive their instruction in a variety of settings during the school day, and teachers want instructional materials that are flexible for group or individual instruction and that can be used in any instructional environment.

The organization and format of the Life Centered Career Education (LCCE) curriculum meets the challenge of these issues for secondary schools in both practical and philosophical ways. Secondary classroom teachers now have access to specific lesson plans for teaching content that typically is not taught systematically, if at all, and that can be used in any setting. The next challenge is that teachers at the elementary and middle school levels who want to teach life skills need to have such materials also so that a K–12 scope and sequence can be laid out for all teachers. When that is done, the ultimate challenge will be to convince those educators who do not have a commitment to life skills education that life-centered outcomes are equally important to academic outcomes.

Gary M. Clark is a professor of special education in the Department of Special Education at the University of Kansas in Lawrence, Kansas, and author of many textbooks and articles on career education. He and Oliver Kolstoe recently completed the second edition of their text, *Career Development and Transition Education for Adolescents with Disabilities,* published in 1995.

intellectual, academic, learning, and personal–social skills widens, which can result in a very frustrating and demeaning situation for students with lesser abilities if they are expected to learn at a regular class level.

- Should all students be subjected to the same curriculum? It is irrational to offer a single core curriculum for all students. Students should have options and alternatives to best meet their individual needs.
- Are the current trends and issues in educational reform enhancing the dropout rate? This issue relates to the high dropout rate that continues despite educational reforms. The factors associated with dropping out need to be better understood so meaningful programs can be instituted for these students.
- Should all students be required to meet minimum-competency standards to qualify for a high school diploma? The minimum competency standards, which were not

even mentioned in the major educational reform reports, are in direct conflict with the philosophy of federal special education legislation, which mandates curricula in determining appropriate education.

The preceding issues are even more relevant today as the movement toward full integration or inclusion of students with disabilities into the mainstream is being vociferously promulgated. Clark and Kolstoe's (1990) point that integration of these students at the high school level can adversely affect their career development and transition planning is valid. This is the critical period of the career preparation stage where students must attain competency levels for the important skills and behaviors needed for successful community and vocational adjustment. Every course these students take at the high school level must enhance their career development. For most students, this will require certain specialized courses to focus on the curriculum areas that will most appropriately prepare them for successful transition. I agree with Clark and Kolstoe, it is irrational to expect all students to respond sufficiently to a single core curriculum. If we expect all students to be exposed to the same unified curricular focus and meet the same competency standards, the dropout rate will, in my opinion, escalate even more and set back the many gains made by the special education field in the past 25 years. This is not meant to imply that special education students should continue to be segregated, rather that we must be careful in too precipitously placing them in general education settings where they will not acquire *all* of the important skills and behaviors needed for successful career development and transition.

 "Having seen one full cycle of transition interest and having researched previous cycles, I am struck with a gnawing thought that some of the youth of today may be no better off—and possibly less better off—than their counterparts were 15 years ago."

(Szymanski, 1994, p. 402)

Issues Identified in the Previous Edition

In the previous edition of this book, several issues were presented that are critical to the successful implementation of a career education approach that could provide a mechanism for functional skills instruction and transition services. Those that are particularly important today are revisited in the following discussion.

Definitions

Our field is expert in reinventing the wheel and in relabeling previous terms and concepts—"old wine in new bottles" so to speak. Over the years, for example, the definitions of several disabilities have been changed, some governmental agencies have changed their names, and several professional organizations have done likewise. Some might wonder if our field suffers from an identity crisis!

Career education was the popular educational reform term during the invigorating decade of the 1970s and into the 1980s. But new federal bureaucrats and politicians establish their own vernacular and abnegate those of their predecessors. Thus, more recent terms such as *transition* and *self-determination* came into vogue and were promoted in the 1980s and into the 1990s. In the very near future, we will probably need to be prepared to welcome another newer buzz word from those who dictate the language and direction of the field.

"The more things change, the more they stay the same!"

(Roessler, Shearin, & Williams, 1993)

Whatever term we use (career education, transition, life skills, functional skills, vocational education, outcome-based education, quality of life education, self-determination, work-based learning), we are talking essentially, and hopefully, about the same major educational goal, namely, preparing students to successfully live, interact, and work in their community.

The term *career education* reflects this major educational goal because it affirms the commitment to emphasize both vocational preparation and the unpaid but productive work activities that one must be able to perform in the home, in community service activities, and in avocational pursuits. Career education reflects our educational focus—to help every student to acquire a satisfactory career and life-style. Unlike the outcome-oriented terms such as *transition, quality of life,* and *self-determination,* career education is a more specifically focused educational intervention to prepare students for a successful transition, quality of life, and to be self-determined, independent individuals. And it requires the active involvement of all educators, not just vocational or special educators.

Career education is generally viewed in one of three ways:

1. As an expansion of vocational education
2. As preparation to function in all adult roles
3. As preparation for all the various work roles, settings, and events in which productive work activity occurs for individuals and which helps them to become a totally functioning person

The latter view was adopted by The Council for Exceptional Children (CEC), which issued a policy paper in 1978 with the following life adjustment, work-focused definition of career education:

Career education is the totality of experiences through which one learns to live a meaningful, satisfying work life. Within the career education framework, work is conceptualized as conscious effort aimed at producing benefits for oneself and others. Career education provides the opportunity for children to learn, in the least restrictive environment possible, the academic, daily living, personal–social and occupational knowledge and specific vocational work skills necessary for attaining their highest levels of economic, personal, and social fulfillment. The individual can obtain this fulfillment through work (both paid and unpaid) and in a variety of other societal roles and personal life styles including his/her pursuits as a student, citizen, volunteer, family member, and participant in meaningful leisure time activities. (CEC, 1978)

A life-centered, work-oriented view has been adopted by Life Centered Career Education (LCCE) because of its focus on preparing students for both the paid and the many unpaid work activities that responsible adults must perform in home, civic, and avocational endeavors. An important concept inherent in this view is that during periods of unemployment, these individuals can still feel worthwhile contributors to their family and community by engaging in productive work activities in the home, doing volunteer and other community work, and being involved in hobbies and other productive avocational activities.

A Decade of Change.   Career education concepts have become embodied in conceptualizations of more recently introduced terms—*transition, functional skills, life skills, self-determination*—and even the more broadened view of vocational education. Halpern (1993) suggests a term that has been bandied about for many years, "quality of life," as appropriate for a conceptual framework for evaluating transition outcomes and three domains: physical and material well-being, performance of adult roles, and personal fulfillment.

Thanks to the bureaucracy, the field is at no loss for inventing new terms and priorities! Often, what is really being promulgated is the repeating saga of "old wine in new bottles." What is needed is for educational leaders and decision makers to move up to the next step and provide the field with specific guidelines, directions, and methods for implementing what they profess.

Instructional Delivery

Many issues or questions relate to the instructional delivery of the career education approach. Some of the important issues are the following:

1. *Should career education be a separate program or infused into the regular curriculum?* Many educators view career education as a separate course that should be taught for 1 or 2 hours each day. Another more appropriate view of the concept is that it should be infused throughout the curriculum and that all school personnel should modify their courses to incorporate career education into the curriculum. Although it is probably easier to develop a separate course, the most preferable way is the more ubiquitous infusion of its concepts and materials into school, home, and community settings.

2. *What functional/life skills need to be taught?* This book has provided some direction to this question by presenting several functional curriculums and resources. In the case of the LCCE curriculum, its 22 competencies have been adopted by many school

districts throughout the country. Some districts have expanded the list of competencies or subcompetencies, depending on the nature of their students and their own situation. The important point is that most of these functional skills have been identified, and many are already being addressed, to varying degrees, in the general and special education curriculums. It is up to each school/district to make decisions about how they will meet this need. Today, with the grave concern about the many problems pervading society—crime, violence, drugs, sex education/life-style, and acquired immune deficiency syndrome (AIDS)—these topics will need even greater attention than in the past.

3. *How much of the curriculum will need to be devoted to functional life skills?* Considerable time will need to be allocated to teaching these skills if students are to really learn and retain them. This will be no easy task with the many pressures to meet so many educational needs in today's society. To adopt the career education approach, functional skills instruction needs to be infused into existing courses, home assignments, and community settings. Career education will need to be a very significant and pervasive part of what is taught. The career education approach will enhance the assimilation and achievement of all students in the mainstream class because its instruction is related to the real world and practical experiences. It is important to remember that much of what is being promoted as necessary for students' career development is already being taught to varying degrees.

Can functional skills instruction be adequately provided only in inclusive settings?

4. *Does career education aid or hinder mainstreaming or inclusive education efforts?* Career education can propitiously enhance the integration of students with special learning needs into general education classes. Most students learn best when the instruction is related to the real world and there are hands-on experiences. An important selling point to regular educators is that career education can be integrated into all classes and for all students. Thus, career education is one vehicle for successful mainstreaming and inclusion. Although an inclusive education is very important, a variety of instructional settings will most likely still be needed, both inside and outside of the school and the regular classroom setting, to provide students with all of the instruction and experiences needed for adult adjustment preparation.

5. *What should be done with present courses, materials, and teaching approaches?* Career education requires educators to take a hard look at what they are doing and how their courses can be modified, materials added or eliminated, and some other teaching methods added. However, it does not call for a wholesale abandonment of present practices. Rather, career education adds greater relevance to the curriculum and requires a more democratic environment. Career education is not the only education students should receive; however, it should be a very significant component of the entire curriculum. School districts must develop more systematic and comprehensive career education plans so that courses, materials, and instruction can be presented in an effective scope and sequence.

A Decade of Change.   Evidence indicates that many educators are changing standard teaching practices to inject more interesting and real-life content and activities into their courses, including more community-based experiences. For example, all four national finalists for the Teacher of the Year award interviewed on one of the national news telecasts in January 1994 cited the incorporation of what we have described as career education as the highlight of their innovative practice, when asked why they thought they were nominated for the award. Other recent TV programs and magazine articles have cited career education activities that are happening in many school districts as innovative school programs and practices in this country. Although the career education approach has not been widely adopted nationwide, it has become a highly desirable practice in many of the more outstanding schools that have parted from the standard method of educating children. The recently passed School-to-Work Opportunities Act is a good example of the impact of the career education approach.

"How can the mainstream improve so dramatically to incorporate an increase in diversity when it has such obvious difficulty accommodating the student diversity it already has?"

(Fuchs & Fuchs, 1994, p. 302)

Although many educators still view career education as a separate course, others have infused or integrated its concepts and materials into their academic-oriented curriculum. There still needs to be a greater emphasis to view career education as an integrated component within the general curriculum and its courses. There has been some positive movement in this direction in the past 10 years, but more work needs to be done.

The increased movement toward inclusive education will still require an appropriate program of services for students with special learning needs. But, as Fuchs and Fuchs (1994) note, there are real concerns about how this can be done. The career education approach is one vehicle for meeting this need. Thus, career education should be viewed as an important contributor to the inclusion effort.

Responsibility

Who is responsible for teaching and promoting career education? The career education approach and the IEP and Individualized Transition Plan (ITP) clearly specify a shared responsibility for the student's education. With the continuing changing role of the special educator as a resource and support specialist, more attention can be directed to family, employer, agency, and community-based experiences to enhance the shared responsibility and needs of students with special learning needs. As more special education students are served in the general classroom, special educators can enrich the student's educational experience by helping the regular class teachers institute career education concepts and materials and community resources that will benefit all of the class members.

"What kind of relationship do we want teachers to have with each other—isolationist and territorial or collaborative?"

(F. Smith, 1989, p. 358)

Both regular and special education teachers are responsible for this effort. But teacher collaboration is not a common practice. In most schools, teachers work alone, planning and preparing their lessons and materials alone, struggling to solve their instructional, curricular, and management problems (Inger, 1993). If real educational progress and restructuring are to occur, it is obvious that a collaborative atmosphere must be established.

A curriculum mapping approach, using a school's curriculum team and/or other personnel, is one method of determining who, where, and when the various skills can be taught. This approach does require, as described earlier, a collaborative effort between school personnel and the student's family, community resources, and various employers in contributing to the students' learning the functional skills.

A Decade of Change.   Many regular class teachers still do not seem to view it as their responsibility to meet the career development needs of their students, particularly those with special learning needs. In several school districts, however, substantial collegial relationships are developing. The emergence of collaborative teams, co-teaching, and the use of cooperative learning and community-based instruction strategies is starting to overcome these barriers. In our experience, if the regular class teacher understands the importance of the student's being in her class and has the support to provide appropriate instruction, integration will be more successful. But, if the student is dumped into the class and the goals are unrealistic, little success is experienced by both the teacher and the student. *Career education, especially for students with special learning needs, makes sense to most teachers because they can see the realistic goals that are being set for each student.* And, in the process, other students in the class also benefit. With the movement toward a more unified educational system, rather than the two disengaged systems of the past, the career education approach offers a vehicle for such an integrated effort.

Partnerships

How can parents, employers, and agencies be more involved? This question has plagued educators for decades. Although some parents will never cooperate with the school, many others will if they are approached properly and if they understand the goals of the educational efforts for their child and how they can contribute. Employers are recognizing more than ever their responsibility to the schools in their community. But they must be approached first and, like the parents, must understand the overall goals of the educational program for the students and how they fit in. The involvement of various community agencies is also important. However, schools must realize these agencies have limited funds, personnel, and resources and often heavy caseloads. Thus, they expect the school to provide the students with substantial preparation for personal independence and employment if they are to help those who will need further assistance and training after leaving the educational system.

A Decade of Change.   Substantial progress has been made in developing important partnerships between schools and their community in many school districts throughout the country. As noted in earlier chapters, this is particularly true with the business community, although not as remarkably in the case of the education sector. The dramatic increase in the involvement of business and industry with school personnel in recent years is a very encouraging development. In the case of agency involvement, Szymanski (1994) warns that the requirement in the Individuals with Disabilities Education Act (IDEA) for multiagency involvement in planning and services can serve as both a blessing and as a curse. Although there is a greater likelihood students will not fall through the cracks as frequently, she cautions that these requirements may threaten to decrease family and individual student control of the transition process.

Much has been written about this topic by the experts, and considerable progress is still needed. The supported employment movement has perhaps made the most significant progress in forming close alliances with the business community. However, closer agency and family partnerships still need considerable improvement.

Personnel Preparation

The previous edition of this book asked if colleges and universities were able and willing to teach career education concepts to all types of educators. We also asked what constitutes an effective delivery system, how it would be carried out, and who would do the training. Because staff development is so critical to make significant changes, we suggested that local school districts take the initiative to train their own staff. And we recommended that state and local administrators needed to convince university trainers to incorporate such training in their personnel preparation programs.

A Decade of Change.   Some progress has been made, but universities are really slow to change. Some university educators, most notably, those belonging to the CEC Division on Career Development and Transition (DCDT), are teaching career education and/or transition concepts and materials. Other educators, mainly those with vocational education backgrounds, are promoting vocational education concepts and materials relative to transition. There is no uniform consensus among university personnel as to the best specific approach; therefore, they teach what they want to teach. In many cases, this is similar to the career education approach advocated in this textbook. One example of a university that is responding to the need is Auburn University, which has initiated a secondary special education teacher training program that incorporates many of the major components of career education and transition described here: functional assessment and curricula, vocational and community preparation, self-determination and family involvement, and interagency collaboration (Browning & Dunn, 1994).

There still seems to be considerable reluctance by school districts to train their own staff or to use university personnel to provide in-service training on career education/transition. As noted in Chapter 3, an in-service/staff development training package with videotapes is available to districts who want to train their own personnel on the LCCE curriculum. Also available is a distance learning course (Brolin, Cook, & O'Keefe, 1994) from the CEC. Funds for the development of these products were provided by the U.S. Office of Special Education Programs (OSEP), Division of Personnel Preparation, which has assumed an important role in promoting the initiation of both in-service and preservice training programs to prepare various types of professionals for transition programs. The agency has distributed funds for special projects and university teacher training programs to several universities committed to training their students in the transition area.

SOME PROBLEMS AND NEEDS

This section addresses some of the problems and needs that are important to implementing the career education/functional life skills approach. Undoubtedly, many other problems exist and could be cited. Described next are some of those that are especially important to the focus of this book.

 Everyone is for change—if they don't have to do it!

Attitudinal Barriers

What is the greatest obstacle to implementing the career education approach advocated in this book? The answer is, unfortunately, attitudes. Everyone is for change, as long as they are the ones who don't need to change. Remember the old adage, "We have met the enemy and they are . . . us?" This continues to be the greatest barrier to meeting the career development/life skills needs of the students in American schools who will not go on to college to become atomic scientists, physicians, lawyers, teachers, CEOs, and the like. It is evident to almost everyone that these students need a practical, functionally oriented curriculum approach so they learn the skills and behaviors to be successfully employed and perform the activities of daily living that will allow them to manage their own personal affairs and have meaningful relationships. Some teachers must abandon the fantasy that job satisfaction comes only by working with the brighter students in the academic and enrichment areas.

The attitudes of and frequent legendary lack of cooperation among many professional disciplines and agencies also presents a serious problem to transition efforts by the schools. Despite the mandates that many of these agencies must interface and work with their local school districts, many shirk their responsibility to the school, which results in ineffective cooperative arrangements. Common among some caseworkers are the attitude that it is the school's responsibility to prepare the student until graduation or dropout time and the complaint that already they have too many clients to serve.

Many agencies even refuse to cooperate with each other. Too many seem more ready to defend their existence and protect their reputation rather than reflect concern for the people they serve.

Some postsecondary agencies that should provide education and training services refuse to accommodate persons with disabilities, as the law mandates, and exclude them as "ineligible" for their services without due justification. There continues to be a need to expose and monitor those agencies that are uncooperative and that fail to provide the services they are responsible for in meeting student needs. Thankfully, there are many outstanding and committed agencies and caseworkers who have provided invaluable assistance and on whom the schools can depend.

The Educational Establishment

It is a well-known fact that American public schools, with a few exceptions, are notorious for their ability to resist change and innovation. Too many continue to perpetuate the mystique that basic academic skills instruction should be the primary criteria of a meaningful education and that all students will miraculously be transformed into successfully functioning citizens and employees of their community. And, as Mellard and Clark found in their National Study of High School Programs for Handicapped Youth in Transition (1992), too many directors of special education and superintendents give first priority to their school's organization and administration, not the important elements of a quality program.

 Despite all the hue and cry for reform, we are still faced with the tremendous challenge of changing the establishment.

In his thought-provoking book entitled *Behind Special Education* (1991), Skrtic paints a dismal picture of the rigid structure existing in American schools and in special education itself. He introduces two terms that he says are important for understanding the structure and functioning of school organizations, *machine bureaucracy* and *professional bureaucracy,* and a third term, *adhocracy,* which is important to understanding special education and educational restructuring. Workers in a machine bureaucracy are tightly coupled links in a chain, each doing one part of a job. Workers in a professional bureaucracy are loosely coupled, doing their own thing such as teaching. Schools are conceptualized, managed, and governed like machine bureaucracies, forcing teachers and other professionals to function in an environment that is structurally nonadaptable at the classroom level and to offer standard programs, which many students with special learning needs (including disabilities) simply cannot fit into successfully.

The adhocracy, according to Skrtic (1991), is premised on the principle of innovation, that is, problem-solving, rather than standardization. Adhocracy uses creative effort to find novel solutions. Skrtic believes that special education itself is not a rationally conceived and coordinated system of services, because it is uncoupled from the basic operation of the school, as well as from other special needs programs. He notes that a basic problem with the special education legislation is

> that it attempts to force an adhocratic value orientation (i.e., engaging in creative effort to find a novel solution) on a professional bureaucracy by treating it as if it were a machine bureaucracy. (p. 184)
>
> [In the process] schools appear to be complying with its procedural requirements because of the adoption of practices that, although they may be well intended and in some respects actually may result in positive outcomes, serve largely to symbolize (e.g., IEPs and resource rooms) and ceremonialize (e.g., IEP staffings and mainstreaming) compliance with the letter of the law rather than conformance with its spirit. (p. 188)

Skrtic's (1991) analysis of the educational system's bureaucracy and why we have such a difficult time meeting students' real needs is an important contribution and insight to those are attempting implementation efforts. We must understand the system in which we are operating and its suppressing factors to best make the changes possible. It is difficult to do justice to Skrtic's fine presentation on the topic; therefore, interested readers should secure his publication for a more accurate, in-depth understanding of his analysis of this problem.

Societal Adjustment Barriers

The follow-up data revealing the high rate of dropouts, unemployment, social and emotional deficiencies, and family problems that students with special learning needs encounter in their school and postschool lives has been available for years. Researchers and experts in the field have been repeating in the literature what has been known and persisted for many decades—simply, that life after school for most students with special learning needs is usually a disaster. And, although some school districts have concerned and committed personnel who want to change, they are often outnumbered by those who do not. Consequently, nothing changes. This is a very discouraging dilemma because the losers in the process are the student, the family, and society.

The educational system, its boards of education, and its educators cannot be completely blamed as the only culprits to instituting a more mechanical approach. Resistance also is mounted by many parents, agencies, employers, and the students themselves who also have a stake in what is offered in the school's curriculum. In Chapter 13, many of the challenges that must be faced in making the necessary changes were identified and discussed.

 Schools need an action plan to begin the change process.

A change to a more functional curriculum approach, for all students, including those with special learning needs, will only occur when the major stakeholders in a community's educational system decide that the major purpose of their efforts is to prepare their students for successful community and adult functioning and back it up with a definitive plan of action (such as the one presented in the previous chapter) that will institute a career development curriculum that will realistically lead to this goal. Such a curriculum must be developed by an influential group such as a district-wide curriculum committee with substantial and meaningful input from various community representatives, parents, and students. The school district will need either to begin from scratch to design such a system or to secure one, such as LCCE, that is already available and can be adapted and modified for its purposes.

The preceding discussion is intended to convey that changing curriculum is not an easy matter, in fact, it is a very complex phenomenon that will not occur serendipitously.

The Individualized Education Program

The IEP is the means by which each student is supposed to be ensured an appropriate education. It is a legal mechanism with specific content requirements, designated developers, and as discussed previously, it must now include transition services that will enable students with disabilities to better ensure their future adult adjustment needs, that is, integrated employment, vocational training, postsecondary education, adult service linkages, independent living, and community participation (NICHCY, 1993; Wehman, 1992). However, in too many instances, IEPs are not being developed and carried out as intended by the federal legislation (Smith, 1990). Roessler, Shearin, and Williams (1993) identified several serious problems based on their literature review of the practice of IEP development:

*   Student assessments either fail to identify student needs or, if they do, are too infrequently the basis for goals in the IEP.
*   IEPs do not reflect input from a variety of perspectives (multiple disciplines) regarding the student's needs.
*   Parents are not involved in the IEP process.
*   IEPs have serious procedural deficiencies.
*   IEPs reflect a narrow range of goals and subobjectives that rarely include plans for achieving adult outcomes.

Regarding the latter problem, Roessler et al. (1993) noted a study by Lynch and Beare (1990), which found only 4% of IEP objectives to be what can be considered functional skills (domestic, community, hygiene, recreation/leisure, and vocational), whereas 86% of the objectives were academic and behavioral management goals. Other studies (e.g., Epstein, Patton, Polloway, & Foley, 1992) have reported similar results. This again reveals the critical need to change policies and practices if students are to gain the behaviors and skills needed for successful adult functioning. Otherwise, as the authors note, "The more things change, the more they stay the same!"

 Most IEPs do not contain functional skills/career education objectives for transition planning and services.

The fact that most IEPS do not contain functional skills/career education objectives for transition planning and services is a serious indictment on the current educational system. Most schools are not responding to the requirements of the federal and state laws, the competency needs of students with special learning needs, and—what is considered critical by many parent groups, organizations, and leaders in the field—the instructional needs that must be provided in the learning environments. Why is this not being monitored appropriately by state educational agencies and those responsible for ensuring these students an appropriate education as mandated by our federal and state laws?

Personnel Preparation Barriers

Many teacher training programs have been unresponsive to the career education/functional skills area. In many institutions of higher education, one faculty member may be given this responsibility, while the remainder teach traditional academic, disability, and behavioral courses to perpetuate the conventional, categorical approach. In several instances, little interface with the regular education program is maintained, despite the current thrust toward inclusive, mainstream education for students with disabilities. Local and state educational agencies will need to work more closely with institutions of higher education if the approach advocated in this book is to be achieved. Teachers need to be oriented and trained in the career education/functional skills area during their preservice education if they are expected to be receptive and feel knowledgeable enough to institute the approach in their courses later. This will not require an unreasonable amount of time and energy.

FUTURE DIRECTIONS

One should probably never be so presumptuous (or preposterous) as to think that he has answers to the age-old problem of making changes in any system. At the same time, one who is advocating such change must be able to provide some suggestions for future directions to those who intend to engage in this frustrating but challenging and rewarding venture. If so, the following major recommendations are presented to help provide future directions toward solving the issues and problems presented in this chapter.

Start at the Top

Administrators at the state and local level have been employed to develop and ensure that the highest quality and most relevant educational services are made available to students under their jurisdiction. Although many school administrators are committed to this goal, others are not for various reasons and are masters at doing nothing or very little of what is needed. These people need to be exposed and replaced by competent, committed professionals who will work diligently with all school staff to make the changes that are necessary for the benefit of the students.

Point of View

There is no question that the intent of programs and legislation that focus on transition both aim for the enhancement of the employability of persons with disabling conditions. Where dedicated professionals have established transition programs, the results have been quite good. Many young people have been able to circumvent or overcome their disabilities and have found jobs.

However, making a living does not guarantee making the living worthwhile. Work is important, but it falls far short of providing the elements needed for a meaningful life. It is values, those affective aspects of living that can ensure a rich life. Without them, life can be very poor, indeed.

It seems ironic that such a basic part of humanness is not proposed or even mentioned in the transition legislation and is often given short shrift in many transition programs.

Indeed, many people have contended that values should not even be included in public school curricula.

Yet it is hard to conceive of a world that eschews honor, integrity, loyalty, courage, compassion, and the other values that make society viable. Certainly, the absence of behaviors that reflect those values characterize uncivilized society. And people whose behavior is not guided by values debase society and themselves.

Given this condition, it seems that teaching values should be obligatory in the transition curricula.

In any given classroom, the teacher's behavior should be exemplary, providing a model of values-directed behavior that can be easily understood and copied by the students. The teacher should behave honorably.

Teachers and others have a responsibility to convey to administration the needs of their students and to help plan for their resolution. This will be a challenge because as Skrtic (1991) has noted,

> Professional behavior in schools is governed more by institutionalized, cultural norms than it is by rational, knowledge-based actions designed to improve instructional effectiveness. Things are done in certain ways simply because they have always been done that way. . . . [S]tandard programs are passed on from one generation of teachers to another within an institutionalized context . . . [and] students whose needs fall outside of the standard programs must be forced into them, or out of the classroom—a situation compounded by the rational-technical approach to school management. (1991, pp. 176, 178)

A more proactive stance by laypeople and professionals who want to change the system must be undertaken in the future. *Parents who are movers and shakers should be used by educators to convince administrators to change policies and practices.* Administrators are more likely to be responsive to angry (but reasonable) parents of students

Additionally, the teacher should be quick to reward student behaviors that demonstrate values. Student demonstrations of integrity, honorable or courageous behavior, or other positive values should be noted by teachers, favorably commented on, and reinforced with appropriate rewards. When possible, lessons that teach values specifically can be employed. Although social studies is the obvious venue for those lessons, values permeate all the academic areas. A teacher alert to the desirability of teaching values can seize the opportunity to point out the existence of values' influence whenever or wherever it occurs. Finally, the technique of role playing specific activities in which values play a thematic part allows the teacher (as moderator) and the students as actors to explore alternative behavior routes in response to specific situations. Questions such as "What could John have done that would have been better?" can open the students' thinking to a range of possible behaviors that lead to different results. At the same time, questions

that probe, "How do you feel about that?" can help the students to see situations from other people's points of view.

When we consider the influence of values on how individuals behave, there is every reason to include values clarification in our classes. And when we consider the cumulative effect of each individuals' behavior, we should include values considerations in our curricular offerings. If each person lived a value-directed life, she could be a better person to be around, and this could be a much better world in which to live.

Oliver P. (Bud) Kolstoe is a distinguished Professor Emeritus of Special Education, University of Northern Colorado, and a former President of the Division on Career Development and Transition.

than their own personnel. Teachers must not be reluctant to involve them in the change process when a mountain needs to be moved.

Figure 14.1 contains suggestions offered a few years ago to educational leaders as important actions for state and local educational agencies to adopt in ensuring a meaningful career development/transition effort in their states and local communities. These actions are as important today as they were yesterday. Thus, they are presented to help readers make the changes advocated in this book.

Adopt a Comprehensive Functional Curriculum Model

Schools need to come to grips with how they can offer their students a functional skills/career development curriculum and how it can be infused into the school's ongoing curriculum. Too many schools interpret the transition mandate as primarily an arrangement of services from other agencies and fail to recognize its functional skills/career development curriculum requirements.

The State Education Agency

1. Identify transition as a priority in state plan.
2. Clarify the concept of transition in position paper and/or state guide that promotes a functional curriulum.
3. Designate a state transition coordinator.
4. In-service state staff on transition so they can provide proper guidance to LEAs.
5. Provide enough monies for LEAs to devise programs and train staff.
6. Develop opperational interagency linkages.
7. Promote transition in university training programs and make available to provide technical assistance.
8. Emphasize the need for substantial/meaningful transition objectives in the IEP.
9. Clarify the role of special education teachers in LEA.
10. Conduct informative follow-up studies to discern program needs for transition leading to curriculum.
11. Devise meaningful methods for encouraging parent involvement.
12. Devise means by which meaningful partnerships with business and industry. can be instituted in LEAs.
13. Provide a hotline/information center for LEAs.
14. Provide continuing technical assistance and funding to LEAs that implement meaningful transition programs.
15. Recognize LEAs that develop effective transition programs—model schools.
16. Provide direction to LEAs on how community-based instruction including transportation/scheduling issued can be managed.

The Local Education Agency

1. Designate transition coordinators in schools.
2. Develop transition teams.
3. Clarify roles including resource teaching.
4. Provide funds for staff development training.
5. Provide time for developing the program.
6. Give relief from other duties.
7. Provide personnel with enough information.
8. Give staff opportunity to decide to do transition.
9. Clarify the purpose of education—expected outcomes.
10. Identify a functional curriculum/framework on which they can build a comprehensive transition program.
11. Decide on a definition/conceptualization of transition—narrow or comprehensive?
12. Develop meaningful partners and support from parents and employers.
13. Develop K–12 scope and sequence for transitional efforts.
14. Develop meaningful interagency relationships.
15. Provide rewards and incentives to implementors.
16. Don't be seen as only a special education initiative.

FIGURE 14.1   Transition: What is education's role?

Note. From *Life Centered Career Education: Trainer's Manual and Professional Development Activity Book* (3rd ed., p. 294) by D. E. Brolin, 1993, Reston, VA: The Council for Exceptional Children. Copyright 1993 by The Council for Exceptional Children. Reprinted by permission.

Comprehensive functional skill curriculums that are built on a solid theoretical basis and that have been field tested regarding the utility of their conceptual framework and curriculum materials are badly needed in school districts. A logical scope and sequence must be established so teachers at the middle school/junior high levels know what career development experiences and instruction their students received earlier to avoid duplication. Then, they can build on prior learning to enhance the students' career development and prepare them for a high school level program.

Inclusive education advocates generally support a process approach rather than the conventional standard curriculum and its predefined knowledge-base focus. One of the problems with the standard curriculum is that teachers feel obligated to teach it and the students must learn it. However, when mainstreaming students, teachers are presented with a diversity of students who require a different set of activities and materials. Mainstreaming therefore requires greater planning and effort among teachers and in the process segregates the students within the mainstream and reduces social interaction (Fuchs & Fuchs, 1994).

> Curriculum and instruction are the foundation of restructuring education. Highly focused academic curricula with objectives and attainment targets tied to specific grade levels are not forgiving of students who may learn at a different pace or may learn differently. Inflexible instructional approaches wrongly assume that *all* students can be successful in one approach. Schools or school districts are therefore faced with making decisions regarding how the diverse learners can be best taught, while maintaining high expectations for students within a balanced curriculum. (McLaughlin & Warren, 1992, p. 59)

The options, as these writers point out, are either a unified curriculum or separate or alternative curricula. For some students, this may be a separate alternative curriculum, but for most students, this should be a parallel curricular approach in which a systematic modification of the regular curricula is conducted so the students can be guided by the same learning outcomes that have been identified by the state or local district for all students.

Although the inclusion advocates must be commended for their deep commitment and concern about the placement of students with disabilities in the mainstream, the total educational needs of these students must be considered. Unless dramatic changes occur in the regular curriculum, many important career development/functional skills instructional needs and experiences will never be provided, and continued dropouts and failure will result. Future curricular efforts must be directed to a total educational effort rather than primarily an academic placement focus.

Educational reform approaches such as the LCCE curriculum, the Clark-Kolstoe model, the Dever model, the Cronin-Patton Top Down model, and 20/20 Analysis (Reynolds et al., 1993), which presents a noncategorical alternative to traditional approaches of educating marginal students, can be used to deliver a comprehensive functional skills curriculum. In the process, students should receive the individualized attention they require for learning and a greater emphasis on learning the actual, real-life skills needed to function as a productive citizen of their community.

Establish an Accountability System

The abysmal results of follow-up studies on the adult adjustment of former students receiving special education services have been mentioned several times throughout this book. The statistics never seem to change, yet, the educational process goes on in practically the same manner, despite the constant rhetoric for reform and change. Well-designed follow-up studies of former students are important in identifying curriculum deficiencies so the need for curriculum changes are substantiated and accepted by the educational community. But, as J. R. Johnson and Rusch have found in their review of transition research, "little empirical evidence exists to support relationships between identified best-practices and post-school outcomes" (1993, p. 13).

Several researchers have noted that most of the accountability by schools has been in relation to compliance with and responding to the federal regulations and not with program content, quality, effectiveness, and certain service-delivery costs (D. R. Johnson et al., 1993; Mellard & Clark, 1992; Skrtic, 1991). Management and accountability systems such as the one described by D. R. Johnson et al. (1993), the Transition Information and Planning System (TIPS), are important for gathering in-school follow-along and postschool follow-up data on each student for better program planning. Such data can be analyzed in relation to the school services received, student and family characteristics, student achievement, community contextual factors, and later-life outcomes (D. R. Johnson et al., 1993).

In the near future, much more accountability of the educational system will be required. Two efforts that are underway to help school districts implement more functional skill-oriented curricula are the work of Halpern and colleagues, who have developed a Community Transition Team Model (CTTM) and a project by The National Center on Educational Outcomes (NCEO) at the University of Minnesota. The Oregon CTTM is a systems change approach to improving secondary special education and transition programs at the local community level (Halpern, Benz, & Lindstrom, 1991). Several materials and a computerized management system have been developed to assist in the implementation of the model. The NCEO project staff are working with state departments of education, national policy-making groups, and others to develop indicators of educational outcomes of students (Ysseldyke, Thurlow, & Gilman, 1993). A conceptual model of domains and outcomes has been devised that contains many of the competencies similar to those in the LCCE model with the exception of occupational skills, which does not appear to be addressed.

It is surprising that school districts conduct so little follow-up activity of their former students. It is almost as if they don't want to find out what has happened to their former students! Many special educators, at the high school level, often know their students' outcome because they informally keep tabs on them, especially in small communities. However, an organized data collection system as recommended by Johnson and colleagues is practically nonexistent in the majority of schools. Again, those responsible for this lackadaisical effort should be admonished.

Improve the IEP Content

Earlier in this chapter, the problems that Roessler and his colleagues (1993) found in their study of IEPs were reported. They further note that assessments based on a career education curriculum facilitate the inclusion of a greater variety of goals and objectives in the IEP. By using the LCCE Knowledge and Performance Batteries, they believe the team can better select instructional goals that will better ensure the student's preparation for transition services and adult roles.

A renewed effort to ensure that IEPs contain a more substantive functional skills instructional component will be instituted in the near future. If the career education approach to enhance functional skills instruction and transition services is to occur meaningfully, considerable changes in the current IEP content must be initiated. Several schools are now required to write ITPs, which is one step in the right direction.

Some of the things that teachers can do to improve the content of the IEP are to develop instructional goals and objectives that will achieve the following:

- Help develop the work personality.
- Promote self-awareness and positive self-concepts.
- Stress independence and self-determination.
- Raise expectations.
- Promote educational activities in the home and community.
- Relate the labor market needs.
- Use more community resources.
- Increase the amount of career education activities.
- Use more cooperative learning.
- Incorporate ongoing career assessment with instruction.
- Keep in mind the purpose of education.

In Chapter 7, a method for implementing a substantive IEP approach using the LCCE framework was presented. Many schools have recognized the usefulness of the LCCE competency-based approach to the ITP mandate and have used the competencies and subcompetencies as core elements of their efforts. Several others have used the LCCE approach as their outcome-based education (OBE) program. It is suggested that educators review the LCCE IEP format for possible adoption with modification for their purposes.

FINAL COMMENTS

Without question, this is a propitious time to implement what is being advocated in this book—a more career education/functional skills approach that will better equip students in American schools to make a successful transition from school to adult functioning. Unlike those students who are college bound, most students with special learning needs will not receive the postsecondary education that will ultimately lead them to obtain a well-paying job, acquire acceptable social skills and friendships, and become productive members of their home and community. For too many, their postsecondary education may be acquired in rehabilitation or correctional programs. Thus, it is more critical than ever for elementary and secondary schools to assume greater responsibility for providing both a solid academic and a functional skills education for these students to enhance their chances for employment and productive living opportunities.

Individuals with special learning needs who have disabilities or who are disadvantaged are a greatly underused resource in our society because the educational system, for the most part, has not prepared them to develop and realize their potentials. The result is that the majority end up getting, at best, the secondary labor market jobs that are low paying and lead nowhere. In addition, a disproportionate number of these students get in trouble with the law, end up on welfare, or experience other unfortunate life circumstances. These tragedies do not have to happen, at least for the vast majority.

One other issue that has not been addressed adequately in this book relates to persons from minority groups who have disabilities and are disadvantaged. A report to the President from the National Council on Disability noted that African-Americans constitute 12% of the general population, Hispanic Americans 8%, Asian-Americans/Pacific Islanders 2%, and Native Americans and Native Alaskans 1% (Wright & Leung, 1993). However, this rapidly growing segment of American society has been largely ignored in regard to disability issues, despite the poverty, unemployment, and poor health status of a significant proportion of these individuals (Wright & Leung, 1993). Much more attention will be directed to better meeting the needs of these citizens as we move toward a better educational system.

The injection of a substantial career education/functional skills curricular approach in the kindergarten-to-postsecondary standard curriculum will help to significantly correct the deficiencies in those school districts that have not adequately restructured their programs. Although career education is certainly not a panacea by itself, it is one important future direction that must be earnestly undertaken in the current educational restructuring that is underway in the 1990s.

Let's reverse the disheartening adage noted earlier by Roessler and his associates (1993), "the more things change, the more they stay the same." Let's finally institute the significant changes that have been identified for years as critically needed for all students. We have the methods and the materials to help almost every student to become a worthwhile, self-determined, productive, and independent functioning individual who can have a decent quality of life. *Now, we must meet this challenge rather than talk about it.* Our students are depending on us. It is now up to you.

ACTIVITIES

1. Develop an action plan to present to your administration that will provide the impetus for starting the process of implementing a substantial career education curricular approach in your district.

2. Besides the content contained in your action plan, prepare a compelling presentation to your administration that will convince them to strongly support the action plan you propose. Good luck! (Note: An action plan outline is presented in Appendix H.)

Appendix A

Cooperative Agreement Between the Department of Education and the Division of Rehabilitation Services, State of West Virginia

PREAMBLE

This agreement is designed to improve the cooperative and collaborative efforts between the Department of Education (hereinafter "Education") and the Division of Rehabilitation Services (hereinafter "Rehabilitation"), for the purpose of more effective and efficient service delivery to individuals with disabilities of our state. This cooperative agreement shall assure that each student with disabilities in the state who needs special education, vocational education, and/or vocational rehabilitation services is promptly identified, and the appropriate services including transition services and modifications, when necessary, are made available to the individual. As used in this document, Education refers specifically to vocational education and special education programs.

DETERMINATION OF AGENCY RESPONSIBILITY

The education and vocational training of students ages 3 to 21 who have not graduated and who have been identified as disabled are the responsibility of Education. Special education programs shall continue to be provided to those students who are at least 21 years old and receiving special education services prior to September 1, 1991, until the end of the school year in which they became 23 years of age. Students ages 14 to 21 who have not graduated and who desire vocational training will have equal access to

Note. From *TRIAD Telecommunications Project: Transition Manual* by I. D. Cook and M. T. Urbanic, 1990, Institute: West Virginia Graduate College. Copyright 1990 by West Virginia Graduate College. Adapted by permission.

secondary vocational training, provided reasonable accommodation or modification can be made. In addition, the training must be: (1) realistic in light of actual or anticipated opportunities for gainful employment or supported employment; and, (2) must be suited to the individual's needs, interest and ability to benefit from such training.

Individuals with disabilities shall have equal access to services which are normally provided by public schools for non-disabled individuals (e.g., adult education or continuing education programs), provided that reasonable accommodation or modification can be made. The adult training programs must be realistic in light of actual or anticipated opportunities for gainful or supported employment and suited to the individual's needs, interests and ability to benefit from such training.

For students ages 16 to 21 who have left school by way of graduation and or have exited the school system, the responsibility of vocational services rests with Rehabilitation.

Rehabilitation will provide services which are legally the responsibility of Rehabilitation for those students who are approaching or are of working age and are determined by Rehabilitation to be eligible for services.

Eligibility for Rehabilitation services is based on:

1. The documented presence of a physical or mental disability, which for the individual constitutes or results in a substantial handicap to employment; and,
2. A reasonable expectation that rehabilitation services can benefit the individual in terms of employability.

Each agency will cooperate to provide referral, support and assistance to the agency with responsibility for services. Each agency will participate in the planning of transition services for individuals with disabilities.

STUDENT/CLIENT REFERRAL

The agency first making contact with the individual applicant assumes responsibility to initiate procedures, provide appropriate services, or make referral to the other agency.

INDIVIDUAL EDUCATION PROGRAM/INDIVIDUALIZED WRITTEN REHABILITATION PROGRAM

Education is responsible for providing special education and related services appropriate for each eligible student enrolled in the school system. At the earliest time that a student is identified at an age potentially eligible for rehabilitation services, it is important that Education and Rehabilitation work together on determining what, when, and how services are to be provided. At the time of the development of the Four Year Education Plan, students covered by Section 504 can be identified and referred for appropriate services. Since the Individualized Education Program (IEP) which focuses on educational goals and the Individual Written Rehabilitation Program (IWRP) which focuses on vocational goals have components in common, it is agreed that an essential step for cooperative planning for secondary school youth is the joint development of an IEP/IWRP. Therefore, when support responsibilities are anticipated, the IEP and/or IWRP will be developed corporately and the individual's program components (vocational training, vocational goals, objectives, services, timelines, etc.) and fiscal responsibilities will be specified.

SERVICES

The agency which has responsibility for providing services shall make available appropriate services for the individual. An individual with disabilities may refuse the services from the agency. However, another agency is not obligated to duplicate the services being offered by the responsible agency. (A detailed listing of services and responsible agencies is contained in the Service Responsibility Chart that follows.)

COORDINATED PLANNING

Each agency shall operate in accordance with its respective laws (P.L. 101–476, the Individuals with Disabilities Education Act; P.L. 101–302, the Carl D. Perkins Vocational Applied Technology Education Act; and Vocational Rehabilitation Act of 1973 as amended), regulations and state plan. Education and Rehabilitation agree jointly to plan and develop appropriate areas of their respective state plan.

CONFIDENTIALITY OF INFORMATION

Personnel employed by Education and Rehabilitation and assigned to cooperatively provide services to students with disabilities will have appropriate access to confidential information within the boundaries of the legal constraints of each agency to expedite the provision of vocational services.

LIAISON COMMITTEE

It is agreed that Education (special education and vocational education) and Rehabilitation each shall appoint at least one representative to a liaison committee, which shall meet at least quarterly (February, May, August and November). The liaison committee shall assist in:

1. the exchange and dissemination of information;
2. coordination of each agency's state plan;
3. provision of necessary inservice training between staff of the agencies;
4. utilization of training facilities for students/clients of the agencies;
5. identification of ideas needing additional cooperative planning and action; and,
6. planning for transitional services.

LOCAL AGREEMENTS

The education and vocational preparation of an individual with disabilities to his/her fullest potential is a complex process requiring numerous services from different agencies. The establishment of interagency agreements promotes the effective, efficient and economical provision of services. Each agency will encourage and provide assistance toward the establishment of a similar statement of cooperation between the local educational agencies and local Rehabilitation offices throughout the state.

It is recommended that at the local level, Education (special education and vocational education) and Rehabilitation establish a local liaison committee to meet quarterly. The liaison committee shall assist in:

1. planning for transition services;
2. provision of the necessary inservice training between staff of the agencies;
3. identification of areas needing additional cooperation; and,
4. coordination of local project plans, if applicable.

Communication between agency representatives and the sharing of pertinent educational, vocational, programmatic, and diagnostic information is necessary for cooperative planning. Upon the duly approved cooperative agreement between Rehabilitation and the local educational agency, certified rehabilitation counselors assigned as agents to the school system become an integral part of the educational process.

ARTICULATION

The State Rehabilitation Center, an approved NCAA special option facility, will accept educational diploma credits from all local educational agencies for joint clients served at the Center. Likewise, all local educational agencies will reciprocate in the acceptance of educational diploma credits for joint clients served at the Rehabilitation Center who are returning to local educational agencies for further services. This articulation procedure will be implemented by the joint development of a Four Year Education Plan, IEP, and/or IWRP.

AGREED TO

AGREED TO

_____   _____
President   DATE
State Board of Education and
State Board of Rehabilitation

_____   _____
State Superintendent of Schools   DATE

_____   _____
Director   DATE
Division of Rehabilitation Services

7/13/90

Appendix B
List of Professional Organizations

Organization and Address	Publications	Features
Alexander Graham Bell Association for the Deaf 3417 Volta Place, NW Washington, DC 20007-2778 (202) 337-5220	*Volta Review* *Newsounds*	Follows philosophy of mainstreaming deaf children emphasizing oral-deaf education. Provides information services for parents and professionals. Sponsors children's rights advocacy network. Offers financial aid programs for oral hearing impaired people.
American Association on Mental Retardation (AAMR) 1719 Kalorama Road, NW Washington DC 20009-2683 (202) 387-1968 (800) 424-3688	*American Journal on Mental Retardation* *Mental Retardation* *News & Notes*	Interdisciplinary team of professionals and concerned individuals in the field. Holds national and regional meetings and provides information on latest research and practices.
American Council on Rural Special Education (ACRES) University of Utah 221 Milton Bennion Hall Salt Lake City, UT 84112 (801) 585-5659	*Ruralink* *Rural Special Education Quarterly*	Dedicated to the interests of individuals with disabilities living in rural areas. Provides job referral service, conferences, monographs, and other resources.
American Deafness and Rehabilitation Association (ADARA) P.O. Box 251554 Little Rock, AR 72225 (501) 868-8850 Fax (501) 868-8812	*Journal of the American Deafness and Rehabilitation Association* *The ADARA Update*	Network of professionals and community persons. Holds forums, conferences, and workshops. Provides information on referral service about careers, university programs, and job opportunities.
American Foundation for the Blind (AFB) 15 West 16th Street New York, NY 10011 (212) 620-2155	*Journal of Visual Impairment and Blindness* *AFB News*	Provides information and consultation in education, rehabilitation, employment, and special products.
American Printing House for the Blind, Inc. 1839 Frankfort Avenue P.O. Box 6085 Louisville, KY 40206-0085 (502) 895-2405 (800) 223-1839	*APH Slate*	Provides reading materials: books in braille, large type, and recorded form, educational aids, tools, and supplies.

Organization and Address	Publications	Features
Boy Scouts of America 1325 West Walnut Hill Lane Irving, TX 75015-7079 (214) 580-2430	*Boys Life* *Scouting Magazine*	Developed and promotes the Learning for Life Program, which is being implemented in elementary schools across the country and includes attention to students with special needs.

Clearinghouse on Disability
  Information
Office of Special Education and
  Rehabilitative Services (OSERS)
U.S. Department of Education
Room 3132, Switzer Building
330 C Street, SW
Washington, DC 20202-2524
(202) 205-8241
	OSERS News in Print	Provides information on federal funding, federal legislation, and federal programs serving people with disabilities.

Council for Exceptional Children (CEC) 1920 Association Drive Reston, VA 22091-1589 (701) 620-3660 (800) 845-6232	*Exceptional Children* *Teaching Exceptional* *Children* *CEC Today*	Dedicated to advancing the quality of education for exceptional children and improving the conditions under which special educators work. Has 17 special interest divisions, e.g., Council for Children with Behavior Disorders, Division on Mental Retardation.
Center for Minority Special Education (CMSE) P.O. Box 6107 Hampton, VA 23668		Provides technical assistance for research and documentation proposals in special education, rehabilitation and related services.
Division on Career Development and Transition Council for Exceptional Children (CEC) 1920 Association Drive Reston, VA 22091-1589 (701) 620-3660 (800) 845-6232	*Career Development for* *Exceptional Individuals,* *DCD Network*	A division of the Council for Exceptional Children that addresses and promotes the career development needs of all types of exceptional students.
Epilepsy Foundation of America 4351 Garden City Drive Landover, MD 20785 (301) 459-3700 (800) 332-1000	*Epilepsy USA*	Provides technical, referral, and research information services. Works with Congress and government agencies to advance the interests of people with epilepsy.
National Association of the Deaf (NAD) 814 Thayer Avenue Silver Spring, MD 20910 (301) 587-1788	*Broadcaster* *Deaf American*	Provides and publishes information on deafness and hearing loss. Serves as an advocate and legal consultant for this disability group. Holds regional workshops and youth programs.
National Association of the Physically Handicapped, Inc. Bethesda Scarlott Oaks, #GA 4 440 Lafayette Avenue Cincinnati, OH 45220-1073	*NAPH National* *Newsletter*	Works to advance the social, economic, and physical welfare of the physically disabled. Advocates and supports legislation that benefits people with disabilities.
National Association of Protection and Advocacy Systems (NAPAS) 900 Second Street, NE, Suite 211 Washington, DC 20002 (202) 408-9514 (202) 408-9521 (TTD)		Membership association of the directors of Protection and Advocacy Systems for Persons with Developmental Disabilities and for Persons with Mental Illness and the Client Assistance Program. Provides technical assistance and training for members and staffs. Monitors congressional and federal agency activities related to disability issues and oversight administration.

Organization and Address	Publications	Features
National Association of Vocational Education Special Needs Personnel (NAVESNP) c/o American Vocational Association (AVA) 1410 King Street Alexandria, VA 22314 (703) 683-3111 (800) 892-2274	*The NAVESNP Journal*	Membership organization of secondary and post-vocational professionals concerned with education of disadvantaged students and students with disabilities or other special needs. Five regional divisions provide information consultancy to consumers.
National Center of Youth with Disabilities (NCYD) Adolescent Health Program University of Minnesota Box 721–UMHC Harvard Street at East River Road Minneapolis, MN 55455 (612) 626-2825 (800) 333-6293	*Cydline Reviews Connections*	Serves as a technical assistance and information resource center focusing on adolescents with chronic illness and disability and issues that surround their transition to adult life. On-line computerized data base provides information on current research, model programs, training and educational materials, federal and state law, and legislation.
National Center for Learning Disabilities 99 Park Avenue, 6th Floor New York, NY 10016 (212) 687-7211	*THEIR WORLD NCLD Newsletter*	Provides information and referrals about special education programs and products to parents and professionals.
National Clearinghouse for Professions in Special Education Information Center c/o Council for Exceptional Children 1920 Association Drive Reston, VA 22091 (703) 264-9475 (703) 620-3660 (TDD)		Collects, synthesizes, and disseminates information on career opportunities, personnel supply and demand, and personnel preparation programs for increasing the supply of qualified professionals serving individuals with disabilities. It provides information, technical assistance, and linkages to promote local, state, and national efforts to collect useful information in these areas.
National Council on Disability U.S. Department of Education 800 Independence Avenue, SW, Suite 814 Washington, DC 20591 (202) 267-3846 (202) 267-3232 (TDD)	*FOCUS*	An independent federal agency of 15 members appointed by the President and confirmed by the Senate. Addresses, analyzes, and makes recommendations on issues of public policy which affect people with disabilities.
National Easter Seal Society 70 East Lake Street Chicago, IL 60601-5907 (312) 726-6200 (800) 221-6827	*Washington Watch Line*	A nonprofit community-based health agency dedicated to increasing the independence of people with disabilities. Offers a wide range of services, research, and programs to assist adults and children with disabilities and their families.
National Federation of the Blind (NFB) 1800 Johnson Street Baltimore, MD 21230 (301) 659-9314	*The Braille Monitor Future Reflections*	Provides information, resources, scholarships, and referral services for people with visual impairment.

Organization and Address	Publications	Features
National Information Center for Children and Youth with Disabilities (NICHCY) P.O. Box 1492 Washington, DC 20013 (703) 893-6061 (800) 999-5599	*NICHCY News Digest* *Transition Summary*	Information and referral clearinghouse for families and professionals concerned with disability issues and children and youth ages 22 and under.
National Organization on Disability 910 16th Street, NW, Suite 600 Washington, DC 20006 (202) 293-5960 (800) 248-2253	*NOD Report*	Works to improve attitudes toward people with disabilities, expand educational and employment opportunities, eliminate physical barriers, increase participation in religious, cultural, and recreational activities.
National Parent Network on Disabilities 1600 Prince Street, Suite 115 Alexandria, VA 22314-2836 (703) 684-6763		Provides legislative representation, reference, and referrals. Holds national and regional conferences. Is involved in materials development and distribution. Has a database linking parents to local, state, regional, national, and/or international services.
National Rehabilitation Association 1910 Association Drive, Suite 205 Reston, VA 22091 (703) 715-9090	*Journal of Rehabilitation*	Involved in advocacy, legislative design, and the development of education and training programs for people with disabilities.
National Spinal Cord Injury Association 600 W. Cummings Park, Suite 2000 Woburn, MA 01801 (617) 935-2722 (800) 962-9629		Provides information to injured individuals, families, health care professionals, and other agencies. Holds conventions and seminars.
President's Committee on Employment of People with Disabilities 1331 F Street, NW Washington, DC 20004-1107 (202) 376-6200	*Tips and Trends* *Worklife*	Provides information, referral, and assistance concerning employment and people with disabilities. Holds conferences, seminars, and workshops on issues concerning employment.
TASH: The Association for Persons with Severe Handicaps 11201 Greenwood Avenue N Seattle, WA 98133 (206) 361-8870 (206) 361-0113 (TDD)	*TASH Newsletter* *DC Update*	Dedicated to improving the living, learning, and working environments of people with severe disabilities. Offers information and referral services.
Technical Assistance for Special Populations Program (TASPP)	*TASPP Bulletin* *TASPP Brief*	Assists in improving vocational education programs for youth and adults with special needs.
The Arc 500 E. Border Street, 3rd Floor Arlington, TX 76010 (817) 640-0204 (800) 433-5255	*The Arc Today*	Trains volunteers to work with mentally challenged people, develops models in areas of education, training, and residence, and furthers employment opportunities.
United Cerebral Palsy Association 1522 K Street, NW, Suite 1112 Washington, DC 20005 (202) 842-1266 (800) 872-5827	*UCP News* *Word From Washington*	Involved in research and advocacy. Provides services ranging from preschool to adult work programs.

Appendix C

LCCE Performance Test 17

FORM A: EXAMINER

Knowing and Exploring Occupational Possibilities (Occupational Guidance and Preparation)

Materials for Duplication

Test Question 1:	Occupational Remuneration
Test Question 2:	Job Information
Test Question 3:	Values from a Job
Test Question 4:	Job Categories
Test Question 5:	Investigate Job Opportunities
Want Ads Sheet	
Score Sheet	

Materials Needed

Telephone directories.

Directions

This test can be given in approximately one class period. Answers may be written or given orally, but care must be taken so other students do not overhear responses. Some directions and vocabulary used in this test may be too advanced for some students and may require further explanation. This test assesses the students' ability to:

1. identify remunerative aspects of work
2. locate sources of occupational and training information
3. identify personal values met through work
4. classify jobs into occupational categories
5. investigate local occupational and training opportunities

Note. From *Life Centered Career Education: Competency Assessment Performance Batteries,* by D. E. Brolin, 1992, Reston, VA: The Council for Exceptional Children. Copyright 1992 by The Council for Exceptional Children. Reprinted by permission.

Scoring Procedures

If the test has previously been administered to the student, circle the number of times on the score sheet.

Examples of appropriate responses are provided on the score sheet for items that may have several acceptable answers. Some questions may have only one acceptable response.

For questions requiring demonstrations or role-playing, the examiner must make a judgment about scoring. Further guidelines are presented below.

Written Responses—On the score sheet, circle the example(s) the student has identified. If the student gives an example that seems appropriate but is not listed on the score sheet, record that response on the line provided. Then record the student's score.

Oral Responses—For test questions to which the student responded orally rather than in writing, record the student's response on the score sheet and score the response.

Observed Responses—For test questions requiring the student to perform by demonstrating or role-playing, record the response immediately after the response is made. If the task is not performed appropriately, note the reason for the point loss on the line provided.

Each question, including the subquestions, is worth up to 2 points. A student must attain a total score of 8–10 for mastery. Record the final score on the Student Competency Assessment Record (SCAR).

Allow students to respond to each request before reading the next task.

Question 1:   Occupational Remuneration (Group Administration)

To the Examiner: Students are to provide explanations for differences in occupational remuneration and why people take lower paying jobs. Also, students are to answer a question concerning types of reductions to paychecks. Distribute Test Question 1.

Read to Students: Look at Test Question 1 and read along with me. People get paid different amounts of money depending on the kind of job they have. Lawyers and doctors make more money than dishwashers and food servers. (a) Give one reason why this is so. (b) Explain why people take lower paying jobs when others pay so much better. (c) When thinking of how much money you're going to make at a job, you must also consider what reductions will be made to your paycheck before you get it. An example of a reduction is money taken out for your retirement plan. List two other possible reductions there may be to a person's paycheck.

Question 2: Job Information (Group Administration)

To the Examiner: Students are to use telephone directories to list four local sources (other than school) of occupational information. Distribute Test Question 2 and telephone directories.

Read to Students: Look at Test Question 2 and read along with me. There are many different places you can go to get information about jobs. Using the phone book, find four places in your town or area, other than school, where you could go to find information about jobs or careers and write the four places on the lines provided.

Question 3: Values From a Job (Group Administration)

To the Examiner: Students are to identify personal values met through work. Distribute Test Question 3.

Read to Students: Look at Test Question 3 and read along with me. There are many personal values, or rewards, that a person can get from a job. Why do you think bus drivers work as bus drivers? Besides money, what is another reward each of the following employees get from his or her work?

Question 4: Job Categories (Group Administration)

To the Examiner: Students are to demonstrate the ability to classify jobs into occupational categories. Distribute Test Question 4 and give a simple explanation of each of the four jobs listed on the Test Question.

Read to Students: Look at Test Question 4 and read along with me. Different jobs fit into different categories. Some of these different categories include jobs that require more education or less education, and a lot of sitting or a lot of moving around. (Briefly explain each of the jobs listed below.) Now that I have explained the four jobs listed below, you should be able to see how each of the four jobs fits in a different square. Match the jobs with the job categories given above the squares, and write that job in the correct square.

Question 5: Investigate Job Opportunities (Group Administration)

To the Examiner: Students are to demonstrate the ability to investigate occupational opportunities. Distribute Test Question 5 and the Want Ads Sheet.

Read to Students: Look at Test Question 5 and read along with me. There are two job descriptions listed below. Using the Want Ads Sheet, pick the job ads that would relate to the two job descriptions listed. Write four ad numbers (not the telephone numbers) for each job in the spaces provided. The first job listed is food service/kitchen worker. This is a worker who performs duties related to preparation or delivery of food or to the upkeep of kitchen work areas and equipment. The second job listed is truck driver. This is a worker who drives a truck to transport materials, merchandise, equipment or people.

LCCE PERFORMANCE TEST 17—Form A
Knowing and Exploring Occupational Possibilities
Score Sheet

Student _____   School _____

Examiner _____   Date _____   Previous Admins.   **1 2 3 4 5**

Question	Possible Points		Examples of Appropriate Responses	Score
Occupational Remuneration				
1	.5	a.	.5 pt. for an appropriate response: More education, more training, greater skill, higher demand.	
	.5	b.	.5 pt. for an appropriate response: Don't want to change location, not something they would enjoy doing, too difficult a job, happy with current work situation, don't want to leave family or friends, don't have the skills or training, can't afford to get training.	
	1	c.	.5 pt. for an appropriate response: Federal income tax, state income tax, Social Security, donations, parking fees.	
Job Information				
2	2		.5 pt. for an appropriate response: Library, employment service, Chamber of Commerce, career center, placement center, various private employment agencies, vocational—technical schools.	

Examiner

LCCE PERFORMANCE TEST 17—Form A
Knowing and Exploring Occupational Possibilities
Score Sheet

Student _____ School _____

Examiner _____ Date _____ Previous Admins.   1 2 3 4 5

Question	Possible Points		Examples of Appropriate Responses	Score
Occupational Remuneration				
1	.5	a.	.5 pt. for an appropriate response: More education, more training, greater skill, higher demand.	
	.5	b.	.5 pt. for an appropriate response: Don't want to change location, not something they would enjoy doing, too difficult a job, happy with current work situation, don't want to leave family or friends, don't have the skills or training, can't afford to get training.	
	1	c.	.5 pt. for an appropriate response: Federal income tax, state income tax, Social Security, donations, parking fees.	
Job Information				
2	2		.5 pt. for an appropriate response: Library, employment service, Chamber of Commerce, career center, placement center, various private employment agencies, vocational—technical schools.	

LCCE PERFORMANCE TEST 17—Form A

Test Question 1: Occupational Remuneration

Name _____   Date _____

People get paid different amounts of money depending on the kinds of jobs they have. Lawyers and doctors make more money than dishwashers and food servers.

a.   Give one reason why this is so.

_____

b.   Explain why people take lower paying jobs when others pay so much better.

_____

c.   When thinking of how much money you're going to make at a job, you must also consider what reductions will be made to your paycheck before you get it. An example of a reduction is money taken out for your retirement plan. List two other possible reductions there may be to a person's paycheck.

1. _____

2. _____

Student

LCCE PERFORMANCE TEST 17—Form A
Test Question 2: Job Information

Name _____   Date _____

There are many different places you can go to get information about jobs. Using the phone book, find four places in your town or area, other than school, where you could go to find information about jobs or careers and write the four places on the lines provided.

1. _____

2 . _____

3. _____

4. _____

Student

LCCE PERFORMANCE TEST 17—Form A

Test Question 3: Personal Values from a Job

Name _____ Date _____

There are many personal values, or rewards, that a person can get from a job. Why do you think bus drivers work as bus drivers? Besides money, what is another reward each of the following employees get from his or her work?

a.   Bus driver _____

_____

b.   Carpenter _____

_____

c.   Janitor _____

_____

d.   Hotel maid _____

_____

Student

LCCE PERFORMANCE TEST 17—Form A
Test Question 4: Job Categories

Name_____ Date _____

Different jobs fit into different categories. Some of these different categories include jobs that require more education or less education, and a lot of sitting or a lot of moving around. Now that I have explained the four jobs listed below, you should be able to see how each of the four jobs fits in a different square. Match the jobs with the job categories given above the squares, and write that job in the correct square.

Jobs:
    Emergency Room Doctor
    Fire Fighter
    Receptionist
    Pilot

a. More Education and Sitting	b. Less Education and Sitting

c. More Education and Moving Around	d. Less Education and Moving Around

LCCE PERFORMANCE TEST 17—Form A

Test Question 5: Investigate Job Opportunities

Name _____ Date _____

There are two job descriptions listed below. Using the Want Ads Sheet, pick the job ads that would relate to each of the two job descriptions listed. Write four ad numbers (not the telephone numbers) for each job in the spaces provided.

Job 1:   Food Service/Kitchen Worker

Description: A worker who performs duties related to preparation or delivery of food or to the upkeep of kitchen work areas and equipment.

Ad numbers:

1. _____
2. _____
3. _____
4. _____

Job 2:   Truck Driver

Description: A worker who drives a truck to transport materials, merchandise, equipment, or people.

Ad numbers:

1. _____
2. _____
3. _____
4. _____

LCCE PERFORMANCE TEST 17—Form A

Want Ads Sheet

(Use in Question 5)

Name _____ Date _____

WANT ADS

Hospital Aide–
Must be able to push carts of medicine through hallways. Must be able to lift 25 lbs. or more. Duties: Assisting hospital personnel with patient care. For more information call:
447-2293
1

Dishwasher needed at Lindy's. All shifts available. Part-time or full-time. $5/hr. Call:
937-2569
2

Needed – Carpenter to finish recording studio. Roughing has been done. Need custom cases, cabinets, and other recording essentials. If experienced call:
750-3738
3

Person to drive beef truck for Binghamm's Foods, Inc. Must have grade 2 license with experience. For more info call:
339-2700
4

Delivery person needed immediately! Will drive truck of produce from market to store. Must be able to lift 50 lbs. or more. Good pay and benefits. Truck provided. Call:
773-2653
5

Builder needed to do deck and patio work. 3 mos. trial then steady pay and benefits. Upward mobility in new company possible. Inquire:
953-9927
6

Nurse's Helper –
Courteous, hard working person needed to help nurse care for elderly gentleman. Good pay. Long hours. Interested? Call:
328-4785
7

Open-road transport operator needed to drive 18 wheel rig from Marshall Junction to 14 points of destination. Excellent pay. Day and night shifts available. Loading and unloading required. Interested? Call:
769-2783
8

Chef needed to cook appetizers at Loi's. Must be ACS member and have 2 yrs experience. Excellent remuneration. Call:
937-4672
9

Skilled toy maker needed to craft toys from raw wood stock. Experience preferred. Bring sample of work. Call Chris at Santa's Helpers, Inc.
895-2203
10

Patient Care Attendant –
Westside Geriatric Unit looking for nurse's aides and custodial personnel. Morning, evening, and night shifts available. Call for more information:
945-2600
11

Busboy needed at Tim's Family Restaurant. $4.25/hr Evenings:
435-7567
12

Truck Driver –
Needed for delivering tires from local distributor across country. Good pay. Will drive in team of 2. For more information call Bob at:
256-4895
13

Mess cook for boys' dorm needed immediately. Experience cooking large portions. Salary and benefits. Apply to Western Central Eastern College:
893-1452
14

Craftsman position open at Ferguson's Clocks and Cabinets. Need carpenter experienced at working with differing hardwoods to run molding operations. Pay is $17.50/hr. Call:
225-9090
15

Nurse's Aides –
5 nurse's aides are needed immediately for new burn unit at Mercy Hospital. Experience working with people preferred. Inquiries to Janet at:
335-0478
16

Appendix D

Functional Assessment Resources

Catalogs are available from the following organizations, which contain information on functional assessment inventories, standardized tests, basic skills assessment instruments, transition assessment batteries, and work sample systems.

American Guidance Service
Publisher's Building
Circle Pines, MN 55014–1796
(900) 328-2560

Arkansas Research & Training Center in Vocational Rehabilitation Publications Department
P.O. Box 1358
Hot Springs, AR 71902
(501) 624-4411 Ext. 316

The Council for Exceptional Children
1920 Association Drive, Dept. K3012 1 2
Reston, VA 22091–1589
(703) 620-3660

CTB/McGraw-Hill
2500 Garden Road
Monterey, CA 93940
(800) 538-9547

Curriculum Associates TM, Inc.
5 Esquire Road
N. Billerica, MA 01862-2589

J. E. Stewart
18518 Kenlake Place Northeast
Seattle, WA 98155
(206) 486-4510

Materials Development Center
Stout Vocational Rehabilitation Institute
University of Wisconsin-Stout
Menomonie, WI 54751
(715) 232-1342

McCarron-Dial Systems, Inc.
P.O. Box 45628
Dallas, TX 75245
(214) 247-5945

Supported Employment Technical Assistance Project
B 125 West Fee Hall
Michigan State University
E. Lansing, MI 48824-1316
(517) 355-0166

VALPAR International Corporation
P.O. Box 5767
Tucson, AZ 85703-5767
(800) 528-7070

TALENT ASSESSMENT, INC.
P.O. Box 5087
Jacksonville, FL 32247
(800) 634-1472
(800) 225-0248

Virginia Commonwealth University
Rehabilitation Research and Training Center
VCU Box 2011
Richmond, VA 23284–0001
Attn: Resource Dissemination
(804) 257-1851

Appendix E

LCCE Resources Available from The Council for Exceptional Children

Life Centered Career Education: A Competency Based Approach

Fourth Edition
Donn E. Brolin

The guide contains the most current set of transitional objectives and units for the 97 LCCE subcompetencies. Includes the Competency Rating Scale and IEP Forms with transition components.

No. P180F. 1993. 180 pp.
ISBN 0–86586–241–9. Price $28

Life Centered Career Education: The Complete Curriculum and Assessment Package

Includes over 1,100 lesson plans covering Daily Living Skills, Personal-Social Skills, and Occupational Skills; Knowledge Batteries (10 copies of each of two alternative forms); Performance Batteries; Administration Manuals; and Technical Report.

No. P371. 1992. Price $980

LCCE: Daily Living Skills

Donn E. Brolin

Includes 472 lesson plans covering personal finances, household management, personal needs, family responsibilities, food preparation, citizenship responsibilities, and leisure.

No. P367. 1992. 1,556 pp. Three loose-leaf binders.
ISBN 0–86586–224–9. Price $400

LCCE: Personal-Social Skills

Donn E. Brolin

Provides 370 lesson plans for developing self-awareness, self-confidence, socially responsible behavior, good interpersonal skills, independence, decision-making, and communication skills.

No. P368. 1992. 1,348 pp. Three loose-leaf binders.
ISBN 0–86586–225–7. Price $400

LCCE: Occupational Guidance and Preparation

Richard T. Roessler and Donn E. Brolin

Includes 286 lesson plans to help students explore occupational possibilities; make occupational choices; develop appropriate work habits; seek, secure, and maintain employment; exhibit sufficient physical/manual skills; and obtain specific occupational competencies.

No. P369. 1992. 670 pp. Two loose-leaf binders.
ISBN 0–86586–226–5. Price $300

LCCE: Competency Assessment Knowledge Batteries

Available in parallel forms, each Knowledge Battery consists of 200 multiple-choice questions that cover the first 20 competencies. Primarily a screening instrument, the Knowledge Batteries were designed to pinpoint specific competency deficiencies. Package includes an Administration Manual, a Technical Report, and samples of each form of the test. Also included are two introductory sets of 10 Knowledge Batteries, Forms A and B, to use with students.

No. P370K. 1992. 152 pp.
ISBN 0–86586–239–7. Price $125

LCCE: Competency Assessment Performance Batteries

The Performance Batteries consist of two alternative forms for each of the 21 competency units. Items are primarily performance-based and should be administered to students before and after instructional units have been taught. Performance Batteries are administered individually or with small groups of students. Test materials must be reproduced as needed. Performance Batteries are packaged in a loose-leaf binder along with an Administration Manual.

No. P370P. 1992. 675 pp.
ISBN 0–86586–240–0. Price $225

Additional Sets of Knowledge Batteries

Packages of 10 tests may be ordered separately to be used by students. Students may answer questions directly in the test booklets by circling the correct choice or may use a standard machine-scorable form. Knowledge Batteries may not be reproduced.

LCCE: Knowledge Battery Form A (10 per package)

No. P372. $50

LCCE: Knowledge Battery Form B (10 per package)

No. P373. $50

Life Centered Career Education: The Training Package

Donn E. Brolin

Includes:
    Ten Videotapes
    Trainer's Manual
    Professional Development Activity Book
    LCCE: A Competency Based Approach

No. M5000. 1993. Package Price $975
Ten Videotapes

Session 1: **The Need to Change and the Law** (23:38 min) No. M5001
Session 2: **The LCCE Curriculum (K–12)** (49:36 min) No. M5002
Session 3: **Assessing Functional Skills** (57:48 min) No. M5003
Session 4: **Teaching Daily Living Skills** (58:41 min) No. M5004
Session 5: **Teaching Personal Social Skills** (58:26 min) No. M5005
Session 6: **Teaching Occupational Skills** (58:82 min) No. M5006

Session 7: **Selection, Modification, and Development of Instructional Materials (Part 1)** (29:10 min) **Involving Parents in Functional Curriculum** (Part 2) (27:29 min) No. M5007

Session 8: **Involving Business and Industry (Part 1)** (28:32 min) **Interagency Collaboration (Part 2)** (30:30 min) No. M5008

Session 9: **Curriculum Modification and Change** (56:27 min) No. M5009

Session 10: **Individualized Transition Planning and Implementation** (62:37 min) No. M5010

Tapes may be ordered separately by Stock Number.
Price $100 each

Life Centered Career Education: Trainer's Manual, Third Edition and Professional Development Activity Book

Donn E. Brolin

This two-volume set of training materials includes a 96-page third edition of the Trainer's Manual and a 458-page Activity Book designed for use by all participants who are in training. These training materials provide approximately 30 hours of LCCE in-service training and are designed to support the video presentations. Orientation and directions for conducting each session are outlined in the Trainer's Manual.

No. M5011. 1993. Price $70

Life Centered Career Education: Professional Development Activity Book

Donn E. Brolin

Designed for use by all participants in the training program. Each session includes objectives, key concepts from that session's video, session activities, note-taking pages, resource materials, and assignments for the next session. The Activity Book is packaged in a loose-leaf binder.

No. M5013. 1993. Price $40

Prices may change without notice. Please call (703) 620-3660 to confirm prices and shipping charges.

LCCE On-site Training is also available from CEC. For more information about LCCE workshops and academies call (703) 620–3660.

The Council for Exceptional Children
1920 Association Drive
Reston, VA 22091–1589
(703) 620-3660 (Voice/TDD)
(703) 264-9494 (FAX)

Materials Correlated to the LCCE Competencies/Subcompetencies and List of Publishers

MATERIALS CORRELATED TO THE LCCE COMPETENCIES/ SUBCOMPETENCIES

Competency 1: Managing Personal Finances

Subcompetency 5, 6

Banking Language and Credit Language. Globe Fearon.

These situation-specific work texts give the students the vocabulary associated with banking and credit.

Reading Level: 3.0
Interest Level: 3–12/ABE/ESL

Subcompetency 1–6

Working Makes Sense. Globe Fearon.

Students acquire and practice skills using fractions, percents, and amounts over $100—while learning about employment, banking, and budgeting. Automated teller machines, check endorsement, bank statements, and employee benefits are introduced.

Reading Level: 3.0
Interest Level: 6–12/ABE/ESL

Subcompetency 2

Using Dollars and Sense. Globe Fearon.

Provides consumer-oriented exercises on estimating, using supermarket shelf labels, averaging prices, finding errors on receipts, as well as weights and measures and making change.

Reading Level: 3.0
Interest Level: 3–12/ABE/ESL

Subcompetency 1–6

Living in the Real World. EBSCO.

This program is designed to teach students how to manage money, balance checkbooks, and deal with unexpected outcomes.

Level: Junior-Senior High School

Subcompetency 1–6

Real-Life Math (Stuart Swartz). Pro-Ed.

This program is designed to teach students to deal with personal money management and business transactions. Spirit masters, posters, and audiocassettes accompany the teacher's manual.

Level: Junior-Senior High School

Subcompetency 2

Consumer Skills for Teenagers and Consumer Skills for Living on Your Own. Quercus.

Students learn to prioritize needs and budget with specific amounts.

Reading Level: 2.5–2.6

Subcompetency 1–6

Mathematics for Consumers. AGS.

This text extends basic math skills through their application to important everyday situations such as paying taxes, buying food, banking, etc. Student workbook, blackline masters, teachers manual, and teacher's resource binder accompany the text.

Interest Level: Grades 8–12; adult

Subcompetency 1–6

Practical Math. Fearon.

The text reinforces basic life skills such as the importance of math competence in money management, banking, career choices, everyday living, and more. The classroom resource binder includes blackline masters and work sheets.

Reading Level: Below 4
Interest Level: 7–12; adult

Subcompetency 1–6

Reading for Survival in Today's Society. Scott Foresman.

This text helps students develop functional reading skills with practical readings such as electric bills, consumer information, recipes, and more.

Reading Levels: Volume I, Grades 6–9; Volume II, Grades 8–12

Subcompetency 3

Building Life Skills Text. Lakeshore Learning Materials.

This text, accompanied by a teacher's guide and activity book, teaches students life management skills such as budgeting, health, nutrition, how to shop for food, and more.

Reading Level: 5.0–7.0

Subcompetency 3

Lifeschool. Pacemaker Learning Materials.

This multilevel program is designed to help the teacher meet the basic skills needs for hard-to-reach students. The binder contains 10 modules with lessons, work sheets, and more, which focus on money, housing, groceries, clothing, and more.

Reading Level: Grades 3.5–4.5

Subcompetency 1–6

Math for Everyday Living. Lakeshore Reading Materials.

This microcomputer software—Apple II Family—teaches students to become wise money managers. The program includes lesson disks, backup disks, and reproducible activity sheets.

Reading Level: Grades 3.5–4.5

Subcompetency 1–6

Everyday Consumer English. Lakeshore Reading Materials.

Lessons that introduce students to making a budget, using banking services, shopping at the supermarket, and leasing an apartment also incorporate comprehension questions, grammar exercises, and vocabulary and spelling activities.

Reading Level: Grades 4.5–6.0

Subcompetency 1–6

Math for Successful Living. Gameco Industries, Inc.

This microcomputer software includes five programs, which focus on time cards and paychecks, managing a checking account, budgeting, buying on credit, and shopping strategies.

Level: Grades 7–12

Subcompetency 1–2

Learning Through Reading Series. Book I. Wallet War (N. Bowling, I. D. Cook, & D. Salyers). Science Research Associates.

The *Wallet War* is a part of a series designed to teach students practical life skills while supporting reading skills. The text teaches students how to use food stamps and money wisely. A criterion-referenced pre-post-test, audiotape, and teacher's guide accompany Book I.

Level: Junior-Senior High School

Competency 2: Selecting and Managing a Household

Subcompetency 9, 10

Buying with Sense. Globe Fearon.

High-interest format lets students put math skills to use while following an about-to-be married couple through the process of buying everything they need to set up a home.

Reading Level: 4.0
Interest Level: 6–12/ABE/ESL

Subcompetency 9

Lifeschool. Pacemaker Learning Series.

(See Competency 1 for description.)

Reading Level: Grades 3.5–4.5

Subcompetency 12–13, 15–16

Health. The Pacemaker Curriculum. Globe Fearon.

This practical text covers both physical and mental health. Systems of the body, safety, and urgent topics such as alcohol, drugs, sexuality, and AIDS are addressed. Covers materials required for GED testing.

Reading Level: Below 4.0
Interest Level: 6–12/ABE/ESL

Subcompetency 13, 14

Good Grooming for Guys and Good Grooming for Girls. Globe Fearon.

These two books show how grooming makes a difference in teens' lives.

Reading Level: 4.0–6.0
Interest Level: 6–12

Subcompetency 13, 16

Self-Help Skills Kit. EBSCO.

Fourteen goal areas, including grooming, dressing, and personal safety are covered. A teacher's guide accompanies the kit.

Level: Early childhood–elementary

Subcompetency 13

Personal Care Skills. Pro-Ed.

This program is designed to provide individualized instruction in daily living skills that enable students to be more independent while fostering increased self-esteem. The complete program includes *A Manual of Basic Teaching Strategy,* 13 training manuals, and a tape cassette.

Level: Elementary

Subcompetency 12, 15

Take Care of Yourself. Quercus.

This text includes objectives that cover health vocabulary, distinguishing self-help conditions from those requiring a doctor's care and developing a plan for basic body care involving diet, rest, and exercise.

Reading Level: 2.3

Subcompetency 12

Nutrition Mission. Good Apple.

Reproducibles teach the five basic food groups essential to good health.

Level: Pregrade 2

Subcompetency 12

Building Life Skills Text. Lakeshore Learning Materials.

(See Competency 1 for description.)

Reading Level: 5.0–7.0

Subcompetency 12

Keeping Fit. Janus.

Presents the physical and emotional health benefits of regular exercise.

Reading Level: 3.5–4.0
Interest Level: 6–12/ABE

Subcompetency 12–13, 15

Looking Good. Janus.

This step-by-step guide to good grooming motivates students to take responsibility for their own health, appearance, and self-esteem.

Reading Level: 3.5–4.0
Interest Level: 6–12/ABE

Subcompetency 12–13, 15

Decisions for Health. Steck Vaughn.

This program covers interests of developing and mature student—nutrition, hygiene, safety, and more. Blackline masters are included with the teacher's guide.

Grade Level: 7–12
Reading Level: 3–4

Subcompetency 12, 16

I Am Amazing. AGS.

This program promotes health, safety, and self-esteem. It includes an activity manual, cards, game boards, posters, and an audiocassette.

Level: Preschool–K.

Subcompetency 15

Help! Janus.

Prepares students to handle 10 common minor medical emergencies including electrical shocks and burns.

Reading Level: 2.3–3.0
Interest Level: 6–12

Subcompetency 13, 14

Learning Through Reading Series. Book 2. Cleaning Up Your Act (N. Bowling, I. D. Cook, & D. Salyers). Science Research Associates.

Cleaning Up Your Act is a part of a series designed to teach practical life skills while supporting reading skills. Book 2 teaches personal hygiene and its social implications. A criterion-referenced pre-post-test, audiotape, and teacher's guide accompany Book 2.

Subcompetency 16

Let's Learn About Safety. Good Apple.

Safety education activities, take-home games, home/school materials, and parent information sheets are provided.

Level: Pregrade 2

Competency 4: Raising Children and Meeting Marriage Responsibilities

Subcompetency 17–19

Interpersonal Relations. Globe Fearon.

This module contains information about problem solving, family planning, pregnancy, baby care, aging, and death and dying.

Reading Level: 1.0–4.0
Interest Level: 9–12/ABE/ESL

Subcompetency 17–18

Building Life Skills Text. Lakeshore Learning Material.

Students learn how to care for children, among other things.

Reading Level: 5.0–7.0

Competency 5: Buying, Preparing, and Consuming Food

Subcompetency 20–25

Functional Work Series. Grocery Words. EBSCO.

This computer software program teaches students 100 words needed to read and write grocery lists and to find items in a grocery store.

Level: Ages 10–adult

Subcompetency 20–25

Functional Word Series. Fast Food. EBSCO.

This computer software program teaches students 100 words that will help them order a meal from a fast-food or restaurant menu.

Level: Ages 10–adult

Subcompetency 24

Self-Help Skills Kit. EBSCO.

This kit includes goals for teaching eating, drinking, and more.

Level: Early childhood–elementary

Subcompetency 25

Basic Home Economics. AGS.

This text helps prepare secondary level students for an adulthood of successful independent living. Written for low-level readers, it focuses on the practical application of consumerism, housing, food, nutrition, and more. A teacher's guide, activities, and blackline masters of tests and reinforcement exercises accompany the text.

Level: 8–12; adult

Subcompetency 24

Eating Skills Game. Attainment Company.

A programming guide and workbooks accompany this game, which teaches good table manners.

Subcompetency 20

Learning Through Reading Series (N. Bowling, I. D. Cook, & D. Salyers). Book I. Wallet War. Science Research Associates.

(See Competency 1 for description.)

Level: Junior–Senior High School

Subcompetency 20

Building Life Skills Text. Lakeshore Learning Materials.

(See Competency 1 for description.)

Reading Level: 5.0–7.0

Subcompetency 20

Comparison Shopping. Hartley Coursework.

Grocery shopping is the focus of this computer software game: the student "goes" to the grocery store with a list of things to buy. The learner takes into account unit, price, value, and coupons.

Level: 4–8.

Subcompetency 24–25

The Foods We Eat. Steck-Vaughn.

This activity module helps students recognize, name, and classify foods from all five food groups and encourages them to choose foods that create healthy meals.

Level: Grades K–2

Subcompetency 20

The Supermarket Program. Steck-Vaughn.

This program enhances and strengthens essential language skills while teaching students about health, nutrition, money, and more.

Level: Grades 1–5

Subcompetency 20, 25

Kitchen Math. Gameco Industries, Inc.

This set of 40 work sheets provides practice in applying basic math to shopping, meal planning, and other kitchen-related activities.

Level: Grades 4–12

Competency 6: Buying and Caring for Clothing

Subcompetency 26

Doing Home Laundry. Pro-Ed.

This is a program developed to increase independence in the home and training for employment in a laundry hotel, etc.

Level: Elementary–High School

Subcompetency 27

Building Life Schools. Lakeshore Learning Materials.

(See Competency 1 for description.)

Reading Level: Grades 3.5–4.5

Competency 7: Exhibiting Responsible Citizenship

Subcompetency 29–32

Our Government in Action. Government at Work. It's Our Government. Globe Fearon.

This series of texts is relevant and involving; it demonstrates the role of government and civics in students' everyday lives. The teacher's guide provides teaching suggestions, answer keys, and easily duplicated Work Master sheets.

Reading Level: 2.5–4.0
Interest Level: 6–12/ABE/ESL

Competency 8: Utilizing Recreational Facilities and Engaging in Leisure Time

Subcompetency 33–37

Keeping Fit (2nd Ed.). Globe Fearon.

The physical and emotional health benefits of regular exercise are presented. The personal fitness goals of each character in the story provide incentives and strategies students can use.

Reading Level: 3.5–4.0
Interest Level: 6–12/ABE

Subcompetency 33–37

Reading Schedules. Globe Fearon.

This work text covers different kinds of schedules and how to read them: how to understand abbreviations on calendars, bus schedules, class schedules, and movie/TV listings.

Reading Level: 2.0–3.5
Interest Level: 6–12/ABE

Subcompetency 33–36

Learning Through Reading Series. Book 3. A Night on the Town (N. Bowling, I. D. Cook, & D. Salyers). Science Research Associates.

A Night on the Town is a part of a series designed to teach practical skills while supporting reading skills. Book 3 teaches students how to organize and plan future events. A criterion-referenced pretest-post-test, audiotape, and teacher's guide accompany this book.

Level: Junior–Senior High School

Competency 9: Getting Around the Community

Subcompetency 38–41

Keys to Responsible Driving. Lakeshore Reading Materials.

This microcomputer software—Apple II Family—lets students experience what it is like to be behind the wheel. It includes two disks, backup disks, teacher's guide, and users guide.

Reading Level: Grades 4.0–5.0

Subcompetency 38–40

Getting Around Cities and Towns. Globe Fearon.

These work texts build confidence by showing how to get around one's neighborhood, then progress to more complex skills such as reading building directories, street maps, bus routes, and more.

Reading Level: 2.0–3.5
Interest Level: 6–12/ABE

Subcompetency 39–40

Finding Your Way. Globe Fearon.

These two work texts teach special needs students to find their way around their neighborhood and city.

Reading Level: 2.6
Interest Level: 3–9/ABE

Subcompetency 39–40

Taking a Trip. Fearon.

This work text prepares students for independent out-of-town travel.

Reading Level: 3.2
Reading Level: 4–12/ABE/ESL

Competency 10: Achieving Self-Awareness

Subcompetency 42–45

Janus Job Planner. Janus.

Self-scoring inventories of work interests, values, attitudes, working conditions, self-esteem, and more are the focus of this career-planning tool.

Reading Level: 2.5–4.0

Subcompetency 42–45

Self-Help Skills Kit. EBSCO.

This kit includes goal areas for teaching self-awareness, social speaking, and more.

Level: Early Childhood–Elementary

Competency 11: Acquiring Self-Confidence

Subcompetency 46–50

Feelings. Belonging. Caring. Loving. Relating. Good Apple.

The open-ended activities in this series of books are designed for the students to improve their own self-concept while developing a better understanding of themselves and others.

Level: Grades 2–8

Subcompetency 46–50

Self-Esteem Library. Wieser Educational, Inc.

This series is designed to raise the level of self-esteem in teens.

Reading Level: 4.0–6.0

Subcompetency 46, 50

Discovering Self-Confidence. Globe Fearon.

Shows students how to develop the self-confidence to reach their goals and have the strength to say "no" to peer pressure on drugs and alcohol.

Reading Level: 4.0–6.0
Interest Level: 6–12

Competency 12: Achieving Socially Responsible Behavior

Subcompetency 51–53, 55

Lifeschool 2000: Government and Law and Community Resources. Globe Fearon.

These modules contain lessons about traffic laws, accidents, taxes, consumer rights, citizenship, and immigration law and provide up-to-date information about social welfare programs, emergency services, crime prevention, and others.

Reading Level: 1.0–4.0
Interest Level: 9–12/ABE/ESL

Subcompetency 51–55

All About You Game. Attainment.

A programming guide and a workbook are included with this game, which provides a lively format to discuss personal issues and interpersonal skills, such as how to be more independent, thoughtful, respecting of the rights of others, and how to deal with peer pressure.

Level: Junior–Senior High School

Subcompetency 51–55

Work Behavior Training Program. EBSCO.

This social skills training program for the workplace provides a structured approach to job-related training to help students learn what's expected of them on the job.

Level: Junior–Senior High School

Subcompetency 51–55

Learning Through Reading Series. Book 3. A Night on the Town (N. Bowling, I. D. Cook, & D. Salyers).

(See Competency 8 for description.)

Level: Junior–Senior High School

Subcompetency 52

Following Directions. Lawrence Productions.

This computer software program encourages students to improve their ability to follow directions.

Level: Secondary

Competency 13: Maintaining Good Interpersonal Skills

Subcompetency 56–58

DUSO: Developing Understanding of Self and Others. AGS.

This program is designed to develop social skills, listening skills, a positive self-image, and an appreciation of individual strengths. The materials include a teacher's guide, puppets, activity cards, audiocassettes, blackline masters, and more.

Levels: DUSO I, K–Grade 2; DUSO II, Grades 3–4

Subcompetency 56–58

The Walker Social Skills Curriculum. Pro-Ed. **The Accepts Program: A Curriculum for Children's Effective Peer and Teacher Skills.**

This program, designed to be used by regular and special education teachers, cognitively teaches social skills as subject matter content.

Level: K–6

The ACCESS Program: Adolescent Curriculum for Communication and Effective Social Skills.

This program, designed for use by regular and special education teachers, teaches peer-to-peer skills, skills for relating to adults, and self-management skills. The materials for these programs include a program guide, videotape, and study guide.

Level: Middle–High School

Subcompetency 56–58

Lifeschool: Occupations and Interpersonal Skills. Globe Fearon.

One half of this multilevel program focuses on relating to others, and the other half focuses on specific employment skills. The 10 self-pacing modules consist of work sheets, activities, teacher's guide, and more.

Reading Level: Grades 2.0–4.5

Subcompetency 56–58

Conversation and Friendship Skills. Lakeshore Educational Inc.

This module includes skill books, workbooks, comic books, practice cards, and blackline masters.

Interest Level: 6–12

Competency 14: Achieving Independence

Subcompetency 59–61

Don't Get Fired. Janus.

Thirteen stories portray young employees who jeopardize their jobs by inappropriate behaviors.

Reading Level: 2.5–4.0

Subcompetency 59–61

Read On! Write On! Series. Globe Fearon.

As students progress through the sequential series, they develop thinking, communication, and socialization skills while examining their own values.

Reading Level: 2.5–4.0
Interest Level: 6–12

Competency 15: Making Adequate Decisions

Subcompetency 62–66

Get Hired. Janus.

Thirteen shortcuts to landing a job are presented in a way students can appreciate and quickly use.

Reading Level: 2.5–4.0
Interest Level: 6–12/ABE/ESL

Subcompetency 62–66

Choosing. Good Apple.

This book helps students in determining choices and more through activities that can be integrated into language, writing, and social studies content areas of the curriculum.

Level: Grades 3–8

Subcompetency 64–66

Problem Solving for Job Success Series. Lakeshore Reading Materials.

This workbook series develops students' decision-making skills and teaches strategies for coping with everyday problems on the job.

Reading Level: Grades 5.0–6.5

Competency 16: Communicating with Others

Subcompetency 68–69

Pacemaker Communication Series. Globe Fearon.

These three work texts help students develop communication and socialization skills.

Reading Level: 2.8
Interest Level: 5–12/ABE/ESL

Subcompetency 67–69

Discovering Self-Expression and Communication

This book discusses the dangers of keeping feelings bottled up and teaches students how to express themselves. The eight chapters include Communication, The Message, Nonverbal Communication, The Language of Personal Power, and Listening.

Reading Level: 4.0–6.0
Interest Level: 6–12

Subcompetency 67–69

Communicating. Good Apple.

The open-ended activities in this unit are designed for the students to improve their own self-concept while developing a better understanding of themselves and others.

Level: Grades 3–8

Subcompetency 67–69

Communication Skills Module. EBSCO.

This module is made up of three interactive components including a teletrainer, telephone skills cassettes, and a simply English curriculum. The materials provide realistic instruction that students need to get along on the job, at home, in school, and anywhere else. The telephone trainer may be used to train anyone to use TDD machines to communicate with the hearing impaired.

Level: Ungraded.

Competency 17: Knowing and Exploring Occupational Possibilities

Subcompetency 70–75

Janus Job Planner. Janus.

(See Competency 10 for description.)

Reading Level: 2.5–4.0

Get Hired. Janus.

(See Competency 15 for description.)

Reading Level: 2.5–4.0
Interest Level: 6–12/ABE/ESL

Subcompetency 70–75

Learning Through Reading Series. Book 4. Serious Business (N. Bowling, I. D. Cook, & D. Salyers). Science Research Associates.

Serious Business is part of a series designed to teach practical skills while supporting reading skills. This book teaches what skills are required for getting and keeping a job. A criterion-referenced pretest–post-test, audiotape, and teacher's guide accompany Book 4.

Level: Junior–Senior High School

Competency 18: Selecting and Planning Occupational Choices

Subcompetency 70–75

Janus Job Planner. Janus.

(See Competency 17 for description.)

Reading Level: 2.5–4.0/ABC/ESL
Interest Level: 6–12/ABE/ESL

Subcompetency 76–77

The Job Box. Lakeshore Reading Materials.

A set of 56 books and teacher's guide cover seven occupational clusters and are designed to give students realistic information about opportunities available to them.

Reading Level: Grades 3.0–4.0

Subcompetency 77

Community Helpers. Steck Vaughn.

This activity module teaches children about job duties of people they encounter every day.

Level: K–2

Competency 19: Exhibiting Appropriate Work Habits and Behaviors

Subcompetency 81–87

Learning Through Reading Series. Book 5. The Pay Off (N. Bowling, I. D. Cook, & D. Salyers). Science Research Associates.

The Pay Off is a part of a series designed to teach students practical life skills while supporting reading skills. *The Pay-Off* teaches students the responsibilities and benefits of being a good employee. A criterion-referenced pretest–post-test, audiotape, and teacher's guide accompany Book 5.

Level: Junior–Senior High School

Subcompetency 81–87

Time Incentive Program. EBSCO.

This program is designed to teach punctuality, improve workplace skills, increase accuracy and rate of work, evaluate production, and help ensure job security. The materials include a card rack, time cards, job cards, and instructional guide.

Level: Junior–Senior High School

Subcompetency 81–87

Worktales. Globe Fearon.

This series dramatizes workplace issues such as job stress, sexism, safety, assertiveness, substance abuse, and coping with layoff. A curriculum guide and reproducible activity sheets accompany the series.

Reading Level: 1.8–2.9
Interest Level: 9–12/ABE/ESL

Subcompetency 81–87

Workplace Skills Game. Attainment Co.

This game looks at relationships with co-workers and supervisors, work behaviors, attendance, punctuality, and more.

Level: Junior–Senior High School

Subcompetency 81–87

Social Skills on the Job. AGS.

The materials include a videotape, teacher's guide, blackline masters, and computer disks. The varied interactive materials teach skills that provide a bridge between school and the workplace.

Level: Ages 15 and up

Subcompetency 81–87

Don't Get Fired. Janus.

(See Competency 14 for description.)

Level: Reading Level 2.5–4.0

Subcompetency 81–87

Good Work Habits. AGS.

This workbook is designed to teach 12 good work habits using a story format.

Reading Level: 4.0
Interest Level: 9–12; adult

Subcompetency 81–83, 85

Working I (6 videos) and Working II (2 videos). James Stanfield Publishing Co.

These eight videos illustrate behaviors and attitudes important to getting and keeping a job and developing effective interactions with both supervisors and co-workers.

Level: Junior–Senior High School

Subcompetency 81–87

English for the World of Work. AGS.

This program provides training for the world of work, including seeking, securing, and holding a job. The materials include a teacher's guide, student workbook, blackline masters, and a teacher's resource binder.

Interest Level: 8–12; adult

Subcompetency 81

Following Directions. Lawrence Productions.

(See Competency 12 for description.)

Level: Secondary

Subcompetency 82, 85

Work Habits. Lawrence Productions.

This high-interest, low-vocabulary computer software program is a part of the Job Success Series. It deals with cooperation, attitude, attendance, and more.

Level: Secondary

Subcompetency 81–87

Your Personal Habits. Lawrence Productions.

This high-interest, low-vocabulary computer software program is a part of the Job Success series. It deals with appropriate work habits and behaviors and a variety of jobs.

Level: Secondary

Subcompetency 81–86

Working. I. James Stanfield Publishing Co.

This series of videotapes and the teacher's guide help students learn behaviors and attitudes important to getting and keeping a job. Good grooming habits, punctuality, accepting criticism, conforming to schedules, and other important points are covered.

Level: Junior–Senior High School

Competency 20: Seeking, Securing, and Maintaining a Job

Subcompetency 88–93

The following series of books helps students to meet the challenges of the working world (Globe Fearon, Publisher).

Attitudes for Work

Reading Level: 2.7
Interest Level: 6–12/ABE

Finding a Job

Reading Level: 3.0
Interest Level: 6–12/ABE

Keeping a Job

Reading Level: 3.0
Interest Level: 6–12/ABE/ESL

How to Look Good to an Employer

Reading Level: 5.0–6
Interest Level: 6–12/ABE

Careers: Exploration and Decisions

Reading Level: 5.0–6.0
Interest Level: 6–12/ABE

Get That Job

Reading Level: 12.2
Interest Level: 6–12

The Way to Work

Reading Level: 2.2
Interest Level: 6–12

Subcompetency 88–93

Occupational Notebook Program (I. D. Cook). Opportunities for Learning.

This is a complete program dealing with the practical skills and basic knowledge required to find and hold a job. A realistic appraisal of personal strengths and weaknesses, techniques for locating jobs, what employers look for and expect from their employees, practice in filling out application forms, interview techniques, using transportation, and communication are included. This program is adaptable to the needs of all students, regular or special needs. The materials include a student notebook and teacher's guide.

Level: Junior–Senior High School

Subcompetency 89–90

Get the Job. Quercus.

This is a skill-oriented text relating to completing applications, such as social security card and job applications, and job interviewing.

Reading Level: 2.2

Subcompetency 90

Workplace Simulation. EBSCO.

This is a hands-on program that incorporates all aspects of a job from the interviewing process to evaluating the completed job.

Level: Junior–Senior High School

Subcompetency 90

Get Hired. Janus.

(See Competency 15 for description.)

Reading Level: 2.5–4.0
Interest Level: 6–12/ABE/ESL

Subcompetency 89

Job Application File. Janus.

Student practice on large-size components of typical application.

Reading Level: 2.5–4.0

Subcompetency 90

Job Interview Practice PAK. Janus.

This practice PAK contains materials to create role-play simulations for 30 different jobs.

Reading Level: 2.0–4.0
Interest Level: 8–adult

Subcompetency 88–93

English for the World of Work. Wieser Educational, Inc.
Actual working situations are used in an easy-to-read format that teaches proper English language skills. The text develops communication skills essential for obtaining, keeping, and advancing in a job and is accompanied by student workbooks, blackline masters, and teacher's manual.

Reading Level: 3.7

Subcompetency 90

Job Interview. Janus.

Students are introduced to the basics of interviewing.

Reading Level: 2.5–4.0

Competency 21: Exhibiting Sufficient Physical-Manual Skills

Subcompetency 94

Keeping Fit. Janus.

Presents the physical and emotional health benefits of regular exercise.

Reading Level: 3.5–4.0
Interest Level: 6–12/ABE

Subcompetency 94–97

Take Care of Yourself. Globe Fearon.

Supports important objectives for lifetime health including body systems and immunization.

Reading Level: 2.3–3.0
Interest Level: 6–12

LISTING OF PUBLISHERS

Allyn & Bacon, Inc.
7 Wells Avenue
Newton, MA 02159

AGS
American Guidance Service
4201 Woodland Road
P.O. Box 99
Circle Pines, MN 55014–1796

Attainment Company
P.O. Box 930160
Verona, WI 53593–0160

EBSCO Curriculum Materials
Division of EBSCO Industries, Inc.
Box 11542
Birmingham, AL 35202–1542

Curriculum Associates, Inc.
5 Esquire Road
N. Billerica, MA 01862–2589

Fearon Publishers
500 Harbor Blvd.
Belmont, CA 94002

Gamco Industries, Inc.
P.O. Box 310R
Big Spring, TX 79721–1911

Globe Fearon
4350 Equity Drive
P.O. Box 2649
Columbus, OH 43216

Good Apple
1204 Buchanan St.
Box 299
Carthage, IL 62321–0299

Hartley Courseware
133 Bridge St.
Demondale, MI 48821

James Stanfield Publishing Co.
Drawer CEC
P.O. Box 41058
Santa Barbara, CA 93140

Janus Book Publishers, Inc.
2501 Industrial Parkway W
Haywood, CA 94545

Lakeshore Learning Materials
2695 E. Dominquez St.
P.O. Box 6261
Carson, CA 90749

Love Publishing Company
1777 S. Bellaire Street
Denver, CO 80222

Opportunities for Learning
20417 Nordhoss St.
Chatsworth, CA 91311

Pro-Ed
5341 Industrial Oaks Boulevard
Austin, TX 78735

Quercus
Simon & Schuster School Group
4343 Equity Drive
P.O. Box 2649
Columbus, OH 43216

Saddleback Educational, Inc.
3505 Cadillac Avenue
Building F–9
Costa Mesa, CA 92626

Scott Foresman, A Division of Harper
Lifelong Learning Books
1900 East Lake Avenue
Glenview, IL 60025–9881

Science Research Associates
250 W. Wilson Bridge Road
Worthington, OH 43085

Steck-Vaughn Co.
P.O. Box 26015
Austin, TX 78755

Weiser Educational, Inc.
30085 Commercio, Department 594
Rancho Santa Margarita, CA 92688

Appendix G
Blank Lesson Plan Outline

_ _ _ _ _

LCCE Objective:

Lesson Objective:

Instructional Resources:

Lesson Introduction:

School Activity: Time:

Task:

   1.

   2.

   3.

   4.

Community/School Activity: Time:

Task:

   1.

   2.

   3.

Home/School Activity: Time:

Task:

   1.

   2.

   3

Lesson Plan Evaluation:

Activity:

Criterion:

Career Role:

Career Stage:

Appendix H
LCCE Action Plan Proposal

Name _____

School/Location _____

A. THE NEED TO IMPLEMENT A FUNCTIONAL SKILLS CURRICULUM
1. The Major Objectives and Outcomes of our Educational Programs should be

    a. _____

    b. _____

    c. _____

    d. _____

    e. _____

2. We Need to Integrate a Functional Curriculum into our overall Educational Programs because

    a. _____

    b. _____

    c. _____

    d. _____

    e. _____

3. We Propose the Adoption of the Life-Centered Career Education (LCCE) Curriculum, which (description of)

    a. _____

    b. _____

    c. _____

    d. _____

    e. _____

    f. _____

4. LCCE is being recommended for adoption because it:

    a. _____

    b. _____

    c. _____

    d. _____

    e. _____

    f.. _____

B. CHANGES NEEDED FOR IMPLEMENTATION

1. Curriculum Changes

    a. _____

    b. _____

    c. _____

    d. _____

    e. _____

2. Administrative/Policy Changes

    a. _____

    b. _____

    c. _____

    d. _____

    e. _____

3. Instructional Revisions Needed

    a. _____

    b. _____

    c. _____

    d. _____

    e. _____

4. Parent Involvement Needs and Strategies

    a. _____

    b. _____

    c. _____

    d. _____

5. Employer Involvement Needs and Strategies

    a. _____

    b. _____

    c. _____

    d. _____

6. Agency Involvement Needs and Strategies

    a. _____

    b. _____

    c. _____

    d. _____

    e. _____

7. Possible Barriers and How They Can Be Overcome

    a. _____   _____

    b. _____   _____

    c. _____   _____

    d. _____   _____

C. STEPS TO IMPLEMENT LCCE AND TIME LINES

Steps	Time Line
1. _____	_____
2. _____	_____
3. _____	_____
4. _____	_____
5. _____	_____
6. _____	_____
7. _____	_____
8. _____	_____
9. _____	_____
10. _____	_____

D. FINAL COMMENTS/RECOMMENDATIONS

_____

_____

_____

Date _____

References

Alberg, J., Petry, C., & Eller, S. (1994). *The social skills planning guide.* Longmont, CA: Sopris West.

American Vocational Association. (1990). *The AVA guide to the Carl D. Perkins vocational and applied technology education act of 1990.* Alexandria, VA: Author.

Arc. (1991). *The Americans with Disabilities Act at work.* Arlington, TX: Author.

Banks, J. (1992). A comment on "teacher perceptions of the regular education initiative." *Exceptional Children, 58*(6), 564.

Beck, J., Broers, J., Hogue, E., Shipstead, J., & Knowlton, E. (1994). Strategies for functional community-based instruction and inclusion for children with mental retardation. *Teaching Exceptional Children, 26*(2), 44–48

Beck, S. L. (1988). Career education for students with handicaps. *Monograph 3*(3), 2–8.

Began, W. (1990). LCCE teacher's perspective. *The Career Educator. The University of Missouri-Columbia, 3*(3), 2–3.

Bellamy, G. T. (1985). Transition progress: Comments on Hasazi, Gordon, and Roe. *Exceptional Children, 51*(6), 474–477.

Benz, M. R., & Halpern, A. S. (1993). Vocational and transition services needed received by students with disabilities during their last year of high school. *Career Development for Exceptional Individuals, 16*(2), 197–211.

Bereiter, C. (1985). The changing face of educational disadvantagement. *Phi Delta Kappan, 66*(8), 538–554.

Bigge, J. (1988). *Curriculum based instruction.* Mountain View, CA: Mayfield Publishing.

Board of Education, Sacramento City Unified School District v. Rachel Holland, Div. S-90-1171-DFL Order.

Bocke, J., & Price, D. (1976). Experiential approach for the exceptional adolescent. *Thresholds in Secondary Education, 2*(3), 12–13.

Brigance, A. H. (1987). *Inventory of essential skills.* Billerica, MA: Curriculum Associates.

Brolin, D. E. (1978). *Life centered career education: A competency-based approach.* Reston, VA: The Council for Exceptional Children.

Brolin, D. E. (1983a). Career education: Where do we go from here? *Career Development for Exceptional Individuals, 6,* 3–14.

Brolin, D. E. (1983b). *Life centered career education: A competency-based approach.* Reston, VA: The Council for Exceptional Children.

Brolin, D. E. (1989). *Life centered career education: A competency-based approach.* Reston, VA: The Council for Exceptional Children.

Brolin, D. E. (1992a). *Life centered career education: Competency assessment knowledge battery.* Reston, VA: The Council for Exceptional Children.

Brolin, D. E. (1992b). *Life centered career education: Competency assessment performance battery.* Reston, VA: The Council for Exceptional Children.

Brolin, D. E. (1992c). *Life centered career education: Daily living skills.* Reston, VA: The Council for Exceptional Children.

Brolin, D. E. (1992d). *Life centered career education: Personal-social skills.* Reston, VA: The Council for Exceptional Children.

Brolin, D. E. (1993a). *Life centered career education: A competency-based approach* (4th ed.). Reston, VA: The Council for Exceptional Children.

Brolin, D. E. (1993b). *Life centered career education: Professional development activity book.* Reston, VA: The Council for Exceptional Children.

Brolin, D. E. (1993c). *Life centered career education: Trainer's manual and professional development activity book* (3rd ed.). Reston, VA: The Council for Exceptional Children.

Brolin, D. E. (in preparation). *Life centered career education: Self-determination scale.* Reston, VA: The Council for Exceptional Children. Available in 1995.

Brolin, D. E., Cook, I. S., & O'Keefe, S. (1994). Going the distance with life centered career education. *Rural Special Education Quarterly, 13*(1), 64–67.

Brolin, D. E., & Schatzman, B. (1989). Lifelong career development. In D. E. Berkell & J. M. Brown (Eds.), *Transition from school to work for persons with disabilities.* New York: Longman.

Brophy, J. (1986). Research linking teacher behavior to student achievement: Potential implications for instruction of Chapter 1 students. In B. I. Williams, P. A. Richmond, & B. J. Mason (Eds.) *Designs for compensatory education: Conference proceedings and papers* (pp. 121–179). Washington, DC: Research and Evaluation Associates.

Brown v. Board of Education of Topeka Kansas, 347 U.S. 483 (1954).

Brown, C., Browning, P., & Dunn, C. (1992). *Secondary special education programs in Alabama: A statewide study.* Auburn, AL: A Program for the Study on Disability, Department of Rehabilitation and Special Education, Auburn University.

Browning, P. (1994). Self-determination: An essential ingredient in transition. In P. Browning (Ed.), *Transition III in Alabama: A profile of commitment* (pp. 93–105). Auburn, AL: Auburn University.

Browning, P., & Brechin, C. (1993). Assessment in transition: A functional definition and collaborative program for practice. *Vocational Evaluation and Work Adjustment Bulletin, 26,* 123–127.

Browning, P., & Dunn, C. (1994). Auburn university's teacher preparation program with an emphasis at the secondary level. In P. Browning (Ed.), *Transition III in Alabama: A profile of commitment* (pp. 76–91). Auburn, AL: Auburn University.

Browning, P., Dunn, C., & Brown, C. (1993). School to community transition for youth with disabilities. In R. C. Eaves & P. J. McLaughlin (Eds.), *Recent advances in special education and rehabilitation* (pp. 193–209). Boston: Andover Medical Publishers.

Bullis, M., Bull, B., Johnson, B., & Peters, D. (1994). Young adults who are hearing and deaf in a transition study: Did they and their parents supply similar data? *Exceptional Children, 60*(4), 323–333.

Bullis, M., & Gaylord-Ross, R. (1991). *Moving on: Transitions for youth with behavioral disorders.* Reston, VA.: The Council for Exceptional Children.

Bush, G. (1991). *America 2000: An education strategy.* Washington, DC: U.S. Department of Education.

Byrnes, M. (1990). The regular education initiative debate: A view from the field. *Exceptional Children, 56*(4), 345–349.

Campbell, L. W., Todd, M., & O'Rourke, E. (1971). *Work-study handbook for educable mentally retarded minors enrolled in high school programs in California public schools.* Sacramento: California State Department of Education.

Carpignano, J., & Bigge, J. (1983). Teaching basic thinking skills. In J. Bigge, *Curriculum based instruction* (pp. 187–232). Mountain View, CA: Mayfield Publishing.

Carter, J., & Sugai, G. (1989). Social skills curriculum analysis. *Teaching Exceptional Children, 22*(1), 36–39.

Chadsey-Rusch, J., & Rusch, F. R. (in press). *Transition from school to adulthood for youths with disabilities.* New York: McGraw-Hill.

Chadsey-Rusch, J., Rusch, F. R., & Phelps, L. A. (1988). Epilogue: Analysis and syntheses of transition issues. In D. E. Berkell & J. M. Brown (Eds.), *Transition from school to work for persons with disabilities* (pp. 227–241). New York: Longman.

Clark, D. H. (1993). Meeting special needs—business and education: A partnership that works. *The Journal for Vocational Special Needs Education, 15*(2), 31–35.

Clark, G. M. (1979). *Career education for the handicapped child in the elementary classroom.* Denver: Love Publishing.

Clark, G. M. (1991). *Functional curriculum and its place in the regular education initiative.* Paper presented at the seventh International Conference of the Division on Career Development, Kansas City, MO.

Clark, G. M. (1994). Is a functional curriculum approach compatible with an inclusive education model? *Teaching Exceptional Children, 26*(2), 36–39.

Clark, G. M., Carlson, B. C., Fisher, S., Cook, I. D., & D'Alonzo, B. J. (1991). Career development for students with disabilities in elementary schools: A position statement of the Division on Career Development. *Career Development for Exceptional Individuals, 14,* 109–120.

Clark, G. M., Field, S., Patton, J. R., Brolin, D. E., & Sitlington, P. L. (1994). *Life skills instruction: A necessary component for all students with disabilities.* A position statement of the Division on Career Development and Transition. Reston, VA: The Division on Career Development and Transition.

Clark, G. M., & Kolstoe, O. P. (1990). *Career development and transition education for adolescents with disabilities.* Boston: Allyn & Bacon.

Clark, G. M., & Kolstoe, O. P. (1995). *Career development and transition education for adolescents with disabilities* (2nd ed.). Boston: Allyn & Bacon.

Clark, G. M., & White, W. J. (1980). *Career education for the handicapped: Current perspectives for teachers.* Boothwyn, PA: Education Resources Center.

Cook, I. D. (1974). *Materials handbook.* Institute, WV: West Virginia College of Graduate Studies.

Cook, I. D. (1979). *Curriculum methods and materials for the handicapped in career/vocational education: Part 4. Developing learning activities.* Institute, WV: West Virginia Graduate College.

Cook, I. D. (1987). *Occupational notebook program, teacher's guide.* Chatsworth, CA: Opportunities for Learning.

Cook, I. D. (1993). Task analysis of matching materials to characteristics of learner. *The LCCE professional development affinity book.* Institute: West Virginia Graduate College.

Cook, I. D., & Thurman-Urbanic, M. (1990). *Transition manual: TRIAD telecommunications project.* Institute, WV: West Virginia Graduate College.

Council for Exceptional Children. (1976). Official actions of the delegate assembly at the 54th annual international convention. *Exceptional Children, 43*(1), 41–45.

Council for Exceptional Children. (1978). *Position paper on career education.* Reston, VA: Author.

Council for Exceptional Children. (1992). *Life centered career education: Professional development activity book.* Reston, VA: Author.

Council for Exceptional Children. (1993). Policy on inclusive schools and community settings. Adopted by the CEC delegate assembly, 1993. *Teaching Exceptional Children Supplement, 25*(4).

Council for Exceptional Children. (1994). *Policy manual.* Reston, VA: Author.

Council for Exceptional Children, Division on Career Development and Transition. (1994). *Career Development for Exceptional Individuals,* Fall. Council for Exceptional Children, Division on Mental Retardation and Developmental Disabilities. (1992). *Position paper.* Reston, VA: Author.

Council for Exceptional Children, Division on Mental Retardation and Developmental Disabilities. (1994). MRDD position paper. Dealing with secondary curricula and policy issues for students with MR/DD. *MRDD Express, 4*(3), 3-4.

Crewe, N. M., Athelstan, G. T., & University of Minnesota. (1984). *Functional assessment inventory manual.* Menomonie, WI: University of Wisconsin-Stout, Materials Development Center.

Cronin, M. E., & Patton, J. R. (1993). *Life skills instruction for all students with special needs: A practical guide for integrating real-life content into the curriculum.* Austin, TX: Pro-Ed.

Cutler, B. C. (1993). *You, your child, and special education.* Baltimore, MD: Paul H. Brookes.

D'Alonzo, B. J., & Geordano, G. (1994). Strategies for developing rural transition programs. *Rural Special Education Quarterly, 13*(1), 37–45.

Darley, J. M., & Latane, B. (1968). When will people help in a crisis? *Psychology Today, 2*(7), 54–57, 70–71.

Davis, D. E. (1988). *My friends and me.* Circle Pines, MN: American Guidance Service.

Davis, S. (1992). *Report card to the nation on inclusion in education of students with mental retardation.* Arlington, TX: The Arc.

Davis, S. (1993). *A status report to the nation on inclusion in employment of people with mental retardation.* Arlington, TX: The Arc.

Davis, S., & Wehmeyer, M. L. (1991). *Ten steps to independence: Promoting self-determination in the home.* Arlington, TX: The Arc National Headquarters.

Davis, W. E. (1989). The regular education initiative debate: Its promises and problems. *Exceptional Children, 55*(5), 440–446.

deBettencourt, L. U., & Zigmond, N. (1990). The learning disabled secondary school dropout: What teachers should know. What teachers can do. *Teacher Education and Special Education, 13*(1), 17–20.

Denny, M. R. (1966). Theoretical analysis and its application to training the mentally retarded. In N. R. Ellis (Ed.), *International review of research in mental retardation* (Vol. 2). New York: Academic Press.

Design for ability. (1994). *Workwell, 1,* 28–31.

DeStefano, L., Linn, R., & Markward, M. (1987). *Review of student assessment instruments and practices in use in secondary/transition projects.* University of Illinois at Urbana-Champaign: Secondary Transition Intervention Effectiveness Institute.

Dever, R. B. (1988). *Community living skills: A taxonomy.* Washington, DC: American Association on Mental Retardation.

Dever, R. B. (1989). A taxonomy of community living skills. *Exceptional Children, 55*(5), 395–404.

Diana v. State Board of Education of California, C-70 37 RFP, District Court of Northern California (1970).

Dictionary of Occupational Titles (4th ed.). (1977). Washington, DC: U.S. Government Printing Office.

Didley, D. R. (1987). *Transition: New challenge for special education.* Paper presented at the Annual Conference of the Association for the Severely Handicapped, October 29–30, 1–13.

Dunn, L. M. (1968). Special education for the mildly retarded: Is much of it justifiable? *Exceptional Children, 35,* 5–22.

Egelston-Dodd, J., & DeCaro, J. (1982). National project on career education: Description and impact report. *Career Development for Exceptional Individuals, 5,* 87–97.

Elksnin, N., & Elksnin, L. K. (1991). Facilitating the vocational success of students with mild handicaps. *The Journal for Vocational Special Needs Education, 13*(2), 5–11.

Ellis, N. R. (1970). Memory processes in retardates and normals. In N. R. Ellis (Ed.), *International review of research in mental retardation* (Vol. 4). New York: Academic Press.

Elrod, F., & Gilliland, M. (1991–1992). A call for neo-progressivism in educating economically disadvantaged children with disabilities: A curricular example. *National Forum of Special Education Journal, 2*(2), 19–27.

Encyclopedia of Associations (26th ed.). (1992). Detroit, MI: Gale Research, Inc.

Epstein, M., Patton, J., Polloway, E., & Foley, R. (1992). Educational services for students with behavior disorders: A review of individualized education programs. *Teacher Education and Special Education, 15,* 41–48.

Equal Employment Opportunity Commission. (1991). Part 1630—Regulations to implement the equal employment provisions of the Americans with Disabilities Act. *Federal Register, 56*(144), Friday, July 26, 1991, pp. 35726–35753.

Everson, J. M., & McNulty, K. (1992). Interagency teams: Building local transition programs through parental and professional partnerships. In F. R. Rusch, L. Destefano, J. Chadsey-Rusch, L. A. Phelps, & E. Szymanski (Eds.), *Transition from school to adult life: Model, linkages, and policy* (pp. 341–351). Sycamore, IL: Sycamore Publishing.

Field, S., & Hoffman, A. (1994). Development of a model for self-determination. *Career Development for Exceptional Individuals, 17*(2), 159–169.

Field, S., LeRoy, B., & Rivera, S. (1994). Meeting functional curriculum needs in middle school general education classrooms. *Teaching Exceptional Children, 26*(2), 40–43.

Fisher, M. A., & Zeaman, D. (1973). Attention/retention theory of retardate discrimination learning. In N. R. Ellis (Ed.), *International review of research in mental retardation* (Vol. 66). New York: Academic Press.

Flaxman, E., & Inger, M. (1991). Parents and schooling in the 1990's. *The ERIC Review, 1*(3), 2–6.

Frank, A. R., & Sitlington, P. L. (1993). Graduates with mental disabilities: The story three years later. *Education and Training in Mental Retardation, 28*(1), 30–37.

Fuchs, D., & Fuchs, L. S. (1994). Inclusive schools movement and the radicalization of special education reform. *Exceptional Children, 60*(4), 294–309.

Gaylord-Ross, R. (Ed.). (1988). *Vocational education for persons with handicaps.* Mountain View, CA: Mayfield Publishing.

Gearhart, B. G. (1985). *Learning disabilities: Educational strategies.* St. Louis: Times Mirror/Mosby College Publishing.

Gemmel, S. J., & Peterson, M. (1989). Supported employment and provision of on-going support services: A pilot project. *Career Development for Exceptional Individuals, 12*(2), 123–128.

Gibbs, J. (1987). *Tribes: A process for social development and cooperative learning.* Santa Rosa, CA: Center Source Publications.

Gilhool, T. K. (1973). Education: An inalienable right. *Exceptional Children, 39,* 597–609.

Gillet, P. (1980). Career education in special elementary education program. *Teaching Exceptional Children, 13*(1), 17–21.

Gilliam, J. E., & Coleman, M. C. (1981). Who influences IEP decisions? *Exceptional Children, 47,* 642–644.

Gloeckler, L. C. (1993). Systems change and transition services for secondary youth with disabilities. *OSERS News in Print, 6*(6), 6–12.

Goldstein, A. P. (1988). *The prepare curriculum: Teaching prosocial competencies.* Champaign, IL: Research Press.

Goldstein, A. P., Sprafkin, R. P., Gershaw, N. J., & Klein, P. (1980). *Skillstreaming the adolescent.* Champaign, IL: Research Press.

Graubard, P. S. (1973). Children with behavioral disabilities. In L. M. Dunn (Ed.), *Exceptional children in the schools.* New York: Holt, Rinehart & Winston.

Greenan, J. P. (1986). Curriculum and assessment in generalizable skills instruction. *The Journal for Vocational Special Needs Education, 9*(1), 3–10.

Gysbers, N. C., & Henderson, P. (1994). *Developing and managing your school guidance program* (2nd ed.). Alexandria, VA: American Counseling Association.

Hagner, D., & Daning, R. (1993). Opening lines: How job developers talk to employers. *Career Development for Exceptional Individuals, 16*(2), 123–134.

Hahn, A., Danzberger, J., & Lefkowitz, B. (1987). *Dropouts in America: Enough is known for action.* Washington, DC: Institute for Educational Leadership.

Halloran, W. D. (1993). Transition services requirement: Issues, implications, challenge. In P. Browning (Ed.), *Transition II in Alabama: A profile of commitment* (pp. 1–15). Auburn, AL: Auburn University.

Halpern, A. S. (1985). Transition: A look at the foundations. *Exceptional Children, 51*(6), 479–486.

Halpern, A. S. (1992). Transition: Old wine in new bottles. *Exceptional Children, 58*(3), 202–211.

Halpern, A. S. (1993). Quality of life as a conceptual framework for evaluating transition outcomes. *Exceptional Children, 59*(6), 486–498.

Halpern, A. S., Benz, M., & Lindstrom, L. (1991). *A systems change approach to improving secondary special education and transition programs at the local community level.* Unpublished manuscript, University of Oregon, Eugene.

Halpern, A. S., Dorenz, B., & Benz, M. R. (1993). Job experiences of students with disabilities during their last two years in school. *Career Development for Exceptional Individuals, 16*(1), 63–73.

Halpern, A. S., & Fuhrer, M. J. (1984). *Functional assessment in rehabilitation.* Baltimore, MD: Paul H. Brookes.

Halpern, A. S., Irvin, L., & Landman, J. T. (1979). *Tests for everyday living.* Monterey, CA: CTB/McGraw-Hill.

Halpern, A., Lehmann, J., Irvin, L., & Heiry, T. (1982). *Contemporary assessment: For mentally retarded adolescents and adults.* Baltimore, MD: University Park Press.

Halpern, A. S., Raffeld, P., Irvin, L. K., Link, R., & Munkres, A. (1985). *Social and prevocational information battery.* Monterey, CA: CTB/McGraw-Hill.

Haring, D. (1978, January 1–3). *Learn and earn with project work.* Paper presented at the meeting of the Career Education Workshop.

Haring, N. G. (1982). *Exceptional children and youth.* New York: Merrill/Macmillan.

Harrington, T., & O'Shea, A. (Eds.). (1984). *Guide to occupational exploration* (2nd ed.). Circle Pines, MN: American Guidance Service.

Hauser, S. (1993, November/December). How Herman Miller put the ADA into action. *FM Journal,* pp. 25–27.

Hazel, J. S., Schumacher, J. B., Sherman, J. A., & Sheldon-Wildgen. (1981). *Asset: A social skills program.* Champaign, IL: Research Press.

Heal, L. W., Copher, J. I., DeStephano, L., & Rusch, F. R. (1989). A comparison of successful and unsuccessful placements of secondary students with mental handicaps into competitive employment. *Career Development for Exceptional Individuals, 12*(2), 167–177.

Hendrick Hudson School District v. Rowley, No. 80-1002.

Heskett, J. (1993), Inclusive education for the disabled. *Missouri Innovations in Special Education, 21*(2), 1–2, 8.

Higgins, A., Fowler, S. A., & Chandler, L. K. (1988). Planning school transitions: Family and professional collaboration. *Journal of the Division for Early Childhood, 12*(2), 108–115.

Hobson v. Hansen, 393 U.S. 801 (1968).

Horne, R. L. (1991). The education of children and youth with special needs: What do the laws say? *NICHCY News Digest, 1*(1), 1–15.

House Report No. 101–544, 10, 1990.

Hoyt, K. B. (1975). *An introduction to career education. A policy paper of the U. S. Department of Education.* Washington, DC: Office of Education.

Hoyt, K. B. (1976). *Community resources for career education. Monographs on career education.* Washington, DC: U.S. Office of Education.

Hoyt, K. B. (1980). *Career education for persons with visual handicaps.* Paper presented at the Helen Keller Centennial Conference, Boston.

Hoyt, K. B. (1982). Federal and state participation in career education: Past, present, and future. *Journal of Career Education, 9*(1), 5–15.

Hoyt, K. B. (1983, June). *How to fix the public's schools in eight not-so-easy steps. Working paper.* Council of State Planning Agencies, National Governors Association.

Hoyt, K. B. (1987). Trends in career education: Implications for the future. In *Career education in transition: Trends and implications for the future* (pp. 5–35). Columbus, OH: ERIC Clearinghouse on Adult, Career, and Vocational Education.

Hoyt, K. B. (1993). Reaction to the three solutions for transition from school to employment. *Youth Policy, 15*(6&7), 36.

Hull, D. (1992). Tech prep: Practical application for America's work force. *School Shop/Technical Directions,* March, 17–19.

Iannacone, C. J., Wienke, W. D., & Cosden, M. A. (1992). Social skills instruction in secondary schools: Factors affecting its implementation. *The High School Journal,* December–January, 111–118.

Inger, M. (1993). Teacher collaboration in secondary schools. *Centerfocus, 2,* 1–4.

Jackson, D. A., Jackson, N. F., Bennett, M. L., Bynum, D. M., & Faryna, E. (1991). *Learning to get along:*

Social effectiveness training for people with development disabilities. Champaign, IL: Research Press.

Jackson, N. F., Jackson, D. A., & Monroe, C. (1983). *Getting along with others.* Champaign, IL: Research Press.

Jastak, J., & Jastak, S. (1973). *Wide range employment sample text.* Wilmington, DE: Jastak Associates.

Jenkins, J. R., & Pious, C. G. (1991). Full inclusion and the REI: A reply to Thousand and Villa. *Exceptional Children, 56*(6), 562–564.

Jenkins, J. R., Pious, C. G., & Jewell, M. (1990). Special education and the regular education initiative: Basic assumptions. *Exceptional Children, 56*(6), 479–491.

Johnson, D., Bruininks, R. H., & Thurlow, M. L. (1987). Meeting the challenge of transition service planning through improved interagency cooperation. *Exceptional Children, 53*(6), 533–530.

Johnson, D. R., Thompson, S. J., Sinclair, M. F., Krantz, G. C., Evelo, S., Stolte, K., & Thompson, J. R. (1993). Considerations in the design and follow-up and follow-along systems for improving transition programs and services. *Career Development for Exceptional Individuals, 16*(2), 225–238.

Johnson, J. (1976, March 4–5). *School stores: A vital part of your career education program.* Paper presented at the meeting of the Career Education Workshop.

Johnson, J. R., & Rusch, F. R. (1993). Secondary special education and transition services: Identification and recommendations for future research and demonstration. *Career Development for Exceptional Individuals, 16*(1), 1–18.

Johnson, R. T., & Johnson, D. W. (1982). Effects of cooperative and competitive learning experiences on interpersonal attraction between handicapped and nonhandicapped students. *Journal of Social Psychology, 116,* 211–219.

Johnson, R. T., & Johnson, D. W. (1983). Effects of cooperative, competitive, and individualistic learning experiences on social development. *Exceptional Children, 49,* 323–329.

Johnson, R. T., Johnson, D. W., & Rynders, J. (1981). Effect of cooperative, competitive, and individualistic learning experiences on self-esteem of handicapped and nonhandicapped students. *Journal of Psychology, 108,* 31–34.

Kaufman, J. M. (1985). *Characteristics of children's behavior disorders* (3rd ed.). New York: Merrill/Macmillan.

Kaufman, M. J., Kameenui, E. J., Birman, B., & Danielson, L. (1990). Special education and the process of change: Victim or master of educational reform? *Exceptional Children, 57*(2), 109–115.

Killilea, M. (1960). *Karen.* New York: Dell.

Kirk, S. A., & Gallagher, J. J. (1989). *Educating exceptional children.* Boston: Houghton-Mifflin.

Kohler, P. D. (in preparation). *A conceptual model of effective transition practices.* Champaign: University of Illinois, Transition Research Institute.

Kohler, P. D. (1993). Best practices in transition: Substantiated or implied? *Career Development for Exceptional Individuals, 16, 107–121.*

Kohler, P. D., DeStefano, F., Wermuth, T., Grayson, T., & McGinty, S. (in press). An analysis of exemplary transition programs: How and why are they selected? *Career Development for Exceptional Individuals.*

Kokaska, C. J., & Brolin, D. E. (1985). *Career education for handicapped individuals* (2nd ed.). New York: Merrill/Macmillan.

Kolstoe, O. P. (1976). Developing career awareness: The foundation of a career education program. In G.B. Blackburn (Ed.), *Colloquium series on career education for handicapped adolescents.* West Lafayette, IN: Purdue University.

Langone, J. (1990). *Teaching students with mild and moderate learning problems.* Boston: Allyn & Bacon.

Larson, C. (1981). *EBCE state of Iowa dissemination model for MD and LD students.* Fort Dodge: Iowa Central Community College.

Lichtenstein, S. (1993). Transition from school to adulthood: Case studies of adults with learning disabilities who dropped out of school. *Exceptional Children, 59*(4), 336–347.

Lindsey, J. D. (1993). *Computers and exceptional individuals* (2nd ed.). Austin, TX: Pro-Ed.

Linkenhoker, D., & McCarron, L. (1983). *Adaptive behavior: The street survival skills questionnaire.* Dallas, TX: Common Market Press.

Linthicum, E., Cole, J. T., & D'Alonzo, B. J. (1991). Employment and the Americans with Disabilities Act of 1990. *Career Development for Exceptional Individuals, 14*(1), 1–13.

Lippman, L., & Goldberg, I. (1973). *Right to education: Anatomy of the Pennsylvania case and its implications for exceptional children.* New York: Teachers College Press, Columbia University.

Loyd, R. J., & Brolin, D. E. (1989). Parent's/family members involvement and training in the LCCE curriculum program. In R. J. Loyd & D. E. Brolin, *Life centered career education: Trainer's manual.* Reston, VA: The Council for Exceptional Children.

Luftig, R. L. (1987). *Teaching the mentally retarded student.* Boston: Allyn & Bacon.

Lynch, E., & Beare, P. (1990). The quality of IEP objectives and their relevance to instruction for students with mental retardation and behavioral disorders. *Remedial and Special Education, 11,* 48–55.

Martinez, L. (1993, Spring). Enhancing community and cultural relevance of high school curriculum. *Inclusive Communities Newsletter.* Detroit: Developmental Disabilities Institute, Wayne State University.

McDaniels, C., & Gysbers, N. C. (1992). *Counseling for career development.* San Francisco: Jossey-Bass.

McFadden, D. L., & Burke, E. P. (1991). Developmental disabilities and the new paradigm: Directions for the 1990's. *Mental Retardation, 29,* iii–vi.

McLaughlin, M. J., & Warren, S. H. (1992). *Issues and options in restructuring schools and special education programs.* College Park, MD: University of Maryland and Westat, Inc.

Mellard, D. F., & Clark, G. M. (1992). National high school project. Vol. 2: A quantitative description of comprehensive services and practices for students with disabilities. Final report. Grant No. G008530217 OSERS Department of Special Education. Lawrence: University of Kansas.

Mercer, C. D. (1983). *Students with learning disabilities* (2nd ed.). New York: Merrill/Macmillan.

Mercer, C. D., & Mercer, A. R. (1993). *Teaching students with learning problems* (4th ed.). New York: Merrill/Macmillan.

Mercer, C. D., & Snell, M. E. (1977). *Learning theory research in mental retardation.* New York: Merrill/Macmillan.

Meyen, E. L. (1990). *Exceptional children in today's school.* Denver, CO: Love Publishing.

Mills v. Board of Education in the District of Columbia, 348 F. Supp. 866 D.D.C. (1972).

Minnesota Department of Education. (no date). *Transition: A report on Minnesota youth with disabilities.* St. Paul, MN: Interagency Office on Transition Services, Author.

Minnesota Department of Education. (1990). Outcome-based education gives teachers chance for a larger role in planning. *Education Update, 25*(1), 1.

Minnesota Employment Stabilization Research Institute. (1969). *Minnesota rate of manipulation test.* Circle Pines, NM: American Guidance Service.

Missouri Department of Elementary and Secondary Education. (1992). *A proposal to implement outcome-based graduation in Missouri high schools.* Jefferson City, MO: Author.

Missouri LINC. (1992). *Legislation regarding special populations.* Columbia, MO: University of Missouri-Columbia.

Mithaug, D. E., Mar, D. K., & Stewart, J. E. (1978). *Prevocational assessment and curriculum guide.* Seattle, WA: J. E. Stewart.

Moon, S., Goodall, P., Barcus, M., & Brooke, V. (1986). *The supported work model of competitive employment for citizens with severe handicaps: A guide for job trainers, revised edition.* Richmond, VA: Virginia Commonwealth University, Rehabilitation Research and Training Center.

Moore, E. J., & Gysbers, N. C. (1972). Career development: A new focus. *Educational Leadership, 30,* 1–8.

Moore, S. C., Agran, M., & McSweyn, C. A. (1990). Career education: Are we starting early enough? *Career Development for Exceptional Individuals, 13*(2), 129–134.

National Association for Industry-Education Cooperation. (1993). *Newsletter,* June–July.

National Center for Educational Outcomes. (1993). NCEO finds states active in "outcomes" efforts. *Outcomes, 2*(2), 2.

National Education Association, Educational Policies Commission. (1938). *The purposes of education in American democracy.* Washington, DC: Author.

National Education Association, Educational Policies Commission. (1952). *Education for all American youth: A further look.* Washington, DC: Author.

"National Organization on Disability and *Business Week* salute the members of the Disability 2000 Council." (1993, December 27). *Business Week.*

Naylor, M. (1985). *Role of vocational education in transition services for handicapped youth.* Washington, DC: National Institute of Education.

Neil, S. B. (1977). Clearing the air in career education. *American Education, 13*(2), 6–9, 13.

Neubert, D. A., & Tilson, G. R. (1987). The critical stage of transition: A challenge and an opportunity. *The Journal,* 3–7.

Nevin, A., Johnson, D. W., & Johnson, R. (1982). Effects of groups and individual contingencies on academic performance and social relations of special needs students. *Journal of Social Psychology, 116,* 41–49.

NICHCY. (1993). Transition services in the IEP. *NICHCY Transition Summary, 3*(1), 1–20.

Nihira, K., Foster, R., Shellhaas, M., & Leland, M. (1981). *AAMD adaptive behavior scale (school edition).* Monterey, CA: CTB/McGraw-Hill.

North Dakota Department of Public Instruction. (1990). *Special education in North Dakota: Guide II—Educational programming for students with mild and moderate mental retardation.* Bismarck, ND: Author.

Nugent, G., & Stone, C. (1981). Think it through: An interactive videodisk for the hearing impaired. In *Proceedings of the Johns Hopkins first national search for applications of personal computing to the handicapped* (pp. 49-51). Los Angeles, CA: IIEE Computer Society Press.

Oberti v. Board of Education of the Borough of Clementon School District, C.A. No. 91-2818, D.N.J. (1992).

O'Leary, E. (1989). *A study to identify educational outcome for secondary mildly handicapped students from public high school programs as perceived by parents, employers, and educators.* Unpublished dissertation, University of Illinois, Champaign-Urbana.

Parker, R. (1991a). *The OASIS-2 aptitude survey—2.* Austin, TX: Pro-Ed.

Parker, R. (1991b). *The OASIS-2 interest schedule—2.* Austin, TX: Pro-Ed.

Parker, R. M., & Szymanski, E. M. (1992). *Rehabilitation counseling: Basics and beyond* (2nd ed.). Austin, TX: Pro-Ed.

Patterson, J. B., & Curl, R. M. (1992). Using occupational and labor market information in transition services. In F. R. Rusch, et al., *Transition from school to work: Models, linkages, and policies* (pp. 353–369). Sycamore: IL: Sycamore Publishing.

Pennsylvania Association for Retarded Children v. Commonwealth of Pennsylvania. 334, F. Supp. 1257, E.D.Ua. (1971).

Pennsylvania State University Institute for the Study of Adult Literacy. (1993). *A day in the life.* North Bilerica, MA: Curriculum Associates.

Phelps, L. A. (1976). *Instructional development for special needs learners: An inservice resource guide.* Urbana: Department of Vocational and Technical Education, University of Illinois.

Phelps, L. A., & Maddy-Bernstein, C. (1992). Developing effective partnerships for special populations: The challenge of partnerships and alliances. *The Journal for Vocational Special Needs Education, 14*(2&3), 33–36.

Polloway, E. A., & Patton, J. R. (1993). *Strategies for teaching learners with special needs* (5th ed.). New York: Merrill/Macmillan.

Polloway, E. A., Patton, J. R., Payne, J. S., & Payne, R. A. (1989). *Strategies for teaching learners with special needs* (4th ed.). New York: Merrill/Macmillan.

The President's Committee on Employment of the Handicapped. (1977). *Newsletter,* September. Washington, DC: U.S. Government Printing Office.

The President's Committee on Employment of People with Disabilities. (1987). *Disabled Americans at work.* Washington, DC: U.S. Government Printing Office.

The President's Committee on Employment of People with Disabilities. (1993, October). Washington, DC: U.S. Government Printing Office. *Energize America—Employ Ability.* Washington, DC: U.S. Government Printing Office.

The President's Panel on Mental Retardation. (1963). *Report to the President: A proposed program for national action to combat mental retardation.* Washington, DC: U.S. Government Printing Office.

Purdue Research Foundation. (1968). *Purdue pegboard.* Chicago: Science Research Associates.

Revell, G. (1993). PL 102–569: The rehabilitation act amendments of 1992. *Virginia Commonwealth Newsletter,* Winter.

Reynolds, M. C., & Birch, J. W. (1982). *Teaching exceptional children in America's schools.* Reston, VA: The Council for Exceptional Children.

Reynolds, M. C., Zetlin, A. G., & Wang, M. C. (1993). 20/20 analysis: Taking a close look at the margins. *Exceptional Children, 59*(4), 294–300.

Roberts, J. R. (1945). *Pennsylvania bi-manual work sample.* Circle Pines, MN: American Guidance Service.

Roessler, R. T. (1991a). A problem-solving approach to implementing career education. *Career Development for Exceptional Individuals, 14*(2), 59–66.

Roessler, R. T. (1991b). *Your hit parade.* Columbia, MO: University of Missouri-Columbia, LCCE/Employability Enhancement Project.

Roessler, R. T., & Brolin, D. E. (1992). *LCCE competency units for occupational guidance and preparation.* Reston, VA: The Council for Exceptional Children.

Roessler, R. T., Brolin, D. E., & Johnson, J. M. (1992). Barriers to the implementation of career education for special education. *Journal of Career Development, 18*(4), 271–282.

Roessler, R. T., Loyd, R. J., & Brolin, D. E. (1990). Implementing life centered career education: Contextual barriers and implementation recommendations. *Academic Therapy, 25*(4), 523–533.

Roessler, R. T., & Rubin, S. E. (1992). *Case management and rehabilitation counseling.* Austin, TX: Pro-Ed.

Roessler, R. T., Shearin, A. A., & Williams, E. R. (1993). *From 94–142 to 101–476: The more things change the more they stay the same.* Fayetteville, AR: University of Arkansas.

Rose, E., Friend, M., & Farnum, M. (1988). Transition planning for mildly handicapped students: The secondary school counselor's role. *The School Counselor,* 275–293.

Rusch, F. R. (Ed.). (1986). *Competitive employment issues and strategies.* Baltimore, MD: Paul H. Brookes.

Rusch, F. R., Destefano, L., Chadsey-Rusch, J., Phelps, L. A., & Szymanski, E. (Eds.). (1992). *Transition from school to adult life: Models, linkages, and policy.* Sycamore, IL: Sycamore Publishing.

Rusch, F. R., Kohler, P. D., & Hughes, C. (1992). An analysis of OSERS-sponsored secondary special education and transitional services research. *Career Education for Exceptional Individuals, 15,* 121–143.

Rusch, F. R., Schutz, R. P., Mithaug, D. E., Stewart, J. E., & Mar, D. K. (1982). *Vocational assessment and curriculum guide.* Seattle, WA: J. E. Stewart.

Schloss, P. J., Smith, M. A., & Schloss, C. N. (1990). *Instructional methods for adolescents with learning and behavior problems.* Boston: Allyn & Bacon.

Schrag, J., & Burnette, J. (1994). Inclusive schools. *Teaching Exceptional Children, 26*(3), 64–68.

Schumacher, J. B., Hazel, J. S., & Pederson, C. S. (1988). *Social skills for daily living.* Circle Pines, MN: American Guidance Service.

Semmel, M. I., Abernathy, T. V., Butera, G., & Lesar, S. (1991). Teacher perceptions of the regular education initiative. *Exceptional Children, 58*(1), 9–23.

Shanker, A. (1994). Push to integrate all disabled kids in regular classes is destructive. Associated Press article. Author. Shapiro, J. P., Bowermaster, D., & Loeb, P. (1993, December 13). Separate and unequal. *U.S. News & World Report,* pp. 46–50, 54–56, 60.

Shapiro, J. P., Loed, P., Bouermaster, D., Wright, A., Headden, S., & Toch, T. (1993, December 13). Separate and unequal: Examining special education. *U.S. News and World Report,* pp. 46–60.

Simon, M., Bourexis, P., & Norman, M. (1993). Labor, education departments team for smooth transition. *Counterpoint,* Winter, 14–15.

Sinclair, M. F., & Christenson, S. L. (1992). Home-school collaboration: A building block of empowerment. *IMPACT-Feature Issue on Family Empowerment, 5*(2), 12–13.

Singer, G. H. S., & Powers, L. C. (1993). Contributing to resilience in families: An overview. In G. H. S. Singer & L. C. Powers (Eds.), *Families, disability and empowerment: Active coping skills and strategies for family interventions* (pp. 1–25). Baltimore, MD: Paul H. Brookes.

Sitlington, P. L. (1991). Curriculum-based assessment—What does it mean? *The Career Educator, University of Missouri-Columbia, 4*(1), 1–2.

Sitlington, P. L., Brolin, D. E., Clark, G. M., & Vacanti, J. M. (1985). Career/vocational assessment in the public school setting. The position of the Division on Career Development. *Career Development for Exceptional Individuals, 8*(1), 3–6.

Sitlington, P. L., & Frank, A. R. (1993). *Iowa statewide follow-up study: Adult adjustment of individuals with learning disabilities three vs. one year out of school.* Des Moines: Iowa Department of Education.

Sitlington, P. L., Frank, A. R., & Carson, R. (1991). Adult adjustment among high school graduates with mild disabilities. *Exceptional Children, 59*(3), 221–233.

Sitlington, P. L., Frank, A. R., & Cooper, L. (1989). *Iowa statewide follow-up study: Adult adjustment of individuals with learning disabilities one year after leaving school.* Des Moines: Iowa Department of Education.

Skrtic, T. M. (1991). *Behind special education: A critical analysis of professional culture and school organization.* Denver: Love Publishing.

Smith, F. (1989). Overselling literacy. *Phi Delta Kappan,* January, 353–359.

Smith, S. (1990). Individualized Education Programs (IEPs) in special education. From intent to acquiescence. *Exceptional Children, 57*(1), 6–14.

Smith, T. E. C., & Hilton, A. (1994). Program design for students with mental retardation. *Education and Training in Mental Retardation and Developmental Disabilities, 29*(1), 3–8.

Sonnenschein, P. (1981). Parents and professionals: An uneasy relationship. *Teaching Exceptional Children, 14,* 62–65.

The Sounding Board, 1(3), 1994. School District of the City of Inkster, MI.

Sparrow, S. S., Balla, D. A., & Cicchetti, D. V. (1985). *Vineland adaptive behavior scales.* Circle Pines, MN: American Guidance Service.

Spitz, H. H. (1973). Consolidating facts into the schematized learning and memory system of educable retardates. In N. R. Ellis (Ed.), *International review of research in mental retardation* (Vol. 6). New York: Academic Press.

Starr, M., & Gysbers, N. (1993). *Missouri comprehensive guidance: A model for program development, implementation, and evaluation.* Jefferson City, MO: Missouri Department of Elementary and Secondary Education.

Steelcase, Inc. (no date). *Workwell Magazine, 1,* 28. Grand Rapids, MI: Author.

Steelcase, Inc. (no date). *Employee handbook.* Grand Rapids, MI: Author.

Steele, P., Burrows, R., Kiburz, P., & Sitlington, P. (1990). *An interagency venture: Transitioning for people with moderate and severe disabilities.* Des Moines: Iowa Department of Education.

Stephens, A. (Ed.). (1990). *Implementing career education at the elementary school level.* Columbia, MO: The University of Missouri-Columbia, Missouri LINC.

Stephens, A. (1992). Life after high school: The purpose of transition planning. *Missouri Lincletter,
14*(4), 1–4.

Stephens, T. M. (1978). *Social skills in the classroom.*
Columbus, OH: Cedars Press.

Stodden, R. A., Ianacone, R. N., Boone, R. M. , & Bisconer, W. W. (1987). *Curriculum-based vocational
assessment: A guide for addressing youth with special needs.* Honolulu, HI: Centre Publications
International Education Corporation.

Supported Employment Technical Assistance Project.
(1989). *Traumatic brain injury: Supplemental manual (employment training specialist series).* Lansing,
MI: Michigan State University.

Swisher, J., & Clark, G. M. (1991). Curriculum-based
vocational assessment of students with special
needs at the middle school/junior high school levels. *The Journal for Vocational Special Needs Education, 13*(3), 9–14.

Swisher, J., & Clark, G. M. (1991). *Practical arts evaluation system (PAES).* Jacksonville, FL: Talent Assessment, Inc.

Szymanski, E. M. (1994). Transition: Life-span and life-
space considerations for empowerment. *Exceptional
Children, 60*(5), 402–410.

Talent Assessment. (no date). *The talent assessment
program.* Jacksonville, FL: Author.

Technical Education Research Centers. (1983). *Promoting collaborative planning of career education
for disabled students.* Cambridge, MA: Author.

Thomas, S. W. (1992). Vocational assessment and the
ADA: Issues and approaches for the rehabilitation
professional. In Directions in Rehabilitation (Ed.),
Understanding the Americans with Disabilities Act
(pp. 4.3–4.16). New York: The Hatherleigh Co., Ltd.

Thousand, J. S., & Villa, R. A. (1991). A futuristic view
of the REI: A response to Jenkins, Pious, and Jewell. *Exceptional Children, 57*(6), 556–562.

Tindall, L. W. (1992). Business linkages. In F. R. Rusch,
L. Destefano, J. Chadsey-Rusch, L. A. Phelps, & E.
Szymanski (Eds.), *Transition from school to adult
life: Models, linkages, and policy* (pp. 319–339).
Sycamore: IL: Sycamore Publishing.

Turnbull, A. P., Strickland, B. B., & Brantley, J. C.
(1982). *Developing and implementing individualized
education programs* (2nd ed.). New York:
Merrill/Macmillan.

Turnbull, A. P., & Turnbull, H. R. (1978). *Parents speak
out: Views from the other side of the two-way mirror.* New York: Merrill/Macmillan.

U.S. Department of Education. (1991). *America 2000:
An education strategy.* Washington, DC: Author.

U.S. Department of Education. (1994). *Goals 2000: A
world-class education for every child.* Washington,
DC: Author.

U.S. Department of Education, Office of Special Education Programs. (1992). *Fourteenth annual report to
Congress on the implementation of the Individuals
with Disabilities Education Act.* Washington, DC:
Author.

U.S. Department of Education, Office of Special Education Programs. (1993). *Fifteenth annual report to
Congress on the implementation of the Individuals
with Disabilities Education Act.* Washington, DC:
Author.

U.S. Department of Education, Office of Special Education and Rehabilitative Services. (1992). *Summary
of existing legislation affecting people with disabilities.* Washington, DC: Author.

U.S. House of Representatives. (1990). Report No. 101-
544, 10. U.S. House of Representatives. (1993).
Report No. 103-378.

VALPAR International. (1986). *Prevocational readiness
battery—VALPAR 17.* Tucson, AZ: VALPAR International Corporation.

Vanderbilt/Minnesota Social Interaction Project.
(1993). *Play time/social time: Organizing your classroom to build interaction skills.* Tucson, AZ: Communication Skill Builders.

Wagner, M. (1991). Sticking it out: Secondary school
completion. In M. Wagner, L. Newman, R. D'Amico,
E. D. Joy, P. Butler-Nalin, C. Marder, & R. Cox
(eds.), *Youth with disabilities: How are they doing?
The first comprehensive report from the National
Longitudinal Transition Study of Special Education
Students.* Menlo Park, CA: SRI International.

Wagner, M., D'Amico, R., Marder, C., Newman, L., &
Blackorley, J. (1992). *What happens next? Trends in
post-school outcomes of youth with disabilities.*
Menlo Park, CA: SRI International.

Wagner, M., Newman, L., D'Amico, R., Joy, E.D., Butler-Nalin, P., Marder, C., & Cox, R. (Eds.). (1991).
*Youth with disabilities: How are they doing? The
first comprehensive report from the National Longitudinal Transition Study of Special Education Students.* Menlo Park, CA: SRI International.

Waksman, S., & Messmer, C. L. (1985). *Waksman
social skills curriculum (AIEP Education).* Portland,
OR: ASIEP.

Walker, H., & Sylvester, R. (1991). Where is school along the path to prison? *Educational Leadership, 49*, 14–16.

Walker, H. M., Todis, B., Holmes, D., & Horton, G. (1988). *The Walker Social Skills Curriculum: The ACCESS Program.* Austin, TX: Pro-Ed.

Walker, H. M., Todis, B., Holmes, D., & Horton, G. (1988). *The ACCESS program: Adolescent curriculum for communication and effective social skills.* Austin, TX: Pro-Ed.

Ward, M. J. (1991). Self-determination re-visited: Going beyond expectations. *Transition Summary, National Information Center for Children and Youth with Handicaps, 7*, 2–4, 12.

Ward, M. J. (1992). Introduction to secondary special education and transition issues. In F. R. Rusch, L. Destefano, J. Chadsey-Rusch, L. A. Phelps, E. & Szymanski (Eds.), *Transition from school to adult life: Models, linkages, and policy* (pp. 387–389). Sycamore, IL: Sycamore Publishing.

Ward, M. J., & Halloran, W. E. (1989). Transition to uncertainty: Status of many school learners with severe disabilities. *Career Development for Exceptional Individuals, 12*(12), 71–81.

Ward, M. J., & Halloran, W. D. (1993). Transition issues for the 1990s. *OSERS News in Print, 6*(6), 4–5.

Warger, C. L. (1991). Peer tutoring: When working together is better than working alone. *Research and Resources on Special Education, 30.* ERIC Clearinghouse of Handicapped and Gifted Children, December, 1991.

Wehman, P. (1981). *Competitive employment: New horizons for severely disabled individuals.* Baltimore, MD: Paul W. Brookes.

Wehman, P. (1992). *Life beyond the classroom.* Baltimore, MD: Paul H. Brookes.

Wehman, P., & Hill, J. W. (1985). *Competitive employment for persons with mental retardation.* Richmond, VA: Virginia Commonwealth University.

Wehman, P., Moon, S., Everson, J. M., & Barcus, J. M. (1988). *Transition from school to work.* Baltimore, MD: Paul H. Brookes.

Wehman, P., Parent, W., Wood, W., Talbert, C. M., Jasper, C., Miller, S., Marchant, J., & Walker, R. (1989). From school to competitive employment for young adults with mental retardation: Transition in practice. *Career Development for Exceptional Individuals, 12*(2), 97–105.

Wehmeyer, M. L. (1992). Self-determination and the education of students with mental retardation. *Education and Training in Mental Retardation, 27,* 303–314.

Wehmeyer, M. L. (1993). *Life centered career education: Self-determination scale.* Reston, VA: The Council for Exceptional Children.

Wehmeyer, M. L., Kelchner, K., & Richards, S. (1993). *Individual and environmental factors related to the self-determination of adults with mental retardation.* Arlington, TX: The Arc National Headquarters.

Weisenstein, G. R., & Elrod, G. F. (1987). Transition services for adolescent individuals with mild mental retardation. In R. N. Ianacone & R. Stodden (Eds.), *Transition issues and directions.* Reston, VA: The Council for Exceptional Children, Division on Mental Retardation.

West, L. L., Corbey, A., Stephens, A., Jones, B., Miller, R. J., Wircenski, S. (1992). *Integrating transition planning into the IEP process.* Reston, VA: The Council for Exceptional Children.

Whetstone, M. (1993). IDEAS and transition: Outcomes and answers. In P. Browning (Ed.), *Transition II in Alabama: A profile of commitment.* Auburn, AL: Auburn University.

Wickwire, P. N. (1993). America at school and work in the 1990s: Career education—An opportunity. *Youth Policy, 15*(6, 7), 16–23.

Wilka, J., & Rudrud, E. H. (1992). School transition to employment partnership (STEP): Employability curriculum. *The Journal of Vocational Special Needs Education, 15*(1), 9–13.

Will, M. (1984a). Let us pause and reflect—but not too long. *Exceptional Children, 51,* 11–16.

Will, M. (1984b). *OSERS programming for transition of youth with disabilities: Bridges from school to working life.* Washington, DC: Office of Special Education and Rehabilitative Services, U. S. Department of Education, Office of Information for the Handicapped.

Williamson, P. (1994). Tech prep . . . The win/win program. *Missouri Schools, 60*(2), 11–14.

Winters, K. (1993). *Building bridges from school to work: A background paper for the goals 2000-educate America satellite town meeting.* Washington, DC: Office of Policy and Planning, Vocational and Adult Education.

Wisniewski, L. A., Alper, S., & Schloss, P. (1991). Work-experience and work-study programs for students with special needs: Quality indicators of transition services. *Career Development for Exceptional Individuals, 14*(1), 43–58.

Wolfensberger, W. (1972). *The principle of normalization in human services.* Toronto: National Institute on Mental Retardation, York University Campus.

Wood, M. M. (1986). *Developmental therapy in the classroom.* Austin, TX: Pro-Ed.

Wright, T. J., & Leung, P. (1993). *Meeting the unique needs of minorities with disabilities: A report to the president and congress.* Washington, DC: National Council on Disability.

Ysseldyke, J. E., Algozzine, B., & Thurlow, M. L. (1992). *Critical issues in special education* (2nd ed.). Boston: Houghton Mifflin.

Ysseldyke, J. E., Thurlow, M. L., & Gilman, C. J. (1993). *Educational outcomes and indicators for students completing school.* Minneapolis, MN: College of Education, National Center on Educational Outcomes.

Zadny, J. J., & James, L. F. (1976). Another view on placement: State of the art 1976. *Studies in Placement Monograph No. 1.* Portland, OR: School of Social Work, Portland State University.

Zeaman, D., & House, B. J. (1963). The roles of attention in retardate discrimination learning. In N. R. Ellis (Ed.), *Handbook of mental deficiency.* New York: McGraw-Hill.

Zigler, E. (1966). *Mental retardation: Current issues and approaches.* In L. Hoffman & M. Hoffman (Eds.), *Review of child development research* (Vol. 2). New York: Russell Sage Foundation.

Zigmond, N., & Thornton, H. S. (1985). Follow-up of post-secondary aged LD graduates and dropouts. *Learning Disabilities Research, 1*(1), 50–55.

Name Index

Subject Index

About the Author

Donn E. Brolin is a professor emeritus of educational and counseling psychology at the University of Missouri in Columbia. He received his Ph.D. in special education and rehabilitation psychology from the University of Wisconsin-Madison in 1969. Donn was the first president of the Division on Career Development and Transition (1976–1978) of The Council for Exceptional Children (CEC) and, in 1990, received CEC's prestigious J. E. Wallace Wallin Education of Handicapped Children Award which honors one professional each year who has made outstanding contributions to the education of children with disabilities. His current professional activities and projects focus on educational consulting and writing with a major focus on validating, improving, and expanding the educational materials contained in his *Life Centered Career Education Curriculum* published by The Council for Exceptional Children.